THE

# EPISTLE OF PAUL

TO THE

# EPHESIANS.

BY

KARL BRAUNE, D.D.

GENERAL SUPERINTENDENT AT ALTENBURG, SAXONY.

*TRANSLATED FROM THE GERMAN, WITH ADDITIONS,*

BY

M. B. RIDDLE, D.D.

*Wipf & Stock*
PUBLISHERS
*Eugene, Oregon*

Wipf and Stock Publishers
199 W 8th Ave, Suite 3
Eugene, OR 97401

The Epistle of Paul to the Ephesians
an Exegetical and Doctrinal Commentary
By Braune, Karl
ISBN 13: 978-1-55635-410-6
ISBN 10: 1-55635-410-x
Publication date 4/6/2007
Previously published by Charles Scribner, 1871

THE

# EPISTLE OF PAUL TO THE EPHESIANS.

---

## INTRODUCTION.

### § 1. CONTENTS OF THE EPISTLE.

#### 1. SYNOPSIS.*

#### ADDRESS AND SALUTATION (I. 1, 2).

#### PART FIRST:

#### The Glory of the Church of Christ (I. 3—III. 21).

#### A. THE GROUND AND GOAL OF THE CHURCH (I. 3–23).

a. *Grateful praise of the decree of grace* (i. 3–14). After the opening verse (ver. 3) the triple foundation of the praise, through the election of eternal mercy (vers. 4–6), the carrying out of the eternal election (vers. 7–12), the personal appropriation of salvation (vers. 13, 14).

b. *Exhortation springing out of the Apostle's supplication for the Church as the Body of Christ, who is the Head* (i. 15–23). With *thanksgiving* for the reader's faith and love (vers. 15, 16) there is joined the *petition*, that God would make known to them the glory of their calling and inheritance as well as of His power (vers. 17–19), which glory is manifest, actual and efficient in the exaltation of Christ over all as Head of the Church, that as His Body is the fulness of Him who filleth all in all (vers. 20–23).

#### B. THE EXTENT AND MISSION OF THE CHURCH.

a. *Reminder of the previous condition of death and the glorious new creation* (ii. 1-10). From the Resurrection and Exaltation of Christ the Apostle arrives first at the thought of the similar condition of death in the case of the Gentiles (vers. 1, 2) and the Jews (ver. 3), and then of God's mercy, which has quickened and blessed these miserable ones in, with and through Christ (vers. 4-7), of grace through faith (vers. 8, 9), as new creatures in Christ (ver. 10).

b. *Extolling comparison of the previous and the present condition* (ii. 11-22). After a detailed description of the previous condition without Christ, promise and God (vers. 11, 12), Paul sets forth the fundamental trait of the present status as nearness to God (ver. 13), explaining the nature and origin of the same in and through the Person and sufferings of Christ (vers. 14-18);

---

* [A popular summary is: I. The *doctrinal* part (chaps. I.—III.): The Church is chosen, redeemed, united *in Christ*. II. The *practical* part (chaps. IV.—VI.): *Therefore* let the Church walk in unity, in newness of life as regards personal and relative duties, in the strength of the Lord and the armor of God.—The reader is referred to the able Synopsis of Dr. LANGE in the *general Introduction* to the Pauline Epistles, Romans, pp. 15, 22. In accordance with his view of the twofold theme in each Epistle, he finds the fundamental theme of this Epistle in chap. i. 20–23, the final theme in chap. iv. 1–6.—R.]

sketching the present condition as that of citizens in the kingdom of God, members in His family, as built into the temple and house of God (vers. 19-22).

C. THE OFFICE AND SERVICE OF THE CHURCH (III. 1-21).

a. *The office in and for this church* (iii. 1-13). In spite of bonds (ver. 1) it is an office of that grace (ver. 2), in which God has made known the mystery of Christ (ver. 4), now made manifest (ver. 5): The acceptance of all nations into the kingdom of God through the Gospel (vers. 6, 7); to the humble minister the riches of Christ are entrusted (ver. 8), that thus on earth and in heaven the wisdom of God might be manifested in the Church (vers. 9, 10), according to God's eternal purpose (ver. 11), and that we might be comforted (ver. 12, 13).

b. *The Apostle's petition with an exhortation for the church* (iii. 14–19). Addressed to the Father (vers. 14, 15), it respects strengthening in the inner man (ver. 16), and Christ's dwelling in the heart through faith, in love (vers. 17, 18 *a*) unto the comprehension of love (vers. 18 *b*, 19).

c. *Conclusion in the form of a Doxology* (iii. 20, 21), praising the might of the merciful God (ver. 20), who makes the church in Christ glorious unto eternity (ver. 21).

## PART SECOND:

### The Spirit ruling in the Church of Christ (IV. 1—VI. 20).

A. THEME OF THE WHOLE PART (iv. 1-3): Walk worthy of the calling in love and unity.

B. THREE MOTIVES to the preservation of the unity in the Spirit (iv. 4-6).

*a.* The working of the Triune God in the church (iv. 4-6);

*b.* The gift of Christ to individuals (iv. 7-10): Each one is cared for (ver. 7), Christ has the requisite power (vers. 8, 10): He came from heaven and is exalted thither again;

*c.* The organization and organism of the church (iv. 11-16): The immediate end of the different offices (ver. 11) is the edification of the church (ver. 12), the ultimate aim is likeness to Christ (ver. 13), the operation depends on independence and growth through genuineness in love to Christ (vers. 14, 15), from whom as Head, the Body, richly furnished with members, knit together, grows in the reciprocal service of love (ver. 16).

C. GENERAL CHRISTIAN DUTIES (iv. 17—v. 21).

a. *Principle of the new walk with reference to the antithesis of the old and the new man* (iv. 17-24): The conduct of the heathen is a type of the natural conduct in general (vers. 17-19); after a reminder respecting Christ and Christian instruction (vers. 20, 21), he speaks of Christian conduct in its putting off the old man and putting on the new in deeply inward renewal (vers. 22-24).

b. *Special traits of the new walk* (iv. 25-32). The general basis is: no lie, but truth (ver. 25), the particular points refer to temper, disposition. Anger without sin (vers. 26, 27); as respects act, honesty even to beneficence (ver. 28); as respects speech, no corrupt word, but gracious speech unto edification (vers. 29, 30). The comprehensive conclusion (vers. 31, 32) refers to the evil that must be removed, and to the forgiving love that should exist in the church.

c. *Three points of view for the new walk* (v. 1-14):

(1) Look *above* thyself to follow God (vers. 1, 2)!

(2) Look *into* thyself and think of purity (vers. 3-5)!

(3) Look *about* thyself and be independent as respects evil men and deeds, and be benevolent (vers. 6-14).

d. *Exhortation to a walk with careful consideration of the Christian position* (v. 15-21): Wise carefulness, zealously using the time, precisely the evil time (vers. 15, 16), clear as to the will of God (ver. 17), avoiding drunkenness (ver. 18), but inspiriting with social song, with private melody, continued thankfulness, and mutual submission (vers. 19-21).

D. SPECIAL CHRISTIAN DUTIES *in domestic relations* (v. 22—vi. 9):

a. *Wives and husbands* (v. 22-33), to which is added a comparison with the church and Christ, in order to enjoin love upon the husbands and submission upon the wives;

b. *Children and parents* (vi. 1-4): the former should honor and obey; the latter should in self-discipline train and admonish them for the Lord;

c. *Servants and masters* (vi. 5-9): the former should obey as the servants of Christ, in hope on Him, and the latter should deal with them without threatening.

E. CONCLUDING EXHORTATION (vi. 10-20) to be strong in the Lord (ver. 10), to contend in the armor of God, needed on account of the adversary the devil (vers. 11-13), but sufficient with its particular pieces (vers. 14-17), if prayer and supplication be added (vers. 18-20).

### CLOSE OF THE EPISTLE (VI. 21-24).

A. *Personal Intelligence* respecting Paul and those with him is carried by the bearer of the letter (vers. 21, 22).

B. *Two-fold salutation* (vers. 23, 24): Peace and Love with Faith in and among the members of the church—and grace upon and with them.

### 2. FUNDAMENTAL THOUGHT.

STIER is undoubtedly correct in taking "*the church which is in Christ Jesus*" as the fundamental thought of the Epistle; his plan, however, on account of its trinitarian division, based on ground, course and aim, in each larger and smaller group, is rather artificial than masterly. The church of Christ has its root in eternity, in God's fatherly heart with its thoughts of peace toward a wicked yet beloved world, and lifts its head into eternity again by the throne of God, ramifying into all the institutions given in creation, even the most special, through all the centuries of developing history, and *all this in Christ.*

Such being the contents, it will not suffice to find in the Epistle only the carrying out of the simple grand thought, that God according to His gracious decree formed from eternity in Christ, has called *the Gentiles* out of the deepest darkness into His light and into fellowship with His ancient covenant people (VON GERLACH). [So HODGE substantially.] Still less is the main matter of the Epistle to be sought in *opposition to the prejudice* of the Jews, who did not wish to admit the Gentiles into the church (*Berlenburger Bible*).

[STIER's view is adopted in the main by ALFORD, who accepts the threefold division in all the parts of the Epistle. "But in fact the *trichotomy* respecting the church rests upon another and sublimer yet. Everywhere with him the origin and foundation of the church is in the *will of the Father*, τοῦ τὰ πάντα ἐνεργοῦντος κατὰ τὴν βουλὴν τοῦ θελήματος αὐτοῦ,—the work and course of the church is by *the satisfaction of the* Son, by our υἱοθεσίαν διὰ Ἰησοῦ Χριστοῦ,—the scope and end of the church is the *life in the Holy Spirit*,—δυνάμει κραταιωθῆναι διὰ τοῦ πνεύματος αὐτοῦ εἰς τὸν ἔσω ἄνθρωπον."—R.]

### § 2. THE CHARACTER OF THE EPISTLE.

1. The *language and tone* of the Epistle, as is obvious in the first part (i. 3, 15, 16; iii. 1, 13 ff.), are essentially governed by the fact, that we have here no scientific exposition nor even a dialectic development, but the thoughts roused in the praying soul of the Apostle are uttered in the continuing emotion. The thought did not then appear gradually in its parts and divisions, but as is the rule in contemplation, in its integrity and fulness. The language accordingly has difficulty in compassing the thought, struggling in a fulness and flow of words, in linked sentences, with the presentation of an idea that transcends it, as the first part repeatedly shows us. —Besides it is evident that the church was gathered mainly from among the Gentiles (ii. 1, 2; iii. 11-13; iv. 17-22), and the writer, as the Apostle to the Gentiles, confronts them in the full joyous consciousness of his office (iii. 1, 7, 8).

[BISHOP ELLICOTT, the most grammatical of English commentators, says that "in this Epistle the cases, *especially the genitive*, present almost every phase and form of difficulty; the uses are most various, the combinations most subtle and significant." While the use of particles is simple, "the intertexture of sentences, and the connection of clauses, especially in the earlier portions of the Epistle, try the powers and principles of grammatical and logical analysis to the very uttermost.—In the first chapter more particularly, when we are permitted as it were to gaze upon the evolution of the archetypal dispensation of God, amidst those linked and blended clauses that, like the enwreathed smoke of some sweet-smelling sacrifice, mount and mount upwards to the very heaven of heavens, in that group of sentences of rarest harmony, and more than mortal eloquence, these difficulties are so great and so deep, that the most exact language and the most discriminating analysis seem, as they truly are, too poor and too weak to convey the force or connection of expressions so august, and thoughts so unspeakably profound."—So DEAN ALFORD (Vol. III., *Prolegg.* pp. 24, 25): "These characteristics contribute to make our Epistle *by far the most difficult of all the writings of St. Paul.* All on the surface is smooth, and flows on unquestioned by the untheological reader: but when we begin to inquire, why thought succeeds to thought, and one cumbrous parenthesis to another,—depths under depths disclose themselves, wonderful systems of parallel allusion, frequent and complicated underplots; every word, the more we search, approves itself as set in its exact logical place; we see every phrase contributing, by its own similar organization and articulation, to the carrying out of the organic whole. But this result is not won without much labor of thought,—without repeated and minute laying together of portions and expressions,—without bestowing on single words and phrases, and their succession and arrangement, as much study as would suffice for whole sections of the more exoteric Epistles."—R.]

2. What is wanting in no other *Pauline* Epistle will be missed most of all in the Epistle to the Ephesians, *viz.*, historical references. Only two facts are noticed: the *imprisonment* (iii. 1; iv. 1; vi. 20) and the sending of Tychicus with oral intelligence (vi. 21, 22). This omission in view of the lively interest the writer takes in the church, and desires on the part of the church (i. 15-18; iii. 1, 13-19; vi. 10, 19-22), is all the more remarkable, since he had labored with great zeal in Ephesus for nearly three years (Acts xx. 18, 19, 31) and, on taking leave of the elders of the church in the summer of A.D. 58 or 59, had referred to false teachers about to arise (Acts xx. 29, 30). Of this we find no trace here. No member of the church is saluted either by the Apostle or his companions. Not the slightest hint is given of any false doctrine. For iii. 4 does not refer to opponents attacking his apostolic authority, while iv. 15, 16, relates only to general experience, and v. 6, to moral temptations, not to any particular false teachers.

3. The Epistle is distinguished by its Universalism. This will appear most strikingly from a comparison with the Epistle to the Colossians; other characteristics will thus also become unmistakably evident.

| EPH. | COL. | EPH. | COL. | EPH. | COL. |
|---|---|---|---|---|---|
| i. 1, 2. | i. 1, 2. | iii. 1-3. | i. 24-26. | v. 3-6. | iii. 5, 8. |
| 4. | 22. | 7-9. | 23, 25, 27, 28. | 15. | iv. 5. |
| 7. | 14. | iv. 1. | 10. | 19-22. | iii. 16-18. |
| 10. | 20. | 2-4. | iii. 12-15. | 25. | 19. |
| 15-17. | 3, 4. | 16. | ii. 19. | vi. 1-4. | 20, 21. |
| 18. | 17. | 22-24. | iii. 9, 10. | 5-9. | 22–iv. 1. |
| 21-23. | 16, 18, 19. | 25, 26. | 8, 9. | 19, 20. | iv. 3, 4. |
| ii. 1, 2, 12. | 21. | 29. | 8. iv. 6. | 21, 22. | 7, 8. |
| | ii. 5, 13. | 31. | 8. | | |
| 15. | 14. | 32. | 12, 13. | | |
| 16. | i. 20, 22. | | | | |

In this grouping of the parallel passages in the two Epistles, regard has been had to the list of DE WETTE and MAYERHOFF. The relationship and connection of the two Epistles is greater than the similarity between the Gospel and first Epistle of John (see *Introd.* 1 Jno. § 3, 2. Biblework, pp. 7 ff.) and between the second Epistle of Peter and the Epistle of Jude (see Biblework on the former, § 4, p. 7). But the thorough diversity is even more surprising than the similarity. We often find the very same word, the same form of speech, and yet a different thought; and then, too, the same thought but modified by a special manner (iv. 22–24; Col. iii. 9, 10), or in an entirely different connection (i. 7, 10; Col. i. 14, 20), now presenting different motives, again presented under different motives (i. 3–14; Col. i. 3–8; Eph. i. 16–ii. 10; Col. i. 15–ii. 18). If it be remembered that an agreement consisting merely in single words or phrases is very common indeed, so much so that a comparison between our Epistle and 1 Peter has been attempted with a view of maintaining the dependence of the former on the latter (WEISS, *Petrin. Lehrbegriff*, p. 426 ff.), a considerable number of parallel passages must either be omitted or declared unworthy of consideration, in deducing a conclusion. If, with DE WETTE, reference is made to the ἅπαξ λεγόμενα in our Epistle, to these we may oppose a long list from the Epistle to the Colossians (RUECKERT, p. 300 f.) [comp. ALFORD, *N. T.* Vol. III. *Prolegg.* p. 40], while the Epistles to the Corinthians, recognized as genuinely Pauline despite the most acute criticism, have more than any other. Particular attention, however, should be paid to the phrase: ἐν τοῖς ἐπουρανίοις, which is peculiar to this Epistle (i. 3–20; ii. 6; iii. 16; vi. 12), especially in the last passage. Following up those sections which our Epistle alone has, either with a very faint verbal echo in the Epistle to the Colossians or without any parallel whatever (i. 3–14; iii. 10–21; iv. 5–15; v. 1, 2, 7–14, 23–31; vi. 10–17), we find passages containing the most important, profound, and comprehensive thoughts, sometimes in a throng of streaming words, again in the most delicate and exact coloring. Finally, it must not be overlooked that, while in the Epistle to the Colossians only a single passage can be found (ii. 21) with a reference to the Old Testament (Lev. v. 2), in our Epistle we find: iv. 7–10, a definite quotation with an explanation (Ps. lxviii. 19); v. 13, an indefinite citation (Isa. lx. 1; xxvi. 19); v. 31, a reference to Gen. ii. 24; vi. 2, to Exod. ii. 12, and also allusions, in iv. 25, 26 to Zech. viii. 16 and Ps. iv. 5, in i. 22 to Ps. viii. 7, and in ii. 17 to Isa. lvii. 19. Accordingly we are not at all warranted in inferring from the relationship of the two Epistles, a dependence of this Epistle upon that to the Colossians. If the individuality and independence of the latter cannot be denied, and this we attempt to prove in the *Introduction* to that Epistle (§ 1, 2), then they certainly cannot be denied in the case of the former. We thus reach the conclusion that both Epistles were written at the same time by the same Apostle. Comp. RUECKERT, pp. 291–305; HARLESS, *Introduction*, lxvii.–lxxvii.

DR. LANGE (*Romans*, pp. 21, 22) has accurately noted the difference and peculiarity of the two Epistles. In the Epistle to the *Ephesians* there obtains a grand universalism in entirely peculiar independence: Here, without any reference to personal, temporal, or local relations and circumstances, we are directed on all sides to the glory of the Church of Christ and the true Christianity given in her for each and every nation, without polemics or apology, purely from her origin and appearance, her growth and consummation, her ground and aim,—so that even after the pressing entreaty for the readers' prayers in his so trying position (vi. 19, 20) and the brief reference to Tychicus, who will give further oral intelligence (vi. 21, 22), the conclusion entirely universal in its scope, reverts to the brethren, to those who love the Lord (vi. 23, 24), not ὑμῖν, wishing them grace and peace as in the beginning. Besides the references to the Old Testament remarked above, the well-considered interchange of "ye" and "we" is a manifest proof of the universal tendency, embracing both Jews and Gentiles. The Epistle to the Colossians, on the contrary, concerns itself with one single local congregation, its special relations and circumstances.

[On the difference between the two Epistles, see Introduction to Colossians, § 2, also WORDSWORTH and ALFORD on that Epistle; the latter accepting the priority of the shorter Epistle, speaks of this one as "the flower and bloom of his moments, during those same days, of devotion and rest, when *he* wrought not so much in the Spirit, as the Spirit wrought in *him*"—"the free outflowing of the earnest spirit—to the mere surface-reader, without system, but to him that delves down into it, in system far deeper, and more recondite, and more exquisite: the greatest and most heavenly work of one, whose very imagination was peopled with the things in the heavens, and even his fancy rapt into the visions of God."—R.]

4. The *language* of this Epistle is also for the most part conditioned by this universalism. Hence BENGEL, after his note in i. 3, remarks: *Paulus scribit effectu per adversa sublimato: et singulare hæc epistola specimen præbet tractationis evangelicæ* IN THESI, *hujusque capitis v.* 3–14 *compendium ea evangelicum exhibet; inde nullum speciatim errorem aut vitium refutat aut redarguat, sed generatim incedit; et quantumcunque lucis in epistola ceteroqui parallela ad*

*Colossenses ex historia ecclesiastica petatur, in hac epistola minus opus est*—and on iii. 4: *Est hic liber valde sublimis et tamen omnium lectioni commissus; in hac epistola apertius et sublimius scripsit Paulus, quam antehac in ulla.* The Epistle does not concern itself with matter limited by given historical relations and particular phenomena or individualities, which by its concrete character would lead to shorter sentences and simpler statements. The universality of the subject, preparing from eternity down through the centuries and now developing itself through all centuries and circumstances unto the consummation in eternity, and the enthusiasm of the spirit possessed by this thought, reflect themselves in the fulness of language and the wonderful interlacing of sentences (see especially i. 3–14). The remarkable interruptions and resumptions (as ii. 1–5; iii. 1, 13) can be readily accounted for, with such a subject and in such enthusiasm, by the Apostle's habit of dictating his Epistles. In those parts where the Apostle touches upon given relations, as in the second part (chaps. iv.–vi.) the language and construction, though terse and precise, are yet simple and clear. RUECKERT: "We do not indeed find here the language of scientific statement, or that of sharp censure against prevailing faults, or that of deeply wounded personal feeling, as in the Epistles to the Romans, Corinthians, and Galatians, nor yet that of hearty affectionateness, as in the Epistle to the Philippians; there is nothing of all this in our Epistle, and in these respects no comparison can be instituted."

5. The *opinions* respecting the character of this Epistle stand in remarkable agreement with each other as a whole, aside from isolated exceptions. CHRYSOSTOM: Ἔστι δε νοημάτων μεστὴ ἡ ἐπιστολὴ, ὑψηλῶν καὶ δογμάτων· ὑψηλῶν σφόδρα γέμει τῶν νοημάτων καὶ ὑπερόγκων· ἃ γὰρ μηδαμοῦ σχεδὸν ἐφθέγξατο, ταῦτα ἐνταῦθα δηλοῖ. ERASMUS: "*Stylus tantum dissonat a ceteris Pauli epistolis, ut alterius videri possit, nisi pectus atque indoles paulinæ mentis hanc prorsus illi vindicaret.*" GROTIUS describes the Epistle as "*rerum sublimitatem adæquans verbis sublimioribus, quam ulla habuit unquam lingua humana.*" WITSIUS characterizes it with special accuracy and excellence: "*Ita universam religionis Christianæ summam divina hac epistola exponit, ut exuberantem quandam non sermonis tantum evangelici παῤῥησίαν, sed et spiritus sancti vim et sensum, et caritatis Christianæ flammam quandam ex electo illo pectore emicantem, et lucis divinæ fulgorem quendam admirabilem inde elucentem, ut ebullientem potius, animadvertere liceat; idque tanta copia, ut superabundans illa cordis plenitudo ipsa animi sensa intimosque conceptus autem verba prolata, verba autem priora quæque subsequentia premant, urgeant, obruant.*"—With this the most important of the latest exegetes agree. [LUTHER (in the editions of the New Testament up to 1537) reckons this Epistle among "the best and noblest books of the New Testament, which show Christ to thee and teach all that is necessary and blessed for thee to know, even if thou shouldst never see or hear another book or doctrine." COLERIDGE (*Table Talk*, p. 82): "In this, the divinest composition of man, is every doctrine of Christianity, first, those doctrines peculiar to Christianity, and secondly, those precepts common to it with natural religion." Bishop ELLICOTT (Preface to 1st Edition) pays a tribute to the character of the Epistle, in confessing how far his labors fall below what it demands, using language that finds an echo in the heart of every faithful student of this stupendous revelation." Comp. SCHAFF, *History of the Apost. Church*, Am. ed., p. 326.—R.]

On the other hand the opinion advanced by DE WETTE is altogether untenable: that the Epistle to the Ephesians is really nothing more than a verbose expansion of the Colossian Epistle without individuality in purpose or reference, without position because without respect to false teachers, unworthy of the Apostle, poor in thought with its wordy style, overloaded with parentheses and additions, without connection. [Similarly RENAN (*St. Paul*, p. xx.), proving how the Epistle strikes a "surface reader." Comp. on the contrary SCHAFF, *Apost. Church*, p. 327: "As to style, in no other Epistle do the ideas flow in such an unbroken stream and such involved periods, as in that to the Ephesians. The perverted taste of some modern critics has pronounced this 'diffuseness,' 'verbosity,' *etc.* GROTIUS understood the matter better, when he said: '*Rerum sublimitatem adæquans verbis sublimioribus, quam alia habuit unquam lingua humana!*' The first chapter has, so to speak, a liturgical, psalmodic character, being as it were a glowing song in praise of the transcendent riches of the grace of God in Christ and the glory of the Christian calling."—R.] BEYSCHLAG's passing remark (*Christologie des N. T.*, p. 201), that our Epistle, through its dependence on that to the Colossians as well as through the lack of freshness and terseness of style connected therewith, can raise doubts, but that still it must be regarded as a working up of the Epistle to the Colossians by the Apostle for a wider circle of readers, as well as HAUSRATH'S (*Der Apostel Paulus*, 1865, p. 2) unproven opinion that the Epistle is "a letter to the Laodiceans wrought over by another hand," Rom. xvi. 1–16, being an accompanying letter to Ephesus,* are answered by the facts adduced above (under 2), taken from the two Epistles.

## § 3. THE SIGNIFICANCE OF THE EPISTLE.

1. The exalted significance of the Epistle for all time lies in the fundamental idea and thought of the Epistle: *The Church of Jesus Christ a creation of the Father through the Son in the Holy Ghost, decreed from eternity, destined for eternity*; it is *the ethical cosmos*, which Redemption purposed and has realized in the cosmos instituted in creation; it is the family of God, gathered in the world and in history and still further to be gathered, the object of His nurture and care in time and eternity.—"This age of ours so lost and wandering in every direction respecting the idea and nature of the Church" (STIER), which has stumbled about from the ultra-montane ecclesiasticism demanding unconditional obedience to all its precepts and dogmas, "clear through the rationalistic troops, who prefer to build a Pythagorean ὁμακοεῖον (common audience hall) in the place of the ἐκκλησία, as far as the free churches and churches of the future, which in Rupp's fashion leaves only a ὅμαδος and ὄχλος without ἀκοή" (STIER), accepting even a mere religious fellowship by the side of others,—this erring age must find its bearings, be consoled and uplifted by such a thought as this.

2. *The ground and goal* of the Church is *Christ*: everything depends on the relation to Christ, according to which the relation to the Church is first determined. *Where Christ is, there is the Church*, even though in incipiency, and where the Church in truth is, there also Christ is and works. Christ and the Church of Christ are indeed there only, where His super-terrestrial eternal Personality is apprehended, where this is neither opposed nor in any way denied. [Hence Rationalism can flourish where the ministry is "a moral police," sustaining some Erastian petrifactions, but confessedly cannot found a Church; nor is this Epistle with its profound ecclesiology any favorite with "liberal Christians." This results not so much from the failure to conceive of the Church, as from the inability to sound the depths of the added and essential phrase: "in Christ."—R.] "In Christ!" is the qualification necessarily and involuntarily joined to all truth and all life.

3. The Church is to be recognized as *one, invisibly visible, thoroughly ethical life-sphere of the Holy Ghost*. As above the different national churches of the same confession, variously formed, or deformed and loosely organized, one confessional church [denomination] is to be sought and found, so above the different confessional churches, each professing to be *a* Christian Church, perhaps *the* Christian Church, there is the one Church of Jesus Christ. From this super-terrestrially eternal life-sphere the Church lives and labors and blesses, in the world and in time, among the nations. In her there is carried on an ethical life-process, moving the individual in his inmost and tenderest centre, away from an ever more deceitful estrangement from God to a blessed nearness to God, from enmity and bondage to sonship and heirship with God, from lust of sin through pardon of sin to glorious purity.

4. *As means of grace* we have *the word of God* becoming personal in the individual as well as in the communion, re-echoed in faith and prayer and song, in the heart and in the Church. Yet the word of God is not made so prominent, that the Sacrament is on this account to be lightly esteemed, as the position of baptism (iv. 5) shows.

5. As regards *polity*, it is only required, that *the organs for the ministry of the word* be efficient, that the members of the congregation stand in affectionate helpfulness toward, over and under each other. For the former it is necessary, that both the susceptibility to receive it, and the activity toward the congregation be unimpaired and unincumbered. Of presbyters and

* [PROF. HAUSRATH does not enter into critical questions, but Dr. HITZIG, of Heidelberg, is understood to be preparing a critical work in which the same view will be defended. This theory considers Rom. xvi. 1–16 to be genuine, but addressed to Ephesus before our Epistle was written. RENAN advances the same view in connection with his theory respecting Romans as a circular letter (p. lxxiii.). See my note, *Romans*, p. 425. Against the Laodicean destination, see below, § 5, 3, c. —R.]

bishops already existing nothing is said; nor is there the slightest hint which can be turned against the lay element, but rather every living Christian is regarded as a saint, a sanctified one, and as a member of the Body, whose Head is Christ. [It is significant that this most *churchly* Epistle has so little to support the exclusive claims of any form of church government. This ought to humble the pretensions of *jure divino* sectarianism. Indeed all Christians should be humbled, as we feel how little any one body of Christians fulfils the conception here given of the Body of Christ. It is through such humility that the true church of the future, not indistinctly alluded to here (iv. 13), will be ushered in.—R.]

6. The natural institutions, marital and domestic, established in creation, the *status œconomicus*, as well as *politicus*, find support, dignity and blessing with the *status ecclesiasticus* in the church, so that salvation redounds to their advantage; in fact they thus first attain their rights, in order to serve in turn the growth and good estate of the church. All that is essential for these and for moral relations in general (which have their home in the church, and like all that is human going to rack and ruin in homelessness without her) is here clearly recognized in a profound and extended view, and sketched in grand outline with wonderfully pregnant force.

In these points the exalted significance of this Epistle for all ages of the church will make itself felt.

[7. The character of the Epistle involves certain results in regard to commentators, which are obvious to one who carefully reviews their labors. "As the wonderful effect of the Spirit of inspiration on the mind of man is nowhere in Scripture more evident than in this Epistle, so, to discern those things of the Spirit, is the spiritual mind here more than any where required" (ALFORD). As one example, DE WETTE is cited, who, though so able, has allowed his prejudice against the Epistle (see § 4, 3) to make his commentary on it "hardly better than works of third-rate or fourth-rate men." But the same principle operates in another class of commentators: those who approach it in a believing spirit, but with minds ever on the alert to prevent Paul from saying anything contrary to their pre-conceived theological opinions. This class includes those of the most opposite views. Certainly this mode of dealing with "the writing of men inspired by the Third Person of the adorable Trinity" (ELLICOTT) is unwarrantable. It finds no warrant in the conception of the church here presented, for this implies growth, precluding the notion that in any given post-apostolic century all theological truth was exactly stated, however valuable such statements may be.—R.]

## § 4. THE AUTHOR OF THE EPISTLE.

1. *The Apostle Paul* is designated as the author in the Epistle itself, not only in the address (i. 1), but also in the body of the Epistle (ii. 1), with great emotion, just as in 2 Cor. x. 1: *αὐτὸς δὲ ἐγὼ Παῦλος ἀπόστολος παρακαλῶ*; Gal. v. 2; *ἴδε ἐγὼ Παῦλος λέγων ὑμῖν*, and yet without imitation in a way entirely peculiar: *ἐγὼ Παῦλος ὁ δέσμιος τοῦ Χριστοῦ Ἰησοῦ ὑπὲρ ὑμῶν τῶν ἐθνῶν*. He thus refers to two things which are well known in his life: His *imprisonment*, mentioned in iv. 1; vi. 20 also, and that he is the *Apostle to the Gentiles* (iii. 7; Acts ix. 15; xxii. 21; xxvi. 17, 18). As he speaks in 1 Cor. xv. 9 with humility, and in Gal. i. 1, 12 with confidence and certainty of having received revelations from God, so here also he speaks humbly and yet as certain of his calling and illumination, of the revelation which has been imparted to him (iii. 3, 8, 9), referring explicitly to *σύνεσίν μου* (ver. 4). Those traits may be perceived here, which are found in the Epistles to the Romans (i. 1, 5, *etc.*) and Galatians, and in his life.—Still another fact is to be noted: the sending of Tychicus, who is commended to the church as a beloved brother and a faithful servant in the Lord. This agrees entirely with what is known respecting him from other sources (see on vi. 21).—Finally the character of the Epistle in thought and language confirm the Pauline origin (§ 2).

2. *The testimony of the ancient church* points without exception to the Epistle to the Ephesians as an Epistle of the Apostle Paul. No weight can be laid upon one passage in the Epistles of IGNATIUS, who suffered martyrdom in Rome between A. D. 105 and 108, since in the briefer recension of the text, it is said that Paul remembered them *ἐν πάσῃ ἐπιστολῇ* (*i. e.*, in *every* letter, except in later Greek it cannot mean: in the *whole* letter, see on ii. 21); in the longer recension, however, the passage reads very differently (*πάντοτε ἐν ταῖς δεήσεσιν αὐτοῦ μνημονεύει ἡμῶν*), while

in the shortest (the oldest) it is wanting altogether. The allusions to our Epistle (ii. 8; iv. 26) in the letter of POLYCARP (who suffered martyrdom A. D. 168) to the Philippians (*Cap.* 1: εἰδότες ὅτι χάριτί ἐστε σεσωσμένοι, οὐκ ἐξ ἔργων; *cap.* 12: *ut his scripturis dictum est; irascimini et nolite peccare, et sol non occidat super iracundiam vestram*) can however be regarded as the earliest witness for our Epistle; although the first is slight, the second is quite definite and cannot refer in its conclusion to Deut. xxiv. 15, as MEYER* supposes. The testimony of the *Canon Muratori* belongs to the same period. According to WIESELER (*Stud. u. Krit.*, 1847, pp. 815-857) and TISCHENDORF (*When were our Gospels written*, p. 6), this was composed in the year A. D. 170, according to LAURENT (*Neutest. Studien*, p. 198), before A. D. 160. This authority refers to what was then generally acknowledged, and hence to a much earlier period. It names among the Epistles to seven churches written by Paul, *ad Ephesos* as *secunda*. Nor are definite citations wanting in IRENÆUS, who suffered martyrdom A. D. 202: Eph. v. 30 [*Adv. Hær.* v. 2, 36; also Eph. v. 13 in i. 5, 8, where it is implied that the Valentinians accepted the Epistle as authentic.—R.]; in CLEMENS ALEX. († 220): Eph. iv. 17-19; v. 21 ff., *etc.* [*Strom.* iv. § 65, *Pæd.* i. § 18.—R.]; while ORIGEN († 254) names ἡ πρὸς Ἐφεσίους as Paul's [*Philos.* 6, 54]. Finally EUSEBIUS cites our Epistle among the *homologoumena.*

In addition to this testimony from the church that from the heretics must not be overlooked. MARCION (about the middle of the 2d century) has our Epistle in his Canon, though under the title: *To the Laodiceans.* Comp. § 5, 1. VALENTINUS, "the most profound, most rich in *esprit*, thought and imagination of the Gnostics," who died about A. D. 160, cites it as a Pauline Epistle, and also as "Scripture" (see BLEEK, *Vorlesungen über Kolosser*, p. 187, f.): [Comp. ALFORD, *Prolegg.*, pp. 6 ff.—R.]—Even DE WETTE acknowledges that the ecclesiastical recognition of the Epistle opposes powerfully the grounds for doubt on this subject.

3. Doubts respecting the genuineness of the Epistle were first published by USTERI (*Paulin. Lehrbegriff*, 1824), occasioned by oral expressions of SCHLEIERMACHER, who however in his lectures on the Introduction to the N. T. (pp. 165 ff., 194) only suggests the conjecture, that the Epistle to the Ephesians was written by an attendant of Paul in accordance with his suggestions. DE WETTE in his *Einleitung*, § 146, and yet more decidedly in his *Commentary*, sought to establish these doubts, and to prove the author to have been a gifted disciple of the Apostle in the Apostolic age. His proof did not however find general sympathy, even among the "liberal" theologians, such as RUECKERT (see § 2, 2), who makes the following apt remarks in opposition to this view: "We find in this Epistle again that man, who, exalted high above his times, could have as his equal only a few, and according to history had none such, since its silence would have been impossible, had there been yet another to stand beside him or to walk in his footsteps. Only such a man as Paul can be the author. If then he is not the author, show me the spirit in those times who is equal to him! Such an one could not walk through this world and leave no trace behind; I ask then, who is he and where? In the ranks of the imitators, the compilers, the counterfeiters, he is not to be found; where then shall I look for him? It is Paul and no one else!" The attack of DE WETTE contains also in itself a peculiar contradiction, since it regards the Epistle to the Ephesians as a wordy expansion of the Epistle to the Colossians, denying the author's independence, ascribing to him poverty of thought, and then charges him with the ἅπαξ λεγόμενα and ἅπαξ νοούμενα, which evidence originality and fertility.

[ALFORD meets DE WETTE'S objections thus (*Prolegg.*, p. 9): "Let every one of DE WETTE'S positions be granted, and caried to the utmost; and the more in number and stronger they are, the more reason there will be to infer, that the only account to be given of a writing, so unlike St. Paul's, obtaining universal contemporary acceptance as his, is, that it was his own genuine composition. Then we should have remaining the problem, to account for the Apostle having so far departed from himself: a problem for the solution of which much acquaintance with himself and the circumstances under which he wrote would be required." But ALFORD by no means admits that the problem is reduced to this form by DE WETTE'S objections. Rarely

* [MEYER (4th ed. p. 27) intimates that *in his scripturis* refers to the O. T., because the Apostolic fathers never thus speak of the N. T. There is the more reason for this view just here, because *in sacris literis* occurs immediately before. Still even Meyer admits that the *connection* of the two passages cited by Polycarp may arise from a recollection of our Epistle.—R.]

does even "subjective criticism" offer so contradictory a theory. Comp. HARLESS (*Einleitung*, pp. lxvi. ff.); MEYER, *Einleitung* (4th ed., pp. 22 ff.); DAVIDSON, *Introduction*, I., p. 352 ff. —R.]

The assertion of EWALD, that the Epistle is more rhetorical than Paul *was in the habit* of writing, yet as a whole *very worthy* of the name it bears on its face, placing it nearer to the Apostle than the Pastoral Epistles, and yet ascribing its authorship to a friend and pupil of the Apostle between A. D. 75–80, has no external support and this internal refutation, that no friend and pupil of the Apostle could possibly play such a prank as to represent himself as *Paul*, the Apostle to the Gentiles in bonds, honored with revelation, praying for the church, and requiring their supplications (see 1, above). This is an entirely different matter from the question respecting the Epistle to the Hebrews, left anonymous.

That this Epistle should be rejected by the Tübingen school (SCHWEGLER, *Nachapost. Zeitalter*, ii. p. 330 ff., and by Master BAUR, ZELLER'S *Theolog. Jahrbücher*, 1844, 2, p. 378 ff.; *Paulus*, p. 418 ff.) as a Montanist or Gnostic production, was to be expected from the animus of this school, but in the present state of exegesis and information respecting the character of both Gnosticism and Montanism, can create no uneasiness as far as the Epistle to the Ephesians is concerned. The terms πλήρωμα, ἀρχή, αἰών, κοσμοκράτωρ, κ. τ. λ. in this Epistle are not to be taken according to the Gnostic terminology, and, however it may be wished by some, it is not possible to discover in the phrase πολυποίκιλος σοφία τοῦ θεοῦ (iii. 10), the σοφία returning into the Pleroma, or in iii. 21 the doctrine of the Æons, or in v. 28 the Syzygies of the Gnostics, especially of the Valentinians, or in iv. 13 the Montanist point of view. For there can be found in our Epistle by considerate exegesis as little of the universalistic character of Gnosticism, which is pervaded by the most adventurous theosophistic and dualistic views, teaching about a physical-life process instead of a moral one, as of the opposite Montanism, which on the basis of a prophetic system, ecstatic in form and chiliastic in origin, substitutes asceticism for morality, running off into rigorism; so that the Tübinger are peculiar enough to rest on no other basis than their own assertions, especially as the Epistle to the Ephesians existed before Montanism and even before the Gnosticism of Valentinus, while these systems stand in the most complete antagonism to the fundamental thoughts and detailed statements of the Epistle (see 2). Comp. LANGE, *Apostol. Zeitalter*, I. 1, p. 119 ff.; KLÖPPER, *De origine epp. ad Ephes. et Coloss.*, 1853; RAEBINGER, *De Christolog. Paulin.*, p. 42 ff.

[RENAN calls this Epistle "doubtful." He wavers between the theory of the later origin (on the ground of Gnostic features and the conception of marriage presented here differing from 1 Cor. vii., *etc.*) and one similar to that of EWALD: "That it was composed during his (Paul's) life, under his eye, in his name, is not improbable." He suggests Timothy as the writer, especially as his name is omitted here, joining with this the notion of a circular letter, afterwards called Ephesians, because coming first to Ephesus, *etc.* The two theories contradict each other. As for the latter, if RENAN regards the Epistle as "*chargée de mots inutiles et de repetitions*" (p. xix.), such a quasi-forger would scarcely employ useless words and repeat himself as he does in chap. iv. 25, where he not only forbids lying, but commands to speak the truth. Still the whole theory accords better with the character of the *St. Paul of Renan* than with that of the *St. Paul of history.* There is as much truth as ever in the remark of ELLICOTT: "The objections have been so fairly and fully confuted that they can no longer be considered to deserve any serious attention."—R.]

## § 5. THE READERS OF THE EPISTLE.

1. *The address* (i. 1) contains a definition of the place, to which the Epistle is directed: ἐν Ἐφέσῳ. The circle of readers is accordingly the Church in Ephesus, if this definition be correct. It is wanting, however, in א. B., which belong to the fourth century, and in cod. 67 of the twelfth. In the first, the *Sinaiticus*, it was originally omitted, but it is added by the otherwise skilful corrector, whom TISCHENDORF designates with C. In the *Codex Vaticanus* the original omission was modified at a later date, as TISCHENDORF has shown in opposition to HUG (*Stud. und Krit.*, 1847, p. 133); in cod. 67 it was found originally, but afterwards erased. It is found besides in A. D. E. F. G. K. L. and others. The versions from the *Peshito* (simple

Syriac) and the *Itala*, which may have existed in the second century, all sustain this definition in the address. Our Epistle has been called the Epistle to the *Ephesians* since the middle of the second century (see § 4, 2).

In favor of the Ephesian destination of the Epistle we have also the testimony of TERTULLIAN (*contra Marcion*, 5, 11): *prætereo hic et de alia epistola, quam nos ad Ephesios præscriptam habemus, hæretici vero ad Laodicenos;* (and the same 5, 17): *ecclesiæ vertitate epistolam istam ad Ephesios habemus emissam, non ad Laodicenos, sed Marcion ei titulum aliquando interpolare gestiit, quasi et in isto diligentissimus explorator; nihil autem de titulis interest, cum ad omnes apostolus scripserit, dum ad quosdam.* From this it follows: Since the middle of the second century the same Epistle, which the ancient church designated and cited as the Epistle to the Ephesians was designated and used by Marcion, and not by him only but by the other heretics, (*hæretici*), as the Epistle to the Laodiceans. TERTULLIAN regarded Marcion as the author of this alteration (*interpolare gestiit*), which related chiefly to the title only (ἡ πρὸς Ἐφεσίους) agreeing, as it of course did, with the address (τοῖς οἶσιν ἐν Ἐφέσῳ), and not to the exact contents of the Ephesian or Laodicean letter, from which the materials for the discussion were drawn. Such a proceeding is easily explicable from the passionate, energetic and proud character of Marcion; besides he accepted Paul alone among the Apostles, and only ten of his Epistles in a very mutilated form, feeling himself entitled from his Asiatic origin to decide on this point. In the relations of the Apostle Paul to the Church at Ephesus, and in the universal character of this Epistle (§ 2, 1, 2), beside the parallel Epistle to the Colossians, and in the mention of an Epistle to Laodicea (Col. iv. 16), Marcion had occasion enough to recoin the Epistle to the Ephesians into a suitable support for his opinions and tendencies. With this agrees remarkably what is said in the *Canon Muratorianus* (see WIESELER, *Stud. u. Krit.*, 1847, p. 828; LAURENT, *Neutestamentl. Studien*, p. 198): *Fertur etiam una ad Laodicenses alia ad Alexandrinos Pauli nomine fictæ ad hæresem Marcionis et alia plura, quæ in Catholicam ecclesiam recipi non poterant; fel enim cum melle misceri non congruit.* When then EPIPHANIUS cites Eph. iv. 5, 6, from Marcion's πρὸς Λαοδικέας, and TERTULLIAN opposes Marcion out of a common text, the acceptation of a *partial* mutilation and alteration of the text by Marcion best meets the facts of the case, and it seems better to accept with WIGGERS (*Stud. und Krit.*, 1841, p. 429), that ἐν Λαοδικείᾳ was written and read by Marcion instead of ἐν Ἐφέσῳ (i. 1) to conform with the title (ἡ πρὸς Λαοδικέας), rather than with TISCHENDORF and MEYER, that all closer local definition was wanting [*i. e.* in Marcion's text]. For some kind of local statement is indispensably required after τοῖς οὖσιν, as will appear from a comparison of the Pauline inscriptions which enter into the discussion here (Rom. i. 7; 1 Cor. i. 2; 2 Cor. i. 1; Phil. i. 1). As regards Rom. i. 7, the words ἐν Ῥώμῃ are wanted only in isolated manuscripts. So that the omission of every local definition seems rather to have arisen in consequence of this manipulation of Marcion and in view of the remarkably universal tone of the Epistle.* It was not until the fourth century that BASIL THE GREAT (*Contra Eunom.* 2, 19) announced himself as convinced by manuscripts, that the address of the Epistle to the Ephesians read as follows: τοῖς ἁγίοις τοῖς οὖσιν καὶ πιστοῖς ἐν Χριστῷ Ἰησοῦ. JEROME, who for his part reads ἐν Ἐφέσῳ in the text, remarks on chap. i. 1: *quidam curiosius quam necesse est, putant, ex eo, quod Moysi dictum sit: hæc dices filiis Israel: qui est misit me, etiam eos, qui Ephesi sunt sancti et fideles, essentiæ vocabulo nuncupatos, ut ab eo qui est hi qui sunt appellentur. Alii vero simpliciter non ad eos, qui sint, sed qui Ephesi sancti et fideles sint, scriptum arbitrantur.* The former attempts to prove from the fact of Christians being called οἱ ὄντες, that Christ is first really ὁ ὤν; the latter refers, as TISCHENDORF (N. T. ed. 7, maj. I. p. 441), affirms, to the explanation and opinion of ORIGEN.—Accordingly this Epistle is to be regarded as addressed to Ephesus.

2. *The Epistle itself* and *Paul's relation to the Ephesian Church* are at least not in opposition to this view. During the second missionary journey, A. D. 53 or 54 (Acts xvi.–xviii. 22) on his return from Corinth, Paul came with Aquila and Priscilla to Ephesus; these he left there

* [MEYER (*Einleitung*, p. 9) suggests, too, the influence of the incorrect inference from passages in the Epistle, that it was addressed to those unknown to the Apostle who were moreover beginners in Christianity. On these points see below (2). The propriety of this suggestion will appear when we consider that "subjective criticism" found favor in early days as well as now. The "critical" as well as "theological" discourses of the present time are often enough those of the "seething" post-apostolic centuries.—R.]

and hastened to the feast at Jerusalem. This excellent pair in connection with Apollos labored still further for the gospel. During the third extended journey from A. D. 56 or 57–59 Paul came again to Ephesus and remained there nearly three years (Acts xix.). Although he at first found some sympathy among the Jews, he was obliged to yield to his opponents and betake himself to the Gentiles, until Demetrius, the goldsmith (silversmith), excited an uproar against the Apostle, which drove him from the city. He won both Jews and Greeks for Christ (Acts xix. 10; xx. 21). An intimate relation was formed between Paul and the church, as is shown in the farewell at Miletus (Acts xx. 17–38), on his return to Palestine, when he fell into the imprisonment at Cesarea, A. D. 60 and 61. The church comprised both Jews and Gentiles, but the latter were in the majority, since the tumult which was excited by the silversmiths in their anxiety about their gains, was far more considerable than the Jewish opposition. The city of Ephesus, being the capital of proconsular Asia and celebrated for trade, art and science as well as on account of the temple of Diana, was a place well adapted for the formation of a church of extended activity. It now lies in ruins, and in its place stands a little village called *Ajasoluk* from ἅγια θεολόγου, the holy place of the theologian, in remembrance of the labors of John the Theologian.*

Just such a city as Ephesus would give occasion to the Apostle in his imprisonment, to present his universal and cosmical view in a letter to the dear church. Even though a "more *personal* than official character" (SCHENKEL) may not be found in the address (i. 1): τοῖς ἁγίοις τοῖς οὖσιν ἐν Ἐφέσῳ καὶ πιστοῖς ἐν Χριστῷ Ἰησοῦ, which is similar to that to the personally unknown church in Rome (Rom. i. 7), and to Phil. i. 1, still the whole Epistle is pervaded by a lively interest in this church, the main elements of which are Gentiles (§ 2, 1). The universalism pervading throughout the Epistle throws the special references into the background and refers to the sending of Tychicus for oral communications. When the Apostle (i. 15) writes, he had heard of their faith and love to all saints, this is to be explained by the separation for years; he does not say that he had *only* heard of it. From iii. 2 we can by no means infer the non-acquaintance of the church with the Apostle, nor from iv. 21 the non-acquaintance of the Apostle with the church (see *Exeg. Notes in loco*, and RINCK, *Stud. u. Krit.*, 1849, p. 953 f.)—It might have been expected, that Paul would mention or hint at some special personal relatives in this Epistle; but he does not do it, though the Epistle is one addressed to a beloved church and full of lively sympathy. Yet at the same time he gives no ground for a justifiable doubt, whether this Epistle was written to Ephesus. No fact in the Epistle compels or justifies a belief that it was not intended for Ephesus, as the historical evidences require.

[The Ephesian destination of this Epistle has been denied by CONYBEARE (C. and HOWSON, *Life and Epistles of St. Paul*, Vol. II., pp. 486 ff.). Owing to the great popularity of this

* ["The city stood on the south of a plain about five miles long from east to west, and three miles broad, the north boundary being Mount Gallesius, the east Mount Pactyas, the south Mount Coressus, and on the west it was washed by the sea. The sides of the mountains were very precipitous, and shut up the plain like a stadium or race-course." (LEWIN, quoted in ALFORD). It was, in the time of the Apostle, an influential centre, a point of importance to be won for Christ. It is highly probable that the churches of Colosse and the neighborhood (Col. ii. 1) were founded as the result of intercourse with Ephesus (see *Introd.* to Colossians, p. 6). As regards its history, present condition, the temple of Diana, and the worship of that goddess, see SMITH'S *Dictionary of Geography*, and his *Bible Dictionary*, WINER, *Realwörterbuch*, in all three under the article "Ephesus;" but especially the interesting and vivacious description in CONYBEARE and HOWSON, *Life and Epistles of St. Paul*, Vol. II., chap. 16; comp. EADIE, pp. viii. ff., and the authorities there cited. The classical references are given by ALFORD, *Prolegg.* p. 11. The main facts are as follows: The city was wealthy and well-known, its chief attraction, aside from its importance as a trading point, being the temple of Diana, to whom the city was sacred. This wonder of the world, a Greek building of the Ionic order, was burnt by Herostratus, to gain immortality for himself, on the night of the birth of Alexander the Great (B. C. 355), but was rebuilt at great cost in the course of centuries, one may say, contributions having been made by all Greece and Western Asia. "A many-breasted idol of wood, rude as an African fetich, was worshipped in its shrine, in some portion of which a meteoric stone may have been inserted, the token of its being 'the image that fell from Jupiter'—τοῦ διοπετοὺς" (EADIE). "Oxford in England is not more Oxford on account of its University, than Ephesus was Ephesus on account of the temple of Diana" (HODGE). On the title νεωκόρος, "temple-sweeper," the most honorable designation of the city, see CONY. and HOW., ii. p. 76. The effect of the preaching of the Apostle Paul on this idolatrous worship is stated in Acts xix. 17 ff. It is not necessary to find any allusion to this temple in certain passages in our Epistle (iii. 20, 21), yet it does seem that it is quite as fair to adduce such a possible allusion in favor of the Ephesian destination of the Epistle, as to advance such internal grounds against it as have gained considerable acceptance. At all events the character of the city is not against the genuineness of the commonly received title.—R.]

work, DEAN ALFORD has answered its arguments in detail (*Prolegg.* pp. 13–18). The same popularity required at least a summing up of the question at this point, before passing to the theories mentioned below, so that the reader may see how little real ground there is for the view which these charming authors have made so current. On external diplomatic and historical grounds, only thus much is proven: that so early as the time of BASIL copies existed without having the words ἐν Ἐφέσῳ in the inscription, as indeed these are now wanting in ℵ. B., but not even he, much less the other fathers, doubted that the true title was "to the Ephesians," as it reads in all the older Uncials; that MARCION (not the best authority) called it the Epistle to the Laodiceans. This scarcely amounts to more than a state of things just short of absolute unanimity. The most probable explanation of the fact of this omission is that of ALFORD, who thinks it was occasioned by the catholic subject of the Epistle, made "very possibly by churches among whom it was read, and with a view to generalize the reference of its contents." On internal grounds but one objection deserves an answer, *viz.*, that it is scarcely possible that Paul could have written to such a church where he was so well-known without sending personal greetings. A sufficient answer is this, that in the Epistles addressed to those churches where he was personally unknown (Romans, Colossians) there are most personal greetings to and from individuals; and in every case where he was known few or none (see the close of the various Pauline Epistles). It is to meet these two difficulties that the theories enumerated below have been suggested, though MARCION's position has involved Col. iv. 16 in the problem.—R.]

3. *The attempts* to explain what is singular in this fact, which must always be recognized, fail in four directions.

*a*) Many, following a few manuscripts, some of them important, and BASIL (see 1) reject all local designation, as SCHNECKENBURGER: "to the saints, who really are such," MATTHIES: "to all the saints who are there," CREDNER: "to the saints who are also real believers;" so also WEISS (HERZOG's *Real encykl.* 19, p. 481). This is not only against the usage of the language (see 1), the attempts at translation themselves showing that the words are incomprehensible and meaningless without a local definition, but it also stamps the Epistle as a *Catholic Epistle*, for which it has never been held by the church, not even by WEISS, who limits it to the totality of the churches in Asia Minor, and considers it encyclical (see *ibid.* p. 482). Were this letter a companion to the πρὸς Ἑβραίους, it should have been entitled πρὸς Ἕλληνας rather than πρὸς Ἐφεσίους.

*b*) Others consider it an *encyclical* letter, addressed to Ephesus and yet intended for the vicinity in a narrower or wider circle. JACOB USHER (*Annales V. et N. T. ad a.* 64, p. 686) started this theory, and claimed that Paul has inserted no local name, leaving it to the bearer to add it. [EADIE (p. 24 f.) gives his language in full, as well as a long list of the supporters of his theory.—R.] Following him are a great many authors who suggest the most various modifications of his view. Some consider it a circular letter for Ephesus and its affiliated churches (HARLESS and others), others for Ephesus and the churches connected with it (BEZA and others), or for the Gentile Christians of Asia (STIER, HOFMANN, *Schriftbeweis* I. 1, p. 372) or for these exclusive of Ephesus (KOPPE and others), or for Laodicea and the neighboring churches, such as Hierapolis (BLEEK). [Among the supporters of this "limited encyclical" view which implies the general correctness of the title: To the Ephesians, we must class some of the most judicious of modern historians and commentators, such as TURNER, HODGE, SCHAFF, ELLICOTT, LANGE. Dr. LANGE with some positiveness says (*Introd.* Romans, p. 16) that in Col. iv. 16: "We are to understand rather the Epistle to the Ephesians as intended also for Laodicea, the last of the Ephesian Cycle of congregations." HODGE merely says: "Perhaps the most probable solution of the problem is, that the Epistle was written to the Ephesians and addressed to them, but being intended specially for the Gentile Christians as a class, rather than for the Ephesians as a church, it was designedly thrown into such a form as to suit it to all such Christians in the neighboring churches, to whom no doubt the Apostle wished it to be communicated." ELLICOTT, while holding that the Ephesian destination "is not open to very serious doubt," is led by the authority of ℵ. to adopt the view of USHER, regarding the Epistle as "left studiously general in form, and free from distinctive notices." OLSHAUSEN, MACKNIGHT, and many others, especially CONYBEARE (see above under 2) adopt the encyclical view, without admitting that Ephesus was the primary destination.—R.] But Paul has already shown in Gal. i. 1: "Unto the churches of Galatia," 2 Cor. i. 1: "Unto the church of God which is at Corinth, with all the saints which are in all Achaia," how he designates a circular letter, and gives an example in 1 Cor. i. 2, how he writes when in the address to a local church he has still in mind the adjacent churches, and one in particular. But of this there is no trace to be found here; hence the view that the Epistle to the Ephesians is an encyclical letter seems to be unfounded, and only an arbitrary means of avoiding a greater difficulty, all the more so, when the modern modification is added, that the Apostle had entrusted several copies to Tychicus, so that he could insert the name of the place on the spot (BENGEL, RUECKERT and others). Besides in that case another riddle is proposed: how does it happen that only copies for Ephesus have become known? [Nor does this theory meet the internal difficulty, since Paul in just such an encyclical letter (2 Cor.) goes into details to an extent that forbids our supposing the wider destination to have been any reason for the absence of personal greetings.—R.]

*c*) The opinion, based on Col. iv. 16, and Marcion, that our Epistle is that to Laodicea, is very peculiar, if it be claimed at the same time that it was intended for Ephesus also (GROTIUS, AUGER). The same Epistle could not be addressed to two so different churches. [Comp. Col. iv. 16, pp. 85, 86. The acceptance of "Laodiceans" and "Laodicea" in the title and address is altogether unwarranted,—a mere fiction to meet a single fact of no great importance, and involving various assumptions; and this strange inconsistency that Paul wrote two letters at the same time, one to Laodicea and the other to Colosse, sending no greetings to Laodicea in the letter intended for that point, but in *the other one* (Col. iv. 15) sent elsewhere. Even RENAN rejects it most decidedly. Still this view has been supported by MILL, WETSTEIN, the younger VITRINGA, PALEY, HOLZHAUSEN, and others.—R.]

*d*) Finally we can put on record as pure hypothesis the view of MEYER: *Paul*, with whose circumstances the Asiatic Tychicus, who is used again as "emissary" (2 Tim. iv. 12) and mentioned together with the Ephesian Trophimus (Acts xx. 4), was entirely entrusted, might have had special motives (the Jewish accusation, Acts xxi. 28, 29, and the avarice of Felix, Acts xxiv. 26) in the circumstances of his imprisonment and the watch kept on him for composing (on the score of prudence) a letter to this very church, with which he stood on the *most confident* footing, *without* presenting any personal reference or special circumstances. [This theory of MEYER is based on his opinion that the letter was written during the imprisonment at Cesarea (see § 6). But it ought to be added that MEYER is very positive in accepting the genuineness of the words ἐν Ἐφέσῳ as well as the exclusively Ephesian destination of the Epistle, views which he distinctly re-affirms in the preface to his 4th edition.—It is perhaps well to close this section with a list of some authors who agree with the view advocated by Dr. Braune: *viz.*. that this Epistle was addressed to Ephesus and to no other church: CALVIN, BUCER, WITSIUS, LARDNER, PROF. STUART of Andover, MEYER, DAVIDSON, WIESELER, ALFORD, WORDSWORTH, EADIE, SCHENKEL and very many others.—R.]

## § 6. TIME AND PLACE OF THE COMPOSITION OF THE EPISTLE.

The time and place are dependent on each other. Paul writes as prisoner (iii. 1; iv. 1; vi. 20), hence between A. D. 59 and 64, either at Cesarea or at Rome. As a starting-point we must remember that the three Epistles, to the Ephesians, the Colossians, and to Philemon, were written at the same time. The Epistle to the Colossians (iv. 10-14) shows us the Apostle surrounded by the same companions sending salutations as in that to Philemon (vers. 23, 24). In the Epistles to the Ephesians (vi. 21, 22) and to the Colossians (iv. 7-9) we find the same messenger with the same commission; this, in connection with the many almost *verbatim* parallel passages, places the contemporaneousness of the Epistles above doubt. Now according to 2 Tim. iv. 12, the Apostle sent Tychicus from Rome to Ephesus. At that time Luke was still with him, Demas had forsaken him, Mark was expected, and to Timothy he was writing. This points evidently to some other time than that required by our Epistles. According to Col. i. 1, Timothy was with Paul, as in Phil. i. 1. According to Col. iv. 7-14, as well as Philemon 23, 24, Aristarchus, Mark, Jesus Justus, Epaphras, Luke, Demas were with him. Aristarchus went with them from Cesarea to Rome (Acts xxvii. 2). Timothy, Aristarchus, Tychicus journeyed to Jerusalem with the Apostle (Acts xx. 4). Hence we can infer nothing definite respecting the time of the composition of this Epistle from Paul's companions. The Apostle was a person of great power of attraction, restlessly active, using his helpers as became necessary. Hence constant change. That the coming together of these men about Paul, who was the centre of all missionary activity would be more easily brought about in Cesarea than in Rome, decides nothing; they did come with him to Rome, to him at Rome, and thence were sent out to return thither again. Accordingly special attention has been directed to one point, *viz.*, the passages respecting Tychicus (Eph. vi. 21, 22; Col. iv. 7-9).

The mention of Onesimus in the latter passage is of special importance. The remarks of LANGE (Romans, p. 15) against SCHENKEL, who with MEYER [THIERSCH, HAUSRATH] and others, following the lead of SCHULTZ (*Stud. und Krit.*, 1829, pp. 612–17), holds that the Epistle was written from Cesarea, are quite correct. Even WIGGERS (*Stud. und Krit.*, 1841, pp. 436-450), who after weighing with great circumspection the arguments for Cesarea and for Rome, decides for the former, does not find those drawn from the companions sufficient. It cannot be perceived why Onesimus should have fled to Jerusalem rather than to Rome; since from the intercourse with Rome, and the sea route and the prospects in the metropolis, this was much nearer. Nor can anything be inferred from the expense, since this would scarcely be reckoned with much care. The fugitive would have been afraid of the *fugitivarii*, but not have fled from them. Nor is any proof to be based upon the position of the cities, Colosse and Ephesus. Even the *custodia militaris* does not help us to decide: the confinement in Cesarea would hardly have been stricter than in Rome. Two reasons are decisive in Wiggers' opinion: 1) that, if Tychicus travelled with Onesimus through Ephesus to Colosse, and hence came from Rome, Onesimus would have been mentioned in the Epistle to the Ephesians also; he is not named, and hence was no longer with Tychicus, but separated from him, left behind in Colosse. It is inconceivable however, why Paul ought to have mentioned in a letter to the Ephesians a slave entirely unknown to them, just as in an Epistle to Colosse, where he belonged. 2) Paul could not have said that he had sent Tychicus to Ephesus (vi. 22), if he in going from Rome [to Colosse] must of necessity pass through Ephesus; in that case the route would have led him to Ephesus, not Paul's sending of him. This remarkable reason is rejected even by Meyer, who agrees with Wiggers.

If on the contrary we call to our aid the situation of the Apostle in his imprisonment, it is clear, that in Rome, the capital of the Empire, to which he had already addressed his most important Epistle, the importance of Ephesus, the capital of Asia, would appear with especial strength to his mind, and at the same time the universality of the Gospel, the importance of the Gentile Christian Church there, the fundamental thought of our Epistle. The place of composition, therefore, indicates the time, probably the beginning of the imprisonment. Paul was in Cesarea from A. D. 59, and from the spring of 61 or 62 in Rome. *Hence the Epistle to the Ephesians was written in A. D.* 61 *or* 62. [With the usual variations in chronology the great majority of commentators and historians agree in assigning this Epistle to the early part of the imprisonment at Rome. See MEYER for the best defence of the other view. RENAN, mainly on internal grounds, thinks this group of Epistles, if genuine, was composed at Rome toward the close of the Apostle's life (p. ix.).—R.]

The priority of the Ephesian Epistle to that to the Colossians will doubtless be accepted as most probable (see *Introd. to Colossians*, § 2, 1, p. 8). It is certain that nothing can be inferred in regard to this point from καὶ ὑμεῖς (Eph. vi. 21), because the contrast with the Colossians, as those to whom Tychicus first came, is not indicated at all, nor can it be proven from the context (See *Exeg. Notes in loco*). Nor can the priority of the Colossian Epistle be concluded from the ungrounded opinion that Colosse was the first and immediate goal for Tychicus.* We may rather suppose, that with the universal thought respecting the Church in Jesus Christ, which impelled Paul to the Ephesian Epistle, the application of the universal complex truth to the special necessities of the Colossian Church might first have come into full view, than to claim that through his writing to the church at Colosse, whose needs had been made known to him by Epaphras and

* [These two grounds are advanced by MEYER, who considers the internal, psychological grounds to be altogether indecisive. But the second reason falls to the ground with the theory that the Epistles were written at Cesarea. Were our Epistle referred to in Col. iv. 16, then it was certainly written first.—R.]

Onesimus, Ephesus as capital of Asia had suggested itself to him and the universalism of the Christianity of the Gentile churches, and that he was thus led to write the Epistle to the Ephesians. The former supposition is supported further by an incidental notice. In the address to Colosse Timothy is mentioned with Paul (Col. i. 1); in the Epistle to the Ephesians he is not mentioned and this is the more remarkable, since Timothy was well known in Ephesus (1 Tim. i. 3). Hence it is scarcely probable that he was at Rome when Paul wrote to Ephesus, but he must have been there when he wrote to Colosse. The most simple theory is that Paul had already finished the Epistle to the Ephesians, when Timothy returned from some errand at a distance.* The Apostle then writes to Colosse, and both letters are sent away, the former written probably towards the end of the summer, the latter at the beginning of autumn. Finally HUTHER's proof for the probable priority of the Colossian Epistle, deduced from the fact that in the Ephesian letter "an unmistakable fulness of language prevails," while the Colossian Epistle is distinguished "by a compact brevity," proves rather the opposite: the briefer form is usually the later one, as the shorter catechism follows the larger. Comp. my remarks on the Epistles of John, LANGE's *Comm.*, p. 16. [HAUSRATH thinks that both were written at one sitting as it were, but the whole question involves conjectures merely. The view which accepts the priority of the Epistle to the Colossians admits of the beautiful theory respecting the Apostle's state of mind in writing the two, which ALFORD sets forth (*Prolegg.* pp. 41, 42) but aside from this there is no advantage whatever to be derived from a decision of the question. As to the argument from the contents of the Epistles, it is manifestly inconclusive, since A-LAPIDE, BÖHMER, CREDNER, SCHNECKENBURGER, LARDNER, and many others agree with Braune in assigning the earlier origin on this ground to our Epistle, while SCHLEIERMACHER, HARLESS, NEANDER, WIGGERS, DE WETTE, BLEEK, SCHENKEL reach the opposite conclusion. So too ELLICOTT, DAVIDSON, ALFORD; EADIE is very cautious in accepting this view.—R.]

## § 7. LITERATURE.

Among the numerous commentaries on all or a number of the Epistles of this Apostle we mention:

KOPPE: *Nov. Testam. Vol.* VI., *Eph. ad Galatas, Thess., Ephes.*, Göttingen, 1778. (The 2d and 3d editions, 1791 and 1824, were revised by Tychsen).—J. D. MICHAELIS: *Paraphrase und Anmerkungen über die Briefe Pauli an die Galat., Ephes., Philip., Koloss., Thess., Tim., Tit., Philemon.*, Göttingen, 1750 (2d edition, 1769).—DE WETTE: *Exegetisches Handbuch über das Neue Testament, Band* 2, *Theil* 4, 1843 (2d edition, 1847).—MEYER: *Kritisch-exeget. Commentar über das N. Testament, Abtheilung* 8, 1843; 3d edition, 1859. [The *fourth* enlarged and improved edition (1867) of this invaluable commentary has been used in preparing the additions in the present volume; and Dr. Braune's citations have been carefully compared with it.—R.]—OLSHAUSEN: *Bibl. Commentar über das N. Testament, Band* 4, 1840. [Accessible to the English reader through the translation of Prof. Kendrick].—SCHENKEL in Lange's *Bibelwerk*, 1862. [A second edition appeared in 1867. The work shows the author's ability, but in point of grammatical accuracy leaves no room to doubt the propriety of translating in its stead the commentary of Dr. Braune, altogether aside from the change of theological position on the part of Dr. Schenkel, which made it necessary to offer to the German public a choice between two separate works on the three Epistles to the Ephesians, Philippians and Colossians.—R.]—FLATT: *Vorlesungen über Gal. und Eph.*, published by Kling, 1828.—BAUMGARTEN-CRUSIUS: *Commentar über die Briefe Pauli an die Epheser und Kolosser*, published from his manuscripts and reports of his lectures by Kinnel and Schauer, 1847.—EWALD: *Die Sendschreiben des Apostels Pauli übersetzt und erklärt*, 1857.

Among the special commentaries the following are to be noted: RUECKERT: *Der Brief Pauli an die Ephesier erläutert und vertheidigt*, 1834.—G. CH. A. HARLESS: *Commentar über den Brief Pauli an die Ephesier*, 1834; 2d unaltered edition, 1858. [Pronounced by Ellicott: "one of the best, if not the very best commentary that has ever yet appeared on any single portion of Holy Scripture." Largely used by both author and editor in the present volume.—R.]

*[So HUG, but SCHOTT argues precisely the other way: that Timothy was present when the Colossian letter was written and after he had been sent on some errand, Paul wrote to the Ephesians; so inconclusive is this circumstance.—R.]

STIER: *Die Gemeinde in Christò Jesu. Auslegung des Briefs an die Epheser.* Two vols., 1848, 1849.—Extracts from the same great work for popular use: *Der Brief an die Epheser. Lehre von der Gemeinde für die Gemeinde.* [Elaborate and diffuse, attempting to retain and combine as many interpretations as possible, yet exceedingly valuable.—R.]—MATTHIES: *Erklärung des Briefs Pauli an die Epheser,* 1834.—[HOLZHAUSEN: *Der Brief des Apostels Paulus an die Epheser übersetzt und erklärt,* 1833].

The following should be compared: LUENEMANN: *De epistola, quam Paulus ad Ephes. dedisse perhibetur, authentica,* 1842.—KLÖPPER: *De origine epp. ad Ephes. et Col.,* 1853.—J. P. LANGE: *Geschichte der Kirche,* I. 1, p. 117 ff.—[W. F. RINCK: *Disput. ad authentiam epist. P. ad Ephes. probandam,* 1848.—Also the histories of the Apostolic times by REUSS, LECHLER, THIERSCH, SCHAFF, *etc.*—R.]

For practical exegesis we name: CHRYSOSTOM: 2d Homilies on our Epistle.—SPENER: *Erklärung der Episteln an die Epheser und Kolosser,* 1730.—RIEGER: *Betrachtungen über das N. Testament, Theil* 3, 1833.—[PASSAVANT: *Versuch einer praktischen Auslegung des Briefes Pauli an die Ephesier,* Basle, 1836]. HEUBNER: *Praktische Erklärung des N. Testaments,* Band 4, 1859.—KAEHLER: *Auslegung der Epistel Pauli an die Epheser in* 34 *Predigten.*—On Eph. vi. 1-9, AHLFELD: *Der Christliche Hausstand,* 1851.

[Comp. the lists in the Introduction to the New Testament, *Biblework,* Matthew, p. 19, in the Introduction to the Pauline Epistles, Romans, pp. 27 f., 48 ff.—Of special value here are the commentaries of CALVIN, BENGEL, MEYER, ALFORD (the 4th edition has been used in preparing the additions), WORDSWORTH. Among the earliest English works on this Epistle we mention: PAUL BAYNE, London, 1643; GOODWIN, London, 1681: BOYD, London, 1652 (in Latin); ROLLOCK, Geneva, 1593 (in Latin also).—Later works—EADIE: *A commentary on the Greek text of the Epistle of Paul to the Ephesians,* London, 1853; 2d edition, 1861. (Full, devout, generally accurate, containing a good list of the literature on the Epistle, and abounding in practical remarks which have been largely used in the Homiletical department).—TURNER: *The Epistle to the Ephesians in Greek and English,* New York, 1856.—HODGE: *A Commentary on the Epistle to the Ephesians,* New York, 1856 (republished in London, 1863).—C. J. ELLICOTT: *A critical and grammatical commentary on St. Paul's Epistle to the Ephesians,* London, 1855; 2d edition, 1859. The 4th edition (1868) has been used in preparing the volume. It differs but little from the 2d. (Without a rival in English for concise statement in the department of grammar, accompanied by a good translation, pervaded by a devout tone, and prepared with the greatest care).—J. LLEWELYN DAVIES: *The Epistle of St. Paul to the Ephesians, the Colossians and Philemon; with introduction and notes, and an essay on the traces of foreign elements in the theology of these Epistles,* London, 1866.—Eadie enumerates among the more popular works those of M'GHEE, LATHROP, EVANS, EASTBOURNE and PRIDHAM.—R.]

THE

# EPISTLE OF PAUL TO THE EPHESIANS.*

## I. ADDRESS AND SALUTATION.

CHAPTER I. 1, 2.

1 Paul, an apostle of Jesus Christ[1] by the will of God, to the saints[2] which [who]
are at [in] Ephesus,[3] and to [omit to] the faithful [or believers] in Christ Jesus: [.]
2 Grace *be* to you, and peace, from God our Father, and *from* [omit *from*][4] the Lord
Jesus Christ.

### TEXTUAL AND GRAMMATICAL.

* TITLE: ℵ. A. B. D. E. K. and others: πρὸς Ἐφεσίους, to which F. G. and others prefix ἄρχεται, some versions *incipit*. L. has τοῦ ἁγίου ἀποστόλου Παύλου ἐπιστολὴ πρὸς Ἐφεσίους. [Elzevir has Παύλου τοῦ ἀποστόλου ἡ πρὸς Ἐφεσίους ἐπιστολή, which is followed in the E. V.—R.]

1 Ver. 1.—[*Rec.*, ℵ. A. F. G. K. L., all cursives, some versions, read: Ἰησοῦ Χριστοῦ. B. D. E., some versions and fathers, Lachmann, Tischendorf, Ellicott, Alford: Χριστοῦ Ἰησοῦ. The latter is more usual (see Col. i. 1) and seemingly better adapted to the contents of this Epistle, which would afford grounds for deciding against it. See in *Exeg. Notes*, Braune's reasons for accepting the first reading.—R.]

2 Ver. 1.—[ℵ.[3] A. insert πᾶσιν after ἁγίοις. So Vulgate, Coptic.—R.]

3 Ver. 1.—[See the *Introd.* § 5, for a discussion respecting the words ἐν Ἐφέσῳ. The words are found in all uncial and cursive manuscripts except ℵ. B. 67. They are found in *all* versions without exception. Meyer (p. 8) defends the words as *decidedly* genuine, and with him a number of the best editors. On the other hand, they are omitted in the three manuscripts mentioned above, though supplied by later hands in ℵ. B., and really present in 67, with marks of suspicion. To this must be added, the testimony of Basil that in his time they were wanting in old copies, Marcion's view, the possibility that Tertullian did not know of them, Origen's acceptance of the omission, and the bare possibility that Jerome did not insert them. The discovery of ℵ. and its omission of them has led careful editors, such as Tischendorf, Ellicott and Alford, to bracket them, but there is at present no evidence sufficient to warrant their rejection, while the omission makes a reading so singular as to overbear the ordinary canon respecting the *lectio difficilior*. We must also take into the account the "subjective criticism" of the earlier centuries.—R.]

4 Ver. 2.—[Ellicott aptly says: "The preposition in such cases as this should certainly be omitted, as its insertion tends to make that unity of source from whence the grace and peace come less apparent than it is in the Greek." For the same reason a thorough revision would remove the comma after "Father," as well as the second "to" in ver. 1.—R.]

### EXEGETICAL AND CRITICAL.

Ver. 1. *The Inscription* (address). A. *The writer* (ver. 1 a). **Paul.** Comp. the Introduction to the Epistle to the Romans. BEZA (Acts xiii. 9) explains the fact that he thus names himself in all his Epistles, by saying that he as the Apostle to the Gentiles retains the appellation used by them. JEROME: "The name *Paul* is the token of victory, raised above the first spoils of the church among the heathen." [Comp, SCHAFF, *Romans*,* p. 58.]—**An apostle of Jesus Christ by the will of God.**—We find precisely as here ἀπόστολος Ἰησοῦ Χριστοῦ διὰ θελήματος θεοῦ in 2 Cor. i. 1; Col. i. 1; 2 Tim. i. 1. While in the earliest Epistles to the Thessalonians there is no qualifying phrase, Paul calls himself in Philem. 1, δέσμιος Χριστοῦ Ἰησοῦ, and writes in Phil. i. 1: Παῦλος καὶ Τιμόθεος, δοῦλοι Χριστοῦ Ἰησοῦ; in 1 Cor. i. 1 κλητός is prefixed, in Rom. i. 1 δοῦλος Ἰησοῦ Χριστοῦ is added, in Tit. i. 1 δοῦλος θεοῦ, ἀπόστολος δι' Ἰησοῦ Χριστοῦ are joined together, while in 1 Tim. i. 1, instead of διὰ θελήματος θεοῦ, we find κατ' ἐπιταγὴν θεοῦ σωτῆρος ἡμῶν καὶ Χριστοῦ Ἰησοῦ τῆς ἐλπίδος ἡμῶν. In Rom. i. 1; Gal. i. 1; Tit. i. 1, still further amplifications are appended. In this variety there is nothing arbitrary, but a consideration of the circumstances and relations determines the special form of the inscription in each letter, as in each case must be shown and has been shown. The shortest form, used here by the Apostle, is sufficient to indicate, humbly in unfading remembrance of his wonderful conversion and calling, that he has received his Apostleship without his own merit or worthiness, through the will and grace of the Most High (Gal. i. 15, 16), hence that he had not assumed it for himself or obtained it through the mediation of others. He did not present himself to the Ephesians as a stranger, as in the case of

* [Whenever the name of an Epistle or Gospel thus occurs, in Italics, followed by a reference to page or section, without any other specification, the reference is to the present edition of the "Biblework," or "Lange's Commentary," as it is popularly called.—R.]

the *Roman* church, nor had he to deal with opponents, as in the case of the *Galatians*, nor was he approaching the end of his life, as it appears in the *Pastoral Epistles*. Hence there was no need of such an amplification as in those letters. Still, as he was not writing about a private matter, as to *Philemon*, but of Church and Christianity at large, and the Epistle is an official letter of great importance, the official designation should not be omitted. Comp. the *Introduction*, § 1. 2, § 3.

Ἀπόστολος is an official title. [Comp. *Romans*, p. 59.] See Luke vi. 13 (ἀποστόλους ὠνόμασεν); Mark iii. 14: ἵνα ἀποστέλλῃ αὐτοὺς κηρύσσειν. Hence 1 Tim. ii. 7: κῆρυξ καὶ ἀπόστολος and πρεσβεύειν ὑπὲρ Χριστοῦ, 2 Cor. v. 20; Eph. vi. 20. As an Apostle, one sent out, he is dependent on the Sender, has his authority in Him (against Harless), since κατ' ἐπιταγὴν—Χριστοῦ Ἰησοῦ, 1 Tim. i. 1, does not describe the source, the origin of the Apostolic authority, but only the *corresponding activity*, the *situation in accordance with* the commission. It is no self-glorification, but in ἀπόστολος Ἰησοῦ Χριστοῦ there is expressed the feeling of *dependence*, in κατ' ἐπιταγὴν—Ἰησοῦ that of *attachment*; thus in 2 Cor. iii. 5 he calls himself ἱκανός, "sufficient," but denies his ἱκανότης ἐκ τοῦ θεοῦ, his "sufficiency is of God."

The genitive Χριστοῦ Ἰησοῦ accordingly designates chiefly Him who sends, who gives authority; the subject of the proclamation commanded to the Apostle is indeed the same Lord; but this lies in the nature and Being and position of the Sender, not in the genitive. Paul thus marks the authority which he has in the Christian church. [Ellicott and Alford follow Harless in taking the genitive as one of simple possession, but Eadie thinks it indicates also "the source, dignity and functions of the Apostolic commission," as well as including the idea of authority.—R.]

Finally, the position of the words must be considered. The best and most MSS. read here Ἰησοῦ Χριστοῦ; the same order is found in Gal. i. 1 without variation, but in all other Pauline inscriptions Χριστοῦ Ἰησοῦ is the better attested reading, so that Tischendorf (ed. 7, maj.) reads thus in every case except Gal. i. 1, while Knapp and others read Ἰησοῦ Χριστοῦ, except in Philemon 1. The difference in position expresses a difference of shading in the view. "Jesus" is the personal name of Him who appeared in the form of a servant, referring chiefly to His humanity. "Christ" is the official name of the Mediator, referring to the Divinity of the Son mediating from eternity. Historically the *Apostolic* proclamation begins with the Jesus in the form of a servant, the Son of man, rising to the Christ, the Son of God, as He proved Himself to be. Thus it occurred in the revelation to Paul, whose question the Lord thus answered: "I am Jesus whom thou persecutest" (Acts ix. 5; xxvi. 15; xxii. 8); in the last passage "of Nazareth" is added. He refers back to this most pointedly in Gal. i. 1; hence in that passage the reading is Ἰησοῦ Χριστοῦ without variation. But for this very reason the prevalent designation of Paul as "an Apostle of Christ Jesus" is explicable: for the *exalted* Son of Man, the Christ, who had appeared in Jesus of Nazareth, had called him to be an Apostle, while He had called all the others in the form of a servant. There is, however, no perceptible reason in the church to which he writes, nor in the contents of the Epistle,* nor in the circumstances in which he writes, for giving prominence to this distinction or to the consciousness of it. Hence the better supported reading is the more to be accepted, since, the subsequent context (πιστοῖς ἐν Χριστῷ Ἰησοῦ) might give occasion for substituting the more usual order.

Διὰ θελήματος θεοῦ sets forth the means, as in 1 Cor. i. 9: ὁ θεὸς δι' οὗ ἐκλήθητε; Gal. iv. 7: κληρόνομος διὰ θεοῦ (א. A. B. C.; F. G.: διὰ θεόν). In these cases the preposition διά with the genitive evidently stands in connection with the *causa principalis*, seeming to be entirely= παρά, ὑπό. So in Gal. i. 1, ἀπό and διά are definitely distinguished, and διά is there applied to Christ and also to God. Fritzsche's remark does not meet the case: *est autem hic usus ibi tantum admissus, ubi nullam sententiæ ambiguitatem crearet.* Winer (p. 355†) comes nearer, since διά does not designate the author as such, *i. e.*, as him *from* whom something proceeds, but chiefly as the person *through* whose endeavors or favor, *etc.*, something is imparted to some one. It is precisely the activity and efficacy of the Divine will over against the various difficulties which must be overcome and set aside, "the achieving and penetrating power, the energy" of the same, which is indicated. It does not rest nor repose, as if what comes, only came *hither from* Him or *out of* Him; He must be active, must further in the present. Hence this phrase is not merely a reference to the final and supreme ground and to the important prerogative of his calling, as one divinely authorized, in order to remove all suspicion of intrusion and unwarranted appearance or writing, but it is also a reminder of the continued energy of the free grace of God; what exalts and sustains him and what humbles him, he comprehends here in one; it is as much an expression of humility as of dignity. Here this added phrase has "still another peculiar meaning. For when an Apostle in the Holy Spirit begins to write an Epistle, he knows already with the first word, what will follow further; he has conceived and borne the whole, before he begins his greeting. If we read further, how in vers. 3-11 all the consolation of this Epistle is brought out of the revealed mystery of the gracious good pleasure and will of God, we can mark what the Apostle has already in mind: an Apostle and messenger through the will of God brings no other message than a glad one, the gospel of Redemption unto blessedness. Comp. Rom. i. 10, 11; xv. 29, 32. It is a counsel of grace creating joy and peace, this will of God, through which he also, who from Saul had become Paul, in his call to be an Apostle stands before all who should

* [The contents of the Epistle, especially its fundamental thoughts, seem to me to be strikingly in keeping with the order: "Christ Jesus," so much so as to awaken additional suspicion of an alteration to that form in MSS. of an early date.—R.]

† [The references in the original are to the 6th German edition of Winer, but they have been altered to conform to the 7th German edition, which is now the standard, and to whose pages the last American edition refers in a separate index.—R.]

believe on Jesus Christ unto eternal life, as an example of the mercy that saves sinners (1 Tim. i. 12–16)."—STIER. [ELLICOTT gives especial weight to the latter part of STIER's view, ALFORD to the former, while EADIE clings to the single notion of authority.—R.] Accordingly the remark of MELANCTHON, although accepted by most commentators, does not cover the case: *Vides, quanta cura fuerit Spiritui sancto certos nos reddere de verbo Dei, ut et secure crederemus et non aliud audiremus præter hoc verbum.*

B. *The recipients of the Epistle* (ver. 1 b).—**To the saints who are in Ephesus and the faithful** [or **believers**] **in Christ Jesus.**—Ἅγιοι is applied to Christians according to the analogy of the Hebrew קָדוֹשׁ (Exod. xix. 6; Deut. vii. 6; xiv. 2; 1 Pet. ii. 9) as those consecrated to God, as members of a sanctified fellowship, of the kingdom of God, of the Church of Christ. Although in the nature of the Christian communion there is not merely, the calling and destination but also the condition and furtherance of inward holiness, so that the latter are to be chiefly thought of in connection with an ἅγιος and can never be separated entirely from him, still they are not assumed in the word itself [HARLESS thus restricts it], so that this is not to be regarded as a moral peculiarity (ESTIUS, GROTIUS and others), nor does it express the call in the history of personal salvation and the moral destination, so as to mean: those called to holiness (SCHENKEL). If the former view includes too much, the latter includes too little. The principle of holiness has already come to them and even into them (LANGE); not merely is the goal of their calling held up before them, but the strength to attain to it is conceded and imparted (STIER). So that ἅγιος designates not merely a goal, a destination, but a *relation* into which the man is transferred and with which something is placed in himself.*

The inner side of this relation, the *demeanor* is here designated by πιστός, which means not merely faithful, reliable, but is also=πίσυνος (in any case from πείθω), πιστεύων, *believing*. Comp. PASSOW *sub voce*.† So that it is used, not only in contrast with ἄπιστος (Jno. xx. 27; 2 Cor. vi. 15), but without such a connection (Gal. iii. 9; 1 Tim. iv. 3; Tit. i. 6), even in the address (Col. i. 1). On this account it is not to be applied to *constantia in sanctimonia* (GROTIUS) or *perpetuitas in evangelica fide* (BAUMGARTEN). MATTHIES is as little justified in limiting πιστοί to the enlightened believing nature, and referring ἅγιοι to the sanctified affectionate walk, as is SCHENKEL in applying the latter to the *destination of the life* and the former to the *direction of the heart.* For πιστεύω is not merely a direction of the heart, but a living activity, the acceptance and appropriation of what is proffered together with the devotion of one's own person to the Giver of every perfect gift.

Καί joins πιστός with ἅγιος, as belonging together, like Col. i. 2, and thus are indicated the external relation established from above, and the demeanor of the church corresponding thereto, or "prominence is given both to the external relation and the internal condition of the Christian" (HARLESS). There is no ground for taking the conjunctive particle as epexegetical, as BEZA and others do, appealing to ii. 8; Gal. vi. 16. Although the absence of the article before πιστοῖς renders this admissible, it is decidedly opposed by the fact that the union of ἁγίοις and πιστοῖς is a description of the one church on its *objective* and *subjective* side, of the two important elements in the completion of the idea (BENGEL: *Dei est, sanctificare nos et asserere, nostrum, ex Dei munere credere*): the two notions do not cover the same ground, nor does one replace or explain the other; besides, Paul, least of all, would elevate the *subjective* above the *objective* element, and that too with an apparent exaltation of the Ephesian church, as though the *vocati* were all *fideles.* Because the article is wanting before πιστοῖς, it is not allowable to find indicated in the two words *two* different *grades* or *parts* of the church, as does STIER,* appealing to 1 Cor. i. 2, where he thinks three grades are referred to; and yet dropping "the thought of grades, which is but indistinctly present in the two words," he applies them to two parts, the first of which is thought of in the first part of the Epistle, the other in the second part. The acceptance of such a division would be grammatically inadmissible here (we should then read τοῖς ἁγίοις καὶ τοῖς πιστοῖς), and a similar division of the matter of the Epistle is found in others also; should not then the churches to which they were written, have had these two parts just as in Ephesus, or should not Paul have so thought of them in the letters addressed to them? The distinction is artificial.

Both ideas are further defined: τοῖς ἁγίοις τοῖς οὖσιν ἐν Ἐφέσῳ, πιστοῖς ἐν Χριστῷ Ἰησοῦ. The first marking the objective side of the church by a local qualification, the second, respecting its subjective side, by the life-sphere of faith; each is thus defined more closely according to its nature. On ἐν Ἐφέσῳ, see *Introduction*, § 5 [and *Textual Note* [3]]. Whether it is accepted or rejected makes little change in the sense of the words.—Τοῖς οὖσιν means those who are. In Rom. i. 7; 1 Cor. i. 2; 2 Cor. i. 1; Phil. i. 1, ἐκκλησίᾳ τῇ οὔσῃ or ἁγίοις τοῖς οὖσιν stand in connection with a following statement of the place, as herewith ἐν Ἐφέσῳ. This justifies the presumption that here too it can mean only this; nor does the word admit of any other meaning. It is entirely inadmissible, to explain τοῖς οὖσιν without ἐν Ἐφέσῳ as meaning "actual" (*to the actually holy*); this would read: τοῖς ὄντως, BASIL (τοῖς Ἐφεσίοις

* [Dr. HODGE explains it: "Those who are cleansed by the blood of Christ, and by the renewing of the Holy Ghost, and thus separated from the world and consecrated to God." No doubt this describes the "saints," but it is too extensive a definition of the word as here used. EADIE opposes the restriction of HARLESS, but properly says: "The appellation ἅγιοι thus exhibits the Christian church in its normal aspect—a community of men self-devoted to God and His service." ELLICOTT has a valuable note on the word, agreeing with ALFORD, who says: "It is used here in its widest sense, as designating the members of Christ's visible Church, presumed to fulfil the conditions of that membership."—R.]

† [The classical meaning: *qui fidem præstant*, is accepted by ALFORD, but the particular and theological sense: *qui fidem habet*, is preferable here, and is adopted by HODGE, ELLICOTT, EADIE. The last author thinks the other meaning would require a simple dative after it, as Heb. iii. 2. See his notes for the authorities justifying this meaning in the N. T.—R.]

* [STIER accepts the meaning: *faithful*, which best accords with his peculiar view respecting the two grades in the church.—R.]

ἐπιστέλλων ὡς γνησίως ἡ νωμένοις τῷ ὄντι δὶ ἐπιγνώσεως—ὄντας αὐτοὺς—ὠνόμασεν) to the contrary notwithstanding. BENGEL, who does not accept ἐν Ἐφέσῳ, renders: *qui præsto sunt*, referring to Acts xiii. 1; Rom. xiii. 1. But the passages cited, Acts xiii. 1: κατὰ τὴν οὖσαν ἐκκλησίαν, and Rom. xiii. 1: αἱ δὲ οὖσαι ἐξουσίαι, by the participle of εἶναι mark only present existence and validity (in the churches which are existing there at present, the powers ruling there at present), and BENGEL himself shortly before explains with more exactness: *qui sunt in omnibus iis locis, quo Tychicus cum hac epistola venit*, so that the participle has still a local reference. Such a reference must at all events be retained, and if ἐν Ἐφέσῳ must be omitted, then there is a *lacuna*, either intentional on the part of the writer, as in the case of a circular letter, or occasioned by the transcribers.

Ἐν Χριστῷ Ἰησοῦ is joined to πιστοῖς. The connection with ἐν is not objectionable,* even though πιστὸς ἐν does not occur elsewhere; for in Col. i. 1: πιστοῖς ἀδελφοῖς ἐν Χριστῷ, the phrase qualifies ἀδελφοῖς; so 1 Tim. i. 2: γνησίῳ τέκνῳ ἐν πίστει. But πίστις ἐν Χριστῷ is found in i. 15; Col. i. 4; Gal. iii. 26: μετὰ πίστεως καὶ ἀγάπης τῆς ἐν Χριστῷ Ἰησοῦ, 1 Tim. i. 14; and πιστεύειν ἐν τῷ εὐαγγελίῳ, Mark i. 15. Since ἐν designates the element, the life-sphere, the principle, the *inmost* life-fellowship of the believer, it is not=εἰς (BAUMGARTEN), for it is not the object, aim or direction of the believer that is marked, but his activity and vitality.† Hence it is also not=διὰ Χριστοῦ, for the means are not here discussed, as SCHENKEL thinks, nor is it to be rendered: *fidem in Christo reponentibus* (MEYER), since in that case we should find ἐπί with the dative (WINER, p. 367). The position ἐν Χριστῷ Ἰησοῦ must be noticed, since at the beginning we read ἀπόστολος Ἰησοῦ Χριστοῦ, and so too in the greeting, ver. 2. "The proclamation of the messenger proceeds mainly from Jesus, preaching and proving that He is the Christ—but the faith of the saints rests mainly on the Christ, the Messiah, the giver of the gift of God, of eternal life (Rom. vi. 23). Comp. Col. i. 4; 1 Tim. ii. 5; i. 14, 15."—STIER. "In Christ" is in this Epistle the centre and heart-beat of the apostolic proclamation. Comp. vers. 3, 4, 6, 7, 10, 11, 12, 13, *etc.* [See EADIE's remarks in *Homil. Notes*.—R.] This formula corresponds entirely to the phrases "in Adam," "in Abraham," referring to the efficient fellowship of life. The connection with πιστοῖς must be retained, the more since ἁγίοις has already an added qualification. It is true ἐν Χριστῷ might be joined with ἁγίοις, as in Phil. i. 1. But it does not result from this, that it belongs here not merely to πιστοῖς, but also to ἁγίοις, as SCHENKEL, HARLESS and others think; as if Paul had written: τοῖς ἁγίοις καὶ πιστοῖς ἐν Χριστῷ Ἰησοῦ! One might say with the same reason, that τοῖς οὖσιν ἐν Ἐφέσῳ belonged to πιστοῖς, since the believers also are there.

While Paul writes τῇ ἐκκλησίᾳ in 1 Cor. i. 2; 2 Cor. i. 1; 1 Thess. i. 1; 2 Thess. i. 1; ταῖς ἐκκλησίαις Gal. i. 2; in Rom. i. 7; Phil. i. 1; Col. i. 2, he says: τοῖς ἁγίοις. In the former cases he has in view the unity comprehending the Christian persons, in the latter the persons standing in this unity: this form will, therefore, scarcely support the view, that it bears in itself a more confidential character. (SCHENKEL on Col. i. 2.) For the Romans were strangers to the Apostle, while the Colossians, Corinthians and Galatians were known and dear. Still less is there to be found in this difference an indication that he had founded the church in question or some one else.

Ver. 2. *The Salutation.* [On the Pauline salutations, see Dr. SCHAFF's note, *Romans*, p. 57.] **Grace be to you and peace.**—Χάρις has the same root as χαίρω, χαρά, χάρμα (joy), χαρτός (pleasant), from which also *carus, gratius, gratia, grates* are derived. It means favor, gracious character, loving, obliging devotion to another, such as that of a wife to the husband, the enjoyment of love. See PASSOW *sub voce.* The thought of the Scripture is aptly expressed by the German word *Gnade*, the original meaning of which may be perceived in the expression: *die Sonne geht zu Gnaden* (the sun goes down, goes under), *ein gnädiger Regen* (a rain that falls lightly and penetrates deeply). It is compounded of *ge*, with the signification of strengthening, multiplying (as in *Geräusch, Geschrei, etc.*), and *naden* (down, into the depths). *Gnade, grace,* is therefore condescending love and beneficent kindness of God, the Lord, condescending indeed from the heights of glory into the depths of darkness. Comp. KLING, 1 Cor. i. 3 (*Biblework*). [The English word *grace*, as will be seen from the etymological remark above, has the same root as the Greek word used here, and is its nearest possible equivalent in all its various meanings.—R.]

Εἰρήνη from εἴρω (to knit, to speak, according to PLATO, *Cratylus*, p. 398, D: τὸ εἴρειν λέγειν ἐστι, according to the analogy of *sero, sermo, sermonem nectere*) designates a union after separation, reconciliation after contest and quarrel, since then the speech is no longer against, but to and for each other, since then comes rest and joyousness, παῤῥησία. It is *Friede, peace*, because one is glad and free [*froh und frei*], the actual well-being, corresponding to the Hebrew שָׁלוֹם. [The meaning of the Hebrew word is aptly expressed thus: "Peace, plenty, and prosperity."—R.] First comes χάρις, *grace*, "that which is subjective in God and Christ, which the Apostle wishes to be directed and shown to his readers; the latter is the actual result, which is presented through the bestowal of grace" (MEYER on Rom. i. 7); grace is the ground of sanctification and of peace, peace is the goal of faith; the dative ὑμῖν, "to you," *viz.*, ἁγίοις and πιστοῖς, after χάρις indicates that "grace" first of all becomes their portion, and then "peace" becomes and remains theirs more and more. The thought will be best completed from 1 Pet. i. 2; 2 Pet. i. 2,

* [ALFORD seems to reject this connection. In that case we must accept an elliptical construction: "The saints who are in Ephesus, the believers (who are) in Christ," or take the phrase as qualifying both adjectives; the objections to the latter will be found below.—R.]

† [ELLICOTT thus discriminates between πιστὸς ἐν Χριστῷ and πιστεύειν εἰς Χριστόν: "The latter involves a closer connection of the verb and the preposition, and points rather to an *act* of the will, while the former involves a closer connection of the preposition and the noun, and marks a *state* and condition."—R.]

where πληθυνθείη is added,* even if this word is not in the Apostle's mind; for as ἅγιοι and πιστοί they are already partakers of these, and in Christians there is a growth both of grace and peace.

**From God our Father and the Lord Jesus Christ.**—The preposition ἀπό designates the *coming hither*, without defining more closely the relation of that which comes to him from whom it comes, as is done by ἐκ and παρά, or denoting the activity of him from whom it comes, as in the case of ὑπό. On the further distinction between these prepositions, see WINER, pp. 342 f., 346 f. Here ἀπό therefore means simply *from*, governing both the genitives: θεοῦ πατρὸς ἡμῶν and κυρίου Ἰησοῦ Χριστοῦ. Both grace and peace come from both God and Jesus Christ; in this then God and Jesus are alike. Still in 2 Cor. xiii. 13 Paul says: "the grace of our Lord Jesus Christ," placing it before "the love of God." In the present passage the two are distinguished by closer qualifications. "Our Father" denotes the fatherhood of God; we rejoice as His children "by virtue of the adoption (ver. 5) attained through Christ." With the word "our" the Apostle includes *himself* and the readers, called "you" just before, and all Christians, in humble, sacred joy. Κυρίου without ἡμῶν denotes in general the Lordship of Christ; He is such as Creator (Col. i. 16; 1 Cor. viii. 6; comp. John i. 3), as Propitiator and Redeemer (Acts xx. 28), as the exalted Son of man (Phil. ii. 9-11); and such power as Lord He has from God the Father (i. 22; Matth. xxviii. 18) until the consummation of the plan of salvation (1 Cor. xv. 24, 28), while He in His appearance as Messiah (Χριστός) has God as head (1 Cor. xi. 3) and is "God's" (1 Cor. iii. 23). Comp. HARLESS *in loco*. It is inconceivable how any can [as the Socinians], in opposition to the language and thought alike, make the genitive "Lord Jesus Christ" co-ordinate with "our," and thus dependent on "Father;" but what is not possible for those who are unwilling to perceive Christ in His Dignity above us, and us in our need below Him!

The importance of this benediction will be perceived from the constant repetition of it, even if in manifold forms. The briefest form is found in 1 Thess. i. 1: χάρις ὑμῖν καὶ εἰρήνη; in Col. i. 2 we have: χάρις ὑμῖν καὶ εἰρήνη ἀπὸ θεοῦ πατρὸς ἡμῶν; 2 Thess. i. 2: χάρις ὑμῖν καὶ εἰρήνη ἀπὸ θεοῦ πατρὸς καὶ κυρίου Ἰησοῦ Χριστοῦ. Then as here (i. 2) in Rom. i. 7; 1 Cor. i. 3; 2 Cor. i. 2; Phil. i. 2; Philem. 3. In Gal. i. 3, ἡμῶν occurs after κυρίου, not after πατρός, and something further is appended, together with a doxology. Tit. i. 4: χάρις καὶ εἰρήνη ἀπὸ θεοῦ πατρὸς καὶ Χριστοῦ Ἰησοῦ τοῦ σωτῆρος ἡμῶν. The greetings in the two Epistles to Timothy are the fullest: χάρις, ἔλεος, εἰρήνη ἀπὸ θεοῦ πατρὸς καὶ Χριστοῦ Ἰησοῦ τοῦ κυρίου ἡμῶν. "Mercy" enters between, to indicate the activity of "grace" towards this "peace."

## DOCTRINAL AND ETHICAL.

1. Paul knows and feels himself to be *an Apostle of Jesus Christ*, quite as much as those who were *immediately* called and sent out by Jesus Himself. He too was called and ordained just as immediately in an *extraordinary* manner, as these in an *ordinary* way. On this account he adds, "by the will of God," excluding all human choice and self-will in his call. Hence he is not to be reckoned as the *thirteenth*, but as the *twelfth* chosen in the place of the traitor *Judas*; the election of *Matthias* (Acts i. 15–26), having been occasioned by Peter and consummated by the disciples *before* the outpouring of the Holy Ghost, is to be regarded as a work of haste and precipitancy. [On the other hand, see LECHLER, *Biblework, Acts*, p. 22. The question is discussed in the histories of the Apostolic times. "Paul never represents himself as one of the twelve, but seems rather to distinguish himself from them as one born out of due time, occupying a similar relation to the Gentile world, as the older apostles did to the Jewish." SCHAFF, *Hist. of the Apost. Church*, p. 513. The only practical use made of it in modern times has been in the interest of Prelacy, against the people's choice of ministers.—R.]

2. As Paul places himself upon an entire equality with the other Apostles, although he is pre-eminently the Apostle to the Gentiles (Acts ix. 15; xx. 21; xxvi. 17, 18; comp. LECHLER, *Biblework, Acts*, p. 171), he designates the *Apostolate* as unique in its character, in respect to the immediate call, as well as to its special position and mission in the incipient stages of the Christian Church. This refutes the error of the Irvingites, who believe in the re-appearance of actual Apostles and the re-establishment and renewal of the Apostolate in their churches (SCHENKEL, SCHMOLLER, on Gal. i. 2, *Biblework*). We must not, however, overlook the fact, that Paul in Phil. i. 1 calls himself in connection with Timothy only "the servant of Christ Jesus," and in Rom. i. 1, "servant of Jesus Christ," in Tit. i. 1, "servant of God," first, and then "Apostle;" thus giving priority in these passages to the general official name; including his assistant with himself in Phil. i. 1, while in the two Epistles to the Thessalonians he mentions these without any further qualification. In the Apostolate, as a specializing of the general service of the church, we must regard the general ecclesiastical office as conjoined, finding in the former the basis of all real church offices. It is in fact the historically first form of office in the church, unfolding itself further in the wider course of ecclesiastical development, according to the necessity of the congregation, in conformity with the gifts and tasks of the church. Thus the *diaconate* soon sprang up (Acts vi. 1-7), then other offices (Eph. iv. 11), especially that of "*presbyter*" in both Jewish and Gentile Christian churches. To this correspond the instructions and commissions imparted to the Apostles by the Lord Himself (Matth. xvi. 19; xviii. 18; xxviii. 19, 20, where the promise: "Lo, I am with you alway, even unto the end of the world," is especially to be noted; Jno. xx. 21-23), which are still in force for the ministers of the word, and will be unto the end of the world. In addition, it may be remembered that the Apostle is writing to churches already existing, though in most cases founded by himself, so that he does not place himself with his office and ministry temporal in priority,

* [ELLICOTT and ALFORD supply εἴη, not ἔστω (MEYER), the optative being the more usual form, as is implied in the suggestion of DR. BRAUNE.—R.]

nor as to his rank above the church, but works on and in her, as well as for her.

3. Paul regards the church from a double point of view, as *consecrated to God*, and *believing*. With the first term (ἅγιοι) he sets forth its *objective ground*, with the second (πιστοὶ ἐν Χριστῷ Ἰησοῦ) its *subjective life;* the former marks the *Divine work of salvation*, the latter the *human acceptance and appropriation;* that indicates the *relation* of the church to God, this the *demeanor;* that defines their *worth* (dignity), this their *worthiness;* that is always *first*, impelling to the other, this is always second, having in the first its ground, impulse and power. In the objective factor, in God's arranging and ordering, there is constantly given the power, which will and can and should become efficient, even though only latent at times. Nothing is said respecting the degree and extent to which this power, given in connection with the assembly effected by God, has wrought and been successful in the whole body; from the first feeble beginnings on to the consummation, there are manifold, unmistakable gradations; fluctuations, too, and relapses of a very dubious character. But above the *appearance* in single churches and periods, the eternal and glorious basis must not be misunderstood; here Paul gives an important example to the Ephesians. The Christian must confess in humble gratitude that he is ἅγιος, and in assiduous obedience feel and show himself to be πιστὸς ἐν Χριστῷ Ἰησοῦ.

4. God, who has condescended and given Himself to us as a Father ("grace be unto you from God our Father") with His gifts ("peace"), stands together with Christ ("and the Lord Jesus Christ") toward us as Giver and Dispenser. It is the will of God, who has ordered all things ("by the will of God") to this end, constantly accomplishing His purpose actively through His creatures, inanimate as well as animate and personal, willing and unwilling, yes, resisting even. Accordingly the Lord sends His Apostles, remains together with the Father the constant source of all the benefits of salvation, aye, the element, the life-sphere for all the called and believing ones. Although it remains untouched here, in what relation the Lord Jesus stands to God the Father, it is still clear, that He needs no "grace" and "peace," but is, as the sending Lord and partaker of Divinity, highly exalted above us, and we are deep below Him, poor, wretched, without peace, needing Him, but yet the objects of His mercy, who should become partakers of God.

5. *Grace* and *peace* stand related to each other: in the former God condescends to man, in the latter man lifts himself to God. In *grace*, the Most High comes down into the depths of misery and sin; in *peace*, poor sinful man, taken up, reconciled, pacified, cleansed, draws nigh to his God and Father. Neither is complete at once, each has its development and history: *grace*, not merely forgiveness of sin, but deliverance, enlightening, sanctification, beatification, imparts ever more fully, penetrates ever deeper and wider, exalts ever more gloriously; *peace*, not merely rest, quiet, but union and harmony, strengthens more and more, grows and impels ever higher and more beautifully. This is indicated by the form of the benediction. The victory is decided; it will be followed up, improved, and that more completely—and all this by the *ethical* mode of *faith*, not an indefinite and general one, but the special definite faith in Christ Jesus, the living Mediator of all blessing and salvation.

HOMILETICAL AND PRACTICAL.

Did God make out of Saul, the persecutor of the Church of Jesus Christ, Paul the Apostle of Jesus Christ, then rejoice in humility and think that the same God who has made of thee a Christian, a joyous child of God, will help others to the same privilege; if He succeeded in doing this in your case, is it not even more likely to succeed in that of others?—Do not forget that in dealing with the Apostle of Jesus Christ, thou dealest with the will and work of God.—Take heed in thine office and calling, that thou standest there by the will of God.—Paul, so wonderfully led, so marvellously overcome and so highly favored, sees through all the defects, weaknesses, sins of his churches, their glory, the glory of the people of God, and their life of faith, however weak. Now then, do not starch thyself in thy precious office with proud ignoring of the worth of thy flock; rejoice in the worth of thy ministry, but at the same time in the church of thy Lord; do not depreciate the church of God because of human appearances or on account of individual members, however numerous, since thou dost claim respect for thy office despite thy sinful person. The dignity of the office and the calling is to be recognized, even if the person in office or called permits himself to become guilty of unworthiness.

What is specifically Christian is this, that thou, called and trained by the Father, inwardly deniest the natural Ego more and more entirely, for the sake of the one and unique person, Jesus Christ.—He who is never satisfied in his morality, but humbly strives and believes and hopes, is near to Christ and belongs to Christ. Christless morality, irreligious virtue, or, as it was more faithfully termed in the last century and still is in this, "godless" virtue, calling and thinking itself "free," has only the outward appearance, the garment, is really foolish pride. Thou canst be a broker or agent of morality, then thy part in it is usufructuary, but thou art no owner of it.—From the fact that thou art "holy," *i. e.*, consecrated to God, accepted by Him the Holy One, follows thy faith, which appropriates and believes what is Divine and holy, more and more inwardly to the internal personality. It is therefore not correct to say: Holiness proceeds from faith in Christ; hence Paul calls them believers, too. Nor is holiness merely the goal of Christian striving; he who has God and Christ, the Holy One, has holiness also; it is not put before us as a goal, far or near, but we, as Christians, are in it, as in an element, a sphere, that it may become ours, be in us, increasing and strengthening itself in us.—The *saint* consecrated to God (ἅγιος) says, first in the consciousness and confession of his faith, however: I am God's! The *believer* (πιστός) says: God is mine! But that we are God's always comes first, then that God is ours.—How well has Paul complemented the salutation of the Old Testament: *Peace be with you* (Judges vi. 23; 1 Sam. xxv. 6, *etc.*), by adding or rather prefixing *grace*, which was not wanting in the Old Testament.

STARKE:—A minister of Christ, a teacher of the Gospel, must be installed by the will of God. Mark this, ye runners, who run of yourselves.—Where grace is, there is peace also, even though it be not felt by a believer in his state of conflict. —Since grace and peace come from Christ as well as from God the Father, Christ must be very God as is the Father.

RIEGER:—A believer is already a saint.—My God! I am Thine; therefore am I holy. Uphold me in faith on Christ Jesus!—The chief possession of the saints and believers is grace and peace. This is from the very first the life of their heart; this distributes to them their daily nourishment and strength, and with this, too, they are equipped even unto the end of their course.

HEUBNER:—The call of God to the ministry gives the proper joy in office.—The Apostolic benediction contains all that is worth wishing for.—SCHENKEL:—Neither the consummation of salvation nor the beginning of faith is to be found outside of fellowship with Christ.—Grace is the ground of our faith, peace the hope of our life.

STIER:—He whom the Lord admits among His called saints, has an inextinguishable spark of faith, that may bring him among the elect and faithful. And if there were left of the church only a lodge in a garden of cucumbers, a cottage in a vineyard, a well-nigh devastated, straitly besieged city, and the rest were as Sodom and Gomorrah—if instead of the Ephesus of the days of Paul and John, there remains only the miserable village of *Aja-soluk:* yet shall the besieged city of God remain His preserved city, until He Himself destroys it, and we would not regard His sacred people as rejected either in their dispersion or in their blindness.—Grace and peace, it is just this which is wanting to those who are away from Christ and without God in the world, aliens from the commonwealth of Israel. Grace and peace, it is this which is ever more and more needful for those, who have obtained precious faith in the righteousness which our God and our Saviour Jesus Christ gives. In this double yet single word we have once more: what proceeds from God and what should be effected in us. The first ground of all holiness is the *grace* of the Eternal One, meeting and preventing us; the final goal of all fidelity in faith is complete peace or entire salvation.

[EADIE:—"In Christ Jesus." The faith of the Ephesian converts rested in Jesus, in calm and permanent repose. It was not a mere external dependence placed *on* Him, but it had convinced itself of His power and love, of His sympathy and merits; it not only knew the strength of His arm, it had also penetrated and felt the throbbing tenderness of His heart—it was therefore *in Him.*—"Grace."—As a wish expressed for the Ephesian church, it does not denote mercy in its general aspect, but that many-sided favor that comes in the form of hope to saints in despondency, of joy to them in sorrow, of patience to them in suffering, of victory to them under assault, and of final triumph to them in the hour of death.—"Peace."—A conscious possession of the Divine favor can alone create and sustain mental tranquility. To use an impressive figure of Scripture, the unsanctified heart resembles "the troubled sea," in constant uproar and agitation—dark, muddy and tempestuous; but the storm subsides, for a voice of power has cried, "Peace, be still," and there is "a great calm:" the lowering clouds are dispelled, and the azure sky smiles on its own reflection in the bosom of the quiet and glassy deep. The favor of God and the felt enjoyment of it, the Apostle wishes to the members of the Ephesian Church.—R.]

---

# II. PART FIRST.

## THE GLORY OF THE CHURCH OF JESUS CHRIST.

CHAPTERS I.—III.

### A. The ground and goal of the church.

CHAP. I. 3–23.

#### 1. *Grateful praise of the decree of grace.*

(CHAP. I. 3–14.)

3 Blessed *be* the God and Father[1] of our Lord Jesus Christ, who hath [omit hath][2]
blessed us with [ἐν, in] all spiritual blessings [blessing][3] in [the] heavenly *places* in
4 Christ: According [even] as he hath chosen [he chose] us in him before the foun-
dation of the world, that we should be holy and without blame before him [;] in
5 love: [omit the colon][4] Having predestinated us unto the adoption of children [unto
adoption] by [through] Jesus Christ to [unto] himself,[5] according to the good
6 pleasure of his will, To [Unto] the praise of the glory of his grace, wherein he hath

7 made us accepted [which[6] he freely bestowed upon us] in the beloved: In whom
we have [the or our] redemption through his blood, the forgiveness of sins [our
8 transgressions],[7] according to the riches[8] of his grace; Wherein he hath abounded
9 [Which he made to abound] toward us in all wisdom and prudence; Having made
known unto [to] us the mystery of his will, according to his good pleasure which
10 he hath [omit hath] purposed in himself: [,] That in [Unto][9] the dispensation of
the fulness of times he might gather together in one [to gather up together] all
things in Christ, both [omit both and supply the things][10] which are in heaven, and
11 [the things] which are on earth; *even* in him: [,] In whom also we have obtained
an [In whom we were also made his][11] inheritance, being [having been] predes-
tinated according to the purpose of him who worketh all things after the counsel
12 of his own [omit own] will: That we should be to [unto] the praise of his glory, who
13 first trusted [we who have before hoped][12] in Christ [or the Christ]. In whom ye
also *trusted*, after that ye heard [In whom ye also, having heard][13] the word of
truth, the gospel of your salvation: in whom also, after that ye believed [in whom
*I say* having also believed], ye were sealed with the Holy Spirit of promise [the
14 Spirit of promise, the holy One], Which [Who][14] is the earnest of our inheritance
until [unto] the redemption of the [his] purchased possession, unto the praise of
his glory.

## TEXTUAL AND GRAMMATICAL.

1 Ver. 3.—B. omits καὶ πατήρ, ℵ. inserts καὶ σωτῆρος [after κυρίου, to complete the well-known phrase], which is disapproved by the later reviser [ℵ.[3]].

2 Ver. 3.—["The aorist here ought certainly to be maintained in translation, as the allusion is to the past act of redemption. The idiom of our language frequently interferes with the regular application of the rule, but it is still no less certain that the English preterite is the nearest equivalent of the Greek aorist." A slavish application of this rule has much marred the version of the *Amer. Bible Union*. This section presents a number of cases where the proper rendering of the Greek tense is a matter of some delicacy, though rarely of great difficulty.—R.]

3 Ver. 3.—[The singular should be retained, as in the Genevan, Bishops', and Rhemish versions. Alford and Ellicott (following the Syriac version) render: *blessing of the Spirit*, but this is a correct interpretation rather than a translation. *With* (E. V.) need not be changed to *in*, but the English reader should be reminded that the Greek preposition is ἐν.—R.]

4 Ver. 4.—[See *Exeg. Notes*.—R.]

5 Ver. 5.—[*Unto adoption through Jesus Christ unto himself;* the variations from the E. V. are all necessary; *the adoption of children* is pleonastic; διά should, as a rule, be rendered *through*, and εἰς *unto*. *Himself* is to be retained, because, although the reading is not αὐτόν but αὐτόν, the reference is to God, and this will not appear if the simple pronoun *Him* is substituted. Ellicott's rendering is peculiar: *having foreordained us for adoption through Jesus Christ into Himself*. He justifies the last preposition by the English idiom "adopt into."—R.]

6 Ver. 6.—ℵ. A. B. have ἧς, corrected in the first to ἐν ᾗ, as D. E. F. G. K. L. read; the former is, however, *lectio difficilior*, and it is more likely that the latter arose from it, than the reverse. [The reading of the *Rec.* (ἐν ᾗ) is found in a great majority of cursives, many versions and fathers; it is adopted by Tischendorf and Ellicott. The other is received by Lachmann, Meyer, Alford. It is very difficult to decide, but the above rendering is based on the reading ἧς.—R.]

7 Ver. 7.—[The emphatic article τῶν before παραπτωμάτων is best rendered by the possessive pronoun *our*, as indeed is often necessary in translating the article from the German. *Transgressions* is more exact than *sins*, and thus the distinction between this verse and Col. i. 14 is maintained.—On τὴν before ἀπολύτρωσιν see *Exeg. Notes*.—R.]

8 Ver. 7.—[Instead of τὸν πλοῦτον (*Rec.*, ℵ.[3] D.[3] K. L.) read τὸ πλοῦτος (ℵ.[1] A. B. D.[1]), which is adopted by Lachmann, Rückert, Tischendorf (see his *Prolegg.* p. lv. 7th ed.), Alford, Ellicott. Comp. Winer, p. 64.—R.]

9 Ver. 10.—[Among the multitude of emendations suggested in regard to this part of ver. 10, I have felt that it was only necessary to adopt this one, which literally translates the preposition εἰς. The phrases, *for*, *with a view to*, *in regard of*, *with reference to*, are not more intelligible than the simple *unto*, providing the pointing be properly altered (as above) to indicate the close connection with "purposed." Ellicott omits even the comma.—*Dispensation* was once an improper translation, but is perhaps now the nearest equivalent to the Greek οἰκονομία; *fulfilment* might be substituted for *fulness*, and *seasons* for *times*, but the gain would be slight. The omission of *that* requires a change in the finite construction of the remainder of the verse.—R.]

10 Ver. 10.—[The τε after τα in the *Rec.* is to be rejected, having scarcely any support (ℵ.[3]). A much more difficult question is, whether we should read ἐπί or ἐν before τοῖς οὐρανοῖς. For the first, which is very unusual in this connection, the authorities are: ℵ.[1] B. D. L. and 40 cursives, accepted by Lachmann, Rückert, Meyer, Alford and others; for the second (*Rec.*), A. F. G. K., majority of cursives, fathers, accepted by Griesbach, Scholz, Harless, De Wette, Tischendorf, Ellicott, Eadie, Braune. If the former be adopted, it must be as an ἅπαξ λεγόμενον; and is so remarkable a one, that we may well incline to the latter, especially as a careless copyist would find ἐπί so close at hand. Comp. *Exeg. Notes*.—R.]

11 Ver. 11.—ℵ. B. K. L. [all modern editors]: ἐκληρώθημεν. A. D. E. F. G.: ἐκλήθημεν. which is the easier reading. [Braune takes this verb to mean: *made an inheritance*, not *obtain an inheritance*, as in E. V.—R.]

12 Ver. 12.—[For a justification of this translation now generally adopted, see *Exeg. Notes*.—R.]

13 Ver. 13.—[This view of the construction is the simplest, and most defensible. The participles: ἀκούσαντες—πιστεύσαντες, are best rendered by the English past participles; *after that, etc.* (E. V.), is, too, pronounced in its temporal reference.—R.]

14 Ver. 14.—ὅς according to ℵ. D. E. K. is *lectio difficilior* over against ὅ, A. B. F. [The latter is the reading of the *Rec.*, Lachmann, Rückert, Alford. The former is accepted by Tischendorf, Ellicott, Meyer, who remarks on the readiness with which the latter reading would arise, owing to the neuter πνεῦμα.—R.]

## EXEGETICAL AND CRITICAL.

*Summary.*—It is clear that ver. 3 *opens* the section with thanksgiving and praise for the blessing of Redemption. But in this wonderful chain of clauses (vers. 4-14), so interwoven and intertwined, the divisions and groupings are not easily perceived, so that expositors hold very different opinions. But it is evident, that the three times repeated: "unto the praise of the glory of his grace" (ver. 6), "unto the praise of his glory" (ver. 12), "unto the praise of his glory" (ver. 14), form conclusions, receiving, it is true, in the flow of language in vers. 6 and 12, qualifications for amplification and transition. Accordingly we find in vers. 4-6, the *first* foundation for praise: *the election of eternal mercy;* in vers. 7-12, the *second: the carrying out of the eternal decree;* vers. 13, 14, the *third: the personal appropriation of salvation.* Our view is directed to the *Father* before all time, the *Son* in time, the *Spirit* in eternity. So STIER, who, however, artificially divides each section again into three parts, according to *ground, course* and *goal.*

[ALFORD, who follows STIER, gives this summary: "The preliminary *idea of the Church,* set forth in the form of an *ascription of praise,* vers. 3-14:—thus arranged: vers. 3-6, the *Father,* in His eternal love, has chosen us to holiness (ver. 4), ordained us to Sonship (ver. 5), bestowed grace on us in the Beloved; vers. 7-12, in the *Son,* we have—redemption according to the riches of His grace (ver. 7), knowledge of the mystery of His will (vers. 8, 9), inheritance under Him the one Head (vers. 10-12); vers. 13-14, through the *Spirit* we are sealed, by hearing the word of salvation (ver. 13), by receiving the earnest of our inheritance, to the redemption of the purchased possession (ver. 14).—Dr. HODGE is less satisfactory, see ver. 4 for his exhaustive analysis of vers. 4-6.—R.]

HARLESS: I. The objective act of God, *a*) in the eternal decree of the Redemption of believers, *b*) actualized through the death of His Son (1-7: *παραπτωμάτων*); II. The revelation of this act in the word (7–10); III. The subjective actualization of this act in the Redemption of individuals (11-14).—MEYER takes the salvation (ver. 3) as *a*) foreordained (vers. 4, 5), *b*) effected (vers. 6, 7), *c*) made known (vers. 8-10), *d*) actually appropriated (ver. 11), by Jews (ver. 12), as well as by those who had been heathen (vers. 13, 14).—Others otherwise, always with an overlooking of the incisa so readily perceived.—[Dr. LANGE, who suggests the frequent occurrence of liturgical forms in Paul's Epistles, finds in these verses the most striking example. See his liturgical reading, *Romans,* p. 26.—R.]

Ver. 3. *General opening.*

**Blessed be** [*εὐλογητός*].*—First of all, we must notice the play upon the words: *εὐλογητός—ὁ εὐλογήσας—ἐν—εὐλογία:* The words *εὐλογεῖν* and *εὐλογία* have a two-fold meaning, as in *benedicere* and *benedictio,* to bless and blessing, בָּרַךְ (בְּרָכָה), to *praise,* to laud and to *endow,* all to be traced back to one sense, *to speak or promise good.* So *εὐλογεῖν,* Luke i. 64 (*ἐλάλει εὐλογῶν τὸν θεόν*); comp. xxiv. 53 (*αἰνοῦντες τὸν θεόν*); Jas. iii. 9 (*ἐν αὐτῇ εὐλογοῦμεν τὸν κυρίον*); *εὐλογία,* Rom. xvi. 18 (*διὰ τῆς χρηστολογίας καὶ εὐλογίας*), *decora oratio,* praise, Gal. iii. 8, 9, 14; Heb. vi. 7. The German word *Segen,* blessing, is derived from *signum,* sign, *i. e.,* the sign of the cross in pronouncing the blessing; from this is derived *segnen,* to bless (see JUETTING, *Bibl. Wörterbuch,* p. 171 ff.), and this means not only to wish well (Ps. x. 3; Isa. lxv. 16) in coming (1 Sam. xiii. 10) or in going (Acts xx. 1), but to praise, to thank (1 Cor. xiv. 16; x. 16) and also to assign or impart good or goods (Gen. xii. 2; xxvii. 34, 36). The meaning, to praise, to thank, does indeed become the prominent one, where it is applied to men with regard to God, since man has only words, can only *εὖ λέγειν;* as does that of allotting good or goods, where God's dealings towards men are in question, since with God there is no resting in words, His words are or become deeds. BENGEL: *Antanaclasis: aliter benedixit Deus nobis, aliter nos benedicimus illi.* THEODORET: *εἰδέναι προσήκει, ὡς εὐλογοῦντες μὲν οἱ ἄνθρωποι τὸν θεὸν λόγους αὐτῷ προσφέρουσι μόνους, ἔργῳ δὲ αὐτὸν εὐεργετῆσαι οὐ δύνανται, ὁ δέ θεὸς εὐλογῶν βεβαιοῖ τοὺς λόγους τῷ ἔργῳ καὶ παντοδαπὴν παρέχει φόραν ἀγαθῶν τοῖς εὐλογουμένοις.* It is otherwise, when Jethro says of God: בָּרוּךְ יְהוָֹה (Exod. xviii. 10), or Laban to Eliezer, (Gen. xxiv. 31): בְּרוּךְ יְהוָֹה "thou blessed of the Lord" (comp. xxvi. 29; Matth. xxv. 34, where Jesus as Judge will say to His own: "Come, ye blessed of my Father;" Luke i. 28, where Mary is called *κεχαριτωμένη,* "highly favored," in the same sense). Both meanings appear here in our passage, where the Apostle praises and blesses God (*εὐλογητός*), who has blessed us (*ὁ εὐλογήσας ἐν εὐλογίᾳ*).

The *form* here chosen should be noticed, *εὐλογητός,* which is always applied to God,* not *εὐλογημένος,* since for Him there is no time when He was not and will not hereafter be "blessed," so that God is *κατ' ἐξοχὴν ὁ εὐλογητός* (Mark xiv. 61). Nor is this=worthy of praise, to be praised, but like בָּרוּךְ in a purely passive sense, as the promiscuous use of both forms requires. The *position* of the words also, at the beginning, shows that the emphasis rests upon it; in Rom. ix. 5 the *Person* is put first for the same reason. [So ELLICOTT.] On the sense of *εὐλογητός* it may be remarked, that Paul begins nearly all his Epistles with praise and thanksgiving to God, and that too with a reference to the churches and persons to which, the circumstances in which, and the purpose with which, he is writing; with *εὐλογητός* as here, only in 2 Cor. i. 3 (so 1 Pet. i. 3), usually with *εὐχαριστεῖν,* Rom. i. 8; 1 Cor. i. 4; Phil. i. 3; Col. i. 3; 1 Thess. i. 2; 2 Thess. i. 3; Philem. 4, with *χάριν ἔχειν,* 2 Tim. i. 3. As the received "grace" is returned again in thanksgiving, so is the *εὐλογία* received from the Lord, in the *εὐλογητός* from the praising creature: God is saluted, never blessed, with His own blessing (STIER).

**The God and Father of our Lord Jesus Christ**—*ὁ θεὸς καὶ πατὴρ τοῦ κυρίου ἡμῶν Ἰησοῦ Χριστοῦ.*—Exactly as in 2 Cor. i. 3; 1 Pet. i. 3. Comp. Rom. xv. 6; 2 Cor. xi. 31; Col. i. 3; Rev. i. 6. It is most natural, since the passage does not read: *ὁ θεός, ὁ πατὴρ τοῦ κυρίου,* to join the genitive *τοῦ κυρίου,* "of our Lord," with *θεός,* "God," as well as with *πατήρ,* "Father" (JEROME, THEOPHYLACT, RUECK-

* [The verb is usually omitted in this and similar forms of doxology. "Understand *εἴη* (Job i. 21; Ps. cxii. 2) or *ἔστω* (2 Chron. ix. 8)." So ALFORD, ELLICOTT. It is from this word that Dr. LANGE derives his view respecting Paul's use of liturgical forms; comp. Rom. ix. 5; and the O. T. passages cited above.—R.]

* [This is true in N. T. usage. In the LXX. it is almost universally true, though in Gen. xxvi. 29; Deut. vii. 14; 1 Sam. xv. 13; xxv. 33. as ELLICOTT remarks, *εὐλογητός* is applied to man. The distinction is sufficiently marked to justify Dr. BRAUNE's remark. See HARLESS *in loco.*—R.]

ERT, STIER), as the genitive is not necessarily required as an explanatory addition to πατήρ. It is found without any qualification, in ver. 20; 1 Cor. xv. 24: τῷ θεῷ καὶ πατρί; vi. 23; 2 Tim. i. 2; Gal. i. 1: θεοῦ πατρός; 1 Thess. i. 1: θεῷ πατρί. Besides in iii. 14 many MSS. read: τὸν πατέρα τοῦ κυρίου ἡμῶν Ἰησοῦ Χριστοῦ (though ℵ. A. B. C. omit the genitive), while the established reading in i. 17 is: ὁ θεὸς τοῦ κυρίου ἡμῶν Ἰησοῦ Χριστοῦ, so that the Apostle, as this very Epistle shows, could join this qualifying phrase to "God" as well as to "Father." On this account MEYER is incorrect, in applying the genitive to πατήρ, and not to θεός, on the ground that the former idea alone demands such complementing, and not the latter; nor should he have laid so great weight upon the notion, that the expression: *the God of Christ*, as an isolated one, has not obtained that currency, which it must have done, had it been found in this "solemn formula" also, since Christ's word on the cross (Matth. xxvii. 46: θεέ μου, θεέ μου) and on the day of His resurrection (John xx. 17: ἀναβαίνω πρὸς τὸν πατέρα μου καὶ πατέρα ὑμῶν καὶ θεόν μου καὶ θεὸν ὑμῶν; comp. Rev. ii. 7; iii. 12) suffice to justify this expression and this connection in our "solemn formula." We find too in B. the reading ὁ θεὸς τοῦ κυρίου, κ. τ. λ. Nor can it be asserted, with HARLESS, that if the following genitive belonged to the first substantive also, the reading should necessarily be: ὁ θεός τε καὶ πατήρ; MEYER refers very properly to 1 Pet. ii. 25. Καί binds what is homogeneous; τε adds something accessory (WINER, pp. 404, 408); *καὶ conjungit, τε adjungit*, as HERMANN says.* To be God and to be Father are not ideas which exclude each other, nor do they appear as two, but as a unity; He is here praised, who is not only the God of the Incarnate One, but is also the Father of this Lord, of the Only Begotten, whom He has given; thus is indicated the God-man by whom the blessings of Redemption are mediated. It was not necessary for THEODORET to say: δηλῶν, ὡς ἡμῶν μέν ἐστι θεός, τοῦ δὲ κυρίου ἡμῶν πατήρ. Practically this generally Christian formula has taken the place of the Jewish: the God of Abraham, Isaac and Jacob, even if it were not so intended by the Apostle or Apostles, as RUECKERT supposes.

**Who blessed us** [ὁ εὐλογήσας ἡμᾶς].—The active, over against the passive (εὐλογητός) denotes efficient, active blessing, the aorist the historical fact in the existence and condition of the Church.† Hence "us" should be taken in its wider meaning and applied to Christians, and should not be limited to the Apostle (KOPPE), who afterwards (ver. 15: ἐγώ) begins to speak of himself and his experiences, nor to the Jewish Christians, who are first thought of in ver. 11 (comp. ver. 13); so strong rather is the feeling of the fellowship under the blessing of God, that the Apostle, as the genuine Apostle to the Gentiles, includes with himself and the Apostles as his people, all men, who have become or will become Christians.

**With all spiritual blessings**, ἐν πάσῃ εὐλογίᾳ πνευματικῇ.—This denotes the sphere into which He in blessing has transferred them; He has so placed us in blessing, that we are surrounded, overflowed thereby, and ἐν πάσῃ εὐλογίᾳ. According to WINER (p. 105) this means *every* blessing; πᾶσα ἡ εὐλογία would be the *whole* blessing; see the instructive passage, Rom. iii. 19. There is no variety of blessing, which God has not bestowed upon us, but the entire fulness of the blessing, so that we have nothing more to receive, has not yet been conferred upon us. Comp. Rom. xv. 29: "in the fulness of the blessing of Christ."

The adjective "spiritual" limits the manifold variety to the domain of the spiritual, to what the Holy Spirit effects and imparts. It is recalled also in what follows respecting the adoption (ver. 5) the redemption and forgiveness of sins (ver. 7), the revelation (ver. 9) and thus is expounded the riches of that spiritual blessing, which we already possess, but which we ever need yet more. There is no manner of occasion for supposing an antithesis to the earthly blessings and promises of the Israelites (CHRYSOSTOM, GROTIUS and others), or to their typical possessions and the vain ones of the heathen (SCHÖTTGEN); nor should "spiritual" be explained as=*qui ad animum pertinet* (ERASMUS, ROSENMUELLER); our spirit of itself still belongs to the σάρξ. [See *Romans*, p. 234 f.]* The Apostle is treating of the blessings promised in Joel iii. 1, which are no longer merely promised, since their fulfilment is expressed in "who hath blessed us."

**In heavenly places**, ἐν τοῖς ἐπουρανίοις.

1. Besides this passage the phrase is found in ver. 20; ii. 6; iii. 10; vi. 12, and in all, even in the last named, with a local sense; in the domain of the heavenly; hence in accordance with the nature of the matter, it is not to be taken in any coarse, sensuous signification as measurable, limitable space, but as domain, region.

2. The word itself has in the preposition ἐπί a local reference, like ἐπίγειος (1 Cor. xv. 40), but as this is to be distinguished from καταγειος, καταχθόνιος (Phil. ii. 10), so is the former from ὑπερουράνιος.

3. Τὰ ἐπουράνια at all events is not to be taken as=ὁ οὐρανός, οἱ οὐρανοί or=βασιλεία τῶν οὐρανῶν, but designates more indefinitely, in general, what belongs to heaven in contrast with what

* [MEYER'S view: "God who is also the Father of our Lord Jesus Christ," would require, if a strict construction be insisted on: ὁ θεός, ὁ καὶ πατήρ. as ALFORD intimates. ELLICOTT admits that there are no grammatical or doctrinal objections to the view defended above, but prefers the other, mainly on the ground that the phrase "the God of Christ" is singular. HODGE and EADIE join the genitive to both nouns. —R.]

† [EADIE at first took this aorist as marking "a customary or repeated act," an interpretation he seems to have given up in his 2d edition, where, however, a trace of it is found in a footnote which has no corresponding number in his text. To take it as having the sense of the present, which HODGE seems to favor (though his view would require the perfect in Greek), is untenable. The aorist participle, retaining as usual its aoristic force, "refers to the counsels of the Father as graciously completed in the Redemption."—R.]

* [ALFORD is fully justified in saying: "πνευματικός in the N. T. always implies the working of the Holy Spirit, never bearing merely our modern inaccurate sense of spiritual as opposed to bodily." HODGE apparently accepts both, which is not allowable, even if the correct meaning be given the greater prominence. EADIE concedes the latter meaning in the New Testament, but improperly in every passage cited. He justly opposes the exclusive reference of our passage to *charismata* (WHITBY), alluding to the transitory character of these gifts. THEODORET: "The blessings referred to here are, the hope of the resurrection, the promises of immortality, the kingdom of heaven in reversion, and the dignity of adoption."—R.]

belongs to and is on earth, as appears from vi. 12, where the contest with the powers of darkness "in heavenly places" is spoken of in antithesis to the contest with flesh and blood.

4. The connection of the phrase ἐν τοῖς ἐπουρανίοις with ἐν εὐλογίᾳ πνευματικῇ is demanded by the fact that the latter is joined with εὐλογήσας and dependent on it, and hence the latter cannot belong to the verb as a closer qualification of the act of blessing. Accordingly this added phrase says, that every spiritual blessing, which we have received, springs from a higher world, is to be sought in a heavenly region and thence to be obtained. [ELLICOTT with his usual exactness presents the view here upheld and now generally received; he takes the phrase as "defining broadly and comprehensively the region and sphere where our true home is (Phil. iii. 20), where our hope is laid up (Col. i. 5), and whence the blessings of the Spirit, the ἡ δωρεὰ ἡ ἐπουράνιος (Heb. vi. 4) truly come." We may add from ALFORD: "Materially we are yet in the body: but in the Spirit, we are in heaven—only waiting for the redemption of the body to be entirely and literally there."—R.]

Accordingly it is incorrect:

*a*) To understand by τὰ ἐπουράνια *bona* not *loca*, with CHRYSOSTOM, THEODORET, LUTHER and many others; the idea of *possessions* is already found in εὐλογία (against RUECKERT, STIER). Nor is CALVIN right in saying: *Non multum refert, subaudias* LOCIS *an* BONIS; *tantum voluit indicare præstantiam gratiæ, quæ per Christum nobis confertur, quia scilicet non in mundo, sed in cœlo et vita æterna nos faciat bonos.*

*b*) GROTIUS is in error, in referring it, to a place indeed, but to the *cœlum summum* in contrast to the *regio astrifera.*

*c*) The rendering and explanation: *in heaven* (MEYER, RUECKERT, HARLESS, STIER, SCHENKEL and others), is not exact, passes beyond the word itself; still less is it admissible to refer it to the kingdom of heaven, the kingdom of heaven on earth, the church (ERNESTI, TELLER and others). [With more definiteness it is explained by HODGE: *cœlum gratiæ*, the kingdom of grace here on earth, the heavenly state into which the believer is introduced; a view to which EADIE inclines.—R.]

*d*) To follow BEZA in joining the phrase to God, is as unjustifiable and inadmissible, as to accept with KOPPE the aorist for the future, because the believers walk in heaven already in a certain sense (Phil. iii. 20, to which JEROME and BEZA refer), or *quia non in mundo, sed in cœlo et vita æterna nos faciat beatos* (CALVIN), or *quia hæc (dona) nos et spe et jure in cœlis collocant* (GROTIUS). The explanation of HOMBERG, that it is =εὐλογίᾳ πνευματικῇ καὶ ἐπουρανίῳ is altogether arbitrary and groundless.

**In Christ**, ἐν Χριστῷ, indicates the mediation of the blessing (*Segnen*) which consists in spiritual blessing (*Segen*). Comp. 2 Cor. v. 18 f. It is not *propter Christum* (MORUS, FLATT, MEYER: "in Him was contained the ground why God blessed us," which is after all equivalent to: for Christ's sake). SCHENKEL: "Outside of the fellowship with the Son there is no part in the spiritual blessing of the Father (Rom. viii. 9 f.)." It cannot be overlooked in this Epistle, that this phrase: ἐν Χριστῷ, is "the centre and heart beat of the Apostle's view." It is repeated in ver. 4, 6, 7, 10, 11, 12, 13 ff.; with the Apostle it stands in the same category as: in Adam, in Abraham. Herein (ἐν Χριστῷ) is to be found the difference between the Christian and Jewish Churches, the New Testament and Old Testament people of God. In the case of the former, the blessing was not wanting, nor the "spiritual," for the law is spiritual (Rom. vii. 14); even the "every" was not lacking, since God's Word was there, the forgiveness of sins, though in incipiency, in types, in shadow (Heb. viii. 5: σκιᾷ τῶν ἐπουρανίων, Col. ii. 17); nor yet is ἐν τοῖς ἐπουρανίοις, "heavenly places," altogether new, as though the New Testament first found place and voice there, first established itself there, while the Old Testament pointed only to the earthly Canaan (against STIER).

[ALFORD follows Stier, in accepting a reference to the Trinity in the threefold ἐν, but ELLICOTT's treatment of the phrases seems more exact: "Εὐλογήσας contains the predication of *time* (Donaldson, *Gr.* § 574 sq.), ἐν π. εὐλογίᾳ πνευμ. the predication of *manner*, more exactly defined by the *local* predication ἐν τοῖς ἐπουρανίοις, while ἐν Χριστῷ is that mystical predication which, as Stier well observes, 'is the very soul of this Epistle,' and involves all other conceptions in itself." This accords well with Braune's view, that it expresses the distinctively Christian character of the blessing here spoken of.—R.]

THE FIRST FOUNDATION OF THE PRAISE; VERS. 4–6:

*The Election of eternal mercy.* [DR. HODGE thus analyzes these verses: "Of these (spiritual gifts for which the Apostle blesses God) the first in order and the source of all the others is election, ver. 4. This election is 1. Of individuals. 2. In Christ. 3. It is from eternity. 4. It is to holiness, and to the dignity of sons of God. 5. It is founded on the sovereign pleasure of God (vers. 4, 5). 6. Its final object is the glory of God, or the manifestation of His grace, ver. 6." This agrees with Braune's view, except that he substitutes "the church" for "individuals" under (1), viewing the church as an organism made up of individuals. See below and also *Doctr. Note* 3.—R.]

Ver. 4. **Even as he chose us in him before the foundation of the world** [καθὼς ἐξελέξατο ἡμᾶς ἐν αὐτῷ πρὸ καταβολῆς κόσμου].—Καθώς marks a relation, indeed a conformity of two facts, which correspond to one another: the εὐλογεῖν has taken place in conformity with the ἐκλέγεσθαι; He has blessed entirely as He has decreed in the choosing, the election. So MEYER also. That analogy is in question, according to which from the fact of the blessing a conclusion may be drawn with respect to the election. It is not merely indicated that there is an internal connection between the election and the blessing, but it is definitely stated that this carrying out *corresponds* to the eternal decree of God. BENGEL: *electio respondet, et eam subsequitur, benedictio, et patefacit.* Hence καθώς is not used here as a designation of causality (MORUS, RUECKERT) [HODGE: because], as it is in other passages (WINER, p. 417: [*quoniam*] *quippe, siquidem*); HARLESS takes it as an argumentative particle (=inasmuch) and says that it is related to καθότι, the latter however designating the *causa*, the former the *modus* (Rom. i. 28; 1 Cor. i. 6). [MEYER takes it as argumentative; ALFORD and ELLICOTT as explaining and expanding the foregoing, the latter admitting its causal force at times; EADIE is most exact: "These spiritual blessings are conferred on us, not merely because God chose us, but they are given in perfect harmony with His eternal purpose." However true it may be that "election is the cause or source of all subsequent benefits" (HODGE), it is hardly safe to found such a statement on the particle καθώς.—R.]

Ἐ ξ ε λ έ ξ α τ ο=*He chose us out for Himself;** Paul uses it only three times elsewhere (all in 1 Cor. i. 27, 28). The verb ἐκλέγεσθαι corresponds entirely to the Hebrew בָּחַר, as ἐκλεκτός=בָּחִיר. In the middle form it designates, both in the Old and New Testaments, an act of God, "by virtue of which some rather than others especially belong to God" (HARLESS). Although HOFMANN (*Schriftbeweis* I. p. 223 ff.) will only admit, that in this word respect is had to that on account of which one is chosen, or respect to him who on that account is chosen or accepted, and that the stress is laid each time upon that which the chosen one thus becomes, and not upon *the antithesis* to those who do not *become* this, yet he perceives in the preposition a *preference*, even if only a preference above a mass to which he would otherwise belong. He refers to οἱ ἐκλεκτοὶ ἄγγελοι (1 Tim. v. 21), ὁ υἱὸς τοῦ θεοῦ ὁ ἐκλελεγμένος (Luke ix. 35), ὁ Χριστὸς τοῦ θεοῦ ὁ ἐκλεκτός (Luke xxiii. 35), remarking, that the angels are thus designated as taken by God into His service, and that Christ is not elected out of the sum of humanity, to become what the rest should not become, but chosen to be, what the rest are not. Ἐκλέγεσθαι, does then still mark a preference, a *distinction from* others, who *are* not what the chosen *are*, even if not an *opposition to* those, who do not *become* this.† Respecting the others, in preference to whom the elect belong to God, nothing is indicated here,—whether they are not chosen after all, or no longer do or can belong to the elect; just as it is not said concerning the elect, that they cannot fall away from such a relation to God. Since in 1 Pet. i. 1, the church is termed "elect" and in the conclusion (v. 13) "the Church at Babylon *elected together with you*," and "elect of God" (Col. iii. 12), "for the elect's sakes" (2 Tim. ii. 10), "God's elect" (Rom. viii. 33), etc., are applied to individual Christians, because and in so far as they are members of the Church of Christ, it may be concluded, that the act of election does not concern individuals as its immediate objects, as HOFMANN thinks. It is true that the κόσμος, out of which they are chosen (Jno. xv. 19), is not a sum of individuals, a *multitude;* it is rather an ethical conception. Still less is the Church a plurality, a *colluvies*, it is an organism, a whole. Yet God does have regard to the individuals, with Him the individual, the member, is not lost in the whole. Accordingly the explanation of HARLESS is to be sustained, only it must be remembered, that the *individuals* are not to be thought of as without connection, severed, by themselves alone, or the *others* as those who may not and shall not belong to God. HOFMANN's opposition is right only against this unjustifiable interpolation. It is evident that Paul could apply the word "chosen" only to himself and the members of the Church, because only in the case of these was this fact *cognizable*, and must be, or at least could be, *perceptible* to individuals. Hence we should here, with FRANK (*Theologie der Form. Con.* iv. p. 177), think of the world merely, out of which Christians are taken by virtue of their effectual calling, as in 1 Pet. i. 1; Jas. ii. 5; 1 Cor. i. 27 f., not however of the totality of those called, from whom the elect, as more numerous (Matt. xx. 16; xxii. 14), are to be distinguished. See further in *Doctr. Note* 3. Inadmissible, therefore, is the explanation: *præcipuo in nos amore Deus fuit*, because ἐκλέγεσθαι is also=*imprimis amare vel imprimis beneficiis ornare* (MORUS). Comp. 2 Thess. ii. 13. It is very erroneous to suppose (RUECKERT), that Paul transferred the faith of his nation, respecting the preference of their race to all the nations of the earth, to those who accepted Christianity with joy, and regarded these as the number chosen by God.

The position of the verb emphasizes this electing act of God as the main thing. It is then further defined.

*First*, there is added a designation of the *objects*, ἡ μ ᾶ ς, **US**. By this is meant the Church of Christ, the *congregatio sanctorum*, the "saints," who at the time make up the people of God, in whom the election, consummated in the calling, is perceptible and manifest. About the conduct of individuals, their faith, its degree or perfection, nothing is said, just as little as was expressed or indicated in ἁγίοις (ver. 1). Accordingly the reference is not to individuals in themselves, to the sum of individuals at that time, but to the Church and its growth externally and internally, yet in such a way that each individual may refer it to himself.* RICHTER, therefore, correctly remarks: "God chooses for Himself, out of all, *before* others and *for* others." But it

* [ALFORD prefers to render the verb: *selected*, as best indicating the middle sense, and the choosing *out of* the world. See ELLICOTT *in loco* on this word.—R.]

† [EADIE also discusses HOFMANN's view, which is simply this, that the election is only a choosing *for* and *unto* something, not a choosing *out of*. MEYER says most emphatically regarding HOFMANN's position: "This is impossible from the *notion* of the word. A reference to *others*, to whom the chosen ones would still have belonged without the ἐκλογή, the verb ἐκλέγεσθαι *always* has, and *as a logical necessity* must have it." How true this is, will appear from the unsatisfactory and confusing character of all attempts to explain away this reference.—R.]

* [EBRARD (*Christliche Dogmatik*, § 560) denies the individual reference in the verb ἐκλέγ.. but, as EADIE well remarks: "The choice of a multitude is simply the choice of each individual composing it. That multitude may be regarded as a unity by God, but to Him it is a unity of definite elements or members. On the Divine side the elect, whatever their number, are a unity, and are so described—πᾶν ὃ δέδωκέ μοι, John vi. 39; πᾶν ὃ δέδωκας αὐτῷ, John xvii. 2—a totality viewed by Omniscience as one; but on the human side, the elect are the whole company of believers, but thus individualized—πᾶς ὁ θεωρῶν τὸν υἱὸν καὶ πιστεύων, John vi. 40." Paul says so distinctly that *God chose us out*, as to put men at their wits' end to make Him say anything else.—R.]

is also correct to say: *Sic nos quoque in Christo eramus, priusquam mundus fieret, vigore scilicet electionis æternæ* (MUSCULUS).

*Second qualification:* definition of *modality*, **in Him**, ἐν αὐτῷ, viz., Christ. By this our election is more closely defined and limited: Christ the Person, in whom we are chosen, the life-sphere, the life-element, in which we are the objects of the Divine election. HARLESS may be correct, in saying that it is first stated in what follows, how He has chosen us in Him, but he is incorrect in rejecting all closer definitions of expositors here as *interpolated*, even if they correspond with what follows. BEZA (*in ipso videlicet adoptandos*) is very near the true explanation, but his view is more limited than the subsequent context authorizes. Our union, our external and internal connection, with Christ is marked as the modality of our election. But the act of choice is asserted as a fact: in Him He has chosen us, so that as humanity was made in Adam, as the people of Israel was separated in Abraham, so the Church was chosen in Christ; not, however, that He has merely *determined* to choose us. Accordingly it is entirely improper to read ἐν ἀυτῷ (Alex., MORUS, HOLZHAUSEN), nor is it = εἰς Χριστόν (Ethiop. Vers.), or = δι' αὐτοῦ, τουτέστι διὰ τῆς εἰς αὐτὸν πίστεως (THEOPHYLACT and others), or *per Christum et Christi merita prævisa* (A-LAPIDE, BULLINGER), or *propter Christum* (GLASSIUS, FLATT). Finally, it is arbitrary and incorrect to join ἐν αὐτῷ with ἡμᾶς, since ὄντας is wanting and εἶναι ἡμᾶς ἁγίους follows.

[OLSHAUSEN, ELLICOTT: "In Christ, as the head and representative of spiritual, as Adam was the representative of natural humanity." "In the proper and final sense this can be said only of His faithful ones, His Church, who are incorporated in Him by the Spirit. But in any sense, all God's election is *in* HIM only" (ALFORD). HODGE: "In Christ, *i. e.*, as united to Him in the covenant of redemption;" on the ground of the federal union which precedes the actual union. So EADIE. MEYER is less exact: "The divine act of our election has in Christ its *determining ground.*" "*Outside* this connection of the divine decree of election with Christ we would *not* be chosen; but *in Christ* there lay for God the *causa meritoria* of our election." This is really equivalent to *propter Christum.*—R.]

*Third qualification:* a *temporal* definition, **before the foundation of the world**, πρὸ καταβολῆς κόσμου. Used by Paul only here, but found in John xvii. 24; 1 Pet. i. 20. In Matt. xxv. 34; Luke xi. 50; Heb. iii. 4: ἀπὸ καταβολῆς κόσμου; Matt. xiii. 35: ἀπὸ καταβολῆς. The preposition πρὸ denotes that the election took place before the creation, and, since καταβολή designates the foundation, the groundwork, before the beginning of the carrying out of the well-ordered plan of creation. Thus the reference to the eternity preceding time is made very strong,* stronger than in πρὸ τῶν αἰώνων (1 Cor. ii. 7; comp. 2 Tim. i. 9; Rom. xvi. 25; Col. i. 26; Eph. iii. 9, 11). The election precedes the creation: the fulfilment of the former is justified in creation and its history, in the history of the world. HARLESS: "The plainest parallel is 2 Tim. i. 9: 'who hath saved us, and called us with an holy calling, not according to our works, but according to His own purpose and grace, which was given us in Christ Jesus before the world began.'" OLSHAUSEN (with STIER also) properly rejects the idea of a real, individual existence of believers before the creation in the Divine mind, but Christ's existence with the Father before the creation of the world is unmistakably indicated (STIER). BENGEL: *Hæc præsupponunt æternitatem filii Dei, namque filius, ante mundum factum erat objectum amoris paterni non futurum tantummodo, sed jam tum præsens,* John xvii. 5, 24. [ALFORD (after STIER): "How utterly irreconcilable pantheism is with this, God's election before laying the foundation of the world, of His people in His Son."—R.]

**That we should be holy and without blame before him** [εἶναι ἡμᾶς ἁγίους καὶ ἀμώμους κατενώπιον αὐτοῦ].—The infinitive εἶναι ἡμᾶς adds a supplement to the previous clause, to the phrase ἡμᾶς ἐν αὐτῷ in particular, and is to be taken as epexegetical (WINER, p. 298), giving prominence to the end, purpose and result of the election. The position of εἶναι marks the existence, the actualized reality aimed at in the pretemporal, eternal choice. Chap. iii. 4, 6 (ἐν τῷ μυστηρίῳ τοῦ Χριστοῦ—εἶναι τὰ ἔθνη, κ. τ. λ.) is similar.

Whether we are to understand the then present realization, just begun, or the consummation, begun in the church militant, or the completed reality in the church triumphant, cannot be determined from the adjectives "holy and without blame," but must be found in the phrase κατενώπιον αὐτοῦ, "before Him." It is not necessary to write αὑτοῦ, with HARLESS, STIER and others. BENGEL has remarked (*App. ad Matt.* i. 21), and TISCHENDORF [*Præf. N. T.*, p. 58 f. ed. 7], corroborates it, that before αυτοῦ αυτῷ, αυτόν we constantly find ἀπ', ὑπ', μετ', ἐπ', κατ', never ἀφ', ὑφ', μεθ', ἐφ', καθ', so that in the New Testament the reflexive form αὑτοῦ is never used, but in its stead ἑαυτοῦ. Thus too it happens that αὐτός is referred in quick succession to different subjects, as Mark viii. 22; ix. 27–29 (WINER, pp. 141, 143*). From the Apostle's point of view αὐτοῦ is quite correct, and to be understood of God, even though ἐν αὐτῷ refers to Christ. To the phrase κατενώπιον αὐτοῦ corresponds the Hebrew לִפְנֵי יְהוָה, *coram Deo.* According to this we must accept a reference to the present life, and not to the Judgment. The context at all events gives no support for the reference to the Judgment, which He will hold at the end of days. The parallel passage, Col. i. 22: "to present holy and unblamable and unreprovable in His sight," as well as the "now" (ver. 21), and "if at least ye continue" (ver. 23) refer

---

* [ELLICOTT says that this phrase "here serves to define the archetypal character of the New Dispensation, and the wide gulf that separated the πρόθεσις πρὸ χρόνων αἰωνίων (2 Tim. i. 9) of God with respect to Christians, from His temporal ἐκλογή of the Jews."—R.]

* [The question respecting the use of αὐτοῦ is discussed on this page of WINER'S *Grammar*. The sweeping assertion that it is never used, is not accepted by WINER. It appears, however, that under the influence of GRIESBACH, this pointing became too frequent, the tendency now being against it. ELLICOTT says: "The distinction, however, between the proper use of these two forms cannot be rigorously defined."—R.]

definitely to the present state.* This is confirmed by a comparison with Jude 24: "to present you faultless before the presence of His glory with exceeding joy." We must evidently apply this to the Judgment before God in eternity, but the expression is modified in accordance with this meaning. Hence STIER is mistaken in regarding our passage as applicable "to the last flaming glance of the holy Judge, who can and will be the perfectly righteous and eternal beatifying God alone (Heb. xii. 23)." SCHENKEL too is not satisfied with the reminder that He is the knower of hearts, but refers to His great Judgment day.

[MEYER renders this phrase: *judice Deo*, in connection with his view of the forensic reference of the adjectives "holy and without blame." But the reference to sanctification is to be preferred, and hence if "before Him" does not refer to the last Judgment, it must mean: *vere, sincere* (BEZA, ELLICOTT; so EADIE). ALFORD: "In the deepest verity of our being, thoroughly penetrated by the Spirit of holiness, bearing His searching eye; but at the same time implying an especial nearness to His presence and dearness to Him—and bearing a foretaste of the time when the elect shall be ἐνώπιον τοῦ θρονοῦ τοῦ θεοῦ, Rev. vii. 15."—R.]

With our view then "holy and unblamable" cannot of course mean the complete holiness, which is the original end of the first choosing, as its attained goal before the throne of God, as STIER thinks, or humanity cleansed from all the defilements of sin, which, according to SCHENKEL, is the end of the Divine election. Ἅγιος, *holy*, can scarcely be taken in any other sense than that of ver. 1, designating one consecrated to God. The distinction between its meaning here and ver. 1 is to be found in the qualifications: εἶναι—κατενώπιον αὐτοῦ. This state of consecration is therefore a reality, not merely a being "called," a "name" (although even this latter is not a mere sound, a non-entity), a reality too before God, and not merely before men. Accordingly ἅγιος here must in some way mark the internal effects upon the subject, connected with this state of consecration; so that ἄμωμος is very naturally added.

Ἄμωμος corresponds to the Hebrew תָּמִים, *unblemished*, and is to be rendered neither *irreprehensus* (MORUS) nor *irreprehensibilis* (2 Pet. iii. 14; Phil. ii. 15, where the form is ἀμώμητος), even though this is the original meaning (PASSOW *sub voce*). It is applied strictly to the sacrificial animal (1 Pet. i. 19) which is also consecrated to God.† The two words are joined together elsewhere (v. 27; Col. i. 22); in the first passage they are used of the church ("not having spot, or wrinkle, or any such thing"), in the latter, which is parallel to our verse, καὶ ἀνεγκλήτους is added. Hence we are reminded of Rom. viii. 33: "Who shall lay anything to the charge of God's elect? It is God that justifieth," and have to do with those who are transferred εἰς υἱοθεσίαν (ver. 5), who are partakers of "redemption," "the forgiveness of sins" (ver. 7), among whom all this is inward, living truth, the vital beginning of a glorious conclusion, so that advance is ever made toward holiness (1 Pet. i. 15, 16), and the saying in the Apocalypse (xxii. 11) is verified: "he that is holy, let him be holy still," which indeed finds a further verification in eternity. Thus both a condition, a subjective state, and more especially a *position*, which is to be and has been occupied, *a station* into which they have come and live, are meant, and not merely a *judgment*. The words of KOPPE, which HARLESS recalls, are apt: *non tum ad virtutis studium, quam potius ad dignitatem Christianorum, qua tanquam homines innocentes sibique caros Deus eos tractat, est referendum, idem quod alias in epp. Pauli est δικαιοῦσθαι παρὰ θεῷ.* Accordingly ἅγιος without further qualification does not refer to inward, actual sanctification (STIER). Such limitations as: *nisi confecto nostro stadio* (CALOV.), *quantum quidem hujus in mortali vita per Dei ipsius gratiam et carnis nostræ infirmitatem fieri potest* (CALIXTUS), are as inadmissible as the explanation of BAUMGARTEN-CRUSIUS, that the final end of the matter of Christianity is found in moral worth, or RUECKERT's opinion, that it was the Apostle's peculiarity, to idealize everything.

[Modern English commentators accept the distinction of MEYER respecting these two words: the first presents the *positive*, the second the *negative* side; but there is an unusual agreement among them against the reference to justification, which BRAUNE, MEYER, OLSHAUSEN, HARLESS, KOPPE and others favor. CHRYSOSTOM, THEOPHYLACT, CALVIN, STIER, HODGE, EADIE, ELLICOTT, ALFORD and others, apply the adjectives to sanctification. And with good reason: For an ultimate *result* is here spoken of, and Paul who had stamped the technical sense on so many Greek words before this Epistle was written, would have made the other meaning plain by using such words here. Dr. HODGE deduces very properly these statements: "If men are chosen to be holy, they cannot be chosen because they are holy." "Holiness is the only evidence of election."—R.]

**In love,** ἐν ἀγάπῃ.—Of course, His, God's love. This phrase, at the close of ver. 4, must be connected grammatically with the following participle, thus standing in emphatic position. The Greek is much freer in the position of words than the German; where the latter must help out the meaning with particles, the former requires only change of position; still it never goes beyond bounds in this respect. It cannot be connected with "chose" (OECUMEN., THOMAS, FLACIUS, BAUMGARTEN, FLATT, and others), since it stands entirely too far and too decidedly removed from that verb; and must be regarded as "trailing after it." Nor yet is the connection with "holy and blameless" (AMBROSIASTER, ERASMUS, LUTHER, CALVIN, BEZA, GROTIUS [*evangelii*, τὸ πᾶν is in love], WOLF, RUECKERT [dubiously], MORUS, MATTHIES, HEUBNER [E. V., ALFORD, HODGE], admissible; although ἄμωμος ἐν ἀγαλλιάσει (Jude 24) and ἀμώμητος ἐν εἰρήνῃ (2 Pet. iii. 14) occur, yet it is in such close union as to form one idea; the phrase could be separated from its adjective by "before Him," only in case the latter were adopted to be in-

* [Dr. BRAUNE seems to refer Col. i. 22 to the future Judgment, in his notes on that passage.—R.]

† ["As there is here no sacrificial allusion, direct or indirect (comp. chap. v. 27), it seems best to retain the simple etymological meaning: *inculpatus*" (ELLICOTT).—R.]

cluded with the adjective as one idea, which was to be qualified; but Paul uses ἅγιος καὶ ἄμωμος without any qualification (ver. 27; Col. i. 22), and the proper exposition excludes this connection, which has mainly subserved the Romanist and Rationalistic view. Accordingly most (from the *Peshito* to TISCHENDORF) have upheld the conection with προορίσας as the only admissible one.

[The connection with the adjectives favors the reference to sanctification in those words, giving this sense: we are chosen to be placed "in a state of moral excellence which consists in love" (HODGE). But this author is as little justified in saying that the reference to sacrificial purification occasioned the connection with the following participle, as BRAUNE is, in affirming that the connection with the adjectives has mainly subserved the Romanist and Rationalistic view. Neither of these statements affect the question. ALFORD has an able defence of the ordinary connection. Besides arguing that throughout this long sentence the verbs and particle precede their qualifying clauses, since the verbs are emphatic, giving prominence to God's act, not His attribute, he holds that this qualification is highly appropriate: "ἀγάπῃ, that which man lost at the Fall, but which God is, and to which God restores man by redemption, is the great element in which, as their abode and breathing-place, all Christian graces subsist, and in which, emphatically, all perfection before God must be found." All which is true, but not sufficient to overcome the grammatical objections to this view. Dr. HODGE says that "predestinated" has a subsequent qualification, hence it would be tautological to join "in love," to it, but as ELLICOTT intimates, the two qualifying phrases point to two different attributes; one to the loving mercy, the other to the sovereign power of God. The view of BRAUNE, is that of the *Peshito*, CHRYSOSTOM, THEODORET, THEOPHYLACT, AUGUSTINE, JEROME, BENGEL, KOPPE, STORR, HARLESS, DE WETTE, OLSHAUSEN, HOLZHAUSEN, STIER, TURNER, EADIE, ELLICOTT, MEYER, BLEEK; also GRIESBACH, SCHOLZ, LACHMANN, TISCHENDORF. The list might be enlarged, but is long enough to sustain the last remark of BRAUNE against HODGE's assertion that "the majority of commentators adopt the construction followed by our translators."—R.]

Ver. 5. In love **having predestinated us** [προορίσας ἡμᾶς].—Προορίζειν, to determine beforehand; πρὸ points out, that the determination existed before the thing or person to be destined, and is to be more closely defined only by the context: "before the foundation of the world" (HARLESS, STIER, MEYER, and others), hence beforehand, not before others (BAUMGARTEN). The participle is associated with ἐξελέξατο: ἐξελέξατο τῷ προορίσαι, or καὶ προώρισε. Thus the Greek expresses it, not indicating a chronological sequence; the temporal relation is not touched upon. The aorist indeed denotes the concluded action without reference to the past or present; the matter spoken of is before time. Similarly vers. 8, 11, 13, 20. The participle denotes, therefore, not priority of fact, but only the attendant manner (HARLESS). HOMBERG is incorrect: *postquam nos prædestinavit adoptandos, elegit etiam nos, ut simus sancti.* In that case we should have found at all events, πρότερον προορίσας. When the Apostle says (Rom. viii. 30): "whom he did predestinate, them he also called," without mentioning the election, we must find the latter included in the first ante-temporal act, not in the other act of accomplishment, taking place in time. Nor can it be inferred from Rom. viii. 29: "whom he did foreknow, he also did predestinate," that the predestination was preceded *temporally* by a particular act, that of foreknowing, quite as little as the two notions are to be confounded.

[As regards the relation of priority, ALFORD and STIER, take the "election" as antecedent to the "predestination," the former regarding the ἐξελέξατο in this passage as ranking with the προέγνω in Rom. viii. 29. On the other hand HODGE implies just the reverse, that the election is based on the preceding predestination. ELLICOTT too regards the participle "as *temporal*, not modal, and its action as *prior to*, not synonymous with, that of ἐξελέξατο." He takes it as=*quum prædestinavit*, "after He had," &c., but MEYER says that "*predestinatio* is never elsewhere distinguished from *electio*, as antecedent to it." EADIE too takes the participle as synchronous with the verb, which is safest where there is no grammatical necessity for insisting on the temporal qualification (see, however, WINER, p. 321). It is not well to dogmatize about the order in the Divine mind, especially on so slender a basis as that afforded by the Greek aorist participle.—R.]

The phrase "in love," coming first, marks with special emphasis the motive of the predestination. *In hac epistola regnat* τὸ *amo, amor, amatus; ipsi principio epistolæ congruit* (BENGEL). This precedence is like iii. 18: ἐν ἀγάπῃ ἐρριζωμένοι. What is thus demanded by the thought, and confirmed by the form of language, is certainly not contradicted, as will appear, by what follows: κατὰ τὴν εὐδοκίαν—εἰς ἔπαινον δόξης τῆς χάριτος, which is not added tautologically, as some (MATTHIES and others) suppose.

Ἡμᾶς, "us," is the object, as in ver. 4; but it must be noticed, that we have here, not ἐκκλησία or some such collective notion, but ἡμᾶς. Hence it cannot be said with SCHENKEL: "The *predestination* applies to the whole of the Divine decree of salvation, the *election* to the *individual persons* in whom it is accomplished." So much only is correct, that the thought does not respect individuals as such, a *colluvies*, a *multitudo*, but the church and its members, or the individuals as members of an organism, but in the predestination, just as in the election (ver. 4). Comp. Rom. viii. 29 f. [EADIE makes a far better distinction between προορίσας and ἐξελέξατο: "The end pre-appointed—πρό, is implied in the one; the mass out of which the choice is made—ἐκ, is glanced at by the other." So ELLICOTT.—R.]

**Unto adoption**, εἰς υἱοθεσίαν. This designates, in distinction from τεκνογονία (1 Tim. ii. 15), *adoption* (υἱοὺς θέσθαι, υἱὸν θετὸν ποιεῖσθαι); we are not children by nature, like Christ, but only by grace. *Adoption* is a rich conception, not at all a simple matter, and its actualization has a very significant history; it did not come to maturity at once, but has a development from primary stages, preceded by grand preparatory stages, unto its completion in eternity. To the Old Testament Israel belonged the adoption (Rom. ix. 4, to which are added the glory, the covenants, the giving of the law, the service of the sanctuary, the promises); even the Christians are "waiting for the adoption, the redemption of the body" (Rom. viii. 23). An explanatory parallel to our verse is found in Rom. viii. 29: "He also did predestinate to be conformed to the image of his Son, that he might be the first-born among many brethren;" ver. 30 ("he also glorified") however points yet deeper, so that we must recall the bold words of Peter (2 Pet. i. 4): "that by these ye might be partakers of the divine nature," as well as those of Paul (Rom. viii. 17): "If children, then heirs; heirs of God, and joint-heirs with Christ." Comp. Gal. iv. 5-7; 1 Thes. ii. 12; 2 Thes. ii. 14; 1 Jno. iii. 2. Hence it is not a *formula solemnis ad Christianam religionem adducere* (KOPPE), nor to be referred in general and indefinitely to the benefits, which distinguish Christians from other men (FLATT), nor yet *futura beatitate ornari, adeo amari Deumque redamare* (MORUS), nor can it be said: *υἱοθεσία veniæ peccatorum morte Christi partæ certa spe verissime constat* (TITTMANN).

[HODGE: Sonship in reference to God includes,—1. Participation of His nature or conformity to His image. 2. The enjoyment of His favor, or being the special objects of His love. 3. Heirship, or a participation of the glory and blessedness of God. Sometimes one and sometimes another of these ideas is the most prominent. In the present case it is the second and third." MEYER has a good note *in loco* on *υἱοθεσία*.—R.]

**Through Jesus Christ unto himself,** *διὰ Ἰησοῦ Χριστοῦ εἰς αὐτόν*.—Against the reading *αὑτόν*, see the close of ver. 4. *Διά* with the genitive retains the meaning *per*, through, marking the mediator, cannot therefore be: *propter* (MOLDENHAUER). Comp. John xiv. 6. The person of the Lord must be regarded as that of the mediator. Even though we find in Gal. iii. 26: *υἱοὶ διὰ τῆς πίστεως*, there the subjective mediation which proceeds from the Object of faith, the mediator, is marked, here the objective, to which the former will not be wanting. We take *αὐτόν* as referring to God; should Jesus Christ be meant, the reading must be, *καὶ εἰς αὐτόν*. Hence the explanation is incorrect: *in conformitatem ejus* (*Christi*) *per fidem et bonos mores* (ANSELM and others). But the preposition *εἰς* must retain the sense *unto* or *into* Him, as is required by those passages cited in the last paragraph, which indicate the final end of the *υἱοθεσία*. Hence it is not so much an "explanatory addition" (HARLESS), as an adjoined supplement (STIER). The explanation: *ad gloriam gratiæ suæ* (PISCATOR, MORUS), is in any case insufficient. It is impossible to take *εἰς αὐτόν* as= the Hebrew לוֹ, *sibi* (GROTIUS, WOLF, KOPPE following the paraphrase of BUCER: *Qui prædestinavit pridem nos, ut in filios sibi per Jesum Christum—adoptaret*). PASSAVANT weakens it into: up to God. Nor is it=*ἐν ἑαυτῷ* (CALVIN, BEZA, CALIXTUS); and just as little a circumlocution for the genitive *αὐτοῦ*, qualifying *υἱοθεσία* (RUECKERT). MEYER is excellent: "How rich and entirely Grecian Paul is precisely in his prepositional expressions, by which he *never* represents a mere relation of case."

[Among the various opinions respecting *εἰς αὐτόν*, and the shadings of signification attached to it, the view of ELLICOTT seems most satisfactory: "In these deeper theological passages the preposition seems to bear its primary (*εἰς*=*ἐνς* Donaldson, *Cratylus*, § 170) and most comprehensive sense of '*to* and *into*' (see Rost u. Palm. *Lex. s. v.*); the idea of *approach* (*τὴν εἰς αὐτὸν ἀνάγουσαν*, Theophylact) being also blended with and heightened by that of *inward union*; comp. notes on Gal. iii. 27. We may thus paraphrase, 'God predestinated us to be adopted as His sons; and that adoption came to us through Christ, and was to lead us into, and unite us to God.'" —R.]

**According to the good pleasure of his will,** *κατὰ τὴν εὐδοκίαν τοῦ θελήματος αὐτοῦ*.—*Εὐδοκία* can indeed mean good will, as in Luke ii. 14; Phil. i. 15; ii. 13; 2 Thess. i. 11, or wish, *arbitrium*, or Matt. xi. 26; Luke x. 21. Here however it is equivalent to *βουλή*, ver. 11: *κατὰ τὴν βουλὴν τοῦ θελήματος*, and the sense is that what was ordained in love, He ordained according to (*κατά*) the determination of His will. As *ἐν ἀγάπῃ* (ver. 4) denotes the principle of the ordaining, *εὐδοκία* here cannot mean "good will." It is the substantive answering to *δοκεῖν* (frequentative from *δέχεσθαι*, Ion., *δέκεσθαι*), to seem good, as Acts xv. 22, 25, 28=*beneplacitum*, and is distinguished from *βουλή*, the inclinational* act of willing (while *ἐθέλειν* designates the ethical act), only in this, that it refers more to deliberation, choice. Comp. TITTMANN, *Syn.* I. p. 124 ff. Hence the interpretations of THEODORET (*ἡ ἐπ' εὐεργεσίᾳ βούλησις*), SUIDAS (from Theodoret *ad* Ps. v. 12; *τὸ ἀγαθὸν θέλημα*), BEZA (*benevolentia*), LUTHER, MORUS (*pro benevolo suo consilio*), HARLESS, (according to the kindness of His will), OLSHAUSEN, HEUBNER [EADIE, not MEYER as the German indicates,—R.] and others, are incorrect.

[The two meanings of *εὐδοκία* here under discussion are: 1. *beneplacitum*, mere good pleasure; 2. *benevolentia*. Undoubtedly in this case God's good pleasure was also His *benevolentia*, but to which does the Apostle here refer? The usage of the LXX. favors the latter meaning, but in the New Testament both occur. The context must decide. It favors meaning (1.), for (a) the idea of benevolence in the highest degree was already introduced as a qualification in *ἐν ἀγάπῃ*, admitting that the phrase is to be joined with this verse. (b) The phrases occurring afterwards in vers. 9, 11 point to this meaning, especially *βουλὴν τοῦ θελήματος αὐτοῦ* (ver. 11). (c) The reference being to the actor exclusively and not to the objects of the action, this meaning brings them less into view (ELLICOTT, after DE WETTE). The proper safe-guard against the notion of bare arbitrary decree is found in *ἐν ἀγάπῃ*. So substantially but with an occasional tendency to press the sense too

* [Braune says: *dem gemüthlichen Akt des Wollens*, thus indicating his acceptance of Buttmann's distinction between *βούλομαι* and *ἐθέλω* (the former more an act of inclination, the latter of deliberation, choice). On this see ver. 11. The word *gemüthlich* has no English equivalent, so far as I am aware.—R.]

far, GROTIUS, ERASMUS, CALVIN, BENGEL, FLATT, RUECKERT, DE WETTE, MEYER ("the *free self-determination* independent of all human desert is here meant"), BLEEK, HODGE, ALFORD, ELLICOTT. Nor does this view make the ground for thanksgiving the less, as EADIE implies.—We accept θέλημα here in the simple sense of "will," reserving the discussion of its precise meaning for a subsequent page.—R.] The explanation of CHRYSOSTOM (τὸ σφοδρὸν θέλημα, τὸ μετὰ ἐπιθυμίας θέλημα) is to be rejected.

Ver. 6. **Unto the praise of the glory of his grace,** εἰς ἔπαινον δόξης τῆς χάριτος αὐτοῦ.—Εἰς ἔπαινον points to the υἱοὶ θετοί, who now praise, as those who have been blessed by the sonship and heirship, and renders prominent, that God's ultimate aim is the blessedness of His creatures, of His Own. For εἰς ἔπαινον is to be taken in connection with προορίσας εἰς υἱοθεσίαν—εἰς αὐτόν as forming the conclusion; it reaches unto the praise from him who has been pardoned. The object of the praise is "the glory," but not glory in itself, or God's glory, but "of his grace" (αὐτοῦ not αὑτοῦ, see on ver. 4). Χάρις is ἀγάπη, the latter is however more general, the former more special, marking love, which condescends, like the German *Gnade* (see on ver. 2), or which acts upon χαίρειν, χαρά, making or being χαριέις (lovely). This then is, principally, the object of the praise, which lauds indeed the glory of the grace. This glory is the object of the praise, vers. 12, 14, where we find: εἰς ἔπαινον τῆς δόξης αὐτοῦ. It is remarkable that the article is omitted here before δόξης; but δόξα is not the main idea, but ἡ χάρις αὐτοῦ, and we should render (according to WINER, p. 179): To the praise of His glory in grace (*Gnadenherrlichkeit*), so that δόξα τῆς χάριτος forms one conception. Still it is altogether inadmissible to explain the genitive δόξης as a Hebraism for the adjective ἔνδοξος; Paul was acquainted with that adjective (v. 27; 1 Cor. iv. 10) and did not select it here. This is equally true, whether it be joined with ἔπαινον, as meaning: to glorious praise (GROTIUS, ESTIUS), or to τῆς χάριτος: to the praise of His glorious grace (LUTHER, BEZA, MORUS, KOPPE, FLATT, and others).

[MEYER: "The glorifying of the Divine love (which however is here designated, according to its definite peculiarity, as *grace*, because it concerns what is sinful, ii. 1 ff.) is the final *end*" of the Divine predestination. ELLICOTT: "As CHRYSOSTOM appears rightly to have felt, δόξης is a pure substantive, and serves to specify that peculiar *quality* or *attribute* of the χάρις which forms the subject of the praise."—R.]

**Which he freely bestowed upon us** [ἧς ἐχαρίτωσεν ἡμᾶς].—On the attraction ἧς ἐχαρίτωσεν for ἥν—according to the well-known expression χάριν χαριτοῦν, see WINER, p. 154, and the *Textual Note* [6]. Similar cases, iv. 1; 2 Cor. i. 4. Χαριτοῦν = *gratia aliquem afficere;* but *gratia* may be taken in the subjective or objective sense, so that this means either: He has made lovely, pleasing, or: He has dispensed grace, favor. The word occurs elsewhere in the New Testament only in Luke i. 28 (the salutation of the angel to Mary: χαῖρε κεχαριτωμένη, where either meaning may be accepted, or both combined (STIER *in loco.*) [The objective sense is certainly to be preferred in Luke i. 28; for to take the other view involves at least a quasi-support of very untenable dogmas. On the force of Greek verbs in όω, see EADIE, HARLESS, ELLICOTT.—R.] It also occurs in the LXX. (Sir. ix. 8; xviii. 17), and in the first sense. The reading ἧς supports the first view; the reading ἐν ᾗ the other. For the former was evidently accepted in the Syriac version, and aptly reproduced: *quam effudit super nos*, so that His grace has not remained and does not remain fruitless. So the *Vulgate: gratificavit.* CHRYSOSTOM: οὐ μόνον ἁμαρτημάτων ἀπήλλαξεν, ἀλλὰ καὶ ἐπεράστους ἐποίησεν; THEODORET, *Theophylact*, ŒCUMENIUS to the same effect. A-LAPIDE: *Gratiosos nos reddidit, scilicet gratiam suam nobis communicando et infundendo.* LUTHER: *Angenehm gemacht*, made pleasant. BEZA: *Gratis nos sibi acceptos reddidit;* so STIER and others. The second view is held by BENGEL (*gratia amplexus est*), BAUMGARTEN, KOPPE, FLATT, HARLESS, RUECKERT, SCHENKEL and others. At all events with the perspective reaching "unto the praise of the glory of His grace," we must not leave out of view the result of pardoning, the effect of the χάρις on the χαριτωθέντες, who become χαρίεντες; here, where the Apostle "closes his first circle of thought" (STIER), there is at the same time a reference to the goal aimed at from the pardon. Accordingly "us" applies not merely to Paul and his readers or contemporaries, but to all believers.

[The subjective sense may be involved, but the other seems decidedly preferable. ALFORD says the subjective meaning of χάρις does not seem to occur in the N. T., certainly not in St. Paul. He very properly argues for the other meaning, from the "indefinite aorist, referring to an act once past in Christ, not to an abiding state which He has brought about in us." Also from the context which is all of God's grace. So ELLICOTT, EADIE, MEYER, HODGE. The Romanist expositors find in the other sense a support for their doctrine of *justitia inhærens.*—R.]

**In the beloved,** ἐν τῷ ἀγαπημένῳ.—This contains a reference to ἐχαρίτωσεν. BENGEL aptly says: *Autonomasia, opportuna. Amor plus significat, quam gratia.* 1 Pet. ii. 10: *ubi de iis, qui misericordiam consecuti sunt, ea dicuntur, supra quæ* ὁ ἠγαπημένος, AMATUS *longe eminet;* ἔλεος *necessario præsupponit præviam miseriam, sed amor non item.* The *Beloved*, κατ' ἐξοχήν, (Col. i. 13; Matt. iii. 17), by God the Father, not *ab omnibus* (PELAGIUS), is the Only Begotten, the Son of God by nature, Christ; He is the object of the love (ἀγάπη) of the Father, not needing χάρις, as we; only through the grace of God in Christ do we become objects of His love; as χαριτωθέντες. Accordingly this distinction is not to be made use of in favor of the second meaning of ἐχαρίτωσεν, as is done by HARLESS. The preposition ἐν must be retained as marking our fellowship with Christ, who is our life-sphere; hence it is not = διὰ τόν, *propter* (GROTIUS and others). We are rather reminded of the verse: *Vor dir sonst nichts gilt, als Dein eigen Bild.* [Before thee nothing passes current but thine own image.] In Him, the image of God, we have, not only objectively, but subjectively also, the grace, that we are well-pleasing to God.

[EADIE: "We, as adopted children, are indeed loved, but there is another, the Son, the own Belovèd Son. It was not, therefore, affection craving indulgence, or eager for an object on which to expend itself, that led to our adoption. There was no void in His bosom, the loved One lay in it."—R.]

SECOND FOUNDATION OF THE PRAISE; VERS. 7–12. *The carrying out of the eternal decree.*

Ver. 7. **In whom we have the [or our] redemption through his blood** [ἐν ᾧ ἔχομεν τὴν ἀπολύτρωσιν διὰ τοῦ αἵματος αὐτοῦ].—Comp. Col. i. 14. "We have," "the first present tense of the whole discourse, and very emphatic" (STIER). Hence it immediately follows ἐν ᾧ, "in whom." With this a new circle of thought begins, pointing to the already experienced accomplishment of the Divine eternal decree, even though just begun. The preposition ἐν is to be taken in its strict meaning: for only within the Person of the Beloved, Christ, are we in the possession and enjoyment of redemption. Christ's work is inseparable from His Person; we have redemption, not in His work *without* His Person, but *in* His Person, which with His work is a living unity (OLSHAUSEN). Hence it will not suffice to explain: in *fellowship* with Him (WINER, p. 364, note 7), while it is altogether incorrect to take it as = διὰ ὅν, ἕνεκα οὗ (FLATT, KOPPE), even though the phrase "through His blood" be adjoined, and the explanation be: *cujus morti cruentæ debeo;* so MORUS: *propter quem.* SCHENKEL appears to interpolate *per* δι' οὗ in his explanation: by means of the fellowship with Him through faith. [HODGE seems to have lost the force of the phrase, weakening it into, "*i. e.,* not in ourselves," and then taking "by his blood" as explanatory. ELLICOTT, EADIE, ALFORD all catch more or less of the true view so aptly expressed by OLSHAUSEN.—R.]

*We are having!* Believers, Christians are in possession of a property. The *possession* is marked, not the receiving, or having received; hence ἔχειν is not = *assecutum esse,* or *assequi.*

[EADIE is still better: "We are ever needing, and so are *ever having* it." The objective sense, *there is for us,* adopted by ALFORD, following HARLESS, underlies the expressed and emphatic subjective one; the latter is not merely "an implied import," but the prominent thought.—R.]

The subject treated of is a *bonum novi testamenti* (BENGEL)—τὴν* ἀπολύτρωσιν. This word points to a redemption through ransom. This idea is a prevalent one, even in the New Testament, where our Lord so uses it (Matt. xx. 28; Mark x. 45: to give His life a ransom for many), and Paul, 1 Tim. ii. 6: ὁ δοὺς ἑαυτὸν ἀντίλυτρον ὑπὲρ πάντων, Tit. ii. 14: λυτροῦσθαι, 1 Cor. vi. 20; vii. 23; Gal. iii. 13: ἀγοράζειν, Acts xx. 28: περιποιεῖσθαι. Still the expiation, indicated in the Lord's saying, appears also, as in Rom. iii. 23–25. *Manifesto satis eam mortis vim indicat, quæ sacrificio confertur piaculari* (FRITZSCHE). Here indeed the thought of an expiatory sacrifice seems to be the prominent one, since "through his blood" is added (comp. Levit. xvii. 11, HARLESS). We may however take the blood of Christ as the ransom price. The powers and evils, indicated in the preposition ἀπό, from which believers are and shall be snatched, are according to STIER, the wrath to come (1 Thess. i. 10), the present evil world (Gal. i. 4), the power of darkness (Col. i. 13), all unrighteousness (Tit. ii. 14), vain conversation after the ways of their fathers (1 Pet. i. 18); indeed the *extirpation* and compensation of *all* the evil in which we have involved ourselves with our transgressions (PFENNINGER). Though the word may have in passages, such as iv. 30; Rom. viii. 23; 1 Cor. i. 30, a more general signification, the original reference being supplanted or obliterated, here this is marked by the context. HARLESS indeed is correct, in maintaining against Romanist expositors (such as A-LAPIDE), that it designates not merely a subjective condition; but he should not have based on the presence of the article the statement that abstract nouns without the article merely designate that the generic notion has become real as a subjective possession.

**Through his blood,** διὰ τοῦ αἵματος αὐτοῦ.—MEYER regards this as entirely like ἐν τῷ αἵματι (ii. 13), remarking that Paul was very fond of prepositional variations (2 Cor. iii. 11). The former, however, describes rather the mediation, which may be in constant movement, as here; while the latter points to an existing life-sphere or fact, in which indeed that mediation must be consummated. Hence the Apostle is not influenced by likings or beauty of diction, *etc.,* but by a shading of the thought.—In the Person of Christ as the Only Begotten, is given to us, as to all believers, Redemption by means of His blood, as an offering and ransom-price, and now we are having such a gift. Though Heb. ix. 12-14 is to be compared with our passage, still we may not introduce here, as is done by KOPPE, the sacrificial worship of the ancient nations, according to which through a sinless offering past sins were extirpated and the angered divinity reconciled, as though Paul had made use of this.

[ALFORD: "It is a noteworthy observation of HARLESS here, that the choice of the word, the *Blood* of Christ, is of itself a testimony to the idea of *expiation* having been in the writer's mind. Not the *death* of the victim, but its BLOOD, was the typical instrument of expiation. I may notice that in Phil. ii. 8, where Christ's *obedience,* not His atonement, is spoken of, there is no mention of His shedding His blood, only of the act of His Death." This was the price, τὸ λύτρον. As EADIE well says: "The *nexus* we may not be able to discover fully, but"—"the death of Christ has governmental relations, has an influence on our salvation totally different in nature and sphere of operation, from its subjective power in subduing the heart by the love which it presents, and the thrilling motives which it brings to bear upon it."—R.]

**The forgiveness of our transgressions,** τὴν ἄφεσιν τῶν παραπτωμάτων.—LUTHER joins this with the foregoing thus: *namely,*

* [The article here points to something well known; if the verb ἔχομεν has a reference mainly objective, then this means *the* redemption promised, etc., but if it be subjective, then it means *our* redemption. So CONYBEARE. ELLICOTT objects to this, but sanctions it in the Revision by Four Ang. Clergymen. Such a rendering by no means implies that the ἀπολύτρωσιν is merely subjective.—R.]

the forgiveness of sins, thus taking it, and correctly, as epexegetical (WINER, p. 492). [So the E. V. in the parallel passage, Col. i. 14.—R.] This implies, that the more comprehensive expression, *redemption*, is to be limited, contains more than is involved in the context, ἔχομεν; "the forgiveness of transgressions" renders emphatically prominent one principal element, on which indeed another depends. Accordingly it cannot be said, that the Apostle defines the nature of the "redemption" with this epexegetical addition (HARLESS) [MEYER]. It is just as erroneous to extend the epexegetical phrase on account of the first expression, and to explain "forgiveness of transgressions" as taking away of sins (*Berlenb. Bible*). Paul *now takes out as chief the first thing:* the forgiveness of sins (STIER). FRITZSCHE aptly remarks (Rom. iii. 25) on the distinction between πάρεσις and ἄφεσις:* "*Conveniunt in hoc, quod sive illa, sive hæc tibi obtigerit nulla peccatorum tuorum ratio habetur; discrepant eo, quod hac data facinorum tuorum pœnas nunquam pendes, illa concessa non diutius nullas peccatorum tuorum pœnas lues, quam ei in iis connivere placuerit, cui in delicta tua animadvertendi jus sit.*" Further the genitive of τά παραπτώματα refers only to individual facts, and, since these can neither be undone or extirpated, we must understand pardon alone; OLSHAUSEN is incorrect in laying no weight upon the form παραπτώματα, ἁμαρτίαι (Col. i. 14), and including also the sinful condition, the inborn sinfulness, understanding here absolutely all that is sinful.† Although he is correct in saying that the *appropriation* of this forgiveness of sins as a fact cannot be conceived of, without the transformation of the man proceeding from it as a *consequence*, yet we must still maintain that nothing is said here about the latter, but only that redemption, like the forgiveness, has its complete objective reality entirely irrespective of the subjective state of the individuals (HARLESS). [Accepting this view, which is that of HODGE, EADIE and others, we must deny ALFORD's remark, that this phrase is not to be limited, but is "at least equipollent with ἀπολύτρωσις."—R.]

**According to the riches of his grace.**—Κατὰ τὸ πλοῦτος τῆς χάριτος αὐτοῦ evidently designates the grace of God, not of Christ, as the ultimate ground of the fact of Redemption, and corresponding (κατά) to the depth and importance of the same in its riches. Similarly ii. 7: τὸ πλοῦτος τῆς χάριτος, Rom. ii. 4: πλοῦτος τῆς χρηστότητος, Rom. ix. 23; Col. i. 27; Eph. iii. 16: τῆς δόξης. Hence it is not=*gratia liberalissima* (KOPPE). Instead of τὸ πλοῦτος, attested by ℵ. and B., and to be retained here, ὁ πλοῦτος more frequently occurs. [Comp. *Textual Note* *.] PASSAVANT aptly says: "We have in this grace not only deliverance from misery and curse, not only forgiveness—we find in it the freedom, the glory, the heritage of the children of God, the crown of eternal life."

[ALFORD is not correct in saying this clause of itself prevents the limitation of ἄφεσιν to mere forgiveness. EADIE seems to catch the spirit of the passage best. "Atonement is not in antagonism with grace. For the opulence of His grace is seen not only in its innumerable forms and varieties of operation among men, but also in the unasked and unmerited provision of such an atonement—as the blood of the 'Beloved One.'"—R.] With the forgiveness of sin we gain access to *all* the treasures of Divine grace (GERLACH). Hence the Apostle continues as in the following verse.

Ver. 8. **Which he made to abound toward us** [ἧς ἐπερίσσευσεν εἰς ἡμᾶς].—Ἧς, referring to τῆς χάριτος, which is imparted, not parted, cannot be, as in Luke xv. 17: περισσεύουσιν ἄρτων, a partitive genitive (ERASMUS: *de qua ubertim nobis impartivit*); but is here an attraction for ἥν, since the ἐπερίσσευσε is to be rendered, transitively in accordance with the context (ver. 9: γνωρίσας), and with the accusative like 2 Cor. ix. 8 (δυνατὸς γὰρ ὁ θεὸς πᾶσαν χάριν περισσεῦσαι εἰς ὑμᾶς; comp. iv. 15; 1 Thess. iii. 12). THEOPHYLACT aptly says: ἀφθόνως ἐξέχεε. It is not in accordance with the language or context to take it as instead of ᾗ (*Vulgate: quæ superabundavit*) or ᾗ (CALVIN: *qua redundavit*). [So E. V., but such an attraction of the dative is not found in the New Testament, while the attraction of the nominative (*Vulgate*) is scarcely possible.—R.]—Εἰς ἡμᾶς, into us He has caused His grace to flow abundantly.

**In all wisdom and prudence** [ἐν πάσῃ σοφίᾳ καὶ φρονήσει*].—The word πάσῃ, without the article, designates every one there is (WINER, p. 105). Comp. ver. 2; Col. iv. 12.—Πᾶς sets forth the multiplicity, fulness, always extensiveness, never intensity, force (HARLESS); hence it is not=*summa* (WAHL, RUECKERT). Σοφία καὶ φρόνησις cannot be taken as exact synonymes (KOPPE), nor so distinguished, that the former is used *de præterito et præsenti, de his, quæ Deus facit* (ver. 17), the latter *de futuro, de his, quæ nos faciemus* (ANSELM, BENGEL). *Wisdom* designates rather a normal state of the mind in the centre of intelligence, *prudence* the special turning of the same in different directions; ἡ δὲ σοφία ἀνδρὶ τίκτει φρόνησιν (Prov. x. 23); the latter is subordinate to the former. Besides this formal distinction, the material difference must be considered: Wisdom grasps God's doings, perceives and understands His counsels of grace, prudence is directed to what we have to do, looks at our problem and how to solve it; the former clearly sees the relations ordered by God, the latter regulates our conduct accordingly. Thus every kind of wisdom and prudence is indicated by "all," and "in" marks that God has caused His grace to flow abundantly into us, in the gift of all wisdom and prudence. So also in the parallel passage, Col. i. 9: ἵνα πληρωθῆτε τὴν ἐπίγνωσιν τοῦ θελήματος αὐτοῦ ἐν πάσῃ σοφίᾳ καὶ συνέσει. Accordingly this is not to be taken as= "manifold wisdom" (iii. 10), and, as in ἐν ἀγάπῃ

*[On this distinction, comp. TRENCH, *Synonymes, N. T.*, § 33; COCCEIUS has a special treatise, *De utilitate distinctionis inter πάρεσιν et ἄφεσιν* (Opp. t. vii.) See SCHAFF, *Romans*, p. 128, *Textual Note* 8.—R.]

†[On παράπτωμα see Dr. SCHAFF's note (Rom. v. 15) p. 182, and the subsequent discussions. The positions taken there forbid any such wide reference as that of OLSHAUSEN. ELLICOTT, while not laying much stress upon the distinction between παρπτώματα and ἁμαρτίαι, takes the former as pointing more to sins on the side of commission, *sinful acts*, the latter to sins as the result of a state, *sinful conditions*.—R.]

* [ELLICOTT renders this word: *discernment* or *intelligence*, adding a very discriminating note.—R.]

προορίσας (ver. 5), to be joined with the following γνωρίσας (JEROME, CHRYS., SEMLER [EADIE], and others), nor to be applied to God, to whom indeed φρόνησις (1 Kings iii. 28; Jer. x. 12) may be ascribed, but not πᾶσα in such a way as to mean that not only is all wisdom and prudence in Him, but that He acts, does this or that in *all* wisdom and prudence (HARLESS).

[The view here defended is also that of HARLESS, MEYER and ELLICOTT, the three most exact commentators on this Epistle. Comp. the note of the last named on the *meaning*, *reference* and *connection* of these words. ALFORD follows DE WETTE in referring them to God, taking the same view of the connection as given above, while EADIE refers them to man, but connects them with γνωρίσας. HODGE joins this phrase to the object of the verb instead of to the verb itself, and inexactly renders the preposition ἐν: in connection with, together with; his view of φρόνησις is also objectionable.—R.]

Ver. 9. **Having made known to us.**—Γνωρίσας denotes, as in vers. 4, 5, the manner of the ἐπερίσσευσε (WINER, p. 322), explaining "in all wisdom and prudence." The verb means to make known, without stating any thing as to the means used. Comp. iii. 3, 5; Gal. i. 12; Col. i. 25. [The perfect participle in English is indefinite, and serves best to express the idea of the Greek aorist participle, which here denotes an act coincident, and terminating synchronously with the finite verb (MEYER, ELLICOTT). The best paraphrase would be: in that He made known (ALFORD).—R.].—"Us" means Christians, believers, not merely Paul or the Apostles.

**The mystery of his will,** τὸ μυστήριον τοῦ θελήματος αὐτοῦ.—[The genitive is that of the object: the mystery concerning His will (MEYER, ELLICOTT, ALFORD and now EADIE). On θέλημα see ver. 11.—R.] This mystery is the object made known. He terms it "of Christ" in iii. 10, because He is the Mediator of the same; "of the gospel," vi. 19, because it is thereby proclaimed; "of faith," "of godliness," 1 Tim. iii. 9, 16, because it is comprehended and preserved only by faith, and the fear of God in faith; here "of his will," because it is willed by God. It is the decree of Redemption in Christ. In iii. 9; Col. i. 25, 26; Rom. xvi. 25, 26; 1 Cor. iii. 7–10, its depth and concealment as well as its revelation are described. This decree, a secret from all eternity in the fullest sense for the Gentiles, hinted and adumbrated in Israel by prophecies and types, is now manifest in Christ, to those only, however, who are true believers (1 Cor. iii. 12), to those who are lost, it remains concealed (2 Cor. iv. 3). It is a secret which has become public, ceasing henceforth to be a secret, yet ever having and still retaining in itself what surpasses all reason (HARLESS, STIER).

**According to his good pleasure,** κατὰ τὴν εὐδοκίαν αὐτοῦ, defines more closely the γνωρίσας, "having made known."—Comp. ver. 5. [The making known is thus defined as having taken place in strict dependence, both in time and manner, on the will of God (ALFORD, ELLICOTT). EADIE retains here the meaning *benevolentia*, which is quite inadmissible, more so than in ver. 5.—R.]

**Which he purposed in himself,** ἣν προέθετο ἐν αὐτῷ.—The determination is thus marked as an internal one, so as to give prominence to its freedom; hence we should read αὑτῷ (HARLESS, TISCHENDORF), not αὐτῷ (MEYER). [The latter reading is adopted by ALFORD, EADIE, ELLICOTT, all of them claiming that if the pronoun refers to God (and we cannot well accept any other reference) the reflexive form is necessary. In ver. 5, they urge, another idea had intervened, hence αὐτόν was there sufficiently explicit, but here the immediate connection with the verb and its subject requires the form αὑτῷ. This is opposed to the theory advanced in ver. 5, that this reflexive form never occurs in the New Testament; but it is safer to accept this reading than to refer the pronoun to Christ.—R.]

In the compound verb προτίθεσθαι, *sibi proponere* (BENGEL, PASSOW *sub voce*), the preposition προ is *local* (MEYER): to put before one's self, not *temporal*=beforehand. So also in πρόθεσις, ver. 11; Rom. i. 13; iii. 25; Acts iii. 20 (προχειρίζομαι); 2 Cor. ix. 7 (προαιρέομαι). Accordingly εὐδοκία is not=good pleasure (LUTHER), gracious purpose (HARLESS), and ἐν αὐτῷ is not to be referred to Christ (CHRYSOSTOM, LUTHER: *hervorgebracht durch Ihn*, BENGEL), nor is προέθετο=*ante constituit* (ANSELM), *apud se retinuit* (CALVIN). [As Meyer remarks, this purpose is to be regarded as taking place before the foundation of the world, but the preposition does not express this.—R.]

Ver. 10. **Unto the dispensation of the fulness of times** [εἰς οἰκονομίαν τοῦ πληρώματος τῶν καιρῶν].—This verse follows, setting forth the goal of the πρόθεσις. Εἰς designates the tendency, the aim, as in iv. 30; Gal. iii. 17, 23 (WINER, p. 371), with a view to which He purposed in Himself; hence it is to be closely joined with προέθετο, not with γνωρίσας (BENGEL), which is too remote. Of course εἰς is not =*in* (*Vulgate*), nor *usque ad* (ERASMUS, CALVIN), for which ἕως, μέχρι, would be used. [HODGE and EADIE: *with reference to*, a view of the preposition which MEYER often favors, but which fails to bring out its full force here.—R.]

Οἰκονομία, from οἰκόνομος, is stewardship (Luke xvi. 2); it is transferred to the spiritual sphere in iii. 2, 6; 1 Tim. i. 4. The original meaning is modified in two ways, according as the word in its connection "designated the activity of a governing or subordinate subject; in the first case: arrangement, disposition, in the second: management, execution" (HARLESS). Thus the context in 1 Cor. ix. 17 defines the word in the second sense, of the apostolic office and service. Here God, and that towards which He has formed a purpose, are spoken of; so it here means: unto, with a view to the disposition. LUTHER correctly renders the εἰς of the aim, but limits οἰκονομίαν too much: that it may be preached; so GROTIUS: *ut suo demum tempore publicaret*. THEOPHYLACT (διοίκησις) and the *Vulgate* (*dispensatio*) restrict it too much. RUECKERT's complaint about the omission of the article is entirely unnecessary, as in Rom. i. 1, which is a parallel for our passage, we read: εἰς εὐαγγέλιον θεοῦ, "unto the gospel of God." The article is wanting on account of the following genitive, which defines our word more fully, and is to be joined most closely with it; so λόγον ζωῆς (Phil. ii. 16)=*Lebenswort*, "Word of life," ἡμέρα τοῦ Χριστοῦ, "day of Christ." Comp. WINER, p. 118 ff. According to this, we should take the phrase to mean: *fulfilment—economy*.

The genitive τοῦ πληρώματος τῶν καιρῶν defines then οἰκονόμιαν more closely. "*Verbo πληρόω et πλήρωμα persæpe utitur Paulus ad Ephesios et Colossenses* (BENGEL). According to the well-known investigations of FRITZSCHE (*Ad Rom.* II. p. 473, and a *Dissertation*, Rostock, 1839)—although HOFMANN (*Schriftbeweis*, I. 2, p 118) denies the active and passive senses of the word, seeking to prove that its meaning is: contents, full amount, complement [*i. e.*, the first of the following senses]—πλήρωμα signifies (1.) *id quo res impletur* [this is often called the active sense, but is not strictly so, see on ver. 23.—R.], (2.) *id quod impletur* [the strictly passive sense=τὸ πεπληρωμένον, that which is filled, or the state of having been filled and continuing so, *fulness;* this being the more usual meaning of verbals in μα.—R.], (3.) *implendi actionem* [the proper active meaning], the passive sense being more prevalent than the active. According to this view, the second signification is to be accepted here, as in Gal. iv. 4: τὸ πλήρωμα τοῦ χρόνου, that which is filled, the state of fulness, the fulness of time.

Between the two passages there is however a difference, occasioned by τοῦ χρόνου and τῶν καιρῶν. Here definite καιροί are spoken of. Although we find in Mark i. 15: πεπλήρωται ὁ καιρός, because *one* point of time is referred to, yet in 1 Tim. ii. 6, the proclamation of salvation is said to take place καιροῖς ἰδίοις, and in Luke xxi. 24 καιροῖς ἐθνῶν are mentioned, as in Acts i. 7 χρόνους ἢ καιρούς. And in the passage strictly parallel (ii. 7) it is said that ἐν τοῖς αἰῶσι, τοῖς ἐπερχομένοις, God would show the riches of His grace toward the congregation of the believers. Hence we must apply the word here to different sections of time, linked on to each other, through which the plan of salvation is unfolded, since God ever revealed what and so much as was requisite, to advance the development of His Kingdom, so soon as the end of one period of time in the history of Redemption arrived, and an epoch had fulfilled its task and passed away; while τοῦ χρόνου in the passage from Galatians marks these details in their connection as a totality. The fulfilment of these definite periods and points of time, adapted for the required development, is to be understood here: ὁ ὁρισθεὶς παρὰ τοῦ πατρὸς καιρός (THEODORET), the point of time, with the entrance of which the pre-Messianic periods are closed and the Messianic ages begin.

The genitive τοῦ πληρώματος τῶν καιρῶν indicates then what belongs to οἰκονομία, the external and internal relation to it. Comp. WINER, p. 176 ff. [So ELLICOTT and EADIE: the former has a capital note on this genitive, which he calls a genitive of the *characterizing quality*.—R.] We have therefore here indicated, that the fulfilling of the times stands under the guidance of God Himself, who has determined and ordered the periods and brings them in according to His purpose. Hence we explain it as: *dispensatio propria plenitudini temporum* (CALOV., RUECKERT, MEYER, MATTHIES, STIER [HODGE, ELLICOTT, EADIE] and others). HARLESS takes the genitive as epexegetical, subjoining the special to the general; but οἰκονομία, that which is arranged by the Lord, is not explained by πλήρωμα, a developing process, nor that mode of action by a fact, such as the latter undoubtedly is. SCHENKEL accepts a genitive of the object, as though "the fulness of the times" was the object of "dispensation;" but while ἦλθε (Gal. iv. 4) may be predicated of that πλήρωμα, οἰκονομεῖται cannot be, and οἰκονομία has the καιρούς as the object of its νέμειν, the result of this being the πλήρωμα. LUTHER's rendering is too limited: *dass es gepredigt würde, da die Zeit erfüllt war.* It should not be explained, as if we read ἐν τῷ πληρώματι: *tempore exacto* (WOLF), or *aliquo tempore, suo tempore* (MORUS); nor should it be referred to *extrema tempora* (KOPPE), still less is it=*eorum quæ restant temporum*, or *in reliquis, i. e., novi fœderis temporibus* (STIER * and others). Unpauline as well as unbiblical is USTERI's explanation, the fulfilling of that time has had its ground in the necessary development of the human consciousness, or of the religious spirit of humanity.† God's gracious design applies then to a dispensation, which ordains time and its periods, leading to a point when they are completed. This is still further defined by what follows:

**To gather up together all things.**—[ἀνακεφαλαιώσασθαι τὰ πάντα. Braune: *to gather together again for Himself all things.*]—The verb is derived from κεφάλαιον, the chief point, and means principally, to gather together in one main point, as Rom. xiii. 9, where it is said of the single commandments, that they are "briefly comprehended" in the one command of love (ἐν τῷ λόγῳ τούτῳ ἀνακεφαλαιοῦται), *summatim comprehendere.* But it is acknowledged, that the Apostle, "who does not etymologize, but follows general accords" (HARLESS), might readily have chosen the word, in order to play upon the word κεφαλή, the head, which according to i. 22 is Christ (CHRYSOSTOM, THEOPHYLACT, LUTHER: "comprehended together under one head," CALOV., WOLF, HARLESS, STIER, SCHENKEL, MATTHIES and others). As *recapitulare* passes over *capitulum* to *caput* in its meaning, so too ἀνακεφαλαιοῦν over κεφάλαιον to κεφαλή. [The play on the word is barely possible. Paul's usage favors it, but the context is against it, since "in Christ" follows so soon, and the idea of Christ as Head occurs much further on, the reference here being more to His atonement than to His sovereignty. He is regarded as κεφάλαιον rather than as κεφαλή (MEYER).—R.]

* [ALFORD argues at some length in favor of the reference to the whole gospel dispensation, "the giving forth of the gospel under God's providential arrangements." Against his view, see EADIE.—R.]

† [It is certainly true that God comprehended this development in His plan, and that it was an important factor in carrying out "the dispensation of the fulness of times," though its importance has not been recognized until lately by theologians and church historians EADIE well observes: "The πλήρωμα is regarded as a vast réceptacle into which centuries and milleniums had been falling, but it was now filled." "That fulness of the time in which this economy was founded, is the *precise* period, for the Lord has appointed it; and the *best* period, for the age was ripe for the event." The view of Dr. Braune is so well stated and agrees so entirely with that of the most exact of modern commentators, that further supplement is needless.—R.]

Although the meaning of the preposition (ἀνα, *again*) does not appear in the verb, Rom. xiii. 9, since it would be too artificial to retain it with HARLESS, because of an assumed reference to the local position of the law given in detail Exod. xx. and afterwards summed up and repeated, Lev. xix. 18 (THILO renders Rom. xiii. 9, *repetere*), still there is no ground for not retaining it here (see PASSOW *sub voce*), where the reference is to a gathering of what was dispersed and a renewal of what was ruined, and not originally so. The word may indeed apply to an entirely new fact, but it still refers back to an original status and beginning (MEYER, HARLESS, STIER).* Comp. Col. i. 15-17.

Finally the middle form must not be left unnoticed: God will gather together again for Himself (*sibi*) what He has created for Himself; this supports at the same time the meaning *again*. Accordingly the following explanations are unsatisfactory: *a principio renovare* (*Syriac*), *instaurare* (*Vulgate*), giving an explanation of the character of the gathering together; συγκεφαλαιοῦσθαι (RAPHEL), to subject all things at once to Christ; borrowing the phrase from rhetoric, to recapitulate (JEROME, ERASMUS, BEZA), or from military usage=*in unum agmen cogere* (GROTIUS) or from arithmetic=*in unam summam redigere* (CAMERARIUS, BUCER), although in each of these there is something more or less correct.

The infinitive is to be taken as epexegetical; it brings forward as an explanation the design† which obtains in the "dispensation of the fulness of times" (WINER, p. 300): in order to gather together under one head for Himself. But how? **In Christ.**—Nothing further is said; in the resumptive ἐν αὐτῷ we find an explanation. We must maintain however that ἐν τῷ Χριστῷ refers to the Saviour who appeared in the fulness of time (the article is in any case inserted purposely and for emphasis), thus preparing the way for the statement of the object. *What* then is to be gathered together? All things.

**The things which are in heaven, and the things which are on earth** [τὰ ἐν τοῖς οὐρανοῖς καὶ ἐπὶ τῆς γῆς. See *Textual Note* [10]]. Τὰ πάντα is neuter and universal, the more because this explanatory clause is added. No importance is to be attached to the plural (οὐρανοῖς), since we find in Phil. iii. 20: ἐν οὐρανοῖς—ἐξ οὗ; despite its different regions (2 Cor. xii. 2: ἕως τρίτου οὐρανοῦ) heaven is conceived of as a unity, over against the earth. The well-attested ἐπί is at all events an error of the transcriber or a provincialism, beside which the established ἐπὶ τῆς γῆς could not appear strange. The repeated article denotes the particularity of what is found in both spheres. Heaven and earth have become places of sin (ii. 2; vi. 12); indeed heaven was the first theatre of sin, when a part of the angels fell into sin and from God (1 Tim. iii. 6; 1 John iii. 8; Jas. ii. 19; 2 Pet. ii. 4; Jude 6); thence it came to earth (2 Cor. xi. 3), in ever greater dimensions (1 Cor. x. 20, 21). Thus the state originally appointed by God and the development He wished to be without disturbance, ceased (Rom. viii. 18-24), so that a renewing of the heavens and of the earth was taken into view (2 Pet. iii. 13). The centre of this renewal is Christ and His redeeming work (Col. i. 20), which, however, has its development also, as before His appearance up to the "fulness of times," so afterwards up to His second Advent, when the "restitution of all things" (Acts iii. 21), the *palingenesia* (Matth. xix. 28), will be introduced. Comp. 2 Pet. iii. 10-13.

It is altogether unmistakable that, in accordance with the views of this Epistle as well as the entire organism of Scripture truth, we must apply this to the totality of the creation (HARLESS, OLSHAUSEN, MATTHIES, MEYER, STIER, HOFMANN, *Schriftbeweis*, I. 216 ff., SCHENKEL and others). If we maintain with BENGEL: *Omnia sub Christo fuerant; per peccatum autem facta erat avulsio et divulsio; atque hæc rursum sublata est*, then only such a "restitution of all things" is here treated of, as takes into the account, not the relations of the individual members, of the individuals of the τὰ πάντα, to each other, nor yet the relations of the same in their diversity over against God and Christ, but rather and only the relation of Christ to the totality. We should neither specialize and restrict too much, as does HOFMANN, who excludes good angels and evil men, and others, who apply it only to intelligence, persons,* nor accept an unspecialized thought (HARLESS), indefinitely in suspense and admitting of no specialization, respecting a totality. If it could be inferred from the fact of the angels not needing redemption, that they were excluded here, we should be finally obliged to except redeemed men from this ἀνακεφαλαίωσις and no longer regard them as under Christ, when their redemption was completed. "The reconciliation through Christ is to the Apostle a fact, whose effects permeate the universe, which affects alike the conscious and the unconscious creation, whether it be touched by sin, or not, as is the case with the good angels" (OLSHAUSEN). Here we may certainly apply what BENGEL so aptly remarks on Rom. viii. 19, that *pro suo quodque genus captu*, and *statu* may be appended, participate in this *Anacephalaiosis*, the evil as conquered and rejected opponents, the good angels as participating, ministering friends, the redeemed as accepted children, the rest of creation as subordinate companions, as theatre of the honors. It is precisely "the restoration of the harmony of

* [The force of ἀνά, *again*, should be retained, it would seem, for Rom. xiii. 9, can include such a notion irrespective of the forced assumption of HARLESS. HODGE and ALFORD indeed are timid about admitting it, lest it be turned to an improper use, but there is undoubtedly a restoration implied in Redemption, although restoration falls very far short of the latter idea.—R.]

† [HARLESS takes it as depending on "the mystery of his will." The general idea is the same, but such a connection would give to the intervening words too much of a parenthetical character.—R.]

* [Perhaps the most restricted view is that of Dr. HODGE: "The redeemed from among men, some of whom are now in heaven and others are still on earth." This he defends by a number of reasons, all of which I am forced to consider irrelevant. The great mistake is in his giving too wide a scope to the *anacephalaiosis*, insisting that it means such a gathering together as implies redemption in its fullest sense, for which there is no authority, save the assumed paranomasia in the word. Granting this position, the restriction of τὰ πάντα follows as a matter of course. It would seem to be a far better method to take τὰ πάντα in its appropriate sense, *all things*, even at the risk of limiting a doubtful word like ἀνακεφαλαιοῦσθαι, than to give it the sense of the masculine, which it never has. This restricted view seems to be adopted more from doctrinal than exegetical reasons.—R.]

the Universe" (HARLESS), which is aimed at. CHRYSOSTOM makes the excellent remark; ὡς ἄν περί οἰκίας τις εἴποι τὰ μὲν σαθρὰ τὰ δὲ ἰσχυρὰ ἐχούσης, ἀνῳκοδόμησε τὴν οἰκίαν—οὕτω καὶ ἐνταῦθα πάντας ὑπὸ μίαν ἤγαγε κεφαλήν. That nothing is said of "the restoration of all things," is quite evident. (See *Doctr. Note* 8.)*

**Even in him**, ἐν αὐτῷ, is to be joined to "things in heaven, and things on earth," as "in Christ" is with "all things," since the two clauses are entirely parallel (HARLESS). GROTIUS well says: "*Sed repetendum censuit, quasi diceret: per ipsum, inquam, unum, non per ullum alium; non hoc factum per Mosen, non per philosophos.*" Hence it is not a Hebraism or Syriasm (RUECKERT, who acknowledges the "not feeble repetition"), nor to be joined with the following ἐν ᾧ as pleonastic. Thus, then, the person of Christ is noted as the Mediator and middle-point of this comprehensive reuniting, and that *without* Him such does not and shall not take place. ["Re-asseverating with great solemnity and emphasis (see Jelf, Gr. § 658), the only blessed sphere in which this ἀνακεφ. can be regarded as operative, and apart from which, and without which, its energies cannot be conceived as acting. It forms also an easy transition to the following relative" (ELLICOTT).—R.]

It is arbitrary and unscriptural (MEYER) for CALOV. and others to assume that Christ is as to His Divine nature the Head of angels, as to His human nature the Head of men. This *anacephalaiosis* is not to be applied to the completion of the kingdom of God in the resurrection of the body (THEODORET, JEROME), and still less to the moral uniting of antagonistic endeavors (KOPPE, WAHL); nor should we determine from Col. i. 20, how it is to be conceived of or to take place, but rather confess that our passage says nothing about this.

* [Comp. MEYER *in loco*. He says: "The doctrine of *restoration*, according to which even those who have remained unbelieving, and finally devils, shall yet attain to blessedness, contrary as it is to the whole tenor of the New Testament, finds no support in our passage either (against CHRYSOSTOM and others), where in ἀνακεφαλ, *etc.*, the *exclusion* of the unbelieving and the demoniacal powers and their banishment to Gehenna is self-evident in connection with the Christian consciousness of faith, so that the *anacephalaiosis* does not apply to *every single individual*, but to the whole complex of things heavenly and earthly, which, after the anti-christian individuals have been excluded and transferred to hell, shall be joined in unity under God in the renewed world again, as formerly before sin all in heaven and on earth was thus united. OLSHAUSEN therefore incorrectly thinks our passage (like Col. i. 20) is to be placed in accord with the general type of Scriptural teaching, by finding in the infinitive ἀνακεφ. the *purpose* of God, 'which, in the founding of redemption furnished with unlimited power, has in view the establishment of *universal harmony*, the restoration of *all that is lost*.' Irrespective of the fact that the infinitive is epexegetical, it is altogether unscriptural to assume that in redemption there is purposed a restoration of *all* that is lost, even of the devils. For those passages which speak of the universality of redemption and such sayings as 1 Pet. iv. 6; Phil. ii. 10 f., leave entirely untouched the constant doctrine of the New Testament respecting eternal damnation. As regards the devils, the purpose of God in the economy of redemption was to *conquer* them (1 John iii. 8; 1 Cor. xv. 24), and to deliver them to the punishment of eternal torment already passed upon them (Matt. xxv. 41; Jude 6; 2 Pet. ii. 4; Rev. xx. 1 ff.; comp. BERTHOLDT, *Christologie*, p. 223). In the New Testament there is no single thought of the restoration of devils, as this is conceived of as an impossibility in the case of the radically antitheistic spirits. The prince of this world is only *judged*." No one can accuse MEYER of theological bias, or of ungrammatical exegesis, hence his opinion is quoted entire.—R.]

Ver. 11. **In whom we were also made his inheritance** [ἐν ᾧ καὶ ἐκληρώθημεν].—A comma only is to be placed after "in Him;" "in whom," which refers to it, marks the union with Him (hence not = through whom, KOPPE, FLATT) as the way to the obtaining of the inheritance, which is rendered prominent by the καί; were the emphasis on the subject we should find καὶ ἡμεῖς here, as in ver. 13: καὶ ὑμεῖς. Incorrect: *in quo etiam nos* (*Vulgate*, ERASMUS). [The E. V.: "in whom also" is equally objectionable in connecting καί with ἐν ᾧ.—R.] Prominence is given to the fact, that the plan of God is already in the process of accomplishment, in accordance with the decree and design; καί is not indeed=*really*, it joins with ἐκληρώθημεν, only what is to be inferred from the preceding context: we are destined, and this connection points to the actualization.

Κληροῦν is found here only; the compound προσεκληρώθησαν in Acts xvii. 4. It is derived, not from κληρονομία, but from κλῆρος, lot (Matth. xxvii. 35; Acts i. 26), portion of an inheritance (Acts xxvi. 18; Col. i. 14), used in a spiritual sense, and transferred to men, to the church composed of individuals (1 Pet. v. 3; τῶν κλήρων). Since this usage is well established, and there is no sufficient reason why the passive sense should not be retained here, we explain: we have become κλῆρος (*i. e.*, of God, as the context requires) in Christ. BENGEL: *hic loquitur per personam Israelis; eramus facti* נַחֲלָה κλῆρος *seu* κληρονομία, *sors, hereditas domini.* Deut. xxxii. 9. So also STIER. The context (ver. 12: "that we should be," ver. 14:) "purchased possession" supports the requirements of the language. Hence it is not to be explained with LUTHER: through whom we also have come to an inheritance, nor with most: have become partakers of the inheritance; nor yet *accepimus* (MORUS), *contigit nobis, ut* (KOPPE).

[The view here taken of the verb is ably defended by ALFORD and ELLICOTT, and the ordinary interpretation by HODGE and EADIE. The passive form calls for a passive sense, unless there are very strong reasons to the contrary. It would seem that the other sense is allowable, but the only grounds for adopting it here are (1) the objective character of the whole passage, (2) the parallel passage, Col. i. 12. But the sense: we have become an inheritance, is subjective only in form, presenting as it does something which God has become to us, quite as much as what we have become. The other reason is in itself of little weight, for the parallel is inexact in other respects. We adopt the passive sense, rejecting however the allusion to the lot as indicating God's freedom of choice, and accepting the special meaning given by BENGEL.—R.]

Finally it is clear that the subject ("we") is not put in antithesis to another one, as in ver. 14, and that no limitation is indicated either in the verb or in the following participle, so that according to the context and ver. 1, we may apply it to the Apostle and his readers, to Christians in general, but not to the Apostle alone (KOPPE), nor to him and the Jewish Christians (GROTIUS, BENGEL, HARLESS, STIER, SCHENKEL

[HODGE] and others). [BARNES restricts it to the ministers of religion. MEYER, EADIE, ALFORD, ELLICOTT, agree with BRAUNE.—R.]

**Having been predestinated according to the purpose of him who worketh all things** [προορισθέντες κατὰ πρόθεσιν τοῦ τὰ πάντα ἐνεργοῦντος].—We who have become an inheritance, are predestinated. A comparison with ver. 5: "having predestinated us unto adoption," shows us the progress and the distinction. Here it is further defined by the phrase "according to the purpose" from ver. 9 (ἣν προέθετο), that the predestinated is grounded in Him, in His design, His will. Accordingly He whose design it is, is termed: τοῦ τὰ πάντα ἐνεργοῦντος,* "the God, who ordains, prepares and carries forward to its goal the Redemption," who is "therein the All-efficient, Almighty" (STIER); τὰ πάντα is both what is external and historical in the world's story, as well as in the life of individuals, and what is spiritual and internal (Gal. ii. 8; iii. 5; 1 Cor. xii. 11.)

This working is further defined by the phrase: **After the counsel of his will** κατὰ τὴν βουλὴν τοῦ θελήματος αὐτοῦ. Similar to this is τὰς βουλὰς τῶν καρδιῶν (1 Cor. iv. 5). HARLESS compares: the desire of my heart, the joy of my eyes, the tears of my sorrow, as examples of the exchange of the simple subject into the activity, or peculiarity, or organ of the subject, which is the ground or means of a mental or sensuous manifestation, in order thus with exactness and definiteness to render prominent the close relation between the two. A similar case is 1 Pet. iii. 17: εἰ θέλοι τὸ θέλημα τοῦ θεοῦ. Βουλή is then the decision, the determination which God forms in His will. See above on ver. 5. It is God absolutely free (MATTHIES), His *consilium liberrimum* (BENGEL). Τὰ πάντα is not *ad id negotium, de quo agitur, adstringendum* (GROTIUS), nor are βουλή and τοῦ θελήματος mere synonymes, as has been affirmed without ground of προορισθέντες and πρόθεσις also, nor yet=*voluntas liberrima* (KOPPE).

[The two words βουλή and θέλημα naturally lead to remarks upon the distinction between the verbs from which they are derived θέλειν and βούλεσθαι.† The distinction of BUTTMANN will not apply in the New Testament. He says (*Lexic. sub voce*): "βούλομαι is confined to the *inclination*, θέλω to that kind of wish in which there lies a *purpose* or *design*." But in Matth. i. 19, where both words occur, they cannot be thus distinguished; for Joseph's inclination was not to expose his wife, and this is expressed by θέλων, while his purpose to put her away is expressed by ἐβουλήθη. It is rather in this case, as ALFORD says: "θέλω expresses the mere wish, βούλομαι the wish ripened into intention," in favor of which view he cites BUTTMANN however. TITTMANN on the other hand, while seeming to agree with BUTTMANN, and usually cited as sustaining him, really differs from him. In his *Synonym. N. T.*, p. 134 ff, he says that θέλειν is simply to will (*simpliciter velle*), while βούλεσθαι denotes further the inclination. His citation of Ammonius who remarks that the latter cannot be predicated of brutes, would prove that deliberation also was implied in it. He further adds that he who does anything θέλων, does it spontaneously, while he who does it βουλόμενος, determines to turn his mind to that matter. So PLATO (*Laws*, v.) opposes τὸ βουλητόν τε καὶ ἑκούσιον and τὸ ἀβούλητόν τε καὶ ἀκούσιον. This distinction would justify the remark of BRAUNE (on ver. 5) that βουλή is the act of willing joined with inclination, while ἐθέλειν is the ethical act. Yet TITTMANN and others are scarcely justified in denying to θέλειν any sense of desiring, wishing, *etc.* With the infinitive such a meaning is common, as in the well-known formula: "I would not have you ignorant" (οὐ θέλω δὲ ὑμᾶς ἀγνοεῖν, Rom. i. 13, *etc.*), and in Rom. vii. 15 ff., where the antithesis is μισῶ. Besides the spontaneity of will may, after all, indicate an impulse from the side of the desire; who can decide? One thing is certain, we cannot, save by a species of anthropomorphism, apply such distinctions to God, *e. g.*, 1 Tim. ii. 4: "who will (θέλει) have all men to be saved;" 2 Pet. iii. 9: "not willing (βουλόμενος) that any should perish." We dare not, it seems to me, say that one passage refers to God's spontaneous will and the other to His inclination. In fact any discrimination between the two words for doctrinal purposes is of doubtful propriety, for there is no conflict in God, such as we find in us. Still we need not hesitate to explain "the counsel of His will" as meaning, the definite and deliberate volition of God's free, sovereign, spontaneous will. A pure *voluntas* on His part involves the accordant desire, purpose, determination and volition, all questions respecting priority being out of place. So ELLICOTT, whether correct in his distinction or not, is right in saying that our passage "solemnly *represents* the Almighty Will as displaying itself in action: θέλημα designating the will generally, βουλή the more special expression of it." So MEYER, ALFORD (on 1 Tim. v. 14) make this general distinction: "θέλω is the resting inclination of the will, βούλομαι its active exertion," which is valid enough here. On the whole EADIE is most judicious in his remarks, preserving TITTMANN's distinction, and yet admitting the idea of desire in θέλω. "Θέλημα is will, the result of desire—*voluntas;* βουλή is counsel, the result of a formal decision—*propositum.*" Donaldson's *New Cratylus*, §§ 463, 464. Here βουλή is the ratified expression of will—the decision to which His will has come. The Divine mind is not in a state of indifference, it has exercised θέλημα—will; and that will is not a lethargic *velleity*, for it has formed a definite purpose, βουλή, which it determines to carry out.—R.]

* [ALFORD: "Energizes; but especially in and among material previously given, as here, in His material creation, and in the spirits of all flesh, also His creation." The same author remarks on the repetition of the notion of predestination: "Here first the Apostle comes to the idea of the universal church, the whole Israel of God, and therefore here brings forward again that fore-ordination which he had indeed hinted at generally in ver. 5, but which properly belonged to Israel, and is accordingly predicated of the Israel of the church."—R.]

† [In my note on *Colossians*, p. 35, I refer to Dr. Hitchcock's views on this point. While it is a matter of regret as regards this work as a whole that Prof. Hitchcock, owing to ill health, was obliged to abandon his intention to edit Ephesians, it is especially unfortunate that his studies on this distinction could not be incorporated here. His conclusions, however, agree in the main with those of TITTMANN, as given above.—R.]

Ver. 12. **That we should be unto the praise of his glory** [εἰς τὸ εἶναι ἡμᾶς εἰς ἔπαινον δόξης αὐτοῦ. The *Rec.* inserts τῆς before δόξης on very slight authority.—R.]—This marks the goal, which is set up for those who are "predestinated" in the "purpose," with the further definition: "to the praise of his glory." Comp. ver. 6. Here He Himself and His glory are the object of the praise, as in ver. 14. This expression, three times repeated, and always used at the close of a circle of thought, must be explained each time in the same way, and so that the emphasis which is laid on it be not lessened; accordingly we must retain its force as a designation of the aim or goal, remembering that εἶναι precedes it; a *being* is spoken of, which is attained through a *becoming*, and this status is that of *persons* (ἡμᾶς), who not merely praise with the mouth, in words, but *should be themselves a praise.* Hence the phrase is not all to be regarded as an *incisum* or as parenthetical, nor should we join "that we should be" either with "in Christ" (ZELTNER) or with "who before hoped" (KNAPP, FLATT, HARLESS, OLSHAUSEN and others), as though the thought were: the goal of the predestination is, that we who before hoped, should be in Christ, to the praise and glory of God, or that we to God's glory, hoped before in Christ. MORUS: *ut adeo in Christo spem reponere possimus in laudem honoremque Dei.* This displaces the proper aim, and what it substitutes cannot be an aim; the hope of the Jews, the faith of the Gentiles.

**We who have before hoped in Christ** [or **the Christ**]. — Τοὺς προηλπικότας = *quippe qui antea spem posuerunt* (WINER, p. 127);* it characterizes those who have thus become to the praise of God, by pointing out the way to this. The construction is not singular (1 Cor. xv. 19: ἐν Χριστῷ ἠλπικότες; Rom. xv. 13; ἐλπὶς ἐν δυνάμει πνεύματος ἁγίου, before in ver. 12: ἐπ' αὐτῷ—ἐλπιοῦσιν). "In Christ," ἐν τῷ Χριστῷ, marks this vital fellowship with Him; it is not = εἰς τὸν Χριστόν, towards Him, to Him; He is the ground of the hope.

And now πρό! It points to the state and the period before attaining the appointed goal, hence to the earthly life; it is a designation of the Christian state in the pilgrimage. Hence BENGEL very properly remarks: τὸ *ante refertur ad tempora V. T.*, but he is incorrect in referring "before" to persons as though the Jews were thus indicated (*primum nacti sunt Judæi deinde gentes,* Acts xix. 46). So CHRYSOSTOM, ERASMUS, HARLESS, STIER, MEYER and others. But προελπίζειν ἐν τῷ Χριστῷ is not = προσδέχεσθαι (Luke ii. 25, 28), notwithstanding Acts xxviii. 20; xxvi. 6, 7. This phrase is added to what precedes in order, as in ver. 6, to furnish at *the same time* a point of connection for what follows, a transition; hence at the close (ver. 14) no such addition is made.

[The view defended above is that of DE WETTE,† and of EADIE (in his first edition). Nearly all modern commentators accept at this point a distinction between ἡμεῖς and ὑμεῖς, referring the former to Jewish Christians, the latter to Gentile Christians. (The other view refers the former to Christians in general, the latter to the readers.) I am constrained to differ from Dr. Braune here, and adopt the common opinion. (1) No other view allows to προ its proper meaning. To refer the participle to the earthly life, seems far-fetched. The word would not be an appropriate *characteristic* of all Christians in this connection. Nor is the reference to before the time of writing, worthy of the context. (2) The antithetical καὶ ὑμεῖς (ver. 13) is well-nigh conclusive, especially if it be taken as the direct subject of the verb ἐσφραγίσθητε. The Jews had in the Messianic prophecies a ground for their hoping before, but a *sealing* was more prominent in the case of the Gentiles to whom no such promise had come. (3) The form ἐν τῷ Χριστῷ, instead of εἰς τὸν Χριστόν, is not against this view: "to have hoped *in Christ* was a higher characteristic than to have directed hope *towards Christ,* and designated them as more worthy exponents of the praise of God's glory" (ELLICOTT).—If this view be accepted, then we can with propriety retain the article in translating: *in the Christ,* as indeed BRAUNE himself insists on the emphatic force of the article in the similar phrase, ver. 10. Any emphasis upon it here would tell against his view.—R.]

THIRD FOUNDATION. Vers. 13, 14: *The personal appropriation of salvation.*

Ver. 13. **In whom ye also.**—Ἐν ᾧ, in Christ, *viz.*, "ye were sealed," since the repetition of ἐν ᾧ is justified by the added phrase: "after that ye heard," *etc.* Comp. WINER, p. 545, 1. [For a capital defence of this view of the construction, see ELLICOTT *in loc.*—R.] Evidently neither ἐστέ (MEYER) [ALFORD], nor ἠλπίκατε (ERASMUS, CALVIN, BEZA [E. V., ESTIUS] and others), nor ἐκληρώθητε (ANSELM, KOPPE, HARLESS, OLSHAUSEN)* should be supplied. The last is manifestly too remote, the second could only be προηλπίκατε, and the first is unnecessary. It is impossible to take the participle ἀκούσαντες as a finite verb (*Syriac*, LUTHER: have heard) [*i. e.*, as the predicate of ὑμεῖς]; just as little should ἐν ᾧ be explained as *ideo* (MORUS).

"Ye also" refers to the readers, and places them in antithesis to "we:" that is, the Christians specially addressed, the local church, written to, over against Christendom in general, the church as a whole. There is no ground whatever for the reference to Gentile Christians, which is accepted by nearly all modern expositors, except RUECKERT; nor does the context justify it. [See my note on ver. 12. The passage is markedly antithetical, and this is a ground for the reference to the Gentile Christians. As for the context: while hearing and

* [ELLICOTT objects to this as inexact, observing that "this would imply a participle *without*, not as here *with* the article." He refers to DONALDSON, *Cratylus*, § 304, *Grammar*, § 492 sq. It should be noticed that the perfect participle expresses here as so often a past act continuing to the present, the perfect of *permanent state.*—R.]

† [It should be noticed, that DE WETTE, who is the principal supporter of this view, is also the chief opposer of the Pauline origin of our Epistle. Naturally enough the latter opinion would influence his judgment on this point, for one who believes that this verse was written by a pupil of the Apostle Paul, in all probability a Gentile, would fail to see the appropriateness of giving prominence to the antithesis between Jewish and Gentile Christians accepted by most commentators.—R.]

* [So HODGE, who misapprehends the difficulties attending the construction accepted by BRAUNE.—R.]

believing and sealing belong to all Christians, there was undoubtedly in the previous circumstances of the Gentile Christians, a good reason for emphasizing these facts in their case.—R.]

**Having heard the word of truth,** ἀκούσαντες τὸν λόγον τῆς ἀληθείας.—This points to the external situation, in which the apostolic preaching came to them, and they accepted it. This is by no means a token that they are Gentile Christians (STIER, SCHENKEL and others), but is chiefly applicable rather to the Jews. (Acts xiii. 46, xviii. 5, 6; Rom. i. 16; xv. 8).* That which is imparted, "the word of truth," is so termed on account of its contents (2 Tim. ii. 15), as it is called "of God," on account of its origin (Acts xiii. 46); "of life," 1 Jno. i. 1, on account of its *effect*. In Col. i. 6: "in the word of the truth of the Gospel" (comp. Gal. ii. 5: "the truth of the gospel") the shading of the thought is somewhat different; here the reference is less to the antithesis in Judaism (the "shadow" of the O. T.), as CHRYSOSTOM, STIER think, or to that in heathenism with its lies (A-LAPIDE and others), or to both (GROTIUS), than to Christ, who is the Truth, so that the word as to its contents and origin is τῆς ἀληθείας (HARLESS, SCHENKEL [EADIE, ALFORD, ELLICOTT, HODGE] and others). But the phrase is never = *doctrina vera* (MORUS, KOPPE), *institutio in vera religione* (WAHL).

**The gospel of your salvation,** τὸ εὐαγγέλιον τῆς σωτηρίας ὑμῶν.—This is appositional, defining what precedes, and in such a way that "word" corresponds to "gospel," "truth" to "salvation;" the latter word sets forth the power of saving, which is joined to the gospel, which operates through it (Rom. i. 16; 1 Cor. i. 18; iv. 20); hence it is the contents to be imparted; "salvation" is more comprehensive than "forgiveness of sins," redemption (ver. 7); it is "the certain, complete rescuing" STIER). [ELLICOTT distinguishes between the two genitives; taking ἀληθείας as genitive *substantiæ*, σωτηρίας as "a genitive of the (spiritual) *contents* or *subject-matter, etc.*, 'the gospel which turns upon, which reveals salvation,' thus forming one of that large class of genitives of remoter reference."—R.]

**In whom I say having also believed, ye were sealed** [ἐν ᾧ καὶ πιστεύσαντες ἐσφραγίσθητε]. Ἐν ᾧ, "in whom," stands in the *anaphora* and, as in the beginning of this verse and in ver. 11, refers to Christ; this is required by καὶ πιστεύσαντες, since καί connects with the preceding ἀκούσαντες: "the inward state of being permeated by the word of truth is expressed by the advance from ἀκούσαντες to καὶ πιστεύσαντες, they have heard it and at the same time really appropriated it" (MATTHIES); hence both words have the same reference. Although it is grammatically allowable that ἐν ᾧ be connected with πιστεύσαντες and applied to the gospel (Mark i. 15; πιστεύετε ἐν τῷ εὐαγγελίῳ); yet as a matter of syntax it should be referred to ἐν τῷ Χριστῷ (ver. 12) which is dialectically justified at the same time, because the vital fellowship with Christ is the pre-supposition for the σφραγισθῆναι, and faith is only the condition, the subjective means of appropriation. "Not *in virtue* of faith, but *by means* of faith in virtue of what the word proffers to him who hears and what he apprehends" (DELITZSCH), comes the new life in Christ.

Πιστεύσαντες may be understood, as in Rom. xiii. 11 of the act of acceptance (RUECKERT), or taken as = διὰ τῆς πίστεως, as in ver. 7; διὰ τοῦ αἵματος αὐτοῦ; iii. 12: διὰ τῆς πίστεως αὐτοῦ. Comp. Rom. v. 2; 1 Cor. iv. 15. [It is best taken absolutely.—R.] We may then say with HARLESS: the notion of the participle as to its temporal occurrence coincides with that of the finite verb. MEYER ought not to separate and sever temporally hearing, believing, baptism, reception of the Holy Ghost, although dialectically they are to be sharply distinguished.

[These aorist participles may express either contemporaneous or antecedent action. The latter relation seems to be most in accordance with the nature of the actions referred to. ALFORD takes them as indicating the *terminus a quo*, rendering: *since*, from the time when *ye* heard, *on your believing*, remarking further that the participle is and is not contemporaneous with the verb: "it is not, inasmuch as in strict accuracy, faith preceded baptism, and baptism preceded the gift of the Spirit: but it is, inasmuch as on looking back over a man's course, the period of the commencement of his faith includes all its accidents and accompaniments."—R.]

Ἐσφραγίσθητε is more closely defined by the context. It means in iv. 30; John iii. 33; vi. 27; 2 Cor. i. 22, to seal, to confirm, as σφραγίς (Rom. iv. 11; 1 Cor. ix. 2; 2 Tim. ii. 19) is the attesting seal. By means of the faith which is joined with your hearing, ye have been also sealed and certified in Christ; referring to ver. 11: ἐν ᾧ καὶ ἐκληρώθημεν. The κληρωθῆναι moves on to the σφραγισθῆναι (CHRYSOSTOM); it is not evident, how this should be particularly true of the Gentile Christians, over against the Jewish Christians, among whom Paul reckoned himself.* There is not merely an intended inheritance and an attestation thereto conceded, but this is presented with a certifying seal; since the heritage is in them, they in it, and it growing into them, they are themselves made sure as heirs, are confirmed and certified in this possession. The immediate meaning is, that they have been assured of this grace for themselves; "ye have been assured by the Holy Ghost, as by a letter and seal" (RUECKERT).

The change of person (ἡμεῖς—ὑμεῖς) marks, that they have been *attested* in this possession for others also, strongly enough *designated*, to be recognized as companions. [This is equally true, if "we," "you," be referred to Jewish and Gentile Christians, for it was precisely the gift of the Holy Ghost (Acts x. 47; xi. 17), which demonstrated to Peter, that the Gentiles should be thus recognized.—R.] THEOPHYLACT: ὥστε εἶναι δῆλον, ὅτι θεοῦ ἐστε λάχος καὶ κλῆρος.)

* [It is difficult to see how these passages prove the correctness of Dr. BRAUNE'S statement. The Jews were the first hearers, but of the ὑμεῖς "believing" also is here predicated, the reference being to the same persons; hence these passages which speak of the Jews hearing and not believing, prove rather that ὑμεῖς refers to Gentile Christians.—R.]

* [The sealing was the same in the case of both, but the antecedents of the Gentile Christians, the fact that they had no previous seal of God's covenant, makes this prominent in their case, but this does not require us to find here any definite allusion to circumcision.—R.]

It is only a sequel and an inference, that they have been *secured* from future wrath, ruin, loss and condemnation.* The passive indicates an experience, which does not proceed from themselves, is not developed out of them, but is the act of another, of God. All this is so natural and so accordant with the use of the word, which is a common one in the Old Testament, that there is no reason for supposing here an allusion to heathen customs, such as branding slaves with the name of their master (FLATT), or the *stigmata* of idolatrous worship (GROTIUS), or, because the letter is addressed to Ephesus, to the σφραγίς of Diana (AMETIUS), or to Jewish circumcision (SCHOETTGEN, WETSTEIN, THOLUCK and others). Nor is it equivalent to: the salvation or inheritance (in RUECKERT) is sealed to you; since they themselves are attested documents.

**With the Spirit of promise, the holy One** [τῷ πνεύματι τῆς ἐπαγγελίας τῷ ἁγίῳ].—The dative τῷ πνεύματι, marks that with which they have been sealed, certified; iv. 30; ἐν ᾧ, wherein "ye are sealed unto the day of redemption," denotes the fellowship with the Holy Ghost. The Spirit is here the attesting "seal," that God affixes to those who in fellowship with Christ have heard His word and become believers: πιστεύσαντες designates the subjective means, τῷ πνεύματι the objective. In Rom. viii. 16, without the figure: "the Spirit beareth witness with our spirit, that we are the children of God." [*With* (E. V.) as indicating that the Holy Spirit is the seal, is preferable to *by* (ALFORD, ELLICOTT), which might imply that the Spirit was the Sealer; God is the Sealer, *we* are the sealed, the Spirit is the Seal.—R.]

The phrase τῷ ἁγίῳ compels us to accept a reference to the Holy Spirit; it is added with emphasis, so as to guard against the mistake, that the spirit inherent in the promise was meant.† But because τῆς ἐπαγγελίας is emphasized, it comes first; it is otherwise in John vii. 37: ἐν τῇ ἐσχάτῃ ἡμέρᾳ τῇ μεγάλῃ τῆς ἑορτῆς. Comp. WINER, p. 488 f. Of course we cannot take it as referring to special miraculous gifts of the Holy Ghost (GROTIUS, ESTIUS), as though only those thus endowed were assured of the adoption and inheritance. Nor does it refer to the *donum sanctificationis* (PELAGIUS, Romanists) since τῷ ἁγίῳ denotes, not the *effect*, but the *attribute* of the Spirit.

The genitive τῆς ἐπαγγελίας accordingly cannot possibly designate the promise as that in which the Spirit is immanent, inheres, but refers to that the object of which is the Spirit, *viz.*, the Holy Spirit. BENGEL is excellent: *per verbum promissus erat spiritus sanctus; dato igitur spiritu sancto, ii., qui credidere verbo, obsignati sunt; et qui spiritum sanctum habent, omnem promissionem sibi præstitum iri sciunt.* So most expositors: the *promised* Spirit.‡ "The promise of the Spirit" (Gal. iii. 14) is the promise which has the Spirit as its aim, or its object. The "promise" here should not, however, be limited to Christ's last words (Luke xxiv. 49; Acts i. 4), as is done by BAUMGARTEN-CRUSIUS, nor yet to the Old Testament promises (Joel iii. 1-5; Isa. xxxii. 15; xliv. 3; Ezek. xxxvi. 25; xxxix. 29), as HARLESS supposes, following CHRYSOSTOM; it includes both what is prophetical and apostolical (Luke xxiv. 44-47). The context definitely decides against the view, that the Spirit brings the promise, or that the notion of a *testimonium reddere, obsignare* is found in the genitival connection (THEOPHYLACT [who, however, also gives this correct explanation: ὅτι ἐξ ἐπαγγελίας ἐδόθη.—R.] CALVIN, BEZA.)

Ver. 14. **Who is the earnest of our inheritance** [ὅς ἐστιν ἀῤῥαβὼν τῆς κληρονομίας ἡμῶν].—Ὅς refers logically to τὸ πνεῦμα, marking its personality, which the Apostle has in mind, *constructio ad sensum*), as Matth. xxviii. 19: τὰ ἔθνη—αὐτούς; 2 John 2: τοῖς τέκνοις—οὕς. Comp. WINER, p. 133. [A better explanation of ὅς, than the *constructio ad sensum*, is that of its agreement in gender with ἀῤῥαβών. So MEYER, ALFORD, ELLICOTT. (See WINER, p. 157.) The last named remarks that "τὸ πνεῦμα in its most distinct personal sense is invariably used with the neuter relative."–R.] It is not to be referred to Christ (POLYCARP); that is too remote (WINER, p. 149) and the sense will not admit of it, since the Spirit is the ἀῤῥαβων; 2 Cor. i. 22: "Who hath also sealed us, and given the earnest of the Spirit in our hearts" (v. 5). From the Hebrew עֵרָבוֹן (Gen. xxxviii. 3, 17, 18, 20)=*pignus*,* there probably arose through the agency of Phœnician traders ἀῤῥαβών in Greek, *arrhabo* and *arrha* in Latin (without the *h* also), with the sense of "earnest-money," the beginning of the payment which should take place in full afterwards. Hence HESYCHIUS:=πρόδομα, CHRYSOSTOM: μέρος τοῦ παντός; JEROME: *Arrabo futuræ emtioni quasi quoddam testimonium et obligamentum datur.* It is=ἀπαρχὴ τοῦ πνεύματος, Rom. viii. 23.

What the Spirit promises to vouchsafe to us in the future, in eternity, is indicated by the genitive τῆς κληρονομίας ἡμῶν, "of our inheritance." The inheritance which is the necessary consequence of sonship (Rom. viii. 17; Gal. iv. 7) is an eternal one (Gal. iii. 18; Heb. ix. 15; comp. v. 5; Col. iii. 24). Thus then believers obtain the certainty that they are heirs and have an inheritance in eternity, not through an assurance from without, but chiefly through the *reality of the possession*, not at once in its entire extent, but in an *earnest* (HARLESS). "Our" includes the Apostle, his readers and all Christendom (1 Cor. ii. 12), because it stands at the end of the paragraph, not Gentile and Jewish Christians (STIER, SCHENKEL and others.)

* [HODGE combines the three meanings: (1) To authenticate or confirm as genuine and true; (2) To mark as one's property; (3) To render secure.—R.]

† [MEYER well remarks that Paul wishes to give *emphatic and solemn* prominence to that by means of which the sealing takes place, and hence speaks with a corresponding pathos. This should be preserved in the English rendering as above (so ALFORD).—R.]

‡ [ELLICOTT: "The Spirit which came from, *i. e.*, was announced, by promise." EADIE: "The genitive is almost that of ablation." MEYER takes it as "a genitive of quality, designating the promise as a *characteristic* of the Holy Spirit." ALFORD would retain the article in English: "the Spirit of the promise."—R.]

* [*Pignus*, pledge, differs from *arra*, earnest; the former is restored when the contract has been performed, the latter is a part of the purchase money. The custom of paying "earnest-money" obtains still in legal transactions, but more especially in the popular usage of most nations.—R.]

**Unto the redemption of his purchased possession, unto the praise of his glory,** *εἰς ἀπολύτρωσιν τῆς περιποιήσεως, εἰς ἔπαινον τῆς δόξης αὐτοῦ.*—These two qualifying phrases, introduced by the same preposition, are to be taken as parallel, the first referring to the *objective* aim of the church of God, the second to the *subjective* aim of the redeemed member (SCHENKEL). Comp. vers. 6, 12. Hence *αὐτοῦ* is to be joined to *περιποιήσεως* as well as to *δόξης* (MEYER, HOFMANN), who however in *Schriftbeweis,* II. 2, p. 28, understands it of Christ, when it obviously refers to God the Father, (SCHENKEL). The preposition *εἰς* marks a goal, which is nearer at hand, more definitely described in the phrase "the earnest of our inheritance," than in "ye were sealed," so that the connection with the relative clause is more natural than to pass over it back to the verb of the main clause, ver. 13 (MEYER, [HODGE, ELLICOTT] and others). Thus the explanation of *ἀπολύτρωσις* as *ἡ τέλεια* is required. [That is, as in chap. iv. 30; Rom. viii. 23 (comp. my note *in loco*) the full final redemption, the accomplishment of all that is included in the word (ALFORD).—R.] The context, however, gives a further definition with *τῆς περιποιήσεως* (*αὐτοῦ.*)

Περιποιεῖν=to cause something to remain, to let remain, to deliver; *περιποιεῖσθαι*, to cause to remain for one's self, hence to acquire, to gain. The substantive therefore=acquisition, possession. In 2 Thess. v. 9: *εἰς περιποίησιν σωτηρίας*; 2 Thess. ii. 14: *εἰς περιποίησιν δόξης*, it is acquisition as the genitives indicate; 1 Pet. ii. 9: *λαὸς εἰς περιποίησιν*, it is evidently possession (comp. Matth. iii. 17; Acts xx. 28; Isa. xliii. 21), hence=סְגֻלָּה as the people of Israel were termed, which is elsewhere designated by *περιούσιος* (Exod. xix. 5; Deut. vii. 6; xiv. 2; xxvi. 18, *λαὸς περιούσιος*, LXX. and Tit. ii. 14), *peculium Dei.* Hence the "redemption" applies to God's possession, to the people already acquired by Him, and cannot be the first redeeming act, "the forgiveness of sins" (ver. 7; Col. i. 14; Rom. iii. 24), by which the people are acquired, but must be the completed work, to which the Holy Ghost, as earnest, pledge, points and leads. So most expositors from THEOPHYLACT (*οἵ τινές ἐσμεν περιποίησις καὶ κτῆσις καὶ περιουσία θεοῦ*) and ŒCUMENIUS (*διὰ τὸ περιποιήσασθαι ἡμᾶς τὸν θεόν*) to ERASMUS and the latest time. Hence *εἰς* is not=*ἕως*, *usque ad* (MORUS), nor *ἀπολύτρωσις*=*mors, liberatio a malo* (MORUS), nor is the genitive *τῆς περιποιήσεως* a designation of the effect (LUTHER: to our redemption, that we become His possession; STIER: to the redemption, *that* we *become* and *because* we *are* His possession.)

[It rarely occurs that a passage presenting a number of difficulties is interpreted with so great an approach to unanimity as in this case. Modern English and American commentators, almost without an exception take the same view as BRAUNE. STIER, among the Germans, does not reject it, but puts other meanings upon the passage as usual. EADIE gives his Trinitarian division as follows: "The Father seals believers, and His glory is the last end; in the Son they are sealed, and their redemption is His work, while the Spirit 'which proceedeth' from the Father, and is sent by the Son—is the Seal and Earnest."—For a very full discussion of the word *περιποίησις*, see HARLESS, whose comments have largely contributed in producing the unanimity respecting this passage among modern interpreters.—R.]

### DOCTRINAL AND ETHICAL.

1. *The importance of the doctrine of predestination.* The Apostle speaks in great emotion, as is unmistakably shown by the remarkably complicated structure of his sentences, and with special emphasis, as the repetition and strength of his expressions (vers. 4, 5, 9, 11) equally prove. CHEMNITZ says, in a sermon on Matth. xxii. (in FRANK'S *Theologie der Form. Concord.*, iv. 268): "Therefore (on account of the contests arising out of the doctrine of election) it has occurred to some, that we ought not to preach at all to Christians in the church about the foreknowledge and choice of God, because it is dangerous to both sides, as it is said, leading either to security or despair; but because God has revealed this very doctrine to us so often and in so many parts of the Scripture, we must not put it under the table, may not and should not say, that it is unprofitable, obnoxious or injurious, yet we must so look into it, as not to run too far or climb too high, but have and hold in all simplicity the true understanding and proper use thereof." [It may well be added, that such use is for Christians alone (ver. 5: "us"), and that this use will lead on the one hand to trustful security in view of the fixedness of God's purpose, on the other hand to profound humility in view of the entire freedom of God's choice irrespective of our merit. Others may, nay some must speculate on this subject, but they find no solution of this problem save so far as God's word gives one; and this solution can be fully apprehended only by a believing soul; it is above logic and philosophy, and even technical theology, even as on many subjects, and these the most important, the heart is a better teacher than the head. Still even the most advanced Christian, seeing that God's word alone gives *any* solution, may well say with the martyr Ridley: "In these matters I am so fearful, that I dare not speak further; yea almost none otherwise than the text does, as it were, lead me by the hand" (from EADIE).—R.]

2. *The starting-point.* It must by no means be overlooked, that the Apostle first expresses in praise the *consciousness of salvation*, though in a summary way, and then passes to *predestination.* Even the transition ("even as he chose us") does not place predestination in the first rank; it only marks the actual relation, and that the possession of salvation becomes our portion according to the election and fore-ordination; yet it still remains true, that from the consciousness of salvation we should look into the eternal will of God, and be lifted up to it. This is done in the confession of the *Lutheran* church, *Form. Concord.*, article xi. In that symbol we begin with sin and the natural powers of man (i. ii.), then follows Justification and its consequences (iii. iv.), next the means of grace in the Word

and the Lord's Supper (v. vi. vii.); to these are joined the Christological articles (viii. ix.), and *De ceremoniis ecclesiasticis* (x.) seems to form the conclusion. But last of all there is added further: *De æterna prædestinatione et electione Dei.* See FRANK, *Theologie*, i. 48; iv. 138. The *Reformed* in their confessions (*Basle, Belgic, Westminster, Helvetic* and others) proceed from the speculative *idea of God*, which is neither Pauline, biblical, nor advisable. [This objection as regards abstractness does not hold against the *Heidelberg Catechism.* Still the Lutheran symbols go to the opposite extreme. That the order in the Reformed confessions is Pauline, Dr. Braune unconsciously admits in the order he himself adopts in these notes (ver. 4 follows ver. 3 very closely, be it observed). If it be Pauline, it is Scriptural, though this Apostle is not alone in putting God and His will so prominently in advance. As to its advisableness: some minds demand the Reformed order, which is at all events that of logical statement, of systematic theology. Others object to it, but the great difficulty is not met by any change of position. If we claim that believing hearts, "blessed with all spiritual blessings in heavenly places in Christ," alone are competent for the discussion, we have claimed all that our section warrants us in doing. Let each systematize as he will; we cannot make God's truth dependent on the order of our symbols. Let us be charitable, since some minds are so constituted as to accept or even demand Calvinism, and others prefer to take the difficulty in another form. Let each hold, indeed, that God's truth is objective truth independent of our subjective statements, and hope for the time when a higher synthesis will reconcile what seems now to be contradictory, all the more because neither Calvinism nor Arminianism has solved the problem presented in this chapter, though one may in its efforts embrace more of the facts of the rule of grace and providence than the other. Comp. the *Doctr. Notes* on Rom. ix. in the Bible-work —R.]

3. *The object of the predestination* is set forth in "us" (vers. 4, 5, 6, 8, 9, 12, 14) and "you" (ver. 13), and in such a way that no ground for the predestination is to be found in those predestinated, hence nothing indicates a limitation of it. It is rather to be extended as widely as sin reaches, and the "forgiveness of sins" (ver. 7) is necessary, and the hearing of "the word of truth, the gospel of salvation" (ver. 13) is designed to extend. Hence the whole human race is the object of the predestination, and as the words "we" and "you" require, not in a mass, but down to each individual. This is entirely in accordance with 1 Tim. ii. 4 (πάντας ἀνθρώπους θέλει σωθῆναι), with the Lord's word, John iii. 16 (ἠγάπησεν ὁ θεὸς τὸν κόσμον), and the saying of Peter (2 Peter iii. 9: μὴ βουλόμενός τινας ἀπολέσθαι, ἀλλὰ πάντας εἰς μετάνοιαν χωρῆσαι). It is precisely the section before us which marks the Divine will of mercy as directed towards *all.* We must maintain the *universality of grace*, UNIVERSALIS VOLUNTAS DEI, *quod non tantum prædicatio pœnitentiæ, verum etiam promissio evangelii sit universalis, hoc est, ad omnes homines pertineat* (Form. Conc. xi. 28). The word πάντας (1 Tim. ii. 4) cannot be explained by *cujusvis status atque conditionis homines, tam illustres ac potentes in mundo, quam obscuros* (PISCATOR), neither can we understand under κόσμον (Jno. iii. 16) the elect, on the ground that God never loved the damned (BEZA), nor limit πάντας (2 Pet. iii. 9) by *nempe credentes* (PISCATOR). Thus the Form. Conc. (xi. 23); *et quidem Deus illo suo consilio—non tantum in genere salutem suorum procuravit, verum etiam* OMNES ET SINGULAS PERSONAS *electorum—præscivit—eligit* (comp. *ibid.* § 54). The Lutheran confession, it is true, besides the *universality of the grace* of God notes also with a reference to this section a *particularity* of the *election* of grace, of which not all, good and bad, are the objects, but only the children of God: ÆTERNA *vero* ELECTIO *seu* PRÆDESTINATIO DEI AD SALUTEM *non simul ad bonos et ad malos pertinet, sed tantum ad filios Dei, qui ad æternam vitam consequendam electi et ordinati sunt, priusquam mundi fundamenta jacerentur* (xi. 5). Accordingly we should reject here the double predestination to salvation and damnation, which from the first was taught by LUTHER and MELANCHTHON (following AUGUSTINE, who, however, expressed himself very prudently and only in an infra-lapsarian sense, and GOTTSCHALK in the ninth century with his *duplex sive gemina prædestinatio*), but in an infralapsarian sense, maintained however by ZWINGLE (see HAHN, *Stud. u. Krit.*, 1837, pp. 765–805) and CALVIN in a supralapsarian sense, and revived by the *Jansenism* of the Catholic Church in the 17th century, and by E. W. KRUMMACHER in our day, and also the doctrine of SAMUEL HUBERS, that God has in His Son ordained and elected each and every man to eternal life (see FRANK, iv. pp. 165, 281 ff., HAGENBACH in *Herzog's Real-Enc.*, vi. p. 293 ff.), a doctrine which SCHLEIERMACHER *repeats* in his discussion of the doctrine of election (*Werke Theol.* ii. p. 393 f.) and in his *Glaubenslehre* (§ 119, 2), and also the view of HOFMANN (*Schriftbeweis*, i. p. 257 ff.), followed by LUTHARDT (*Compendium der Dogmatik*, p. 85), which denies the reference of the decree of grace to a definite number. [Dr. Braune seems to avoid a definite statement. Whatever may be deduced from the other passages referred to, Paul here declares that *individual persons* are chosen by God, predestinated unto adoption. How many those persons are is a question which when asked of the Son of God led only to personal exhortation. Who they are, manifests itself only in the exercise of faith, though even this is not always manifest to others (nor, as in the case of infants, is this a decisive test). Practically, the question is respecting our personal appropriation of the blessings of redemption, which are according as (καθώς, ver. 4) the election. Logically and theologically, the fact that some are partakers of blessing and others not, when taken in connection with the statement of vers. 4, 5, leads to the conclusion, that of God's free will some have been chosen and others *not chosen.* The negation is, however, all that any ought to deduce from our passage. The difficulties arising from this conclusion cannot be fully met save by a heart so trustful in its affection to the God and Father of our Lord Jesus Christ, as to know it to be right because He has so ordered. The same difficulty meets us in God's providential dealings, aye, in the workings of

His natural laws, for as a brilliant author has well said: "Nature is a terrible Calvinist." Paul concerns himself here only with the positive side, which presents but one difficulty, viz. that of fully responding in love to the gracious fact.—R.]

4. The *Subject of the predestination is God*, the Father of our Lord and Saviour Jesus Christ (ver. 3), and that, too, in His "love" (ver. 4) according to "the good pleasure of His will" (vers. 5, 9), or "the purpose of Him who worketh all things after the counsel of His will" (ver. 11); reference being made to His "grace" (ver. 11), and "the mystery of His will" (ver. 9) being recognized as the subject of the revelation. A duplex state in God Himself is by no means indicated, but rather excluded. In Him there are not two wills, one revealed, according to which God wills the salvation of all men, and another secret (*occulta illa et metuenda voluntas Dei ordinantis suo consilio, quos et quales prædicatæ et oblatæ misericordiæ capaces et participes esse velit*), nor do His mercy and justice exist merely *beside* each other, the latter respecting the damned and the former the elect. It is not that God is gracious, and at the same time just, or just and yet gracious, but in that He provides a satisfaction for His justice, He is gracious, and because He will satisfy His grace, He appeases His justice, so that justice as satisfied is the ground of grace, and grace as to be satisfied is the ground for the satisfaction of justice (FRANK, iv. 191). The secret will is not here asserted beside the revealed, nor can the secret will detract aught from the revealed: the latter, "as the real, unlimitedly efficient" will, stands "constantly over against the apparently contradicting secret" will and "conditions and controls" "the reality of the secret will." "A secret will *in abstracto*, not having at the same time in itself as substantial elements the substantial determinations of the revealed will, does not exist" (FRANK, iv. pp. 198–200). "The Scriptures, however, teach, that the Providence of God has not such a manner and meaning as if a master cook determines he will strangle some of the pheasants lying before him and let others fly, a figure Gerson uses, but predestination comprises in itself *totum decretum redemptionis, vocationis, justificationis, gubernationis et glorificationis*, as Paul throughout the first chapter of the Epistle to the Ephesians thus treats and expounds this doctrine in detail" (CHEMNITZ in FRANK). The omnipotence and executive energy of God is conditioned and bound by His will, by His Nature, as well as by the regulations He has Himself established, which will be spoken of hereafter (notes 6, 7, 8). It is not the Absolute in itself, nor yet the *purely Absolute One*, but the self-conditioning Unconditioned One. Accordingly the Scriptures and the Lutheran Confession distinguish from the *prædestinatio Dei ad salutem*, taken as identical with the *electio*, the *præscientia Dei*, according to which He *prævidet et novit etiam mala, sed non ea ratione, quasi Dei voluntas propitia illa sit, ut fiant* (Form. Conc. xi. 6); *principium autem et causa mali non sit ipsa Dei præscientia, Deus enim non creat, procurat, efficit aut operatur malum, sed neque illud juvat aut promovet* (*Ibid*. 7).

[The theory of the self-conditioning of God is a favorite one with many German theologians. Such self-conditioning may be assumed as the basis of creation, especially the creation of free moral agents, but the mystery yet remains: an Almighty God from whose freedom none of His creatures dare detract aught, and moral, yet sinful, men, from whose freedom of will God will detract nothing. If foreknowledge be assumed as the basis of the predestination, the difficulty is increased: "If God foresaw this faith and holiness, then these qualities were either self-created, or were to be bestowed by Himself; if the former, the grace of God is denied, and if the latter, the question turns upon itself—what prompted God to give them the faith and holiness which He foresaw they should possess" (EADIE). Braune only hints at this explanation, however. Sir WM. HAMILTON's "Philosophy of the Unconditioned" encounters the problem* as directly as Calvinism. Assuming as we must that "God's grace fits men for heaven, but men by unbelief prepare themselves for hell," we still insist: that St. Paul here teaches the entire freedom of choice on the part of God, that choice being in accordance with the nature of the Sovereign Chooser; and at the same time in ver. 13 assumes the free faith on the part of those addressed, while the state of blessing which moves his thanksgiving is expressly said to be in accordance with the choice of God. So much a fair exegesis allows, as Dr. Braune himself admits in his exegetical notes. "Whether this doctrine be identified with Pagan Stoicism or Mohammedan fatalism, and be rudely set aside, and the world placed under the inspection of an inert omniscience; or whether it be modified as to its end, and be declared to be privilege, and not holiness; or as to its foundation, and that be alleged to be not gratuitous and irrespective choice, but foreseen merit and goodness; or as to its subjects, and they be affirmed to be not individuals, but communities; or as to its result, and it be reckoned contingent, and not absolute; or whether the idea of election be diluted into mere preferential choice:"—"such hypotheses leave the central difficulty still unsolved, and throw us back on the unconditioned and undivided sovereignty of Him 'of whom, to whom, and through whom are all things,'—all whose plans and purposes wrought out in the Church, and designed to promote His glory, have been conceived in the vast and incomprehensible solitudes of His own eternity."—EADIE.—R.]

5. *The end of the predestination* is defined in a threefold way:

a. *For the predestinated:* "unto adoption" (ver.

* [EADIE, whose notes on this subject are as judicious as they are apt, quotes from Sir Wm. Hamilton (*Discussions*, etc. p. 598): "It is here shown to be as irrational as irreligious, on the ground of human understanding, to deny, either, on the one hand, the fore-knowledge, predestination, and free grace of God, or, on the other, the free will of man; that we should believe both, and both in unison, though unable to comprehend even either apart. This philosophy proclaims with *St. Augustine*, and Augustine in his maturest writings: —'If there be not free grace in God, how can He save the world? and if there be not free will in man, how can the world by God be judged?' (*Ad Valentinum Epist.* 214.) Or, as the same doctrine is perhaps expressed even better by *St. Bernard:* 'Abolish free will and there is nothing to be saved: abolish free grace, and there is nothing wherewithal to save.' (*De Gratia et Libero Arbitrio.*)" See the list of authors of all opinions given by EADIE, pp. 28, 29.—R.]

5), in which "redemption, the forgiveness of sins" (vers. 7, 14) are given to them in grace ("His grace which He freely bestowed upon us," ver. 6), so that they as the "possession" of God (ver. 14) become partakers of the inheritance (ver. 11), of the salvation which the gospel brings (ver. 13) and "holy and without blame" (ver. 4).

b. *For the entire world*, in the history of which through various periods of development ("dispensation of the fulness of times," ver. 10), it is accomplished: "to gather up together all things in Christ."

c. *For God the Lord:* "unto the praise of the glory of His grace" (ver. 6), "unto the praise of His glory" (vers. 12, 14). The aim is accordingly as much *moral* as *religious*, and as much *individually-personal* as *world-historical*. The synthesis of the moral and religious factors, which is in the main peculiar to the Sacred Scriptures (SCHENKEL), appears all the more prominently here, as the emphatic εἰς ἔπαινον is at once both religious and moral. The same is true of the glory of God and the blessedness of man, and so much so that it is not correct to affirm that the glory of God and it alone is "the final and most exalted end of the creation and redemption of the world" (SCHENKEL).

What is world-historical must be combined with what is personal, the individual life with the whole; it is however unmistakable, that the relation of the creature to the Creator is arranged in order to regulate the demeanor of the former, and that the whole is wrought upon by the individual parts becoming the object of activity, as these are wrought upon through the whole, and thus the totality is brought to completion.

6. *The Mediator is Christ*, "our Lord and Saviour" (ver. 3), "the Beloved" (ver. 6), and it is "through His blood" (ver. 7) thus in conformity to His eternal *Person* and His relation to God, as well as according to His atoning and redeeming *sufferings* in time. *Æterna igitur prædestinatio in Christo et nequaquam extra mediatorem Christum consideranda est* (Form. Conc. xi. 65). Since then God, who is the Father of our Lord and Saviour Jesus Christ, the Beloved, formed the decree of redemption in Christ, He must be conceived of as existing before the purpose, and hence the Person of Christ as that eternal person, in whom the Father chose us, as He created us in Him despite the foreseen fall. Accordingly Christ is the *causa meritoria* of our election, both of the purpose and its accomplishment, to which latter the suffering of death, mentioned in ver. 7, especially refers. Although the Reformed agree with the Lutherans in formal statement on this point, all their symbols describing the election of grace as taking place *in Christo* and *propter Christum*, yet they deviate from scriptural truth, in regarding Him as the object of the predestination: *ut ipse quoque* ἐκλεκτός (Helvet. Conf. V.), and not as *fundamentum ipsam electionem præcedens*, not as *causa meritoria*. So that they not only refer with *propter Christum* to the idea of satisfaction, which should not be the *causa impulsiva*, rather merely the condition chosen by God for the actualization of the predestination in eternal blessedness, but also with *in Christo* wish to designate only the medium of the accomplishment. According to this view only for those elected by God's mercy is there a Christ and an atoning death, and it cannot be perceived whence there should then arise any necessity of the atoning act of redemption for the satisfaction of Divine wrath; for the grace has not to be rendered possible, but the determined gracious purpose has only to be carried out. Comp. SCHNECKENBURGER, *Vergleichende Darstellung*, I. p. 192 ff.; FRANK, IV. p. 192 ff. [It is scarcely fair to take the strongly partisan work of HEIDEGGER (*Formula Consensus Helvetica*, 1675, see *Biblework*, Romans, pp. 191, 192) as a representative of the Reformed Confessions on this point. There has been, since the days of the Reformation, a tendency in the Reformed Church to bald forensic statements on this point, but to-day the full significance of the phrase: "in Christ," is perhaps better understood than ever before.—R.]

7. *The means of grace* in carrying out the decree of redemption the Apostle indicates with γνωρίσας, "having made known" (ver. 9), and calls them also: "the word of truth, the Gospel of your salvation" (ver. 13). To neither designation of the Divine word is there attached any limitation as respects the sphere of its effect, while the genitives describe rather, partly ("of truth") an efficient truth, calculated for all, as the purport of this word, partly ("of your salvation") the power and effect, which it bears in itself and exercises. At all events we should maintain, as respects this chapter, what is said in the *Form. Conc.* xi. 16, 29, 33 (where the German version has "*verleiht*," the Latin expressing it more weakly: *largiri vult*, though meaning quite as much): For it should not be thought, that God spoke thus: Externally through the word I call all of you, to whom I give my word, into my kingdom, but in my heart I do not intend it for all, but only for a certain few; for it is my will, that the greater part of those whom I thus call through my word should not be enlightened and converted, but be and remain condemned, although I declare otherwise respecting them in the invitations of my word. "*Hoc enim esset Deo contradictorias voluntates affingere*" (xi. 24). [This is the old difficulty in another form. It is a difficulty of fact, too. For a large portion of those who have the word of God in their hands and hear it, even while it is the Gospel of salvation to those who sit beside them, are "not enlightened and converted." Why not? The question is not a merely theoretical one, but comes out of agonized hearts often enough. An answer which charges God with folly, or which accepts His purpose as thwarted, will not satisfy the heart, however theologians may philosophize; the resting place in this strait, as in all others, is in God. "He worketh all things after the counsel of His will"—but is "the God and Father of our Lord Jesus Christ."—R.]

8. *The condition* of the saving effect of these means the Apostle marks with ἀκούσαντες, to which he adds with emphasis καὶ πιστεύσαντες (ver. 13), and with προηλπικότας ἐν τῷ Χριστῷ. The Formula of Concord aptly states these thoughts (xi. 17): *Decrevit etiam se spiritu sancto*

*suo per verbum annuntiatum auditione perceptum et memoriæ commendatum velle in nobis efficacem esse, et corda ad veram pœnitentiam agendam inflectere et vera fide conservare.* There is at least nothing to be derived from these propositions in favor of the *Synergism* of Melanchthon and his followers. The word of God develops in the hearer that power which he has placed in it, and in this power he apprehends, being himself first apprehended, what is bidden him, and thus gains hope and confidence through the power of the word which has become vital and active in him. But it is indicated definitely enough that man can resist; he is not forced to hear and accept what is proclaimed, nor to believe in it and hope in it. Since God will save only in Christ, and only through the Word will create faith and hope in Him, this does not accord with the statement of the Reformed and the Predestinarians, that God wills nothing which He does not do. If the Ninevites could avert His punitive will by repentance, so His gracious will may be thwarted through resistance. This is Scriptural truth, and it is confirmed by Christian experience, which knows of no necessity for obeying the will of God, but too well of a possibility of resisting it (FRANK, IV. p. 205). The *gratia irresistibilis* of AUGUSTINE is a fiction arising from an abstract conception of the purely Absolute. The unconditioned yet self-conditioning Personality of God does not will, as the predestinarians think that He wills, but with a self-restraining almightiness within the sphere of redemption, so that salvation is not gained without His will, but the proffered salvation is lost through man's own fault against His earnest gracious will, which He offers in His Word. Both must be maintained: God has willingly given men of His will and conditioned Himself, in placing conditions before men in the hearing and believing of His Word, and man has the power of continued resistance, so that an entire *apocatastasis* of all things, the ultimate salvation of all, although God's revealed will points thereto, is scarcely conceivable, as ORIGEN, SCHLEIERMACHER and others suppose. A final resistance is to be maintained as possible. NITZSCH, *System*, p. 416.

9. *Assurance of election* is definitely pointed out in vers. 13, 14: "ye were *sealed* with the Spirit of *promise*, the Holy One, who is the earnest of our inheritance," and although in consequence of faith (πιστεύσαντες), still on the ground of the promise of the Holy Ghost and the resulting bestowal of the same—in the means of grace, the word, and baptism (which, though not expressed, is to be understood) and through which Christ's merit, that is and suffices for all, is attributed to us. On the ground of the certainty, that God's word is true, that God has loved the *world*, that Christ has died for the sins of the *whole* world, and that God has called you also, *must* have called you, because He has loved you in Christ, and I have been baptized, accepted as a child, endowed with the Holy Ghost, renewed, regenerated, even though it be but germinally, potentially, I am certain of my election before the foundation of the world, and my inheritance in eternity. [Rightly enough the doctrine of election is for the comfort of believers, but they will derive far more comfort from a more definite conception of the matter. If "baptismal regeneration" is a ground for the assurance of election, then many thus assured are not sanctified in this world, and such an assurance is not likely to further such a result. The Augustinian view is here the practical one.—R.]

10. *The possibility of apostasy* is indicated by the phrase "unto the redemption of the purchased possession." It marks chiefly the goal to which the Holy Ghost, as "earnest of our inheritance," points. But the Christian has the consciousness, that his life-development is an ethical, not a physical, process, that he can withdraw himself, can resist the Divine will, can fall and fall away too. God *will* preserve us to the end and complete His work on and in us, *si modo non ipsi nos ab eo avertamus* (*Form. Conc.*, xi. 32, 75). Hence the warnings in the hortatory part of this Epistle (chap. iv.–vi). Comp. Heb. vi. 4–6, where the fall of the regenerate is assumed, and only the return of such is called impossible. Accordingly there inheres in the reference to election and the possession of salvation a strong means of incitement to sanctification, on the ground and in virtue of the existing ethical matter of fact in *faith*. [An "earnest" is generally a safeguard against failure to fulfil the agreement, nor does the preposition εἰς (ver. 14), rendered "until" in the E. V., indicate any possibility of failure, but rather with its strong final sense, and that too in parallelism with "unto the praise of his glory," implies the very opposite. The doctrine of the perseverance of the saints stands or falls with that of personal predestination, and both are parts of the theological system, which makes "His glory" the chief end.—R.]

11. *Concluding remark.* A mystery remains here until eternity. It is analogous to a *miracle*, which is not such in the sight of God nor of the redeemed any longer, but only for those in lower stages. Thus it is with the mystery of God's will, which is ever dissolving and in the higher degrees of revelation becomes ever more manifest. The completion of revelation like that of the inheritance lies beyond this world. Hence we have not contradictions,* that inhere in the Scripture or the truth, but only those which belong to human statement, and are such to our understanding. Let us then be humble! [This is the best guard against dogmatism. Especially let those who hold those views of Divine Sovereignty which are most humbling learn the lesson!—R.]

## HOMILETICAL AND PRACTICAL.

Begin always with thanksgiving to God, and neither forget nor overlook the benefits He has conferred upon you; but above all consider the spiritual gifts with which He has blessed you and yours.—The beginning, middle, and end of the Christian life, or its ground, path and goal, is the praise and adoration of God. Before God created men, He willed that they should be His children; it is just in being or becoming God's

* [The position to be taken is not that the future will reconcile propositions which *are* contradictory, but which *seem to be* contradictory, the whole question transcending the limits of human thought.—R.]

children, that we foster the human in us, and we should be Christians, in order to be really men. He who does not fully *become a man*, is no proper Christian or child of God. The ultimate end of God is His glory; this is attained, when we become holy and blameless. He wills His glory only in our blessedness; the Father's honor is linked with the children's blessedness.—Everything is to be *traced* back to the will of God: what is manifest, revealed, experienced is the guide into the secrecy of God and His will; we must let ourselves be led from His revealed will into His secret will.—God accomplishes His will, but only according to the purpose of His will; hence not in a physical, chemical, "natural" process, but in an ethical life-process of men created after His image and for sonship with Him does He effect the desired and determined redemption of the same.—In Christ, the Beloved, is the counsel of salvation formed, in Christ it is to be carried out, and in such a way that Christ dies for the sake of sinners as a sacrifice of reconciliation, as an atoning sacrifice, and with the forgiveness of sins is begun that redemption, which leads to the throne and heart of God, since the Spirit of God works on our spirit, and His work not being in vain, confirms us in sonship, in regeneration and renewal even unto the inheritance. The process is from above to beneath, then from within to without, in order to lead from the depths up on high. The mystery of the Divine will is not in itself an incomprehensible, inconceivable enigma, entirely uncomprehended; it is only a mystery for us, rising so far above us, who cannot fathom its depth nor measure its infinitude, considering the majesty and the kindness of the same. For *our* reason it is a mystery; not *contrary to*, but above our reason; the reason of man and of God are two very different things. The mystery of the Divine will is only the manifestation of what is conditioned, limited, finite and imperfect in our knowledge, which bears to what in itself is clearest of all the same relation as the eyes of night birds to bright daylight. It is a proof of a *Divine* revelation, if we seem, when confronted with His will and truth, to be transferred to a shoreless sea, a fathomless depth. That is at once the mystery and the revelation of God. Without revelation knowest thou nothing of God, canst know nothing of Him; whoever rejects the revelation in Christ, in the sacred Scriptures, rejects also the science of God Himself; to him the mystery of God ever becomes a riddle without solution, while the Christian ever knows and feels it with greater joy. It is not unreasonable to believe on the mystery in God, since this disappears ever more and more; like children, we grow into the truth which was at first so mysterious.—As Christ is the point of beginning for the Father's gracious decree in eternity, so He is the middle-point of its accomplishment in history, and the terminal point in its consummation.—All things, the creation of heaven and earth, the maintenance and administration of the world are subordinate and subservient to the counsel of God's grace respecting our redemption in Christ: the Father is concerned for His children, not for His servants and His possessions; these are employed and rightly placed, when the children are cared for.—The word of revelation must be proclaimed and accepted: this is the chief duty of men ordered by God.—Here believers have no lack of germs, beginnings, earnest; but fruit, completion, full payment come not here, but above.

STARKE:—The wealth of the elect is inconceivable, indescribable, incomparable.—See the final point of this election of grace, and its tokens too. Prove yourselves thereby, ye Christians!—Believers have sonship with God through Christ, not from their own worthiness: it brings with it the noblest treasures, yes, the eternal inheritance.—The forgiveness of sins is the most glorious fruit of Christ's redemption; it is the basis of all other benefits: for where it is, there is life and blessedness.—The fountain of grace will never be drained, but is and remains inexhaustible, so that of its fulness we receive grace for grace.—Christ is the true ladder whose top touches heaven and its end the earth, thus linking and binding heaven and earth, God and men. Let him, who will be united to God, hold to Christ.—Angels and men stand again in friendship through Christ. Hence Christ is concerned with the angels, not that He must gain something for them of which they do not stand in need, but that they may have friendship again with men, when these again attain to grace.—The work of our election and salvation is full of wisdom, because it has taken place according to the counsel of Him who is wisdom itself; it is pure grace, because it appertains to an inheritance; infallible, because it is founded on the purpose of the Almighty; full of righteousness, because all comes to us through Christ, the righteous. Excellent tokens of the Divine truth of the Christian religion: it brings that with it, which the whole world cannot give and which makes man blessed, in the germ here in time, in perfection in eternity. This makes believers joyful in all tribulation, even in martyrdom.

RIEGER:—*They shall be blessed* is the sum of all the promises of the Old Testament; *He has blessed us* is the Gospel laud for the fulfilment of these promises in the New Testament. With these spiritual blessings in heavenly places the gospel conquers the whole world and the earthly mind, in which Jews and Gentiles lay captive.—In this are the honor of God and our salvation inseparably joined: God seeks His honor or the praise of His glory in us through our pardon.—In the Old Testament, it was often said: the Lord do thee good for Abraham's sake, for His servant David's sake; but now all is in and through the Beloved, who became the propitiation for the sins of the whole world. Once obtain in Him the forgiveness of sins, and then all other spiritual blessings flow without ceasing.—By the frequent phrase: according to His good pleasure, according to the counsel of His will, the Apostle bows down our mistrustful heart, so apt to strive for the mastery with the Holy One of Israel.—In the repeated expressions: through Himself, in whom, in Christ, the Apostle manifests an unusual zeal and care, to bind us ever to Christ, to accustom us to seek and find our glory in this alone, that we belong to Christ and are numbered in His inheritance; we may have reason hereafter to praise more the *truth* of God, like the

*Jews*, descending from the fathers, whose are the promises; or to magnify rather His mercy, like the *Gentiles*, who unexpectedly have been favored with the gracious call. It is *a word of truth*, searched by every one, who is of the truth, concerned about the truth, that thus he may be helped to the truth; it is *the Gospel of our salvation*, not only bringing us tidings of it, but containing a Divine power for actual blessing, through the faith to which it inclines the heart, giving also the Spirit, which affords what redounds to our own certainty and steadfastness in the truth, serving at the same time as a witness to others, that we have attained a position in true grace, and especially assuring us of our preservation, which we are to enjoy as the redeemed possession of the Lord, but which with the crown thereto appertaining we will lay at the feet of Him, who has accepted us to the praise of His glory.

BENGEL:—*Ultra hoc beneplacitum nobis neque in salutis nostræ neque in ullis operum divinorum causis rimandis ire licet. Quid philosopharis de mundo optimo? Cave, ne tute sis malus!*

KLEUKER:—The entire Pauline theology rests mainly on what he calls the *Divine mystery*, terming its execution the *economy* of God. No Apostle speaks with such a sweep and fulness of spirit, as Paul, whose revelation is in this economy.

GERLACH:—The riches of Divine grace in the forgiveness of sins makes itself known to us chiefly through the illumination, which thus becomes ours, the knowledge of God and our salvation,—this we include under *wisdom;* under *prudence* especially the insight into our condition and the life of the world, the practical, Christian wisdom for living. In neither should we think merely of the one-sided intellectual knowledge.

HEUBNER:—Christ, the eternal Son of God, has been the ground, why God created the world, and delivered and blessed the fallen world. Christ is the eternal ground of the Divine complacency toward the world, the ground of our blessedness.—The highest grace is Redemption. God decreed it, Christ accomplished it, earning it. It is of a purely spiritual character, the forgiveness of sins. That is true redemption, which releases us not from earthly need, but from anxiety and disquietude of conscience, from enmity to God, from incapacity for good and fear of hell. It is the fundamental condition of all other possessions, which we have through Christ. The *general* decree of God is the basis of the calling of individuals; for God overlooks no one. Man can bring either honor or shame to God, as a child to its parents. Christians should bring honor to God, He desires to get honor through us before the world.—The Holy Spirit is the seal of Christians, the stamp which they receive, that they are real children of God, the token by means of which they appear and pass current as Christians before the celestial spirits. Without this *character* ("express image") faith is vain and all Christianity mere sham. How many sham Christians there are, who have not this seal!—This Spirit is to the Christian the strongest proof also of eternal life, because in itself it is something eternal, imperishable.

PASSAVANT:—The eternal counsel of the Father respecting the election of souls is first carried out and consummated in the Son and through Him in the course of time. It is a work and miracle of love, unsearchable and unfathomable, carried on at once on earth and in heaven, in a human breast, and in a Divine heart. This election does not rest in man or angel, not in the will of man or angel's thought; not in human or angelic holiness or righteousness, purity or greatness or fidelity, not in any virtue, glory or love of the creature.—By nature we are not the children of God; even though so many may, flatly and godlessly enough, think and affirm otherwise, calling God Father and All-father.—But God now makes us His children; He has exalted us to the joys, the blessednesses, the treasures, the eternities, the glories of the heavenly nature; we are children, beloved children, heirs of God, heirs of heaven! This is the doing of the Lord's grace.—Nothing makes so poor in all true good and worth and blessing, as sin and all that belongs to and proceeds from sin.—The gospel traces our thoughts and feelings back to and into ourselves, so that we perceive the cunning of our hearts and the deceit of sin, and come to the footprints of God, to the springs of what is eternally true and good. It reveals to us, what we were, what we are, and what we should become; what are our deepest needs, the eternal ones; what our internal injury, the worst of all; what our heaviest sorrows might be, here and hereafter. It reveals to us, where the true, certain aid is, where salvation, light, peace, life are, a Divine salvation, an unerring light, an eternal peace, an everlasting life.—It is out of this light, that its opponents and enemies have borrowed or stolen all the rays of truth and wisdom, which shine here and there in their proud writings and philosophies.—It is the Holy Spirit, who gives man to God in this life, and gives God to man in eternal life; who here sketches the features of the children in likeness to their heavenly Father, and will complete the picture in eternity: who begins their redemption here with their release from the servile yoke of the creature, and will complete it in the unity and love of the Creator.

STIER:—An Apostle *prays* for his church, *teaches* and *exhorts* out of the promise and petition of his apostolic prayer, but does not lord it, does not establish eternal forms, does not urge and carry to excess the external phenomena of the church, which is forming itself deeply and inwardly in view of its goal.—Each after his manner! As Christ is now our Head in another way than that of the holy angels, so is He in another way Lord and King, and *Crown*, too, of the material world also. The condemned and evil spirits lie at His *feet* in another manner than the adoring saints and angels—yet still all really, all finally before Him.

BEECHER*:—Those who are willing are always the elect, those who will not, are not elected. Many men are wrapped up in the doctrines of election and predestination, but that is the height of impertinence. They are truths

* [This is no doubt HENRY WARD BEECHER. Dr. Braune gives no further clue to the discovery of the original passage than the single word "Beecher," which might apply to any one of a large family. As this is the only American citation in any part of the volume, it is retained, even though at the disadvantage of being a translation of a translation.—R.]

belonging to God alone, and if you are perplexed by them, it is only because you trouble yourself about things which do not concern you. You only need to know that God sustains you with all His might in the winning of your salvation, if you will only rightly use His help. Whoever doubts this is like the crew of a boat working with all their might against the tide and yet going back hour after hour; then they notice, that the tide turns, while at the same time the wind springs up and fills their sails. The coxswain cries: pull away boys! wind and tide favor you! But they answer: What can we do with the oars, don't the wind and tide take away our free agency?

SCHELLING:—It is a *vacuity of ideas*, that ventures to call itself Rationalism. Not to hate one's enemies, not to persecute them, but to do them good, aye, to *love* them, is *above* Reason. The supreme commands of a generous morality, exalting humanity, could not be fulfilled, if man could not act *above* Reason. Why then should not God act above Reason? In this sense it is by no means irrational to say,—the will of God as respects the human race estranged from Him is *above* Reason. We can, with J. G. Haman, answer the good-natured people who want to have a rational God *after their notions:* whether they have never noticed, that God is a genius, *who asks very little about what they call rational or irrational.*

HOFACKER:—The wide range which Christmas Day opens to our eye of faith: 1) How *far back;* 2) How *high up;* 3) How *far ahead* it teaches us to look.

AHLFELD:—Thank the Lord, who hath blessed thee with all spiritual blessings in heavenly things! 1) *For what* should I be thankful? 2) *How* should I thank Him?—(Sermon for Whitsunday): The Holy Ghost, as Steward of the possessions of Christ, pours out His treasures upon us. He (1) *proclaims,* (2) *entails,* (3) *seals* to us salvation in Jesus Christ.

PALMER:—Our election in Christ: 1) It is an eternal one, but linked to the temporal Incarnation of Christ; 2) It is a mysterious act of God, but each may have a clear consciousness respecting it; 3) It has taken place without our help, but does not permit us to be idle.

KAPFF (on St. Thomas' Day):—What a mighty strengthening of our faith lies in the Divine election! 1) in its goal, 2) in its ground, 3) in the mode of its accomplishment.

[SCHENKEL:—The eternal election of the Christian: 1. A work of Divine love; 2. With the effect of presenting him ever more and more pure and holy before God.—Jesus Christ the Saviour of the world: He is (1) the Centre of the world's history, (2) the Key to the understanding of the mystery of God's providential rule.—How in the Person of Jesus Christ, beginning and end, heaven and earth harmoniously unite.—No predestination save unto holiness, no election outside of the Mediator, Jesus Christ.—All events in time depend on the decree of God in eternity.—The Holy Ghost as the earnest of our heavenly inheritance: 1. A balm of consolation for the weak; 2. A weapon of victory for the strong.—R.]

[EADIE:—Ver. 3. We bless Him because He has blessed us.—Christianity is the dispensation of the Spirit, and as its graces are inwrought by Him, they are all named "spiritual" after Him.—Ver. 4. The pulsation of a holy heart leads to a stainless life, and this is the avowed purpose of our election.—Sovereignty is but another name for highest and benignest equity.—Ver. 5. The returning prodigal does not win his way back into the paternal mansion. This purpose to accept us existed ere the fact of our apostacy had manifested itself, and being without epoch of origin, it comes not within the limits of chronology. It pre-existed time.—Adoption has its medium in Christ: but it has its ultimate enjoyment and blessing in God. Himself is our Father.—*His* household we enter—*His* welcome we are saluted with—*His* name and dignity we wear—*His* image we possess—*His* discipline we receive—and *His* home, secured and prepared for us, we hope forever to dwell in. To *Himself* we are adopted. The origin of this privilege and distinction is the Divine love.—Ver. 8. A mystery is not to be flung abroad without due discrimination. The revealer of it wisely selects his audience, and prudently chooses the proper time, place and method for his disclosure.—Ver. 10. This *re-capitulation* of all things is declared a second time to be in Christ—a solemn and emphatic re-assertion. His mediative work has secured it, and His mediatorial person is the one centre of the universe. As the stone dropped into the lake creates those widening and concentric circles, which ultimately reach the farthest shore, so the deed done on Calvary has sent its undulations through the distant spheres and realms of God's great empire.—Ver. 11. His desire and His decrees are not at variance, but every resolution embodies His unthwarted pleasure.—Ver. 13. The gospel is wholly truth, and that very truth which is indispensable to a guilty world. And it comes as a word, by special oral revelation, for it is not gleaned and gathered: there is a kind and faithful oracle.—The gospel is good news, and that good news is our salvation.—That seal unbroken remains a token of safety. Whatever bears God's image will be safely carried home to His bosom.—Ver. 14. The earnest, though it differ in degree, is the same in kind with the prospective inheritance. The earnest is not withdrawn, nor a totally new circle of possessions substituted. Heaven is but an addition to present enjoyments. The prelibation will be followed by the banquet.—"We have redemption" so soon as we believe; we are ever having it so long as we are on earth; and when Jesus comes again to finish the economy of grace, we shall have it in its full and final completion.—All issues "to the praise of His glory," His grace having now done its work. The church receives its complement in extent at the very same epoch at which it is crowned with fulness of purity and blessedness. "May it please Thee of thy gracious goodness shortly to accomplish the number of Thy elect, and to hasten Thy kingdom," is an appropriate petition on the part of all saints.—R.]

2. *Exhortation springing out of the Apostle's supplication for the Church as the body of Christ, who is the Head.*

(CHAP. I. 15–23.)

15 Wherefore [For this cause] I also, after I [having] heard of your faith [or the
faith which is among you] in the Lord Jesus, and love [the love which *ye have*][1]
16 unto all the saints, Cease not to give thanks for you, making mention of you[2] in
17 my prayers; That the God of our Lord Jesus Christ, the Father of glory, may give
unto you the spirit of wisdom and revelation in the knowledge [in full knowledge]
18 of him: The eyes of your understanding being enlightened; [Having the eyes of
your heart[3] enlightened,] that ye may know what is the hope of his calling, and
19 [*omit* and][4] what the riches of the glory of his inheritance in the saints, And what
*is* [*omit is*] the exceeding greatness of his power to us-ward who believe, according
20 to the working of his mighty power [the might of his strength],[5] Which he [hath][6]
wrought in Christ, when he raised him from the dead, and set *him* [in raising him
from the dead and making him sit][7] at his own right hand in the heavenly *places*,[8]
21 Far [over][9] above all principality, and power, and might, and dominion [lordship],
and every name that is named, not only in this world, but also in that which is to
22 come: And hath put [And subjected] all *things* under his feet, and gave him *to be*
23 the head over all *things* to the church, Which is his body, the fulness of him that
[who] filleth all[10] in all.

## TEXTUAL AND GRAMMATICAL.

[1] Ver. 15.—ℵ.[1] A. B. and some other authorities omit τὴν ἀγάπην; ℵ.[3] adds it. The omission is an evident error of the transcriber. [K. L., nearly all versions, most fathers support the longer reading, which is adopted by Tischendorf, Meyer, Ellicott and the great majority of editors and commentators. The repetition of τήν readily accounts for the omission, while there is little reason for accepting an insertion from Col. i. 4.—In the above emendations Ellicott has been followed. *For this cause* is adopted in preference to *wherefore* (the rendering for διό) and *on this account* (which is more modern). The more indefinite participial construction, *having heard*, is necessary here; *the faith which is among you* is more exact than *your* faith (see *Exeg. Notes*), while *the love which ye have* brings out the force of the second τήν.—R.]

[2] Ver. 16.—[The *Rec.* reads: μνείαν ὑμῶν ποιούμενος, on the authority of D.[3] E. K. L. (F. G. transposing: ποιούμενος ὑμῶν), most cursives, Vulgate, Syriac versions, Coptic, most fathers; accepted by Tischendorf (but not in all editions), Griesbach, Ellicott, Wordsworth (De Wette and Braune tacitly). In ℵ. A. B. D.,[1] and about 10 cursives, ὑμῶν is omitted; accepted by Rückert, Lachmann, Meyer, Alford. The question is a delicate one: Was the word inserted where the meaning is so obvious, or was it omitted because occurring so immediately before? The variation in position favors the former theory, but a similar omission by nearly the same authorities in 1 Thess. i. 2 is almost decisive for the latter. See *Exeg. Notes* for the interpretation of Meyer and Alford, resulting from the acceptance of the briefer reading.—R.]

[3] Ver. 18.—Instead of καρδίας (ℵ. A. B. D. E. F. G. K. L. and others) a few [*Rec.*, fathers, no uncials] have διανοίας, an evident gloss from iv. 18. [There should be merely a comma after *enlightened* in the English text.—On the reasons for rejecting the absolute construction followed in the E. V., see *Exeg. Notes*.—R.]

[4] Ver. 18.—Καί is omitted in ℵ.[1] A. B. [D.[1] F.; by Lachmann, Rückert, Alford, Braune. It is found in ℵ.[3] D.[3] E. K. L., nearly all cursives. retained by Tischendorf, Meyer, Ellicott, Eadie. The probability is against its genuineness, yet it may have been omitted because καί follows in ver. 10.—R.]—A very few authorities substitute τί for τίς.

[5] Ver. 19.—[On this choice of words, see *Exeg. Notes*.—R.]

[6] Ver. 20.—[Braune apparently accepts the reading ἐνέργησεν, which is sustained by ℵ. D. F. K. L. (So *Rec.*), accepted by Ellicott among other careful critics. The perfect ἐνήργηκεν (A. B.) is adopted by Lachmann, Tischendorf, Meyer, Alford, mainly for the sufficient reason that the more usual aorist would scarcely have been altered to the perfect, while the succeeding aorists might readily occasion the alteration *from* the perfect.—Hence we render: "hath wrought." —R.]

[7] Ver. 20.—ℵ. A. B. and others read: καθίσας [adopted by Rückert, Lachmann, Alford. Tischendorf varies. The *Rec.* reads ἐκάθισεν, with D. F. K. L. and most cursives. So Eadie, Ellicott, and Meyer (apparently); but the change to the finite verb looks more like the attempted relief of the construction.—R.]

[8] Ver. 20.—Instead of ἐν τοῖς ἐπουρανίοις in ℵ.[1] and most authorities, ἐν τοῖς οὐρανοῖς [an evident gloss] is found in B. with a few minor authorities.

[9] Ver. 21.—[*Far above* (E. V.) involves more than is expressed by the Greek word ὑπεράνω, according to the most exact commentators.—R.]

[10] Ver. 23.—[The *Rec.* omits τά before πάντα, but on altogether insufficient authority. No important alterations have been made in the rendering of this clause, because it is almost impossible to change the literal rendering of the E. V., without substituting an explanation for the translation: Braune's view would require: all things in all (persons), but the difference of gender he accepts cannot be expressed in an English rendering.—R.]

## EXEGETICAL AND CRITICAL.

*Summary.*—After the praise of God on account of His grace towards Christendom, to which the readers of this letter belong (ver. 13) has been expressed (vers. 3–14), there follows on account of this very grace the Apostle's thanksgiving for the readers' faith and love in his prayers (vers. 15, 16), out of which he gives prominence to the *petition*, united with his thanksgiving, that God would make them know the glory of their calling and inheritance as well as of His power (vers. 17–19), which He has shown and will show in the

Redemption through Christ, the Head of the church (vers. 20-23).

It is not proper to find here, as OLSHAUSEN does, after an "effusion of love," only a "thanksgiving for the faith of the readers," as far as ii. 10, without perceiving the profound, rich instruction contained in these verses. But it is not precisely a prayer for the readers which follows, as HARLESS says; he only mentions what he does when thinking of the church. This prayer and supplication to God about and for souls is the apostolic ministry in faith, care and joy; and the *whole Church should know it* and should infer from this petition, how weak and needy she is in and of herself, even though born a heavenly seed for heaven; and how necessary earnest, persevering prayer and supplication on her part always is, for her preservation and prosperity.

[After praise comes prayer (EADIE). ELLICOTT: "I ever give thanks, and pray that you may be enlightened to know the hope of His calling, the riches of His inheritance, and the greatness of His power, which was especially displayed in the Resurrection and supreme exaltation of Christ."—ALFORD, following the Trinitarian division of STIER: "*The idea of the Church* carried forward, in the form of a prayer for the Ephesians, in which the fulfilment of the Father's counsel through the Son and by the Spirit, in His people, is set forth, as consisting in the *knowledge* of the hope of His calling, of the riches of His promise, and the power which He exercises on His saints as first wrought by Him in Christ, whom He has made Head over all to the Church."—R.]

*The Apostle's Thanksgiving* (vers. 15, 16).

Ver. 15. **For this cause,** διὰ τοῦτο, refers to what precedes, and on account of the close connection of the individual parts with each other, to vers. 3-14. So most ancient and modern commentators (ŒCUMENIUS: διὰ τὰ ἀποκείμενα ἀγαθὰ τοῖς ὀρθῶς πιστεύουσι καὶ βιοῦσι καὶ διὰ τὸ ἐν τοῖς σωθησομένοις τετάχθαι ἡμᾶς); it is not merely an appendage to vers. 13, 14, because the thanksgiving and petition apply to the *readers* only (MEYER, RUECKERT), nor to the last clause (ver. 14: "to the praise of His glory"), as GROTIUS thinks. But it treats of more than thanksgiving, of petition, supplication, not merely of the readers, but also of all Christendom (εἰς ἡμᾶς, ver. 19; comp. vers. 20-23).

[The reference to the whole preceding paragraph is defended by HARLESS (so CHRYSOSTOM, WINZER, SCHENKEL and many others). It accords best with Braune's exegesis of vers. 13, 14, to accept this view, but EADIE, ELLICOTT, HODGE follow THEOPHYLACT, in referring it to vers. 13, 14. ALFORD: "On account of what has gone before, since ver. 3; but especially of what has been said since ver. 13, where καὶ ὑμεῖς first came in." The more restricted view seems preferable, but we must then accept an expanded reference in ver. 19.—R.]

**I also,** καὶ ἐγώ.—The unexpressed fellowship in which Paul thus marks himself, as ver. 13 (καὶ ὑμεῖς), is to be inferred from the context, from the clause ἀκούσας—οὐ παύομαι εὐχαριστῶν. He thinks of the Christians, who have spoken of the readers' Christian state with joy and thanksgiving, and "expects, that all Christians, especially they themselves to whom he writes, would do the same" (HARLESS). Hence it is not= *even* I also, a believing Israelite (BAUMGARTEN); such arrogance he would have opposed, not possessed. Nor is it=also I, your Apostle (STIER) [EADIE]; He places himself as a member of the body of Christ, who is the Head, in the Church, not above it. [DE WETTE unwarrantably joins καί with the preceding διὰ τοῦτο. ALFORD objects to the view of MEYER ("Paul knows that he *cooperates* with the readers in his prayerful activity"), preferring to take καί as marking the resumption of the first person after the second. ELLICOTT thus expresses Braune's view: "Κἀγὼ is thus faintly corresponsive with καὶ ὑμεῖς, and hints at the union in prayer and praise which subsisted between the Apostle and his converts."—R.]

**Having heard,** ἀκούσας.—This marks nothing further than that he had heard, and accordingly indicates only, that what has been heard has been spoken of, hence that the Apostle was not in Ephesus, when he heard. GROTIUS is therefore correct: *loquitur apostolus de profectu evangelii apud Ephesios, ex quo ipse ab illis discesserat.* So THEODORET, HARLESS, MEYER and others. Nothing is said respecting acquaintance or non-acquaintance (against OLSHAUSEN [who thinks the larger part were probably unknown to him—R.]); it is used in the former case, Philem. 5, in the latter, Col. i. 4; Rom. i. 8. BENGEL: *Hoc referri potest non solum ad ignotos facie, sed etiam ad familiarissimos, pro statu eorum præsenti.* It is therefore not=*scire, comperire* (HAMMOND), as though it described personal observation, since it is the very opposite; but at the same time nothing can be inferred from this against the composition of this Epistle for the Ephesians, nor that he wrote the letter before his personal acquaintance, nor yet that he had other churches in his mind at the same time (STIER).*

**Of the faith which is among you in the Lord Jesus,** τὴν καθʼ ὑμᾶς πίστιν ἐν τῷ κυρίῳ Ἰησοῦ.—To this Col. i. 4 is parallel: "your faith in Christ Jesus," *etc.* Accordingly τὴν καθʼ ὑμᾶς πίστιν here seems to be equivalent to τὴν πίστιν ὑμῶν there [so E. V.]. But "faith among you" differs somewhat from "your faith;" the relation of the faith to the subjects is different: in the first case, in accordance with the notion of the preposition (κατὰ τὴν πόλιν, Luke viii. 39, κατʼ οἶκον not=ἐν οἴκῳ, see WINER, p. 374), which is *distributive*, the faith is merely to be found there, within the church, even though each one does not have it, and believers and unbelievers dwell side by side, in the other case, however, the faith is the possession of the individuals; WINER, p. 146, *fides, quæ ad vos pertinet, apud vos (in vobis?) est.*† Such cir-

* [On the other hand, the aorist must not be taken as frequentative, so as to show from such a sense, that he had frequent communication with them as a well-known church. Even EADIE, who at first adopted this view, citing Kühner and Buttmann in support of it, is disposed to defer to the judgment which WINER (p. 260) pronounces against it. HODGE seems to have been led into the same error.—R.]

† [MEYER admits no distinction between the two passages, while EADIE, finding this form singular in the New Testa-

cumlocutions have their special shadings of thought, as τὴν ἀπὸ σοῦ ἐπαγγελίαν (Acts xxiii. 21), τῇ ἐξ ὑμῶν ἀγάπῃ (1 Cor. viii. 7), *promissio a te profecta, amor qui a vobis proficiscitur*, are not exactly equivalent to *tua promissio, amor vester.* Comp. WINER, p. 181. STIER is excellent: A hint that a gracious treasure of faith and love is indeed present within the church, yet not certainly active in every member of it. [So ALFORD.] The notion of the *substantive* is not, however, thereby modified, as though the objective nature of faith were to be understood here, and the individual quality of faith in the particular persons, in Col. i. 4 (HARLESS) [ELLICOTT]; with the Apostle the faith in Ephesus as among the Colossians remains the subject of thanksgiving; and the genitive indicates nothing about individual *quality*, only the possession of the individuals, still less any thing about *purity* or impurity (MATTHIES); nor is any hint given respecting *fides qua* or *fides quæ creditur.*

It is indeed here as there more closely defined as the faith "in the Lord Jesus," as Gal. iii. 26. The preposition marks the foundation of the faith: founded in the Lord Jesus, or its life-sphere, without placing any other aim of the faith. There is no reason for understanding here εἰς θεόν from 1 Pet. i. 21: "who by him do believe in God" (BENGEL: *fidem erga Deum in domino Jesu;* GROTIUS: *fidem in Deum fundatam in Christo*); "in the Lord" is not="through Him," nor ἐν=εἰς (KOPPE, FLATT). The article τήν is wanting before ἐν τῷ κυρίῳ, because the qualifying phrase adds an integral element to πίστις, which as anticipated is joined *immediately* (Rom. iii. 25; 2 Cor. vii. 7). ["Christ-centred faith" (ELLICOTT).—R.] Comp. WINER, p. 128. The position of the words does not permit our connecting ἐν τῷ κυρίῳ with ὑμᾶς (WINZER); besides πίστις requires further definition more than ὑμᾶς.

**And the love which ye have unto all the saints,** καὶ τὴν ἀγάπην τὴν εἰς πάντας τοὺς ἁγίους.—[See *Textual Note* [1].—R.] This sets forth the first and immediate manifestation of the faith. CHRYSOSTOM aptly says: πανταχοῦ συνάπτει καὶ συγκολλᾷ τὴν πίστιν καὶ τὴν ἀγάπην, θαυμαστήν τινα ξυνωρίδα. *Quisquis fidem et amorem habet, particeps est totius benefactionis* (BENGEL). This love is, however, more closely defined as "unto all the saints." On the article [which here specializes love.—R.] see WINER, p. 126. "Paul had here first the idea of love *in itself* and then *added* in his thought τὴν εἰς πάντας" (MEYER). Ἅγιοι are Christians. Hence: "*all saints*" (iii. 8, 18; vi. 18, 24) points to *brotherly love* as *character Christianismi*, John xiii. 34 f.; 1 John v. 1. As little as this notion is to be enlarged here into universal philanthropy, as CALVIN would do, and as is the case in 1 Cor. xiii.; Gal. v. 6; 1 Tim. ii. 1; Tit. iii. 2, also in 2 Pet. i. 7 (ἐν τῇ φιλαδελφίᾳ τὴν ἀγάπην), so little and still less is brotherly love to be narrowed down, with THEODORET, to *liberality*. At the same time we should not overlook the emphasis resting on the word "all," permitting no distinction as respects condition, rank, possessions or internal endowment, either mental or spiritual.

Ver. 16. **Cease not to give thanks for you,** οὐ παύομαι εὐχαριστῶν ὑπὲρ ὑμῶν.—Thus or εὐχαριστῶ πάντοτε, 1 Cor. i. 4; Phil. i. 3; Col. i. 3; 1 Thess. i. 2; Phil. 4; comp. WINER, p. 323. Paul never ceases to be a giver of thanks. [The participle points to a state supposed to be already in existence. EADIE: "As one giving thanks for you I cease not." ULPHILUS: *non cessans gratias dico.*—R.] The phrase ὑπὲρ ὑμῶν, as in ver. 2: 1 Tim. ii. 1, marks the protection of prayer, like that of a shield *over* the assailed (WINER, p. 359) while περὶ πάντων ὑμῶν (Rom. i. 8) denotes the position of the protector around the protected.

**Making mention of you,** μνείαν ὑμῶν ποιούμενος, adds a limitation; he thanks constantly whenever he thinks of them; but that happens daily.—**In my prayers,** ἐπὶ τῶν προσευχῶν μου.—This indicates that Paul has and takes occasion to think of them from his prayers.* Comp. WINER, p. 352; 1 Thess. i. 2; Rom. i. 10. Praying is the Apostle's daily doing, and therewith arises the thought about his church, changing his prayer into intercession. The subject of his thought and petition is not, therefore, precisely the faith and love of the Ephesians (MEYER [ALFORD] who rejects ὑμῶν), but themselves, with their necessities indeed, which determine the purport of the petition.—"No thanksgiving without petition, so long as perfection and completion are not yet there" (STIER).

*The Apostle's petition as to its purport.* Vers. 17-19.

Ver. 17. **That,** ἵνα, has its parallel in ὅπως, Phil. vi. and must retain, as in iii. 16, the signification of the purpose, design. Comp. WINER, pp. 418 f., 428 f. The Apostle's will, in the very thought of his prayer, is directed to this, that God *should* give (MEYER, SCHENKEL). Hence there is no reason for weakening the force of ἵνα here into: that He *may* give (WINER, p. 273), as if it introduced only the object, the purport of the petition (HARLESS, STIER); for although Paul did not regard his request "as *causa* of Divine favors," nor purpose "*thereby*" to bestow upon others the gift of grace, yet still in his petitions offered in the name of Jesus (John xiv. 13; xv. 16; vi. 23) he has the design as well as the hope, that they should take place.† BENGEL: *Argumentum precum pro veris Christianis.*

---

ment (though frequently used for the possessive genitive in later classical Greek), makes it denote more characteristic possession, differing thus from nearly all the commentators.—R.]

* ["In ἐπί with a genitive, the apparent *temporal* reference partakes somewhat of the *local* reference of juxtaposition," BERNHARDY. So ALFORD, ELLICOTT, and now EADIE who formerly omitted the *sub-local* reference. The preposition "serves to express the concurrent circumstances and relations, in which and under which an event took place."—R.]

† [On the force of ἵνα comp. TITTMANN, *Syn.* N. T., II., p. 35, ff., who is perhaps the ablest defender of the frequency of its ecbatic signification. But many of the instances he cites are very doubtful. The eventual or ecbatic sense (indicative of result) is not defensible here. The very best explanation of the force of ἵνα after verbs of praying, *etc.*, is given by ALFORD (on 1 Cor. xiv. 3): "The idea of *purpose* is inseparably bound up in this particle, and can be traced wherever it is used. At the same time, prayer being a *direct seeking* of the fulfilment of the purpose on account of which we pray—not like many other actions, *indirectly* connected with it,—the *purport* and *purpose* become *compounded in the expression.*" This *sub-final* force is accepted by ELLICOTT, denied by EADIE and by MEYER, who rejects everything short of the strict final

**The God of our Lord Jesus Christ,** ὁ θεὸς τοῦ κυρίου ἡμῶν Ἰησοῦ Χριστοῦ.—Here we must hold (see ver. 3 f.), that he is speaking of the Incarnate One, the God-*man*, to whom God is God, worshipped by Him also (STIER). It does not suffice to say, that the meaning is, God sent Him, He bore witness of God and returned to God (HARLESS) [apparently HODGE also].

**The Father of glory,** ὁ πατὴρ τῆς δόξης. This parallel clause is far more difficult than the last. First of all, πατήρ, corresponding to θεός, is to be retained in its established meaning, "Father," hence not to be taken in the sense of *causa* (GROTIUS), *auctor* (ὁ μεγάλα ὑμῖν δεδωκὼς ἀγαθά, CHRYSOSTOM and others), source, origin (MATTHIES, SCHENKEL). The genitive, τῆς δόξης, designates the possession, the character of the Father, to whom the glory belongs, which is = כָּבוֹד, the Divine glory and majesty; it is like "the God of glory" (Acts vii. 2; Ps. xxix. 3), "the Lord of glory" (1 Cor. ii. 8), "the King of glory" (Ps. xxiv. 7); comp. also "the Father of mercies" (2 Cor. i. 3). Hence: the Father full of glory. As parallel to the genitive: "of our Lord Jesus Christ," we must also in connection with "glory," think of Him, in whom it was manifested. BENGEL: *Pater gloriæ, infinitæ illius, quæ refulget in facie Christi; imo gloriæ, quæ est ipse filius Dei, unde etiam nobis hereditas gloriosa obtinget* (ver. 18). HARLESS: Father of glory, because the glory presses upon the Apostle, which God has revealed to men in His Son.

Though *the Greek Fathers* go too far (δόξαν γὰρ τὴν θείαν φύσιν ὠνόμασεν), yet "the Father full of glory," following "the God of our Lord Jesus Christ," is evidently not without a reference to Christ and of such a kind, that the Apostle's first phrase conceives rather of the God-*man*;* the second of the *God*-man. This explanation accordingly is not a curiosity (RUECKERT), needing no contradiction (OLSHAUSEN), nor is it *obscurius et remotius* (A-LAPIDE). It is much more of a curiosity, to wish to connect thus: *Deus qui est domini nostri Jesu Christi pater, gloriæ;* since then ὁ θεός and τῆς δόξης must be taken together, while τοῦ κυρίου—ὁ πατήρ is inserted between them (VATABLE). The conjecture of PISCATOR, that πατήρ and θεός were first written in interchanged positions, is very bold. Still it cannot be said that our phrase is = *pater gloriosus* (CALVIN and others), or *cui debetur honor, venerandus,* or *præstantissimus* (WAHL and others), or the Almighty Father (KOPPE).—ŒCUMENIUS aptly remarks: πρὸς τὸ προσκείμενον ὀνομάζει θεόν. The designation of God in this passage corresponds entirely with the fervor and confidence of the Apostle's petition respecting the affairs of the kingdom of Christ.

**May give unto you,** δῴη ὑμῖν.—Δῴη the optative; John xv. 16: δώῃ the conjunctive; the Ionic conjunctive form is not sufficiently attested in the New Testament, and δῷ is preferred [in that passage, B. giving it here also.—R.] The optative as *modus optandi* is here, especially in *oratio obliqua* (MATTHIES), used in the place of the conjunctive (WINER, p. 273). In 2 Tim. i. 16, 18 we find a similar usage. [MEYER and ELLICOTT regard the optative as chosen to follow the present here, because the answer belongs to what is hoped for, *etc.*, the latter finding in its use a support for his view of the sub-final force of ἵνα. But the view of ALFORD (and EADIE) is preferable: The optative "is used when the purpose is not that of the writer as *he is writing*, but is described as that of himself or some one else *at another time*," thus falling in effect under the rule of the *oratio obliqua*.—R.]

**The spirit of wisdom and revelation,** πνεῦμα σοφίας καὶ ἀποκαλύψεως, is the object of the preceding verb. The omission of the article before the genitives points to the close connection with the governing substantive, to which also the article may be wanting, without its becoming indefinite, as the genitives contain the closer definition; Luke xxiii. 46: εἰς χεῖράς σου παρατίθεμαι τὸ πνεῦμά μου (WINER, p. 118 f.). God gives as a Father to His children, who have become such through Christ, of His Spirit; hence the reference may well be to the Holy Ghost; but since they have already been sealed with this (ver. 13), this efficient, personal, power recedes rather, and we are to understand the spirit wrought or to be wrought by the same in Christians. So Gal. vi. 1; 2 Tim. i. 7. So OLSHAUSEN, STIER: Something of God, yet manifesting itself as in man. Hence we are not to understand the human spirit of itself, or the human heart (RUECKERT: God give you a wise heart, open to His revelation), nor yet precisely the Person of the Holy Ghost (BENGEL: *idem Spiritus, qui est promissionis, in progressu fidelium est etiam sapientiæ et revelationis; sapientia in nobis operatur sapientiam,* REVELATIO *cognitionem;* MATTHIES, MEYER).* Evidently Paul is speaking of a gift for all Christians; hence *Charisms* are not meant, as 1 Cor. xii. 8; xiv. 12; vi. 26 (OLSHAUSEN).

Both "wisdom" and "revelation" point to universal gifts to Christians, and to what is or comes to pass in them, hence to something subjective. By "wisdom" we understand a continued condition, by "revelation" the single glances afforded us, into the truths of Christianity, into the will of God in special circumstances and situations of life, into the human heart, into the course of time, into eternal life. The former includes the φρόνησις, "understanding," joined with it in ver. 8; the latter is "the very necessary private revelation for every Christian" (STIER), as 1 Cor. ii. 10. Paul adds the special to the general in the same way (Rom. i. 5; v. 15; xi. 29). Accordingly we are not to consider the second an objective medium for the first (HARLESS); in that case, the position would be reversed (MEYER).† Comp. Col. i. 9.

---

sense. The ecbatic sense is rare, it must be admitted, and due to "Hebrew teleology," which reverently accepted a prophecy as fulfilled.—R.]

* [It is perhaps unwise to press any Christological reference upon this phrase upon the ground of its parallelism with the preceding one, though this is preferable to the many distorted views, which have been adopted through fear of an Arian interpretation.—R.]

* [EADIE and HODGE defend the formal reference to the Holy Spirit here, but it seems better with ALFORD and BRAUNE to accept πνεῦμα as "the complex idea, of the spirit of man indwelt by the Spirit of God, so that as such, it is His special gift." This intermediate or complex sense is that suggested in my Excursus, *Romans*, p. 235, B., but too often overlooked.—R.]

† [These genitives are also characterizing genitives, it would seem. EADIE takes the latter as indicating the mode by which

**In the full knowledge of him** [ἐν ἐπιγνώσει αὐτοῦ].—First the meaning of the words. In ἐπίγνωσις the preposition, which "renders prominent the *intension* of the verbal notion to its object" (HARLESS), must not be overlooked, and the distinction from γνῶσις must be maintained. It is *major exactiorque cognitio* (GROTIUS,) *plena et accurata cognitio* (WAHL). 1 Cor. xiii. 12 is instructive: "Now I know (γιγνώσκω) in part; but then shall I know (ἐπιγνώσομαι) even as also I am known" (ἐπεγνώσθην).* Hence it is not = *agnitio* (CALOVIUS and others), nor can it be of any force here, that γνῶσις designates the higher, the charismatic form of knowledge, 1 Cor. xii. 8; xiii. 8 (OLSHAUSEN), since this technical term designates the character, not the *degree* (MEYER). The context, vers. 18, 19, evidently determines that the knowledge of God is here referred to, and does not permit αὐτοῦ to be referred to Christ (BEZA, ERASMUS, LUTHER and others); nor can it remain undetermined (CALVIN). Finally ἐν, "in," designates the sphere within which that is accomplished, which has been spoken of: it cannot possibly be taken as = εἰς (*Vulgate*, LUTHER and others), or = *per* (ERASMUS and others), or = *una cum* (FLATT). [HODGE most unwarrantably renders the preposition ἐν, "together with."—R.]

The *connection* with the verb "give" is clear then: The knowledge of God is a status or circle of life, wrought already by the Spirit and word of God, in which he should and must be, who will and shall receive the spirit of wisdom and revelation, since this does not take place without means, Col. i. 9, 10. Advance is made from truth to truth, from knowledge to knowledge. The connection with what follows: πεφωτισμένους ὀφθαλμούς (CHRYSOSTOM and others), is impossible, both grammatically and logically, on account of the appended εἰς τὸ εἰδέναι ὑμᾶς, which is joined at the close of ver. 18, just as ἐν ἐπιγνώσει αὐτοῦ here in ver. 17; the two phrases correspond to each other. But the connection with ὑμῖν is quite as impossible, as with ἀποκαλύψεως (a suggestion of KOPPE's); it is contrary to the *usus loquendi* and introduces erroneous thoughts: for it is not to those, who have known, who are real worshippers, that He gives such a spirit, as He does not give the spirit through knowledge, but rather knowledge *through* the Spirit, nor does revelation consist only in the knowledge of God, although this is the beginning, centre and main point to which all comes and returns. [EADIE follows KOPPE, the result being a confusion respecting these phrases, which is very uncommon with him.—R.]

Ver. 18. **Having the eyes of your heart enlightened** [πεφωτισμένους τοὺς ὀφθαλμοὺς τῆς καρδίας ὑμῶν].—This is added without a conjunction, seeming to be in apposition, with the emphasis on the participle; the *being enlightened* is, what God should give. Τοὺς ὀφθαλμούς, eyes, He need not first give; BENGEL: *articulus præsupponit oculos jam præsentes*. But the Apostle wishes that the eyes may be given in a new quality (HARLESS). Accordingly we should not render: enlightened eyes (LUTHER); in that case we should find, τοὺς ὀφθαλμοὺς τοὺς πεφωτισμένους. It is arbitrary to correct the reading into πεφωτισμένοις (PISCATOR and others), as though it belonged to ὑμῖν. It is untenable to accept an accusative absolute (BEZA, KOPPE, MEYER [E. V., EADIE), and to refer the participle to ὑμῖν, so that the accusative of the noun is made to contain the closer definition; for then the recipients would have been, which is contrary to Scripture and to fact, enlightened before they received the Spirit of wisdom and revelation; the reference to the *effect:* so that you are illuminated as respects your eyes—is grammatically impossible. Nor should εἶναι be interpolated (FLATT).

[The interpretation: so that you are illuminated as respects your eyes, is that of MEYER, who does not defend the accusative absolute. ELLICOTT and ALFORD, whose rendering is given in the English text, refer the participle to ὑμῖν, as a lax construction, taking the noun as an accusative of limiting reference. Notwithstanding Dr. Braune's objection, this seems the best solution. The clause "serves to define the result of the gift of the Spirit, and owing to the subsequent infinitive, which expresses the *purpose* of the illumination, not unnaturally lapses into the accusative" (ELLICOTT). See ALFORD for similar constructions. The accusative absolute which also expresses a result, is a very doubtful construction, see MEYER *in loco*, and on Rom. viii. 3. The appositional construction, which makes our clause the object of δώῃ, is open to fewer grammatical than logical objections. The enlightenment as regards the eyes of the heart ought not to be put as correlative or co-ordinate with the gift of the Spirit of wisdom, *etc.* This objection holds, however, the meaning of our clause may be enlarged, as is done below, and by HARLESS and others. Braune's view, it should be added, is supported by RUECKERT, MATTHIES, MEIER, HOLZHAUSEN, HARLESS, OLSHAUSEN, DE WETTE and others; apparently by HODGE, who does not notice the construction preferred in this note.—R.]

The value of the gift is well described by GREGORY NAZIAN.: εἰ γὰρ σκότος ἡ ἄγνοια καὶ ἡ ἁμαρτία, φῶς ἂν εἴη ἡ γνῶσις καὶ ὁ βίος ἔνθεος. According to v. 8, compared with iv. 18; 2 Cor. iv. 4; Heb. vi. 4, the light of life is meant, that illumination which is already connected with sanctification and rooted in experience (HARLESS, STIER), so that it cannot be referred to merely intellectual insight (RUECKERT and others). [Yet "*the eyes* of the heart" are spoken of, giving prominence to the perceptive side.—R.]

The eyes are τῆς καρδίας ὑμῶν, "of your heart," and this is the centre of life (HARLESS), the core of the personality (OLSHAUSEN), and not merely mind or soul, without disposition. Matth. xxiii. 15: τῇ καρδίᾳ συνῶσι. Comp. iv. 22; Rom. i. 21; 2 Cor. iv. 6. *Cor est, quo tan-*

the wisdom is imparted, which appears illogical. Dr. HODGE does not clearly indicate what view he adopts, but apparently inclines toward that accepted above.—R.]

* [The use of the verb in this passage, applying it in the second instance to God, contradicts the position taken by EADIE, that ἐπί has in our word an *additive* force, referring to the successive increments of knowledge, for in that case it could not be applied to God, as indeed he affirms ἐπίγνωσις never is.—R.]

*tas res percipimus* (BENGEL).* It is thus marked by this qualifying phrase, that we, in spite of our old nature, are renewed and made susceptible of that wisdom and revelation, that is the light for which the eyes of our heart are prepared; our heart should become secure and full of the Spirit. Thus this apposition is defended from MEYER's objections.

**That ye may know,** εἰς τὸ εἰδέναι ὑμᾶς.—This sets forth the aim of the enlightening, toward which progress is made "in the knowledge of Him;" the latter is to be developed. Thus to the ground and outgoing there corresponds the aim, in which the beginning now appears in its extent; the deeper *insight* after the hearing of the proclamation, after the first faith and knowledge and understanding, is here treated of.†

**What is the hope of his calling,** τίς ἐστιν ἡ ἐλπὶς τῆς κλήσεως αὐτοῦ.—The *first* object of this insight is "the hope of His calling." "His," αὐτοῦ, according to the context, is to be understood of God; Rom. xi. 29: the "calling of God." He calls; this call is not without effect; and this is the hope, the cause of which is the call. The re-echo in us of this call of God on us is hope, hoping; the Christian's hope lies, not in the eternal "election," but in the temporal "calling." So "joy of the Holy Ghost" (1 Thess. i. 6), "trial of affliction" (2 Cor. viii. 2). Hope is the Christian's advantage (ii. 12; 1 Thess. iv. 13; Rom. v. 2), and a hope that "maketh not ashamed" (Rom. v. 5; viii. 24). To know the character of such hope is not a small matter (against STIER). Τίς points then to the character, the quality of this hope. PASSOW *sub voce.* It is therefore not = πόση, ποταπή, *quanta* (STIER, OLSHAUSEN, SCHENKEL), but *qualis, cujusnam naturæ* (HARLESS, MEYER and others). Nor is ἐλπίς = *res sperata* (OLSHAUSEN, STIER [EADIE] and many others), although it can mean this (Col. i. 5: "laid up;" Heb. vi. 18: "set before us;" Gal. v. 5: "wait for the hope of righteousness"), which MEYER [with ELLICOTT] denies. It is inconceivable that κλῆσις should be = those called (SCHUETZE). LUTHER renders: "your calling," putting the effect for the cause: "his calling." [With ALFORD, EADIE, and ELLICOTT it is better to take τίς in the simple meaning "what," *quæ* (*Vulgate*), without referring either to quality or quantity. As regards "hope," the objective sense must be admitted in the N. T., but the bald *res sperata* does not express the signification here. ALFORD thinks the controversy mere trifling: "If I know *what* the hope is, I know both its essence and its accidents." Even ELLICOTT admits an objective aspect: "the grounds, the state of the hope." HODGE supports the subjective sense. On κλῆσις, see *Romans*, pp. 280, 281.—R.]

**What the riches of the glory of his inheritance in the saints** [τίς ὁ πλοῦτος τῆς δόξης τῆς κληρονομίας αὐτοῦ ἐν τοῖς ἁγίοις].—The *second* object of the insight is the object of the Christian hope, the inheritance, to which "the calling of God" helps us, hence "His:" He gives it, it is from His own. As Divine, eternal life, participation in the kingdom of God, heirship with Christ (God Himself is our portion), it has a "glory" and this glory has "riches," so that it is an important object for our more profound observation. So Col. i. 27: "the riches of the glory of this mystery." It is a weakening of the ideas, to resolve these substantives into objectives: what is the riches of the glorious inheritance (LUTHER), or: what is the glorious riches of His inheritance (STIER). [As MEYER well says: "What a rich, sublime cumulation, setting forth in like terms the weightiness of the matters described;—and not to be *diluted* by any resolving of the genitives into adjectives."—R.]

"In the saints" is added after "His inheritance," without the article (τῆς ἐν τοῖς ἁγίοις), and hence conceived of as most closely connected with his inheritance, which is to be found *in* (LUTHER: *an*) and *among* the saints, the called Christians not outside of them. So Rom. ix. 3: "my kinsmen according to the flesh;" 2 Cor. vii. 7: τὸν ὑμῶν ζῆλον ὑπὲρ ἐμοῦ. Comp. Col. i. 12 (εἰς τὴν μερίδα τοῦ κλήρου τῶν ἁγίων ἐν φωτί); Acts xx. 32 (δοῦναι τὴν κληρονομίαν ἐν τοῖς ἡγιασμένοις πᾶσιν); xxvi. 18. The Apostle does not say "in you," "us," but states it altogether objectively in humility and wisdom. He speaks indeed of the inheritance of God in Christians, but not of the glory of the portion, nor its riches in the saints, so that we must understand here chiefly the children of God, who are partakers of the inheritance (vers. 11, 14), even though only in its incipient stages; "the riches of the glory" become indeed perceptible even here, but unfold themselves fully only in eternity, which is the more to be included, since here and hereafter are less divided than light and darkness. Accordingly we are not to consider the object of the inheritance to be principally and solely the present kingdom of God on earth (HARLESS), or on the other hand the future kingdom of God to be established at the second Advent (MEYER); nor is the connection of ἐν τοῖς ἁγίοις with an ἐστιν to be supplied (KOPPE and others) possible, since not ὁ πλοῦτος, but only κληρονομία, is in, on and among the saints.* To join αὐτοῦ with

* [ELLICOTT says of the phrase, "the eyes of your heart:" "A somewhat unusual and figurative expression, denoting the inward intelligence of that portion of our immaterial nature (the ψυχή) of which the καρδία is the imaginary seat." Comp. MEYER, ALFORD, HARLESS and STIER.—R.]

† [Dr. HODGE divides the prayer of the Apostle into three leading petitions: 1. For adequate knowledge of Divine truth; 2. For due appreciation of the future blessedness of the saints; 3. For a proper understanding of what they themselves had already experienced in their conversion. This is well enough for homiletical purposes, but it is very unsatisfactory as an exegesis of the passage, since it places as co-ordinate three clauses, which hold very different relations to each other, destroying altogether the proper final force of εἰς, besides being open to other objections. ALFORD rightly takes εἰς τὸ εἰδέναι as setting forth the purpose of the πεφωτισμένους, not of the πνεῦμα σοφίας What is now described is *involved in* the latter, not its *object*, but that of the former.—R.]

* [This interpretation should not be lightly passed over, since it is sustained by WINER (in earlier editions, not in 6th and 7th), DE WETTE, MEYER and ELLICOTT. The reason for adopting it is the assumption that the article should precede our phrase, were it joined directly with κληρονομίας αὐτοῦ, since that expression is so complete in itself as to admit of no qualification forming one conception with it (which is the condition of the omission of the article). Our phrase would then, according to ELLICOTT, define the sphere in which the riches, *etc*., are peculiarly found, felt and realized. To this view, however, there are grave objections. It is awkward to begin with; it disturbs the grammatical parallelism of the clauses, and logically it represents Paul as praying that they might know what great things are already among Christians,

*ἐν τοῖς ἁγίοις* (STIER) is inadmissible, because far-fetched. The reference is not to the totality of morally good beings in the other world (RUECKERT), or in the holiest of all (CALOVIUS), as Heb. ix. 12; nor should prominence be given to the thought, as inhering in the text: God inherits the saints (MEYER, ŒTTINGER, STIER), although they belong to Him, and He to them. This is the carrying out, extension and expansion of the thought, but not an exegesis of the words set before us.

Ver. 19. **And what the exceeding greatness of his power to us-ward who believe** [*καὶ τί τὸ ὑπερβάλλον μέγεθος τῆς δυνάμεως αὐτοῦ εἰς ἡμᾶς τοὺς πιστεύοντας*].—The *third* object of the insight is *the power of God*, which leads from the calling to the inheritance. The "exceeding greatness" of this power is a worthy object of profound insight (2 Cor. iv. 7: ὑπερβολὴ τῆς δυνάμεως); it must and can also be experienced, since it makes itself felt "to us-ward," to those "who believe" in the present, hence, without limiting the circle of those who believe, or passing beyond it, not to all in general, but only to those who admit and consent to this condition appointed by God. Since the preposition designates the direction towards the believers, and the present participle the present time, and the article before the participle marks that word as the ground, condition of the activity (ver. 13; 1 John iii. 23), and since only experiences of the power of God are spoken of, from which "the exceeding greatness" is to be inferred, we must here hold fast to the proofs in this earthly life (CHRYSOSTOM or to HARLESS, STIER), and not apply it to the future (MEYER, SCHENKEL, who however adds, that the beginning of the consummation manifests itself in this life).*

**According to the working of the might of his strength,**† *κατὰ τὴν ἐνέργειαν τοῦ κράτους τῆς ἰσχύος αὐτοῦ*.—In this collocation of words the proper subject is *ἰσχύς*, as *δύναμις* just before, giving prominence to a characteristic, the *strength* (*ἰσχύς* from *ἴς* = seat of elasticity, sinew, muscle, nape of the neck, stem of a tree, hence *vis*); *δύναμις* is *brachium divinum*, *ἰσχύς* its muscles; *κράτος* is the power manifesting itself, the *ἐξουσία*, which rules (*κρατεῖ*); *ἐνέργεια* (*ἐν ἔργῳ*), *efficacia* (ERASMUS), the actual efficiency (HARLESS). So BENGEL, CALVIN: *robur est quasi radix, potentia autem arbor, efficacia fructus.* There is no chance throwing together of words, but an order corresponding to the thought: regard is to be paid chiefly to the efficacy, the effects, in which the power of God's strength allows itself to be perceived and felt. [The language is intended to exalt our ideas of God's power in connection with this "eminent act of His omnipotency."—R.]

*Κατά* with the accusative is *juxta, secundum*, according to, thus designating the norm and standard as well as the motive and occasion (WINER, p. 375 f.). Comp. iv. 7; i. 5, and *κατὰ νόμον* (Luke ii. 22), *κατὰ χάριν* (Rom. iv. 4). The two notions, "according to" and "by virtue of" are related (1 Cor. xii. 8, 9). The simplest connection and that most readily understood by the hearer, is that with "us who believe." We believe only by virtue of the efficacy of the power of God in Christ and upon our souls. [The meaning of the preposition is something less than *propter* and something more than *according* to. On the connection see below.—R.]

So CHRYSOSTOM, who truly and beautifully says: *τοῦ ἀναστῆσαι νεκρὸν πολλῷ θαυμασιώτερον τὸ πεῖσαι ψυχάς.* Just on this account, because we believe only by virtue of the efficacy of God's power, which has enough obstacles to faith to overcome in us, we can understand, how great the power of God is. Since believing is not a momentary affair, but a *status*, preserved by the same power, which produced it, the aorist participle *πιστεύσαντες* is not necessary (BLEEK), and no room is given for the monstrous thought, that faith according to the power of God is spoken of. It is inadmissible to connect, either with the verb *ἐστι* which is understood, or with "the exceeding greatness" (SCHENKEL), or with all the points introduced by "what" (HARLESS), or with "may know" (MEYER). [Dr. HODGE also defends the connection of this clause with *πιστεύοντας*, but it is doubtful whether this is correct. For though undoubtedly expressing a truth, yet it places the rest of the chapter in grammatical dependence on an incidental idea. It has also a suspicion of polemical purpose (against Pelagianism) attached to it, besides pressing too strongly on *κατά* the sense of "in virtue of." It is better then with DE WETTE, EADIE, ELLICOTT, ALFORD and others, to accept a reference which Braune does not mention, *viz.*: to the whole preceding clause: "not however as an explanation (Chrys.) or an amplification (Calv.) of this power, but in accordance with the full ethical force of *κατά*, as a definition of its mode of operation (Eadie), a mighty *measure*, a stupendous *exemplar* by which its infinite powers towards the believing, in its future, yea, and its present manifestations, might be felt, acknowledged, estimated and realized" (ELLICOTT).—R.]

---

This last objection MEYER, who on all possible occasions adopts a reference to the future kingdom of God at the second Advent, avoids by saying that Paul conceives of it as present (*vergegenwärtiges*). Nor does the absence of the article interfere with the other interpretation. Comp. HARLESS and ALFORD for a clear statement of the case. We give the paraphrase of the latter: "*His inheritance in*, whose example and fulness, and embodying is in *the saints*." EADIE and HODGE apparently restrict "inheritance" to the future blessing, the former expanding this idea with his usual felicity as a practical expositor.—R.]

* [ELLICOTT agrees with SCHENKEL in taking the primary reference to be to the future, but admits a secondary present reference, which MEYER denies. See the beautiful climax ELLICOTT gives in his note. But the other view is preferable, on the grammatical grounds urged by Braune, and because of the comparison with the *resurrection* of Christ. See HODGE, who quotes CALVIN'S remarks against the notion that this language would be frigid hyperbole if applied to our experience in this life. Dr. HODGE, however, incorrectly takes our clause as a third petition. ELLICOTT and MEYER again supply *ἐστί*, with which they connect *εἰς ἡμᾶς*. It is better, with most, to join it with *δυνάμεως αὐτοῦ*.—ALFORD retains "to us-ward" as better indicating the prominence which belongs to "us" in the fact of its *direction*. "But it is not the power which works faith in us, except in so far indeed as faith is a portion of its whole work: here the *πιστεύοντες* are the material on which the power works."—R.]

† [ALFORD and ELLICOTT prefer "strength of his might;" the former says: "The latter (*ἰσχύς*) is the attribute subjectively considered; the former (*κρώτος*) the weight of that attribute, objectively esteemed." Most commentators accept this distinction; the question is only, whether the inherent strength (*ἰσχύς*) is best expressed in English by the word *strength* or *might*. The former seems preferable.—R.]

*The Apostle's petition as to its ground.* Vers. 20–23.

Ver. 20. **Which he hath wrought in Christ**—Ἣν ἐνέργησεν,* analogous to ἀγάπην ἀγαπᾷν, ii. 4, is to be referred to ἐνέργειαν. WINER, p. 210 [The cognate accusative]. Nor is ἐν τῷ Χριστῷ, without a reference to εἰς ἡμᾶς, ver. 19: in Christ is accomplished that efficacy of God, which is powerful toward us. ["In Him" as our spiritual Head (ELLICOTT and others).—R.]

**In raising him from the dead**, ἐγείρας αὐτὸν ἐκ νεκρῶν, marks a fact of his working. [The aorist indicates that the act is contemporaneous with that of the preceding verb. ALFORD justly warns against the danger of regarding, "with the shallower expositors, Christ's resurrection as merely a *pledge* of our *bodily* resurrection, or as a mere *figure representing* our *spiritual* resurrection,—not as *involving* the resurrection of the church in both senses." Both HODGE and EADIE fall somewhat short of the full conception thus expressed.—R.]

**And making him sit at his own right hand in the heavenly places** [καὶ καθίσας ἐν δεξιᾷ αὐτοῦ ἐν τοῖς ἐπουρανίοις].—Thus the exaltation, beginning with the resurrection, was completed (1 Pet. iii. 21 ff.). Instead of the better supported participle, ἐκάθισεν has been generally substituted, because the Greeks disliked the spinning out of long relative and participial sentences, and easily passed over into the finite verb (WINER, p. 533, b.).† Ἐν δεξιᾷ αὐτοῦ denotes the participation in dominion, the σύνθρονος of the Father (Mark xvi. 19; Rom. viii. 34; Acts vii. 55; Phil. iii. 20 f.; Matth. xx. 21; Mark x. 37). Comp. also 1 Sam. x. 25; 1 Kings ii. 19, in the earthly relations, which are transferred to Christ, Ps. cx. 1. The phrase ἐν τοῖς ἐπουρανίοις (see on ver. 3), which is the antithesis of ἐκ νεκρῶν, designates space, or as HOFMANN (*Schriftbeweis*, II. 1, p. 334) intimates, the relation to the world; ἐν δεξιᾷ αὐτοῦ distinguishes Him from spirits, ἐν ἐπουρανίοις locates Him and them alike. We may with as little right understand here the *status cœlestis* (HARLESS and others) as the central place of Divine glory and revelation, the highest, inmost heaven (STIER, SCHENKEL), since the word is used of Satan also (vi. 11, 12).

[The various *local* expressions used in the context seem decisive as to the meaning of ἐπουρανίοις. It refers to heavenly places, is more indefinite than ἐν τοῖς οὐρανοῖς, but was chosen here probably on account of the details in ver. 21 (ELLICOTT).—ALFORD reminds us, that "the fact of the universal idea of God's dwelling being in heaven, being only a symbolism common to all men, must not for a moment induce us to let go the verity of Christ's bodily existence, or to explain away the glories of His resurrection into mere spiritualities. As Stephen saw Him, so He veritably is: in human form, locally existent, over above," *etc.*—R.]

Ver. 21. **Over above all principality, and power, and might, and lordship, and every name that is named** [ὑπεράνω πάσης ἀρχῆς καὶ ἐξουσίας καὶ δυνάμεως καὶ κυριότητος καὶ παντὸς ὀνόματος ὀνομαζομένου].—The word ὑπεράνω (iv. 10: πάντων τῶν οὐρανῶν; Heb. ix. 5), the opposite of ὑποκάτω (κλίνης, Luke viii. 16; τῆς συκῆς, Jno. i. 51; τῶν ποδῶν, Mark vi. 11; Matth. xxii. 44; Rev. xii. 1), can only mean "over, above" [so ELLICOTT, ALFORD] without marking any particular eminence, GREEK FATHERS, BEZA, ESTIUS [EADIE] or dominion (BENGEL), although the latter inheres in the nature of the case (MEYER). It is to be connected with "setting," and with its genitives ("all principality," *etc.*) forms the detailed description and explanation of the phrase, "at his right hand in the heavenly places;" the two belong together, the first being more closely defined by the second.

Of these four names the first three occur in the same order in 1 Cor. xv. 24, the first two occur in our Epistle, iii. 10, and in Col. i. 16, after εἴτε θρόνοι εἴτε κυριότητες, joined with εἴτε also and in the same order, in 1 Pet. iii. 22: ὑποταγέντων· αὐτῷ ἀγγέλων καὶ ἐξουσιῶν καὶ δυνάμεων. On the other hand in Rom. viii. 38: ἄγγελοι and ἀρχαί, like ζωή and θάνατος, δύναμις, ὕψωμα and βάθος, are contrasted with each other by οὔτε—οὔτε; so that we can infer nothing thence respecting our passage.* A certain consistency is noticeable in the use of these words. Besides the reference to angels is quite obvious, being required here by the context, especially ἐν τοῖς ἐπουρανίοις. CALVIN. *Cur non simpliciter nominavit angelos? Respondeo, amplificandæ Christi gloriæ causa Paulum exaggerasse hos titulos, ac si diceret; nihil est tam sublime aut excelsum, quocunque nomine censeatur, quod non subjectum sit Christi majestati.* According to HOFMANN (*Schriftbeweis*, I. p. 34)† we cannot understand here a *climax descendens* (MEYER, STIER). These designations for the world of angels were given through the higher position of the angels as the messengers of God (Ps. ciii. 20 f.; Heb. i. 6 f., 13 f.), as holy (Ps. lxxxix. 5; Dan. viii. 13). Since the context points to the resurrection of Christ, the Crucified, and His exaltation to a participation in the government of the world, as a fact, in which we see the efficiency of God, according to which He works on us also, in order to make us His children and heirs of His glory, we may well apply these terms to good as well as bad angels, aye, we can scarcely limit the reference to the angels, who reach also into this world, the αἰὼν οὗτος, especially as both πάσης and the concluding phrase "every name that is named," which corresponds entirely with "nor any other creature" (Rom. viii. 38), warrant an unbounded

* [See *Textual Note* 6, where the reading ἐνήργηκεν is accepted. MEYER notes its distinctive sense here in referring to an act completed, as viewed by the writer.—R.]

† [ELLICOTT, adopting the reading ἐκάθισεν, says the change to the finite verb, is especially designed to enhance the importance of the truth conveyed by the participle, referring to the same page in WINER. The main thought at first is that of the resurrection, but the Apostle is speedily absorbed with the other, which accords so well with the ground-tone of the Epistle.—R.]

* [The variation in the text of Rom. viii. 38 indicates certainly that the early transcribers referred δυνάμεις to angels, since there is no other motive for the change in its position; the correct reading however seems to justify a reference to earthly powers, so that as remarked above we gain nothing decisive from that passage.—R.]

† [HOFMANN denies any reference to gradations in rank, admitting only a designation of various relations to God and the world, but this distinction does not seem to be tenable.—R.]

extension, limited only to power and might. HARLESS only concedes this, preferring however the reference to *good angels* alone, as does MEYER, who then refers "name" to every thing created. In such universality is the passage understood by ERASMUS, RUECKERT, STIER [ALFORD] and others. With STIER we must understand under the first four designations, personalities, not merely principles, forces, factors, recognizing them in "every name that is named," the transition to the impersonal (τὰ πάντα). Accordingly the following views are to be rejected: the reference to devils alone (SCHOLZ), to Jewish hierarchs (SCHÖTTGEN), to heathen (VAN TILL) human potentates (MORUS); the affirmation of a polemical purpose, not at all indicated, against angel-worship (BUCER, ESTIUS, HUG), or a preservative purpose against possible infection through false *gnosis* (OLSHAUSEN [HODGE, though not decidedly]); also every attempt to define the different grades of these groups of angels, and the explanation of "name" as a summing up of a *nomen dignitatis potentiæve* (ERASMUS and others); it is not even to be limited to names of "such a character" (HARLESS).

[It is on some accounts safest to take the four terms here introduced in the widest, most indefinite sense. Still it would seem best, if any limitation is made to refer the words to *good angels* alone, including of course under that term all created heavenly intelligences. The prevailing reference in these words is to angelic powers, to good (Eph. iii. 10; Col. i. 16; ii. 10) and bad (vi. 12; Col. ii. 15; 1 Cor. xv. 24; comp. Rom. viii. 38) alike. The preceding local definition would not exclude the latter, as Christ is placed "over above" all these (besides ἐν τοῖς ἐπουρανίοις is apparently applicable to bad angels also, vi. 12). But the "verse relates to Christ's exaltation in heaven rather than His victory over the powers of hell." Then without attempting any closer definition of these *classes*, we may still admit a *descensive* order throughout: First the Exalted One, then the various gradations of heavenly Intelligence, then "every name that is named," a view which is favored by the apparent regularity in the order (comp. Col. i. 16). "Every name that is named" includes more than persons, in this view, more than titles of honor: Every thing which can bear a name. No less comprehensive sense seems admissible.—ALFORD accepts the most universal reference for the four terms under discussion, but adopts rather too abstract a sense.—ELLICOTT refers to the list of authors in HAGENBACH, *History of Doctrine*, § 131. —R.]

**Not only in this world, but also in that which is to come** [οὐ μόνον ἐν τῷ αἰῶνι τούτῳ ἀλλὰ καὶ ἐν τῷ μέλλοντι].—This qualifies "named," establishing the pre-eminence of Christ above all that is ever named in both this world and that to come. BEZA: *præstantiam non esse temporariam, sed æternam.* We find a parallel in "things present," "things to come" (Rom. viii. 38). Yet the expression here is not purely=now and hereafter [HODGE], but designates the present time as the first age, disappearing in the transition to the future glory, the future as the eternal glory beginning with the return of Christ. Paul takes the reference to time from the system of the world ruling in each period, thinking at once of pre-messianic and post-messianic, terrestrial and celestial worlds. Excellent, but rather abrupt is BENGEL's remark: *αἰών denotat hic non tempus, sed systema rerum et operum suo tempore revelatum et permanens.* It is then=*always* (HARLESS) with respect to this institution of the history of salvation (STIER).* Comp. my remarks on αἰὼν οὗτος and μέλλων, *Biblework*, 1 John ii. 18, p. 73 f. The connection with καθίσας (CALVIN and others) is incorrect and also the remark of BENGEL, following CHRYSOSTOM: "*Imperia, potestas, etc., sunt in futuro, sed tamen* NOMINANTUR *etiam in seculo hoc; at ea quoque, quæ in præsenti ne nominantur quidem, sed in futuro demum nobis nomine et re patefient, Christo subjecta sunt.*"

Ver. 22. **And subjected all things under his feet** [καὶ πάντα ὑπέταξεν ὑπὸ τοὺς πόδας αὐτοῦ].—Even if we retain the participle in ver. 20, we must here accept the transition from the participle to the finite verb. The words themselves are not difficult. Evidently, and in this the advance of thought consists, πάντα, "all things," is to be applied to all that is created, and ὑπέταξεν, "subjected," with its closer definition, refers of itself as well as on account of Ps. viii. 6 (comp. iii. 6) to conflict and opposition, which was suggested already by the passage (Ps. cx. 1) evidently in mind in ver. 20: "set him at his own right hand." The Lord Himself had quoted Ps. viii. 3. The same Psalm (ver. 6) is used with special emphasis in 1 Cor. xv. 27; Heb. ii. 6–8. Should the Psalm refer to the glory of the first Adam (Gen. i. 26-28) and its restoration, as is definitely indicated in the Epistle to the Hebrews (ii. 6-8), then we must suppose here, that Paul is led by such thoughts to the use of this passage, especially as the context requires it, treating as it does of what shall occur to us, in accordance with what has occurred to Christ. *Dominium nunc illi uni (Christo) tribui potest, quandoquidem per Adamum primum potestatem dignitatemque a Deo concessam nostrum genus amisit* (PETER MARTYR). There is therefore no tautological repetition here, but from above descensively the Apostle marks, after a sketch of the *dignity* of Christ (SCHENKEL), the *sovereignty*, which subjects all things, even the unconscious creation (OLSHAUSEN). This representation is not merely *emphatic*, or only a reminiscence (MEYER), but καὶ τὴν προφητικὴν ἐπήγαγε μαρτυρίαν (THEODORET). So HARLESS and STIER in the main.

[The notion of opposition should not be too strongly pressed, though it is undoubtedly implied. As regards the allusion or citation from Psa. viii. 6, if it be regarded as a mere allusion the difficulty disappears; if it be a veritable citation, then we must adopt one of two conclusions:

* [Alford remarks: "Not only *time* present and to come, but the present earthly condition of things, and the future heavenly one." ELLICOTT: "With regard to the meaning of αἰών it may be observed that in all passages where it occurs, a *temporal* notion is more or less apparent. To this in the majority, an *ethical* idea is limited. In a few passages like the present a *semi-local* meaning seems also superadded, causing αἰών to approach in meaning to κόσμος, though it still may be always distinguished from it by the temporal and (commonly) ethical notions which ever form its background." Comp. chap. ii. 2; Gal. i. 4.—R.]

either the Psalm is in a certain sense *Messianic*, or Paul quotes in the *accommodating* manner which virtually destroys any specific meaning the Scriptures have. I prefer to adopt the former alternative, little fearing that too many Psalms will be accepted as Messianic. Paul's allusion is due to a direct reference under the guidance of the Spirit to a passage in the O. T. which in its primary application to man involves a secondary and more profound application to Christ. In the grant of terrestrial sovereignty the Psalmist saw and felt the antitypical mystery of man's future exaltation in Christ" (ELLICOTT).—R.]

**And gave him to be the head over all things to the church** [καὶ αὐτὸν ἔδωκεν κεφαλὴν ὑπὲρ πάντα τῇ ἐκκλησίᾳ].—Thus is set forth the *office* (SCHENKEL) of Christ, and the sphere of His efficiency. Αὐτὸν is in emphatic position, Him. Such an one, thus placed [thus exalted, thus glorified]. We must regard Him too as a gift, a present. Διδόναι is not=τιθέναι, the Apostle might otherwise have said ἔθηκεν or κατέστησεν; it is quite different in 1 Cor. xii. 28: "And God hath set (ἔθετο) some in the church." He gave Him to be "Head over all things to the church." We say with equal exactness: He gave Him to be Head, or as Head for the Church. As Head! not as καρδιά, but as κεφαλή. In the head lies the organizing power. SCHUBERT (*Geschichte der Seele*, p. 163) describes the relation of head and body "as a figure of a love, descending from above to beneath, grasping and moving the corporeal, and of a longing rising from below to above, the work of which it is, to constantly transform the lower nature of that which longs into the higher nature of that which is longed for." MARTIN BOOS boldly says: "Christ dwelling in our humanity is as active as in that which He assumed from Mary." GERLACH beautifully says: "At once Ruler and Member of His Body." "Head" designates elsewhere superiority also (1 Cor. xi. 3).

The qualifying phrase "over all" is governed by "gave him to be head," and marks the might (ὑπὲρ) of this Head; πάντα is all without limitation, He is Head over *all—to the church*, to Christendom; "Head" is not to be supplied again (MEYER). The presence of κεφαλὴν ὑπὲρ πάντα between ἔδωκεν and τῇ ἐκκλησίᾳ does not at all alter the construction (against HOFMANN, *Schriftbeweis*, II. 2, p. 117). The sense is precisely this: "Christ is such a Head of the Church, that He is for all that the Lord over all, over devils, world, *etc.*" (LUTHER). The whole economy of Creation stands at His disposal as the basis and sphere of activity for the economy of redemption (BECK). Accordingly ὑπὲρ πάντα is not to be joined *per trajectionem* to αὐτόν (*Syriac*, GREEK FATHERS, ERASMUS and others), nor is ὑπὲρ πάντα to be taken as meaning: above all the good which God has given stands this that He gave Christ as Head of the Church (CHRYSOSTOM), nor is it=*præcipue*, μάλιστα πάντων (BAUMGARTEN), nor=ὑπερέχουσα πάντων, *caput summum* (BEZA, RUECKERT: *Oberhaupt*, OLSH.: the prophets also were heads); nor are we to understand it of *bona virtutum* (ANSELM), or *dona gratiæ*, nor is "the natural limitation to be found in τῇ ἐκκλησίᾳ" and this dative taken as *in commodum ecclesiæ*, for the Church (HARLESS). It is altogether unwarrantable to take the neuter for the masculine (JEROME, WAHL).

[The view of Braune is in the main that of modern English commentators. We must reject any sense of the verb but the simple one of "give," since the dative follows. Christ is given to the church—and given as *Head*, for the next clause renders this view imperative. The only trouble then is with "over all things;" what is His relation to them? Evidently that of Head also. No other view is admissible exegetically; the question becoming thus a purely grammatical one: Shall we accept a brachyology and understand a second κεφαλήν before τῇ ἐκκλησίᾳ (MEYER, STIER, HODGE approvingly): "gave Him the Head over all things (to be the Head) to the church," or take κεφαλήν as a species of tertiary predicate (ALFORD, EADIE, ELLICOTT): "gave Him as Head over all things to the Church." The latter seems to be Braune's view, and is certainly the simpler grammatically. Nor does it throw out of view the grand thought that Christ is Head of the Church. ALFORD: "CHRIST is Head over all things: the Church is the BODY of Christ, and as such is the fulness of Him who fills all with all: the Head of such a Body, is Head over all things; therefore when God gives Christ as *Head* to the Church, He gives Him as *Head over all things* to the Church, from the necessity of the case."—R.]

The choice of the word ἐκκλησία for the Christian Church (iii. 10, 21; v. 23, 25, 27, 29, 32; Phil. iii. 6; 1 Cor. vi. 4; xii. 28) is very apt. GERHARD (*Loc. ed. Cotta.* X. 3, 20): *Chemnitius notat σύγκλησιν de primoribus, magnatibus, consulibus et eorum conventu, διάκλησιν de colluvie promiscuæ multitudinis quando fit congregatio ab agris, ἐκκλησίαν vero de civibus, quando σύνοδος τῶν κατὰ τὴν πόλιν celebratur, eorum scilicet, qui certis legibus sibi devincti unius reipublicæ cives sunt. Appellatio igitur ecclesiæ ad populum Dei translata ostendit*, ECCLESIAM DEI NON ESSE COLLUVIEM PROMISCUÆ MULTITUDINIS, *sed eorum, qui certis legibus a Deo vocati et sibi invicem sunt obstricti. Athenis erant usitati duplices conventus, ἐκκλησίαι et ἀγοραί vel ἀγοραίαι. Illæ significabant* CONVENTUS ORDINATOS, *quando universitas civium, eorum scilicet, qui jus civitatis habebant, ordine, justo, a magistratu convocati congregabantur; hæ vero significabant congregationes promiscuas et inordinatas, quando promiscua multitudo hominum in civitatibus et oppidis sine observatione ordinis in unum coibat.—Appellationi igitur ecclesiæ ad populum Dei translatæ inest significatio εὐταξίας καὶ εὐνομίας, qualis est in aristocratia civili, cui opponitur δημοκρατία, ἀκαταστασίας καὶ ἀταξίας plenissima.—Ut civitas non consistit ex medico et medico, aut ex rustico et rustico, sed ex medico et rustico, sicut Aristoteles in ethicis loquitur*, ITA QUOQUE ECCLESIA NON CONSTAT EX PASTORE ET PASTORE SEU EX AUDITORE ET AUDITORE, SED EX DOCENTIBUS ET DISCENTIBUS, ATQUE INTER IPSOS AUDITORES SUNT VARII VITÆ STATUS ATQUE ORDINES.

Accordingly the ἐκκλησία has two main features in it, one the *ordained unity* and the other the *calling*, which includes in itself a separating out (ἐκλέγεσθαι) from the world not yet called or rejecting the call, and which is consummated through *intellectual* means. See further under *Doctr. Note* 5.

Ver. 23. **Which is his body,** ἥτις ἐστὶν τὸ σῶμα αὐτοῦ.—The pronoun ὅστις has an "explanatory element," introducing the statement of a reason, and is=the old German *als welcher*, "as which." So Rom. ii. 15: οἵτινες= *ut qui* (BEZA), *qui quidem ostendant* (CASTALIO); LUTHER renders it quite well: *damit dass sie beweisen*, and here: *welche da ist*. [ALFORD: *which same;* EADIE, ELLICOTT: *which indeed.* MEYER: "*ut quæ*, defining the attribute as belonging to the being of the church"—is perhaps too strong —though true enough.—R.] He is the Head of the church, since it is His Body, τὸ σῶμα αὐτοῦ (ii. 16; iv. 4, 12, 16; v. 23, 30; Col. i. 18, 24; ii. 19; iii. 15; Rom. xii. 5; 1 Cor. vi. 15; x. 17; xii. 13, 27). From this citation of passages, in all of which this view of the Apostle is contained, the frequency of the figure, especially in this Epistle, may be seen. The membership making up the whole, the indispensableness of Christ and the vital fellowship with Him are marked. We must also remember, that here, on account of the ἥτις, only that is treated of, which the church is and has in Christ, and not what He has in it; this is only an inference, though a correct one, and remains in the background, should it enter at all.

[The questions, what constitutes the church? who are true members of the true church? do not enter here; but that Paul here teaches a mystical union, above and beyond any federal or representative union, or ethical union of thought and feeling, seems perfectly clear. We call this a figure, but is it not the reality, and the organic unity of the body the figure? Really and truly the church is the body of Christ, and out of this truth spring many lessons respecting our personal union with Christ. ALFORD: "It is veritably His body: not that which in our glorified humanity He personally bears, but that in which He, as the Christ of God, is manifested and glorified by spiritual organization. He is its Head; from Him comes its life; in Him, it is exalted; in it, He is lived forth and witnessed to; He possesses nothing for Himself,—neither His communion with the Father, nor His fulness of the Spirit, nor His glorified humanity,—but all for His Church, which is in the innermost reality, HIMSELF." Comp. Col. i. 24, which admits of no satisfactory explanation, unless we accept the fact that the Apostle was conscious of such a union as this.—R.]

**The fulness of him who filleth all in all** [τὸ πλήρωμα τοῦ τὰ πάντα ἐν πᾶσιν πληρουμένου.]—As respects syntax, this is the intrusion of an apposition, forming a parallel clause, in order to express without a figure, what has just been figuratively explained: "fulness" corresponds to "body," "of Him filling all in all" to "His."

On πλήρωμα, comp. ver. 10 and PASSOW *sub voce*. Words ending in —μός as a rule represent the abstract action of the verb, those in —μα the concrete effect, so "that they are for the most part equivalent to the perfect participle passive" (BUTTMANN), like πρᾶγμα, σπέρμα, κήρυγμα, especially here σῶμα (*id quod σώζεται*). The word is not=πλήρωσις, the act of filling, but is to be taken in the passive sense: all that, or with which any thing is filled, the fulness. So here. [This simple passive sense is adopted by FRITZSCHE, DE WETTE, OLSHAUSEN, STIER, MEYER, and by ALFORD, EADIE, ELLICOTT ("that which is filled, the filled-up receptacle)." As the word was a favorite among the Gnostics (in after times however), so it has been a favorite plaything with commentators since, who have thrown not a little confusion upon its meaning. The simple passive sense is the most natural one; though perhaps not the most usual one, it is certainly allowable. The active sense, the filling up is adopted by HARLESS, who says there is no other sense used in the New Testament, in which view HODGE seems to acquiesce. But what is meant by the active sense: *implendi actionem*, or *id quod res impletur?* ELLICOTT speaks of the latter as passive, while HODGE evidently regards it as active (so Braune apparently under 2 below). ALFORD deems it a transition from the abstract sense, denying any active sense to such nouns, but saying that what is thus termed is "a logical transference from the effect to that which exemplifies the effect." From this it is evident how impossible it is to speak intelligibly about the word in its active and passive senses, until this meaning: *that by which any thing is filled*, is properly labelled. That is the work of the grammarian, yet it is evident that it is active or passive, according to the point of view: "whether one thinks first of the container, and then of the contained, or the reverse." HARLESS and HODGE are not justified in saying that the word is always used actively in the New Testament, though this sense is a common one.* It would give here the meaning *complement*, or *supplement*, which seems appropriate in view of the figure of Head and Body. But, on the other hand, this gives a sense which is so remarkable as to raise doubts; for how can Christ be filled by the church? Then again, we are almost forced by this interpretation to take the following participle in a passive sense, which is objectionable grammatically and logically. These reasons are strong enough to lead us to adopt the passive sense, which may be done without any fear of running counter to the *usus loquendi* of the New Testament.—R.]

Nor does the difficulty lie in the genitive: τοῦ πληρουμένου, which refers to Christ. The participle is middle, and, as usage requires in the case of such correlated words, is used in the same sense as the preceding noun: of Him who fills from out Himself, through Himself (WINER, p. 242), or fills for Himself (FRITZSCHE: *qui sibi complet*). [The latter sense is adopted by MEYER (in 4th edition, Braune quotes him as accepting a deponent sense), ELLICOTT, EADIE. This reciprocal sense seems to have escaped the notice of Dr. HODGE, who agrees with ALFORD in accepting the active sense, though he admits it is favored only by classical usage. Certainly the active meaning of the participle is not so justi-

* [In many of the instances specified by HODGE, the passive sense is equally allowable. For example, chap. i. 10, "the fulness of the times" may as well be taken as meaning the state of being full on the part of the appointed periods of time, as that which fills up those periods, and so in Gal. iv. 4; Eph. iii. 19: "the fulness of God" affords a much better sense if taken passively (see in *loco*), while Mark viii. 20: "the fulnesses of how many baskets," refers not to what fills up the baskets, but "the state of fulness as respects the baskets."—R.]

fiable as the passive sense of the noun πλή-ρωμα.—R.] The present tense must also be taken into the account: He is conceived of in the process of filling; whether He succeeds, the result will show; the process is now *going on.*

The real difficulty lies in τὰ πάντα ἐν πᾶ-σιν, "all in all." The object τὰ πάντα, is of course, in accordance with what precedes, to be referred to the entire world of creatures, which Christ fills, naturally as a soul the body, the former however working out beyond the latter, not exclusively in and upon it, and not only working, but being actively present, hence not as blood fills the heart, or water a vessel. "All" is filled by Christ, as is the Church, His Body, hence not mechanically, chemically, or the like. The most difficult point still remains: ἐν πᾶσιν, "in all." The preposition ἐν joined with πλη-ροῦσθαι and πλήρωμα must designate that *in* which He fills; if this is inconceivable, then the Apostle must and would have expressed himself otherwise. Accordingly the neuter cannot be accepted here, since then *idem per idem* would be asserted, or an exaggeration occur: *Alles in Allem* [*all things in all things*, see below under (7.)—R.] Following the rule, that those cases which belong to both genders (πάντων, πᾶσι) are to be taken as masculine, unless the context absolutely requires the neuter, we render: *in Allen*, "in all persons" (so LUTHER originally, but "*in Allem*" afterwards crept in); it thus marks His filling efficiency in persons, in heavenly spirits and human souls, of which also His relation as Head of the Church obliges us to think. He is the central Personality, working through all things, working in all. Such a Head has the Church, the central sphere of the world which is to be perfected (STIER).* This explanation is in no particular without supporters, but there is also no incorrect explanation possible which has not been made here.

(1.) The *connection* is viewed incorrectly, by joining the parallel clause "the fulness," etc., with "him" (ver. 22), and taking "which is his body" as parenthetical (ERASMUS), when it is too important to admit of this. BENGEL, too, following SEMLER, is incorrect: "*Hoc neque de ecclesia prædicatur, ut plerique censent, neque, ut aliis visum, cum* DEDIT *construitur, sed absolute ponitur accusativo casu, uti* τὸ μαρτύριον, 1 Tim. ii. 6. *Est enim epiphonema eorum, quæ a ver.* 20 *dicuntur, innuitque apostolus, in Christo esse* PLENITUDINEM *patris omnia implentis in omnibus.*"

(2.) Πλήρωμα is taken in the active sense as *supplementum.* So the GREEK FATHERS, ESTIUS, CALVIN, BEZA ("*ut sciamus Christum per se non* INDIGERE *hoc supplemento, ut qui efficiat omnia in omnibus revera,*" even HARLESS, who holds with BAEHR as the undoubted result of investigation, that πλήρωμα is used in the New Testament only in its active sense, says: "She is the fulness of Christ, not as though she were the glory which dwells in Him, but because He permits His glory, as in all, so to dwell in her; she is the glory, not of one who would be in want without her, but of Him who fills all in all parts," so HOFMANN (*Schriftbeweis*, II. 2, p. 118–120). Even STIER points to this, bringing it over out of the *middle* form; yet this is not *se implere, se supplere,* but *sibi.* It is quite as incorrect to take it as= πλῆθος (HESYCHIUS, WAHL: *copia cultorum Dei sive Christi*, SCHÖTTGEN: *multitudo, cui Christus præest*).—RUECKERT, too, who is helpless here, is in error, in taking the Church, πλήρωμα, as the means of filling for Christ's executive efficiency, since the Church can do nothing without Him.—The explanation of CAMERON is a curiosity: full bodily mass.*

(3.) The participle τοῦ πληρουμένου is taken as *passive* (CHRYSOSTOM, *Vulgate*); ἀντὶ τοῦ πληροῦντος (THEODORET, ŒKUMENIUS, OLSHAUSEN, HARLESS); as *deponent* (MEYER). BENGEL remarks: "*i. e.*, πληροῦντος; *sed major vis mediæ vocis, in denotanda relatione ejus, qui implet et eorum, qui implentur*"—quite correct!

(4.) The *meaning* of the verb is certainly not: to make complete (*Vulgate*, ESTIUS: *adimpletur*).

(5.) As regards the *subject* of the verb, HARLESS, referring to THEODORET: τοῦ μὲν Χριστοῦ σῶμα, τοῦ δὲ πατρὸς πλήρωμα—οἰκεῖ ἐν αὐτῇ τῇ (ἐκκλησίᾳ) καὶ ἐμπεριπατεῖ κατὰ τὴν προφητικὴν φωνήν says: it *must* be referred to Christ, while STIER, who founds his proof less on the passage in question than on the organism of the Epistle, says: God *must* be considered the subject. [So ALFORD, but the great majority of commentators adopt the other reference.—R.]

(6.) Τὰ πάντα has been limited to the members of the Church, to members of the body of Christ (ESTIUS, STIER), to the spiritual results wrought by Christ, or the Christian's faculties of soul (GROTIUS: *Christus in omnibus* (*credentibus*) *implet omnia, mentem luce, voluntatem piis affectibus, corpus ipsum obsequendi facultate*), to different peoples, nations (FLATT, MORUS).

(7.) The preposition ἐν is taken as instrumental (MEYER). [ALFORD: "The thing with, or by, or in which as an element, the filling takes place. So that the expression will mean, *with all,* not only gifts, not only blessings, but things." So ELLICOTT, who thus explains the whole verse: "The Church is the veritable mystical Body of Christ, yea the recipient of the plenitudes of Him who filleth all things, whether in heaven or in earth, with all the things, elements, and entities, of which they are composed." This view accepts πᾶσιν as neuter, and is on the whole preferable to every other interpretation, unless that of Braune be an exception. See above.—R.]

* [This interpretation is very plausible, and commends itself especially on account of the view it takes of the preposition ἐν. As τὰ πάντα immediately precedes, too much stress should not be laid on the rule mentioned above respecting the choice of the masculine. But I fully share in Dr. Braune's dislike for the *instrumental* sense of ἐν (taking it as=*per*). One who has been puzzled by the E. V., which accepts this as one of its most usual significations, and seen how often commentators pass over it without notice, must feel that for so small a word, it has suffered more at the hands of its friends than any other in the Greek Testament. It is a good rule: never render ἐν, *by* if any other possible meaning accords with the context. ALFORD and ELLICOTT refer to chap. v. 18, in support of the instrumental sense, but it is very doubtful even there. If we take ἐν=*in* here, then the πᾶσιν must be accepted as masculine, for the neuter would not allow of any intelligible meaning, especially in view of the well-known phrase τὰ πάντα, the *universe.* See under (7) however.—R.]

* [HARLESS takes πλήρωμα as expressing the *Divine glory*=*Shekinah*, but that is objectionable for reasons both lexical and logical.—EADIE refers to the view of MICHAELIS and BRETSCHNEIDER (=*quasi templum in quo habitat, quod occupat et regit, ut anima corpus*), but this and kindred interpretations are all either too limited or too specific. Just here it becomes us to be cautious.—R.]

(8.) Πᾶσιν is taken as neuter and rendered: *in all parts* (HARLESS and others), or in all places, everywhere (FLATT). BENGEL (*neutrum, masculini potestatem*) does not belong here, nor does he waver; he refers it to μέλεσι τοῦ σώματος αὐτοῦ, to persons. It is also taken adverbially: ἐν παντί (JEROME: *sicut adimpletur imperator, si quotidie ejus augetur exercitus—ita et—Christus—sic tamen, ut omnia adimpleantur in omnibus, i. e., ut qui in eum credunt, cunctis virtutibus pleni sint*). Indeed, πάντα ἐν πᾶσιν has been taken adverbially (SCHÖTTGEN: *omnia omnino*), or referred to the eternal (HOLZHAUSEN).

(9.) It is entirely groundless to find a polemic purpose here, especially an account of the word πλήρωμα used afterwards by the Gnostics also (MEIER, BAEHR).

(10.) Quite as groundless is the assumption that the ubiquity of the glorified Body is taught here (CALOVIUS).

## DOCTRINAL AND ETHICAL.

1. God, whose power and glory is so exceeding great (ver. 19), at whose command and disposal are all things, even Christ, whom He raised and exalted above all heavenly and earthly, personal and unpersonal powers (vers. 20–22), works *freely*, but without arbitrariness, *conditioning* Himself, upon men—not without faith (ver. 19), not without Christ (vers. 22, 23), so that the prayer also (vers. 16, 17: ἵνα), which is offered believingly in the name of Christ, has a prospect of being granted. Precisely in the *work of Redemption* is manifested the worshipful glory of God, who in self-conditioning love moderates Himself, lowers and limits Himself, in order to employ and to show His unbounded love, to impart of His nature and to make blessed. His whole power, strength, might and efficacy stand in the service of His love.

2. *Christ*, who as to His human nature has in His Father His God (ver. 17), is our Lord, the Head of His Church, at the right hand of God in glory, of unlimited power over angels and men, ministering and hostile spirits, as well as over the economy of the creation and of salvation. He cannot be put down to the level of Divine humanity and God likeness. Yet our section says nothing of His state of humiliation, speaks only of His state of exaltation, beginning with the resurrection from the dead, refers to the humanity, which He assumed, appropriated, and did not afterwards relinquish,* only that in what the Father did in Him, we might have a standard for what the Almighty God, who through Him is our Father, will and shall do and work in us (vers. 19, 20: εἰς ἡμᾶς—κατὰ τὴν ἐνέργειαν—ἐν τῷ Χριστῷ). He is the Head, to whom there will not be wanting a body, which He will prepare for Himself; He cannot be a "mere Head." But he has also no *vicar*, such as the Pope. *Sancta enim Christiana sive Catholica ecclesia consistere absque* ISTO *capite optime potest et constitisset certe rectius, ac melius cum eo ageretur, nisi diabolus illud caput in medium projecisset et exaltasset* (*Articles of Smalkald*).

3. *The connection between creation and redemption* is presupposed here; the two spheres do not fall asunder; Christ, the acme in both, holds them together; the former must serve the latter (vers. 21–23).

4. *Respecting the angels*, who are included in ver. 21. "over above all principality, and power, and might, and lordship," it is only indicated that they are *personalities*, and affirmed that they *have power and might*. From the series of these designations, which can scarcely be taken as a descending climax [though this is the most plausible hypothesis—R.], nothing can be inferred as to the ranks or groups of angels.* ["On the nature of angels, consult the able treatise by TWESTEN, *Dogmatik*, Vol. II. especially § 1, 4, the essay by STUART, *Bibliotheca Sacra* for 1843, p. 88–154, EBRARD, *Dogmatik*, § 228 sq., Vol. I. p. 276, and the remarks of LANGE, *Leben Jesu*, Part II. p. 41 f." (ELLICOTT).—All that is expressed is well set forth by WESLEY: "We know that the king is above all, though we cannot name all the officers of his court. So we know that Christ is above all, though we are not able to name all His subjects."—R.]

5. *The Church*. On this subject our section teaches more. As regards its origin the name ἐκκλησία (ver. 22), "the calling of God" (ver. 18) show what is indicated by "Head" or "gave Him to be Head" (ver. 22) viz.: The Church results not from a physical or purely world-historical process without the creative power and fatherly love of God; it is His work, His gracious gift, and indeed His Word is efficient therein, Christ, also, as the Eternal Word, as the power organizing the whole (τὸ σῶμα), through the word, as the *intellectual* means of the ingathering. The *extent* of the Church is also pointed out in two directions:

*a*) *On earth*: "the faith which is among you in the Lord Jesus" (ver. 15) and "to us-ward who believe" (ver. 19)—the faith in Jesus, wrought in men through the word, describes the domain of the Church: *where* (καθ' ὑμᾶς) faith is there is the Church, the congregation, even if it is wanting in particular persons or in many. The extent is not to be limited by Donatist or Anabaptist notions of the Church; she has, according to the purity of the word, the power of the preaching, the vitality of the faith, her degrees, *quo purior et sincerior est verbi prædicatio, eo etiam purior est ecclesiæ status* (JOHN GERHARD, *Loc.* XI. p. 195). But it should not be said, that there is no Church where sinners are and are tolerated (*Anabaptists*, SCHWENKFELD and others).

*b*) *On earth and in heaven*: "the fulness of Him who filleth all in all" (ver. 23); she is not merely a temporal institution, within the visible world, she embraces men after as well as before death. "Of all the names which the Church can and does bear, not one is so immeasurably

* [We must hold fast, especially in view of the local reference in ver. 20 to the truth of Christ's actual bodily presence in heaven, over against the Lutheran doctrine of the ubiquity of His humanity (Form. Conc. ii. 8). Comp. the implied opposition to this dogma in the Heidelberg Catechism, Q. 47, 48, 80 (apparently inserted afterwards). The Eucharistic controversies of the 16th century made of this a battle-field.—R.]

* [The so-called revelations of modern "spiritualism" do not seem to have shed much light on the few passages of Scripture which treat of angels. Nor do they attempt to do so. One might infer something from this fact, as to the question whether these revelations, granting them a supernatural origin, have the same origin as the statements of Scripture.—R.]

deep and yet so transparently clear, so sharply defined and yet so inexhaustibly rich, at once so real and spiritual, external and internal, obvious and mysterious as this one: she is the *Body of Christ.* It is this name and no other, which the New Testament Church has not in common with the Old Testament Church, and in which all her superiority over the latter is included; *time and eternity, suffering and glory, blessing and curse,* for all over whom the name of Christ is named, lie in its lap, and itself a riddle, to be first solved hereafter, yet all the riddles proposed to us by the present life find in it their solution" (DELITZSCH).

The *completion* of the Church is an object of the Divine government of the world, and has begun here in Christendom by the path of faith, to which the inheritance in the saints is certain (vers. 18, 19, 23).

6. *Faith* has its *ground* "in the Lord Jesus (ver. 15), its place of manifestation in the Church (καθ' ὑμᾶς, ver. 15), its *worth* and its *position* before love (ver. 15), its *importance* and *value* for God, who requires it as the condition of salvation (ver. 19: "to us-ward who believe"), from which may be inferred at the same time, that it has different *degrees*, since the Apostle joins together himself and others, also since the participle is present, that it is not to be conceived of as an act once for all, but as "a continuing *life-movement* to be constantly renewed."

7. Beside faith stands *love*, which is germinally included in the former, since this "is an act of self-emptying and surrender to a gracious God," who is Love. But it is not to be regarded as a virtue, by means of which we become well-pleasing to the beloved Love; it comes into existence with faith, which lays hold of the righteousness of Christ, and thus attains to righteousness before God, and is the mother of all virtues.—In the phrase "unto all the saints" no limitation can be perceived, since he who loves *all* the members of the Church, the orthodox and the erring too, will imitate his Lord Jesus, the Good Samaritan of the world in Samaritan love (Luke, x. 37: "Go thou and do likewise"). The context leads only to this emphasizing of love.

8. *The ground of hope* is the calling of God and its *goal* the "inheritance" of God. It comes from above, points and looks upward; it lifts us out of the natural ego and above the visible world about us.*

9. *Knowledge* is both *path* (ἐν ἐπιγνώσει, ver. 17) and *goal* (εἰς τὸ εἰδέναι, ver. 18); it is a matter capable of growth, for it has but to ponder the thoughts of the eternal, creative God. Man's knowledge is not perfect within the domain of creation, still less can he know the things of the invisible world. Only by *living* in a sphere does he gather knowledge of what is found there; knowledge comes from experience of occurrences. Without a disposition of the heart the sense of the understanding is not enlarged and sharpened. *Sensible, mental, spiritual* knowledge refers to life-spheres, in which he who knows must move. Only the believing, loving, longing one knows and grows in knowledge unto knowledge.

10. *The prayer of the Apostle* has it *starting-point* in what God has given, and its *goal* in what God should give. From thankful acknowledgment, he proceeds to requests, petitions; with the faith and love of the church before his eyes, he rises to supplication for the spirit of wisdom and revelation, for wider knowledge of what God is, on behalf of their inner life. This occurs daily. Thus have we all, ministers and members of the church, especially the former, to learn, in order to practise it, what furthers the Kingdom of God in general and in particular: *such prayer is a means of grace* full of blessing for those who offer it, as well as for those for whom it is offered.

11. The *consummation* in the case of individuals is *conditioned* by the church and conditions its consummation. Hence "His inheritance in the saints" (ver. 18). Outside the church we do not advance, nor salvation become ours, whatever we may be, or accrue to us, wherever we stand; it is a gift, for which we must be prepared. The fulness of the gift and our perfection finally coincide.

### HOMILETICAL AND PRACTICAL.

It is a joy, when in social circles one hears from another, just as of city and state events, so especially of the kingdom of God, the church of Christ, of the faith and love of Christians.—We should not judge the faith of particular persons in a church, but rejoice in the faith within the church, though it be only among the minority; so long as there is believing preaching, supplication for all that concerns the church, order in the administration of the sacraments, grace at table and family worship, use of the best hymns, since we have so many poor ones, and many another sign of faith in the Lord Jesus Christ in the church, a stranger who does not know the individuals at all, may and ought to rejoice therein and speak thereof.—Love to *all* Christians! As we must pray every Sunday for love toward *all men*, so love to *all Christians* is not so easily brought about. The orthodox, pietists, and those who deal earnestly with God's word and the confessions of the church, are least likely to encounter love from those, who regard themselves as precisely the liberal Christians; such fall in much more readily with those who are against the Church of Christ than with these. Always reckon among "all Christians" those first, who are to you the most unpleasant, thus you will best perceive the weight of this injunction and your own weakness.—Who of us always begins his prayers with thanksgiving, as did the Apostle? We rather pray for what we lack, than thank for what we have received. This should not be.

Men rejoice much, if they are thought of at a distance; they part well-nigh always with the

* [MEYER: "Notice here, too, the three fundamental elements of subjective Christianity: *Faith* and *Love* and *Hope* (vers. 15, 18); in *faith* and *love* the illumination through the Holy Ghost should ever bring more and more to our knowledge the glory of our *hope;* for the Christians' πολίτευμα is in heaven (Phil. iii. 20), whither their entire "minding" and "seeking" is directed. The centre of Christianity is still faith with its love, in connection with which, however, *hope* ever, encouragingly and inspiritingly, holds up the constant *goal.*" He adduces this against WEISS, who seeks to discover here special prominence given to hope "entirely after the Petrine mode," which as that author thinks makes "hope" the centre.—R.]

request: Remember me! It is something beyond this, when such remembrance rises into intercession, and one remembers the absent, not merely pleasantly or listlessly, in conversation with men, but devoutly in prayer to God.—Without knowledge we do not attain to knowledge; only in the light do we see light. The Apostle does not indeed preach the Word of learning or science, but still it is spoken against ignorance, indiscretion, narrowness. Only that the centre of man, the *heart* and temper with the will be open to the light, to knowledge!—As the fear of God is the beginning of wisdom (Ps. cxi. 10), so the starting point for this is insight into our misery and poverty; poor human beings generally swell out with their own worth, and just in this way fritter away what they have of God's gifts. We must in the end seek our worth above, if we would find it; else we get into a pitiful satisfaction.

The three most important objects of our knowledge: 1. God's *call*—in our need; 2. God's *heritage*—in our *heart;* 3. God's *strength*—in our *longing* and *striving.*—As the world needs revelation beside the wisdom from experience, so a man also needs besides wisdom and prudence the private revelation to teach what and how he should act and suffer and bear.—Our hope rests on Christ in God. What the Father, to whom Christ in His holy humanity prayed, praying as to His God, has done to Him, *in* and *upon* Him, when He exalted Him from the dead to His right hand, that shall occur to thee, since He works *upon thee,* yet only in proportion to thy faith in thy Saviour.—Be, become and remain a member of the Church which is His Body! Those are *beheaded* rather, who deny the Lord to save their heads, than those who in holy martyrdom lost their heads, to remain with their Head.

STARKE:—Faith has to do with the gospel, love with the law. Faith takes, love gives; the former has the benefits, the latter the duties.—We must not seek the saints only in heaven, for they are certainly already on the earth. The imperfection of sanctification and holiness does not deny the truth of these things.—See here, how a preacher should remember his congregation before God in prayer!—As it is one of the signs and duties of a faithful teacher, now to thank and now to pray to God for his congregation, so it is not less the characteristic of a good hearer, to give the teacher, whose intercession he will confidently expect as a blessing to himself, great cause for thanksgiving.—The possessions of our glorious inheritance are so great and excellent, that no man can understand them without the illumination of the Holy Ghost.—The mere science of the letter in Divine things, obtained by the natural powers of godless people is no real enlightenment nor proper knowledge of Jesus Christ.—The call to the kingdom of God must stand at the basis of every external calling which we have in our sphere of life, that we may master it.—Conversion is a great and almighty work of God, hence not the power of man, nor consisting in a mere thought of the brain, but is a great change of soul, since all its powers are turned away from sin and the world to heaven and God.—Lazarus was awakened by Christ with a word, but how many sermons did He use to awaken the spiritually dead Jews, and yet they would not let themselves be awakened. God's power and grace for the conversion of man is in itself infinite, yet He will force no man, but leaves him the freedom to resist.—The Christian Church is the Body of Christ and hence closely united with Him. She receives all her fulness from Him; from Him, the Head, flows all strength into the members. Although she here finds herself surrounded with much weakness and misery, yet is she still glorious in her Head, who already reigns in glory.

A. H. FRANCKE:—This then is also wisdom, to know that we cannot be wise unless there be a God and we can receive it from Him in answer to *prayer.* The Apostle does *not* say, he wishes that a university might be established in the city of Ephesus, in which many professors would take positions, that by this means the people might be made wise,—but: that the God of our Lord Jesus Christ, the Father of glory, may give unto you the spirit of wisdom.

RIEGER:—Beside the glances into the distance and the hope of our calling in the invisible and eternal, beside the insight into the economy of God, without us, we must not disregard the insight into the necessary truths learned by experience of God's work of grace within us, that each do their part in making the heart steadfast and full of confidence and love. If a man thinks of the depth of his fall, the throng and deceit of his foes, the powerful hindrances to his salvation, then he may well desire to look into the greatness of the power of God, which is employed in his calling and preservation unto blessedness.—In faith we can most precisely notice, how God applies His transcendent might and yet how man is not overcome by it in a violent manner, but is so disposed, that he can maintain his convictions, his love for light, his obedience under its influence.—Believing is opposed by the love of our own life so deeply inherent in us, by so many offences occurring to us in the world's ways; therefore it requires the working of His mighty strength. This power of God and its effect is indeed still concealed in us, covered up by our weaknesses, and behind the curtain of the flesh not yet fully to be judged; but in Jesus Christ it has already attained to victory.—The Head and the Body together make a whole; in the church is seen the fulness of Him who filleth all in all; Christ applies the fulness of the Godhead dwelling in Him to the completing and perfecting of this His church; He does not leave her until He has also fulfilled all that is well-pleasing to God, and presented her, blameless, filled with all the fruits of righteousness.—He who stands in vital fellowship with Him, has all things.—All that is not yet disclosed to you, remains yours still in this fulness.

PASSAVANT:—Do you detect no result of this Divine power in you, no new life from God, or no hunger and thirst after deliverance out of the old nature into the new nature of the friends of the Lord; oh, do not trust yourself, do not trust thy best thoughts, thy most beautiful feelings, thy noblest strivings, thy best beliefs, for there is also a vain, a false, self-made, fancied faith, a faith leading to God as little as coming from God.—Are they holy and good, those powers, Jesus is still more holy and glorious above them; and have they on God's account, as is the case, as angels of light an influence upon the worlds of God, upon the earth, upon us, they receive from Christ their power and strength, they stand under His supreme influence; He directs them, He equips them. Are they unholy and evil, those powers, even here Jesus will have power and maintain authority; will punish their evil nature, will restrain their corrupting influence and destroy their power, aye, has already, as the Dying and Crucified One, broken and destroyed their power.—*All in all:* In the angels of His power, in the glorified righteous, in His saints, and all the Blessed, their only clear and heavenly radiance, their Divine joy, their eternal peace, their blessedness, their glory. All in all: Among the angels of disobedience, about the unrighteous, the ungodly and the damned, for all the Light shining with eternal rays of anxiety and terror through their darkness; the eye, that with a flame of fire searches forever through their inmost nature; the power, that always from without and from within tends them with a rod of iron; the word, the eternal word, judging and condemning them in their own hearts, ever anew, ever more penetratingly, more irrevocably, more awfully. All in all: In all His worlds, from the lowest to the highest degrees, in all powers and glories, from the smallest to the most exalted of constellations, of suns, which excel all others in clearness and glory. He is the Divine, infinite fulness of light, of life, from out which they gladly rise in His heavens.

Heubner:—Thanksgiving and prayer are the inward emotions of a holy mind, the inward holy choir.—Only what proceeds from God's revelation, which is attested to man by the illumination of the Holy Ghost, is true wisdom. Every one must have his own revelation of Christianity, for he should not believe on the testimony of a stranger.—The Christian knows not only his misery, but also his blessedness, how rich and glorious is the inheritance ordained by God for the saints, and from the greatness of his blessedness he knows the greatness of Divine grace. All this can be known and valued only by an enlightened eye, because it has not the dazzling glitter of earthly things. The evil spirit blinds man, so that he does not perceive how great is the blessedness won by Christ, so that he in his blindness thinks this disturbs his happiness and lays a yoke upon him.—God's mental power shows itself in what He has made out of man, in the transformation of the single sinner as well as of the heathen world. What philosopher could have suspected this? What did Apollonius accomplish? Nothing, save that the next generation held him to be what he was, a charlatan.—The resurrection of Christ is a token of spiritual life, of the regeneration of humanity, to take place through the Risen and Exalted Christ.—Christ is the Lord of the whole world of spirits, visible and invisible; He has authority over all ruling powers in heaven and on earth. Paul's words are an amplification of Matth. xxviii. 18.—This heavenly King is given to the Church as Head; she is committed to Him *in specie;* over her He has immediate oversight and care; she is to Him the dearest of all, because He has bought her with His own blood.—The Church is the Body of Christ, she is a communion, entirely permeated by His Spirit, the members being animated and controlled by His Spirit; she is the very centre of His efficiency.

Stier:—The most powerful and yet most humble way of exhorting is with this introduction: I pray for thee!—No thanksgiving without petition, so long as perfection and completeness are not yet there.—Our state of grace does not indeed begin with this deeper insight, but only through this does it indeed advance: may all preachers then learn from the Apostles, to work properly in their sermons and in their congregations for this end.—The Spirit of God cannot begin entirely without knowledge, nor work through dim feeling toward new will and life.—Illumination is not itself as yet sanctification, but is the immediately vital transition thereto from faith, which is at first, in and before experience, a matter of knowledge.—*To know God*—the highest aim of all wisdom of the spirit.—In the heart is all decided, faith, insight, desire, will.—The Apostle unfolds and portrays the supremacy of the Exalted One in the domain of *power*, especially in the kingdom of grace, of the Spirit, making alive again the dead in sin on the earth, *in the church.*—In this world there are many names before God and Christ, that we do not know or name, but hereafter we shall learn them.—Church is the assembly or unity of those called to the fellowship of salvation in Christ; it is the growing, developing body of Christ.

Leupold (*Sermons for Whitsunday* on vers. 15-19): *The heavenly gifts, in which the children of God rejoice with praise to-day.* 1) The *grace* of God, enriching us in the knowledge of salvation; 2) The *power* of God, causing this knowledge to become a might; 3) The *faithfulness* of God, carrying forward the good work already begun to the blessed goal.—*How do we prove ourselves thankful for the outpouring of the Holy Ghost and His gifts?* 1) By our knowing His gifts better; 2) ever imploring them more faithfully for ourselves and others; 3) by letting ourselves be filled by them and their power become more perceptible and precious in us.—*What are the Christian's festival petitions?* 1) That he may grow in the knowledge of salvation; 2) that he may grow in fellowship with the Saviour and all saints; 3) that he may not forget to give thanks for the unmerited favors of God.—*The high significance of the Pentecostal gift:* 1) It comes from the Lord; prayer is its condition; 2) In it the Lord comes to us; knowledge of God and His plan of salvation, of Christ and His saving work, is its proof; 3) Through it we come to the Lord; living faith, working in love is its crown.—*The fellowship of believers, holy and glorious:* 1) The spirit of revelation endows it; 2) Faith in the Lord Jesus founds it; 3) Love to all saints strengthens it; 4) Fraternal intercession crowns it.

Winter (vers. 20-23):—*The ascension of Christ His exaltation to the right hand of God in heaven:* 1. Let us so consider it. 2. Let us perceive the transcendent consolation therein inherent for us: *a*) now is He properly attested as our Saviour and Deliverer; *b*) now we know, not only that He still lives, but has power to defend us and His kingdom; *c*) now we may cheerfully go there too. 3. The high and holy duties proceeding from this: *a*) that we obey Him in all things; *b*) commit to Him ourselves and our whole life; *c*) seek not what is below, but what is above, and have our conversation in heaven.—*Christ all in all!* 1) The Lord of all in heaven; 2) the Almighty Head of His Church on earth.

[HODGE:—In praying that the Ephesians might be enlightened with spiritual apprehensions of the truth, the Apostle prays for their sanctification. In praying that they might have just conceptions of the inheritance to which they were called, he prayed that they might be elevated above the world. And in praying that they might know the exceeding greatness of the power exercised in their conversion, he prayed that they might be at once humble and confident,—humble, in view of the death of sin from which they had been raised; and confident, in view of the omnipotence of that God who had begun their salvation.

[EADIE:—Ver. 15. Community of faith begets community of feeling, and this brother-love is an instinctive emotion, as well as an earnest obligation. In that spiritual temple which the Spirit is rearing in the sanctified bosom, faith and love are the Jachin and Boaz, the twin pillars that grace and support the structure.—Ver. 16. The Apostle, though he had visited them, does not felicitate himself on his pastoral success among them, but gives thanks on this account to God.—The Apostle gave thanks, and his thanks ended in prayer.—Ver. 17. It is only when the prayerful study of the Bible is blessed by spiritual influence that wisdom is acquired.—This knowledge of God concerns not the works of His creation, which is but the "time-vesture" of the Eternal; but the grace and the purposes of His heart, His possession and exhibition of love and power.—Ver. 18. If the spirit of wisdom and revelation in the knowledge of God be conferred, then the scales fall from the moral vision, and the cloudy haze that hovers round it melts away.—Not only had they been the objects of God's affection—but also, and especially, of God's power. Infinite love prompted into operation omnipotent strength.—Ver. 19. If the resurrection of Jesus be the normal exhibition of Divine power, other similar exhibitions are pledged to Christ's people.—Ver. 20. The specimen and pledge of that power displayed in quickening us, is Christ's resurrection. 1. It is transcendent power. 2. It is power already experienced by believers. 3. It is resurrectionary power, displayed in restoring life. 4. The resurrection of Jesus is in this respect not merely a specimen or illustration—it is also a pledge. Present spiritual life and future resurrection are both involved.—Jesus was placed at the Father's "right hand." 1. It is the place of honor. 2. It is the place of power. 3. It is the place of happiness—happiness possessed, and happiness communicated.—Ver. 22. The brow once crowned with thorns now wears the diadem of universal sovereignty; and that hand, once nailed to the cross, now holds in it the sceptre of unlimited dominion. He who lay in the tomb has ascended the throne of unbounded empire. Jesus, the brother-man, is Lord of all: He has had all things put under His feet—the true apotheosis of humanity.—The history of the church is a proof extending through eighteen centuries; a proof so often tested, and by such opposite processes, as to gather irresistible strength with its age; a proof varied, ramified, prolonged, and unique, that the exalted Jesus is Head over all things to the church.—Ver. 23. Head and body are correlative, and are organically connected. There is first a connection of life—at the same time a connection of power,—and, in fine, a connection of sympathy.—The Head of the Church is at the same time Lord of the Universe. While He fills the Church fully with those blessings which have been won for it and are adapted to it, He also fills the universe with all such gifts as are appropriate to its welfare—gifts which it is now His exalted prerogative to bestow.—R.]

---

### B. The extent and mission of the church.

CHAPTER II. 1–22.

1. *Reminder of the previous condition of death and the glorious new creation.*

(CHAP. II. 1–10.)

1 And you *hath he quickened,* who were dead in trespasses and sins [You also who
2 were dead in your[1] trespasses and your sins]; Wherein in time past ye [Wherein
ye once] walked according to the course of this world, according to the prince of
the power [or powers][2] of the air, [of] the spirit that [which] now worketh in the
3 children [sons] of disobedience: Among whom also [even] we all had our conver-
sation [way of life] in times past in the lusts of our flesh, fulfilling the desires [do-
ing the wishes] of the flesh and of the mind [thoughts]; and [we] were by nature[3]
4 the children of wrath, even as others [the rest:—]. But God, who is [being] rich

5 in mercy, for [because of] his great love wherewith he loved us, Even when we were
dead in sins [our trespasses], hath [*omit* hath][4] quickened us together with Christ,
6 (by grace ye are [have been] saved;) And hath [*omit* hath] raised *us* up together
[with *Him*],[5] and made *us* sit together [with *Him*] in [the] heavenly *places* in
7 Christ Jesus: That in the ages to come he might shew [That he might shew forth
in the ages which are to come][6] the exceeding riches[7] of his grace, in *his* [*omit his*]
8 kindness toward us, through [toward us in][8] Christ Jesus. For by grace are ye
9 [have ye been] saved through faith;[9] *it is* the gift of God [the gift is God's]. Not
10 of works, lest any [that no] man should boast. For we are his workmanship
[his handiwork are we][10], created in Christ Jesus unto [for] good works, which
God hath before ordained [God before prepared] we should walk in them.

## TEXTUAL AND GRAMMATICAL.

1 Ver. 1.—[The pronoun ὑμῶν is found in ℵ. B. D. F.; accepted by Lachmann, Tischendorf, Meyer, Ellicott. It is omitted in *Rec.*, K. L.; bracketted by Alford, rejected by Braune, but it seems unlikely to have been inserted, since the articles are sufficiently explicit. They justify at all events the above rendering.—On *also* instead of *and*, the meaning of *in*, and the anacoluthon, see *Exeg. Notes*.—R.]—B. reads ἐπιθυμίαις instead of ἁμαρτίαις.

2 Ver. 2.—[The word ἐξουσίας is generally taken collectively. It means here either *empire* (so Ellicott renders) or *powers* (Four Ang. clergymen). The latter least disturbs the E. V., and gives an excellent sense.—*Of* must be inserted before "spirit," to show that it is not in apposition with "prince," as the E. V. assumes.—*Sons* is more literal than "children," and serves to distinguish υἱοί from τέκνα (ver. 2).—R.]

3 Ver. 3.—Instead of τέκνα φύσει [*Rec.*] in ℵ. B. and others, A. D. E. F. G. and others read φύσει τέκνα; an evident transposition, to take φύσει from between two words belonging together. [Most modern editors retain the order of the *Rec.*—Alford accepts ἤμεθα (ℵ. B.) instead of ἦμεν (*Rec.*, A. D. F. K. L., most editors).—Ellicott has been followed in the emendations of the English text.—R.]

4 Ver. 5.—[The aorist should be rendered by the English past, here and ver. 6, while the peculiar and emphatic ἐστε σεσωσμένοι, ye have been and (still are) saved, seems to require the perfect here, where a series of past acts are brought in review.—We substitute *our trespasses* for *sins*, because παραπτώμασιν is usually rendered thus, the article having in this instance almost the force of our possessive pronoun.—B. has a number of various readings in this verse, inserting ἐν before τοῖς παραπτώμασιν, which is an evident gloss. On *in* see the parallel expression, ver. 1.—R.]

5 Ver. 6.—[*In Him* is preferable to *together*, bringing out more exactly the force of συν in the compound verbs.—R.]

6 Ver. 7.—The whole verse is wanting in ℵ.; yet added very early. [The order of the E. V. is unfortunate, since the emphasis rests on the verb *shew forth*. The fuller expression: *the ages which are to come*, seems to be required by the full form of the Greek.

7 Ver. 7.—[The *Rec.* (with D.[3] K. L.) gives the masculine form. The neuter is found in A. B. D.[1] F., added in ℵ., accepted by nearly all modern editors.—R.]

8 Ver. 7.—[The E. V. as so often incorrectly renders ἐν, *through*. The comma should be omitted, as the phrase is either part of a compound modal clause, or closely joined with "toward us."—*His* before *kindness* is altogether unnecessary.—R.]

9 Ver. 8. [The article τῆς before πίστεως is found in ℵ. D.[3] K. L., most cursives, *Rec.*; accepted by Tischendorf, Meyer, Eadie. Bracketted by Alford. It is omitted in ℵ. B. D. F. G.; rejected by Lachmann, Ellicott (not in eds. 1, 2, but in 3, 4) and Braune. The weight, though not the majority, of authorities seems to be against it.—Alford renders the last clause of the verse: *God's is the gift*, following the Greek order, but Ellicott's rendering: *the gift is God's*, better accords with the English usage respecting emphatic position.—R.]

10 Ver. 10.—[This transposition brings out the emphasis resting on *His*, required by the Greek order, and has the additional advantage of showing that the participle *created* agrees with *we*.—The changes in the latter part of the verse are demanded by the generally admitted interpretation of the passage.—See *Exeg. Notes*.—R.]

## EXEGETICAL AND CRITICAL.

*Connection and Summary.*—After the Apostle has been led, by his petition for enlightenment respecting the glory purposed from eternity and already begun, to the carrying out of this purpose in the Church of Christ, the Body of which He is the Head, and in such a manner too, that i. 23, "so grand and solemn in matter and in manner," is adapted to form "a full-toned conclusion" (MEYER), his look is again turned to his readers to notice the "mighty working of the Father, through the resurrection and ascension of the Son, done once for all, and yet taking place in every one called into the Church" (STIER). First of all he is moved by "a glance at the similar condition of death in the case of the Gentiles (vers. 1, 2) and of the Jews (ver. 3)" (STIER) and then by the thought of God, who out of mercy has quickened and blessed the wretched in, with and through Christ (vers. 4–7): of grace through faith (vers. 8, 9), new-creating in Christ (ver. 10)!

[Braune, as will be seen below, arranges this section into paragraphs: Vers. 1–3, the condition of death out of Christ; ver. 4, the Deliverer; vers. 5, 6, the deliverance; ver. 7, the purpose; vers. 8-10, the means of bringing about the deliverance.—HODGE, who is always clear in his analysis, finds three principal topics treated of in this section:—(1) The spiritual state of the Ephesians before their conversion, vers. 1-3. (2) The change which God had wrought in them, vers. 4-6. (3) The design for which that change had been effected, vers. 7-10. He then enters into details.—ALFORD: "The power of the Father in quickening us, both Gentiles and Jews, in and with Christ (1-6); His purpose in manifesting this power (7); inference respecting the method of our salvation." This follows STIER's view, who refers the preceding clause to God.—R.]

Hence the connection of the beginning of this chapter (καὶ ὑμᾶς συνεζωποίησε, ver. 5) with "wrought" (i. 20, BENGEL) or "gave" (i. 22, HARLESS) is inadmissible. Nor is καὶ ὄντας ὑμᾶς to be joined with εἰς ἡμᾶς τοὺς πιστεύοντας (i. 19, KNATCHBULL and others) or with πληρουμένου (i. 23, CALOVIUS, KOPPE and others); nor is it necessary to complain here again, that a well-continued thread of discourse can scarcely be found in this Epistle (RUECKERT). Although these grammatical connections are to be rejected, there is still an internal relation: as the petition (i. 15-19) passed over into the typical and consolatory view of the exaltation of Christ, this section by applying this to the readers in effect continues the subject.

*The condition of death out of Christ* (vers. 1-3). The construction is not easy at first sight, but otherwise regular: καὶ ὑμᾶς ὄντας (ver. 1)—ὁ θεός (ver. 4)—συνεζωοποίησεν (ver. 5). The expansion of the object (vers. 1-3) alone occasions the beginning of a new sentence (ver. 4), as ὁ δὲ θεός shows, indicating as do *autem, inquam* the *epanalepsis* (WINER, p. 412); in consequence the object already described (vers. 1-3) is again repeated in briefer statement (ver. 5). So THEOPHYLACT and most ancient and modern expositors. [ELLICOTT thus states the same view: "Ver. 1, after having its structure interrupted by the two relatival sentences, vers. 2, 3, is renewed in ver. 4 (not ver. 5, SCHOTT) by means of δέ resumptive (Herm. *Viger*, No. 544), and there further elucidated by the interpolated nominative Θεός, expanded in application by the more comprehensive ἡμᾶς, and concluded in ver. 5."—HODGE (more popularly, but less exactly): "He dwells so long, in vers. 2-4, on the natural state of the Ephesians, that he is obliged, in ver. 5, to repeat substantially the beginning of ver. 1, in order to complete the sentence there commenced." The objection to the E. V.: *hath he quickened*, aside from the wrong tense, is that "he" has no antecedent, if ii. 23 refers to Christ, within reasonable distance.—R.]

Ver. 1. **You also,** καὶ ὑμᾶς, applies the discourse to the readers, without opposing ὑμᾶς to any others, than the genus, the whole church, as members of which they here come into special consideration, since they also have experienced, what has been experienced by the whole, and are a proof of the truth before uttered. [In rendering καὶ ὑμᾶς, "you also," it is not implied that they are contrasted with other Christians; it is chosen rather to avoid the simple connection with what precedes which is expressed by "and you," and to give prominence to the word "you;" not thus introducing "a special exemplification of the general act of grace in ver. 23," but implying a parallelism between the physical death in the case of Christ and the spiritual death in their case, as indeed the governing verb συνεζωοποίησεν (ver. 5) suggests.—R.]

**Who were dead in your trespasses and your sins,** [ὄντας νεκροὺς τοῖς παραπτώμασι καὶ ταῖς ἁμαρτίαις ὑμῶν. See *Textual Note* [1]].—Ὄντας, depending on συνεζωοποίησε, in view of the ποτέ occurring in the subsequent relative clause, is evidently=*cum eratis* (BENGEL), the condition in which God found them, when He quickened them (MEYER). They were dead through sins; the dative is ablatival, marking the *causa efficiens* (GROTIUS, MEYER). Hence it is not equivalent to νεκροὶ τῇ ἁμαρτίᾳ (Rom. vi. 11), ye *are* dead for sin (CAJETAN), nor with GROTIUS=ἐν τοῖς παραπτώμασι (Col. ii. 13, the parallel passage, in which the status, the element is emphasized).*

That Paul makes a distinction between παράπτωμα and ἁμαρτία, and what it is, is shown in Rom. v. 12-19. There the sin of Adam is termed τὸ τοῦ ἑνὸς παράπτωμα (vers. 15, 17, 18) or παρακοή (ver. 19), and through one man ἡ ἁμαρτία has come into the world (ver. 12). Comp. Rom. v. 20 with vii. 10-13. Παράπτωμα is applicable to the first sin of the seduced first man; the idea of *mis*deed is contained in it, of a deed not considered, *temere commissum, i. e., a nolente facere injuriam*, while ἁμαρτία, with its manifestations αἱ ἁμαρτίαι reaches further and deeper (TITTMANN, *Syn.* I. p. 45 ff.).* There is here an ascent from *desertio boni* to *perpetratio mali* (AUGUSTINE). To this view approximate HARLESS [HODGE] (actual sins and manifestations of sin in word, deed or otherwise), OLSHAUSEN (actions of sin and the more internal sinful motions of the soul in desires and words), JEROME (*delicta cogitatione inchoata* and actual sins).† The distinction: the *mental* errors and obscurations, the *moral* sins and vices (MATTHIES), is unfounded; neither should we apply the former to the *Jews* and the latter to the *Gentiles* (BENGEL), nor with STIER first think of the law of the State, of the conscience, well-known to the heathen also, and then of the outbreaks of corruption itself. We may not, however, take the two as purely synonymous (KOPPE), or deny a *real* distinction by affirming merely a two-fold representation, fall and transgression (MEYER).—The article points to the sins committed by the readers, Rom. v. 12: ἐφ' ᾧ πάντες ἥμαρτον. Hence ὑμῶν is an unnecessary explanatory gloss. [It is to be retained on diplomatic and critical grounds, but does not affect the sense.—R.]

Under νεκροί we should understand the dead, made dead; it recalls ἐκ νεκρῶν (i. 20); Christians are no longer dead. But the natural sinful condition, according to the Scripture from Gen. ii. 17 on, is really a death, because it is without life from and in God (iv. 18). It is therefore not=miserable (KOPPE and others), nor does it refer to *physical* death, as though it were equivalent to *certo morituri* (MEYER), which does not spare them now. *Spiritual* death alone is spoken of, since God is the source of life (Ps. xxxvi. 10) and without Him men are in the shadow of death (Matt. iv. 16; Luke i. 79; Matth. viii. 22; Luke xv. 24, 32; Rom. vii. 9, 10). So nearly all expositors. [No weakening of the sense is admissible; comp. *Doctr. Note* 3, d.—R.]

Ver. 2. **Wherein ye once walked** [ἐν αἷς ποτὲ περιεπατήσατε].—Ἐν αἷς, which

---

* [EADIE infers from ver. 2, "in which," that these datives represent not simply the instrument, but at the same time the condition of death. The general notion of the dative, the *where-case*, is not opposed to this. HODGE. ELLICOTT and ALFORD accept the causal sense, the latter justifying the use of *in*, to express this ("sick *in* a fever"). There seems to be doubt enough as to the exact force to warrant us in retaining the preposition supplied in our version.—R.]

* [ALFORD doubts the universal applicability of TITTMANN'S distinction, but accepts it as correct here, where both words are used. In Rom. v. 12-19 (see pp. 176. 182, *Romans*) there is a very marked distinction between the words, but here it is less observable. We must however attribute to ἁμαρτία a more generic sense than is found in the concrete παράπτωμα.—R.]

† [ELLICOTT: The former, the more *limited* term, *viz.:* particular and special acts of sin; the latter, the more *inclusive* and abstract, embracing all forms, phases and movements of sin, whether entertained in thought or consummated in act." So EADIE, though not very decided in his preference.—R.]

connects with ἁμαρτίαις, the word just preceding and forming a climax, denotes the *causa* of the condition of death as a developed condition, as a desired element. Ποτὲ περιεπατήσατε joined with νεκρούς is an *oxymoron*, like 1 Tim. v. 6: ζῶσα τέθνηκεν. Περιπατεῖν ἔν τινι (iv. 17; v. 2; Rom. vi. 4; 2 Cor. iv. 2; Col. iii. 7) has been transferred from the Hebrew (הלך) and designates *walking* as to the mode of life (WINER, p. 32); in English it designates the being at home, having entrance and exit, having one's doings and movements, having one's residence (Matth. xvii. 22: they abode in Galilee"). [EADIE: "The ἐν marks out the sphere or walk which they usually and continually trod, for in this sleep of death there is a strange somnambulism. Col. iii. 7."—R.]

**According to the course of this world** [κατὰ τὸν αἰῶνα τοῦ κόσμου τούτου].—Κατά now defines a relation of those walking to a power. This relation qualifies the walk more closely as one directed thereby, dependent thereon, determined thereby; "according to," "by virtue of" are the two significations required here (STIER), which are combined in: corresponding to. This power is designated by τὸν αἰῶνα τοῦ κόσμου τούτου, "the course of this world." This combination is peculiar, the words themselves are frequent, seeming to be used indiscriminately: 1 Cor. ii. 6 (σοφία τοῦ αἰῶνος τούτου); iii. 18 (σοφὸς ἐν τῷ αἰῶνι τούτῳ); ver. 19 (σοφία τοῦ κόσμου τούτου); i. 20 (σοφία τοῦ κόσμου); John xii. 31 (ὁ ἄρχων τοῦ κόσμου τούτου); 1 Cor. ii. 6 (τῶν ἀρχόντων τοῦ αἰῶνος τούτου); 2 Cor. iv. 4 (ὁ θεὸς τοῦ αἰῶνος τούτου). But the distinction is clearly obvious. Αἰών (PASSOW *sub voce*, HARLESS *in loco*), from αἴω=ἄημι, ἄω, to breathe, is related to ψυχή, with which Homer joins it, referring to life and time (*ævum*); hence also ἀπ' αἰῶνος, ἀπ' αἰώνων. In the New Testament the notion of time predominates, of periods of time, and the tendencies controlling them, their character, view and mode of life, their spirit. Κόσμος is the created, but fallen, apostate world, more definitely: humanity. The former may occur in the plural, the latter not. Hence BENGEL is very correct: *Ille hunc regit, et quasi informat; κόσμος est quiddam exterius: αἰών subtilius.* "TEMPUS *dicitur non solum physice, sed etiam moraliter, connotata qualitate hominum in eo viventium; et sic αἰών dicit longam temporum seriem, ubi ætas mala malam ætatem excipit.*" Acts xiv. 16; 1 Pet. i. 18. In αἰών here the notion of the tendency of time predominates, and means more what we call the course of the world than lapse (*Verlauf*); the course includes both the time and its character, as does αἰών also. Hence: according to, corresponding to the course of this world. The αἰών is in itself ethically indefinite, hence αἰὼν πονηρός (Gal. i. 4) and the demonstrative οὗτος or a genitive as here τοῦ κόσμου τούτου. Κόσμος is the external appearance, the external continuance of the world of men, αἰών its course, current, impulse (STIER); the latter may change, vary, in different periods, the former remains, and as the latter is estranged from God, so is this.*

It is incorrect to take the two words as purely synonymous, as though it were τὸν κόσμον τοῦτον (KOPPE). We regard as arbitrary the view that they are=τὸν αἰῶνα τοῦτον τοῦ κόσμου (RUECKERT), or: τὸν κόσμον τοῦ αἰῶνος τούτου (BRETSCHNEIDER). It is impossible to explain this designation from the gnostic doctrine of Æons, and to understand the devil thereby (SEMLER). LUTHER's rendering: *Lauf* [so E. V.: "course"] is more apt than: spirit of the age (MATTHIES), tendency of the age (OLSHAUSEN), life (HARLESS), duration of time (MEYER), course of time (SCHENKEL).

**According to the prince of the powers of the air** [κατὰ τὸν ἄρχοντα τῆς ἐξουσίας τοῦ ἀέρος].—Here Paul evidently passes to what stands behind the course of this world, influencing it, working through it. Κατά places this clause as parallel to the preceding, and τὸν ἄρχοντα refers to the master, the prince.* The genitive τῆς ἐξουσίας denotes the power belonging to and at the command of this prince (Matth. ix. 34; xii. 24; Mark iii. 22; Luke xi. 15). This power, which is to be considered as collective, is further defined by the genitive τοῦ ἀέρος, "of the air," most closely connected with it. Ἀήρ, which in its etymology reminds us of αἰών and in its nature of πνεῦμα, is the air, the atmosphere, surrounding the earth, breathed by all, acting upon the κόσμος, the world of men, standing in many relations to and exerting great power and influence upon their life; hence the power which the prince controls, is brought into connection with "the air," is described by "of the air," because in this are found the place and character of the power, its medium, element, region and domain, its means and mode; the figurative and literal meanings coalesce, the air as a cosmical and pneumatic reality (STIER); we too say: it lies in the air, in the time, thus denoting a quiet, profound and powerful operation. Thus Satan with his kingdom is sharply characterized, his nature spreading widely miasmata of corrupting power, from which even those truly living can scarcely withdraw or defend themselves, miasmata from diabolical choke-damp (as in the French Revolution) even to the most refined ethereal poisons of classical, æsthetic literature (vi. 11, 12; Col. i. 13). So ŒCUMENIUS has described the devil's power as ὑπὸ τὸν οὐρανόν, οὐχ ὑπὲρ τὸν οὐρανόν, concluding thus: φύσις γὰρ τοῖς πνεύμασιν ἡ ἐναέριος διατριβή.

We reject therefore those explanations, which take ὁ ἄρχων τῆς ἐξουσίας as *princeps potentissimus* (CLARIUS), or the genitive as appositional=ὅς ἐστιν ἐξουσία (FLATT), or *cui est potestas* (ERASMUS and others), or as the object=*imperium* (GREEK and LATIN FATHERS and others); those taking τῆς ἐξουσίας τοῦ ἀέρος as *potestatis*

* [ELLICOTT finds an ethical meaning predominant here in αἰών. "In such cases as the present the meaning seems to approach that of 'tendency, spirit, of the age' (Olsh.), yet still not without distinct trace of the regular *temporal* notion, which, even in those passages where αἰών seems to imply little more than our 'world' (comp. 2 Tim. iv. 10), may still be felt in the idea of the (evil) *course*, development, and progress ('*ubi ætas mala malam excipit*'), that is tacitly associated with the term."—R.]

* ["The world and the church are now tacitly brought into contrast as antagonistic societies; and as the church has its own exalted and glorious Head, so the world is under the control of an active and powerful master, thus characterized" (EADIE). The reference to a personality is to be found in this word, though ἐξουσίας as a collective noun includes the evil spirits whose prince is Satan.—R.]

*aëriæ* (*Syriac*, BUCER and others); or those taking τοῦ ἀέρος only figuratively (CALVIN, BEZA), or=τοῦ σκότους (although we find: ἐσκοτίσθη ὁ ἀήρ, Rev. ix. 2), either tropically *pro obnubilatione mentis* (COCCEIUS, STORR and others), or *pro concreto* as darkened spirits, men and bad angels (FLATT), or by metonyme, *continens pro contento*, the earth surrounded by the atmosphere (HILARY, BULLINGER and others), or merely as the region=ἐν τῷ ἀέρι (BAUMGARTEN, not -CRUSIUS), or only as a designation of quality=ἀέριος (A-LAPIDE, CALIXTUS and others), or referring it to the "prison," 2 Pet. ii. 4 (AUGUSTINE); nor can we suppose here a remnant of rabbinical tradition (MEYER), or echoes of a Pythagorean view of the world (MEYER, SCHENKEL), or the influence of Alexandrian gnosis (ELSNER and others). Out of such "muddy pools" or untenable speculations Paul would not have drawn his doctrine. Comp. *Doctr. Note* 3.

[HARLESS and STIER are very full on this clause. The most extended comments easily accessible to the English reader will be found in EADIE, whose opinion approaches very nearly to that of Braune. The simplest explanation is that of ALFORD, who thinks the phrase "of the air" is drawn from "the persuasion and common parlance of mankind," without conveying any teaching respecting demonology. In any case the genitive ἀέρος is to be regarded as a genitive, not of quality, but of *place*, either literal or figurative, or both, as Braune holds. HODGE, while not definitely deciding, seems to favor the untenable view, that "of the air" is="of darkness." EADIE: "The κόσμος of the New Testament is opposed to God, for it hates Christianity: the believer does not belong to it, for it is crucified to him and he to it. That same world may be an ideal sphere, comprehending all that is sinful in thought and pursuit—a region on the actual physical globe, but without geographical boundary—all that out-field which lies beyond the living church of Christ. And, like the material globe, this world of death-walkers has its own atmosphere, corresponding to it in character—an atmosphere in which it breathes and moves. All that animates it, gives it community of sentiment, contributes to sustain its life in death, and enables it to breathe and be, may be termed its atmosphere. Such an atmosphere belting a death-world, whose inhabitants are νεκροὶ τοῖς παραπτώμασι καὶ ταῖς ἁμαρτίαις, is really Satan's seat. His chosen abode is the dark nebulous zone which canopies such a region of spiritual mortality, close upon its inhabitants, ever near and ever active, unseen and yet real, unfelt and yet mighty, giving to the κόσμος that 'form and pressure'—that αἰών—which the Apostle here describes as its characteristic element." —Comp. STUART, *Biblioth. Sacra*, 1843, p. 140; HAGENBACH, *Stud. u. Krit.* I. p. 479; CUDWORTH, *Intel. System*, II. p. 664.—R.]

**Of the spirit**, τοῦ πνεύματος, is in apposition to τῆς ἐξουσίας τοῦ ἀέρος, "of the power of the air." While the last phrase sets forth his external dominion, the parallel phrase denotes his internal efficiency. BENGEL is excellent: *principium illud internum, ex quo fluunt actiones infidelium, oppositum spiritui fidelium filiorum Dei.* It is therefore not a personality, but an influence which has become a ruling mode of thought, disposition, a πνεῦμα ἐνεργοῦν (RUECKERT, STIER). Comp. Winer, p. 589. Hence it is not to be joined in apposition to τὸν ἄρχοντα and a hypallage accepted as in iii. 2; 2 Cor. iii. 7; Luke viii. 32; xxii. 20. So CALOVIUS, KOPPE, RUECKERT; similarly FLATT. But τοῦ πνεύματος is also not dependent on τοῦ ἀέρος, as HOFMANN (*Schriftbeweis* I. p. 455) thinks, taking ἐξουσία in accordance with Luke xxiii. 7 as the region of dominion, so that the air of the spirit working in the disobedient is the atmosphere formed by his nature. Nor is it to be taken collectively, just as ἐξουσία τοῦ ἀέρος is the complex of demons (GROTIUS and others). It is the spirit, which through its ruler, the devil, exists outside of individuals, defines them, works in them, the *spirit of the age* [*Zeitgeist*].

[The apposition with ἐξουσίας is at all events to be accepted, with the majority of modern commentators. But here the two views present themselves: (1) the reference to the evil principle, which must be taken objectively as the article requires (MEYER, ELLICOTT), as Braune holds, or (2) to the aggregate character of the individual πνεύματα (EADIE, ALFORD). The former is open to the objection, that it represents Satan as the prince of a principle, and the latter assumes a collective sense which is quite unusual. If we accept a tacit antithesis to the Spirit of God, and remember that this spirit is here conceived of as distinct from its influence on men, (1) will be the safer view.—R.]

**Which now worketh**, τοῦ νῦν ἐνεργοῦντος.—This spirit is to be regarded as efficient, not as effected, *affectus mundanus* (SCHMIDT); νῦν being put in advance and "in the children of disobedience" appended for emphasis. "Now" expresses the fact that it has not ceased to work, after no longer working in them, the readers (ποτέ); it now works in the children of disobedience, subjects of its activity are not wanting; it might be explained with OLSHAUSEN by ἐν τῷ αἰῶνι τούτῳ. From this danger always springs for the believers. Hence it is not: now still, *ad huc* (MEYER and others), nor: *nunc maxime* (BENGEL: *qui evangelium per incredulitatem spernunt, manent mancipia spiritus illius et amplius capiuntur;* STIER: "more now, since accomplished redemption proffers itself"). RUECKERT also, with FLATT, refers to the extraordinary, specially dangerous power of the Satanic kingdom in the age of Redemption (2 Thess. ii. 2 ff.; 2 Cor. iv. 4). [So DE WETTE].

**In the sons of disobedience**, ἐν τοῖς υἱοῖς τῆς ἀπειθείας.—Thus are those designated who are οἱ ἐξ ἀπειθείας (comp. Rom. ii. 8: οἱ ἐξ ἐριθείας), who are dependent on, springing from, nourished by disobedience, as v. 6; Col. iii. 6. It is a Hebraistic expression. [It marks "the essential and innate disobedience of the subjects, a disobedience to which they belong as children to a parent" (ELLICOTT).—R.] "Disobedience" emphasizes the immoral nature of unbelief, which is precisely disobedience, contumacy, among the heathen also, who resist the secret voice of God in their conscience (Rom. ii. 14, 15) as well as among the Jews who resist the revealed will of God in the word of the prophets, and among both, in resisting the apostolic announcement. MEYER should not be willing to refute the explanation: unbelief (LUTHER, BENGEL, HARLESS, STIER).*—The preposition ἐν, "in," marks the internality of this Satanic working: in their souls (MEYER). They are the "fulness" of the devil, on whose part there is a "spirit," efficient unto destruction, which the disobedient and unbelieving mood already present in man comes to meet.

Ver. 3. **Among whom even we all had our way of life in times past** [ἐν οἷς καὶ ἡμεῖς πάντες ἀνεστράφημεν ποτέ].—The emphasis rests on καὶ ἡμεῖς "even we;" in antithesis to "you" (ver. 1), the readers, whom he describes as previously heathen, he places himself and the Jewish Christians,† and that too without exception ("all"). Ἐν οἷς, according to grammatical rules, refers to "the children of disobedience" (ver. 2); thus declaring that those who were formerly Jews belonged also to the children of disobedience; ἐν οἷς is=ὧν καὶ ἡμεῖς ὄντες, in order to lay down the ethical category for the Jews (MEYER). So the same corruption and its universality are predicated of the Jews, over against the Gentiles. Comp. *Doctr. Note* 3. We should not then render it *inter quos*, or explain that although the Jews were actually locally among the Gentiles, they did not live there as children of disobedience. The reference to παραπτώμασιν, "trespasses," ver. 1 (*Syriac*, JEROME, BENGEL, STIER and others), is at once impossible, if ὑμῶν be retained there, and in any case inadmissible on account of "in the lusts of our flesh," which denotes the element or sphere of the verb, so that this cannot be found in ἐν οἷς. The grammatical connection cannot be decided by the parallel passage, Col. iii. 7: ἐν οἷς—περιεπατήσατε, since parallelism will not contravene the requirements of grammar.

**In the lusts of our flesh** [ἐν ταῖς ἐπιθυμίαις τῆς σαρκὸς ἡμῶν].—The repetition of ἐν in the same clause occurs also in 2 Cor. i. 12: ἐν ἁγιότητι καὶ εἰλικρινείᾳ—ἐν σοφίᾳ—ἐν χάριτι ἀνεστράφημεν ἐν τῷ κόσμῳ, where the first phrase answers to the last in our verse, and the last to our first. BENGEL remarks on the verb: *hoc quiddam speciosius quam ambulare.* STIER finds it sharper and stronger than περιεπατήσατε, used of the Gentiles. LUTHER: "ye have walked"—"we have had our walk." [So substantially the E. V.] This ἀναστρέφεσθαι refers more to an unquiet, refractory, quarrelsome course of conduct, περιπατεῖν is rather an indolent letting one's self go according to habit. The qualifying phrase; "in the lusts of our flesh," also sharpens the affirmative here, in comparison with that respecting the Gentiles. Among the latter the power of the evil spirit works, as respects the Jews prominence is given to their own disposition and will. Israel had already the proper ἄρχων in the theocracy, in its discipline another ἐξουσία, the moderating and helping air of a better spirit, being by no means given over in the same degree to the course of this world (STIER).—HARLESS sets forth very well the order of the significations of σάρξ; 1) what is *material*, 2) *external*, not mental, 3) what is *ruled by matter*, and in so far *sinful*, 4) what is *sinful*, opposed directly to the Spirit of God, 5) *Humanity* in all these aspects. [Comp. the Excursus in *Romans*, pp. 235 ff. The word is here used in its ethical sense: the *whole human nature* turned away from God, in the supreme interest of self, devoted to the creature.—R.]

**Doing the wishes of the flesh and of the thoughts** [ποιοῦντες τὰ θελήματα τῆς σαρκὸς καὶ τῶν διανοιῶν].—Ποιοῦντες, placed first for emphasis, defines more closely the preceding verb. [A participle of manner.—R.] The children of disobedience to whom they belonged, do the wills, τὰ θελήματα,* not merely single ones, which the flesh has, and those τῶν διανοιῶν, as real servants, slaves in fact. The plural denotes the confused, opposing multiplicity; a united, self-contained will is not spoken of. But these are not mere ebullitions of the flesh. "The διανοιεῖσθαι is the internal self-activity of man, conscious of his nature as self-determinable, and the διάνοιαι are the manifold productions of this" (HOFMANN, *Schriftbeweis*, I. p. 563). He appears as the slave of his inborn nature and of his selfish thought; the two are turned to various objects, and in his desires create a diversity. The understanding or the reason stands in the service of the flesh, falls into subtleties, seeking reasons, excuses, ways and means for the "lusts of the flesh," helping the desire to strengthen into determinations and activities of the will. Διάνοιαι are "opinions of the will representing themselves as prudent, deceitful grounds of volition." COGITATIONES *callidius peccandi studium inferunt*, CARO *cœco ruit impetu* (BENGEL). The plural marks the sundering, the confusion of the διάνοιά into the unhappy and treacherous diversity (HARLESS, STIER); the flesh makes a heap of reasonings (*Berlenburger Bible*). The context determines this view, as MEYER correctly remarks, but the form chosen subserves the context, corresponding well to its purpose; but it should be noted, that διάνοιαι is used by Paul only here, and θελήματα only in his speech, Acts xiii. 22, there too of God's will. It is incorrect to regard διάνοιαι as loose fancies (MATTHIES),

* [The connection between "unbelief" and "disobedience" is undoubted. but the former does not come into any special prominence here. The word here "characterizes the world not as in direct antagonism to the gospel, but as it is by nature—hostile to the will and government of God, and daringly and wantonly violating that law which is written in their hearts" (EADIE).—R.]

† [The reference to Jewish Christians has been accepted by the vast majority of commentators, both on account of the particular antithesis (ὑμᾶς, ver. 1) and the general distinction which seems to attach to these pronouns in this Epistle. But DE WETTE, EADIE, ELLICOTT, ALFORD oppose this reference here, on the ground that πάντες will not admit of this limitation. In every case Paul refers to both, when he uses ἡμεῖς πάντες.—Perhaps it is safest to follow this usage here, for the doctrinal teaching remains the same, whether we suppose the Apostle is emphasizing the fact that all Christians are children of wrath by nature, or even the Jews who thought themselves children of promise by nature.—The meaning of οἱ λοιποί at the close of the verse will of course be modified by the view taken of ἡμεῖς.—R.]

* [ELLICOTT says of this word: "It here probably denotes the various exhibitions and manifestations of the will, and is thus symmetrical with, but a fuller expansion of ἐπιθυμίαις." So MEYER. EADIE similarly; the latter inclinations, the former the resolves into which they ripen. and which are further divided.—The use of the word seemed to justify our finding in it an element of desire, though the E. V. is too decided in its rendering.—R.]

sensuous thoughts without the basis of sensuous desire (OLSHAUSEN), or corrupt imaginations (HASE).

[The distinction between the two classes of θελήματα is thus expressed by EADIE: "The 'desires of the flesh' are those grosser gratifications of appetite which are palpable and easily recognized; and the 'desires of the thoughts,' those mental trespasses which may or may not be connected with sensuous indulgences." ELLICOTT: "The worldly sensual tendency of our life on the one hand, and the spiritual sins of our thoughts and intentions on the other." Both EADIE and HODGE restrict σάρξ (in the second clause, not in the first) to the animal part of our nature, but this scarcely seems justifiable, especially as the wider meaning gives so good a sense. Nor is the latter exact in taking *διανοία* as including "the whole thinking and sentient principle, so far as distinguished from the animal principle," still less in referring it here "more to the affections." MEYER says *διάνοιαι* bears to *σάρξ* in this case the relation of the special to the general.—The article before *σαρκός* and before *διανοιῶν* would justify the rendering "our flesh," "our thoughts," but the literal translation is sufficiently explicit, "thoughts" being the nearest equivalent to *διάνοια*.—R.]

**And we were by nature the children of wrath** [*καὶ ἤμεν τέκνα φύσει ὀργῆς*].—*Καὶ ἤμεν* is most naturally taken as i. 19-22: *ἐγείρας—καὶ καθίσας—καὶ ὑπέταξεν*, or *ἐγείρας—καὶ ἐκάθισεν*—and joined with *ποιοῦντες*, as a participle resolved into the finite verb. Since *ἤμεν* comes first, it is emphatic. [The change of construction gives emphasis to this verb also, marking that they "were," not that they "are," and further, as EADIE suggests, indicating unmistakably, that what they "were by nature" was not the result of what they had been doing.—The insertion of "we" in the English text will serve to indicate this emphasis.—R.] The Apostle has noted the *action* in the preceding clause, he now notices the *state* of the Jews, which is perceptible and perceived from the action, and hence put in the second place, this like the other being more sharply expressed than in the case of the heathen. This is parallel to "the children of disobedience," among whom he has already reckoned them (*ἐν οἷς*) but among whom they are now characterized as "by nature children of wrath." The phrases: "son of perdition" (2 Thess. ii. 3), "child of hell" (Matth. xxiii. 15), "Son of peace" (Luke x. 6) are similar. Paul says *τέκνα*, not *υἱοί*, not to weaken it into "little children," but to indicate the relation to birth.

The genitive *ὀργῆς* without the article must be connected as closely as possible with *τέκνα*, "children of wrath." [Not mere liable to wrath, but under it, as the figure implies.—R.] The Hebrew phrase בְּנֵים־לַיהוָֹה (2 Sam. xii. 5: *υἱὸς θανάτου* in the LXX., comp. Ps. lxxix. 11; cii. 21) may have occasioned the expression, but does not modify the explanation in the N. Testament, nor justify a weakening of the meaning, only marking the dependence of *ὀργή*, which the context (ver. 4) defines as that of God. So v. 6; Col. iii. 6; Rom. i. 18; comp. *Doctr. Note* 1.

*Φύσει* is not so emphatic as *ἤμεν*, nor even as *τέκνα*, denoting only a closer qualification of the latter, as regards origin, by nature. *Φύσις* (from *φύω*, to become, to arise, as *natura* from *nasci*, *ingenium* from *geno*, *gigno*) refers to birth, origin, and is that which has grown as distinguished from what has been effected, has the ground of its being, as it is in its own development, not in the accessory influence of others (HARLESS, STIER). [So EADIE, ALFORD, HODGE, ELLICOTT and the vast body of commentators. The last named finds the exact meaning in Gal. ii. 25; Rom. ii. 14; Gal. iv. 8, to be respectively (*a*) transmitted inborn nature; (*b*) inherent nature; (*c*) essential nature. The first is the meaning here, see below.—R.] So in Gal. iv. 8; Rom. ii. 24 (comp. Acts xvii. 28) *φύσει* points to the ground and origin of the present status. The meaning of these words necessarily is: we were from birth those who were forfeited to the Divine wrath, *iræ Dei devoti atque obnoxii, quasi ad eam rem ab ipsa natura effcti* (BEZA). Indeed *ἡ φύσις* is something living, developing itself, but from its beginning, in accordance with the principle inherent in it, so that there is included here also the natural development, further determined by man in his unregenerate state.

Standing in contrast to this *φύσει* is the Divine *θέσις* of God's work of revelation and of His covenant with the people of Israel, according to which they should not be "children of wrath," and also might not have been. "As belonging to the people of God, the Jews were בְּנֵים־לַיהוָֹה, but aside from this, consequently as belonging to the Adamite humanity, they were *τέκνα ὀργῆς*" (HOFMANN, *Schriftbeweis*, I. p. 565), hence *φύσει*. It is aptly mentioned that CHEMNITZ remarks: *Dicit, eramus et nos, Judæi scilicet. Dixerat enim Rom.* xi. 16: *si radix sancti, ergo rami. Ne ergo intelligatur, Judæos natura esse sanctos, dicit; eramus et nos Judæi filii iræ, sicut cæteri* (HARLESS). The position of *φύσει* between *τέκνα* and *ὀργῆς* suggests too: we were children —that is, *φύσει*, not *θέσει*, *ὀργῆς*, and yet might and should have been *διαθήκης* (*cum putaremus nos esse liberos liberos Dei.* BENGEL)! [The doctrine of original sin is here plainly implied (EADIE, HODGE, ALFORD, ELLICOTT, and others), the implication being an "even more convincing assertion of that profound truth." The opposition of BARNES and STUART, so far as it has an exegetical basis, finds some justification in the forcing of a direct theological statement on our passage. But the attitude here taken as respects this fearful fact of a *universal natural state of condemnation*, is precisely that which the Scriptures hold toward the question of the existence of God: it is not proved, but assumed. Comp. *Doctr. Notes* 1, 3, 4; EADIE *in loco; Romans*, Dr. SCHAFF's exhaustive notes on v. 12-21, especially pp. 178-180, 191-195; the last reference is to a *resumè* of the theories of original sin.—R.]

Accordingly "children of wrath" is not to be taken as merely a Hebraizing phrase for "worthy of wrath," *ira rei, digni* (THEODORET, RUECKERT and others), nor *proprii iræ* (STRIEGEL), objects of wrath (FLACIUS). Nor is *ὀργή=pœna* (GREEK FATHERS). Quite as little is *φύσει=ἀληθῶς, γνησίως* (ŒCUMENIUS), or: *natura, indole gentis* (CLER-

ICUS), still less: *paternæ traditionis consuetudine* (PELAGIUS), since it is the very opposite of συνήθεια. Moreover we should not think of a relation produced by the development of a *nativa indoles* (MEYER), or of the customary actual life of sin, "a doing of the wills of the flesh and of the thoughts," which had become habitual, making them "the children of wrath" (SCHENKEL). BLEEK says more circumspectly: the reference here is *not merely* to the inborn character, but also to the natural development springing from the man himself. To explain it of the natural condition of man in ante-christian life (ERASMUS and others) leaves undecided the main question, whether or not the φύσει designates an inborn relation. HOLZHAUSEN's connection of φύσει with ὀργῆς (wrath springing from the ungodly natural life) is entirely too inverted.

**Even as others,** ὡς καὶ οἱ λοιποί.—In 1 Thess. iv. 13, this designates the Gentiles, who have not become Christians. Λοιποί are passed over, without any further characteristics; according to the context the word classes together here men with and men without Christ, who have not submitted themselves to the working of Christ, resist it; such can be among Christians even. We may easily suppose, however, that Paul means the yet unbelieving Jews, over against the "we all," who have become believers in Christ; this would render prominent that while the Jewish Christians who have been rescued from the condition of death are no longer "children of wrath," these are and remain so, like the heathen, the "children of disobedience." So STIER, while nearly all expositors refer it either to the Gentiles (MEYER and others) or to all except those mentioned before (HARLESS and others); the latter is unquestionably more correct than the former, since just here the Gentiles are not in question, and to refer it to these alone, would be as if ver. 3 had been appended. The extension to other nations is, however, unnecessary, since all men are either Jews or Gentiles, and what has been said of the previous life of Christians from among the Gentiles or Jews, applies to the whole of the human race. It marks in a tender, sparing manner those Jews unconverted to Christ as "children of wrath," as the Gentiles not converted to Christ are "children of disobedience," in whom Satan works. [Those who refer ἡμεῖς πάντες to *all Christians*, of course take οἱ λοιποί as including all the rest of mankind, *not Christians;* but the universality of sin and guilt remains the indirect (and more convincing) assertion of the passage, whatever reference be adopted.—R.]

Ver. 4. *The Deliverer.* **But God,** ὁ δὲ θεός.—This is not antithetical, but resumes the discourse, begun with the object and then lengthened out, in order to permit the subject to follow, as we would say in German: *hat also Gott.* [We have no word so strictly resumptive as the German *also*, or the Greek δέ, as used here, hence the E. V. supplies both subject and verb in ver. 1, and resumes here with "but," which may bear a resumptive meaning.—R.] See on ver. 1. The δέ is required here by the antithesis in which the subject stands to the object; otherwise we have found οὖν here (MEYER and others). [HODGE makes the antithesis too strong: "notwithstanding our guilt and misery." —R.]

**Being rich in mercy** [πλούσιος ὢν ἐν ἐλέει].—Πλούσιος stands first for emphasis; our Epistle frequently mentions the riches in God (i. 7; Rom. x. 12: πλουτῶν). [Ὢν does not seem to be causal here (HODGE: "because He is rich in mercy"), but rather to state (in the form of a secondary predicate of time) the general principle under which the Divine compassion was exhibited (ELLICOTT, ALFORD); "being rich in mercy." The special ground follows.—R.] The connection "rich in mercy" is like Jas. ii. 5 ("rich in faith"); 1 Cor. i. 5; 2 Cor. ix. 11. So πλῆθος τῶν οἰκτιρμῶν σου, Ps. li. 1; lxix. 16. But ἔλεος is somewhat more than οἰκτιρμός (*ὁ ἐλεῶν subvenire studet misero et si potest, vere subvenit, sed qui intra fines doloris se tenet, is tantum οἰκτείρει;* TITTMANN, *Syn.* I. p. 70).

**Because of his great love wherewith he loved us** [διὰ τὴν πολλὴν ἀγάπην αὐτοῦ ἣν ἠγάπησεν ἡμᾶς].—The preposition (διά) marks the ground of His doings (vers. 5, 6), on account of this, *propter multum suum amorem.* LUTHER is therefore incorrect: *through* His *great* love. Prominence is given, not so much to the greatness, as to the riches, the manifold character of the love of God. The construction, ἣν ἠγάπησεν ἡμᾶς, is like John xvii. 26; Mark x. 38. WINER, p. 210.—The great love of God (αὐτοῦ) is added by Paul, after the expression respecting the riches of His mercy, which he had placed first on account of the context over against the condition of death in the case of Gentiles and Jews alike, because there was to be found in men themselves no ground at all for their salvation. Mercy was in God the movement of His love, which belongs to His Being; that men should be helped, required the entire *fulness* of the love of God. MISERICORDIA *removet miseriam,* AMOR *confert salutem* (BENGEL). CALVIN incorrectly joins διὰ τὴν πολλὴν ἀγάπην with πλούσιος ὢν [HODGE apparently]; the latter is an attribute of God, the former is an adverbial qualification of συνεζωοποίησεν. "Us" must be applied here to entire Christendom, after the necessary statements about "you" (vers. 1, 2) and "us" (ver. 3). *Aperta satis hæc verba sunt et cognitu facillima, si tantum et creditu facilia ea plerisque dominus redderet* (BUCER)! STIER refers it to the Jews, on which view see next verse. [It is=ἡμεῖς πάντες, if that phrase be accepted in its wider reference.—R.]

*The Deliverance;* vers. 5, 6.

Ver. 5. **Even when we were dead in our trespasses** [καὶ ὄντας ἡμᾶς νεκροὺς τοῖς παραπτώμασιν].—After ἡμᾶς (ver. 4) the object is again repeated, with a reference to what has been said in vers. 1-3, in admiration and wonder at the Divine grace, mercy and love. Now however we read καὶ ὄντας ἡμᾶς, while before we had καὶ ὑμᾶς ὄντας (ver. 1), καὶ ἡμεῖς (ver. 3); the emphasis therefore rests on ὄντας, and καί puts this state of death with another ὢν in a certain relation to πλούσιος ὢν ἐν ἐλέει. Accordingly the distinction between those dead, between "you" and "us" falls into the background behind the existence, the reality of this condition.

[Against MEYER, who takes καί as the simple copula, and RUECKERT, who deems it resumptive, we are fully justified in taking it as *intensive*, retaining *even* (E. V.) therefore; so ALFORD, ELLICOTT and most.—The dative is precisely as in ver. 1.—R.] What he has said in ver. 1 of the heathen: "dead in trespasses," is true of both therefore: it is the briefest expression, and quite sufficient after the previous explication of the object, especially as he mentions παραπτώματα, in which the reality of the condition of death is perceptible. The article denotes that the sins are the sins of the "dead" themselves (MEYER). [Hence *our* trespasses.]

This statement cannot indeed be referred to entire humanity; though it be done *for* all men, yet it is only done *in* Christians; and that is what is spoken of here. But it is just as little to be limited to Jewish Christians (STIER); the interchange of ἡμεῖς and ὑμεῖς (vers. 5, 7, 8) springs from the liveliness of the discourse, the interest in the readers and the purpose of the Apostle. Καί is of course not=καίπερ, *quamvis* (CALVIN, SCHENKEL). [For a making alive could only be from a state of death, not in spite of it.—R.]

**Quickened us together with Christ,** συνεζωοποίησεν τῷ Χριστῷ.—The construction is clear; the dative is governed by the σύν in composition. A fact in the past is clearly denoted as having taken place upon Christ and upon us. The meaning is also indicated by the antithesis or object: the dead He has made alive; were these not physically, but spiritually dead, then a spiritual life is meant. The preposition σύν does not denote contemporaneousness, but only fellowship: in the fellowship with the Risen One God quickened us also: Him hath He raised from the dead, us from our death, but not without Him, the Risen One. The verb itself does not determine any thing more definite regarding the life; the tense marks only the act of God as having taken place. Nothing further is added. Accordingly this fact is to be taken altogether objectively, without a subjective reference, altogether generally, without further qualification, as Col. ii. 12, 13, 20; iii. 1, 3; Rom. vi. 4-6; it is simply: He quickened us together with Christ. THEODORET: κεφαλὴ ἡμῶν ὁ συνεδρεύων, ἀπαρχὴ ἡμῶν ὁ συμβασιλεύων· τὴν γὰρ ἡμετέραν ἐνδέδυται φύσιν. Comp. i. 7, 22, 23. Though the life of Christ the Risen One is completed, and ours just begun, beginning in the Spirit, yet the two stand in an internal connection (2 Cor. v. 15), the latter, like the former, is the Father's act, in which the whole, the full life is implied and granted.

Accordingly it is first of all incorrect to apply συν to the re-animation of the Jews and Gentiles *together* (BEZA), or: *sicut ad exemplum* (ANSELM, GROTIUS). Then the reference is not to physical death and the actual resurrection life (MEYER), or to the forgiveness of sins (RUECKERT), or only to the first degree of life, from which the subsequent ones advance (OLSHAUSEN), or to justification and regeneration (BODEUS); nor are the aorists to be justified by recalling God's prescience (JEROME), or by introduced hope (AUGUSTINE, ERASMUS), or by a prophetic view, as if it had already taken place, were as good as certain (MEYER), nor is the fact of the actual accomplishment of this act of love in the readers, the Christians to be set aside by an emphasizing of the objective act in Christ (HARLESS).*

**By grace ye have been saved** [χάριτί ἐστε σεσωσμένοι].—In lively discourse, with a direct application to the readers, this is joined parenthetically to the general, objective fact of new life in Christ. The emphasis rests on χάριτι, which comes first; it refers to "His great love," is God's grace, thus dismissing all thought of claim and merit on the part of man. The clause emphasizes the fact of the deliverance from death into life, from wrath into love. Ye are (ἐστε)! This means more than the simple ἐσώθετε. ["Ye have been and are saved," the perfect of permanent state, implying that God's grace abides.—R.] *Videmus, ut nunquam sibi in prædicanda gratiæ amplitudine satisfaciat; ideoque identidem pluribus verbis inculcat, nihil esse in salute nostra, quod non sit Deo tribuendum certe qui ingratitudinem hominum rite expendet, non fastidiet hanc parenthesin quasi supervacaneam* (CALVIN).† It is not interpolated from what follows (GROTIUS), nor is the grace of Christ (BEZA) referred to.

Ver. 6. **And raised us up with him and made us sit with him in the heavenly places in Christ Jesus** [καὶ συνήγειρεν καὶ συνεκάθισεν ἐν τοῖς ἐπουρανίοις ἐν Χριστῷ Ἰησοῦ].—After thus specializing, Paul expands what was expressed in συνεζωοποίησεν. Here the first verb gives prominence to the negative side, and the second, with "in heavenly places," to the positive side of the quickening; the former marks the disappearance of the condition of death, the latter the permanent participation in what is heavenly. The liveliness of the discourse causes the introduction and repetition of καί, καί; they are not to be rendered: both—and. "In heavenly places" (comp. on i. 3) sets forth the antithesis to "the power of the air;" "at His right hand" (i. 20) could be predicated only of Christ (BENGEL:

* [EADIE emphasizes the subjective side: "The object of the Apostle, however, is not merely to affirm that spiritual life and resurrection have been secured by such a connection with Jesus, but that having been so provided, they are really possessed." This makes the "life" here referred to strictly spiritual. But a reference to physical resurrection seems to be involved (ALFORD, ELLICOTT). The aorist, retaining its proper force, has occasioned some difficulty. While the reading ἐν (B.) is to be rejected, and "in Christ" is not the exact sense, we must still hold that this thought underlies our verse. "What God wrought in Christ He wrought *ipso facto* in all who are united with Him" (ELLICOTT); not to the exclusion of a reference to the actual quickening in the case of believers. "When He was raised physically, all His people were *ideally* raised in Him; and in consequence of this connection with Him, they are, through faith, actually quickened and raised" (EADIE).—Dr. HODGE finds in the last fact that two other aorists follow a reason for limiting this verb to the beginning of the work of restoration, and yet says, ver. 6: "In its widest sense the life, which in ver. 5 is said to be given to us, includes the exaltation expressed in this verse. It is, therefore, only by way of amplification that the Apostle, after saying we are made partakers of the life of Christ, adds that we are raised up and enthroned with Him in heaven." If the latter position be correct, the verb is not to be limited here.—R.]

† [ELLICOTT: "This emphatic mention of grace (grace, not works) is to make the readers feel what their own hearts might otherwise have caused them to doubt.—the real and vital truth, that they have present, and actual fellowship with Christ in the quickening, yea, and even in the resurrectionary and glorifying power of God."—R.]

*Christo sua manet excellentia*), but "in heavenly places" of Christians also. "In Christ Jesus," following "with Christ" (ver. 5), introduces the mediation in the fellowship with Him; with this Col. ii. 12, 13 should be compared. [EADIE takes "in Christ Jesus" as qualifying "in the heavenly places," but this is scarcely allowable. —R.]

Accordingly, "raised with him," is not an advance from "quickened" toward "made us sit" (OLSHAUSEN) [EADIE], the first two expressions occur Col. ii. 12, 13 in inverted order. We should not interpolate *spe* (GROTIUS) or *jure et virtute spirituali* (BENGEL), nor are the aorists to be taken as futures from a prophetic view (A-LAPIDE), nor should we refer them to *summa et universa felicitas* (KOPPE), or to something spiritual, which is not yet objectively and really given. Comp. Col. iii. 1-3; Phil. iii. 20; Rom. vi. 6-10. Though ἐν Χριστῷ Ἰησοῦ is not=*per et propter Christum*, yet it cannot be denied that fellowship with Him is indicated (HARLESS), in accordance with the συν in the verbs.* But it may not be affirmed that on account of this "wonderful union" of the redeemed with the Redeemer, all the occurrences, through which the Redeemer passed after His death until His glorification, are spiritually and morally, hence in this life, consummated in the converted (SCHENKEL). Comp. *Doctr. Note* 2.

[EADIE also takes the three aorists as referring to what takes place in this life, and as marking successive steps: "The dead, on being quickened, do not lie in their graves." ELLICOTT is very cautious here: "As συνεζωοποίησεν, though primarily spiritual and present, may have a physical and future reference,—so here conversely, a present spiritual resurrection and enthronement may also be attended to," the primary reference being, as he thinks, to what is future and objective. ALFORD seems most correct: "God vivified us together with Christ: in the one act and fact of His resurrection He raised all His people—to spiritual life, and in that to victory over death, both spiritual and *therefore necessarily* physical also. To dispute therefore whether such an expression as this is past (spiritual), or future (physical), is to forget that the whole includes its parts.—The three aorists are proleptical as regards the actualization in each man, but equally describe a past and accomplished act on God's part.—The disputes as to whether these are to be taken as present or future, actual or potential, literal or spiritual, will be easily disposed of by those who have apprehended the truth of the believer's union in and with Christ." This last statement finds a striking confirmation in the fact, that many a commentator begins by limiting the sense, and ends by including the entire meaning.—R.]

Ver. 7. *The purpose*.—**That he might show forth,** ἵνα ἐνδείξηται.—The verb stands emphatically first. Ἐνδείκνυσθαι (Rom. ii. 15; ix. 17, 22; 1 Tim. i. 16; 2 Tim. iv. 14; Tit. ii. 10; iii. 2) has, like ἔνδειξος (2 Cor. viii. 24) the signification of an efficient, active showing, a making known through communicating, giving, causing to experience. It is not a mere φανεροῦν, γνωρίζειν, *declarare* (OLSHAUSEN, MEYER and others. [EADIE inclines to the singular meaning: give a specimen of, which is not in accordance with the emphasis resting on the word. —R.]

**In the ages which are to come,** ἐν τοῖς αἰῶσι τοῖς ἐπερχομένοις.—The plural marks a series, the word αἰῶνες, periods of time, stretching over "generations" (iii. 21), standing over against "the course (αἰών) of this world (ver. 2), not mere καιροί, occasions, moments of time (i. 10); ἐπερχόμενοι points to coming periods, *i. e.*, according to the context, those periods (*temporibus instantibus*) following each other with the fact of Redemption in the resurrection of Christ as the starting-point; lastly the preposition ἐν marks these as the spaces of time in which the showing takes place, in which there is really an advance. BENGEL: *Plurale, contra unum seculum malum, cui secula beata superveniunt potenter. Congruit hæc locutio menti Pauli de die novissimo non proxime instante.* Even in the earliest Epistles there is not wanting the thought of the long development of Christianity, whose blossoming in the Apostolic Church and in the first Christians as first fruits and representatives, lets us perceive the fulness of their Lord (1 Thess. iv. 15-17; comp. v. 1; 2 Thess. i. 7; comp. ii. 3 ff.). It is neither the age succeeding the resurrection, the age of the *parousia* (GROTIUS, MEYER), nor αἰὼν μέλλων (HARLESS). [These limitations are rejected by EADIE, ALFORD and ELLICOTT, HODGE who agree with Braune in referring the phrase to the successive periods of time between the resurrection and the Second Advent of Christ. The plural forbids the limitation to any one age, the present participle renders any remote future reference improbable. The Second Advent is rarely alluded to in this Epistle (ALFORD), though as usual MEYER finds it here also.—R.]

**The exceeding riches of his grace,** τὸ ὑπερβάλλον πλοῦτος τῆς χάριτος αὐτοῦ.—The neuter form τὸ πλοῦτος is well established here, as in iii. 16, and occurs several times (iii. 8; Phil. iv. 19; Col. ii. 2). On ὑπερβάλλον, see notes on i. 19. It denotes, over against the wrath of God (ver. 3) and the power of Satan (ver. 2) the triumphant superior power, hence it is not=περισσεύειν (i. 8). Comp. Rom. v. 20. Evidently as in the case of those realities, so is the power of this grace efficient, already imparted. Rom. ix. 23.

**In kindness toward us in Christ Jesus** [ἐν χρηστότητι ἐφ' ἡμᾶς ἐν Χριστῷ Ἰησοῦ].—"In kindness" designates the mode of showing the grace, "the friendly, condescending kindness" (HEUBNER), which expressed itself in Christ's Incarnation and in Himself. TITTMANN (*Syn.* I. p. 195): *Est benignitas Dei ad benefaciendum hominibus potius parata, quam ad puniendum; differt a voce χάρις; in hac enim certe in N. T. imperat notio benevolentiæ et gratiæ, quæ nihil merentibus bene facit.* It is therefore not here (as TITTMANN thinks, p. 142): *ipsum beneficium in nos Dei benignitate per Jesum Christum;* it is not χάρισμα, but χάρις is active "in kindness," the condescending love scatters out of the fulness of its

* [The force of συν in the two verbs is brought out in our rendering of this verse. A neater version would probably be: "And with Him raised us up, and made us sit in the heavenly places in Christ Jesus."—R.]

possessions; that is, its "kindness." [EADIE says of the four terms here used respecting the source of salvation: ἔλεος, ἀγάπη, χάρις, χρηστότης, "the first respects our misery; the second defines the co-essential form of this—ἔλεος; the third characterizes its free outgoing, and the last points to its palpable and experienced embodiment." He finds an evident alteration in χάρις, χρηστότης, Χριστός.—R.]

'Εφ' ἡμᾶς is connected with "in kindness," as χαρὰ ἐν πνεύματι ἁγίῳ (Rom. xiv. 17) and similar cases. See WINER, p. 126. This occurs with anarthrous substantives, which receive further definition; ἐπὶ denotes the object of the kindness, as Luke vi. 35. The phrase: ἐν Χριστῷ 'Ιησοῦ without τοὺς or ὄντας is therefore not to be referred to ἡμᾶς. Were it grammatically admissible, the thought would not be against it, since it corresponds with "to us-ward who believe" (i. 19). As, however, it stands here without any word to connect it with ἡμᾶς, it must be taken as qualifying the verb ἐνδείξηται.* *Notanda repetitio nominis Christi, quia nihil gratiæ neque amoris a Deo sperari vult, nisi ipso intercedente* (CALVIN). Comp. *Doctr. Note* 2.

*The means of the deliverance.* Vers. 8-10.

Ver. 8. **For by grace have ye been saved through faith,** τῇ γὰρ χάριτί ἐστε σεσωσμένοι διὰ πίστεως.—This is a completed, more closely defined, repetition of the parenthetical clause (ver. 5). Γάρ is connective. *Non* IGITUR *ait, sed* ENIM, *quia ab effectu ad causam concludit* (BENGEL): because He in the course of time brings into manifestation nothing else than the exceeding riches of His grace. Ye are saved by grace. Τῇ χάριτι, not merely χάριτι (ver. 5), to denote the category; the article referring to the grace mentioned in ver. 7, the wealth of which is so exceeding, marking thus the grace in question (MEYER). The dative expresses, as Rom. iii. 24 (αὐτοῦ χάριτι διὰ τῆς ἀπολυτρώσεως), the motive, διά with the genitive here states the subjective means,† in the passage just referred to, the objective. Comp. WINER, p. 204 f. The emphasis rests on "by grace," which is placed first, being the *causa efficiens;* the *causa apprehendens* follows, as a modal qualification. On the nature of "faith," see *Doctr. Note* 5.

**And that not of yourselves: the gift is God's** [καὶ τοῦτο οὐκ ἐξ ὑμῶν, θεοῦ τὸ δῶρον].—"And that" refers back to the idea of the preceding verb: "ye are saved," in the sense of *et quidem* (PASSOW, sub οὗτος, 12); and *this in addition* I say, or *and this*, being saved through faith, comes not out of yourselves. Thus the value of διὰ πίστεως is put below that of τῇ χάριτι; salvation has not its origin in faith or the believing one (οὐκ ἐξ ὑμῶν); he has indeed only to accept it. Hence there is at once added to the negative the positive (not parenthetical, HARLESS) expression: θεοῦ τὸ δῶρον, God's is the gift, *i. e.*, the salvation; the genitive being=ἐκ θεοῦ (Phil. iii. 9) or ἀπὸ θεοῦ (Phil. i. 29), and τὸ δῶρον=δωρεάν (Rom. iii. 24; v. 15, 17), *gratis*, as a present of grace.

[The reference to salvation is adopted by CALVIN, RUECKERT, HARLESS, OLSHAUSEN, MEYER, DE WETTE, STIER, EADIE, ALFORD, ELLICOTT, and every commentator of note since the days of BENGEL, except HODGE.* Of course on doctrinal grounds there is no objection to the reference to faith, for, as ELLICOTT remarks, "it may be said that the clause καὶ τοῦτο κ. τ. λ. was *suggested* by the mention of the subjective medium πίστις, which might be thought to imply some independent action on the part of the subject." But since the next verse: "not of works," cannot be referred to faith, and an unnecessary parenthesis, creating some confusion and destroying the obvious parallelism between ἐξ ὑμῶν and ἐξ ἔργων, is the result of this view, it seems far better to accept the other reference. The gender of τοῦτο is not decisive in favor of this; but when it stands so near to πίστεως, it does seem strange that it should not be feminine, were the latter its antecedent.—R.]

Ver. 9 takes up the negative side again: **not of works**, οὐκ ἐξ ἔργων, used by Paul repeatedly (Rom. iii. 20; iv. 2; xi. 6; Gal. ii. 16; iii. 2; v. 4; Tit. iii. 5). Without the article, because in this respect there are no saving, meritorious works; it is God who rescues, and He is determined thereto by no works or virtues of men. There is not here, nor should there be, any thought of the works of the Mosaic law (BLEEK). Thus the phrase "not of yourselves" is more closely and sharply defined. Accordingly we should not accept a parenthesis from καὶ τοῦτο to ἐξ ἔργων (GRIESBACH) or καὶ τοῦτο—τὸ δῶρον (BEZA), or θεοῦ τὸ δῶρον (LACHMANN, HARLESS), nor refer καὶ τοῦτο to διὰ τῆς πίστεως and then to infer τὸ πιστεύειν on this account (FATHERS, ERASMUS and others).

**That no man should boast,** ἵνα μή τις καυχήσηται.—This is the manifest end (ἵνα) of this ordering of grace, established and desired by God Himself. Comp. 1 Cor. i. 29 ff.; iv. 7;

* [It is joined by some to χρηστότητι, but this seems a strange collocation. ELLICOTT takes the whole expression as "a single compound modal clause," "in kindness toward us" defining accurately the manner in which God displays "the riches of His grace," while "in Christ Jesus" specifics as it were, the ever-blessed sphere to which its manifestations are confined, and in which alone its operations are felt. The same author very properly remarks on DE WETTE'S "melancholy want of appreciation" of the repeated mention of the name of Christ.—R.]

† [The variation in the reading does not affect this statement, since διὰ πίστεως would mean, through faith, taken abstractly, while τῆς πίστεως would mean *your* faith. As regards the meaning of "grace," it preserves the same wide sense as in ver. 5. and is "not to be regarded specially and technically as in the scholastic theology, and divided into *gratiæ præveniens, operans, co-operans;* the first having for its object *homo convertendus;* the second, *homo qui convertitur;* and the third, *homo conversus sed sanctificandus*" (EADIE). The force of the perfect as expressing both a terminated action and a present state should not be overlooked: Ye have been saved, and ye are actually now in a state of salvation.—R.]

* [Dr. HODGE presents four reasons for preferring the reference to faith. 1. "It best suits the design of the passage." Grant it, but that is of little weight when the other reference accords better with grammar and syntax. 2. "The other interpretation makes the passage tautological." Paul uses a great deal of such tautology. 3. "The antithesis between faith and works is preserved." But regard for an antithesis found in the Epistles to the Galatians and Romans should not outweigh regard for the parallelism of our own passage. 4. "The analogy of Scripture is in favor of this view." Very true, but as it represents *elsewhere* faith as the gift of God, so it represents *everywhere* that salvation is the gift of God.—It is to be regretted that so judicious an author had not stated the difficulties attending his view as well as these arguments in its favor.—R.]

2 Cor. x. 17 f.; Rom. iii. 27; iv. 2. Ἵνα is not to be taken as=ὥστε or as imperative (KOPPE). [MACKNIGHT objects that this is not a worthy end, therefore ἵνα is not telic. But it is only one end, and then it implies a great deal more than the mere stopping of man's boasts. The implied antithesis is: that God should have the glory, as ver. 10 indicates.—R.]

Ver. 10. **For his handiwork are we**, *αὐτοῦ γάρ ἐσμεν ποίημα*.—The genitive stands first with special emphasis; if there should be any boasting, He should be boasted of by us, His work.* Hence the connection by means of *γάρ*, for the reason is given why no one should boast. *Gratia tollit naturam.* What we are to understand by *ποίημα*, the Apostle sets forth in the following participial clause belonging to *ἐσμέν:*

**Created in Christ Jesus for good works.** —*Κτισθέντες ἐν Χριστῷ Ἰησοῦ*, "created in Christ Jesus," is like 2 Cor. v. 17: *εἴ τις ἐν Χριστῷ, καινὴ κτίσις*. Comp. Gal. vi. 15. The fellowship with Christ is the mediation conditioning the creative efficiency of God. "God's work" is a creation in Christ, by means of which there becomes a "new man" (ver. 15). A double creation is therefore not spoken of, the physical, that of the protoplast, in "His handiwork" (TERTULLIAN, GREGORY NAZ. and others), and the spiritual, that of the new birth in "created," nor are both creations to be regarded as united here (PELAGIUS, ERASMUS, MATTHIES, RUECKERT), so that we both as Christians and as men are God's work. Salvation alone is in question. Thus much only is true, that the expressions respecting the physical first creation are transferred to this ethical one, which is a new birth (Tit. iii. 5), a real creation (ver. 15; iv. 21, 22).

The preposition *ἐπί* with the dative marks both the end and the result; Gal. v. 13: *ἐπ' ἐλευθερίᾳ ἐκλήθητε;* 1 Thess. iv. 7; 2 Tim. ii. 14; WINER, p. 368. It is not=*εἰς ἔργα ἀγαθά*, hence not merely the end and aim of salvation [HODGE], (SCHENKEL). [ALFORD: "Just as a tree may be said to be created for its fruit."—R.] *Ἐπὶ ἔργοις ἀγαθοῖς* is in antithesis to *ἐξ ἔργων*, denoting that those created in Christ Jesus do perform good works, as "a peculiar people, zealous of good works" (Tit. ii. 14); such works are therefore not the cause but the consequence of being delivered.† Hence we read here not *ἔργοις* or *ἔργοις νόμου*, but, what is much more significant, *ἔργοις ἀγαθοῖς:* good works are performed only by the regenerate.

**Which God before prepared that we should walk in them**, *οἷς προητοίμασεν ὁ θεός, ἵνα ἐν αὐτοῖς περιπατήσωμεν*.—As regards the construction it should first be remarked that the difficulty lies in *οἷς* and in the meaning of the verb *προητοίμασεν*, which requires an object in the accusative, as well as in the reference of the preposition *προ*. The relative *οἷς* can belong only to *ἔργοις ἀγαθοῖς*, and since *προετοιμάζειν* cannot be taken as neuter (BENGEL) and there is no *ἡμᾶς* added, it must be explained by attraction (*Vulgate, Syriac*, down to BLEEK); *ἐν αὐτοῖς* follows, as in John v. 36. [That is, the relative is the object of the verb, which would be in the accusative (*ἃ*) were it not attracted into the case of its antecedent *ἔργοις ἀγαθοῖς;* so E. V. and the vast majority of commentators.—R.] *Προετοιμάζειν* (Rom. ix. 23) is to prepare beforehand, here of things, as *προορίζειν* of persons (i. 11). [See below however.] The *προ totam rem Deo tribuit* (BENGEL), implying that they should be performed. It should be borne in mind that we do not find: *ἐπὶ τοῖς ἔργοις ἀγαθοῖς, οἷς* —; the individual good works are not regarded as prepared before, but only *ἔργα ἀγαθά* in general. Christians are new-created for these; they are performed by the Christians not according to arbitrary choice; they are determined, as by the law, so by the Holy Ghost (GROTIUS: *quasi in mari aliquis et viam præsignaret et simul ventos daret ferentes*); they are given, to them is the Christian directed, equipped therefor with strength and desire.

God Himself has thus prepared before "good works," and that too with the design, to the end: "that we should walk in them," as prepared beforehand by God, as in the element in which the Christians' walk moves, in which the regenerate should prove themselves alive. This final clause is in antithesis to: "lest any man should boast" (ver. 9). HOFMANN, who (*Schriftbeweis*, II. 1, p. 365) rejects rightly the explanations, ordained before, predisposed in God's counsel, and accepts the proper conduct of humanity to God as once for all present in Christ, says excellently in further exposition (*ibid.* II. 2, p. 294): Our walk in Him is a walk in them (good works), so that *ἐν αὐτοῖς* has the emphasis, and *ἡμεῖς* is not missed in the first clause.

Accordingly *οἷς* cannot be referred to *κτισθέντες* and explained as masculine: for whom, to whom He has before ordained (ERASMUS, and necessarily RUECKERT also). It is altogether impossible to accept a Hebraism and construct thus: *ἐν οἷς ἵνα περιπατήσωμεν προητοίμασεν ὁ θεός* (BENGEL, KOPPE); but *προετοιμάζειν* is not= *velle, jubere*. Nor should *ἡμᾶς* be supplied from the context and the clause rendered: to which, or: for which He has prepared us before (LUTHER, RUECKERT but doubtfully, SCHENKEL). Nor should the verb be taken as neuter (BENGEL): for which He has already prepared, so that nothing is wanting (STIER). Nor should we say that God has prepared the circumstances for them (*bonos socios, præceptores, confessionarios, concionatores, sancta exempla aliaque incitamenta et occasiones*), as do MICHAELIS and OLSHAUSEN, following Catholic expositors. Nor does *προ* stand related to "created unto good works," as though the preparation of the works preceded the new creation of the man, and the men were redeemed for the works and for their sake, and the walk in good works were the final and supreme aim of the Divine revelation of grace and saving dealings with man (MEYER, SCHENKEL).

---

* [ALFORD: "The English reader is likely to imagine a contrast between 'not of *works*' and 'for we are His *workmanship*,' which can hardly have been in the mind of the Apostle." The word *ποίημα* becomes in Latin and English *poema, poem;* the same notion of poetry being the truest, highest work or creation, is found in other languages.—R.]

† [EADIE well sums up the argument of the Apostle, that salvation is not of works: 1. The statement that salvation is of works involves an anachronism; 2. Involves the fallacy of mistaking the effect for the cause. 3. Even such good works can have in them no saving merit, for we are His workmanship.—R.]

[The view of Braune is open to serious doubt in one point alone. The attraction from the accusative is by far the best solution of the grammatical question. The verb, which is not neuter, does not mean "predestinated," but "prepared before." Comp. *Romans*, p. 321. That notion is a fair inference, but does not necessarily belong to the word, as even HODGE admits. It may be allowed too that "good works" without the article does not of necessity refer to definite, particular actions, which God has appointed for the several believers. But the force of προ is not sufficiently taken into the account in the view advocated above, while HOFMANN'S explanation seems to be an attempt to avoid a theological difficulty rather than a fair exegesis. Προορίζειν is distinguished from προετοιμάζειν, not by a difference of objects (as Braune holds, following HARLESS), but as follows: The end comes more into view in the former, the means more in the latter (so FRITZSCHE, LANGE, *Romans*, p. 320, EADIE, ELLICOTT). As the temporal relation to "created" seems to be the only proper reference in the preposition προ, we should accept this explanation: God, *before* we were created in Christ, *made ready* for us a sphere of moral action, a road, with the intent that we should walk in it, and not leave it; this sphere, this road, was "good works" (ELLICOTT).—Or yet more definitely, with ALFORD: As trees are created for fruits which God before prepared that they should bear them: *i. e.*, defined and assigned to each tree its own, in form, and flavor, and time of bearing. So in the course of God's providence, our good works are marked out for and assigned to each one of us. This does not seem to be open to the objection that it makes the works the supreme end of God's saving dealings. —EADIE: "These good works, though they do not secure salvation, are by God's eternal purpose essentially connected with it, and are not a mere offshoot accidentally united to it."—R.] BENGEL says aptly: ***Ambularemus, non salvaremur aut viveremus.***

DOCTRINAL AND ETHICAL.

1. THEOLOGICALLY: *God's nature* is designated by: "who is rich in mercy, for His great love" (ver. 4). Precisely as in 1 John iv. 16: "God is love" (comp. my notes, *Biblework in loco*, p. 146 f.). What He will ever more and more manifest and prove, is "the exceeding riches of His grace in kindness" (ver. 7). All salvation is traced back to "grace" (vers. 5-8), to "love" (ἀγάπη) now condescending in its entire fulness to the deepest misery, the lost condition of sinners (χάρις), in order to help (ἔλεος) as a master and to minister (χρηστότης) as a servant. How then can there be room for "wrath?" Ὀργή (from ὀρέγω, allied with reach, rack, stretch, and ὀργάω, to swell, to be full) designates first of all, appetite, emotion, then passion, anger. God is indeed holy love, hence precisely not an apathetic personality, not an epicurean *natura divom semota ab rebus nostris sejunctaque longa*, not a pagan or Turkish εἱμαρμένη, nor a modern moral order of the world, or mere "Providence," "Heaven," or the philosophical Absolute, or the common numb Deity. He loves, He must also be angry with what is unholy, evil; He has wrath, not as a man, *active et initiative*, but *passive et consecutive*. His wrath is the zeal of love against corrupting evil, the energy in the conduct of God against that relation to Him, established with the fall of the creature from Him; in the creature's sin God's wrath brings forth itself (STIER).—One thing besides should be especially considered. By "we," described in ver. 3, the Israelites are meant: precisely these, though chosen, are called on account of the apostasy of the human race, "children of wrath." Accordingly all, the entire fallen race, are the object of the wrath of God, even the elect, just as all are the object of His grace, as even these have been, who, because they will not let themselves be saved, are cast away. In mercy and anger is He the same God, and has before Him the human race in like manner undivided, in order to save it as the object of His love. Comp. FRANK, *Theologie der Form. Conc.*, IV. p. 194 ff.

2. CHRISTOLOGICALLY: The *Mediator*, in whom alone the fallen race, now a prey to the corruption of sin, is and can be an object of love to God, and through whom alone, yet certainly, the purpose of salvation conceived in Him, is consummated, is Jesus Christ, the Risen One, who, as the Sinless One, was not forfeit to death, but overcame it. The text only indicates this latter thought; but it distinctly asserts: *only in Him* is life, renewal, power, blessedness, without Him there is none of this (vers. 10, 5–7). In this entirely unique Person, including in Himself all that man needs for a renewal well-pleasing to God, presenting in His resurrection and exaltation, not merely a type, but the dynamic principle for the elevation of humanity to sonship with God—in this Person is set forth all that is specifically Christian in Christianity.

3. HAMARTOLOGICALLY: *a*) *The essence of sin is disobedience* ("sons of disobedience") to the will of God, and *obedience* to the *flesh* ("doing the wishes of the flesh and of the thoughts").

*b*) The *universality* of sin. It extends itself over the whole human race without exception. Gentiles (vers. 1, 2) and Jews (ver. 3), and among these (ἡμεῖς πάντες) to those also who like the Apostle were "taught according to the perfect manner of the law of the fathers, and zealous toward God" (Acts xxii. 3); for fleshly self-will and obstinacy mingles itself as a ruling power, even in the most refined forms, with human virtue and honorableness.

*c*) The *variety* of sin does not condition a variety in the extent of guilt. To the Apostle the heathen world was a wrestling place of demons: Satan ruled it; there all goes according to his will; and the Apostle calls the Gentiles "sons of disobedience." The people of Israel, notwithstanding its theocracy, consists in his esteem of "children of wrath," as he designates them much more sharply. The guilt increases with the less considerable sins, if the favors received, which have been despised or neglected, are greater: so there may be less guilt with greater sins, and a far greater guilt with sins less great externally, because there is a greater sinful corruption.

*d*) The *corruption* of sin. Although some may hold for truth in Eph. v. 14 ("Awake thou that sleepest and arise from the dead"), only "thou that sleepest," together with Rom. v. 6: "when we were yet without strength," the phrase "were dead" (vers. 1, 5) here may not be overlooked. The Romanists indeed say (*Conc. Trid. Sess.* VI. cap. 1): *liberum arbitrium minime extinctum esse, viribus licet attenuatum et inclinatum*, and MÖHLER speaks only of the *sleep* of sin (*Symbolik*, p. 100), but Paul says, in accordance with his Lord in the parable of him left "half-dead" (ἡμιθανῆ, Luke x. 30), that we are dead to what is good, robbed of the "life," which includes strength and activity in connection with entire satisfaction, *i. e.* happiness, and hence are powerless, inactive, cramped in our life-movement, troubled, dissatisfied and unhappy; it is therefore not merely a feeling of unhappiness, not merely the corruption of the intellectual, but also of the moral, in fact of all the powers of life, so that physical death cannot fail, nor yet the ἀπώλεια, eternal destruction. Indeed the physical life is so affected, that sin is the heritage of every child of man from birth, it is forfeit to death as well as to sin.

[EADIE: "While admitting the scriptural account of the introduction of sin, many have shaped their views of it from the connection in which they place it in reference to Divine foreknowledge, and so have sprung up the Supralapsarian and Sub-lapsarian hypotheses. Attempts to form a perfect scheme of Theodicy, or a full vindication of the Divinity, have occupied many other minds than that of Leibnitz. The relation of the race to its Progenitor has been viewed in various lights, and analogies physical, political and metaphysical, with theories of Creationism and Traducianism, have been employed in illustration, from the days of Augustine and Pelagius to those of Erasmus and Luther, Calvin and Arminius, Taylor and President Edwards. Questions about the origin of evil, transmission of depravity, imputation of guilt, federal or representative position on the part of Adam, and physical and spiritual death as elements of the curse, have given rise to long and labored argumentation, because men have looked at them from very different stand-points, and have been influenced in their treatment of the problem by their philosophical conceptions of the Divine character, the nature of sin, and that moral freedom and power which belong to responsible humanity. The *modus* may be and is among the deep things of God; but the *res* is palpable: for experience confirms the Divine testimony that we are by nature 'children of wrath,' *per generationem*, not *per imitationem*." Comp. the history of the Doctrine, *Romans*, pp. 191 ff.—R.]

These *walking* dead ones (vers. 2, 3) stand in the relation of slaves in Satan's kingdom, and so long as they are without help from above, they wallow ever deeper and deeper into misery and death. They have in Satan an ἄρχοντα, "prince," who works and rules in opposition to Christ, the Head of the Church. He has his personal wicked will as ruler, according to which (κατά) unconverted sinners walk; he has in the existing tendencies of the age in the world, urging themselves as a norm, an assistant of his power, which surrounds all men, penetrates all, unperceived and unregarded (ἐξουσία τοῦ ἀέρος), which works as a spirit in the sons of disobedience (ver. 2). The lusts of the flesh also and its glory, of the "thoughts," the selfish thought, are channels of his influence, of the flow of his spirit into the children of wrath, to which he is himself forfeit and to which all are exposed, who do not permit themselves to be converted and redeemed. This truth is as startling as it is humbling. In and with the world-historical progress under God's gracious guidance Satan as the prince of darkness carries on his activity to the destruction of men.*

4. ANTHROPOLOGICALLY: Man appears here:

*a.* As the *creature of God* (αὐτοῦ ποίημα), in which however there is but a side reference to the fact of man's creation. Paul uses this (ver. 10) only as a substratum for his remarks respecting man's renewal and regeneration in Christ, holding this truth firmly however, just here, where man's ruin in sin is spoken of. This must never be forgotten: Every man, not merely Adam and Eve, those too who are born, are God's creatures. Even though the substance is given, out of which man is begotten and born, it exists only as the creative inworking of God. And although man is to be regarded continually as the creature of God, this does not exclude the second causes by means of which God since the close of the Hexaëmeron continues the work of creation (see FRANK, *Theol.*, F. c., I. p. 52), so that the Apostle can say: "by nature children of wrath." There is a two-fold nature, the original, created by God, the degenerated, corrupted by sin. So far as we are God's work and creation, is the nature of the body and the soul in organism and powers, good; but intruded sin has corrupted their nature which was in itself good. This leads to the second point.

*b.* *As a member of his race* (φύσει) and that from the point of time when his "nature," a production within humanity, begins, hence from his birth. As respects this he is "flesh," doing the wishes of the flesh and of the thoughts, is "dead in trespasses and sins." For humanity is a living whole and in it every individual partakes of the character of the whole. This permits no one to be a non-participant in the consequences of the first sin, and each individual has his natural share in the corruption thereof. There is however, notwithstanding, in him a capacity for being converted, redeemed, saved, which distinguishes him from the fallen angels, who do not possess this, and also from *lapis* or *truncus*, negatively, in that he holds himself not passively, but aggressively against God, and positively, in that he has been created by God for renewal in Christ, and has from the creation on such an *aptitudo* (see FRANK, p. 140 ff.). To his doings

* [In our section, immediately following i. 22, 23, the world is marked in distinct and telling contrast to the Church. "The Church has its head—κεφαλή; the world has its—ἄρχων. That Head is a man, allied by blood to the community over which He presides; that other prince is an unembodied spirit—an alien as well as a usurper. The one so blesses the church, that it becomes His 'fulness,' the other sheds darkness and distress all around him. The one has His Spirit dwelling in the church, leading it to holiness; the other, himself the darkest, most malignant, and unlovely being in the universe, exercises a subtle and debasing influence over the minds of his vassals, who are 'children of disobedience.' Matt. xiii. 38; John viii. 44; Acts xxvi. 18; 2 Cor. iv. 4." EADIE.—R.]

and his character there belongs however no activity or relation to the salvation given in Christ, although he can and will have a consciousness of his unhappiness as a "child of wrath," and has accordingly a certain knowledge (*obscura scintillula ejus notitia quid sit Deus*), or a *memoriter* knowledge of God and a longing for the removal of his need, and hence too will try in his conduct and plans many a way to help himself, without ever finding the right way and the effective means. He will rather be deceived by the lusts and be oftener and more powerfully moved by the wills of his flesh and of his selfish thought under the evil influences of his surroundings.

c. *As a child of his age* ("according to the course of this world") and his *nation*, breathing in the atmosphere of his time and his tribe, determined and swept on by the stream of the present, to which he belongs.

d. *As member of a world*, in which outside the Divine power the power of the kingdom of darkness secretly, noiselessly exercises its force all about and in the individual men, who are unbelieving and unconverted. Man has an individual, moral, national position, but stands related also to the cosmical power of the evil one as well as to the eternal power of God working above and within the world.

5. SOTERIOLOGICALLY: *a*) The essence of salvation ("ye have been and are saved") out of the condition of death, wrought and strengthened by sin, is "life:" hence "quickened together" (ver. 5). Life is a gift, a gratuity of grace (*δῶρον*, ver. 8), but not so complete at once, that it only needs to be offered and taken into possession; it is a new creation (ver. 10), a creative renewal. Salvation is also conceived of as deliverance from the power and dominion of this world and its prince, as exaltation and redemption into the kingdom of God; hence "raised us up with Him, and made us sit with Him in heavenly places."

*b*) *The cause of salvation is God*, who quickens, raises and exalts, and especially His grace (vers. 5, 8). Comp. 1. This salvation is so little a life developing itself out of the natural character, that it is called a "gift of God," which is only to be received.

*c*) *The Mediator is Christ.* See 2.

*d*) The *condition* is faith: "through faith." The context shows that the object of faith is the Person of Christ (vers. 5, 6, 7, 10), in whom God and God's grace are known and grasped, grasped and known. The nature of faith is evidently thus defined, that it is no work, since in this salvation works are denied as antecedent ("not of works," ver. 9), and good works are designated only as subsequent thereto (ver. 10), but also, that it does not spring of itself on the soil of our heart or spirit, since salvation comes "not of yourselves:" faith is not from the natural man. But since salvation is the impartation of life, and that too in creative manner, faith itself must be conceived of as an accepting activity, an ethical act, or an ethical course of action, having its corresponding development. Still nothing further is predicated on this point.

["It is the uniform doctrine of the New Testament, that no man is saved against his will; and his desire to be saved is proved by his belief of the Divine testimony. Salvation by grace is not arbitrarily attached to faith by the mere sovereign dictate of the Most High, for man's willing acceptance of salvation is essential to his possession of it, and the operation of faith is just the sinner's appreciation of the Divine mercy, and his acquiescence in the goodness and wisdom of the plan of recovery, followed by a cordial appropriation of its needed and adapted blessings, or, as Augustine tersely and quaintly phrases it—*Qui creavit te sine te, non salvabit te sine te.* Justification by faith alone is simply pardon enjoyed on the condition of taking it." EADIE.—R.]

*e*) The *course of salvation*, according to vers. 5, 6: "quickened us together with Christ," "and raised us up with Him and made us sit with Him" "in Christ," as well as ver. 10: "created in Christ Jesus," is to be thus understood: that the salvation, given personally and actually in Christ, begins in man with a reviving, which is a "dying to sin" (Rom. vi. 1 f.), beginning first of all in the individual and having in him first its growth and development, but then extending itself over whole races and unfolding itself ever more gloriously in them, not indeed as a natural life left to itself, but as continually evoked and furthered by the supernatural grace in its riches (ver. 7), always in Christ, out from Christ, never away from Christ, beyond Christ, but on toward and up to Him.

6. ETHICALLY: *a. The worth of morality* transcends all intellectual power. If ever a people was great in the latter respect, it was the Greeks, and yet to them applies what is said in vers. 1, 2: despite all science and art, despite all progress in the department of human mental culture and the earthly life, so that they have been for centuries the masters of the leading civilized nations, they have fallen and persisted in moral corruption.

*b. The nature of morality* is "good works," which God prepared before; they have been given since the beginning of the creation: in the written law the unwritten laws have been rendered, fixed and secured against alteration. The new creation in Christ has resumed and continued the first, not obsolete creation, not however as supplementing a defective one, but as renewing one disfigured and destroyed in man. God's dealings ordered from the beginning by Him are alone spoken of.

*c. The basis of morality*, which is the proper bearing of man towards the will of God, rests in the proper relation of man to God, into which he is transferred as a new creature in Christ. Since this is brought to pass through faith, faith itself is the basis of true Christian morality. From what is said respecting the people of Israel, it is manifest that even the law of God and many other salutary institutions can be in force, without helping or furthering this, if faith be lacking. But works cannot and may not be lacking to faith, if it is genuine: they are essential in the life of faith; even though not necessary for the sake of justification and to the attainment of eternal life, they are still necessary proofs of faith, and necessary on account of the *mandatum, ordinatio et voluntas Dei.* Since good works are not created by God, but Christians created for them, and since Christians should perform them of their own free will under the impulse of the Spirit, faith must be the basis for these, the same faith by means of which the man becomes a new man. [The Gospel says "Live and do this," not "Do this and live," and the old maxim: *bona opera non præcedunt justificandum, sed sequuntur justificatum*, is here again proven Scriptural, as experience proves it the only possible order. The many battles on this point, the ever-recurring tendency in theology and in the heart of the Christian, to mix, confuse, contrast and oppose faith and works, find in the plain, pellucid statement of the Apostle their proper rebuke. Alas, such simple words have too often been tortured by expositors to support their theories.*—R.]

### HOMILETICAL AND PRACTICAL.

Despite the amiable qualities and social virtues in the character, lovely mental gifts in the life of those who are not born of God, not born of His Spirit; they are still walking dead men, dead in the living body, in which the outer man is nobly upheld while the inward man perishes day by day.—Through trespasses and sins, through many, but little sins, little meannesses, trifling impurities, petty jealousies, which creep in secretly, lightly, unnoticed, and work so successfully for the death of man's soul,—it occurs that one otherwise honorable can be inwardly more corrupt, more thoroughly ruined, than one who has committed some great crime. Among the twelve disciples of Jesus, one was Judas the traitor!—Consider the experience of all Christians: only after conversion do they perceive the abomination of sin, its origin and its end, destruction. Here can man only *reflect*.—Most men appear well, but if they had at one time the thoughts and feelings which so often steal in upon them, in externally manifest and accomplished deeds before their eyes, their body would seem to them like a shroud, and their heart like a corpse, of a beloved one indeed, yet full of stench.—The spirit of the age of this world is never a good spirit. It does indeed occasionally appear to be so here and there, as in the time of the Reformation. This was born of God's Spirit and Word, and yet it was furthered by carnal hostility to the Pope, evil desires after the ecclesiastical possessions, after the treasures of the monasteries; godless movements against godless oppression; if God the Lord had not helped it by special events and circumstances, it would have been repressed or polluted—by the spirit of the age!—In evil there is system, progress, growth, development; a prince too and rulers, spirit and law; evil, darkness is a kingdom also, and at its head is a prince, the chief of the devils; from frivolous, temperate sinners to premeditated villains, and from sinful men to fallen angels, and among these there is gradation and connection, a kingdom, without peace and happiness, it is true.

Selfishness is a destructive pervading disease of one's own Ego, which dies of it. To live for self and only for self is a poor, pitiable life. What kind of a wife is that who will not live for her husband? what kind of a man is he who will not live for his calling? what kind of a human being is that who will not live for his God, but only for his lusts, capable of no sacrifice, except petty alms if he is rich; noble before men, before God a tatter, honored before men and yet the object of Divine wrath and of His sentence to perdition?—It is a sad contradiction among men, that they speak of the "dear God" [the common German phrase: *der liebe Gott*] and say, He is love, while no one is to them more uncomfortable and obnoxious than the Church, which makes this a matter of earnest, preaching of the love of the Father in Christ the Crucified and Risen One; they are tolerant toward sins in themselves and others, aye, toward vile sins, fornication, suicide, if there is any respectability about it, but tolerant toward the living and active members of the church they are certainly not, that is impossible for them. What then *do* they think of the love of God?—You may as little undervalue faith as the rudder, however small it is in a large ship. All labor in the rigging, in the masts and sails, at stem or stern, helps nothing even in the best of weather, much less in swell and storm, if the rudder is not in order and rightly used; so without faith you toss about in life, aimless, helpless, hopeless.—God did not first make the members and then out of them the body; man was at once entire. So too man is not born piecemeal, though small and weak, he is yet an entire human being. It is so with the new birth also. Conversion affects the whole man, is however only the first step, not perfection, is a beginning pointing and impelling toward advance and completion.

LUTHER:—That for which each thing is created, it does without law and compulsion. The sun shines by nature, unbidden; the pear-tree bears of itself, voluntarily; three and seven *ought not* to be ten, they *are* ten already. There is no need that one should say to God, He should do good, for He does all the time willingly and gladly of Himself. So too one should not command the righteous man, that he should do good works, for he does it without this, without command and compulsion, because he is a new creature and a good tree.—He should not be driven thereto, if his faith be not fancied and feigned.

STARKE:—He who does not walk in God's way, following the guiding star of God's will, gets other blind guides, and is induced to cut such capers, that he is plunged into extreme corruption.—The saints are free confessors of their sins, having no desire for hypocrisy to justify themselves.—All men are equally corrupted by original sin, although the corruption breaks out in various ways.—Evil lust is the root of all sins, even of sin itself.—Reason is a glorious gift of God, as the deprival of the same, madness, is a great misery and judgment. But it is much weakened and darkened through the fall, and hence inclined to many errors and prejudices, permitting itself to be abused.—Art thou poor in soul, here thou mayest find an inexhaustible

* [As a specimen of the mode by which human inferences and hypotheses can be added to Scripture to pervert it, take the declaration of the Council of Trent. *Sess.* VI. *cap.* 16: "The Lord's goodness to all men is so great that He will have the things which are His own gifts to be their merits"—*ut eorum velit esse merita quæ sunt ipsius dona* (from EADIE).—R.]

treasure of God's mercy, making us rich in Him.—Our salvation comes from God's compassionate love alone.—We are really quickened in Christ, by Christ and with Christ. Therefore we have a real not a fancied life, and there is as great a difference between a natural and a regenerated man as between those physically dead and alive.—Believers not only become blessed in the future, but they are really blessed, although their blessedness is still imperfect.—Without grace no one can believe, and without believing no one can partake of grace.—We are God's work as regards creation; but if we do not become so as regards sanctification and the application of redemption, we remain outside the fellowship with God.—Regeneration is a real creation and the source of all spiritual life.

RIEGER:—Living men cannot exactly understand that they are to regard themselves as *dead* through trespasses and sins. Weak they prefer admitting as applicable to them; and indeed the word of God does occasionally describe us as weak, as sick. But the Spirit of God does not mean this, as men gladly explain it. They confess themselves weak with the persuasion that they can make themselves better and become strong by self-improvement. The word of God, however, means a weakness, in which self-help is no longer possible, where the hope of recovery rests solely on the presence and power of the physician. As certainly as the body without the soul is dead, so certainly is the soul without the Spirit dead.—The walk and the occupation with which man commonly conceals this death, do not make the harm less, but rather the more dangerous.—That the time, the existing course of the world, the principles, opinions and habits arising therein, can operate largely in man, bearing him into much which he would not reach by himself, making his exit and freedom very difficult, should a longing for something better actually arise within him; this is quite readily perceived. But that a prince, a ruler of darkness, an expert power, extending as far as the air and clouds, lurks therein, that we do not know of ourselves, nor do we want to believe it, though it is proven by the word of God. The devil himself has the best interest in the fact that so little of his business is suspected among the dealings of men.—At first flesh and Reason can be for a while in conflict. Reason accuses the lusts of the flesh of being vile and unbecoming to man; but there is no power to free itself from them; and the flesh reproaches the reason with this inability and the consequent falsity of its assumed virtues, and so the two prefer to make peace with each other. The reason is reconciled with the flesh, helps to justify and excuse its lusts, paints a better external appearance for them, while the flesh for the sake of the praise occasionally crawls into a form not too coarse.—What will God yet do in future ages, that the riches of the grace of Christ may be yet more confidently proven, more gladly believed, and more uninterruptedly enjoyed!

PASSAVANT:—Our whole nature desires life, life is our thirst, we hate death! So often and so long as we trespass against the law of our conscience or God's law, is all holiness and righteousness dead within us; there lives then no love of God, no Spirit of the Lord, no joy in Him, no heavenly peace, no Divine life in us, that is, no real life.—If God's breath does not breathe afresh upon us with the power of the Divine nature, then education however careful, culture however refined, is mere patchwork and tinsel, no pure truth, no pure power from God, no new birth, no heavenly life.—We can learn from the reports of the gospel messengers, in what forms, in what follies and enormities the kingdom of superstition and unbelief has down to our days, multiplied and established itself. Every recollection of the holy and eternal, every trace, every presage of the unknown God in the human soul, has been degraded and distorted into the silliest and most infamous fictions and lies, into the most miserable and sinful abortions of idolatrous forms and worship.—Notice the language of Scripture. One and the same word in the text signifies unbelief and disobedience, for both these poisonous plants proceed from one and the same bitter root of the heart. You do not look with pleasure on Him, whom you will not obey; you do not keep Him in mind, nor inquire after Him.—Is thy obedience poor, then thy faith is not earnest; is thy faith not vital and genuine, then there is no child-like, earnest obedience.

HEUBNER:—Those are dead, who have died to all that is good and godly, in whom the spirit is benumbed and the flesh alone is active. There are grades of death as well as of life. Spiritual death manifests itself in the entire lack of knowledge respecting spiritual things, of desire, love, power for good; all taste for the Divine, all longing for God is wanting. This death is the result of sin. Christianity found the world dead and reanimated it. To be without God, without Christ, is death. The first stirring of life is anxiety about ourselves, the consciousness of misery and sin.—Fearful is the power, which the course, the spirit of the world, maintains over man. It distorts all his ideas. We must agree with it, if we would have peace, honor, respect and power; those who oppose it, are regarded with wrath. The *origin* of this spirit is in the prince of darkness. He who stands outside of Christ, stands in fellowship with Satan; for he thinks and lives in accordance with the maxims of the evil spirit.—"Prince of the power of the air!" This description is apt, because the evil spirit is not a visible member of human society, and yet is *about us*, in our circle, in the sublunary world.—Satan was therefore the ruling power in heathenism, and accordingly this cannot be regarded as a healthful and normal development of religion. His influence still continues.—To deny this activity of Satan is to bring water to his mill.—The bodily resurrection of Christ has as a consequence a spiritual resurrection of men.—It is contrary to the proud consciousness of man, to live by the grace of God, and yet he cannot live by any thing else than grace. All is of grace: that we may hear the gospel, God opens our understanding, and makes our hearts willing to believe.—What would have occurred had Christ not come? Socrates, Plato, Pythagoras appeared 4–500 years before Him—what had they helped the world? He who thinks that others would have come after them, who would have helped, will wait in vain forever.—On the one side Paul excludes works, on the other he requires them.

STIER:—God not only raised Him from the dead, but the dead in Him.—The air which exhales from earth the old villain who hides therein and uses it, thoroughly knows how to turn and pour in opposition to the gales from heaven.—*Mercy* removes misery and death, Love appears instead of wrath, blessing, delivering, saving.—First life, the new creature, then we may speak of walk and good works.—Life, as just begun, is not complete, does not stand still, but grows, develops, forms and employs itself. It proceeds from the Risen One continually as the Spirit of sanctification.

SPURGEON:—*Spiritual quickening:* Jairus' daughter, the young man at Nain, Lazarus, 1) Illustrations of the different circumstances in which those who are really dead are to be found; 2) Illustrations of the various means of grace through which they are quickened by the power of the same Spirit; 3) Illustrations of experiences through which those who have been made alive pass after their quickening.

LANGBEIN:—The glorification of Christ, the glorification of Redeemed ones: 1) God has quickened us together with Him, 2) raised us together with Him, 3) transferred us into heavenly places in Him.—*Gesetz und Zeugniss:* Bow thy knees and rejoice over the great gracious plan of God: 1) that we fully survey it in Christ, 2) that each of us has his place in it, 3) that it has become actual in many respects through the word and faith and in the Holy Ghost.

[SCHENKEL:—Sin a fountain of death in apparent life.—The kingdom of Satan in its dreadfulness and nothingness.—The blessedness of the Christian: 1) It has a firm basis, that of grace; 2) It leads them to a certain way, that of faith.—Our hope that in the course of ages God will manifest Himself yet more gloriously by means of the grace and truth made known in Christ. "Faith opens our eyes, ears, mind and heart; giving us (1) the heavenly desire, (2) the Divine knowledge, (3) the Divine taste, (4) the truth of life" (from PASSAVANT).—R.]

[EADIE:—Ver. 1. The epithet "dead" here implies: 1. Previous life; 2. Insensibility; 3. Inability. He cannot because he will not, and therefore he is justly responsible.—Ver. 2. They did not pursue indulgences fashionable at a former epoch, but now obsolete and forgotten. Theirs were not the idolatries and impurities of other centuries. No; they lived as the age on all sides of them lived—in its popular and universal errors and delusions; they walked in entire conformity to the reigning sins of the times.—Ver. 3. *Si Deus non irascitur impiis et injustis, nec pios justosque diligit* (LACTANTIUS).—Ver. 4. Though mercy has been expended by God for six milleniums, and myriads of myriads have been partakers of it, it is still an unexhausted mine of wealth.—The love is great—a great God is its possessor and great sinners are its objects.—Ver. 5. Life may be feeble at first, but the sincere milk of the word is imbibed and the expected maturity is at length reached. Its first moment may not indeed be registered in the consciousness, as it may be awakened within us by a varying process.—Ver. 6. The quickened soul is not merely made aware that in Christ, as containing it and all similar souls, it is enlivened, and raised, and elevated, but along with this it enjoys individually a conscious life, resurrection and session with Jesus.—Ver. 7. All the grace in this kindness shown in the first century is a lesson even to the nineteenth century. What God did then, He can do now and will do now; and one reason why He did it then was, to teach the men of the present age His ability and desire to repeat in them the same blessed process of salvation and life.—Ver. 8. Look at salvation in its origin—it is "by grace;" in its reception—it is "through faith;" in its manner of conferment—it is a "gift."—Ver. 9. If man be guilty, and being unable to win a pardon, simply receives it; if, being dead, he gets life only as a Divine endowment; if favor, and nothing but favor, has originated his safety, and the only possible act on his part be that of reception; if what he has be but a gift to him in his weak and meritless state—then surely nothing can be further from him than boasting, for he will glorify God for all.—R.]

---

### 2. *Extolling comparison of their previous and their present condition.*

CHAP. II. 11-22.

11 Wherefore remember, that ye *being* in time past Gentiles, [that once[1] ye, Gentiles] in the flesh, who are called [the] Uncircumcision by that which is called the
12 [or by the so-called] Circumcision in the flesh made [wrought] by hands; That at
that time[2] ye were [ye were at that time] without Christ, being aliens [alienated]
from the commonwealth of Israel, and strangers from the covenants of [the] pro-
13 mise, having no hope, and without God in the world: But now in Christ Jesus, ye
who sometime [once] were far off are made [were brought][3] nigh by [in] the
14 blood of Christ. For he is our peace, who hath [*omit* hath] made both one, and
hath broken down the middle wall of partition *between us* [and broke down the

15 middle wall of the partition,]; Having abolished [or done away][4] in his flesh the
enmity, *even* the law of [the] commandments *contained* [*expressed*] in ordinances;
for to make in himself of twain [that he might create the two in himself[5] into] one
16 new man, *so* making peace; And that he might reconcile both [And might reconcile them both][6] unto God in one body by [in one body to God through] the cross,
17 having slain the enmity thereby [on it]: And [he] came and preached peace to
you which [who] were afar off, and [peace][7] to them that [those who] were nigh.
18 For through him we both have [our][8] access by [in] one Spirit unto the Father.
19 Now therefore [So then] ye are no more [longer] strangers and foreigners [sojourners], but [ye are][9] fellow-citizens with the saints, and of the household of God;
20 And are built [Built up] upon the foundation of the apostles and prophets, Jesus
21 Christ [Christ Jesus][10] himself being the chief corner *stone;* In whom all the
building[11] fitly framed together groweth [is growing] unto a holy temple in the
22 Lord: In whom ye also are [being] builded together for a habitation of God
through [in] the Spirit.

## TEXTUAL AND GRAMMATICAL.

[1] Ver. 11.—[ℵ.[3] D.[3] K. L., and a number of versions and fathers support the order of the *Rec.* (ὑμεῖς ποτέ), which Braune seems to prefer, but Lachmann, Tischendorf, Meyer and English editors accept the reading of ℵ.[1] A. B. D.[1] (ποτὲ ὑμεῖς). The former arose from a regard for euphony in all probability. The pointing adopted above accepts τὰ ἔθνη ἐν σαρκί as in simple apposition to ὑμεῖς, a view strengthened by the correct reading (see Ellicott).—The usage respecting the article in English differs from that in Greek, as the alterations in this verse indicate.—R.]

[2] Ver. 12.—[The *Rec.* inserts ἐν before τῷ καιρῷ, with D.[3] K. L., and some versions, but it is omitted in ℵ. A. B. D.[1] F., by most fathers; rejected by nearly all modern editors (Hodge retains it without remark) as an explanatory gloss, the preposition being more usual and perhaps more correct in such cases.—The same gloss occurs in the *Rec.* again (iii. 5).—R.]

[3] Ver. 13.—[The *Rec.* reads ἐγγὺς ἐγενήθητε, on the authority of D. F. K. L., Greek fathers; accepted by Meyer, Ellicott and others, on the ground of the contrast with μακράν. Lachmann, Alford, Braune, and others accept the order of ℵ. A. B., versions, which is quite as well supported.—On the emendations see *Exeg. Notes*.—R.]

[4] Ver. 15.—[As Braune adopts the construction favored by the E. V., only verbal changes have been made in the first half of this verse. But it is doubtful whether this is correct. The other prominent opinions require the following renderings: "Broke down the middle wall of the partition—*to wit*, the enmity—in His flesh, having made void the law of the commandments *expressed* in decrees" (Ellicott). This joins ἔχθραν in apposition to μεσότοιχον, and ἐν τῇ σαρκὶ αὐτοῦ to λύσας. The other view, that of Meyer, De Wette, Hodge (and preferred in the additional notes), accepts the apposition, but joins "in His flesh" to "abolished:" "Broke down the middle wall of partition, to wit, the enmity, having in His flesh done away the law," *etc.* In any case we ought to put a comma instead of a colon at the close of ver. 14.—R.]

[5] Ver. 15.—[The *Rec.*, ℵ.[3] D. K. L., most cursives and fathers read: ἑαυτῷ, accepted by Meyer, and most commentators. ℵ.[1] A. B. F., 10 mss.: αὐτῷ, accepted by Lachmann, Alford. The authorities are about equally divided, the latter being the more difficult reading, too difficult in fact, since the pronoun must be referred to Christ, and that would be intolerably harsh with this reading. Besides the Greek ε might easily be dropped, either from the interchange of forms, or after ἐν, as Meyer suggests.—The E. V. is very unfortunate in the structure of its clauses here, making two co-ordinate final clauses differ as widely as possible in form.—R.]

[6] Ver. 16.—[We may render here: *both of us* with equal correctness.—*Reconcile again* may be the true meaning, but I hesitate in adopting it.—*In one body* is to be closely connected with *both*. *To* instead of *unto* (E. V.) for the simple dative.—*Through* best expresses the sense of διά.—*On it* is more exact than *thereby*, the reference being to the cross.—We might put a period at the close of this verse, but the insertion of the subject in verse 17, indicates the want of close connection.—R.]

[7] Ver. 17.—ℵ. A. B. D. E. F. G. and others: εἰρήνην τοῖς ἐγγύς. The emphatic repetition is well attested, and an omission by the transcribers is more probable than an insertion. [So all modern editors and commentators, even the most conservative as regards the *Recepta*.—R.]

[8] Ver. 18.—[The article here is almost equivalent to the possessive.—The E. V. again renders ἐν, *by*.—R.]

[9] Ver. 19.—[The *Rec.* omits ἐστέ, with D.[3] K. L., versions and fathers; but it was probably deemed superfluous, instead of emphatic; it is found in ℵ. B. (both ἀλλά ἐστε), A. C. D.[1] F., accepted by modern editors.—R.]

[10] Ver. 20.—[The *Rec.* reads Ἰησοῦ Χριστοῦ on the authority of C. D. E. F. G. K. L., several versions and a number of fathers; accepted by Scholz, De Wette, Meyer, Ellicott. ℵ.[2] A. B., the Vulgate and other versions, some fathers, support the order: Χριστοῦ Ἰησοῦ; adopted by Tischendorf, Lachmann, Alford and others. ℵ[1] has only τοῦ Χριστοῦ, which Braune seems to favor. On the whole the order of the *Rec.* should be given up.—R.]

[11] Ver. 21.—[The *Rec.* inserts ἡ between πᾶσα and οἰκοδομή (ℵ.[2] A. C., some cursives), but it is omitted in ℵ.[1] B. D. E. F. G. K. L., most cursives, and is rejected by nearly all modern editors. The briefer reading is difficult, and the change was an easy way of avoiding it, just as following the *Rec.* now-a-days saves a little trouble to the commentator.—R.]

## EXEGETICAL AND CRITICAL.

*Detailed description of their previous condition.* Vers. 11, 12.*

Ver. 11. **Wherefore remember.**—Διό, "wherefore," refers, like i. 15: διὰ τοῦτο, to the preceding section (STIER, BLEEK), since the object of "remember" is their previous quite as well as their present condition, or the "creating" of those who were "dead." *Talis recordatio gratum animum acuit et fidem roborat* (BENGEL), taking into view not merely the obtained riches, but also the poverty and misery from which they were released. The reference to vers. 5-10 (MEYER) is not correct, since ver. 5 resumes the object of vers. 1-3, and ver. 4 contains the subject, nor that to the last thought only (CHRYSOSTOM), since this sums up the whole. [ELLICOTT suggests the reference "to the declaratory portion of the foregoing paragraph, vers. 1-7; vers. 8-10 being an argumentative and explanatory addition.—R.]

* [Dr. Hodge gives the following analysis of this paragraph: I. Their former relation,—1. To the Church as foreigners and aliens. 2. To God as those who were far off, without any saving knowledge of Him, or interest in His promise—vers. 11, 12.—II. The means by which this alienation from God and the Church has been removed, *viz.*, by the blood of Christ. 1. Satisfying the demands of justice it secured reconciliation with God. 2. Abolishing the law in the form of Mosaic institutions, it removed the wall of partition between the Jews and Gentiles—both are united in one body and reconciled to God—vers. 13-18.—III. The Ephesians are therefore united with God and His people. 1. They are represented as fellow-citizens of the saints. 2. They are members of the family of God. 3. They are constituent portions of that temple in which God dwells by His Spirit—vers. 19-22.—R.]

**That once ye, Gentiles in the flesh,** ὅτι ὑμεῖς ποτὲ [ποτὲ ὑμεῖς] τὰ ἔθνη ἐν σαρκί.—(See *Textual Note* 1.] The ἦτε (ver. 12), introduced by the resumptive ὅτε after the apposition, belongs here, so that it need not be supplied. "Ye" means those who are now Christians (σεσωσμένοι), and that they have been "Gentiles in the flesh" is marked by ποτέ. Accordingly τὰ ἔθνη ἐν σαρκί is a predicatory appositional phrase. The article marks the designation as one well-known, the substantive, which in itself has no dishonorable meaning, being used with a reference to גּוֹיִם, and thus with the additional notion of a fault. Accordingly, Paul adds, "in the flesh." This is not κατὰ σάρκα (vi. 5; Rom. ix. 3, 5; 1 Cor. x. 18), which denotes a relation, while here a status is spoken of, one which has been, but is no longer existing (ποτέ). Joined without the article it forms with "Gentiles" one conception: *Goim* in the flesh, denoting what is external: Ye former heathen in the flesh, in the natural condition, uncircumcised, without a sign of the covenant, not even externally, in the flesh, endowed with the known sign of the people of God. [Σάρξ is taken in this its simple meaning by nearly all later commentators (MEYER, ELLICOTT, ALFORD, HODGE, EADIE, for the very good reason that the context plainly points to it, especially ἐν σαρκί just below. Braune's view of the construction is also the usual one.—R.] Otherwise we must take τὰ ἔθνη without any reference to heathenism and the therewith connected deficiencies, as the *nations excepting Israel*, and find its quality denoted in the added phrase, as designating what was defective in them. BENGEL: *hoc considerate Paulus conjungit cum* GENTES; *nam Judæi gentes simpliciter dicebunt præputium, non præputium in carne*—Gentiles, not Gentiles in the flesh. Hence it is incorrect to take ἐν σαρκί = *natalibus, origine carnati* (GROTIUS); for this they would continue to be. Nor does it designate the carnal mind, the unholy life (AMBROSE, ANSELM, CALOVIUS), nor has it a typical reference (STIER) for which Heb. vii. 16; ix. 10, give no occasion.

**Who are called the Uncircumcision by that which is called [the so-called] Circumcision in the flesh wrought by hands** [οἱ λεγόμενοι ἀκροβυστία ὑπὸ τῆς λεγομένης περιτομῆς ἐν σαρκὶ χειροποιήτου.].—Ἀκροβυστία, "uncircumcision," is evidently in apposition to "Gentiles in the flesh," and οἱ λεγόμενοι, already prepared for by τά before ἔθνη, is placed first for emphasis. The nations are called "Uncircumcision" on account of heathenism, the absence of the sign of the covenant in the flesh. The abstract noun, denoting here the essential point, is here a name also; hence it stands for the concrete = the uncircumcised. Col. iii. 11; Gal. ii. 7; 1 Cor. vii. 19, and περιτομή = the circumcised. In the phrase "who are called the Uncircumcision," the fact that they *were* (LUTHER) and are so termed, is stated here objectively, while in ὑπὸ τῆς λεγομένης περιτομῆς, instead of τῶν λεγομένων, which *is* called, instead of *are* called, it is indicated that the thing and the name do not coincide in the same way, *i. e.*, by the so-called circumcision, the so-called circumcised.* Accordingly the added phrase "in the flesh," corresponding precisely with "in the flesh" in the last clause, marks the externalness, in the flesh where it takes place.

Χειροποιήτου, "wrought by hands," is added with special emphasis, forming the antithesis to ἀχειροποιήτῳ, Col. ii. 11, and to what is perfect, wrought by God (Heb. ix. 11, 24; Acts vii. 48; xvii. 24). It has a typical reference, as the passages in Hebrews plainly affirm, so that this reference is not contained in ἐν σαρκί, which is not opposed to ἐν πνεύματι, either here or in the previous clause (STIER). Hence we should connect closely "circumcision in the flesh," and explain: which is made by hands in the flesh (MEYER, BLEEK). There is indeed a special significance in circumcision, which is mentioned by Moses (Deut. x. 16; xxx. 6), and the prophets (Jer. iv. 4; ix. 24, 25; Ezek. xliv. 7, 9). This the Apostle does not wish to undervalue; he only does not permit it to pass for something merely external, over against that of the heart, wrought by God (Phil. iii. 3: Rom. ii. 29; Col. ii. 11), to which that wrought in the flesh points.† He marks here the Jew in the people of Israel; the Jew, who remains satisfied with this external mark of the covenant with Israel, is a so-called circumcised one, and exalts himself without reason arrogantly above the uncircumcised and unclean nations. How miserable must be the condition of the heathen, who are despised by the Jew! So much the more glorious is it that they as Christians are now exalted above the latter. Hence we should not accept here a repugnance toward the Jews (RUECKERT), or an advantage of the Gentiles (CHRYSOSTOM), or the opinion, that uncircumcision was no detriment to the Gentiles, and circumcision no advantage to the Jews (CLARIUS). *In ea æqualitate, quam antea commemorat apostolus, nunc latentem inæqualitatem profert, ut Gentes, quo longius a Deo abfuerant, eo plura se gratiæ Dei debere fateantur* (BEZA).

Ver. 12. **That ye were at that time** [ὅτι ἦτε τῷ καιρῷ ἐκείνῳ].—Ὅτι, "that," is a resumption of the first ὅτι (ver. 11), and connects with "remember," adding to the *status miserabilior* of the heathen, already defined, the inner side. The verb placed first for emphasis marks the past, and τῷ καιρῷ ἐκείνῳ, the dative of time (Luke xii 20: ταύτῃ τῇ νυκτί; WINER, p. 205) renders it even more prominent than ποτέ (ver. 11).

**Without Christ,** χωρὶς Χριστοῦ.—Χωρίς *ad subjectum, quod ab objecto sejunctum est, refertur,* ανευ, *ad objectum, quod a subjecto abesse cogitandum est* (TITTMANN, *Syn.*, I. 93 ff.). Thus χωρὶς Χριστοῦ affirms: the heathen are in a condition, where they are deprived of Him: *vos eratis*

* [The Gentiles were called and really were the ἀκροβυστία: the Jews were called the περιτομή, but were not truly so" (ELLICOTT).—R.]

† [Here again ELLICOTT is excellent. He renders: *performed by hand in the flesh*, to bring out the connection more accurately, and calls the phrase "a tertiary predication added by the Apostle reflectively rather than descriptively; 'the circumcision,—yes, hand-wrought in the flesh; only a visible manual operation on the flesh, when it ought to be a secret spiritual process in the heart; only κατατομή, not περιτομή.' "—R.]

*procul a Christo; ἄνευ Χριστοῦ esset; Christus non aderat vobis.** "Christ" refers to the promised One, the eternal Son of God; since a time is spoken of when He had not appeared in the form of a servant. Hence the name "Jesus" is not inserted. Christ, by means of ἐπιδημία νοητή (OLSHAUSEN), as the Angel of the Covenant (RUECKERT), dwelt already in the people of Israel (see 1 Cor. x. 4), and the people of God stood in an attitude of longing, hope, trust and faith, towards the coming One. The antithesis is in ver. 13: "in Christ Jesus." Hence we have here the summary which is expanded in the succeeding clause; this is not then a first point followed by a second and third (SCHENKEL), but ἀ κεφάλαιον. [HODGE takes the following clauses as a confirmation of this phrase, but ELLICOTT, more correctly, as an elucidation of its significance.—R.] It is incorrect also to explain it as = *sine Christi fide vel notitia* (ANSELM, CALOVIUS).

**Being alienated from the commonwealth of Israel,** ἀπηλλοτριωμένοι τῆς πολιτείας τοῦ Ἰσραήλ.—This is the first of two co-ordinate members of one thought; it describes the external relation, the other the internal. We have marked here, a separation from the πολιτεία of the people of Israel, which has become and will become ever greater, and at the same time an internal estrangement (comp. iv. 18; Col. i. 21). The word indicates, if not an original fellowship, still an earlier nearness and equality. BENGEL: *Abalienati, non: alieni; participia præsupponunt, gentes ante defectionem suam a fide patrum, imo potius ante lapsum Adami fuisse participes lucis et vitæ.* So RUECKERT, OLSHAUSEN, STIER. [MEYER does not think this notion of a previous fellowship is here implied. ALFORD: "Gentiles and Jews were once united in the hope of redemption—this was constituted, on the apostasy of the nations, into a definite πολιτεία for the Jews, from which and its blessings the Gentiles were alienated." To which ELLICOTT adds: "The Gentile lapsed from it, the Jew made it invalid (Matt. xv. 6, comp. Chrysostom); and they parted, only to unite again (ἔθνη καὶ λαοὶ Ἰσραήλ, Acts iv. 27) in one act of uttermost rebellion, and yet, through the mystery of redeeming love, to remain thereby (vers. 15, 16) united in Christ forever."—R.]

By πολιτεία (ARISTOTLE: τῶν τὴν πόλιν οἰκούντων τάξις τις) we necessarily understand here according to the context the constitution of the State, the external polity, from which the Gentiles were ever further removed; a reference to the theocracy also is of course included. Hence too the theocratic name of honor, of "Israel" (Gen. xxxii. 28), not "of the Jews." *Tota respublica Israelis spectabat Christum* (BENGEL). Comp. John i. 48; Rom. ix. 4, 6; 2 Cor. xi. 22; Gal. vi. 16. The genitive τοῦ Ἰσραήλ denotes the possessor, the usufructuary, of the *πολιτεία*. [So ELLICOTT, who rightly insists that the word marks their *religious* and *spiritual*, rather than their national or political distinctions. HODGE and ALFORD accept as more simple the view of HARLESS, that the genitive is that of the identical nation: "the commonwealth which is Israel." ALFORD notices that the word "alienated" requires an objective reality as its reference, hence the meaning mentioned next is to be rejected.—R.] Certainly we should not refer this to the civil constitution (ANSELM, GROTIUS), for which a Roman or Greek could have no desire; what the Gentiles, who became Christians, lacked previously and now possessed, was certainly not "places of honor" or "citizenship in the Jewish State" (HARLESS). We should not then think of citizenship (BULLINGER, CALVIN).

**And strangers from the covenants of the promise,** καὶ ξένοι τῶν διαθηκῶν* τῆς ἐπαγγελίας.—This clause is closely connected with the preceding (καὶ), as a formula. So too the words correspond: "strangers" to "alienated," "covenants" to "polity," "promise" to "Israel." "Strangers" respects what has come to pass in the course of development or the internal position, which that development furthers (BULLINGER: *eandem rem significat utraque, nisi quod posterius prius*); "covenants" designates the repeated renewal of the covenant from Abraham to Moses (Gen. xii. 2 f. 7; xiii. 15; xv. 18; xvii. 20; xxii. 16 ff.; xxvi. 2 ff.; xxviii. 13 ff.), to the prophets; the context speaks merely of the time before Christ. All these repeated agreements, however, serve the *one* promise given to Abraham referring to all nations as well as characterizing the covenants, and reechoing again and again. So in Rom. ix. 4: "the covenants" and "the giving of the law" are placed side by side. Hence this is not to be referred to the two covenants, the old and the new (CALOVIUS and others), or to the two tables of the law (BEZA and others).

**Having no hope,** *etc.*—Here again we have two clauses connected and belonging together. Ἐλπίδα μὴ ἔχοντες, "having no hope," owing to the absence of the article, denotes that they have no hope of any kind; not merely a definite hope, but all hope is denied in their case. Hence we should not understand it of the resurrection and eternal life (BULLINGER, GROTIUS), or of the promised possessions (ESTIUS, BENGEL), as the object of the hope, nor indefinitely of deliverance (HARLESS). At most we might join to it from the following ἄθεοι, in accordance with Acts xxiv. 15: "toward God," πρὸς (εἰς) τὸν θεόν. In 1 Thess. iv. 13 we find the expression used as absolutely as here. The negative μή is used with the participle in this

* [On this distinction EADIE remarks: "Not to contradict this refinement, we might add, that ἄνευ, allied to *in*, *un*, *ohne*, might, in a general sense, signify privation; but χωρίς marks that privation as caused by separation. The Gentiles are viewed as being not merely without Him, but far away from Him. Their relation to Him is marked by a great interval—χωρίς. But, as Ellicott says, 'this distinction must be applied with caution, when it is remembered that χωρὶς is used forty times in the New Testament, and ἄνευ only three times.'"—The connection of this phrase with ἀπηλλοτριωμένοι: "that at that time, being without Christ, ye were excluded from theocratic privileges" (DE WETTE, following the punctuation of LACHMANN, EADIE, though not decidedly in his second edition), is properly deemed harsh by ELLICOTT and ALFORD, though it ought not to be termed "clumsy beyond precedent' by the latter, since there are no clumsy tricks possible in interpretation that have not found a field for their exhibition in Biblical Exegesis (?)!—R.]

* [The genitive seems to be one of *privation*, or inverted possession. Bernhardy, *Syn.* iii. 49, p. 171; Kühner, ii. 163. Comp. WINER, p. 185, who takes the genitive here as one of separation, properly following the noun ξένοι. ELLICOTT: genitive of the point of view.—R.]

clause, which is dependent on μνημονεύετε, "remember," as a subjective negative. WINER, p. 441. Accordingly this clause is not to be put in dependence upon the preceding "strangers," *etc.* (BENGEL: *si promissionem habuissent, spem habuissent illi respondentem;* HARLESS); the clause would thus also be loosened from its close connection with the following one: καὶ ἄθεοι ἐν τῷ κόσμῳ.

**Without God.**—Ἄθεος is stronger than χωρὶς θεοῦ, corresponding to θεὸν οὐκ ἔχει (2 John 9; 1 John ii. 23), = "not having God." The essence of heathenism is Atheism (Rom. i. 21 ff.); the worship of devils and εἴδωλα (1 Cor. x. 20; xii. 2) does not take the place of God; "for polytheism is atheistic," and that philosophy is first correct, which throws this off in its thoughts respecting God. BENGEL: *non statuerant, nullos esse deos* (Acts xix. 35): *sed verum Deum ignorabant; tantum aberat, ut haberent* (1 Thess. iv. 5). He who is ἄθεος is, not merely as respects religion, but also as respects morality, God-less, and heathen immorality is different from Jewish immorality. Hence HARLESS should not wish to exclude this, as if it were true enough but not pertinent here, where the distinction from the people of Israel is set forth, they being however included also under sin. MEYER, against the context, weakens the idea, by taking it as passive: God-forsaken. [Of the three senses of ἄθεος: *active* (opposed to God), *neuter* (ignorant of God, without the subordinate notion of impiety, which Braune prefers), and *passive* (forsaken of God, without God's help), the latter seems most prominent here, and is accepted by HODGE, EADIE, ELLICOTT, ALFORD, mainly on the ground that the whole passage is passive in its character. This is the gloomiest view, and hence the more probable one, though the others stand so closely related to it, that it is hardly correct to term this a weakening of the idea.—R.] The connection with the preceding clause is evident, God is the God of hope (Rom. xv. 13; 2 Thess. ii. 16). Comp. *Doctr. Note*, 2.

**In the world,** ἐν τῷ κόσμῳ, sets forth the antithesis to "the commonwealth of Israel," denoting the "ungodly where" (MEYER), and marking in any case the fearful element of ἄθεος, the place, where a "sure hope, a firm hold" is so urgently needed (OLSHAUSEN), the place without the Creator in the service of nature and the creature, without a Redeemer in need and sin, without consolation and salvation in vanity and nothingness. Hence it is not=*inter ceteros homines, in his terris* (KOPPE), in profane humanity, the heathen world (MEYER), or in the world created and ruled by God (GROTIUS, RUECKERT).

Finally it must be remarked in regard to the structure of this sentence, that the two pair of clauses which unfold the meaning of "without Christ," each contain two related connected thoughts, and the two in the first pair stand in such a relation to the two in the second pair, that the first corresponds to the fourth and the second to the third. [The various correspondences as well as the relation to the leading clause of the verse are aptly expressed by EADIE: "Being *Christless*, they are described in regular gradation as being *churchless*, *hopeless*, *godless* and *homeless*."—R.]

Ver. 13. *Fundamental trait of their present condition.*—**But now, in Christ Jesus** [νυνὶ δὲ ἐν Χριστῷ Ἰησοῦ].—The thought of this verse is still in dependence on "remember" (ver. 11); the Apostle however breaks off into the independent, antithetical form. "But now" is in contrast with "once" (ver. 11), "at that time" (ver. 12), and as there the past was described by "without Christ," so here the present by "in Christ Jesus;" the latter form being fuller than the former, because the Promised One has come, the eternal Son of God has become man.* The Apostle does not refer to "the 'now' of the present 'simply,' but to the present in their fellowship with Christ" (HARLESS). Still we need not supply either ἐστε (BAUMGARTEN-CRUSIUS) or ὄντες (CALVIN), nor connect the phrase exclusively with "now" (HARLESS); both belong to ἐγενήθητε below, in fact to the whole sentence.

**Ye who once were far off were brought nigh in the blood of Christ,** ὑμεῖς οἵ ποτε ὄντες μακρὰν ἐγενήθητε ἐγγὺς ἐν τῷ αἵματι τοῦ Χριστοῦ.—The position of the words obliges us to regard ἐν Χριστῷ Ἰησοῦ as rendered specially prominent, as a general definition of modality, and ἐν τῷ αἵματι τοῦ Χριστοῦ, "in the blood of Christ," as a special one, so that the latter is to be taken as a more precise explanation of the former; it is not then in apposition with it; both belong to the verbal notion "were brought nigh." Then again "ye" has *now* another qualification than before: "who were once far off," as corresponding to ver. 12 ("alienated"—"strangers"). Comp. ii. 17; Acts iii. 39; xvii. 27 ("though He be not far from every one of us"); Mark xii. 34 ("Thou art not far from the kingdom of heaven"). These words have a reference figuratively to our relation to God; the heathen are thus spoken of in prophecy (Isa. xlix. 1; lx. 3, 4; lxvi. 19; lv. 5; lvii. 19) in their relation to both God Himself and His people. BUCER: *qui hactenus non fuisti populus domini, jam estis populus domini.* The distance and nearness include both the relation to God and that to His people; hence should not be referred either to the former alone (MATTHIES), or to the latter alone (RUECKERT, OLSHAUSEN, BLEEK). BENGEL: *procul a populo Dei et a Deo.* It is not sufficient to say: *longe eratis a cognitione Dei veri et a spe vitæ cœlestis* (GROTIUS), still less: μακράν *homines miserrimi,* ἐγγύς, *felicissimi* (KOPPE). The approach is something which develops (ἐγενήθητε), has a history;† the means rest in and proceed from what is expressed by: "in the blood of Christ." This is almost="through his blood," διὰ τοῦ αἵματος αὐτοῦ (i. 7); the prepositions ἐν and διά are, however, both used in Col. i. 16: ἐν αὐτῷ—δι' αὐτοῦ. The latter denotes the cause, through which any thing takes place, comes into position or existence, the former the permanent ground,

* [The reference to the personal Messiah, to Jesus of Nazareth, who is the Christ, seems to be quite certain (comp. ELLICOTT and EADIE).—R.]

† [The verb is the aorist passive, expressing the effect of a definite event in the past, though the idea of *becoming* or being gradually brought is not to be forgotten. They were brought nigh, they became nigh through the instrumentality of another.—R.]

on which it has its continuance.* (WINER, p. 362. The word "Christ" here has special significance: it marks the Son of God beside the word "blood," which marks "the form of a servant."

*Closer explanation respecting the nature and genesis of their present condition.* Vers. 14–18.

Ver. 14. **For he is our peace** [αὐτὸς γάρ† ἐστιν ἡ εἰρήνη ἡμῶν].—The position is emphatic, "He," not the unemphatic subject, but He Himself (WINER, p. 142). [He and none other; so most commentators.—R.] His Person is "our peace." The article marks the peace as well-known, more closely defined. BENGEL aptly says: *pax, non modo* PACIFICATOR; *nam* SUI *impensa pacem peperit et ipsi vinculum est* UTRORUMQUE. The allusion to passages in prophecy (Mic. v. 4; Isa. ix. 5, 6; lii. 7; liii. 5; Zech. ix. 10, *etc.;* also Ps. lxxii.) is unmistakable. This is denied by BAUMGARTEN-CRUSIUS. The Messiah is indeed called שָׁלוֹם, not merely Prince of Peace, εἰρηνοποιός. The genitive ἡμῶν, "our," merely denotes that the peace belongs to them, does not say whether the peace is among themselves or between them and God. This is determined by the context. On the nature of this peace, see Doctr. Note 3 *b*.

**Who made both one**, ὁ ποιήσας τὰ ἀμφότερα ἕν.—He is therefore "the peace" through an act (ὁ ποιήσας with αὐτός, *quippe qui fecit*), which is set forth here only generally: made one, ἓν ποιεῖν. Here we find a closer definition of the idea "peace," not of "our," as the neuter requires. Τὰ ἀμφότερα, like τὰ μωρά, ἀσθενῆ, κ. τ. λ., 1 Cor. i. 27 f., designates the general: what is of two kinds, "what opposes because sundered" (MATTHIES). The annulling of an existent variance is thereby noted as the nature of the peace. Hence we may not say that the neuter is=τοὺς ἀμφοτέρους (vers. 16, 18), τοὺς δύο (ver. 15), as KOPPE, MEYER and others think, nor does the neuter ἕν define the neuter τὰ ἀμφότερα (BENGEL). ["Both" is usually referred to "Jews and Gentiles." This is a legitimate inference, but Braune holds that the statement here does not require any specific reference.—R.]

**And broke down the middle wall of the partition** [καὶ τὸ μεσότοιχον τοῦ φραγμοῦ λύσας].—The indefinite notion of "making one" is now more closely defined; καί adds in a figure the main point; hence it is not epexegetical (MEYER). [The explanatory or epexegetical force of καί is accepted by EADIE, ALFORD, ELLICOTT. It is correct, if the previous clause has a distinct reference to the Jews and Gentiles: who made both Jews and Gentiles one, *viz.*, in that He broke down, *etc.* There seems to be nothing gained by adopting Braune's view, while the other most obviously suggests itself.—R.]

Τὸ μεσότοιχον, τοῦ φραγμοῦ (like ἕρκος ὀδόντων)=the partition wall of the fence, that is, the partition wall which is in the fence, denoting in the figure of an independent object a quality and effect of the hedge. [So HARLESS]. The leading idea is found in the first noun, the wall set up between the two, the Gentiles without the promise and covenant of God, and the Jews, the people of promise, which contains in itself the notion of separation; the participle applies to it. Therefore τοῦ φραγμοῦ is not the genitive of apposition (MEYER) or to be resolved into τὸν φραγμὸν τὸ μεσότοιχον ὄντα (GRIMM, *Clavis, sub voce*); in that case we would have found here τὸν φραγμὸν τοῦ μεσοτοίχου. LUTHER too is incorrect: and has broken down the hedge, which was between. Nor is it=μεσότοιχον διαφράσσον (GROTIUS and others). Unserviceable here also is the distinction of BENGEL: *paries disjungit domos, sepes regiones.* From Matth. xxi. 33; Isa. v. 2, we are shown that φραγμός (in agreement with ver. 15) refers to the law, that is, to its quality or effect in separating the people of God, which permits it to be regarded as a partition wall. We may also refer it to the temple in which a type of the spiritual is presented, and to which the expressions here selected point; there was there a court of the Gentiles (Acts xxi. 28), though only in latter times, in the last temple; a vail, which separated like a wall, rent first at the death of the Redeemer. Hence the word λύσας is aptly chosen (John ii. 19; Matth. v. 17; Gal. ii. 18; 1 John iii. 8; 2 Pet. iii. 10).*—All reference to the separated residence of Jews in cities, as in Frankfort, Rome and elsewhere (GRONOW and others) and the like is to be rejected.

Ver. 15. **Having abolished (done away) in his flesh the enmity, even the law of the commandments expressed in ordinances** [τὴν ἔχθραν, ἐν τῇ σαρκὶ αὐτοῦ, τὸν νόμον τῶν ἐντολῶν ἐν δόγμασιν καταργήσας. See *Textual Note* [4]]. The Apostle now adds, without a connecting particle, the meaning of the figure: he construes it thus: τὴν ἔχθραν ἐν τῇ σαρκὶ αὐτοῦ καταργήσας, but during the dictation inserts after αὐτοῦ the phrase τὸν νόμον τῶν ἐντολῶν ἐν δόγμασιν, the banner of this enmity; these two objects in the accusative representing two sides of one object, hence very well allowing the dependence on κατηργήσας. To τὸ μεσότοιχον corresponds τὴν ἔχθραν, denoting simply the literal reality, the division, the hostile separation and antagonism of Jews and Gentiles, and, since there is nothing to indicate any limitation, but as the context rather points to enmity of man towards God which is active behind this hostility of the Jews and Gentiles, including this latter at the same time (ver. 16). [So ALFORD and ELLI-

* [The strictly instrumental sense does not belong to ἐν, even here, where it seems so natural. At all events the idea of *immanent* instrumentality is as much as can be conceded in that direction. ALFORD rightly prefers "in" as more comprehensive: "The symbol of a fact *in* which—the seal of a covenant *in* which—your nearness to God consists." HODGE accepts "by" as the proper rendering without question.—R.]

† [This particle introduces a confirmatory explanation of the preceding verse (so most commentators).—R.]

* [EADIE, ALFORD, ELLICOTT follow DE WETTE in taking τοῦ φραγμοῦ as the genitive of possession: the wall which pertained to, or belonged to the fence. This view has the advantage of giving a wide reference to φραγμός. ALFORD finds a primary allusion to the rending of the vail of the temple, a view which is supported by the complex idea of peace running through our passage. He takes φραγμός (of which μεσότοιχον is the instrument) as=the whole legal system, ceremonial and moral, which made the whole separation,—of Jew from Gentile,—and in the background of both from God. (So ELLICOTT.)—R.]

COTT: "The enmity due not only to Judaical limitations and antagonisms, but also and, as the widening context shows, more especially to the alienation of both Jew and Gentile from God."—R.] BUCER: *Vera tamen inter Judæos et ethnicos inimicitia, i. e., diversitas erat, quod illi verum Deum colerent, hi minime.* It is incorrect to refer it exclusively to the enmity against God (GREEK FATHERS, HARLESS and others) or to the enmity between the Jews and the Gentiles (AMBROSIASTER, ERASMUS, BLEEK [EADIE, HODGE] and others), or to understand only the cause of division that is the law (LUTHER, CALVIN and others). It is correct however to understand that the Apostle places by the side of the existing fact, τὴν ἔχθραν, the cause of the same, τὸν νόμον τῶν ἐντολῶν ἐν δόγμασι.

The law has its contents in "commandments:" αἱ ἐντολαί, the injunctions to be regarded and executed, are both the purely moral and the ceremonial commandments of God (Matth. xv. 3; xxii. 36, 38; Rom. vii. 8-13), called also "of men" (Tit. i. 14); the plural marks plurality, and points also to divisions. This is rendered prominent by the phrase ἐν δόγμασιν, joined closely without the article to ἐντολῶν, and defining its quality. Similarly: πίστις ἐν τῷ κυρίῳ (i. 15), ἀγάπη ἐν πνεύματι (Col. i. 8), σοφία ἐν μυστηρίῳ (1 Cor. ii. 7). Comp. WINER, pp. 129, 206. Δόγμα, used of regal orders (Luke ii. 1; Acts xvii. 7), of apostolic determinations (Acts xvi. 4), means here as in Col. ii. 14 the statutes of the law; δογματίζεσθαι, in Col. ii. 20, is to be ordered or to order one's self. The idea of a mandate is always contained in it. ERASMUS: *Ostendens legem imperiosam appellat illam* τῶν ἐντολῶν (ἐντέλλουσαν)—*quomodo? non persuasione et lenitate aut promissis, sed præceptis quæ vocat* DOGMATA. Every ἐντολή appears then in a special, mandatory precept. [This view of the phrase is now the common one. ALFORD: "The law of decretory commandments." For the other interpretations, see HARLESS and EADIE *in loco*.—R.]

Of this there is predicated καταργήσας (ἀργὸν=ἀεργὸν ποιεῖν, Rom. iii. 31; 1 Cor. xiii. 11): to make unavailing, to do away, to deprive of power. The ideal worth remains intact, so also the theocratic obligation; but in so far as the law imperiously binds the heart and will with casuistic ordinances for all cases, it is done away. In this too lies the cause of the enmity against God and men. [EADIE takes "law," *etc.* to mean the ceremonial law. HODGE more correctly: "The idea probably is that the law in all its compass, and in all its forms, so far as it was a covenant prescribing the conditions of salvation, is abolished." He extends it to all the law of God, written in the heart as well, while admitting a special reference to the Mosaic law.—R.]

This doing away took place "in his flesh." As the decisive, main qualification it stands in an emphatic position. It means more than "in Himself," denoting the real "likeness" to our "flesh," in which He began His sanctifying, expiating sorrows, which slew what was opposed, which helped the right to full right, in active obedience to the law even to the acme, of the death on the cross, the passive obedience, thus, though without sin, bearing, feeling, overcoming the "enmity" with the "law," thus "by virtue of His fleshly life under the law, which He gave to death, in order to receive it back from death living, glorious, free in spirit for us all" (DELITZSCH), putting the law with its ordinances into inactivity, at the same time in His bodily life burying it. BENGEL construes incorrectly: *Est quasi stilo lapidari scriptum: Christus. carne sua inimicitiam, dogmatibus evangelicis in totum orbem deditis legem præceptorum sustulit;* this is simply untrue historically, impossible logically, unnecessary grammatically, and too artificial. [It seems scarcely correct to render "*by* His flesh" (HODGE: "*i. e.*, by His death"), since this leaves out of view the life of Christ as a satisfaction of the law. Besides ἐν rarely means simply *by*. ALFORD and ELLICOTT however thus limit it: "in His *crucified* flesh."—The question of connection is more disputed. The article would precede, if it should be joined to ἔχθραν. HARLESS, DE WETTE, MEYER, EADIE, HODGE agree with Braune in joining it with καταργήσας, in emphatic position. To this ALFORD, who, with ELLICOTT and many of the earlier commentators, joins it with λύσας, objects, because it makes the instrumental predication precede the verb. If ἔχθραν is governed by καταργήσας, the question is decided at once, while in any case this view seems preferable; the general sense remaining the same, although the allusion to the vail of the temple becomes more prominent, if Alford's view be accepted.—R.]

MEYER and others take τὴν ἔχθραν by itself as in apposition to μεσότοιχον, detaching it from what follows; in that case τὸν νόμον τῶν ἐντολῶν ἐν δόγμασιν would stand before ἐν τῇ σαρκὶ αὐτοῦ. [This is also the view of EADIE, HODGE, ALFORD, ELLICOTT. While it does not introduce any *material* difference into the interpretation of the passage, it modifies its form very considerably. And it seems the preferable view. The objection Braune raises is met at once by saying that his own interpretation assumes an afterthought influencing the order (see beginning of this verse). The emphatic phrase: "in His flesh" thus takes an emphatic position, whatever be its connection. The emphasis is altogether lost in the E. V., as any reader may perceive. This view allows of a nicer discrimination between the accusatives, introduces a needed explanation of the figurative expression: "middle wall," while ἔχθραν is more usual after the verb λύειν than after καταργεῖν. HODGE thus paraphrases: "He is our peace, because He has made the two one, by removing the enmity or middle wall which divided the Jews and Gentiles, and this was done by abolishing the law." This is correct, but omits the important description of the law and the emphatic: in His flesh." Comp. *Textual Note* 4.—R.]

STIER incorrectly joins ἐν δόγμασιν to νόμον; but then the article τόν would necessarily have been prefixed (1 Thess. i. 8) or ἐντολῶν have preceded νόμον (Col. i. 8). Nor is "in his flesh" to be joined with "enmity" (CHRYSOSTOM), as though only a natural hatred among his people, among his kindred, were referred to. It is incorrect to understand νόμος τῶν ἐντολῶν as referring only to *adiaphora* (GROTIUS), to the ceremonial law (BENGEL) [EADIE], or to the moral law alone (CALOVIUS), or *δόγματα* as referring to *philosophorum doctrinas* (GROTIUS), since the readers are not *homines triti in philosophorum Scriptis;* quite as little can the doctrine of Christ be denoted thereby (BENGEL and others), or *nova præcepta* (FRITZSCHE). Finally καταργήσας does not point to the removal of the theocratic obligation (SCHENKEL).

**That he might create the two in himself into one new man** [ἵνα τοὺς δύο κτίσῃ ἐν ἑαυτῷ εἰς ἕνα καινὸν ἄνθρωπον].—Ἵνα introduces a final clause, giving here the purpose of *καταργήσας*, which defines *λύσας* more closely, and with this explains *ποιήσας*. He has done away the law in its commandments; destroyed the separating elements clinging to it, that He might κτίσῃ. Thus the *ποιήσας* is further defined as creating. The objects of this creation, τοὺς δύο, are the two great masses of people regarded as two individualities, as two, not a greater number of separate individuals beside each other, each of whom stands or falls for himself (OLSHAUSEN); still less is there involved a series of various specimens of the different races. The masculine denotes the persons, in distinction from the more general idea of the neuter (*τὰ ἀμφότερα*, ver. 14); the choice of words corresponds. That *ἀνθρώπους* is not inserted, is not to be explained by the wider scope, as BENGEL thinks: *eleganter omittit homines, antea enim vix humanum nomen tuiti erant.* Ἐν ἑαυτῷ places the Person of Christ again in the foreground: *Ne alibi quam in Christo unitatem quærant* (CALVIN). [HODGE: "In virtue of union with Him,—union with Christ being the condition at once of their unity and of their holiness." In His Person, at all events.—R.] The ground of the existence and permanence is in Him; He is the Author (κτίσῃ) and foundation, and at the same time the life-sphere, Creator and Second Adam, Progenitor of the new race, which stands in original peace with God. It is therefore not =*δι' ἑαυτοῦ* (GREEK FATHERS), in order to exclude angels or other powers, as those through whom what is asserted was effected. But still less is it=*per suam doctrinam* (GROTIUS).

In this creation (*κτίσῃ*, vers. 1, 10) there is a purpose εἰς ἕνα καινὸν ἄνθρωπον. Ἐν ἑαυτῷ conditions *ἄνθρωπος* in the singular. Comp. Gal. iii. 28: *πάντες γὰρ ὑμεῖς εἷς ἐστὲ ἐν Χριστῷ Ἰησοῦ*; John x. 16. By εἷς καινὸς ἄνθρωπος is indicated: *ὁρᾷς οὐχὶ τὸν Ἕλληνα γενόμενον Ἰουδαῖον, ἀλλὰ καὶ τοῦτον κἀκεῖνον εἰς ἑτέραν κατάστασιν ἥκοντας οὐχ ἵνα τοῦτον ἕτερον ἐργάσηται, τὸν νόμον κατήργησεν, ἀλλ' ἵνα τοὺς* δύο *κτίσῃ*. It is very superficial and perverted to take "one new man" as a third, which is neither heathenism nor Judaism, without thinking of the *moral* renewal of *persons* (BAUMGARTEN-CRUSIUS). The preposition marks the purpose or tendency, and thus the creation as one not yet concluded; humanity, consisting of personally free individuals, is potentially renewed in Christ, but not yet actually.

[ALFORD: "Observe, not that He might reconcile the two to *each other* only, nor is the Apostle speaking merely of any such reconciliation: but that He might incorporate the two, reconciled in Him to God, into one *new* man,—the old man to which both belonged, the enemy of God, having been slain in His flesh on the cross. Observe, too, *one* new man: we are all in God's sight, but one in Christ, as we are but one in Adam."—R.]

Hence: **So making peace,** ποιῶν εἰρήνην.—The present participle stands first for emphasis, marking a continued activity of Christ. The act of union does not therefore coincide with the act of creation. Hence BUCER is incorrect: *pace facta.* Since *εἰρήνη* has no limitation joined with it, that peace (between Jews and Gentiles) which the context indicates as the most immediate reference, is to be meant, but that which is implied also in "new man" (toward God) is not to be excluded (SCHENKEL [EADIE, HODGE], and others). HARLESS should not term the note of CHRYSOSTOM (*πρὸς τὸν θεὸν καὶ πρὸς ἀλλήλους*) correct only in the first half.

Ver. 16. **And might reconcile them both** [Καὶ ἀποκαταλλάξῃ τοὺς ἀμφοτέρους].—Καί connects this clause with *ἵνα*, on which the verb depends; so that this too belongs to the purpose of *καταργήσας*. The emphasis is on the verb which comes first. This compound occurs only here and in Col. i. 20, 21, and is a strengthened *καταλλάσσειν*, as *ἀπεκδέχεσθαι* and *ἀποκαραδοκεῖν*, not merely to expect, but to await, to expect with perseverance. The preposition *ἀπό* has the meaning "again" in composition (see PASSOW *sub voce*), but only when the notion of the verb itself includes this in some measure, as *ἀποκαθίστημι* of what is healed, restored (Matth. xii. 13; Mark iii. 5; viii. 25; Luke vi. 10; Acts i. 6); certainly the notion "again" is near at hand in that of reconciliation, because separation and enmity are not original, and the reconciliation leads away from the present status back to the original one. Hence the strengthened notion is "reconcile again." [So CALVIN, ALFORD, ELLICOTT; but EADIE and MEYER object.—R.] *Qui ita deposuerunt immicitiam, ut amicitia successerit, neque quidquam reliquum sit, quin concordes vivant ἐν ἑνὶ σώματι, cujus est unum caput Christus* (TITTMANN, *Syn.* I. p. 105).*—The *object* of the reconciliation: τοὺς ἀμφοτέρους. [The article renders the object definite: *them both* or *both of us.*—R.] Since Paul does not say *δύο*, which is a mere numeral, but *ἀμφότεροι*, which denotes diversity, he renders prominent the difficulty and importance of the reconciliation.

**In one body to God through the cross** [ἐν ἑνὶ σώματι τῷ θεῷ διὰ τοῦ σταυροῦ].—"In one body" denotes the sphere in which the reconciliation is consummated: over against "both" there is now only "one body," in which they are; each does not need a separate one. To supply "being," *ὄντας*, in thought is the simplest interpretation. The phrase refers,

* [Against TITTMANN'S distinction, according to which *διαλάσσω* refers to the cessation of mutual enmity, and *καταλάσσω* is employed in cases where the enmity has existed only on one side, see EADIE; comp. USTERI, *Lehrbegriff*, p. 102; FRITZSCHE, *Romans*, I. p. 276; THOLUCK, *Bergpredigt.* p. 192; TRENCH. *Syn. N. T*, 2d part, p. 137; and especially the notes of Drs. LANGE and SCHAFF, *Romans*. p. 166 f., and 2 *Corinthians*, p. 98 f. We must hold fast here: That the reconciliation is with God, that the ground of it is what Christ did on and through His cross, viz., removed from us the Divine wrath against sin, of which we were the objects in consequence of sin.—R.]

like ἐν ἑαυτῷ, ἐν τῇ σαρκὶ αὐτοῦ, αὐτὸς γάρ (ver. 14), to His Person, as the only one in which both are redeemed, to an organism (σῶμα, not σάρξ) in its outward appearance, thus to the body of Christ, the Church. [So HODGE, ALFORD, ELLICOTT.] It is not, *sicut Latinis collegia vocantur corpora*, corporation=Society (GROTIUS).

The end of the reconciliation is τῷ θεῷ. It is not God that is reconciled with men,* but men with God. What has all along been implied, conceived of in general, left indefinite in the words "peace" (vers. 14, 15), "the enmity" (ver. 15), "new man" (ver. 15), is now definitely expressed as the other side. The added qualification of the reconciliation: "through the [or His] cross" refers to the death on the cross, in which the ἱλασμός, the *atonement*, is marked as the act, which is the condition of the at-onement. Comp. *Doctr. Note* 3.

Hence it is not justifiable to take ἐν ἑνὶ σώματι as=εἰς ἓν σῶμα (DELITZSCH), or to refer it to the body of Christ on the cross (CHRYSOSTOM, BENGEL: *cruci affixo*, HARLESS, HOFMANN and others), since then διὰ τοῦ σταυροῦ would be altogether unnecessary or should be joined with the following ἀποκτείνας (HOFMANN, *Schriftbeweis*, II. 1, p. 381); nor is the thought to be completed thus: Christ has reconciled in one single body, or made one single body (His own) to a unity, including them in the same fellowship with God; there is no reference to the antithesis of *many* sacrifices before and outside of Christ. GROTIUS interprets διὰ τοῦ σταυροῦ incorrectly: *Simul intelligit doctrinam cruce sanctam; sed crucem dicere malint, ut intelligamus, quanto res ista Christo steterit*; STIER too misinterprets: the power and fear of the cross which is to be preached. Nor can we accept a reconciliation of "both" with each other, taking "to God" as dative *commodi: ut Deo serviant* (GROTIUS).

**Having slain the enmity on it** [ἀποκτείνας τὴν ἔχθραν ἐν αὐτῷ].—The aorist participle defines the mode of consummating the reconciliation, explaining τοῦ σταυροῦ, on which account ἐν αὐτῷ can refer only to this: the Crucified One, who was slain, the Dying One, slays and has slain "the enmity," which includes here as in ver. 15 both the enmity between "both" and against God, the latter being more prominent here, the former in ver. 15. On the cross the chief matter was, that He who had been rejected by both Jews and Gentiles should through a propitiation in Himself reconcile both to God. It is incorrect to exclude from τὴν ἔχθραν enmity toward God (SCHENKEL, MEYER) or of the Jews and Gentiles against each other (RUECKERT, HARLESS, HOFMANN), for the peace of these with each other does not condition their peace with God, indeed enmity against God participates in the hate these have toward each other, which the law occasions and furthers. [ALFORD and ELLICOTT adopt this wide or complex reference. HODGE however says: "The enmity is that which subsisted between God and man." Many doubt the propriety of predicating ἔχθραν of God, who certainly has ὀργήν. Comp. *Romans*, p. 165. In the passage there commented on, the active sense of the adjective must be accepted, I think, but that does not seem so bold and harsh as to say that ἔχθραν is "God's enmity." The wider reference is better sustained by the context, and of itself tones down the objectionable form without at all interfering with the implied truth respecting God's anger against sin and the satisfaction rendered on the cross.—The view of MEYER is accepted by EADIE, though there seems to be a confusion in his language. But this limited meaning does not "at all satisfy the solemnity of the sentence, or of the next two verses." Enmity here is "that between man and God, which Christ did slay on the cross, and which being brought to an end, the separation between Jew and Gentile, which was the result of it, was done away" (ALFORD). The fact that our participle is aorist, and in all probability denotes an antecedent act, is no objection to this view, as EADIE seems to think, since what Christ did on the cross (here spoken of) necessarily precedes what He designs doing through His cross ("reconcile them both in one body to God"), and the enmity of man against God was as fully and effectually destroyed in that act as that between Jew and Gentile. MEYER's position takes this distinction of enmity as the basis of the "one body," in which both are reconciled to God, but this seems to condition the latter on the former.—R.] It is a perversion to understand τὴν ἔχθραν as the law (KOPPE and others). Comp. on ver. 14. Ἐν αὐτῷ cannot be referred to ἐν ἑνὶ σώματι (BENGEL, HOFMANN).

Ver. 17. **And he came and preached peace** [καὶ ἐλθὼν εὐηγγελίσατο εἰρήνην].—Since the verb is not dependent upon ἵνα, but independent, it cannot be joined with ver. 16. Καί connects rather with ver. 14: He Himself is our Peace and announces that Himself (HARLESS). What intervenes explains the former statement, by showing its meaning and truth in His doings even unto death: He has established peace, therefore He is our Peace. This is to be regarded as pre-supposed in ἐλθών. Accordingly His coming is after His resurrection. BENGEL is excellent: *Veniens a morte, profectione ad inferos, resurrectione, victor lætus ipse ultro nuntiavit.* To this the verb εὐηγγελίσατο, "preached," refers, which is not a predicting of the future, but a message from one who is present, who has come. Ἐλθών is added descriptively, and is in accordance with the promise (John xiv. 18): "I come to you," denoting there His continued presence, *insigne verbum* (BENGEL). CHRYSOSTOM well says: οὐ δι' ἑτέρου ἔπεμψεν, οὐδὲ δι' ἄλλου τινὸς ταῦτα ἐμήνυσεν, ἀλλ' αὐτὸς δι' ἑαυτοῦ. The Risen One is Himself an actual announcement of the attained victory and peace; He is present in the coming of the Holy Ghost, and also with His messengers and their gospel. So in 2 Tim. i. 10, where the ἐπιφάνεια of the Risen One and His gospel are spoken of.

Thus the proffering and appropriating of the

* [Inasmuch as "the cross" is here spoken of, we must admit a secondary reference to the propitiary sacrifice of Christ as the condition or ground of the reconciliation. If then we ask respecting the *nexus* between this ground and the result, there must enter a thought of God's wrath (ver. 3) against sin. One thing remains clear—whatever was objectively necessary that men might be at peace with God and with each other was effected by the death of Christ, and what is necessary in the subject is, to take hold of Christ by faith, as to be "in Him" (ver. 15) a member of the "one body" (ver. 16).—R.]

established peace is emphasized, and "preaching peace" is distinguished from "being peace." Evidently we should understand both peace with one another and with God. Accordingly it is incorrect to regard ἐλθών as redundant (GROTIUS and others), or to refer it to the Incarnation (CHRYSOSTOM, ANSELM, HARLESS); the expression can by no means be referred merely to the resurrection and the salutation of peace (BENGEL), or to the coming in the Holy Spirit (OLSHAUSEN, SCHENKEL), or in the Apostles (AMBROSE, CALVIN and others); nor can it be=caused to be proclaimed (GROTIUS), since ἐλθών is found here and is not redundant. "Peace" should not be limited to the relation to God (CHRYSOSTOM, HARLESS [HODGE]) or of the Jews and Gentiles toward each other (BLEEK, MEYER). [The repetition and emphasis are against this.] As regards the matters here treated of, we should not compare here John x. 16; xii. 20–23; Matth. viii. 11; xxiv. 14, as though this were that which He "came and preached." We should rather be reminded of the renewal of the Apostles, the conversion of Paul, and of Rom. viii. 9, 10; 14-17; xv. 18; 2 Cor. xiii. 3, 5; Gal. ii. 20; Eph. i. 13. [So EADIE, ALFORD, ELLICOTT (and HODGE, except as regards the comprehensive sense of "peace").—R.] The tense of the verb εὐηγγελίσατο defines the point of time of the conversion of individuals; then Christ brought it to them.

**To you who were afar off and peace to those who were nigh,** ὑμῖν τοῖς μακρὰν καὶ εἰρήνην τοῖς ἐγγύς.—This is to be taken in accordance with ver. 13. The readers, as originally Gentiles are those "afar off," and on this account they come first, as indeed historically such were converted to the Church, the Jews, "those nigh," falling into the background. The repetition of εἰρήνην before this last term marks their need of this, notwithstanding their nearness; ὑμῖν however comprises both, since both (Jews and Gentiles) were in the Church, though the latter constituted the main element.* Comp. Acts xvi. 23. The double εἰρήνην is derived from Isa. lvii. 19. There שָׁלוֹם שָׁלוֹם refers not inaptly but emphatically, like the double ναὶ ναί, οὒ οὔ (Matth. v. 37; Jas. v. 12), to Gentiles and Jews, and hence the repetition. The dative depends on the verb, not on εἰρήνη as dative *commodi;* the interpretation of HARLESS compelling him to accept this view of it: the purport of His message was a peace which respected all, Jews as well as Gentiles. [So HODGE, but the other is far simpler, and accepted by MEYER, EADIE, ALFORD, and most.—R.]

Ver. 18. **For through him** [ὅτι δι' αὐτοῦ].—Ὅτι is here evidently=*quia;* it is *probatio ab effectu* (CALVIN).* The purport of the εὐηγγελίσατο cannot be thus introduced (KOPPE); this is set forth in "peace," and it cannot be preached, that (ὅτι) we have, but only: because we have, or: that we may have. The nature of the "peace" is not to be explained by this clause (RUECKERT); this has been already defined. The truth of the assertion: "came and preached" is shown in a reality (ἔχομεν), the reality of the result of this preaching (τὴν προσαγωγήν); because the preaching of *Christ* is spoken of, δι' αὐτοῦ stands first. Were the proclamation the main matter, then ἔχομεν would have taken the first place. "Through Him" denotes the mediation by means of the entire Divine-human Person; it is not="through his blood" (OLSHAUSEN). [HODGE suggests this, but not to the exclusion of other thoughts. —R.]

**We both have our access in one Spirit unto the Father** [ἔχομεν τὴν προσαγωγὴν οἱ ἀμφότεροι ἐν ἑνὶ πνεύματι πρὸς τὸν πατέρα].—Προσαγωγή here, iii. 12 and Rom. v. 2 (εἰς χάριν) is the presupposition to the entrance into the holiest (Heb. x. 19) and "into the everlasting kingdom of our Lord" (2 Pet. i. 11) and the occasion of the drawing near (Heb. x. 22); it is not merely the right and permission to do so, but a fact in which we rejoice as a reality (1 Pet. iii. 18) that has become ours (ἔχομεν); the drawing near should not be wanting; ἐσχήκαμεν (Rom. v. 2) gives prominence to the appropriation as a continuing fact, ἔχομεν denotes only the present possession, the acceptance which has taken place. The underlying figure is according to Heb. x. 19-22 the entrance into the most holy place. In προσαγωγή STIER finds indicated a free approach and an ever closer approach. [The active, transitive sense: *admission, introduction,* is preferred by ELLICOTT, EADIE, and HODGE apparently, following THOLUCK (Romans v. 2), while ALFORD prefers the intransitive sense, *access,* which does not differ greatly from the other, certainly does mean merely liberty of approach, and leave the actual enjoyment of the privilege out of view. "Introduction" certainly does not bring out the idea of "repetition, present liberty of approach," as "access" does.—MEYER and EADIE remark that it means more than "door," John x. 9. Comp. *Romans,* pp. 160, 161.—R.] We need not with CHRYSOSTOM (οὐκ εἶπεν πρόσοδον· οὐ γὰρ ἀφ' ἑαυτοῦ προσήλθομεν, ἀλλ' ὑπ' αὐτοῦ προσήχθημεν) and MEYER think of a προσαγωγεύς to the king. [This thought need not be peremptorily rejected, however, though the other is on the whole preferable (ELLICOTT, EADIE, ALFORD).—R]. The notion of "leading into" [MEYER] does not suit the other passages, iii. 12; Rom. v. 2.

The words: οἱ ἀμφότεροι ἐν ἑνὶ πνεύματι placed in juxtaposition, mark strongly the removed division, the unity, that too in the fellow-

* [This seems doubtful in view of the repeated εἰρήνην, which interposes between ὑμῖν and τοῖς ἐγγύς. ALFORD is better: "Not '*to us*' (*i. e.*, in the second category), for fear of still upholding the distinction where he wishes to merge it altogether."—"Though those 'who were nigh' were the first who heard the proclamation based on the commission—'beginning at Jerusalem,' yet those 'who were afar off' are mentioned first, as they had so deep an interest in the tidings, and as the invitation of Gentiles into the Church—a theme the Apostle delighted in, proving, as it did, the abolition of class privileges, and the commencement of an unrestricted economy—was the result and proof of the truths illustrated in this paragraph."—R.]

* [ELLICOTT says correctly that the particle is not merely explanatory, nor yet strongly causal, 'because we have,' but with more of a demonstrative or confirmatory force, "as it is a fact that we have."—ALFORD finds in this verse a proof of the wide reference of the words "peace" and "reconcile" in the previous verses. "Here clearly the union (not reconciliation, nor is enmity predicted of them) of Jew and Gentile is subordinated to the blessed fact of an access to God, having been provided for both through Christ by the Spirit."—R.]

ship of the Holy Spirit. They are not merely within the body of Christ, members of the Church, but are animated and impelled by the Spirit ruling there, which He has sent. "In one Spirit" refers to "in one body;" the two expressions being parallel. It is certainly not = *unanimis voluntate*, ὁμοθυμαδόν (ANSELM). [The reference to the Holy Spirit scarcely admits of a reasonable doubt. But the preposition is not instrumental. To take as such destroys the parallelism with "in one body," and confuses the relations of this clause. It is greatly to be regretted that this verse, so explicit and discriminating in its designations of the work of the Trinity in our salvation, should be thus confused. Dr. HODGE, whose notes on this verse are otherwise so excellent, does not bring out fully the correct interpretation of this preposition. "The Holy Spirit is, as it were, the vital sphere or element in which both parties have their common πρωσαγωγή to the Father" (ELLICOTT).—R.] "Unto the Father," *ad Patrem ut ad Patrem. Hoc versu fit mentio Christi, Spiritus, Patris, eodem ordine, quo* ver. 12, 1 Cor. i. 3, 5; *aliter* Acts i. 4, 5 (BENGEL). The choice of prepositions is remarkably apt: πρὸς τὸν πατέρα διὰ Χριστοῦ ἐν πνεύματι, *Unto* the Father *through* Christ *in* the Spirit.

*Sketch of their present condition.* Vers. 19-22.

Ver. 19. **So then ye are no longer** [ἄρα οὖν οὐκέτι ἐστέ].—Ἄρα οὖν is very often used by Paul (Rom. v. 18; vii. 3; viii. 12, *etc.* WINER, pp. 414, 519); it is = *hinc ergo* [accordingly then, comp. on Gal. vi. 10.—R.]; ἄρα draws a conclusion from vers. 14-18; οὖν continues the discourse. Οὐκέτι, "no longer," is placed immediately after ἄρα οὖν, for the sake of emphasis.

**Strangers and sojourners,** ξένοι καὶ πάροικοι.—LUTHER's rendering: *Gäste und Freundlinge*, unnecessarily transposes the words. The expression proceeds from the more remote, ξένοι, to the less remote, πάροικοι. The former is the antithesis of ἐπιχώριος, and thus of the following συνπολῖται. So "brethren" are termed (3 John 5*) "strangers;" it is = גֵּר. The latter word, πάροικοι = תּוֹשָׁב, which is often joined with the former (Lev. xxv. 35, 40). Lev. xxii. 10, 11, where the LXX oppose πάροικος ἱερέως and οἰκογενεῖς αὐτου, forbidding the former and permitting the latter to eat of the holy things, seems to have been in the Apostle's mind. Πάροικοι is then here the opposite of οικεῖοι, and means *inquilini* (from *incolo, incolinus*), *qui domicilium in aliquo loco habent sine jure civitatis, hospites in urbe aliqua* (GROTIUS). The frequent figurative descriptions of the kingdom of God as the city or house of God (1 Tim. iii. 15; Gal. iv. 26 and Heb. iii. 6; xii. 22) here evidently pass over into each other (συνπολῖται—οἰκεῖοι); there is not however a union or a mixing of these figures, but the πολιτεία is regarded as a more extended household. It inheres in the matter itself, that the citizens of the kingdom of God, have now filial and household privileges with Him, His whole people become themselves the holy house, the temple in which His Spirit dwells (HARLESS, STIER). The figure of the house and building predominates (vers. 20-22). We should not think of proselytes (STIER), nor take ξένοι καὶ πάροικοι as the antithesis to συνπολῖται τῶν ἁγίων, which is enhanced in meaning by οἰκεῖοι τοῦ θεοῦ (MEYER). [The plausible parallelism of HARLESS and BENGEL, adopted by Braune, is doubted by ALFORD and ELLICOTT, but accepted by EADIE.—R.]

**But ye are.**—The repetition of ἐστέ, in accordance with the best authorities (see *Textual Note* 9), is emphatic, like Rom. viii. 15; 1 Cor. ii. 6, 7; Heb. xii. 18, 22.

**Fellow-citizens with the saints** [συνπολῖται* τῶν ἁγίων].—Among "the saints" we can include only those who have been thus termed from the beginning of the Epistle, Christians. BENGEL (*Israëlis cfr.* iii. 18), STIER, BLEEK, and others, have taken occasion from ver. 12 to refer it to the spiritual Israel; but this word being without closer qualification scarcely admits of this. RUECKERT understands the Jewish Christians alone under the term. Still less are we to think of the patriarchs (CHRYSOSTOM), or the angels (CALVIN, and others), or to include them here. Still the notion should be extended as it has been by ZANCHIUS: *omnium vere sanctorum, qui unquam fuerunt futurive sunt.* [So EADIE. ALFORD: "Not *angels*, nor *Jews*, nor *Christians then alive* merely, but the saints of God in the widest sense, all the members of the mystical body of Christ, the commonwealth of the spiritual Israel." ELLICOTT: "The members of that spiritual community in which Jew and Gentile Christians were now united and incorporated, and to which the external theocracy formed a typical and preparatory institution." This view, which is that of MEYER, HODGE and many others, is preferable, notwithstanding the objection of Braune, since ver. 13 could not fail to remain in the Apostle's mind.—R.]

**And of the household of God,** οἰκεῖοι τοῦ θεοῦ.—This means those who belong to the house, to the family, whose Head and Father is God. To the right of citizen is added that of the house, of the child, of the heir, ye are not merely menials, servants, but members of the family, children. They have a relation of fellowship not merely to "the saints," but to "God" also. Οἰκεῖος by itself would mean only *domesticus*, one who dwelt in the same house, as 1 Tim. v. 8, and as οἰκιακός, Matt. x. 36, so that it would remain undecided in what precise relation he stood. The genitive τοῦ θεοῦ, "of God," in accordance with συνπολῖται τῶν ἁγίων, obliges us to apply it to the most intimate relation, that of a child. It is incorrect to understand, according to Gal. vi. 10: οἰκείους τῆς πίστεως, *religionis socii* (WINER, who compares οἰκεῖοι φιλοσοφίας, *philosophiæ addicti*), here *familiares*,

* [The E. V. makes an antithesis in this passage which the original does not at all warrant; "to brethren, and that strangers," is the literal rendering.—R.]

* [The word would ordinarily be spelled συμπολῖται, but ℵ. A. B.[1] C. D. E. F. G. support συνπολῖται, which is adopted by Tischendorf and most later editors and commentators (MEYER studiously retains the other orthography).—The word belongs to later Greek, and is considered rather inelegant. ALFORD says the compound verb is found in the purest Attic writers, and the noun in Euripides, *Herac.* 826. Certainly the compound is necessary to express the Apostle's meaning, even though it belong in itself to the *fatiscens Græcitas.*—R.]

intimate friends (THEODORET: προσοικειωθέντες, relatives); quite as little should we take the family here as the stones of the house in which God dwells (HARLESS), even though the next verse passes to that figure.

Ver. 20. **Built up upon the foundation,** ἐποικοδομηθέντες ἐπὶ τῷ θεμελίῳ.—The participle characterizes the οἰκεῖοι as members, who are themselves first wrought, and inserted in the whole as "living stones" (1 Pet. ii. 5), and that too upon the foundation which is laid. *Vulgate* and BENGEL: *superædificate*. [We have the noun *super-structure*, but not a corresponding verb. The phrase "built up" is the nearest equivalent. "Having been built up" has perhaps too strict a reference to the past act.—R.] The aorist denotes the act of *being* built upon, and the context refers only to what has already been attained, not to the further building, which is emphasized in 1 Cor. iii. 10, but first mentioned here in ver. 22. Hence we have here ἐπὶ τῷ θεμελίῳ, not: ἐπὶ τὸν θεμέλιον (Rom. xv. 20), nor yet: ἐπὶ τοῦ θεμελίου (= from the foundation, over the foundation; see WINER, p. 350), which would point to the further building. The dative here is not then "accidental" (MEYER). [ELLICOTT remarks on the assertion of Meyer, that the dative of rest, instead of the genitive of rest, is accidental: 'the former denotes absolute and less separable, the latter partial and more separable super-position." The apparent exception (i. 10: ἐπὶ τοῖς οὐρανοῖς) is a reading of doubtful authority.—R.]

There is here no leap from one figure (that of the family) to another (that of a building); it is only on the other side of the same figure, which has in the temple its deeper or higher unity. Comp. Numb. xii. 7; Heb. iii. 2-6; 1 Tim. iii. 15; 2 Tim. ii. 19-21: 1 Cor. iii. 9, 10; Col. ii. 7; Jude 20; Acts xx. 32. [If there be a transition it is quite easy and natural, "the employment of a term in a double meaning. 'House' has a similar twofold signification with us, as the 'house of Bourbon," or 'house of Stuart,'—phrases in which the word is employed in a secondary and emphatic signification. We speak too of such houses being 'built up' by the wisdom or valor of their founders. In such cases, as Alford says, there is a transition from a political and social to a material image" (EADIE).—R.] Whether θεμέλιος is masculine, as in 1 Cor. iii. 10, 11, 12; 2 Tim. ii. 19; Heb. xi. 10; Acts xxi. 14, 19, or neuter, as in Acts xvi. 26, can be determined as little from the text as Rom. xv. 20; 1 Tim. vi. 19; nor can it be decided on the ground that the neuter is used only metaphorically, which would be inadmissible here (HARLESS), but rather from the fact that the masculine seems to be the prevalent usage with Paul.

**Of the apostles and prophets,** τῶν ἀποστόλων καὶ προφητῶν.—These genitives set forth who has laid the foundation; 1 Cor. iii. 10: θεμέλιον ἔθηκα; Rom. xv. 20: ἐπ' ἀλλότριον θεμέλιον οἰκοδομῶ. For: *testimonium apostolorum et prophetarum substrictum est fidei credentium omnium; per illos jactum est fundamentum* (BENGEL). Comp. iii. 5, 6, 7. It is not then a genitive of apposition, which would designate the Apostles and Prophets as the foundation (CHRYSOSTOM, A-LAPIDE, ESTIUS, [BAUMGARTEN-CRUSIUS, OLSHAUSEN, DE WETTE, HODGE], and others), for Christ is not *primus inter pares* (1 Cor. i. 12, 13; iii. 11) and Rev. xxi. 14 is a vision, in which the name of Christ is not mentioned, and the names of the Apostles are only inscribed on the foundations. Nor is it a possessive genitive (ANSELM, BEZA, [BUCER, COCCEIUS, ALFORD], and others), for Christ can at least not be the foundation, where He is represented as the corner-stone.

[This view may be now considered the usual one. It is adopted by BULLINGER, CALVIN, CALIXTUS, GROTIUS, BENGEL, KOPPE, FLATT, RUECKERT, HARLESS, HOLZHAUSEN, BLEEK, MEYER, EADIE, ELLICOTT, SCHENKEL. This takes the genitive as that of "originating cause." The only possible objection to it is that urged by ALFORD against the introduction of those who form parts of the building as agents; but on this very foundation they rested even if they laid it. To take the genitive as *appositional* is grammatical enough, and does not necessarily involve doctrinal difficulties, while it avoids confusing the foundation and the corner-stone, as the possessive sense does; but the whole analogy of Scripture figures seems to be against it. The simplest, least embarrassed view is then: "The doctrine of the Apostles, *i. e.* Christ *preached*, is the θεμέλιος; Christ *personal* the ἀκρογωνιαῖος; Christ mystical the πλήρωμα" (ELLICOTT). This view elevates evangelical preaching, while it sends us back of councils and creeds to Christ for our doctrine.—R.]

The context, which admits only of the preaching of the Christ already come, the order of the words and the omission of the article before προφητῶν, thus denoting a single category, compel us to think chiefly of the Apostles alone (HARLESS, STIER, HOFMANN, II. 2, p. 103),—who are prophets also (iii. 11): the first term referring more to their personal testimony respecting what they have seen and heard, the latter more to the testimony communicated through the Spirit,—and not to the Old Testament prophets (GREEK FATHERS, JEROME, ERASMUS, CALVIN, CALOVIUS, RUECKERT, [BARNES], and others), or to the New Testament prophets, subordinate to the Apostles (PELAGIUS, BENGEL: *qui apostolis sunt proximi*, KOPPE, MEYER, SCHENKEL, BLEEK). [The reasons for a reference to New Testament prophets seem far more decisive than those which support the identity of Apostles and prophets in this passage. The absence of the article is not conclusive. So EADIE, HODGE, ALFORD, ELLICOTT. The reference to the Old Testament prophets is untenable; comp. EADIE and ALFORD *in loco*.—R.] Of Montanism with its continuation of the Apostolate by means of prophets, ZELLER and his teacher BAUR alone can think. On the significance of the view here set forth, see *Doctr. Note* 6.

**Christ Jesus himself being the chief corner-stone** [ὄντος ἀκρογωνιαίου αὐτοῦ Χριστοῦ Ἰησοῦ. See *Textual* Note [10]].—*Participium* ὄντος *initio commatis hujus, valde demonstrat in præsenti tempore* (BENGEL), and marks the *being so*. Ἀκρογωνιαίου, to which some codices add λίθου, occurs only here and 1 Pet.

ii. 6: λίθον ἀκρογωνιαῖον, from Isa. xxviii. 16; comp. Matt. xxi. 42: λίθος—ἐγενήθη εἰς κεφαλὴν γωνίας. *Lapis angularis, ut duos parietes ipse medius contineret* (JEROME) καὶ τοὺς τοίχους συνέχει καὶ τοὺς θεμελίους (CHRYSOSTOM), is the stone, which upholds the connection of the single ones with the whole, gives support to the whole edifice, is the most important stone, designating here the importance and indispensableness of Christ above the Apostles, just as in 1 Cor. iii. 11 Christ is termed the foundation, and the Apostles those who have in preaching laid this foundation and built others upon it. The foundation on which the Ephesians have been built is the preaching of the Apostles, but Christ is the corner-stone, who gives support to the whole and to the parts, Christ Himself, the living historical Christ. It must not be supposed that the Apostles personally are a foundation; they themselves need the corner-stone and are also built upon it. The various readings (see *Textual Note* [10]) do not alter the sense, only αὐτοῦ marks somewhat more strongly the Person of Christ, and τοῦ in ℵ., or Ἰησοῦ in the others the historical Christ. Αὐτοῦ is not to be referred to θεμελίῳ (BENGEL and others). The article is naturally wanting after αὐτοῦ, since no reference to what precedes is intended; the "corner-stone" is not for the "foundation;" that would be the support of the foundation; the support of the edifice is spoken of. A reference to the union of Jewish and Gentile Christians (THEODORET, ESTIUS and others) is too remote according to the context, ver. 19: "ye no longer are."

Ver. 21. **In whom,** ἐν ᾧ.—This is to be referred then to the Person of Christ, not to "corner-stone" (ESTIUS, KOPPE and others), or "foundation" (HOLZHAUSEN), ἐφ' ᾧ or ἐφ' οὗ the building might be raised. It is not then: above which (BEZA: *Super*), nor: on which (LUTHER), nor yet: through whom (FLATT: *per*), but like i. 10: ἐν τῷ Χριστῷ, who is the point of union and support of the framing together and growing, without which the building falls, dissolves, and does not grow (RUECKERT, HARLESS, STIER), [ALFORD, HODGE, EADIE and most.—R.]

**All the building,** πᾶσα οἰκοδομή.—Although πᾶσα ἡ οἰκοδομή is the least sustained reading, and the article should be rejected, and the use of πᾶς with and without the article according to Rom. iii. 9 (πᾶν στόμα—πᾶς ὁ κόσμος) is such that the former would mean; the *whole* building and the latter: *every* building, yet here we must in accordance with the context interpret: the *whole* building, as πᾶς οἶκος Ἰσραηλ (Acts ii. 36), which however can be regarded as a proper name not requiring the article see WINER, p. 106. ŒKUMENIUS reads πᾶσα οἰκοδομή and explains: ἡ καθόλου ἐκκλησια. IGNATIUS uses πᾶσα ἐπιστολή, πᾶσα ἐκκλησία in the sense of the whole letter, the whole church. The later Greek usage justifies this explanation and the omission of the article.

[Those commentators who are unwilling to accept the poorly supported reading of the *Rec.*, as a rule take refuge from the incongruous interpretation: every building, which usage favors, in some such explanation as Braune gives. MEYER, whose grammatical accuracy rarely leads him astray, in this case insists on a strict interpretation. ALFORD: "Are we then to render ungrammatically, and force words to that which they cannot mean? Certainly not"—"the account to be given of such later usages is, that gradually other words besides proper names became regarded as able to dispense with the article after πᾶς, so that as they said first πᾶσα Ἱεροσόλυμα (Matth. ii. 23), and then πᾶς οἶκος Ἰσραήλ (Acts ii. 36), so they came at length to say πᾶσα κτίσις (as we ourselves, 'all creation' for 'all *the* creation') and πᾶσα οἰκοδομή, when speaking of one universal and notorious building." ELLICOTT accepts this view, but doubts the existence of another distinct instance in the New Testament. EADIE thinks the passages cited above and Luke iv. 13; Acts vii. 22; Col. i. 15, at least show a transition to a larger usage. MEYER's grammatical haste leads him into an unwarranted exegesis, for what warrant is there for calling separate congregations οἰκοδομη.—R.]

Οἰκοδομή is like 1 Cor. iii. 9, *building*, the edifice in the process of erection, which grows into a temple, especially as ver. 22: συνοικοδομεῖσθε εἰς κατοικητήριον, marks decidedly the process, requiring the substantive idea of this verse to be that of a building going up. [Hence our word is chosen, not οἶκος.—R.] Our verse then contains an entirely general thought, which ver. 22 applies to the Ephesian church, in the figure of a temple, of the Church as one whole on one foundation; the view that every Christian is a temple of the Holy Ghost (2 Cor. vi. 16), and every congregation also such an one, being quite remote. Hence it does not mean: *every* building (MEYER), nor "every part of the building," walls, roof, *etc.* (CHRYSOSTOM), since it is not these parts, but the building as a whole that grows into a temple. [Comp. however EADIE *in loco*.—R.]

**Fitly framed together is growing** [συναρμολογουμένη αὔξει].—The present αὔξει, instead of αὐξάνεται, like αὔξῃ (Col. ii. 19), is rare but classical, denoting together with the present participle the process, which the Apostle considers merely as a spectator; the participle sets forth the form of the growth. Συναρμολογεῖν from ἁρμός, groove, joint, member (*armus, artus*), as Heb. iv. 12, occurs only here and in iv. 16, and according to this and the parallel passage Col. ii. 19 is = framed together, incorporated together. The figure is derived from the organism of the body.—Αὐξάνειν (sometimes transitive = *augere*, as in 1 Cor. iii. 6, 7; 2 Cor. ix. 10, but usually intransitive) is used most exactly of plants (Matth. vi. 28; xiii. 32), but of men also (Luke i. 80; ii. 40; 1 Pet. ii. 2), of a nation (Acts vii. 17), of the word of God (Acts vi. 7; xix. 20), of faith (2 Cor. x. 15), of growth in grace (2 Pet. iii. 18; comp. Col. i. 10); John the Baptist uses it in a purely external sense of Christ (Jno. iii. 30: δεῖ αὐξάνειν). The growth is not then merely an outward extension, but respects the number of the called and their progress toward perfection (NITZSCH). Hence GROTIUS is incorrect: *quorum jam mœnia surgunt;* the citizens themselves are largely involved. BENGEL: *crescit coagmentata, Vulgate: constructa,* but these renderings are insufficient.

[ALFORD: "Both participle and verb imply

that the fitting together and the growing are still going on: and the only way which we in English have to mark this so as to avoid the chance of mistake, is by the auxiliary verb substantive, and the participle. The bare present, 'growth,' is in danger of being mistaken for the abstract quality, and the temporal development is thus lost sight of: whereas the other, in giving prominence to that temporal development, also necessarily implies the 'normal, perpetual unconditioned nature of the organic increase' (ELLICOTT)."—R.]

**Unto a holy temple,** εἰς ναὸν ἅγιον.—The goal of the growth is set forth in the figure of the temple in Zion. It is mere playing with the text to refer it to the temple of Diana, which *cedere debet* (BENGEL) to this. [MEYER remarks: "This is not to be translated: unto *a* holy temple; for the notion of *several* temples was foreign to the Apostle in consequence of the Jewish national peculiarity, but: unto *the* holy temple, which does not require the article." This accords with the extensive reference advocated above.—R.]

**In the Lord,** ἐν κυρίῳ.—This phrase is to be joined with "holy," characterizing the sacredness of their temple as inward, vital, proceeding from, effected and nourished by Him.—[So HARLESS, USTERI, DE WETTE, HOFMANN, BLEEK.—R.] Unquestionably Christ is meant, as the Apostolic *usus loquendi* (WINER, p. 118) and the context which refers back to ἐν ᾧ, demand; He is the Mediator, in whom the members become οἰκεῖοι τοῦ θεοῦ. Hence ἐν κυρίῳ is not to be taken as the simple dative (BEZA, KOPPE [MACKNIGHT] and others), or joined with ναόν = κυρίου, *i. e., Dei* (BENGEL). Others rightly refer it to Christ, but incorrectly join it with ναὸν ἅγιον as one notion (STIER), or with αὔξει (MEYER), in spite of ἐν ᾧ. [The construction last named is rendered still more objectionable by taking ἐν = "through" (GROTIUS, WOLF, and SCHENKEL, who has a fondness for this instrumental sense of the proposition). HODGE suggests the same view, but prefers that of MEYER, which is tautological. ELLICOTT objects to the connection with ἅγιον, that it "gives perhaps a greater prominence to the special nature of the holiness than the context requires" He therefore prefers the view of STIER, taking the phrase as a kind of tertiary predicate, almost = "and it is a holy temple in the Lord, and in Him alone." ALFORD thinks this more in accordance with the Apostle's style, and it is favored by ἐν πνεύματι, ver. 22. So EADIE.—R.]

Ver. 22. **In whom ye also** [ἐν ᾧ καὶ ὑμεῖς].—*Per anaphoram iteratur* ἐν ᾧ (BENGEL), which is to be joined to "Christ Jesus Himself," as i. 13. It is not to be connected with κυρίῳ (HARLESS, MEYER, SCHENKEL) because the whole clause is parallel to the preceding one; still less however to "holy temple" (CALIXTUS, MATTHIES [EADIE] and others), since they are not built in a temple for a habitation. "Ye also" places the readers as being Christians, without any reference to their coming out of heathenism, as BAUMGARTEN-CRUSIUS and BLEEK suppose, in connection with the whole ("the whole building"). This is in accordance with the parallelism of the application in ver. 22, which is not tautological, but marks a dialectic advance. [Most commentators take "in the Lord" as the antecedent of the relative. "You also," not "even you," "καί with its ascensive and slightly contrasting force marking the exalted nature of the association in which the Ephesians shared" (ELLICOTT).—R.]

**Are being builded together,** συνοικοδομεῖσθε.—This is indicative, not imperative (CALVIN and others), according to the context, which says what the readers, and the church in general, *are*, not what they *ought to be*. The preposition συν, as in συναρμολογουμένη, makes the connection with each other and with the whole; hence not merely with each other (MEYER), nor only with "the whole building" (HARLESS). The verb points to internal edification more strongly than αὔξει, denotes the process of becoming built, *magis magisque coaptari* (BUCER); hence with LUTHER we should retain: *miterbaut* WERDET, not *seid* (PASSAVANT). ["Are being builded together" is the nearest English equivalent. The preposition refers to the close and compact union of the component parts of the building (ELLICOTT).—R.]

**For an habitation of God,** εἰς κατοικητήριον τοῦ θεοῦ.—This sets forth the goal, as in ver. 21. The word here chosen in the stead of ναόν occurs only here and in Rev. xviii. 2, marking the place of dwelling (LUTHER: *Behausung*), while ναόν marks the place of worship. In this there is implied a significant advance, which explains the idea of the church. Comp. *Doct. Note* 5. The genitive τοῦ θεοῦ designates the Master of the house, who goes in and out, doing, regulating, taking care of everything, even to the smallest and most external matters. Hence this is not the same idea as in the previous verse with only a change of expression (MEYER, SCHENKEL), though it is not to be referred to *individual* Christians (HARLESS) and quite as little to be taken as dependent on αὔξει, ἐν ᾧ καὶ ὑμεῖς συνοικοδομεῖσθε being regarded as a parenthesis (GRIESBACH, KNAPP), so that the sense would be: that a dwelling of God might arise (KOPPE, RUECKERT).

**In the Spirit,** ἐν πνεύματι.—This, being parallel to "in the Lord," which qualifies "holy," defines more closely the phrase, "of God," His relation to the "habitation": It is God, who dwells in you, in His church, in the Spirit as the element of His presence, hence in the Holy Spirit. The comparison with χαρὰ ἐν πνεύματι ἁγίῳ (Rom. xiv. 17), ἀγάπη ἐν πνεύματι (Col. i. 8) should not be so decidedly rejected as inappropriate by MEYER, as though this were possible only with abstract terms. Eph. iv. 1: δέσμιος ἐν Χριστῷ or κυρίῳ, 1 Thess. iv. 16: νεκροὶ ἐν Χριστῷ are by no means abstract. Comp. on the idea of this verse, 1 Cor. iii. 16: ναὸς θεοῦ ἐστὲ καὶ τὸ πνεῦμα θεοῦ οἰκεῖ ἐν ὑμῖν; 2 Cor. vi. 16; Rom. viii. 11. As the Church is a temple, which is holy not merely outwardly, but "in the Lord," so it is also a dwelling of God, where He does not dwell as the Shekinah in the temple, but in the Spirit, in His, the Holy Spirit, who is the Regent in this edifice, as He is efficient in its growth and occupation. So RIEGER, HARLESS, STIER. It is not then = πνευματικόν (*Greek Fathers*, RUECKERT and others), in accordance with 1 Pet. ii. 5: *οἶκος πνευματικός*; nor is *ἐν* = *διά* (THEOPHYLACT [E. V.] and others), nor is the connection with the verb admissible: by virtue of, by means of the Holy Ghost ye are built together (MEYER, SCHENKEL, BLEEK). [HODGE also prefers this view, which disturbs the parallelism, giving the phrase an unwarranted emphasis. The view of RUECKERT is against the whole sense of the passage (ALFORD). Against MEYER'S objection to the interpretation of Braune, see ELLICOTT *in loco*. Comp. EADIE, and *Galatians*, v. 5, against the distinction of HARLESS respecting the use of the article with *πνεῦμα*. The reference to the Holy Spirit is undoubtedly the correct one and thus the verse brings the Trinity into view.—R.]

### DOCTRINAL AND ETHICAL.

1. *The Trinity*. Ver. 18 points to the Trinity: To the Father through Christ in the Spirit. But the allusion in ver. 22 is more obscure. [Yet ALFORD correctly says of the latter part of this section: "Thus we have the true temple of the Father, built in the Son, inhabited in the Spirit; the offices of the three blessed Persons being distinctly pointed out; God THE FATHER, in all His fulness, dwells in, fills the church: that church is constituted an holy temple to Him in THE SON, —is inhabited by Him in the ever-present indwelling of the HOLY SPIRIT."—R.]

2. *The* ANTHROPOLOGY of this section.

a. *Heathenism in distinction from Judaism*. The *heathen* are termed those "*afar off*," the *Jews* those "*nigh*." The latter had the theocracy and a covenant of God with them, repeated in many ways, and containing a glorious promise; the former were without hope and without God. For neither in the idol deities of the people, nor in the fancied deities of the philosophers and the educated, did they have the living God; neither nature (Rom. i. 19, 20; Acts xiv. 17; xvii. 27), nor conscience could reveal to them the mercy, and the holy and sanctifying love of God, as this had become evident to the Jews in theocratic training and guidance. The heathen with their *natural* gifts wallowed ever more deeply in the creature, the Jews with their *gracious* gifts relied more and more on God's election, proudly exalting themselves, as did the former. Such distinctions, defining the relation of God to the nations and of the nations to God, define at the same time differences in the moral conduct of the Gentiles and the Jews. The former, left to themselves, did not see the arm of God shown to be so strong in nature, or the finger of God warning in the conscience, but fell into the mire, into the starless night of vile immorality; heathenism becomes ever worse and worse (Rom. i. 18–32); modern heathenism, which not only struggles to be free from the arm of God's power, but tears itself away from the heart of God with its thoughts of peace, is even more loathsome. Judaism falls away into externality ("the so-called circumcision in the flesh," ver. 11; Rom. ii. 14-29) throwing the *theocratic* feature into the background and out of practice, but giving prominence and power to the *national* element; modern Judaism has lapsed into the most frivolous emptiness.

b. *Heathenism* and *Judaism are alike* in this, that external position, neither in *natural* endowments nor in the gifts of revelation, decides as to the *personal* state of salvation. Whether one is a "stranger," as a heathen, or a "sojourner" as a Jew, amounts to nothing; he ought and must still be and become "of the household of God." Let him who enjoys the gifts of grace, think rather how to use them, to make them efficient in himself, than in false delight to despise others who lack them. In natural endowments there are indeed ways and means to the knowledge of God, which He can carry further unto eternal salvation, through Christ in the Holy Ghost however. We may not with philosophers, such as Hegel, place upon an equal footing the Jews with their theocracy, or the mission of preserving salvation, and the heathen, with their *cosmocracy*, or *anthropocracy*, the mission of moulding in its naturalness the subject attaining salvation, and regard both as united in the Theanthropos Christ, thinking then that they shall all become Christ's, God-men, instead of new men, God's men. Still less should we with Abelard, Zwingli and others, make exceptions arbitrarily, placing Socrates, Plato, Cicero and others, among the patriarchs and prophets, Apostles and believers, in heaven, as though we could act as judges in such a matter. Here it is best to keep within bounds, as did Paul, who sticks to what is evident, making no final judgment respecting individuals and their personal state of safety, nor overlooking the distinctions in what is similar.

c. *The continued validity* of these two forms. This antithesis is perceptible, not merely before Christ, but also in the Church which He established. They are not forms historically concluded, but active categories of human error, showing themselves constantly anew. Man suffers from a defect, though in the rich possession and masterly use of the most important natural endowments, if he is estranged from his Creator, and even in the possession, use and enjoyment of noble gifts of grace, if he has not attained to personal fellowship of life and heart with the Giver. Such a defect does not remain quiescent, but impels to restless opposition and enmity towards God and Man. The onesidedness urges ever deeper into discord, as the abuse of the gifts of nature or of grace is changed into the destruction of the same, coming home upon him who has enjoyed them.

d. *Natural and gracious endowments* do not *exclude* each other. The latter direct, purify, elevate the former, making them more productive. Human nature loses nothing, but gains much by means of the latter, if they are but rightly used: the Divine in the human, the Divinity in humanity is thus nurtured. It is thus that the state of things will be brought about when neither the individual, nor nations as a whole, will stand in hostile antagonism to one another, but will complement each other in peaceful contact, furthering each other's interests through the fulfilment of their calling in life or history, of their ministry with the gifts entrusted to them.

3. CHRISTOLOGY.

a. *Without Christ* the distance from God in the case of the Gentiles is not overcome, nor does the nearness to God in the case of the Jews become fellowship with God. Without Him a man or a people is either "stranger" or "sojourner," and the advance from "stranger" to "of the household of God" is not through the "sojourner." As little as sonship of itself develops itself from slavery, so little avail circumcision, Mosaic law, theocracy, promise; only creative renewal (ver. 15) is of avail among Jews as well as Gentiles, and this is accomplished only through Him and in Him.

*b. He is our Peace*, He, in His Person; and this peace is here defined by its antithesis, "enmity" (ver. 15), by the hostility of Gentiles and Jews (ver. 11), by the estrangement of the Gentiles from God and His law, as well as the distance and separation from God the Father (vers. 12, 18) and the externality of the Jews (ver. 11)—as concord, as unity concluded and secured in agreement, in friendly intercourse. This peace is not a sensation, but a possession. HOFMANN (*Schriftbeweis*, II. 1, pp. 374) refers to the etymology, deriving the word from εἰρη and ἰρις, the circle, the place of assembly, or it may be traced to εἴρω, to speak, quiet, friendly, independent intercourse in speech. STIER (*Reden Jesu*, V., p. 224 on Jno. xiv. 27) compares it with שָׁלוֹם, and reaches thus the notion of prosperity, welfare. In this concord with its intercourse is found welfare, complete and symmetrical development. Hence the possession of this peace is at the same time a *status*. The first and main thing is peace with God; on this is based and depends necessarily the peace with our neighbor. Where the latter appears, the former is certainly efficient; hence Paul can here give special prominence to it in accordance with the context. He who has Christ, can speak of *His* peace (Jno. xiv. 27), has peace.*

*c. The work of Christ culminates in the death of the cross* (ver. 13: "made nigh in the blood of Christ;" ver. 16: "might reconcile them both to God through the cross"), having for its end the *reconciliation* with God and among each other (ver. 14: "who made both one;" ver. 16: "having slain the enmity;" ver. 17: "came and preached peace:" ver. 18; "we both have our access in one Spirit unto the Father"), comp. Col. i. 20-22; Rom. v. 10; 2 Cor. v. 18-20. Enmity is to be overcome only on the side of man, on the part of God "wrath" (ii. 3). We have only the popular expression: ἱλάσθητί μοι (Luke xviii. 13) and 2 Macc. i. 5; vii. 33: viii. 29: καταλλάσσεσθαι ὑμῖν.—*Non Deus inimicus erat hominibus, sed homines inimici erant Deo. Non cœpit homines amare, qui cum eo reconciliati essent, sed quia ab æterno homines amavit, idcirco decrevit homines sibi inimicos per Christiani secum reconciliare. Reconciliatio, morte Christi effecta, non est duplex seu mutua, sed simplex, h. e., Christus morte sua non Deum, hominum amantissimum, cum hominibus, sed homines, Deo inimicos, cum Deo reconciliavit* (WEBER). The enmity against God was extirpated by, through and in Christ; the attracting power of His Person, especially of His cross is so great, that man is won by Him for God. Thus the Father of Christ becomes the Father of men and the contending nations and creatures become peaceful children in one church and one Spirit. This is the reconciliation. It rests upon the *propitiation*, removing the wrath of God, which is however only the energy of His holy love for sinners against sin. But this is not treated of in this section. By this reconciliation of men resting on the atonement their relation not merely to *God* but also to the *law* is changed. In that He fulfilled the law in deed and in truth, performed God's will and suffered in obedience, He rendered it powerless in its single ordinances, dissolving its separative features; it thus gained through Him internal validity and importance, so that it no longer burdens men, but they stand and walk in and on the same as a common soil within salutary bounds. Here too all depends on His Person and our relation to Him (ver. 15: "in His flesh;" ver. 16: "in Him;" ver. 18: "through Him;" ver. 21: "in whom"—"in the Lord"); in Him and through Him that takes place which ought to take place both for us and in us. *Ipsa natura suscipienda erat, quæ liberanda* (AUGUSTINE). *Neque Christo imputari potuissent peccata nostra, nisi tum naturæ ejusdem vinculo tum voluntaria sponsione nobiscum unitus esset, neque justitia Christi nobis imputaretur; nisi in unum cum Ipso corpus coaluissemus* (TURRETINE).—He guards against that humanitarianism, which is only the glory of the flesh, as well as against a godless cosmopolitism ["without God, in the world"]; He creates new, real men, who as the children become the possessors and rulers of the world.

4. *The law* here is the Mosaic law. This follows from the description: τῶν ἐντολῶν ἐν δόγμασιν (ver. 15), from the figure: τὸ μεσότοιχον τοῦ φραγμοῦ (ver. 14), and also from the statement that Christ has abolished this "in His flesh;" for it was precisely to this law that He was subject in the flesh; this was the "hedge" of the vineyard of God, the people of Israel; it was this which split the will of God into ordinances difficult to be grasped, and multiplied by casuistry most enormously. But here where the subject is not merely the enmity of the Jews against the Gentiles and against God, an enmity denoted by and connected with the law, but quite as much the enmity of the Gentiles against the Jews and against God, this too being joined with the law, we must admit a secondary reference to the law in the conscience. Rom. ii. 14, 15 permits such a reference, the connection requires it and the nature of the case explains it: the *bad* conscience is the still active conscience, so far as it is still *good.* The bad conscience is the justly judging conscience, is enmity, not as it should be with sin and the sinful subject, but with God, before whom it puts to shame, with our neighbor, from whom it divides us; the sinner against the law excuses himself and accuses God and men, by always finding the circumstances, relations, surroundings more to blame than himself. The voices of a bad conscience became for the heathen Furies, but not so easily Eumenides.

* [There is little necessity for seeking to sunder the two ideas, peace with God, peace among men, in this paragraph, since the complex notion alone meets the requirements of a fair exegesis. The doctrine to be deduced is one eminently Biblical: Right relations to God are the basis of right relations with man; the former involve the latter of necessity, while the latter constitute the evidence and indicator of the former. The complex notion of peace becomes a simple one, when thus regarded as simple because "He is our peace."—R.]

*Nitimur in vetitum.* He too, who holds to the law and to conscience, is an object of enmity for the frivolous world; where the law appears powerful, there is in the world discord, opposition—within the heart, in individuals and in the whole, and externally also. Thus enmity toward God and men clings to the law. We do not wish to have the will of God about us, above us, before us, and to know and feel ourselves under the law with its single decrees; it is impossible for us to have the law in us and peace at the same time, unless we have God Himself. Only fellowship of life with God in Christ removes the enmity which attaches to the law, as it appears in its commandments and ordinances over against the natural man.

5. *The church* is essentially a *fellowship*, closely united and *organic*. Her *support* is in Christ, her *beginning* in the pure and powerful Word of God, in His Apostles and prophets, her *design* respects every man and every nation, her *task* is not merely the worship of God, but abiding fellowship with God, and accordingly each individual must be prepared in the work of the Holy Ghost, freed from his singularity and framed into the whole (vers. 19-22). She is "the assured residence and abiding working-place" of God, from which He will and does work further into His world. In the world He indeed already has His real, immanent, continued presence, but in the church He is present in an extraordinary manner; she is His palace, His immediate surroundings, His family, while the world is His broad kingdom on which He operates from this, and which is subservient to it. Certain as the permanence of the church is, she is still in process of growth; not yet complete. But she is real, not merely ideal.

6. *The Holy Scriptures* are referred to in the expression: "the foundation of the Apostles and prophets" (ver. 20). There is here evidently a reminiscence of the words of Christ (Matt. xvi. 18: "Thou art Peter," *etc.*), in which He promises to build His church, not upon the person of Peter, but upon Peter's confession of the Person of Christ. The foundation of the church, the beginning of this building is not the persons of the Apostles, but their witness of Him, the preaching of the Apostles. *Scripture* is not the producer, but the product, not before the church, but within and for her. The *word of God* springing up in the Apostles, as prophets of God, as men to whom revelation was imparted by the Holy Ghost, and *preached* by them, is the *foundation*, but what is given in fixed form in the Scriptures is the *norm* for the church. She has her *support* and deepest ground in Christ, her beginning in the preaching of the Apostles, but her rule in the standard of truth contained in the Apostolic and prophetical Scriptures, the sufficiency of which is such, that no tradition is needed in addition. ["And no other foundation can suffice. When philosophical speculation or critical erudition, political affinity or human enactment supplants it, the structure topples and is about to fall. The opinions of Luther, Calvin, Cranmer, Wesley, Knox, or Erskine (and these were all "pillars"), are not the foundation; nor are the edicts and creeds of Trent, Augsburg, Dort, or Westminster. Such writings may originate sectional distinctions, and give peculiar shape to column or portico, shaft or capital, on the great edifice, but they can never be substituted for the one foundation" (EADIE).—R.]

### HOMILETICAL AND PRACTICAL.

Ponder this: What thou wast and wouldst have been without Him? what thou wast and hast become through Him? what thou wast and shouldst and shalt become, if thou abide with Him?—God is near thee, nearest of all, yet hast thou at first not noticed or known this at all, and still dost thou forget it and fail to feel it; many a one does not learn it and perishes, but he who learns it gains what is most glorious, the everlasting salvation of the soul, God's gifts, God Himself, as joint-heir with Christ. The moon is by no means so valuable to thee as the sun; it is nearer to the earth with its powerful influence notwithstanding its distance, than the near moon with its borrowed light. So is Christ nearer than Luther; He makes for thee spring with fruit abiding eternally.—See now, what it has cost Him, to bring thee near to God, who is so nigh, to win thee for Him! He must die, that thou mightest live in God and God in thee.—Do not deny it, underneath all hast thou enmity to God; in order not to be obliged to acknowledge His wrath, thou feignest friendship and love to Him, and still wilt not allow Him to rule in thee.—The foundation of religion is not a doctrine but a life, not the Apostles' life, but Christ and He alone, in His Person and in His life and death, His work and suffering. He disturbs the peace, the false one, in order to establish one which is real and eternal.

The Church of Christ is God's house and our own home, in which we should be children and become heirs. Here we are not only instructed, as in a school, but educated, in order to go out into the world and do what is good and useful; here not only is religion protected from the world, but we ourselves from irreligion.—In the church each one should feel, that the might of the whole is at his command, to be used for himself, to be efficient in him, quite as much as that he must serve with assiduity the whole; thus he himself will grow and thrive. The temple becomes a home: First worship Him, then live with Him. Is the home but a hovel at first, a hovel is still home. Do not take offence at the outward appearance of the church, but look at the internal loveliness!—Builded together on the one cornerstone, Christ, so that we are changed from servants or slaves into children and heirs. We are to become free! God hates the slavery of the world, or hireling service no less than we do tyranny. See to it that with thy hatred of tyrants and raving about freedom thou dost not still remain a slave.—In the Church of Christ we first really become men, the grace of God in Christ leads us directly to nature and to true humanity.

STARKE:—Where a soul will have hope toward God, it must have a testament or promise of God as its foundation.—Our life must properly be nothing else than a continued going out of ourselves and going to God. The great glory of Christians as citizens of the city of God and members of His household. What was Roman citizenship in comparison? Acts xxii. 28. Thus we are assured of all possessions, liberties, privileges and protection. Ps. lxxxiv. 5.—What glorious and wonderful thing does not attach to the Church of God? Nothing is more majestic, because it is His temple; nothing more worthy of veneration, for He dwells therein; nothing more ancient, for the patriarchs and prophets labored thereon, nothing more solid, for Jesus Christ is its foundation, nothing firmer and stronger, for He is its corner-stone, nothing more exalted, for it reaches into eternity and the bosom of God, nothing more well-ordered and arranged, for the Holy Ghost is the architect; nothing more beautiful and agreeable in its variety, for stones come from all quarters, Jews and Gentiles, from every age, land, race and condition, nothing more roomy, for all the elect and righteous of all generations have a place therein, nothing more sacred, for it is consecrated to the Lord, nothing more divine, for it is a living edifice animated by the Holy Spirit.

Passavant:—God was not far off, but they were far from Him,—with heart and life far from Him in their darkness. How often are we—notwithstanding revelation and the knowledge of the Lord—far from God in our hearts and lives, while we are "in the world!" And that is the beginning and end of all heathenism. We are of a heathen race and always bring again into all our worldly—yes, Christian concerns, undertakings, plans and labors—something, much, that is Pagan.—Instead of making the holy law of their God serve as a sacred and salutary safeguard from the Gentiles, their customs, sins and enormities, the Israelites turned their hearts toward hate and bitter enmity against all the nations about them.—Though both Greek and Roman occupied the most beautiful isles, the loveliest home; yet were they still on an earth foreign to them and not yet confirmed as their property; above them was a heaven, though so glad and beautiful—still—unknown and strange; under them unknown depths and abysses full of night and horror. As really homeless they walked the earth, not knowing whence they were or whither their living and dying would lead them! The holiest and sweetest of the Here and the Hereafter remained closed and strange to them. With all their advantages of form, of culture and customs,—with all the beauty and brilliancy, in which many of them are to-day still patterns for us in earthly things,—they were, over against the Israelites, at most like guests, suffered to remain or kindly received beside the children and members of the household.—Ask thy heart, thou who art called, and mayhap art, a Christian; hast thou really given thyself to thy God? Hast thou transferred every hall, chamber, nook and corner, all the heights and depths of thine inner man to Him for a living, pure, spiritual indwelling? Art thou His temple?—[Christ our peace; 1) In time and in eternity; 2) Before God, in His Judgment; 3) In all sufferings, in all anxieties of life; 4) In need, in death; 5) In God's rest, in His love.—Jesus Christ: 1) The cause, 2) Ground, 3) Strength of all peace.—It is Christ's Cross, that atones for Christians; His blood sanctifies them; His Spirit impels them; His love permeates them; His name unites them in one and the same grace.—R.]—

Rieger:—The wretchedness of Paganism is not represented now-a-days in its full extent.—The matter is now inverted; first the heathen are granted a fortunate fate in eternity, that thus afterwards the difference between nature and grace, faith in the gospel and walking by the feeble light of conscience may be altogether ignored.—The distinction between Jews and Gentiles was brought about by man, but fixed by God Himself, and guarded by the entire ecclesiastical polity of the Jews as by a hedge. Then indeed the human heart took occasion from this for much pride and mutual enmity. This too must then be interrupted and removed by another Divine interposition, which took place in the sending of His Son.—He who thoroughly believes the word of the Apostle, accepting Christ as the Alpha and Omega, the beginning and the end, in the matter of our salvation, is not only in connection with the foundation, but is in love built in with all the living stones beside Him; abides too for the further work of the good Spirit, who is the master-builder of this edifice, but also the future Possessor and Ruler of every well-erected habitation.

Heubner:—Quesnel distinguishes three kinds of looking back at former sins: a longing, faithless one, destructive of grace, a distrustful, disquieting one, hindering the course of grace, a penitent, thankful one, increasing grace.—Without Christ we can be alive in no church; without Him there is no holy kingdom of God on earth. Christ transfers us into the state of the pious, into the congregation of the saints; with Him we are in a state, embracing all true Israelites, in the kingdom of the just and blessed. Heavenly citizenship is a favor from Christ. Without Him man has no part in the covenant of promise, in the covenant with God, which gives salvation. Christianity is the eternal covenant with God. Without Christ we are without hope.—Without Christ we are without God, because the true God has not yet become ours. First with Christ is God rightly known and revealed; we know that He is *our* God, who cares for us sinners and desires our salvation. Outside of Christianity God remains as it were only a general idea.—The Personality of God is illustrated by nothing so well as by the Personality of His Son. Losing Christ is losing God, denying Him leads to Atheism. Who can read this description of the heathen condition without horror? Yet that is the picture of many baptized people; they live without Christ, they have fallen away from Christ and that leads to apostasy from God. An unhappy withdrawing of the heart from God continues, unless we are brought nigh through Christ.

Christ's death is the nations' peace! Who can quarrel and fight with others under the cross of Christ?—The whole of mankind should be one man, one holy body whose Head is Christ. Humanity must be held together by one Head, else unity is impossible. Who is available for this, if God had not given such an one? The highest union of men is that of becoming one in Christ; then they make one family, one household.—Since the establishment of Christianity, God no longer knows any distinction of nations; all have the same access to the Father, because Christianity gives one Spirit to all. That is the business of Christ, the Only-Begotten, to bring the wandering children to the Father, and to reconcile those divided. He is the only and the indispensable Guide. He, who imagines that he will go alone to the Father, will be rejected, because he comes as a self-righteous one. But he, who clings to Christ, will not be rejected.—Men lost through sin the heavenly family-right or the fellowship with angels, through Christ they obtain it again. Without Him eternal banishment were our fate. Now we belong again to the house and family of God.—The Christian Church is the only edifice, that will last. What others, the free-masons for example, boast of as their building amounts to nothing; it will perish.

STIER:—There was a little light even in the midst of heathenish darkness, just as on the other hand *Israel* with all the light of the law and the promise sat for the most part in the shadow of death.—The enmity between Israel and the Gentiles was at bottom only the prominent manifestation of the enmity of the flesh against God's truth and love, against the Spirit already in the law itself. The same hate and antagonism to the Living One manifested itself in the scorn and hatred of Israel on the part of the Gentiles, led to false glorying in their pre-eminence on the part of the Jews. Something analogous continues to exist everywhere, where Christ has not made all new and free.—Christ is humanity, on that account He can represent it.—Let us hold fast to the words of the Apostles and prophets as the foundation of the Church, but recognize the words respecting Christ as the pith and marrow of the teaching.

[EADIE:—Ver. 11. The exercise of memory would deepen their humility, elevate their ideas of Divine grace, and incite them to ardent and continued thankfulness.—Ver. 12. The Jewish nation—had the Messiah—not Jesus indeed—but the Christ in promise. He was the great subject—the one, glowing, pervading promise of their inspired oracles. But the Gentiles were "without Christ."—"The commonwealth of Israel" is that government framed by God, in which religion and polity were so conjoined, that piety and loyalty were synonymous, to fear God and honor the king were the same obligation.—They had hope of nothing a sinner should hope for; their future was a night without a star. They were godless, having no one to cry to, to trust in, to love, praise, and serve. "In the world," dark, hostile and under Satan's dominion.—Ver. 15. Deep hostility lay in their bosoms; the Jew looked down with supercilious contempt upon the Gentile, and the Gentile reciprocated and scowled upon the Jew as a haughty and heathenish bigot.—One *new* man—the Gentile is not elevated to the position of the Jew; but Jew and Gentile together are both raised to a higher platform than the circumcision ever enjoyed. Spiritual blessing in itself, and not merely pictured in type, is possessed by the Jew as well as the Gentile.—Ver. 16. Jesus reconciles us to God by turning away the Divine anger from us. God has shown infinite love to the sinner, and infinite hatred to his sin, in the sufferings of the cross, so that we tremble at His severity, while we are in the arms of His mercy.—Ver. 18. Christians do not approach some dark and spectral phantom, nor a grim and terrible avenger. It is not Jehovah in the awful attitude of Judge and governor, but Jehovah as a Father.—Ver. 20. That man, "Jesus," who was the "Christ," the Divinely appointed, qualified, and accepted Saviour, unites and sustains the Church. Is He not in His truth, His blood, His power, His legislation, and His presence to His Church, Himself "the chief corner-stone?"—Ver. 21. Every stone is in its place, and fits its place. One's ingenuity devises what another's activity works out. As Fergusson says—"By taking bond with Christ the foundation, they are fastened one to another."—Jehovah dwelt in His temple: 1. To instruct His people; 2. To accept the services of His people. God inhabits this spiritual fane for spiritual ends—spiritual sacrifices are still laid on the altar to God.—The Church is one, holy and Divine; it rests on Christ—is possessed by God—filled with the Spirit—and is ever increasing.—R.]

[The so-called Circumcision occasionally finds a parallel in the externalness of a so-called church.—Hand-wrought ordinances are a fruitful source of pride.—In discovering the condition of men out of Christ we must reverse the order of the Apostle: we see that they are "in the world," learn that they are "without God," and despite their stout denials conclude with certainty that they have "no hope."—Near the cross, near each other.—Christ came to destroy the works of the devil; He destroys partition-walls, which we are slow to class with these works. Christ came to abolish Jewish casuistry and hair-splitting distinctions and ordinances, but how much of this remains in His church. Such things have not tended to make peace.—The peace Christ preaches is no armed neutrality. As disbanded armies give laborers for a country's prosperity, so the activities once employed in hostility against God and man, are turned to edification.—*We have* our access, do we really enjoy it?—Let men sneer at the "saints"—it is a term of privilege, not of presumption, implying here the highest citizenship, the most exalted adoption, while in itself it means that God is making us sinful ones holy like Himself, that we may the more enjoy the blessings of His household.—Let us hold to that church, whose foundation and corner-stone are here set forth, and then despite all the mistakes of the past and imperfection of the present, we shall see in her the reality described in the figures of verse 21, and find in our own experience that we, together with this corner-stone, "are being builded together for a habitation in the Spirit."—R.]

### C. The office and service of the church.

CHAP. III. 1–21.

1. *The office in and for this church.*

(CHAP. III. 1–13.)

1 For this cause I Paul, the prisoner of Jesus Christ [Christ Jesus][1] for [in behalf
2 of] you Gentiles, If [indeed] ye have heard of the dispensation of the grace of God
3 which is given me to you-ward: How that [That] by revelation he made known
unto me the mystery [the mystery was made known[2] to me]; ([*omit* parenthesis]
4 as I wrote [have written] afore in few words; Whereby, when ye read, ye may understand my knowledge [In accordance with which, while reading, ye can perceive
5 my understanding][3] in the mystery of Christ,) [*omit*)] Which in other ages [generations][4] was not made known unto [to] the sons of men, as it is [has been][5] now
6 revealed unto [to] his holy apostles and prophets by [in] the Spirit; That the Gentiles should be [are] fellow heirs, and of the same body [fellow members], and partakers [fellow-partakers] of his [the][6] promise in Christ [Christ Jesus][7] by [through]
7 the gospel: Whereof I was made [became][8] a minister, according to the gift of the grace of God given unto [which was given[9] to] me by the effectual working [ac-
8 cording to the working] of his power. Unto me, who am less than the least of all saints, is [was] this grace given, that I should preach among [to preach to][10] the
9 Gentiles the unsearchable riches of Christ; And to make all *men* see what *is* the fellowship [dispensation][11] of the mystery, which from the beginning of the world [*lit.*, from the ages] hath been hid in God, who created all things by Jesus Christ
10 [*omit* by Jesus Christ]:[12] To the intent that now unto the principalities and powers in [the] heavenly *places* might be [made] known by [through] the church the
11 manifold wisdom of God, According to the eternal purpose which he purposed
12 [wrought] in Christ Jesus our Lord: In whom we have [our] boldness and [our][13]
13 access with [in] confidence by the faith of [through our faith on][14] him. Wherefore I desire that ye faint not [I beseech *you* not to faint][15] at my tribulations for you, which is [are] your glory.

#### TEXTUAL AND GRAMMATICAL.

[1] Ver. 1.—['Ιησοῦ is omitted in ℵ.[1] D.[1] F.; it is brackerted by Alford. The order in A. B. C. D.[2 3] K. L. is Χριστοῦ 'Ιησοῦ, so the corrector in ℵ. For the inverted order of the E. V., there is no authority.—R.]

[2] Ver. 3.—ℵ. A. B. C. D. and others [many cursives, most versions, including the *Syriac* and *Vulgate*] read ἐγνωρίσθη; the internal grounds (Stier notices the agreement with i. 9, the distinct reference to the Trinity, the great probability of an alteration from ver. 5) are not stronger than the external. [The reading of the *Rec.* (ἐγνώρισε) supported by D.[3] K. L., and some minor authorities, is considered an explanatory gloss by most modern editors.—R.]

[3] Ver. 4.—[This verse must be thus recast to conform to the exegesis of Dr. Braune, which agrees exactly with that of Ellicott, Alford and others.—R.]

[4] Ver. 5.—[The preposition ἐν is an explanatory interpolation, having no uncial support, rejected by all modern editors. —R.]

[5] Ver. 5.—[The Greek aorist is joined with νῦν, but in English we cannot say: as it was now revealed. Since *now* is emphatic, we must adopt the English perfect, as indeed is frequently necessary.—R.]

[6] Ver. 6.—[The *Rec.* inserts αὐτοῦ. It is rejected by most modern editors, since the more important MSS. (ℵ. A. B. C. D.[1]) with a number of minor authorities are against it.—On *are* instead of *should be*, see *Exeg. Notes.* The words: *fellow-heirs*, *fellow-members*, *fellow-partakers*, are analogous to the unusual Greek compounds, seemingly coined by the Apostle. Tischendorf (on the authority of some of the best MSS., (ℵ. A. B.[1] and others in the various instances) adopts the forms: συνκληρ., σύνσω., σύνμέτ., instead of the more euphonic and usual forms. So Ellicott.—R.]

[7] Ver. 6.—[Modern editors generally accept Χριστῷ 'Ιησοῦ (ℵ. A. B. C., cursives and versions) instead of τῷ Χριστῷ (*Rec.*, D. E. F. G. K. L.; most cursives) —R.]

[8] Ver. 7.—The reading ἐγενήθην is found in ℵ. A. B. D.[1] F. G. and others; ἐγενόμην [*Rec.*, C. D.[3] K. L.] being the more usual form, was likely to creep in.

[9] Ver. 7.—[The *Rec.* has: τὴν δοθεῖσαν, on the authority of D.[3] K. L., most cursives, many versions and fathers; adopted by Tischendorf, Meyer, Braune. The genitive: τῆς δοθείσης is found in ℵ. A. B. C. D.[1] F. G., 10 cursives and a few versions; adopted by Lachmann, Rückert, Alford, Ellicott and most later critics. The latter is better sustained; the presence of the genitive in ver. 2 casts a doubt on it, but to my mind not sufficient to warrant adopting the accusative.—The longer form substituted above brings out better the connection between *given* and what follows.—R.]

[10] Ver. 8.—[*Rec.* inserts ἐν before τοῖς ἔθνεσιν, on the authority of D. F. K. L., most cursives, versions and fathers; retained by Ellicott and Eadie. The suspicion of an alteration from Gal. i. 16 (a parallel passage) is very great, and as its omission, supported by ℵ. A. B. C., presents a *lectio difficilior*, it is rejected by Lachmann, Tischendorf, Meyer, Alford, Braune and others.—The *Rec.* also inserts τῶν after πάντων against all our manuscript authority.—The rendering: *to preach*

is more literal, conforms better with the sense of the aorist: *was* given, as well as with the infinitive construction retained in ver. 9.—R.]

[11] Ver. 9.—[The reading κοινωνία (*Rec.*) instead of οἰκονομία (ℵ. A. B. C. D. F. K. L.) is an explanatory gloss, supported by no important authority and rejected by all critical editors.—Πάντας is omitted in A. ℵ.[1] (afterwards added). *Men* need not be supplied, since the *personal* reference is not marked.—ℵ. (with a few minor authorities) omits ἐν after τῷ θεῷ.—R.]

[12] Ver. 9.—[The longer reading of the *Rec.* is supported by D.[3] K. L., a number of cursives, and a few fathers; διὰ Ἰησοῦ Χριστοῦ is omitted in ℵ. A. B. C. D.[1] F. G., a few cursives, the best versions and many fathers. It is therefore rightly rejected by critical editors.—R.]

[13] Ver. 12.—[The second τήν is omitted in ℵ. A. B. (rejected by Lachmann, Rückert, bracketted by Alford); but nearly all cursives and fathers support it, together with ℵ[3] C. D. F. G. K. L. (though with some variations in position); accepted by Tischendorf, Meyer, Ellicott and most.—R.]

[14] Ver. 12.—[This emendation gives the correct sense better than the literal but harsh and equivocal rendering of the E. V.—R.]

[15] Ver. 13.—[Dr. Braune's exegesis requires the following rendering: Wherefore I pray (God) that (I) faint not," etc. See *Exeg. Notes*.—The *Rec.* has ἐκκακεῖν, with C. D.[3] F. K. L. Ellicott (with A. B.[1] D.[1] E.) ἐνκακεῖν, while most editors accept the form ἐγκακεῖν (ℵ. B.[2]). Comp. my *Textual Notes* on Gal. vi. 9. Meyer does not accept the view that the first named is a doubtful word, but thinks it was in oral use and first introduced into writing by Paul; the other reading being an attempt at improvement. He is almost alone in this opinion.—R.]

## EXEGETICAL AND CRITICAL.

*Connection and Summary.* With τούτου χάριν the Apostle refers to what precedes (ii. 19–22), not exclusively to ver. 22 (Bleek, also Meyer), which is only a conclusion, although a comprehensive one. The reference to vers. 11–22 (Stier) is preferable to that of Bleek, yet the first part of that section contains merely an antithesis which has been overcome and is past. Without any fear of a relapse he now looks forward and points to the end and *aim.*—From the fact that the church, "of the family of God," is built together in Christ "unto an habitation of God in the Spirit," there proceeds as a result: *the Apostle's intercession and exhortation* (vers. 14–19)* the weight and indispensable consideration of which rest upon the *office*, not the *person*, although person and office do and must include each other; if the former rightly regards and administers the latter, the latter makes its importance felt chiefly in its bearer. Hence vers. 1–12 treat of the apostolic office as the appointed *subject* of the intercession and exhortation. Ver. 1 describes the present efficient *bearer* of this office *in general;* ver. 2 defines the office as a *gift of God's grace*, which according to vers. 3, 4 has been imparted in a *special manner* and according to ver. 5 *now for the first time*, having as *its task* the *reception of all nations through the proclamation of the gospel* (ver. 6). Vers. 7, 8 *a* mark the *service* and the *unworthiness* of its recipient, ver. 8 *b*, 9, the *extent* of the task allotted to this gift; ver. 10 points to the *aim;* ver. 11, back to the *beginning* and foundation; ver. 12, to the *carrying* out of the task already begun. So Stier in the main.

Ver. 1. *The person holding the office.* **For this cause.** Τούτου χάριν is an emphatic expression, occurring elsewhere only in iii. 14; Tit. i. 5. It is stronger than διό, διὰ τοῦτο, introducing something special. [It means *for this reason* and is aptly rendered in the E. V.]—To this strong expression corresponds: **I Paul,** ἐγὼ Παῦλος.—The phrase is found also in 2 Cor. x. 1; Gal. v. 2; Col. i. 23; 1 Thess. ii. 18; Philemon 19 (and ver. 9). Similarly ἐγὼ Ἰωάννης, Rev. i. 9; xxii. 8; xxi. 2 (*Rec.*). He mentions his name, not on account of his person (ver. 8), but because of his office and the importance of what he is doing.

**The prisoner of Christ Jesus** [ὁ δέσμιος Χριστοῦ Ἰησοῦ].—In iv. 1 alone do we find ἐν κυρίῳ, elsewhere always (2 Tim. i. 8; Philemon i. 9) as here, with the genitive. It is undoubtedly the genitive *auctoris, causæ.** Winer, p. 178. So δεσμοὶ τοῦ εὐαγγελίου, "bonds of the gospel" (Philemon 13) are bonds which belong to the service of the gospel, ὀνειδισμὸν Χριστοῦ (Heb. xiii. 13) is reproach which Christ bore, παθήματα τοῦ Χριστοῦ (2 Cor. i. 3). Our phrase is not = for Christ's sake, *propter Christum.* A special emphasis rests on the expression. In the Epistle to Philemon written at the same time (ver. 1), it even stands in the place where "Apostle" is usually found, and in ver. 9 ("as Paul the aged, and now also a prisoner of Christ Jesus") it is similarly used. Here it is not a predicate, but in apposition to the subject already so emphatically named, not an adjective, but a substantive added for the sake of description. Bengel aptly remarks: *legatus, isque vinctus.* As if he would say: I Paul, the prisoner, not of the emperor, nor of the soldier, but of Christ Jesus, whose Apostle I am. So, following Rieger, Passavant and Stier. Meyer approaches this view (= δοῦλος Χριστοῦ).

[The phrase is taken as a predicate (εἰμί being supplied) by very many from Chrysostom to Beza, Koppe, Meyer. The Syriac version sustains this view, which simplifies the construction very greatly, but is open to great objection: (1) It makes "for this cause" and "on behalf of you" tautological; (2) disconnects vers. 2 ff. from ver. 1, since they then do not explain it; (3) the article could only occur in the predicate with special emphasis; this emphasis is unpauline and inconsistent with "if indeed ye have heard" (Alford).—Other verbs are supplied in some codices. Meyer formerly accepted a *brachyology:* I Paul, the prisoner of Christ Jesus, (am a prisoner) for you Gentiles, but gave it up as untenable in his 2d ed. See further below.—R.]

**In behalf of you Gentiles,** ὑπὲρ ὑμῶν τῶν ἐθνῶν.—This added phrase justifies the above interpretation. Paul is imprisoned *for* the Gentiles, suffers to their benefit, as is said also in Phil. i. 7, 12 ff.; Col. iv. 3. Although Paul had to suffer on account of his proclamation

* [According to the usual view, ver. 14 is a resumption of ver. 1, all that intervenes being a digression. Dr. Braune takes another view of the construction (see his note at the close of ver. 1), but is forced to accept a connection of thought which amounts to the same thing.—R.]

* [Χριστοῦ standing first perhaps implies that it was the Messiahship of Jesus which caused his imprisonment (Alford).—R.]

of the gospel among the Gentiles (Acts xxi. 21, 28 f.; xxii. 21 ff.), yet ὑπέρ is not=*propter* (GROTIUS).* It refers to ὑμᾶς (ver. 2) and is rather *ad evangelium gentibus annuntiandum* than *annuntiatum* (FLATT). BENGEL: "*Pauli studio erga gentes incensi sunt persecutores, ut vincirent illum; et vincula ipsa profuere gentibus*, ver. 13; 2 Tim. ii. 10." Here then everything "odious" is to be rejected from the term, differing thus from the expression: "once Gentiles in the flesh" (ii. 10). OLSHAUSEN is excellent: "He here makes mention of his bonds, in order to bring into stronger prominence the glory just described in contrast with the present condition of the church." HARLESS also remarks: "Paul would have the Gentiles led to none other than Him, whose chains he wore, and would thus give a proof of the glory of such fellowship, exalted above suffering and shame." STIER: "The bonds should especially show that proof of the office which proceeds from *internal efficacy*; the bonds themselves also *preach* to the Gentiles, and themselves *reveal* to the Apostle something new."

At this point the sentence breaks off, and is resumed again in ver. 8, since it is peculiar to the *naive* style of the Greeks, to place the name in the nominative in a sentence, the end of which is not immediately contemplated, and since ἐμοί (ver. 8) is in a strikingly emphatic position, so that it refers back to ἐγώ (ver. 1) and thus indicates the resumption of the interrupted construction. So ŒCUMENIUS, GROTIUS.

[Notwithstanding Dr. Braune's preference for this view of the construction, it seems to be untenable. (1) Though examples of such a change of case may be found, Origen affirms that it is a solecism. (2) There is no natural connection of thought afforded by this view, while "for this cause" loses its meaning; the grace was not given for this cause, *i. e.*, because they were built in. (3) Ver. 8 has another obvious connection, *viz.*, with vers. 6, 7, so that according to this view "the leading thought of the antapodosis in ver. 8 is clumsily forestalled in vers. 6, 7" (ALFORD).—R.]

Most however (from LUTHER to WINER, p. 526 f., BLEEK) find in ver. 13 a return to the thought of our verse, and in ver. 14 a resumption and continuation. [This view is supported, among others by THEODORET, BENGEL, FLATT, LACHMANN, RUECKERT, HARLESS, DE WETTE (who however regards the construction as "scarcely Pauline"), OLSHAUSEN, EADIE, HODGE, ALFORD, ELLICOTT. It is the simplest view, except that of MEYER, and not open to any grave objection. (1.) It makes the τούτου χάριν of ver. 14 take up the same emphatic phrase from ver. 1. (2.) It gives to that phrase as well as to the whole chapter an appropriate meaning, while a long digression or parenthetical statement is not unpauline. In view of the truth he has just uttered (ii. 19-22), he is about to pray for them, but other thoughts come in. He is a prisoner (ver. 1), that too in behalf of the Gentiles; the thought of his office leads him away (vers. 2-12), when at length he comes back to the thought of imprisonment (ver. 13) with a request that they would not despond on account of his sufferings—then he resumes (ver. 14). The whole seems Pauline, and need occasion no difficulty.—R.]

BAUMGARTEN-CRUSIUS accepts an anacoluthon without any subsequent continuation. CALVIN [*legatione fungor*] and others supply πρεσβεύω (from vi. 20); others κεκαύχημαι (from Phil. ii. 16); while such supplements as *postulo, hoc scribo* [CAMERARIUS], *cognovi mysterium* [JEROME], *sum captivus adhuc, etc.*, are quite ancient, and occur in some copies. A prevalent view (from the *Syriac* to MEYER and SCHENKEL) accepts εἰμί as the proper supplement; but it can scarcely be asserted, that Paul, τούτου χάριν, just on this account, *is* the Apostle to the Gentiles, the prisoner of the Lord, and that too κατ' ἐξοχήν. [See above.]

[Among other untenable views there should be mentioned that of ZANCHIUS, CRAMER and HOLZHAUSEN, who suppose the resumption to take place in ver. 13. Against this may be urged the simple διό, the want of connection thus given to ver. 14 with its strong τούτου χάριν, and "the insufficiency of such a secondary sentiment as that in ver. 13 to justify the long parenthesis full of such solemn matter, as that of vers. 2-12" (ALFORD).—To take the whole chapter as parenthetical is still more objectionable. In that case the digression were too long, and the parts of the chapter would not find their proper connection; besides chap. iv. does *not* resume the thought begun in our verse.—R.]

Ver. 2. *The apostolic office is a gift of grace.*

**If indeed ye have* heard**, εἴ γε ἠκούσατε.—It is evident, first of all, that εἰ *cannot* be regarded as purely hypothetical, since it is written by the prisoner "in behalf of you," and also since the object they have learned: "the dispensation of the grace of God," will not admit of such a view. It is not necessary, however, to take it as=ἐπεί, *since*, Acts iv. 9; Rom. xi. 21; 1 John iv. 11; see WINER, p. 417. The same is true of εἴ γε in iv. 21; for there, immediately after ver. 20 ("but ye did not so learn Christ"), expressing accurate knowledge of the church, we find: εἴ γε αὐτὸν ἠκούσατε, "if indeed ye have heard him." The particle occurs elsewhere only in Col. i. 23; Gal. iii. 4 (2 Cor. v. 3, we have in various readings both εἴ γε and εἴπερ). It does not necessarily indicate a doubt, as does εἴπερ (HERMANN, *ad Viger.*, p. 833), and hence is more like ἐπείγε, though it must not be regarded as precisely equivalent. In the form there is expressed an uncertainty, an assumption, which challenges a self-scrutiny in the case of every reader or hearer. ["Assuming that;" ALFORD, ELLICOTT, not in itself implying the rectitude of the assumption made, which depends on the context.—R.] The context, however, confirms the truth of the assumption, that they have heard. This turn of expression is therefore a rhetorical,

* [It was indeed the fact that he was a prisoner *on account* of the Gentiles, but this is not the prominent thought here. Hence EADIE may or may not be correct in saying: "In writing to the Ephesians he could not forget that the suspicion of his having taken an Ephesian named Trophimus into the temple with him, created the popular disturbance that led to his capture and his final appeal to Cæsar, his journey to Rome, and his imprisonment in the imperial city."—R.]

* [This seems to be one of those cases where the Greek aorist is properly rendered by the English perfect.—R.]

"a more elegant and suggestive reminder" (MEYER) of the preaching of Paul, as if he had written: "for ye have heard;" or "since ye have heard." ESTIUS: "*εἴγε non est dubitantis, sed potius affirmantis.*" Or we may say with STIER, that it is pre-supposition, not without a slight touch of irony, in case it were otherwise; or still more correctly: in case they would not consider the Apostle as the Apostle of the Lord for them; not to have recognized Paul, not to have received his teaching would be equivalent to not having heard. Hence it is not correct to conclude from these words, that the Epistle was not written to Ephesus (see *Introd.* § 5, 2). Nor does this phraseology render it necessary to accept a wider, partially unknown, circle of readers (HARLESS, STIER, BLEEK and others). The assumption of CALVIN is inadmissible: "It is credible, that when he labored in Ephesus, he was silent on these topics." Nor is it at all necessary to do violence to the verb, and render it: *firmiter retinetis* (PELAGIUS), *intellexistis* (ANSELM, GROTIUS and others). The reference is simply to preaching, especially that of Paul; hence this is termed ἀκοή (Rom. x. 16 f.). [See *Romans, in loco*, p. 349.—R.]

**Of the dispensation of the grace of God** [τὴν οἰκονομίαν τῆς χάριτος τοῦ θεοῦ].—Οἰκονομία here follows the close of chap. ii. with its οἰκοδομή. There the building of "an habitation" is treated of, here the establishment of a household, a νέμειν (STIER). See on i. 10. This is a matter belonging to God, or still more closely to "the grace of God." Hence it is to be regarded not as an apostolic function (PELAGIUS, ANSELM, LUTHER: *office*. [HODGE] and others), but as a Divine arrangement. It must also be remembered that we find here, not χάρισμα, but χάρις. This χάρις is then more closely defined:

**Which is given me to you-ward.**—Τῆς δοθείσης μοι, as in Rom. xii. 3; xv. 15; 1 Cor. iii. 10; Gal. ii. 9, with ὑμῖν 1 Cor. i. 4. Hence it is not to be understood of the Apostolic office exclusively; although the context here points to that (εἰς ὑμᾶς, as in Gal. ii. 8, εἰς τὰ ἔθνη). Εἰς ὑμᾶς marks the readers as the object about which the Apostle's position and activity was concerned, and is neither=ὑπὲρ ὑμῶν, *vestra causa* (MORUS), nor=ἐν ὑμῖν, *in vobis* (*Vulgate*) or *inter vos*, but upon, towards you; as εἰς ἡμᾶς, i. 19: hence it is not merely: with respect to you (RUECKERT). ["To you-ward," though now unusual, expresses very well the precise shade of meaning.—R.]

Thus the apostolic office is described as a gift of God's grace, yet not so imparted and conferred that a "dispensation" is not necessary in addition, but so that the person himself (μοι) is especially prepared for it. Here we must include all that God had done for and in Paul, from childhood on (Gal. i. 15), near and in Damascus (Acts ix. 1 ff.; xxii. 3 ff.; xxvi. 12 ff.); in Jerusalem (Acts xxii. 21) and elsewhere (Gal. ii. 8; 1 Cor. xv. 8-10; 2 Cor. xii. 1-10). So RUECKERT especially. To regard this as merely *munus apostolicum gratiose, immerito beneficio Divino creditum* is too superficial. Nor can we in accordance with Col. i. 25: "the dispensation of God which was given to me for you," explain it thus, that the administrative office of the Divine grace was committed to him (ANSELM, GROTIUS and others); here τῆς δοθείσης belongs to χάριτος, here the matter is regarded under a different aspect, and the context is different, since "heard" is the governing verb, and the office is not heard.

[This view of οἰκονομία is defended by EADIE, ALFORD, ELLICOTT (HODGE mentions it, though he thinks it differs from his own merely in form). The only remaining question is respecting the genitive. It is obviously not that of the subject, but either that of the object, "the material with respect to which the dispensation was to be exercised" (ALFORD) or that of "the point of view" (ELLICOTT). These scarcely differ here, but some such sense is favored by the passive verb ἐγνωρίσθη (ver. 3 where the *Rec.* has ἐγνώρισε).—R.]

*The method of communication.* Vers. 3, 4.

Ver. 3. **That,** ὅτι, gives prominence to a particular part of what they have heard, the essential part of the dispensation of the grace of God. [ALFORD: "Epexegesis of the fact implied in ἠκούσατε τὴν οἰκ., *viz.*, of the fact that: as we say 'how that.'" *That* is the literal rendering, "how that" is a rather inelegant exegesis.—R.]

**By revelation was made known to me** [κατὰ ἀποκάλυψιν ἐγνωρίσθη μοι].—The emphasis here rests on "by revelation," since it comes first. As neither τινα nor τήν is added, the reference is not to some particular event, definite in itself, but not more closely indicated (Acts ix. 1 ff., as OLSHAUSEN thinks, or Acts xxii. 21), nor to some occurrence definitely designated, but rather to the mode of making known. It is an adverbial qualification of ἐγνωρίσθη=ἀπεκαλύφθη (ver. 5), or like Gal. i. 15, 16. Κατά denotes, as in κατ' ἄνθρωπον (Rom. iii. 5 and frequently), κατὰ χάριν (Rom. iv. 4), a mode which obtains or prevails (WINER, p. 375). [So MEYER, ALFORD, ELLICOTT, HODGE apparently.—R.] Even δι' ἀποκαλύψεως (Gal. i. 12) does not point to a single revelation (STIER). [Comp. *in loco*. ELLICOTT says the allusion in the phrase as it occurs Gal. ii. 2 "is rather to the *norma* or *rule*, here to the *manner*."—R.] It might be interpreted (according to PASSOW, *sub voce*, II. 3, p. 1598 *b*) like ἔρχεσθαι κατὰ θήραν, to go hunting, or 2 Tim. i. 1: ἀπόστολος κατ' ἐπαγγελίαν, apostle for the proclamation; indeed G. HERMANN explains Gal. ii. 2: for the explanation, proclamation, presentation. But ἀποκάλυψις is only what occurs to man from God, not what men have to impart to one another. The word μοι, placed last, indicates that he treats of something which does not distinguish him personally, but which belongs to his office: "Revelation" and "apostles and prophets" are correlatives; γνωρίζειν is the general making known, but ἀποκάλυψις denotes that by means of which the official personages thus endowed are immediately distinguished, by means of which the Apostles become prophets. See ver. 5 and *Doctr. Notes* on ii. 20.

**The mystery,** τὸ μυστήριον, altogether indefinite, is, like i. 9, the decree of salvation and grace in Christ (STIER), the renewing of humanity through Christ, especially moreover the calling of the Gentiles (ALLIOLI). To refer it to the latter exclusively (most commentators from CHRYSOSTOM to HARLESS, MEYER, SCHENKEL, BLEEK) is not admissible, even though ver. 6 follows.

[On the *precise reference* of the word "*mystery*" in this chapter. The great majority of commentators, including HODGE, EADIE, ALFORD, ELLICOTT, accept the more restricted view just mentioned, but admit the wider reference in ver. 4 (and many in ver. 9). The reasons for so doing are quite strong: the *purport* of the mystery is set forth in ver. 6, the dispensation of grace spoken of is "to you-ward," a leading thought of the Epistle has been this calling of the Gentiles to fellowship with the Jews. Nor can it be urged against this, that it presents a matter unworthy of this designation and not at all mysterious. THOLUCK (Rom. xi. 25) thus classifies the meanings of our term: (1) "Such matters of fact, as are inaccessible to reason, and can only be known through revelation: (2) such matters as are patent facts, but the process of which cannot be entirely taken in by the reason." In the latter sense, the calling of the Gentiles was a "mystery," is so still in view of the separatism, which to the Gentile mind is in some aspects yet stronger. Evidently the indefinite reference, which leaves this special fact out of view, is inadmissible, while ver. 4 seems to require the wider meaning. Accordingly the alternating reference has been accepted to meet these requirements. To my mind it is unsatisfactory: (1.) It seems unlikely that a word should thus vary so speedily, when there is so little to mark a difference. (2.) The difficulty in construction is thus increased: the E. V. accepts a parenthesis so as to connect vers. 5, 6 with "mystery" in our verse, and thus leave the wider reference of ver. 4, undisturbed; but this is altogether arbitrary, since the relative clause (ver. 5) is to be joined directly with "mystery" (ver. 4) in accordance with the common structural usages of the Apostle. (3.) Since then the grammatical connection is such, the purport of "the mystery of Christ", is set forth in ver. 6, and the alternating reference has lost its one great object, *viz.*, the extension of the meaning in ver. 4.

It seems best then to accept Braune's view, but with somewhat more definiteness in statement. "The mystery" throughout is one mystery, but in view of the universalism of the Epistle and the current of thought in this section, it here appears as complex, precisely as the notions of "enmity" and "peace" in the preceding section: the mystery of redemption, whose centre is the Person of Christ, whose object and purport is Christ, taking that term as including the Body of which He is the Head, which He has redeemed, and in which the Gentiles are "fellow-members" (*σύσσωμα*, ver. 6); the latter thought being the special reference throughout, though never to the exclusion of the wider thought, since ver. 6 itself with its compounds of *συν* compels us to think of the one inheritance, body and promise which the gospel presents. VAN OOSTERZEE well remarks (LANGE'S *Comm.* 1 Tim. iii. 16, p. 47): "Paul knows *one* only great mystery," the chief truth of which as revealed to us is the Person of Christ in its connection with the Body of Christ, as the passage in the Epistle to Timothy itself teaches, and as is not obscurely hinted in v. 32 of our Epistle. With this thought of union as the ruling one, no wonder the special reference to the union of Jews and Gentiles comes in without in the least disturbing or excluding the more general one.—R.]

**As I have written afore in few words** [*καθὼς προέγραψα ἐν ὀλίγῳ*.—The English perfect brings out the force of the verb best, though it is not a literal rendering. The parenthesis of the E. V. is altogether unnecessary, the linking of clauses by relatives being common in this Epistle.—R.] *Καθώς* indicates that Paul has written only as "it has been made known to him by revelation," of course, from God. This the context demands (vers. 2, 4). This writing has therefore great importance. The verb refers to what is written already. The phrase *ἐν ὀλίγῳ*, *in brief*=*διὰ βραχέων* (CHRYSOSTOM, Heb. xiii. 22); in Plato: *δι' ὀλίγων*, as in 1 Pet. v. 12. The preposition is, at all events, local: in little space=*συντόμως*, Acts xxiv. 4; xxvi. 28 (*ἐν ὀλίγῳ* sc. *χρόνῳ*). *Pauca tantum attigi, cum multa dici possent* (WETSTEIN). Accordingly we must apply it to the whole Epistle up to this point; in comparison with the wealth of the truth revealed, its fulness, its wide-reaching, deep-moving efficiency, what he writes is to him always little and brief. He thus speaks in modesty respecting his writings, not as though the time for a more thorough treatise failed him (SCHENKEL). The reference is to such passages as i. 9 ff.; 17 ff.; ii. 4 ff.; 11 ff., not to one passage especially,* as those expositors must hold, who limit "mystery." Since he is speaking of local precedence alone, not of temporal, "written before" cannot be referred to a *previous* Epistle (CHRYSOSTOM, CALVIN:—*ferre omnium consensu*) as *προειρήκαμεν* (Gal. i. 9), *προλέγω*, *προεῖπον* (Gal. v. 21), point to something spoken at a previous time; so 2 Cor. xiii. 2; 1 Thess. iii. 4; *προεγράφη* Rom. xv. 4 must be understood of a prophetic writing with respect to the future. But Rom. iii. 9: *προῃτιασάμεθα*, as in the present instance, relates to what precedes, in the same Epistle. The explanation: *paulo ante* (THEODORET, CALVIN, ESTIUS and others) is incorrect.

Ver. 4. **In accordance with which, while reading, ye can perceive.**—*Πρὸς ὃ δύνασθε—νοῆσαι* must at all events be joined together. *Πρός* with the accusative denotes the measure (Rom. viii. 18) as well as the norm (2 Cor. v. 10; Gal. ii. 14). Comp. WINER, p. 378. The relative *ὃ* refers to what was written briefly before, as the measure by which to reckon, on which to measure; *hoc non refertur præcise ad* PAUCIS, *sed ad totum noëma et πρός notat analogiam ex ungue leonem* (BENGEL). Accordingly it is not to be applied merely to what was written before (MEYER: *προέγραψα*), or to *ἐν ὀλίγῳ* (STIER); nor is it = *prout* (JEROME), nor = *ἐν ᾧ* (KOPPE), nor = *ἐξ οὗ* (FLATT), since what precedes is neither the source or ground, but can only be

* [ALFORD refers it to i. 9 ff., EADIE to ii. 13-22; HODGE and ELLICOTT accept the wider reference. The last author refers *καθώς* to the *fact* that the mystery was made known to the Apostle, not to the manner in which it was made known, but Braune's view seems preferable.—R.]

the measure. [EADIE prefers the sense "in reference to which," but "in accordance with" is adopted by ALFORD, ELLICOTT (whose note *in loco* on this preposition is a marvel of neatness and exactness) and others, favored by HODGE, who adds: "what he had written might be taken as the standard or evidence of his knowledge."—R.]

With δύνασθε (BENGEL: *moderate et liberaliter positum verbum*) Paul refers cautiously to the *ability* which can be affirmed of every one; of the *willingness* he says nothing, that must come in afterwards. Modestly he points to what they can do, leaving to them the doing, neither commanding nor demanding it. The subject is each and all in the Church. Δύνασθε stands first very properly, since it is the emphatic word. The *conditio sine qua non* is indeed ἀναγινώσκοντες, *reading*, while ye read; not *attendentes* (CALVIN). Nor does he say: ἀκούοντες, hearing; he conceives of each one reading for himself. The present tense suggests repeated reading (GROTIUS). To the Greek reading [as the word indicates] was a second perception following the first perception of the author; to the Roman and German the immediate thought is of connecting the letters and joining the words (*legere, lesen*). [The present participle here indicates an act contemporary with that of the perception: *while reading*.—R.] Νοῆσαι is not exactly equivalent to συνιέναι; they differ as do our "perceive" and "understand." Comp. Mark viii. 17; TITTMANN, *Syn.*, I. p. 191. The readers *perceive* that which Paul *understands*. It is not a knowledge possible through reflection (RUECKERT), but a kind of immediate perception (iii. 20; Rom. i. 20; Heb. xi. 3; Matt. xv. 17)*

**My understanding in the mystery of Christ.**—Τὴν σύνεσίν μου ἐν τῷ μυστηρίῳ τοῦ Χριστοῦ.—These words are to be taken together as the object of νοῆσαι (MEYER). Σύνεσις used with σοφία (Col. i. 9), has a πληροφορία (Col. ii. 2; 2 Tim. ii. 7), is *vox media* (1 Cor. i. 19), and marks an especial knowing, that penetrates and commands its subject, as in the case of a master of the science (Jno. iii. 11). "The mystery of Christ" (Col. iv. 3) is the mystery, which has Christ for its object and purport; Christ Himself is the *concrete* Divine mystery. Col. i. 27 (MEYER, STIER).† It is evident that μυστηρίου is not an absolute secret, since there is an "understanding" with respect to it. See i. 9. BEZA: "*Optimo vero jure de se ista prædicare apostolum, re ipsa cognoscet, quisquis perspexerit, quam sublimiter et prorsus divine totum illud argumentum ab initio epistolæ pertractarit.*" In the connection in which Paul writes, in virtue of his office and by writing labors in and for the Church two things are evident and properly placed together; that he urgently directs the Church to what is written as a standard for their judgment respecting him, as the Apostle, by whom it is said to them, and ascribes to them unconstrained ability and freedom for examination.

Hence the inferences drawn from this passage against the genuineness of the Epistle are inadmissible. It is not necessary that he should refer to his *labors* among them, since his σύνεσις is under discussion, and both the subject-matter itself and his mode of treating it in this Epistle are well adapted to make them aware of this. 1 Cor. xiv. 37; 1 Jno. iv. 6. Comp. Introd. § 5, 2. [See EADIE on the reasons for professing such a knowledge of the mystery. MEYER properly intimates that this verse is worthy of the Apostle, (against DE WETTE, SCHWEGLER), and that an imitator would never have written it. In fact an imitator would have probably thought of it as DE WETTE does!—R.]

Ver. 5. *The period and persons concerned in the communication.*—**Which**, ὃ, refers to "the mystery of Christ" (ver. 4), not to "the mystery" (ver. 3); in which case we should have to regard what follows καθώς as a parenthesis (WETSTEIN, [E. V.], and others). [Dr. HODGE seems disposed to regard ver. 4 as a parenthesis, but the relative forms a direct connection. The other construction is an attempt to avoid the difficulty which arises in taking ver. 6 as the purport of the "mystery of Christ."—R.]

**In other generations.**—The dative ἑτέραις γενεαῖς, is a temporal qualification, which is of very common occurrence; see WINER, p. 205. So ii. 12; Matt. xii. 1: τοῖς σάββασι; Luke xiii. 14: τῷ σαββάτῳ. The word γενεά designates the lineage, the family, Matt. i. 1, 17; also in a spiritual sense, Matt. xvii. 17; Mark ix. 19. Then a generation, Matt. xxiv. 34; Luke i. 48; xxi. 32; Phil. ii. 15; and also an age, Acts xiv. 16; xv. 21; Luke i. 50; Col. i. 26 (ἀπὸ τῶν αἰώνων καὶ τῶν γενεῶν); here the temporal idea is the prominent one, only a shorter period of about 33 years is meant. There is no ground for taking it as = time, era (SCHENKEL); and still greater objection to retaining the meaning: lineage, and taking it as an ordinary dative, so that "the sons of men" is an epexegesis, which sets forth *in concreto* what is meant by the "generations" (MEYER). The antithesis "now" demands a temporal definition here. Yet it must be noticed, that the word "generations" is chosen on account of the various stages of revelation to the patriarchs, Moses, David and the prophets.

[MEYER, in his 4th edition, gives up his former opinion, adopting the usual view of our word, mainly on the ground that νῦν requires an antithetical temporal qualification here. Still he correctly insists on the meaning "generations," over against "times" or "periods." HODGE apparently inclines to the earlier view of MEYER.—The word is used in the LXX. to translate the Hebrew word דּוֹר, which admits of the temporal signification, now generally attached to γενεαῖς in this passage. ELLICOTT remarks

* [The aorist infinitive, according to DONALDSON (*Grammar*, § 427, 8) "describes a single act either as the completion or as the commencement of a continuity." Hence ALFORD says that here "the act is regarded as one of a series, each of which, when it occurs, is sudden and transitory." Comp. ELLICOTT *in loco*, who does not press the aorist here; and WINER, p. 313, where the idiomatic use of the aorist infinitive after δύναμαι is mentioned. The view of Braune is in any case allowable.—R.]

† [So ALFORD, ELLICOTT and others. EADIE prefers to take the genitive as one of the object, but Braune does so, and yet reaches MEYER'S explanation. In any case "the mystery" here refers to the whole wonderful scheme or purpose of Redemption in Christ, of which He is Himself the centre. See note on ver. 3.—R.]

that in one case (Isa. xxiv. 22) even יָמִים is thus rendered.—R.]

**Was not made known,** *οὐκ ἐγνωρίσθη.*—This in distinction from ἀποκαλύφθη is something more general and indefinite. BENGEL: *Notificatio per* REVELATIONEM (ver. 3) *est fons notificationis per præconium.* REVELATIO *est quiddam specialius;* NOTIFICATIO *fit ad reliquos etiam auditores,* REVELATIO *tantum ad prophetas.*

**To the sons of men,** *τοῖς υἱοῖς τῶν ἀνθρώπων.*—Only here and in Mark iii. 28. *Latissima appellatio, causam exprimens ignorantiæ, ortum naturarum* (BENGEL, who adds with over-nicety: *de statu vetere loquitur idiotismo linguæ hebraicæ*). The antithesis is found in "His holy apostles and prophets," which moreover compels us to give prominence to the "need of men born of men" (HARLESS), while ἐν πνεύματι suggests the lack of the *regeneration,* correlated to *revelation* (STIER); so that under the term בְּנֵי־אָדָם we must include also the Old Testament men of God, such as Abraham (Gal. iii. 8), and even the prophets (Rom. ix. 24-29; xv. 9-12), whom JEROME would exclude. BENGEL, however, is incorrect, when he says: *denotari præcipue* PROPHETAS *antiquos, v. g. Ezechielem, qui sæpe dicitur* בֶּן־אָדָם; thus he is described not as a prophet, but as a man born of men. [EADIE thinks the phrase was suggested by the word γενεά. "Sons succeeded fathers, and their sons succeeded them; so that by 'sons of men' is signified the successive band of contemporaries whose lives measured these fleeting γενεαί."—R.]

**As it has been now revealed.**—Ὡς contrasts now (νῦν) and formerly. On account of this ὡς, we must take οὐκ ἐγνωρίσθη as = οὐχ οὕτως ἐγνωρίσθη, "*not thus made known,*" and supply here in thought: "through their words and works" (CHRYSOSTOM). Comp. *Doctr. Notes.* It is only asserted that the knowledge of the mystery in former times is not to be regarded as at all equal to the knowledge which now exists; the latter is immeasurably deeper, richer, clearer than the former. It is incorrect to interpret ὡς as=while, and to infer that the mystery was not all known before (BLEEK); that cannot be asserted.

**His holy apostles and prophets.**—The *Apostles* are ἅγιοι, because they are Christians; Paul can have no hesitation in affirming of the Apostles, what he had already said of the whole Church (i. 1); of course a higher degree is involved here, especially since they, as well as the Old Testament prophets, who are called "holy," Luke i. 70; Acts iii. 21; 2 Pet. i. 21 (various reading), are termed "prophets." The Apostles also were of themselves naturally only "the sons of men," but like the Christians a holy ἐκλογή. "His," according to the context (ver. 2), must be understood of God, and "apostles and prophets," especially on account of the word "now," must be interpreted as in ii. 20. It is incorrect to regard τοῖς ἁγίοις as qualified by what follows as an appositional phrase. [So LACHMANN, BISPING].

**In the Spirit,** *ἐν πνεύματι,* is to be joined with the verb, and defines the modality of the revelation and its communication. It cannot be joined either with "prophets" (CHRYSOSTOM)* or with "holy" (MEIER), still less with what follows (ERASMUS). It is not however = διὰ τοῦ πνεύματος, 1 Cor. ii. 10 (LUTHER: *durch den Geist*). [E. V., HODGE, ELLICOTT, MEYER], but denotes the life-sphere, within which the revelation is accomplished: one must live in the Spirit to be a partaker in the revelation. BENGEL: *cujus donum Novo Testamento reservatum ad Christum glorificandum.* The glory of the revelation and the importance of the Apostolic office so overpower Paul here, that he forgets himself altogether.

[OLSHAUSEN: "It is certainly peculiar, that Paul here calls the Apostles, and consequently himself among them, 'holy Apostles.' It is going too far when De Wette finds in this a sign of an unapostolic origin of the Epistle; but still the expression remains an unusual one. I account for it to myself thus—that Paul here conceives of the Apostles and Prophets, as a corporation (comp. iv. 11), and as such, in their official character, he gives them the predicate ἅγιος, as he names believers, conceived as a whole, ἅγιοι or ἡγιασμένοι, but never an individual."—R.]

Ver. 6. *The purport of the mystery.* **That the Gentiles are** (*εἶναι τὰ ἔθνη*).—The infinitive, standing here in emphatic position, is epexegetical of μυστήριον, "mystery," hence not to be joined with "revealed" (FLATT), or with "made known," nor is εἰς τό to be supplied; and it should not be taken as = γίνεσθαι. ["A mystery is not a secret design, but a secret fact" (ALFORD); hence "are," not "should be." So most commentators.—R.]

**Fellow-heirs.**—*Συγκληρονόμα,* not as in Rom. viii. 17 (Χριστοῦ), but "of the saints" (ii. 19), the believing Israel. Comp. i. 14, 18; Gal. iii. 29. *With* the saints they are heirs of God (Rom. viii. 17), as His children. That is the highest privilege.—**Fellow-members** [of the same body].—*Καὶ σύσσωμα* denotes, by means of a peculiarly formed word, the membership in that body, the Head of which is Christ (i. 23; ii. 12, 16).—**Fellow-partakers of the promise,** *καὶ συμμέτοχα τῆς ἐπαγγελίας.* [See *Textual Note* [6].] This denotes participation in the promise (i. 13; ii. 12; Gal. iii. 14), the fulfilment of which is already begun, but by no means completed as yet; βασιλεία γὰρ ἐπήγγελται παρὰ τοῦ πατρός (ŒCUMEN.). It refers neither in general to *res* or *bona promissa,* nor in particular to the Holy Ghost alone, as BENGEL, [EADIE] and STIER think, who find a reference to the Head, Christ, in "fellow-members," and to the Father in "fellow-heirs," and thus to the Trinity as in iv. 4-6, 18, 21, 30; v. 1, 2, 18; 2 Cor. xiii. 13. There is as little ground for this as there is indication of a climax (JEROME, PELAGIUS, SCHENKEL: heir, possessor, partaker). For "fellow-heir" comprises the whole, on the ground of the relation to God as a Father, who

* [This is a mistake borrowed from DE WETTE. See ALFORD *in loco.* This view of the connection is that of KOPPE and HOLZHAUSEN. It is admissible enough grammatically, but why define "prophets" by so self-evident a qualification, or distinguish them thus from "apostles;" for the adjective "holy" must then be limited to the latter term.—That the two terms "apostles" and "prophets" refer to the same persons can scarcely be accepted; see on ii. 20.—R.]

has prepared an inheritance for His children; the two added terms respect their relation among each other: the first arising from the relation of the community to which dependence attaches, the other springing directly from the personality regarded as self-inclusive; the first marks the membership in the Church, the relation to it, the second the independence of the individuals, their relation in and of itself. Hence it cannot be said, that what is already sufficiently expressed by the term "fellow-heir," is repeated twice afterwards, once figuratively and the second time literally (MEYER). or that Paul creatively rummaged in the language (KAHNIS), or that the first term contains a personal and substantive reference (HARLESS), which is further indicated by the other two. [ELLICOTT's view resembles that of Braune, but is more clearly expressed: "The general fact of the συνκληρονομία is re-asserted, both in its *outward* and *inward* relations. The Gentiles were fellow-heirs with the believing Jews in the most unrestricted sense: they belonged to the same corporate body, the faithful; they shared to the full in the same spiritual blessings: the ἐπαγγελία."—R.]

**In Christ Jesus through the Gospel.**—"In Christ Jesus," defines "are" more closely and, like this, relates to all three of the preceding words. It cannot be joined with "promise" (KOPPE, BAUMGARTEN-CRUSIUS). Thus Paul indicates that all is communicated only in Him, the God-man. Hence "through the Gospel" is added, in order to point to the means by which that objectively given in Christ, already proffered and prepared, is brought to the individual, is presented for his subjective appropriation. Because Paul is speaking of his office and calling, he must add this also.

*The ministry and unworthiness of the recipient;* vers. 7, 8 *a.*

Ver. 7. **Whereof I became a minister** [οὗ ἐγενήθην διάκονος].—"Whereof" refers to "Gospel" (Col. i. 23, 25).—Διάκονος (Col. i. 7) is a synonym of ὑπηρέτης (1 Cor. iv. 1; Matt. xxvi. 58; Mark xiv. 54, 65; Jno. vii. 32, 45 f., *etc.*); and according to its etymology (διὰ—κόνις,* dust), like the latter (ὑπὸ—ἐρέτης, rower), designates a servant of a lower order, while οἰκόνομος (1 Cor. iv. 1; Tit. i. 7; 1 Pet. iv. 10) denotes one as related to the property, συνεργός (1 Cor. iii. 9; 1 Thess. iii. 2), as related to the works of his Master, δοῦλος (vi. 6; Col. iv. 12; Rom. i. 1; vi. 16; 1 Cor. vii. 21; Gal. i. 10; Phil. i. 1), in his dependence on his Master, λειτουργός (Rom. xiii. 6; xv. 16) in his devotion. It is incorrect to assert that διάκονος describes the servant in his activity for the service, ὑπερέτης in that for his Master (HARLESS). [See MEYER and ELLICOTT against HARLESS].—Ἐγενήθην marks more strongly than ἐγενόμην [*Rec.*] his becoming a servant, refers to a development, even if not as ŒCUMENIUS (οὐδὲν γὰρ ἐγὼ ἔργον ἐμὸν συνεισήνεγκα τῇ χάριτι ταύτῃ), RUECKERT and others think; that thought is found in the context, not in the word.

* [According to BUTTMANN (*Lexic.* under the word διάκτορος) this word is derived from διάκω, or διήκω, to hasten. The Ionic form is διήκονος, and the α is long. hence it is not a compound with διά. ELLICOTT refers to Benfey, *Wurzellexicon* for remoter difficulties.—R.]



**According to the gift of the grace of God** [κατὰ τὴν δωρεὰν τῆς χάριτος τοῦ θεοῦ].—Κατά marks the fact that Paul's becoming a minister of the Gospel had for its norm the grace of God. Δωρεά (iv. 7; Rom. v. 17), the single gift, like δῶρον (ii. 8), marks the free present. "The grace of God" sets forth the nature, purport of the gift. [The genitive is one of apposition or identity; the grace *was* the gift.—R.] LUTHER accordingly is incorrect: according to the gift out of grace, as if this were the source, the dispenser, while the gift itself was something else, such as the gift of tongues (GROTIUS), the Holy Ghost (A-LAPIDE, FLATT). It is in accordance with the context to think of the Apostolic office [HODGE, EADIE]; but the grace of God, which Paul had received, prepared him for this; He cannot use for His service persons as they are. He must convert and transform them for this end (ii. 10).

**Which was given to me.**—TISCHENDORF retains τὴν δοθεῖσαν in spite of the *Cod. Sin.* [See *Textual Note* 9. The received reading makes "given" agree with "gift;" the other with "grace," the sense being the same in either case.—R.]

**According to the working of his power** [κατὰ τὴν ἐνέργειαν τῆς δυνάμεως αὐτοῦ].—"According to the working" (i. 19) marks that the gift has been bestowed, not according to the receptivity of the recipient, but according to the efficiency of the Giver. [This prepositional clause depends on τῆς δοθείσης μοι, defining the mode of giving. This justifies the seeming tautology: "the gift given to me." MEYER, whom ELLICOTT cites in favor of connecting the phrase with the leading verb, now adopts this simpler view. Dr. HODGE accepts without remark the incorrect rendering of the E. V., which, not content with the instrumental sense it imposes so frequently on ἐν, here gives κατά the same sense: *by.*—R.] "Of His power" gives prominence to God's power, and throws Paul's person into the back-ground; yet recalls the fact, as he himself does in ver. 8, that it is precisely the persecutor who has become an Apostle, the narrow-minded, proud Pharisee who has been transformed into the most large-hearted and humble servant of the Gospel to the Gentiles (STIER). CALVIN: *In hoc dono prædicat Dei potentiam, ac si diceret: nolite respicere, quid sim meritus, quia dominus ultro mihi sua liberalitate hoc contulit, ut sim apostolus gentium, non mea, dignitate, sed ejus gratia. Nolite etiam respicere qualis fuerim; nam domini est, homines nihili extollere. Hæc est potentiæ ejus efficacia, ex nihilo grande aliquid efficere.*

Ver. 8. **To me, who am less than the least,** ἐμοὶ τῷ ἐλαχιστοτέρῳ.—The pronoun in the dative stands first, somewhat remarkably; we might rather expect: αὕτη ἡ χάρις ἐδόθη τῷ ἐλαχιστοτέρῳ πάντων, this very grace is grace to less than the least of all. But the pronoun refers to ver. 1, and must be joined with it. It is scarcely possible that after the grammatical and logical conclusion of the sentence begun in ver. 1 (ver. 7: τῆς δυνάμεως αὐτοῦ) another entirely new sentence should begin in ver. 8, only to introduce a parenthetical thought, especially as the sentence closes with ver. 12, beyond which the supposed parenthesis must be continued. [The objections to this view of the connection will be found in my note at the close of ver. 1. Dr. Braune's difficulty suggested above is not so singular in a writer like Paul as the resumption by means of a dative. As regards the logical connection, ELLICOTT remarks: "No addition was required to the former period; the great Apostle however so truly, so earnestly felt his own weakness and nothingness (2 Cor. xii. 11), that the mention of God's grace towards him awakens within, by the forcible contrast it suggests, not only the remembrance of his former persecutions of the Church (1 Cor. xv. 9, 10), but of his own sinful nature (1 Tim. i. 15) and unworthiness for so high an office." The transition always seems natural to one who is familiar with Paul's modes of thought.—R.]

STIER attempts to transfer the double comparative into the German: *dem Gerinsteren.* BENGEL: *Notio nominis* PAULUS *cumulata per comparativum superlativo superiorem; quo se sanctis vix accenset; elegantissima modestia.* A similar double comparative is found in 3 Jno. 4: *μειζοτέραν.* Comp WINER, p. 67, where he compares the Latin *minimissimus, pessimissimus.* [To this we may add *excelsior*, now almost naturalized in English; a word constructed precisely like Paul's double comparative. The rendering of the E. V. cannot be improved.—R.] Comp. 1 Cor. xv. 9: *ἐλάχιστος τῶν ἀποστόλων.* Here he cannot sufficiently express himself; here he speaks of the service of the Gospel in general. Accordingly he adds:

**Of all saints**, *πάντων ἁγίων, i. e.* Christians; he does not say of "Apostles," nor yet "of men," two interpretations, the latter of which is designed to exclude angels, without any ground. According to Phil. iii. 6; 1 Tim. i. 13, Paul's persecution of the Church of Christ is the strongest expression of sin in him, so that, according to the context, compared with all Christians, he regards himself as the most unworthy, because he is conscious of his sin and guilt, feeling that since God's grace has helped him, there is no one whom it cannot and may not help.

**Was this grace given**, *ἐδόθη ἡ χάρις αὕτη.*—This is the grace which lies at the foundation of his vocation as Apostle (STIER), not the Apostolic office itself (RUECKERT).—*Αὕτη*, "this," points forward to what follows, which sets forth wherein this grace consists. What he has set forth in ver. 6 as the purport of the mystery, as the mission of the Apostles in general, he now represents as that which is committed to him. There is not therefore here a parenthesis and exclamation of joy: "to me less than the least, is this grace given!" so that what follows is to be joined with "gift," ver. 7 (HARLESS); for vers. 2-12 do not form an interpolation, but the sentence begun in ver. 1 is entirely broken off, and *αὕτη* does not refer to what precedes, nor is ii. 6 to be compared with this construction.

*The magnitude of the mission;* vers. 8 *b*, 9.

Ver. 8 *b*. **To preach to the Gentiles** [*τοῖς ἔθνεσιν εὐαγγελίσασθαι.*—"An explanatory and partly appositional clause," ELLICOTT.—R.] The infinitive here sets forth the mission of the gift of grace, as in ver. 6 it indicated the purport of the mystery. See WINER. p. 298. The dative, which in accordance with the context stands first for emphasis, is a more difficult reading than if *ἐν* were inserted, as in Gal. i. 16. [See *Textual Note* [10].] Yet to Paul was committed the task of preaching to the Gentiles (Gal. i. 16; ii. 8; 1 Tim. ii. 7; Acts ix. 15; xxii. 21; xxvi. 17), not merely *among* the Gentiles; he should do what he could, the completed solution of the problem belongs to God.

**The unsearchable riches of Christ**, *τὸ ἀνεξιχνίαστον πλοῦτος τοῦ Χριστοῦ.*—THEODORET is excellent: *καὶ πῶς κηρύττεις, εἴπερ ὁ πλοῦτος ἀνεξιχνίαστος; Τοῦτο γὰρ αὐτο, φησι, κηρύττω, ὅτι ἀνεξιχνίαστος.* Rom. xi. 32. "Of Christ" is not an abbreviated form for the grace, the goodness of Christ, but refers rather to the fulness of the glory (HARLESS). [ALFORD: "The fulness of wisdom, righteousness, sanctification and redemption—all centred and summed up in Him."—R.] BUCER: *Jam evangelium exponit investigabiles divitias Christi, non illas quidem, quas nemo nostrum percipere potest, sic enim frustra prædicaretur nobis evangelium; sed quod quisque pro modulo dono suo tantum percipiat opum cœlestium, quantum ad salutem, consequendam satis est.* There is ever indeed an immeasurable remainder, and poor needy souls seek in vain to exhaust it (*Berlenburger Bible*). Comp. ver. 19; 1 Cor. xiii. 9-12. [Exhaustless "both in its nature, extent and application" (ELLICOTT).—R.]

Ver. 9. **And to make all see**, *καὶ φωτίσαι πάντας.*—This adds to "preach," a further task of the Apostle, which is accomplished by means of the preaching of the gospel; what the gospel can do (2 Cor. iv. 4: *τὸν φωτισμὸν τοῦ εὐαγγελίου*) this the evangelizing Apostle effects, whose word enlightens as a "word of prophecy," which is a "light shining in a dark place" (2 Pet. i. 19). He is bidden "to open their eyes, and to turn them from darkness to light" (Acts xxvi. 18). See i. 18; Heb. vi. 4; x. 32; Ps. cxix. 130. The object is "all," which according to the context, means the Gentiles hearing him; there is no reference to the Jews (PELAGIUS, HARLESS, STIER), since *πάντας*, "all," following the emphatic *τοῖς ἔθνεσιν* (ver. 8) cannot receive any emphasis. Since, however, no such accusative as "eyes" is added, the verb "enlighten" refers to the whole man, spirit, heart, conscience, not merely to the perceptive faculty (SCHENKEL), nor is it = *docere* (BENGEL). It is more than "make known," almost equivalent to *ἀποκάλυψις*, revelation (STIER).* As to what he enlightens the Gentiles then follows:

**What is the dispensation of the mystery**, *τίς ἡ οἰκονομία τοῦ μυστηρίου.*—See on i. 9, 10. The "mystery" here is not merely the calling of the Gentiles (ver. 6), but as in ii. 3; here "the actual accomplishment of the plan hitherto formed in secret" (STIER) is treated of. [HODGE favors the same view. ELLICOTT:

* [ALFORD: "Not merely externally to teach, referred to *his work*—but internally to enlighten the hearers, referred to their *apprehension*." HODGE takes the verb as equivalent to "teach;" EADIE is much better.—R.]

"The dispensation (arrangement, regulation) of the mystery (the union of Jews and Gentiles in Christ, ver. 6), which was to be humbly traced and acknowledged in the fact of its having secretly existed in the primal counsels of God, and now having been revealed to the heavenly powers by means of the Church." So MEYER, ALFORD and most. See on ver. 3, however. —R.]

**Which from the beginning of the world hath been hid in God who created all things** [τοῦ ἀποκεκρυμμένου ἀπὸ τῶν αἰώνων ἐν τῷ θεῷ τῷ τὰ πάντα κτίσαντι].—Τοῦ ἀποκεκρυμμένου is like σεσιγημένου, Rom. xvi. 25; comp. 1 Cor. ii. 7; Col. i. 26. It has been hid ἀπὸ τῶν αἰώνων (Col. i. 26; = ἀπ' αἰῶνος, Luke i. 70; Acts iii. 21; ἐκ τοῦ αἰῶνος, Jno. ix. 32), since the ages, from the beginning of the same; since there were men and angels, it has been revealed to none of them; before that there was no one, from whom it could be hid (MEYER). It was concealed "in God who created all things." Thus God is marked as the Creator of the universe with all that therein is, of heaven and earth. BENGEL: *Antitheton ad creaturas, etiam excellentissimas*, ver. 10. There is no ground for limiting "all things," and referring it either to the *moral* creation* (CALVIN, GROTIUS, MORUS, and others), which is forbidden both by the meaning of the word and by the aorist (κτίσας), or to the moral world (HOLZHAUSEN). Evidently, however, Redemption and creation are thus placed in relation and connection with each other; BENGEL takes the latter as *fundamentum omnis reliquiæ œconomiæ, pro protestate Dei universali liberrimæ dispensatæ;* STIER regards the former as *fundamentum creationis rerum omnium*, even of angels. We can and must join together Creation and Redemption, as decrees, dare not separate them, even though the act of creation self-evidently precedes the act of Redemption and the acts of revelation, and is ordered with a view to these.

[The only question that arises in regard to this passage is this, Why is the creation introduced in this connection? HODGE deems it a mere expression of reverence, but this is unsatisfactory. ALFORD thinks the fact here expressed "involves His perfect right to adjust all things as He will," thus the concealment is justified (so RUECKERT). To this MEYER properly objects, that there is no logical connection of this kind, and ELLICOTT says: "A reference to God's omniscience would more suitably have justified the concealment." OLSHAUSEN's view, that Redemption is itself a creative act seems equally irrelevant. It is either added to enhance the idea of God's omnipotence (ELLICOTT), or better with MEYER, EADIE, and others, to indicate that God in creating the world included in His purpose and arrangement that development which forms the purport of the mystery.—R.]

*The end with a glance at the final cause and also at the present;* vers. 10-12.

Ver. 10. **To the intent that now**, *etc.*—Upon what ἵνα depends will be best determined after the whole verse has been explained. Γνωρισθῇ νῦν is the order in the Greek, hence the former word is emphatic and corresponds with "hath been hid," just as "now" does with "from the beginning." Comp. WINER, p. 269. [We might render: "In order that there might be made known now," (the last word having a secondary emphasis).—R.]

**Unto the principalities and powers**, ταῖς ἀρχαῖς καὶ ταῖς ἐξουσίαις.—Thus the objects to which it is made known, are marked as of importance. See i. 21. [The repetition of the article adds solemnity without distinguishing two classes.—R.]

**In the heavenly places**, ἐν τοῖς ἐπουρανίοις, describes them more closely as to locality (comp. i. 3); hence they are not earthly and human, either heathen priests, Jewish rulers or Christian church authorities, but angels, and good angels, who desire to look into these things (1 Pet. i. 12). CALVIN: *Quid enim egregium de evangelio prædicaret apostolus aut de gentium vocatione, si nunc primum diabolus innotuisse diceret?* The context does not permit us to apply the terms to bad angels (AMBROSIASTER), nor even to consider them as included (BENGEL, OLSHAUSEN, HOFMANN, *Schriftbeweis*, I. p. 361 f., BLEEK), since it treats of a designed making known of the wisdom of God to His praise.* That Paul did not concisely say "angels," arises from the fact that here, as in i. 21, he wishes to give prominence to their power and elevation, here to glorify the Church, as there to glorify Christ, hence the agency of angels in the world of nations is not indicated (HOFMANN). In order to mark that a *cosmical* relation is under discussion here as in i. 10, the "powers" are termed ἐν τοῖς ἐπουρανίοις. This added phrase is so joined with "principalities and powers" as to form a single conception; hence does not indicate the modality of the verb "made known" (MATTHIES). This is done by the next phrase.

**Through the church**, διὰ τῆς ἐκκλησίας.—This is the theatre of the glory of God, of the Divine works (BENGEL), see 1 Cor. iv. 9. It is a communion in heaven and on earth, the militant and triumphant church, and as such an object of interest to the good angels (Matth. xviii. 10; Luke xv. 7, 10; 1 Cor. xi. 10; Heb. i. 14). LUTHER renders: *an die Gemeinde*, on the church, which does not accurately present the means employed, as it makes of the church only an object of observation or a place of instruction, while the preposition διά presents it as an instructress, who makes known, not in words indeed, but by acts, conduct and character.

**The manifold wisdom of God**, ἡ πολυποίκιλος σοφία τοῦ θεοῦ.—Ποίκιλος occurs with νόσοις, Matth. iv. 24; Mark i. 34; Luke iv. 40, with ἐπιθυμίαις 2 Tim. iii. 6, with ἡδοναῖς Tit. iii. 3, with δυνάμεσι Heb. ii. 4, with διδαχαῖς Heb. xiii. 9, with πειρασμοῖς Jas. i. 2: 1 Pet. i. 6, with χάριτος 1 Pet. iv. 10; iii. 7 (various reading) and means "various;" so that the special word πολυποίκιλος, occurring only here means multifarious, strengthening the idea of "manifold." Accordingly it cannot be = very wise (KOPPE),

* [The correct reading takes away the only support which this view could have from text or context.—R.]

* [A reference to both classes is excluded "not so much by ἐν τοῖς ἐπουρανίοις, as by the general tenor of the passage; evil angels more naturally recognize the *power*, good angels the *wisdom* of God" (ELLICOTT).—R.]

nor mean merely the wisdom which adjusts the antagonism between law and grace (HARLESS), but it refers "to those wondrous ways operating on the Church" of that God "who imparts reconciliation and actually edifies the church" (so STIER, who incorrectly limits it to the Holy Ghost), to the different treatment of different men, the various means He employs, so that He is "to each eternally another and yet to each eternally the same" (LAVATER). Rom. xi. 33, 34. The "wisdom," is indeed one, it is only its manifestation that is so manifold (ANSELM); certainly it is not that of Gnosticism (BAUR). What is said of the Old Testament in Heb. i. 1 ("sundry times and divers mannners") is true in the highest degree of the New Testament economy.

[ALFORD: "It is all *one* in sublime unity of truth and purpose: but cannot be apprehended by finite minds in this its unity, and therefore is by Him variously portioned out to each finite race and finite capacity of individuals—so that the Church is a mirror of God's wisdom—chromatic, so to speak, with the rainbow colors of that light which in itself is one and undivided." ELLICOTT: "The variety of the Divine counsels, which nevertheless all mysteriously co-operated toward a single end—the call of the Gentiles, and salvation of mankind by faith in Jesus Christ." "That the holy angels are capable of a specific increase of knowledge, and of a deepening insight into God's wisdom, seems from this passage clear and incontrovertible."—R.]

It is evident then that this clause of design depends with its ἵνα on the clause: "What is the dispensation of the mystery." The arrangement, management and guidance of this edifice (οἰκον νέμειν) is of precisely that kind (τίς), so planned, that (ἵνα) through the church as a collection of believing saints out of every land and condition the wisdom of God should in continued acts become perceptible and manifest to the participant and active angelic world in the most multifarious manner; that is the purpose of the "dispensation of the mystery, which from the beginning hath been hid in God who created all things." The mystery has not been hid from the ages, in order that God's wisdom might be revealed later (MEYER, SCHENKEL, [EADIE] BLEEK), nor has God created all things, that this might be made known through the Church (HARLESS); this purpose and design does not form a closer definition of "mystery" nor of "God," but of His "economy." Nor is the ground of this purpose found in the task set before the Apostle Paul (STIER), his preaching and enlightening, but in that which he has to preach and about which he has to enlighten, which remains after him and his labor, upon which he entered as fellow-laborer; hence in the economy of God itself.

[This view of Braune is certainly plausible, but it is not preferable to that which he mentions last, *viz.*, that this verse is joined with the "preaching" and "enlightening" of vers. 8, 9 (so OLSHAUSEN, DE WETTE, HOFMANN, HODGE, ELLICOTT, ALFORD, who however thinks the reference is to ἐδόθη, if one word must be singled out). The objection that this ascribes too much to Paul's own preaching (MEYER) is scarcely valid in view of the current of thought and the fact that the "manifold wisdom" did manifest itself through the preaching of the Apostle to the Gentiles. OLSHAUSEN: "Paul contrasts the greatness of his vocation with his personal nothingness, and he therefore traces the design of his mission through different steps. First, he says, he had to preach to the heathen; then to enlighten all concerning the mystery; and both, in order to manifest even to angels the infinite wisdom of God."—To take ἵνα as ecbatic is altogether inadmissible. The connection with "created" is accepted by some who adopt the longer reading and refer this then to the moral creation. HARLESS however adopts the same connection in a supralapsarian sense. As this is the only passage in the New Testament which can be made to assert this view, it may be here remarked: (1.) This is singular and involves a theory of creation which, however logical, becomes too terrific to be admitted on the strength of a doubtful exegesis. (2.) It joins a marked final clause to a participle which depends on another participle which depends on an infinitive which depends on a leading verb. (3.) The *present* manifestation is the end of a present operation, *viz.*, the preaching and making known. (4.) The end of creation is distinctly stated in Col. i. 16 to be the personal Christ: εἰς αὐτόν, "unto Him," as *causa finalis*, "all things were created."—R.]

Ver. 11. **According to the eternal purpose**, κατὰ πρόθεσιν τῶν αἰώνων, evidently defines "might be made known," not "manifold" (ANSELM), nor "wisdom" (KOPPE), certainly not vers. 3 and 5 (FLATT). The making known takes place according to the purpose "before the foundation of the world" (i. 3). The genitive marks the relation to the ages, that this purpose will be retained during these, will remain in force and regulate them. Col. i. 20: αἷμα τοῦ σταυροῦ, 2 Cor. xi. 26: κίνδυνοι ποταμῶν are similar; see WINER, p. 176. [ALFORD: "The genitive is apparently one of time, as when we say it has been an opinion of years:" "The duration all that time giving the αἰῶνες a kind of possession. If so, the sense is best given in English by '*eternal*,' as in E. V." ELLICOTT: "The purpose which pertained to, existed in, was determined on in the ages." Two things we may hold fast to: (1.) The general correctness of the rendering "eternal." (2.) The utter groundlessness of any Gnostic reference.—R.]

**Which he wrought in Christ Jesus.**—Ἣν ἐποίησεν refers of course to πρόθεσιν, not to σοφία (LUTHER: which He has shown), nor to ἐκκλησία (ERASMUS): Πρόθεσιν ποιεῖν means either to *form* a purpose (Rev. xvii. 17; γνώμην ποιεῖν, Mark xv. 1: συμβούλιον ποιεῖν), or to *execute* one. The context points to the carrying out, which is however just begun: the mystery has already become clear in the gospel, it is no longer as before, and ver. 12, with its emphatic "we have," gives prominence to the present time. Hence it is incorrect to render: "which He purposed" (CALVIN, RUECKERT, HARLESS, HOFMANN, *Schriftbeweis*, 1, p. 230); in that case we would find the verb in the middle voice (ἐποιήσατο), which is used in a periphrasis like this (WINER, p. 240).* To combine the two (STIER) is altogether improper; we must choose one or the other.—"In" denotes, that *outside* of Him who existed before all (Χριστῷ) and has now become incarnate (Ἰησοῦ) and *without* Him God's purpose is not accomplished.

The added: **Our Lord,** τῷ κυρίῳ ἡμῶν, pointing to the time of His appearing, is added on account of the ἐκκλησία, the ἡμῶν, whose Head and Lord is Jesus the Christ. [ALFORD is forced by his view of the verb to apply the whole to Christ in His pre-existence, which is very unusual.—R.] It is now explicable why the angels through such a church obtain wider knowledge of God's wisdom. At the same time the phrase introduces what follows.

Ver. 12. **In whom we have,** ἐν ᾧ ἔχομεν.—[The relative has here a slightly demonstrative and explanatory force (MEYER, ELLICOTT).—R.] Here "we" evidently means those who are really in Him; our fellowship with Him is the fundamental thought. For the gifts which are afterwards mentioned, do not inhere in Him, as do Truth, Love, Life, but are states of mind resulting from fellowship with Him or ripened relations.

**Our boldness and our access in confidence** [τὴν παῤῥησίαν καὶ τὴν προσαγωγὴν ἐν πεποιθήσει. See *Textual Note* 13.]—On the first term see my remarks on Jno. ii. 28, LANGE'S *Comm.*, p. 82.† It is used by Paul besides in vi. 19; Col. ii. 15; Phil. i. 20; 2 Cor. iii. 12; vii. 4; 1 Tim. iii. 13; Philem. 8; and is found in Heb. iii. 6; iv. 16; x. 19, 35. Here it means the free, joyous spirit of the redeemed, and must not be limited either to *libertas dicendi* (VATABLE), or to prayer (BENGEL). Καὶ τὴν προσαγωγὴν ἐν πεποιθήσει, "our access in confidence," forms a single conception; the last term is not to be joined with "boldness;" for that does not require as a closer definition what it has essentially in itself. "Access" (ii. 18) however requires it, since this may be feeble, timid, anxious, uncertain of acceptance.‡

The "confidence" (πεποίθησις, only in Phil. iii. 4; 2 Cor. i. 15; iii. 4; viii. 22; x. 2), which expresses itself after the boldness (comp. Rom. viii. 38, 39 with 31-37), is the childlike confidence in which the subject of grace approaches God. The phrase, therefore, is not to be joined with "we have" (MEYER, SCHENKEL). [The latter view of the connection is adopted by ELLICOTT and ALFORD. While the other is admissible, there seems to be a gain in thought from joining it with the verb; see below —R.]

**Through our faith in Him** [διὰ τῆς πίστεως αὐτοῦ].—The preposition marks that by means of which the fellowship we have with Him is brought about, and is a closer definition of ἔχομεν, "we have." Τῆς πίστεως αὐτοῦ (only in iv. 13) like Rom. iii. 22, Gal. iii. 22, means faith on Him, *viz.*, on Him, in whom "we have," *etc.*, on "Christ Jesus our Lord" (ver. 11). This faith is the subjective means of the union and the continued fellowship (Rom. v. 1, 2). [ELLICOTT taking "in confidence" as a predication of manner defining the tone and frame of mind in which the "access" is enjoyed and realized, makes the following distinctions between the three qualifying phrases: "in whom" makes the objective ground of the possession, "through our faith in Him" the subjective medium *by which*, and "in confidence" the subjective state *in which* it is apprehended. EADIE: "That faith whose object is Jesus is the means to all who are Christ's, first, of 'boldness,' for their belief in the Divine Mediator gives them courage; secondly of 'access,' for their realization of His glorified humanity warrants and enables them to approach the throne of grace; and thirdly these blessings are possessed 'in confidence,' for they feel that for Christ's sake their persons and services will be accepted by the Father."—R.]

Ver. 13. *Conclusion.* **Wherefore I beseech** διὸ αἰτοῦμαι:—This refers to ver. 12 ("we have our boldness and our access"); he proves this in petition, of course, to God. [See below however.] The middle voice, upon which however too great stress must not be laid (Col. i. 9; Jas. i. 6), denotes the praying for himself

[The reference seems rather to be to the whole paragraph: "Since I am the appointed minister of so great a matter" (ALFORD; so EADIE, ELLICOTT and now MEYER). The other view is perfectly grammatical, but joins this verse to a secondary thought, while the wider reference brings us back, as if the steps were being retraced, to ver. 1: "the prisoner of Jesus Christ in behalf of you Gentiles," the next verse passing further back to "for this cause."—R.]

**Not to faint.** μὴ ἐγκακεῖν.—Dr. Braune's rendering is: I pray (God) not to become dispirited, *i. e.*, that I become not dispirited: others I pray (God) that you faint not; while most accept the view which supplies ὑμᾶς as the object of the verb and the subject of the infinitive:

* [ALFORD supports the sense: "constituted," urging that Paul would have used a more definite verb to express the idea of executing the purpose, and further that the aorist seems to point back to a definite act of origination, while the perfect would better express the continued execution. The latter remark has some force, but does not outweigh the arguments supporting the other sense: (1) That the name of "Jesus," the historical Saviour, follows immediately; (2) that the next verse is an explanatory confirmation of the *accomplished*, not the *purposed* design (MEYER). It may be added that this meaning is more common in the New Testament (ii. 3; Matth. xxi. 31; John vi. 38; 1 Thess. v. 24 and elsewhere) than the other, which occurs only in Mark xv. 1; Rev. xvii. 17 (not Acts xvii. 17, as Braune has it in the German, repeating a typographical error, which has been allowed to remain in several editions of MEYER). Notwithstanding WINER'S distinction, in neither case do we find the middle. ELLICOTT properly renders the verb: *wrought*, instead of using the too definite "fulfilled." In support of Braune's view, the following names may be mentioned: THEODORET, GROTIUS, OLSHAUSEN, DE WETTE, MEYER, CONYBEARE, ELLICOTT, HODGE, EADIE.—R.]

† [Dr. Braune there refers to the mistaken conception of the term arising from one of those etymological jumbles so common in all languages. The sense is *Freimüthigkeit*; Luther however rendered it *Freydigkeit*, *Freidigkeit* (derived from *frei*, free). This was soon confounded with *Freudigkeit*, *freudig*, joyful); a sense which has influenced English commentators as well. The joyous element is present indeed, but not so prominent as this mistake has made it.—R.]

‡ [ELLICOTT clings to the transitive meaning here also, though admitting some uncertainty in regard to it. The union with "boldness" requires the transitive sense. "We may confidently say, that so important an objective truth as our introduction to God by Christ would never have been thus coupled to a mere subjective quality in ourselves" (ALFORD). Still it is not so purely subjective as "boldness."—R.]

"I beseech you not to faint." See below.—R.] The subject according to the context, especially "in my tribulations," is the Apostle. It is precisely the result of his prayer to God and his intercourse with Him that he is courageous and in high-hearted joy even in tribulations.—**In my tribulations for you** [ἐν ταῖς θλίψεσίν μου ὑπὲρ ὑμῶν].—The word θλίψις definitely shows that the subject is the Apostle; so does the expression ὑπὲρ ὑμῶν, which is to be closely joined with θλίψεσίν μου. Accordingly Paul does not ask the readers not to faint (*Vulgate*, LUTHER, MEYER, BLEEK, and many others), but prays to God for himself.

[This view of the verse is supported by such able commentators as BENGEL, RUECKERT, HARLESS (who however altogether unwarrantably joins ὑπὲρ ὑμῶν with αἰτοῦμαι) OLSHAUSEN, TURNER, BAUMGARTEN-CRUSIUS, and is favored by the *Syriac* version, THEODORET and JEROME. Still the majority of commentators from CHRYSOSTOM to the latest English expositors, reject it. With good reason too, for (1.) it seems unpauline to insert such a prayer here; he rejoiced in suffering (Col. i. 29) and gloried in infirmity (2 Cor. xi. 30), and was speaking of high privilege little likely to suggest faint-heartedness in himself. (2.) The next clause presents, a motive (MEYER), which is irrelevant if the prayer is for himself. (3.) Notwithstanding Braune's remark, μου would be superfluous in that case. (4.) Grammatically it is far simpler to supply ὑμᾶς as the object of the finite verb and the subject of the infinitive, than to supply θεόν as the object and then ἐμέ as subject-accusative; two words necessary to define the thought would scarcely be omitted, and the view we oppose necessarily requires two different words. If, as is natural, only one is to be supplied, that one must be ὑμᾶς.—'Εν therefore denotes the sphere in which the faint-heartedness of the Ephesians might possibly be shown (ELLICOTT); the article is not necessary before ὑπέρ, since the close connection of thought is similar to that in ver. 1: "prisoner for you Gentiles."—R.]

**Which are your glory** [ἥτις ἐστὶ δόξα ὑμῶν].—Ἥτις put for αἵτινες by the attraction δόξα ὑμῶν (WINER, pp. 157, 505). The tribulations of the Apostle for the church are the honor, fame and glory of the same; it would be a detriment, distress and disgrace to the church, to have a founder and leader, who in tribulations became discouraged and despondent; but they confess a faith, for the proclamation of which the Apostles must bear heavy sorrow, yet compared with which sorrows are not to be dreaded, and they have a leader, whom they may joyously and confidently follow. This clause is not to be referred to "faint not" (HARLESS, SCHENKEL and others), nor is it to be left indefinite in an oratorical sense (RUECKERT). It is thus that he prays first for himself (ver. 13) and then (ver. 14) for the Ephesians (RHENFERD). Thus he closes the section concerning himself and his office, in order to pass to a supplication for the church.

[The reference of this clause to "tribulations" is to be maintained and is best indicated by restoring the plural form in English: which are (seeing that they are) your glory. The view of Braune stands or falls with that taken of the former part of the verse. It must be apparent that the other explanation is more satisfactory here. ELLICOTT well remarks too: "Glory accrued to the Ephesians from the official dignity, not the personal dignity of the sufferer." Both because God so loved them as to give His Son first, and then to send His servants to suffering, (CHRYSOSTOM) and because these tribulations were the tokens of the freedom of the gospel (EADIE), are these "your glory." He has now returned to his starting-point (ver. 1), and resumes the thought there broken off in ver. 14.—R.]

## DOCTRINAL AND ETHICAL.

1. *The idea of substitution* is more *ethical* than doctrinal, and finds a sphere in the whole human life, in its narrowest and widest circles. The Apostle suffers for his Church; his suffering is for her advantage. So the child lives at the expense of its parents; the child for whom no one suffers is a miserable creature, and the parents who do not suffer for their child, nor take sorrow on themselves to avert them from their offspring, are no true parents. So benefactors suffer for their wards, and suffering for them, remove their pain and need. So the shepherds of the people. The suffering of human life is in its widest range *vicarious*. Where this really exists, without some subtle selfishness, there it is without vanity, desire to please, ambition or vain-glory, there, just as one does his duty to his neighbor, faithful in the least, does he also bear and with joy *dares* suffer! And it is just he who has felt the truth of the vicarious sufferings of Jesus Christ, who can thus do. The Romanists acknowledge such vicarious suffering only in the case of the saints, we find it in all departments of our social life. As Paul was a martyr, so is every teacher, every mother. But they are only martyrs, *i. e.*, witnesses of the everlasting mercy and the everlasting redemption, Christ Jesus is the author of redemption, the mediator of mercy.

2. *The official service in the Church.* On this subject this section contains important suggestions of various kinds.

*a.* First of all Paul feels that he is "the prisoner of Christ Jesus:" he has orders, powers, duties, rights and authority *from the Master; quum verbum Christi—porrigunt* (*ministri*), *Christi vice et loco porrigunt* (*Apology Aug. Conf. Art.* vii. viii. § 28), *non repræsentant suam personam* (the same, § 47).

*b.* The office is a *gift of grace* (vers. 2, 7); *beneficium seu gratia, non judicium seu lex* (*Apology*, vi. § 6); it stands and falls with the church, so that "a priority attaches neither to the church before the office, nor to the office before the church; rather the office has never existed without the church, as the church has never existed without the office" (HARNACK, *Die Kirche, ihr Amt, ihr Regiment*, § 41).

*c.* The office must be distinguished from the *general calling of Christians* as a special call of the church, but not separated from it ("less than the least of all saints," ver. 8); there is no specific difference, and the ministers of the church remain members of the body of Christ, just as the private Christian does; both belong together and are included in the organism of the church. Hence the communicative "we have" (ver. 12). Here however is the distinction of the New Testament office, that it is not united with a class, family, or with definite persons, like that of the Old Testament. It is filled from among the "saints."

*d.* In its *nature* the office is a διακονία (ver. 7: οὐ ἐγενόμην διάκονος), *ministerium*, not a lordship; the free inquiry of the individual member in private must not be abridged (ver. 4). "For the Apostles did not receive *a mandatum cum libera*, *i. e.*, an entirely free and unlimited authority and power, but a certain [*i. e.*, definite] authority (*Apology*, xiv. § 18).

*e. The gift* of this office is God's Word, and its *task* is the preaching of the same: "Gospel" (ver. 6), "to preach to the Gentiles the unsearchable riches of Christ, to make all see what is the dispensation of the mystery" (vers. 8, 9); hence we must not preach our own words! So far it is *juris Divini*, belonging to the economy of salvation as a continuation of the apostolic ministry; not however of the *apostolate* * with apostolic dignity and authority, for the Apostles as persons *have no successors*. For this office too we must distinguish the empirical establishment of church offices, which is a matter of ecclesiastical regulation and *juris humani*. [These principles are of great importance, but the trouble has been that "ecclesiastical regulation" exalted itself to such a degree as to assert for its creatures the *jus Divinum*.—R.]

*f.* The *equipment* for and in this office is the work of the Holy Ghost, who vouchsafes the "revelation" (ver. 3), in whom the mystery is revealed (ver. 5), who furnishes the necessary "knowledge" (ver. 4).

*g. Oral preaching* and the Holy Scriptures belong together ("ye have heard," ver. 2; "when ye read," ver. 4) in the Apostle's method, just as the congregation should hear and read, both in public and in private.

*h.* This office lays claim to the *person* of the minister, not merely to his strength and his time; the office is not conferred upon him just as he is; it does not make demands upon him merely when an official discharge of duty is concerned. Hence the Apostle says: "I became" (ver. 7), "the grace to God which was given to me (vers. 2, 7, 8)" according to the working of his power (ver. 7), so that he who is "less than the least" (ver. 8) has still "boldness" and "access with confidence" (ver. 12). [Comp. here the note of Eadie, p. 231, from Baxter's *Reformed Pastor*.—R.]

3. As regards Revelation, Paul only declares, that it was *actually* the possession of himself and the Apostles (ver. 3, 5). We find moreover at the same time an expression of the necessity of revelation: "the mystery" would never have become "the gospel," had the Apostles been wanting in that understanding and clearness necessary to preach and explain the mystery. Evidently the personal intercourse of the Apostles with the Lord was not sufficient for this purpose, they needed the revealing Spirit, just as Paul required the appearance of the Lord. Nothing is said respecting the *mode* of revelation in the Apostles, except that it did not consist in a single act, but in a continuous one, which could have its pauses and its ebbings, but never ceased entirely. In the church however, it is plainly stated (ver. 6), the revelation respecting the "mystery" is mediated "through the gospel," and is therefore joined with the words of the preached gospel.

4. Hence there results the duty of the private Christian, neither to absent himself from the common public service, so that he may hear, nor to neglect private closet worship, so as to read. Upon this is based the obligation of the church to circulate the Scriptures through the agency of Bible Societies, and the crime of the Roman pontiff in forbidding and hindering this. * "The old complaint continues still: *sed nos non habemus aures, sicût Deus linguam* (Stier).

5. *The difference in the Holy Scriptures.* Old and New Testament, are defined in ver. 5, very much according to the saying of Augustine; *et in vetere novum latet, et in novo vetus patet.* Both treat of the "mystery," which is the purport of the gospel, as it was the subject of prophecy. The difference is only in clearness respecting this; the former lacks it, the latter possesses it. In the former the full universal idea of the gospel lies hidden, as, in a bud, in enigmatical visions and figures. The hope of the Old Testament prophets had not that clearness of understanding which belongs to the New Testament Apostles and congregations, but the intensity of the consciousness of salvation and of the sense of God's mercy was not less then than afterwards, hence not less perfect in itself, only less distinct in form and expression; so that we may in the light of the gospel and the adult church understand the prophets of the Old Testament better than they did themselves, and yet be not more perfect than they. Hence we can only say with Jerome: *aliud est in spiritu ventura cognoscere, aliud ea cernere opera completa*, or with Calovius: *distinguendum inter cognitionem generalem et specialem.* The contrast of the Old and New Testament is not under discussion, as Harless remarks, but that bestowal of the Holy Ghost upon the Apostles, which introduced them into the entire already existing truth of redemption, and which was accordingly something actually different from the previous inspiration.

6. Carefully as the Apostle demands the reading of what he has written (ver 4: "while reading," *etc.*), he yet places it before them as a measure and norm ("in accordance with which"). The *preached* word, when written, became yet more objective and permanent, as a

* [Hodge: "You could no more appoint a man an Apostle, than you could appoint him a saint. Neither inspiration nor holiness come by appointment. An Apostle without inspiration is as much a solecism as a saint without holiness. Rome, here as everywhere, retains the semblance without the reality, the form without the power. She has Apostles without inspiration, the office without the grace of which the office was but the expression. Thus she feeds herself and her children upon ashes."—R.]

* [Bayne (from Eadie) on ver. 4: "Here he confuteth the papists, on account of their cursed practice in taking away the key of knowledge—the reading of the Scriptures; in which fact they are like the Philistines, putting out the eyes of Samson, and taking away the smiths, not leaving a weapon in Israel."—R.]

genuine expression of the truth, accomplished by the clarifying reflection of the collected spirit (comp. PETERSEN, *Idee der Christlichen Kirche*, 2, p. 181 ff.). The propositions: it is true, because it is in the Scriptures, and it is in the Scriptures because it is true, supplement each other.

7. *The Church* is to be conceived of as a communion rising above the limits of time and of the history of humanity on the earth; it reaches into eternity. But it is also to be regarded as a sphere of the operations of God and of the revelation of His glory, which has a significance, not merely terrestrial but cosmical: a place of the revelation of the Lord, which is the high school of angels (ver. 10); we are not indeed the professors at whose feet the angels must sit as scholars, but it is God who leads them onward in the knowledge of His wisdom; we are but the means of instruction. They attend the work of Redemption from the beginning: Matth. i. 20; ii. 13, 19; Luke i. 11, 26 ff.; ii. 9 ff. Matth. iv. 11; Luke xxii. 43; Matth. xxviii. 2 ff. 1 Tim. iii. 16.

8. Creation and Redemption stand in internal connection (ver. 9); the former was not willed by God without the latter, and is arranged and ordered with reference to it.

9. The strength of the consciousness of sin (ver. 8) is here intensified by means of the contrast with the high office; it is not conditioned by special and peculiar sin, but by his especially clear and profound self-knowledge in the light of the gospel of Jesus Christ, which it was his duty to preach. HARLESS: "Into the inmost depths of the soul each one sees only for himself; what he sees *in* himself, he does not see *on* others; what he sees there says to him, that sin dwells in him (Rom. vii. 17) and that the wrath of God is upon him, and that now when God's grace has saved him, he has nothing which he has not received (1 Cor. iv. 7); the hearts of others are searched not by him, but by God." It cannot be affirmed, then, to be a constantly recurring phenomenon, that the most powerful witnesses to Christian truth have been led there through previous and great errors and wanderings; it is however true that such must have obtained a deeper knowledge and experience of corruption in their own hearts, passing through hard and humiliating struggles. Conversion in their case is no greater act of God's grace than in that of others; they feel it as such, however, more vividly and overwhelmingly: Has the Lord helped me, then I know not whom He is unable and unwilling to help!

10. The *ground-tone* of the Christian is "boldness" (ver. 12), which has a two-fold reference: 1) backwards to the accusing guilt and forwards to the exalted goal; 2) downwards to the threatening world and upwards to the Ever-Present One. In the first aspect this "boldness" is fearless and undoubting confidence, that sin is forgiven, its power broken, and its eradication assured, according to the promise; in the other it is the joyful assurance of the favor and nearness of God, which cannot be disturbed by circumstances the most adverse.—Hence with this "boldness" is joined "the access in confidence" to the throne of the Most High, in the prayer, certain of a hearing, to be preserved in grace and mercy, and to obtain help against the evil without us and the sin within us. [Or taking the other view of the passage, such "boldness and access" possessed "in confidence" so exalts, that he who suffers comforts those who sympathize; the sympathy of Christ not only rises above human sympathy in consoling power, but makes the sufferer able to remove in turn the reflected sorrow in the hearts of sympathizing friends.—R.]

11. Concerning *faith* it is only stated here, that it is the medium of the blessed condition of the child of God (ver. 12: "through our faith in Him"); it alone gives a courageous spirit, constancy and joyous confidence; without it "we have" none of these.

### HOMILETICAL AND PRACTICAL.

That is an elevating sight—a man who has overcome sorrow and compelled it to grant him joy, strength, comfort, as a star in the night joyously twinkles for the traveller. It is sad enough, when a man, an heir of eternal life, a child of a Heavenly Father, permits himself to be overcome by sorrow and cast forth like a faded leaf from the tree, to be trodden under foot, instead of affording shade.—The cause of sorrow was to Paul a cause of joy: on account of the Gentiles, to whom he preached the gospel, he was persecuted, and this persecution turned out for their advantage.—Paul was like a sword in the contest against error and falsehood and godlessness; life was the workshop, God the Lord was the master, who formed it, but suffering was the anvil and hammer, by means of which it became solid and sharp; and that was good for the church.—That sufferer is right and sets God right before others, who is like a farmer, that knows the bright sky is ever behind the cloud of sorrow, and finds in streaming rain a blessing from above, and thus praises and thankfully accepts what city folks call "bad weather."—See to it that you know what gifts are given to you and for what. For in this is the task which you have to do; are you uncertain whether others have rightly profited by you, still be certain of this, that you have done your duty.—Joy in the ministerial office must be greater than the sorrow over the injuries which accompany it. Your calling among men is a gift of God to you and you should be a blessing of God to others.—God does not bestow His gifts of grace perfect and complete out of heaven, as one hangs up a picture in his room; but He produces them in our lives, like a harvest, for while the field is prepared, the seed sown and harrowed in, and sunshine and rain, day and night are ordained.

The Scriptures lay claim to be heard on one matter alone. God's everlasting mercy in Jesus Christ: Is that of importance to you, then the Bible is also: only there is this made clear to you.—About what is spiritual, Divine, eternal, you find no such information anywhere else, whether among the Greeks or the Germans or the English, as in the prophets and Apostles of Jesus Christ; they are greater than all the world's philosophers and poets.—It is wonderful how the mystery of Christ, the theme of the symphony of the Holy Scriptures gradually passes from the faint twilight through the gray morning of the prophets to the bright day in the birth and death of Jesus Christ, and the church, like a Memnon-statue, give a clear note in the beams of the rising sun.—"In a few lines!" often enough a mere phrase. Not so here: the rich contents, the deep insight, the pleasure in the communication, the love to the Church—all these conspire to make what is written brief, all too brief. Here the preacher may learn: *much matter, few words!*—Hear in the congregation, read in the closet! Walk in the Spirit and search in the Scriptures! Shun not solitude, but seek God there! These are three exhortations and three rules for the growth of the inner man.—If you do not consider yourself worse than others, you have not yet known yourself or God.—You should not lose joy or power in your calling, when you recognize in humility your own insignificance, the office is ever greater than its incumbent and rather holds him than he it.—He who with the microscope of God's word, honestly searches and knows his own heart and life, will have in the same word, a telescope to help his gaze toward the furthest heaven, the world of angels and the life eternal, in blissful gratitude.

STARKE:—Papal Rome and what belongs thereto is as cruel as heathen Rome was, since it arrests and imprisons so many real Christians.—Let no one run into the important office of the preacher, unless God has sent him there.—Reason knows nothing of the mystery of Christ; it is a revelation from God.—God did not at once make known the secrets of His will in all their extent and present distinctness, but it pleased the Divine Wisdom to proceed therein gradually.—Each book of the Bible is like a jewel in a golden crown; Paul's Epistles, however, have this excellence, that they lead more richly, powerfully and emphatically to Christ. Hence we must use them like daily bread for the nourishment of our souls. Happy are they who in such a perusal can say: the longer, the dearer!—The calling of the Gentiles remains full of mysteries, for thus God has shown His grace, power and truth.—Why should he who is endowed with office and gifts in Christ's Church exalt himself? He is what he is, and has what he has, not of merit, but all of grace.—The gospel has to do with the unsearchable riches of Christ: away with all else from the pulpit, such as mere human science, pleasant stories, fables, *etc.*—Learn also, O my soul, with the angels the manifold wisdom of God; learn it in the church, and watch how wonderfully God has gathered, called, upheld and protected it; learn it in thyself, and notice how wondrously He has led thee through this world.—Those teachers should be ashamed who attempt to force from the flock with knocks and scoldings, what would be so much better gained by more winning ways, by requests and entreaties.—When faithful shepherds have weak and timid sheep they must strengthen them with the consolations of the word of God and thus instil courage.—The tribulations of its teachers are no disgrace to the Church, but honor and glorious strengthening. For the power of the Spirit and of the truth manifests itself most gloriously, when on this account one is willing to suffer also.

RIEGER:—The chain and the soldier, with which and to whom Paul was bound made him the prisoner of the Emperor, but the willingness of spirit with which these bonds were borne was from Jesus Christ; hence he was "the prisoner of Christ Jesus," who also was near him and had an oversight of all that occurred to him. To know and make known God in His unsearchable love is more than to investigate all the works of His hands.—God will not give up His right as Creator, His purpose, which he had in the foundation of the world, with respect to the Kingdom of His Son, but through Redemption will save the Creation, and restore it to its original goodness.—How greatly is the manifold wisdom of God made known through the Church, in the gathering of it from all tribes and tongues, in the adorning of it with so many and varied gifts, in overruling all events for its good, in enduring so many tares, in the unfailing fulfilment of all the declarations of God.

HEUBNER:—Every one has a criterion of his Christian knowledge, in his proper perception of the purpose of God in Christ and the indispensableness of Christ. In our day this is often willingly changed. Many would make of Christianity, something local, temporal, and thus degrade it.—Christ is inexhaustible for mind and heart; we find all in Him. If we would speak of Him, the theme is never exhausted. Let us never make of this rich Christ a poor one!—What Christ has instituted must truly be something transcendent, and not so common that every intellect can discover it; else the angels would not be able to look into it and be satisfied therewith.

PASSAVANT:—Paul will not speak or teach from his own wisdom or his own inspirations; he will not give or recommend any thing, that is from his own thought or mind or will; at this he trembles, against this his whole conduct and life in the service of his Lord speaks. Nor will he speak a single word of any wise or learned one of this world, any birth or abortion of their little brain and great conceit; as little will he borrow from their idle word.—Divinely great was the light, which appeared, on so many pages of the Psalms and Prophets, respecting the calling of the Gentiles; yet even to the Old Testament seers themselves this, like many other things in the future universal economy of salvation, remained largely in the dark; much both in general and in particular was still concealed. Still less than they, did the people to whom they prophesied, perceive this mystery. Besides this, up to the times of Christ and afterwards, the view of most of them was disturbed by their inborn enmity and profound contempt for the Gentiles.—Among these "holy Apostles and prophets" none seem to have viewed the mystery of Christ with so clear, profound and quick a glance as did the Apostle Paul.—The great Apostle knows nothing save grace, will know nothing save grace.—The richer my life, my experience, my knowledge of grace, the richer the gifts, the joys, the richer my eternity, the nearer to the eternal building of God, so much the less can I understand it all, so much more deep and unfathomable are these depths.—"The highest of sciences is Christianity!" says a friend of God; "little as Christians devote their attention and study to it! the highest, most enlightened of the angels have made it their study, and learn from it to perceive God in a manner worthy of Him; and those, for whom such a master-piece is wrought, do not know it nor deem it worth their knowledge." Others, on the contrary, search therein in an ungodly spirit alone, their wit will guess everything, their intellect explain all, even arrange all; will blame and criticise, will approve and deny, will break up and break off,—and the powers on high in eternal light wait patiently, until light and knowledge comes to them respecting these things.

Stier:—The bonds themselves preach to the Gentiles; they reveal even to the Apostle himself something new.—The *reading for one's self* is pre-supposed and recommended in the case of each individual.—Missions are the continued, God-given, gracious and spiritual life of the church, her impulse of growth. They re-act as powerfully, widely and thoroughly as the preaching of the gospel on the church of the baptized, since from them we first learned the idea of the *Inner Mission*, or as the English say still more beautifully: *Home Missions.*

Ziel (on Eph. iii. 8-21):—The Apostle Paul was a rich man in his prison: 1. Rich in the unsearchable riches of Christ, to the proclamation of which the grace of God had called him (vers. 8-12); 2. Rich in his fervent love to the brethren, which revealed itself in his supplication for them (vers. 13-19); 3. Rich in his unswerving confidence in God, who can do exceeding abundantly above all we can ask or think, and with whose praise he is full (vers. 20, 21).

[Eadie:—Ver. 8. The riches of Christ are the true wealth of men and nations. And those riches are unsearchable. Even the value of the portion already possessed cannot be told by any symbols of numeration, for such riches can have no adequate exponent or representative. The latest periods of time shall find those riches unimpaired, and eternity shall behold the same wealth neither worn by use nor dimmed by age, nor yet diminished by the myriads of its happy participants.—Ver. 9. If we gaze upon a landscape as the rising sun strikes successive points and brings them into view in every variety of tint and shade, both subjective and objective illumination is enjoyed. No wonder that in so many languages light is the emblem of knowledge.—At the fittest time, not prematurely, but with leisurely exactness, were created both the human materials on which redemption was to work that peculiar and varied mechanism by which its designs were to be accomplished.—Ver. 10. In the proclamation of the gospel to the Gentiles, with its strange preparations, various agencies and stupendous effects—involving the origination and extinction of Judaism, the incarnation and the atonement, the manger and the cross, the spread of the Greek language and the triumph of the Roman arms—"these principalities and powers in heavenly places" beheld with rapture other and brighter phases of a wisdom which had often dazzled them by its brilliant and profuse versatility, and surprised and entranced them by the infinite fulness of the love which prompts it, and of the power which itself directs and controls.—Ver. 11. In all this procedure, which reveals to princedoms and powers God's manifold wisdom, the Divine eternal plan is consistently and systematically developed in Christ.—R.]

[Hodge:—"Through faith of him." How may I come to God with the assurance of acceptance? The answer given by the Apostle, and confirmed by the experience of the saints of all ages, is, 'By faith in Jesus Christ.' It is because men rely on some other means of access, either bringing some worthless bribe in their hands, or trusting to some other mediator, priestly or saintly, that so many fail who seek to enter God's presence.—R.]

[Schenkel:—It is a grace to be able to suffer for the sake of the kingdom of God and the advantage of our brethren: for thus to suffer is a blessing 1) for one's own heart, 2) for the church.—The glory of the Apostolic office: 1. As to its ground, resting on revelation; 2. As to its end, to effect a knowledge of the mystery of God.—The preaching of the gospel: 1) As to its purport, it is about the unsearchable riches of Christ; 2) As to its end, the enlightening of a darkened world.—The Christian Church, the bond which links heaven with earth.—R.]

---

### 2. *The Apostle's petition with an exhortation for the church.*

(Chap. III. 14–19.)

14 For this cause I bow my knees unto the Father of our Lord Jesus Christ [*omit*
15 of our Lord Jesus Christ],[1] Of [From] whom the whole [every] family in heaven
16 and [on] earth is named, That he would grant[2] you, according to the riches[3] of his
glory, to be strengthened with might by [through] his Spirit in the inner man;
17 That Christ may dwell in your hearts by [through] faith; that ye, being rooted
18 and grounded in love,[4] May be [fully] able to comprehend with all saints what *is*
19 the breadth, and length, and depth, and height;[5] And to know the love of Christ,
which passeth knowledge [or the knowledge-surpassing-love of Christ], that ye
might be filled with [may be filled up to] all the fulness of God.

## TEXTUAL AND GRAMMATICAL.

[1] Ver 14.—[The phrase: τοῦ κυρίου ἡμῶν Ἰησοῦ Χριστοῦ, which follows πατήρ in i. 3; Col. i. 3; 2 Cor. i. 3; Rom. xv. 6, should be rejected here. The *weight* of diplomatic authority is against it (omitted in א.[1] A. B. C. 17, 67; found in א.[3] D. F. K. L. and all other cursives). A number of fathers reject it (Jerome expressly speaks of the omission), while the best versions retain it. It is scarcely credible, as De Wette urges, that it was omitted because coming between πατέρα and πατριά, since it really disturbs the rhythmical connection; while on the other hand no addition would be more likely than this from the common formula. If internal grounds have any weight, it must be rejected. So Lachmann, Tischendorf, Rückert. Harless, Meyer, Olshausen, Alford, Ellicott; Eadie inclines to this view. Reiche and De Wette retain it, as does Hodge, who says: "the majority of recent editions and commentators retain them," a statement surprisingly unwarranted.—R.]

[2] Ver. 16.—[The *Rec.* reads δῴη with D. K. L., and most fathers, but δῷ (א. A. B. C. F.) is to be preferred. Comp. i. 17.—R.]

[3] Ver. 16.—[Here also as in i. 7; ii. 7; iii. 8, the *Rec.* gives the masculine form (D.[3] K. L., cursives), but א. A. B. C. D.[1] F. support the neuter.—R.]

[4] Ver. 17.—[Another view of the construction requires the following translation: "That Christ may dwell in your hearts through faith, ye having been rooted and grounded in love, in order that," *etc.* See *Exegetical Notes.*—R.]

[5] Ver. 18.—[The order of the *Rec.* (βάθος καὶ ὕψος) is sustained by א. A. K. L., most cursives; adopted by Tischendorf, Ellicott, Meyer and Braune, as *lectio difficilior.* B. C. D. E. F. G., most versions, give the reverse order, which as more natural and prevalent (Rom. viii. 39) is open to suspicion. It is accepted by Lachmann, Alford and others.—R.]

## EXEGETICAL AND CRITICAL.

Ver. 14. *The connection.* **For this cause,** τούτου χάριν.—Thus Paul connects with ver. 1, where the construction is interrupted. Still with ὑπερ ὑμῶν (ver. 13) he has already resumed what was expressed in ver. 1, and with "which are your glory," referred to the previous current of thought (ii. 22: "ye are builded together"). Comp. iii. 1. [EADIE: "The prayer must be regarded as immediately following that section, and its architectural terms and allusions will thus be more clearly understood." MEYER however explains: on this account that you faint not, *etc.*—R.]

*The prayer*, vers. 14, 15.

**I bow my knees,** κάμπτω τὰ γόνατά μου.—So Phil. ii. 10. It describes τὴν κατανενυγμένην δέησιν (CHRYSOSTOM). BENGEL: "*Si præsens adfuisset Paulus, genua flexisset, exardescente pectore.* Acts xx. 36. Here the reference is to *genua mentis* (JEROME); the idea of "praying" is so prominent, that the accusative sometimes follows the verb γονυπετεῖν (Matth. xvii. 14; Mark x. 17).

**Unto the Father,** πρὸς τὸν πατέρα.—The phrase is found thus without any qualification in ii. 18; v. 20; Col. i. 12. [On πρός, denoting the direction, see WINER, p. 378. The metaphorical sense of the phrase justifies the preposition; were the idea merely that of bending the knee, a dative would probably follow.—On the phrase: **of our Lord Jesus Christ**, see *Textual Note* [1].—R.]

**From whom every family in heaven and on earth is named.***—Ἐξ οὗ πᾶσα πατριὰ—ὀνομάζεται is a paronomasia to πατέρα, which cannot be reproduced, except as Luther (1545) has so beautifully and correctly expressed it: *Der der rechte Vater ist über Alles, was da kinder heisst;* all editions from 1522–1541 read: *was Vater heisst.* Evidently "from whom," ἐξ οὗ, refers to "Father," from Him (ἐξ) originates the name borne (ὀνομάζεται) by him who stands at the head of a group, πατριά, which is thus termed from πατήρ. The etymology must be well considered here. While φυλαί (מַטּוֹת) designates the tribes descending from the sons of Jacob, πατριαί (מִשְׁפָּחוֹת) denotes the families in the several tribes, descending from the sons of Jacob's sons; οἶκοι (בֵּית־הָאָבוֹת) is yet more special in its meaning. Hence the reference here is to larger groups. The word designates a lineage, family, springing from one father and bearing his name. [EADIE: "Every circle of holy and intelligent creatures having the name of πατριά takes that name from God as Πατήρ." So ALFORD, ELLICOTT.—R.] Accordingly something concrete and living is treated of, so that it is not=πατρότης, Fatherhood (THEODORET, JOHN *of Damascus*, ANSELM, LUTHER, 1522–41; MEYER: He is the original Father, the Father of all fathers; THOLUCK, *Sermon on the Mount*, p. 394; NITZSCH, *Prakt. Theol.* I. p. 269).

Πᾶσα without the article (WINER, p. 110) necessarily refers to the multiplicity of the families: *every* family. BENGEL is excellent: *omnis, angelorum, hominum celerorum, ex ipso, ut patre, pendens;* as David's family from David (Luke ii. 4) and from Abraham, so the blessing comes, like that of a father upon all the families of the earth (Acts iii. 25). The phrase: "in heaven and on earth," ἐν οὐρανοῖς καὶ ἐπὶ γῆς, joined closely to πατριά without the article, points to the world of angels and of men, referring to the groups dependent on heads and chiefs. We must then understand here classes of angels (comp. on i. 21), since the angels also are called sons, children of God (Job xxxviii. 7; Luke xx. 36) and call God their Father, not merely their Creator, and races of people as national families, although "children of disobedience" (ii. 2; v. 6) are not wanting. For "all angels, all Christians, aye, all children of men are God's children, for He has created them all" (LUTHER) in Christ, the Son of filiation. The word πατριά, which by the addition of πᾶσα and ἐν οὐρανοῖς καὶ ἐπὶ γῆς, has received an extension of meaning reaching far beyond bodily descent, must be understood not merely in a natural, but also in an *ethical* sense, as indeed the idea: "Father" is thus used. Since "fatherhood" has not a concrete meaning it cannot be translated by this word, but STIER thus attempts to preserve the concrete force, *der rechte Vater uber Alles, was nach Vätern heisst.*

It is incorrect and ungrammatical to understand by it the *whole* world family (MEYER, OLS-

* [ELLICOTT renders: "From whom every race in heaven and on earth is thus named," while the German text of Braune runs thus in a literal translation: "whose name every family in heaven and on earth bears."—R.]

HAUSEN and others), or only two groups, angels and men (CALVIN), or the saints in heaven and the elect on the earth (CALOV.),* since in that case the article would be found before ἐν οὐρανοῖς and before ἐπὶ γῆς, as in the first case it should stand after πᾶσα. It is incorrect to ignore altogether the idea of groups, families, which Luther's version throws into the background, and to make of God an "All-father" (MEYER). LUTHER has given occasion to this mistake, but corrected it through his translation; for he says there that God is Father over all, that is called children, of course maintained, cared for, as we are, in Christ. It respects more the *right* Father than the *right* children (HARLESS). Finally all polemical reference, such as against the particularism of the Jews (CALVIN), angel-worship (MICHAEL), must be rejected. The passage is *ironical* rather. Comp. *Doctr. Note* 2.

Ver. 16. *The purport of the supplication.* Vers. 16, 17.—**That he would grant you.**—Ἵνα δῷ ὑμῖν marks the *purpose* and consequently the *purport* of the supplication, indicating at the same time the confidence of him who prays, that He who is implored will fulfil his request. Comp. i. 17. [The subject and the purpose thus blended as so often when ἵνα follows a verb signifying (even metaphorically) to pray.—R.]

**According to the riches of his glory.**—Κατὰ τὸ πλοῦτος τῆς δόξης αὐτοῦ defines the δῷ more closely, as a rich and glorious giving. He should *give*, not merely announce, according to, in the proportion of His riches in glory. See i. 7, 17; Col. i. 11. "Glory" here embraces the whole glorious perfection of God (MEYER); there is no ground for limiting it to power (GROTIUS) or grace (CALVIN).

**To be strengthened with might.**—Δυνάμει, "with might," placed first for emphasis, cannot anticipate either the phrase "by his spirit," or "in the inner man," nor can it be an instrumental dative (MEYER), nor does it refer to the will or moral being over against knowledge (HARLESS), which also belongs to the inner man and is given prominence in vers. 18, 19. It qualifies the verb "strengthened," κραταιωθῆναι, which is antithetical to the term ἐγκακεῖν, "faint" (ver. 13) thus not merely excluding discouragement and weakness, but marking also the external efficiency, the influence on the world, the overcoming as well as the standing fast, like ἀνδρίζεσθε before κραταιοῦσθε (1 Cor. xvi. 13). See vi. 10; Col. i. 11; 1 Pet. v. 10. Hence the passage does not refer to mere passivity, so that δυνάμει is merely a strengthening of the verb (RUECKERT). LUTHER is incorrect: "That he may give you strength—to become strong." [The instrumental sense is adopted by ELLICOTT, HODGE, ALFORD, EADIE and many others. Braune's view virtually resolves the dative into an adverb. ELLICOTT: It defines "the element or influence of which the spirit is the '*causa medians*.'" The contrast with ἐγκακεῖν, though plausible, must not be pressed. EADIE, who finds a reference to the figure of the temple in ver. 18, sees an architectural allusion here. —R.]

**Through his Spirit** [διὰ τοῦ πνεύματος αὐτοῦ].—The means of imparting such strength is indicated thus (αὐτοῦ=θεοῦ, who is implored); God's Holy Spirit makes us strong within, and thus prepares not only the actual fellowship in the kingdom of God, but also the powerful demonstration of the same; hence BENGEL well says: *δυνάμει bene congruit cum mentione spiritus.*

**In the inner man.**—[Εἰς here is not=ἐν, nor=in regard of (MEYER, WINER, DE WETTE, HODGE: as to), but "to and into," marking "the direction and destination of the prayed for gift of infused strength" (ELLICOTT).—R.] Ὁ ἔσω ἄνθρωπος (so also Rom. vii. 22) is the antithesis of ὁ ἔξω ἡμῶν ἄνθρωπος (2 Cor. iv. 16), which "perishes," while "the inward man is renewed day by day." It is not something physical, but moral, hence too, not=νοῦς, which can have a "vanity" (iv. 17), of which "corrupt" can be predicated (1 Tim. vi. 5), which is impossible in the case of the inner man. It is rather="the hidden man of the heart" (1 Pet. iii. 4) and refers to the concealed, displaced and obscured image of God within us. Accordingly the Apostle says εἰς τὸν ἔσω, to become strong so far as to reach within to this; the preposition thus marking the aim towards which the becoming strong should be constantly and renewedly directed. See WINER, p. 389. Accordingly "the inner man" cannot be used interchangeably with "the new man" (iv. 24); the latter is the new creature, in which the former lives again, rises anew out of the death of sin which has come upon it: "the inner man" does not stand in antithesis to the "body," but includes so much of it as God in the creation has prepared and designed for the life in glory, in the new creation for the resurrection of the body. See *Doctr. Note* 3. [Comp. LANGE, *Romans* vii. 7–25, especially my Excursus, pp. 232–236.*—R.]

* [So BODIUS and HODGE, both insisting upon the exclusive reference to the redeemed. The argument of the latter rests altogether on the incorrect reading he accepts. Admitting that the omission of the article favors the rendering: "every family," he adds that it may still be omitted where the sense is "the whole family," provided the context is so clear as to prevent mistake. But it is not so clear, else the great body of commentators would not have mistaken it; hence the condition is not met. Besides the context does not teach, except critical judgments are to give way to exegetical preferences, "that those who are here contemplated as children, are those who are by Jesus Christ brought into this relation to God." "Consequently" it ought not to be affirmed that "the word πατριά cannot include any but the subjects of redemption."—Undoubtedly there is an underlying thought of redemption; "it is not in virtue of God's creative power that the Apostle here prays to Him, but in virtue of His adoptive love in Christ" (ALFORD). The thought of an "All-Father" is remote enough, but any unnecessary limitation of πᾶσα πατριά is at the same time a limitation of the wider results of Redemptive Love so frequently hinted at by Paul and not very remote here (ver. 10). ALFORD: "The Apostle seems, regarding God as the Father of us His adopted children, to go forth into the fact, that He, in this His relation to us, is in reality the great original and proto-type of the paternal relation, wherever found." And in an ethical sense this relation may be readily conceived of as existing in heaven among other than those redeemed from earth.—R.]

* [Dr. HODGE, very sweepingly, intimates that all those interpretations which distinguish this "inner man" from the renewed man, belong to "the theory of Semi-Pelagianism, embodied and developed in the theology of the Church of Rome." But this is based on a mere assumption, viz., that this view of "the inner man" as the seat of spiritual influences implies the actual sinlessness and unfallen status of "that inner man," an implication distinctly denied by many of the supporters of this theory, among whom are expositors,

Ver. 17. **That Christ may dwell in your hearts through faith.**—This verse forms an explanatory, further developing, parallel to the infinitive clause of ver. 16. We have here a second petition, in continuation of the first, hence Luther is not altogether incorrect in inserting an epexegetical "and." [See below.] *Κατοικῆσαι* denotes a permanent indwelling of one taking entire possession, as Col. i. 19; ii. 9; Matth. xii. 45; Luke xi. 26; 2 Pet. iii. 13; Jas. iv. 5. The expression *οἰκεῖν*, Rom. vii. 20 (ver. 17: *ἐνοικοῦσα*), viii. 9; 1 Cor. iii. 16, is weaker. Here it stands first for emphasis and refers to *κατοικητήριον*, ii. 21, 22. Comp. John xiv. 21-23. BENGEL is excellent: *in perpetuum.* It corresponds to "strengthened with might," which precedes it; as the former is marked as an effect from without, from above, by "*into* the inner man," so the latter is distinguished by "*in* your hearts," as an internal condition.

*Διὰ τῆς πίστεως* [almost=through *your* faith] denotes in any case a power of the Spirit which has been appropriated by the Christian; accordingly the previous petition was *διὰ τοῦ πνεύματος*, "through the Spirit," to whom the initiative belongs, the Spirit of Christ, preparing for Him (BENGEL: *ubi spiritus Dei, ibi etiam Christus*), while *πίστις*, "faith," is wrought by the Spirit in the human spirit, is the power of man, awakened, directed, strengthened by the Holy Spirit, to appropriate Christ, to become Christ's. Hence it is neither *idem per idem* (MATTHIES), nor something entirely different (RUECKERT), nor yet a consequence from what precedes, independent of *δῷ*, but dependent on *κραταιωθῆναι* (BLEEK).

[The connection has been much discussed. MEYER (following CALVIN: *declarat, quale sit interioris hominis robur*) takes the clause as Braune does: parallel to the last clause of ver. 16, with an explanatory force. DE WETTE explains the infinitive as one of design, an opinion to which EADIE formerly inclined. Notwithstanding Braune's objection, the simplest explanation is that of BLEEK, adopted previously however by ALFORD and ELLICOTT among others. This accepts the clause as one expressive of the *result* ("so that") of the inward strengthening. The emphasis resting on the infinitive seems to demand this (ALFORD). This is a somewhat lax construction, but clearly admissible (WINER, p. 298).—The view which connects "the inner man" with this verse (*Syriac*, AMBROSIASTER, PELAGIUS): "In order that Christ may inhabit the inner man by the faith which is in your hearts," is altogether untenable. On *καρδία*, comp. i. 18; DELITZSCH, *Bib. Psychologie*, II. p. 203 f.: "the seat and centre of the moral life viewed on the side of the affections." CALVIN: "*Partem etiam designat ubi legitima est Christus sedes; nempe cor: ut sciamus, non satis esse, si in lingua versatur, aut in cerebro volitet.*—R."]

*The end of the supplication;* vers. 18, 19 *a.*

Ver. 18. **That ye.**—*Ἵνα*, "that," is placed after the closer definition of the subject, as *ἕως*, 2 Thess. ii. 7, and as *ἵνα* is put after the object in 2 Cor. ii. 4; Gal. ii. 10; Acts xix. 4. Similarly 1 Cor. xi. 14, 15; xiv. 7 (*ἐάν*), 16 (*πῶς*). [So Rom. xi. 31, where however Dr. Lange denies the trajection. This view of the construction is accepted by BEZA, CAMERARIUS, GROTIUS, CALIXTUS, SEMLER, STORR, ROSENMUELLER, FLATT, MEIER, MEYER, WINER (eds. 6, 7), BUTTMANN, SCHENKEL, HODGE. It is however adopted by none of the ancient versions except the Gothic, is rejected by ORIGEN expressly. The other view joins this clause to what precedes, as a consequence of the indwelling of Christ, accepting an irregular nominative. So in the main: CHRYSOSTOM, ERASMUS, LUTHER, ESTIUS, MORUS, KOPPE, RUECKERT, MATTHIES, HARLESS, OLSHAUSEN, B-CRUSIUS, DE WETTE, BLEEK, EADIE, ELLICOTT, ALFORD. Our preference is for the former construction. See below.—R.]*

who cannot be classed among the advocates of Semi-Pelagianism. I append the statement of ELLICOTT, which agrees with my own view, referred to above: "The expression *ὁ ἔσω ἄνθρωπος* (Rom. vii. 22) is nearly identical with, but somewhat more inclusive than *ὁ κρυπτὸς τῆς καρδίας ἄνθρωπος* (1 Pet. iii. 4), and stands in antithesis to *ὁ ἔξω ἄνθρωπος* (2 Cor. iv. 16); the former being practically equivalent to the *νοῦς* or higher nature of man (Rom. vii. 23), the latter to the *σάρξ* or *μέλη*: see BECK, *Seelenlehre*, III. 21, 3, p. 68. It is within this *ἔσω ἄνθρωπος* that the powers of regeneration are exercised (HARLESS, *Christl. Ethik*, § 22 *a*), and it is from their operation in this province that the whole man ('*secundu interna spectatus*,' Bengel) becomes a *νέος ἄνθρωπος* (as opposed to a former state), or a *καινὸς ἄνθρωπος* (as opposed to a former corrupt state), and is either *ὁ κατὰ Θεὸν κτισθείς* (chap. iv. 24), or *ὁ ἀνακαινούμενος εἰς ἐπίγνωσιν κατ' εἰκόνα τοῦ κτίσαντος αὐτόν* (Col. iii. 10), according to the point of view under which regeneration is regarded. The distinction between this and the partially synonymous terms *πνεῦμα* and *νοῦς* may perhaps be thus roughly stated: *πνεῦμα* is simply the highest of the three parts of which man is composed; *νοῦς* the *πνεῦμα* regarded more in its *moral* and intellectual aspects, '*quatenus intelligit, cogitat, et vult*;' *ὁ ἔσω ἄνθρωπος* the *πνεῦμα* or rather the whole immaterial portion, considered in its *theological aspects*, and as the seat of the inworking powers of grace." To which may be added that owing to the fact that *πνεῦμα* has also a second meaning (the human spirit as inwrought upon by the Divine Spirit), Paul does not use it in Rom. vii. 7-25, but rather *νοῦς* and *ὁ ἔσω ἄνθρωπος*. This view of the phrase is adopted by EADIE and ALFORD, and may be regarded as the prevalent one in Germany, perhaps now among English commentators.—R.]

* [EADIE thus states his view: The change of syntax indicates a change of connection, and the use of the irregular nominative makes the transition easy to the form adopted with *ἵνα*. The clause thus changed becomes a species of independent proposition, giving a marked prominence to the sense, and connected at once with the preceding context as its result, and with the following context as its starting idea. So ELLICOTT, who in his translation puts a dash before and after the clause. The course of thought then is: "Christ dwelling in their hearts—they are supposed, as the effect of this inhabitation, to have been now rooted and grounded in love; and as the design of this confirmation in love—they are then and there qualified to comprehend," *etc.* This construction is certainly admissible, although HARLESS is fanciful in accounting for it by the reference to both the dative and genitive which precede. MEYER presents the forcible objection that the present participles would occur were this the connection. When to this it is replied, "that the clause does express the state which must ensue upon the indwelling of Christ before what is expressed in the next clause can in any way be realized, and that therefore the perf. part. is correctly used" (ELLICOTT), I find in this but a confession of that subordinate relation of the clause to the next one, which is implied in the other view. If the ideas are so nearly similar, a trajection seems a better explanation, than to complicate the relation of the clauses further (we have already a leading clause in ver. 14, a clause of purport in ver. 16, containing a finite verb followed by an infinitive, on which infinitive a clause of result depends, ver. 17. The view under discussion would make an irregular sub-subordinate clause of result to be followed (ver. 18) by a clause of design, which the other view would append directly to the purport of the prayer). On the other hand this metathesis is open to objection. Such a trajection implies an emphasis on the words thrown in advance, and it is asserted that there is no necesssity for such emphasis here, but this is no real objection, since the words *can* be emphatic (notwithstanding ALFORD's denial). Again, it is said that the premised words in all such cases form the objective factor of the sentence and are not connected with

**Being rooted and grounded in love.**—The perfect participles, ἐρριζωμένοι καὶ τεθεμελιωμένοι, denote a state, in which they already are and continue to be, which is the pre-supposition, in order that they may be able to know. This state is effected by what has been prayed for in vers. 15, 16; hence according to the sense and the context it is impossible to connect these participles with what precedes (CHRYSOSTOM, LUTHER: "and to become rooted and grounded through love," RUECKERT, HARLESS, BLEEK and others), even if it were grammatically admissible to join a nominative to ὑμῶν, as in iv. 23: ὑμᾶς—ἀνεχόμενοι—σπουδάζοντες. Col. ii. 2; iii. 16. See WINER, p. 532. This position gives especial weight to the participles, which introduce two figures borrowed from a tree and a building. They mark that a profoundly penetrating life (ἐρριζωμένοι) and a well-grounded, permanent character (τεθεμελιωμένοι) are necessary. [The first may be regarded as used "without any other allusion to its primitive meaning than that of *fixedness, firmness* at the *base* or *foundation*" (ELLICOTT).—R.] Comp. 1 Cor. iii. 9; Col. ii. 7.

The double figure strengthens the notion of the relation to love; this latter (ἐν ἀγάπῃ) is made prominent by being placed first. "In" marks "love" as the soil, *in* which they are rooted, and as the foundation, *on* which they are grounded. This implies moreover that it is not their own love which is referred to, but one which corresponds with the soil afforded to the tree, the foundation given to the house; and this would undoubtedly be, in accordance with the context, the love of Christ (BENGEL), were not all closer definition wanting, even the article. Accordingly this substantive rendered general by the absence of the article corresponds with the verbal idea: in loving, *i. e.* in that love, which is first God's in Christ and then that of men who become Christians, who are rooted in Him and grounded on Him through faith. [The reference to the Christian grace of love (EADIE, ALFORD, ELLICOTT) is preferable, since it does not lay too much stress on the absence of the article, as is done by both MEYER (*in amando*) and HARLESS (*subjective*, because anarthrous), and does not confound two things (God's love to us and our love in response), either of which might be represented as soil and foundation, scarcely both.—R.] But it is not necessary to supply "in Christ" (HARLESS) in thought, as if "in love" could be instrumental and the preposition could be repeated with two different references and used in joining two distinct definitions. Nor should it be limited to "love of the brethren" (CALVIN, SCHENKEL, BLEEK and others), as is still further evident from what follows.

**May be fully able to comprehend** [ἵνα ἐξισχύσητε καταλαβέσθαι].—Καταλαβέσθαι here means more than a mere intellectual apprehension, a perception, as in Acts iv. 13; xxv. 25; x. 34, but pre-eminently an inward experience: it corresponds with γνῶναι, which is conjoined to it with τε, but differs from it however, the first word denoting the inward experience, the latter the spiritual perception. [The tense of this verb perhaps implies the singleness of the act, and the voice the exercise of the mental power, a *dynamic* middle (KRUEGER), indicating the earnestness or spiritual energy with which the action is performed (ELLICOTT).—R.] The verb ἐξισχύσητε, placed in emphatic position, adds the idea of exertion, an energetic pressing through; BENGEL: *evaleatis*.

Something important is treated of, which cannot be comprehended in solitude, for one's self alone, but only in fellowship: **with all saints,** σὺν πᾶσι τοῖς ἁγίοις.—Like all science, the science of God's love, the study of God, is a joint labor.

**What is the breadth and length and depth and height,** τί τὸ πλάτος καὶ μῆκος καὶ βάθος καὶ ὕψος.—The lively, roused spirit of the Apostle here borrows the figure of a body, a mathematical magnitude [*sacra illa Pauli mathematica*], as in Job xi. 8, 9, it is applied to God's wisdom and perfection; it is instead of and = τί τὸ μέγεθος, what is the greatness. Since the article occurs but once, the unity of the object referred to is strongly indicated. Very naturally the "breadth" comes first, to this the "length" corresponds; then the "depth" is the nearest dimension, and the "height" closes the series: what is the object then whose dimensions Paul notices here? It is not directly designated, and hence must be taken from the context. The added clause connected with this by τε points at once to "the love of Christ." The dimensions set forth here then become clear: "breadth" refers to the nations lying beside each other on the earth, over all of whom the love of Christ will extend itself; "length," to the successive ages during which it will reach; "depth," to the misery and corruption of sin, into which it will descend; "height" to the glory at God's throne and near His heart to which it would elevate all.

To return to ver. 9 and accept "the mystery" as the object (CHRYSOSTOM, CALOVIUS, RUECKERT, HARLESS and others) is as unfounded as to find a reference to "the fulness of God" (ver. 19), and with Rev. xi. 1; xxi. 15, 16, to understand the Church of Christ, the temple of God (BENGEL, STIER, [EADIE], and others), or merely to supply "of God" or "of Christ" (MATTHIES, and others); HOLZHAUSEN alone suggests "our love!" Arbitrary as many of the explanations of the four dimensions undoubtedly are, the opinion of MEYER, that *every* special interpretation is unpsychological, only opening the door to subjective speculations, is equally unjustifiable. *Abusus non tollit usum.* The thought of the Apostle is clear: Loved and loving thou knowest the love of Christ. Certainly it is not: In the love to the brethren thou wilt know God's love. Comp. 1 John iv. 10, 16; John xv. 9-11.

[This simple view of the object whose dimensions are here predicated is held in the main by CALVIN, CALIXTUS, MORUS, STORR, HODGE, MEYER, ELLICOTT. EADIE strangely enough opposes it because τε follows: see his notes for a good *resumé* of opinions. ELLICOTT says: "The consequent clause, without being dependent or explanatory, still practically supplies the defining

---

the subject as here (ELLICOTT). ELLICOTT's remark is true as regards the other cases where ἵνα is trajected, but in 2 Thess. ii. 7, ἕως is put after the subject, which if not strictly parallel, is certainly analogous.—R.]

genitive: Paul pauses on the word ὕψος, and then, perhaps feeling it the most appropriate characteristic of Christ's love, he appends, without finishing the construction, a parallel thought which hints at the same conception (ὑπερβάλλουσαν), and suggests the required genitive." ALFORD, less correctly, leaves the object indefinite: "of all that God has revealed or done in or for us," a view which results from his insisting on the subordinate character of the clause introduced by τε. This little word really settles the question the other way.—An allusion to the temple of Diana (MACKNIGHT, CHANDLER) is exceedingly improbable, and the reference to the Christian Church finds no support in the context, foregoing or subsequent. AUGUSTINE gives the fanciful explanation: *sacramentum cruces*, which ESTIUS elaborates. Comp. that of SEVERIANUS (in ALFORD), and the various homiletical applications given in *Hom. Notes.*—R.]

Ver. 19. **And to know the knowledge-surpassing love of Christ** [γνῶναί τε τὴν ὑπερβάλλουσαν τῆς γνώσεως ἀγάπην τοῦ Χριστοῦ].—Γνῶναί τε adds something closely related, giving prominence to the perception of what has become a matter of internal experience. The object is "the love of Christ," obviously Christ's love, not our love to Him. To the former alone is the attribute "knowledge-surpassing" applicable. BENGEL: *Suavissima hæc quasi correctio est; dixerat: cognoscere, statim negat cognitionem idoneam haberi posse.* The participle, which is here placed between the article and substantive, must evidently be taken as an adjective, governing with its comparative meaning the genitive which follows, *superiorem cognitione.* See WINER, p. 324. It is = ὑπέχουσαν πάντα νοῦν, "which passeth all understanding" (Phil. iv. 7). Comp. Phil. iii. 8-10. It is an oxymoron, like 1 Cor. i. 21, 25; 2 Cor. viii. 2; Gal. ii. 19; 1 Tim. v. 6, and refers to an (adequate) apprehension of the love of Christ which surpasses knowledge (*i. e.*, the particular abstract knowledge, which is possible to man of himself). HARLESS: "Love fully solves the mystery of love; only love experiences love and knows love. The γνῶσις of the reflecting understanding finds its limit here; the γνῶσις of love understands the love of Christ, which otherwise far transcended γνῶσις." LUTHER (1522–41): also to know the love of Christ, which yet exceeds all knowledge; in 1545 the incorrect rendering first appeared, which goes too far in the attempt to popularize the Scriptural language: and to know that to love Christ is better than all knowing. This is contrary both to the language and the context. Yet it cannot be said, that the love of Christ is the object of a knowledge, which never attains its full end (RUECKERT). Against this is the previous expression: "that ye may be able," as well as the remainder of the verse. [Nor can we accept the view of HARLESS and OLSHAUSEN: "that ye may know that the love of Christ is knowledge-surpassing," since the participle, which is properly taken as an adjective, is thus twisted into an infinitive, and since the Apostle's prayer is thus unnecessarily shorn of its fulness.—R.]

*The final end of the supplication;* ver. 19 *b.*

**That ye may be filled up.**—This phrase connects itself with "that ye may be able . . to know," and designates the highest, last favor which the Apostle implores for the Church. With what are they to be filled?

**To all the fulness of God** [εἰς πᾶν τὸ πλήρωμα τοῦ θεοῦ.]—Εἰς designates that toward and unto which the becoming filled proceeds, and πᾶν τὸ πλήρωμα, *meta est* (BENGEL), to which the Church should attain, when it is filled. It is therefore in her, not without her. Hence the Apostle is treating of a fulness in them which God grants, and which is unincumbered, unabridged. They must themselves, through the experience and knowledge of the love of Christ, be prepared, expanded, strengthened and fitted to receive πᾶν τὸ πλήρωμα, "all the fulness," which God will impart, has determined and ordained to impart. What God imparts is indeed in Him, from His own character and glory He imparts. LUTHER: "That is according to the Hebrew mode of speech as much as to say, that we are filled in every way, by which *He makes full*—that He alone completely rules and works in us."

It is a bolder expression than 2 Pet. i. 4: "partakers of the Divine nature." Comp. iv. 13; Col. ii. 9, 10. CHRYSOSTOM: πληροῦσθαι πάσης ἀρετῆς, ἧς πλήρης ἐστὶν ὁ θεός. THEODORET: ἵνα τελείως αὐτὸν ἔνοικον δέξησθε. It is not to be limited to the presence of grace (HARLESS), or to *charisms* (MEYER), nor to be pantheistically extended or applied to the universe, filling itself in God, *i. e.*, reaching the highest expression of its perfection, and reflecting itself in the Church, so that in it there is no more defect to be discovered (SCHENKEL). A fulness of God, which complements His Godhead, as though God's Being were first perfected through the Church, is as little the subject treated of as a pantheistic deification of men. See i. 23. The Apostle undoubtedly refers to the persons and personal culture of the individual members of the Church. See *Doctr. Note.* 4.

[MEYER and DE WETTE take πλήρωμα in the sense of πλῆθος, and the genitive as that of origin. But the GREEK FATHERS, and OLSHAUSEN, ALFORD, ELLICOTT, HODGE, among late commentators, prefer to take πλήρωμα in the strict sense of *id quo res impletur*, and the genitive as a possessive, implying: "that ye may be so filled as God is filled," the reference being not to charismatic gifts, but to the spiritual perfections of God. The only objection is, that such a fulness could not be realized here in a state of imperfection, but εἰς shows that a standard is here set up, and none but a perfect one would be thus held before them. The other view is too tame for the climactic position and force of the clause. ALFORD: "All the fulness of the Godhead abides in Christ, Col. ii. 9. Christ then abiding in your hearts, ye, being raised up to the comprehension of God's mercy in Him and of His love, will be filled, even as God is full—each in your degree, but all to your utmost capacity, with Divine wisdom, might and love."—R.]

## DOCTRINAL AND ETHICAL.

1. The fervency of the *worship* (κάμπτω τὰ

γόνατά μου) does not lose itself in the joyous sense of the love of God (πρὸς τὸν πατέρα), but becomes more deep and clear in love to the neighbor, in unselfish *supplication*, which in the scale of prayer rises above the lowest grade, which is a cry of need, a cry for help, above the grade of a pupil, the petition for supply of needed good and protection from threatening evil, and approaches in its best feature the master-prayer of thanksgiving, which is so often forgotten, and of praise, that so often is not understood.

2. *The Father* who is here supplicated is not the All-father of the 18th century or of the rationalists, nor the Father of the heathen. For He is not that weak father, who on account of His goodness consents to withdraw all the demands of His righteousness; nor is He merely the Creator, as if He were, like Jupiter, a father of the trees and animals, of the flowers of earth and the stars of heaven, as well as of angels and men, and as if the idea of "Father" included only that of the Creator, who calls into being. The father is more than the begetter, he is also the provider, the teacher, the guardian in preserving sacred love. Where such paternal care exists, it comes from God, it points to Him, the original Father. Even the most scanty traces of such fatherhood, *i. e.*, of such companies with a father at their hand, point to Him, who has ordained and still sustains such relations. The children may be lost and not permit Him to work within them; still traces of Him, kindnesses from Him are so little wanting, that even among the heathen "an altar with this inscription, To the unknown God," points to them. The Church sings and speaks of a λόγος σπερματικός, and sees a great family in different groups, in different circumstances, conditions and attitudes, but at the head, over all and for all the One Father in Christ.

3. *The inner man* (ὁ ἔσω ἄνθρωπος) is the remnant of the man created in the image of God, which is found in all men, even though extremely disfigured or shrivelled up into insignificance. On this account is Redemption possible, man is capable as well as in need of redemption. Hence the inner man is to be thus distinguished from the new man (ὁ καινὸς ἄνθρωπος): the former is the remnant of the original man as created by God in His own image, the latter is the beginning of the regenerated man, new born in Christ; that is still present in all men, this not yet existing in all, though it might and should be; that is found without the Church also, this begins only within it; the former is the starting-point for the latter, the latter is the result of the reviving of the former obtained in Christ; that is the first creation, conceived in retrospect, this the "new creature," conceived as rising; the former is accordingly of *nature*, which God in holy love has created, preserved and guided, the latter of *grace*, in which He has had mercy upon the former. But universal as the need of redemption and the capacity for redemption are, man is, on account of this need and in spite of this capability, not in a condition to *win* the gracious right of sonship, or *obligated thereto* (SCHENKEL), but on account of this need notwithstanding this capability only in a state to receive the gift of renewed sonship. See *Exeg. Notes*, ver. 16.

4. In the *economy of salvation,*—in which our passage, being addressed to believers, presupposes justification and antecedent repentance, and regards only the growing renewal, the strengthening of the inner man, his growth in the grace and truth of Christ—the Father constantly, at every stage, takes the initiative, and the recovering man takes no step forward without power received from God. Hence the supplication, that He would "grant" and that too "through His Spirit" to the inner man: thus the renewal within begins from above. Then the awakened, renewed power of the inner man appears in faith, in dependence draws Christ into himself, into his heart, as a guest into his house, for continued intercourse with Him, carefully directing himself by Him in all respects. The inner man, when once he has actually, with saving effect, become the *object* (εἰς) of the working of the *Holy Ghost*, becomes the *subject* of transforming activity in *faith*, which like a screw binds Christ to the soul. Though we may not, with the mystics, accept a union *essentialis et corporalis*, still we should not, with the rationalists, deny the *conjunctio substantiæ hominis fidelis cum substantia sanctæ trinitatis* and affirm only a dynamic or operative presence of Christ.

5. *The work* of salvation is a difficult one, and demands the power of God and man. *Of God:* hence Paul prays (ver. 16): "that he would grant you according to the riches of His glory." Of *man:* hence ver. 18: "that ye may be fully able."

6. *Knowledge and Love are not to be separated.* There is not merely an "illumination" before conversion and repentance, but also after justification through faith. In the enjoyment of the love of Christ, which we experience, our love is strengthened, forgetting itself and yet with a profound remembrance of itself it knows what it has experienced, denying itself it is thus strengthened to a clear knowledge of the love of Christ. Human things one must know, in order to love but Divine things one must love, in order to know (PASCAL). Love, hastening before, ever gains new material and light for knowledge. "The more I love, the more I *find* that I ought to love Thee."

7. *The connection of faith and love* is also presupposed here, and in such a way that the former is the mother's lap for the latter; the faith in that love of God in Christ, which we experience and enjoy, must impel to love, to love in return again and again.

8. *Christ's Love* surpasses all knowledge and understanding, that only toilsomely attains to seeing. HOFMANN: "There is really but one love in the world, because but one actual entering in of person into person. The eternally personal God, who is Love, who has entered into humanity as the personal Christ, who in the Holy Ghost personally flows into the personal life of men, so that we *have Him* and *are His*, He loves and is loved. Only where this archetypal fountain of love exists, can man exercise toward his fellow man a copied love." Only so far as it is felt, can it be known in our weakness.

9. *The completion of fellowship with* God points into eternity, from the militant to the triumphant church; there the children become heritors,

are taken on His throne and heart. Here many radial lines already proceed from the circumference, grace, peace and joy, truth and freedom, sonship and the sense of sonship, life-power and life-fulness, yet they come together in the center only above. Let us only hold fast to the unity of the family of God in heaven and on earth, the oneness of the Father through Christ in the Holy Ghost.

## HOMILETICAL AND PRACTICAL.

Had not the Apostle said so, no one would have discovered from his tone, that he was in bonds and chains, looking death in the face. To him affliction is a clear winter night, in which the stars of promise only shine the brighter. Has he tears in his eyes, they become a telescope to carry his sight into the far distant heavens, to open heaven to him and permit him to gaze into the depth of its wonders. It does not occur to him, to pray for release; he asks only for the perfecting and ennobling of the church.—In outward woe he thinks, feels and prays about inward weal alone; in evil, that concerns himself, about the good of the church alone.—God, the true Father, is not nearer to heaven with its angels and saints than to earth with its sons of men; were we but nearer to Him!—He is the Rich One, who can and will give; we are the poor ones, who should receive and—*will not!*—It were better if thou didst not care so much how to adorn the outer man through the spirit of the world and of fashion; God can through His Spirit re-animate and strengthen the inner man.—Above all see how it stands within thee, so that what God has created after His image in thee be not stunted and starved out. Thine outer man may laugh and sing and dance, while the inner man laments and sighs and goes to destruction.

Christ wishes to dwell with thee, not as a mere passing guest; so order thy work and recreation and mode of life after His example, that it may please Him to dwell there and not to hasten away. He is willing to belong to thee; it is not enough then that thou hearest Him, hearkenest to Him, thou must also belong to Him as His possession, must submit thyself and all thou hast to His disposal.—Bind thyself in faith to Him and hold communion with those who believe in Him, that thou mayest grow in the knowledge of His love. Root thyself ever deeper in that love, ground thyself ever more firmly upon it.—Do like Ernest the Pious, who in 1636 had a medal struck in commemoration of his marriage with Elizabeth Sophia of Altenburg, with this inscription on the one side: *Christum lieben ist das beste wissen* (Loving Christ is the best knowledge), and on the other: *Gott, lehr erkennen mich und Dich* (God, teach me to know myself and Thee)!—Holy love alone lets us understand and use the Scriptures ever better and better! If we look at God's word and world without love; we see them only remotely.—Three-fold aim of Christian supplication: 1. Strengthening of the inner man; 2. Knowledge of the love of Christ; 3. Fulness of Divine glory.

STARKE:—In praying the outward posture is indeed of little importance; it is left to Christian liberty to take this or that position with the body; yet no kind of posture seems better fitted for fervent, earnest prayer, than kneeling.—Thou hast indeed a merciful, gracious and loving Father: Thinkest thou, He can ever forsake thee? That is an idle thought. As little as He can take Love out of His heart so little can He forget thee. See, what is the best thing a teacher can ask for his flock; but also what thou too, O soul, must seek after, to be strengthened through the Spirit of God in the inner man.—It is not enough to have come into a state of grace through conversion, there must be added a strengthening and fortifying, which however is not the work of man, since Christ is the Author and Finisher of our faith. Though our sins were so broad, so long, so deep, so high, as heaven and earth, yet is the grace and mercy of God deeper, broader, higher and longer, so that it cannot be measured.—The mystery of the love of God is incomprehensible: in future perfection we will understand it. Because we still await that time, let us meanwhile imitate such love in its depth, by helping those who are in the deepest misery and least deserving; in its breadth, by showing to all men without distinction, for God's sake, kindness and affection, in its length, by never ceasing or becoming weary; in its height, by looking up to God, devoting to Him all our efforts, and having His glory as our purpose.—In Christianity more depends upon taking in faith, than upon giving and doing in love. For the more we take of the fulness of God, the more we can give.

A. MUELLER:—He who lets Christ dwell in his heart, only that he may have from Him a household blessing or a joyful consolation, *sells* Him his heart; but he who surrenders himself to Christ out of pure love, at the same time thinking himself unworthy of the least look of His grace, *gives* Him his heart.

RIEGER:—God oftentimes indeed begins in a very small way in His works of grace, because He will effect nothing according to absolute power, but so as to lead men to faith and obedience.—Christ dwelling in the heart and His Spirit lay claim also to the members of the body, putting them into the service of righteousness, to bring forth fruit unto God in holiness.—Being rooted and grounded in love we obtain the ability to comprehend, not merely to know, but also with other powers of soul so to appropriate something as to be filled therewith. Faith widens the heart, so that more and more can be grasped. But with these enlarged views, which are imparted to us, we should not sunder ourselves from other saints, nor attach to anything such an immoderate value, as to sever the bond which unites us with other saints, but apply all to the edification of the body of Christ.

HEUBNER:—It is a truly proud misery of Kant's, his denying kneeling as a slavish Orientalism. He can scarcely have felt the impulse of a praying heart. Lichtenberg judges very differently, when he says: "When the body falls upon its knees, the spirit lifts itself to God."—We have too little bending of the knee; the Catholics perhaps too much, so that a Catholic may occasionally be recognized by the looks of his clothes at the knees. Spener wished that kneeling devotion was more common among us.—What a comfort for fatherless children and widows, what hope for affectionate fathers, to know that their dear children have in heaven a better Father than themselves. Still the human relation can best teach the true "Father-theology."—A church can be good outwardly and apparently and yet be without inward life. This inward life comes from the Spirit of God. Christianity should be learned not by heart, but in the heart. *—Christ will dwell, not in stone churches, but in living hearts; the heart should live and move in Him, His Spirit should animate our spirit in constant intercourse with Him.—When Christ dwells in the heart, every one has his Christ in his neighbor.—*Breadth:* the Church of Christ should stretch itself over the whole circle of the earth, over all lands. The *length* refers to time; she continues throughout all centuries. The *depth* points to her foundation; she has it in the unfathomable abyss of Divine mercy, and her *height* reaches into heaven, it is unassailable, for the church on earth and in the spirit world is one. This is the greatness and the origin of the spiritual temple.—Love to Christ, a simple heart full of faith and love to Him, is better than all science. This love has an unconditioned value, is in itself the highest: not so with knowledge; it can give a kind of enlightenment, without at all affecting the heart. The heart excels the understanding. Science should not be over-estimated, and made an idol. Science can never conquer the enemies of the Kingdom of God, she should be a handmaid. The true science is only where the cross is. Only the *theologus crucis* is the *theologus lucis.*

PASSAVANT:—With a narrow heart we cannot pray with confidence. Hence everything demands that we should receive Divine riches, which enlightens our mind, expands our heart and makes God great in us.—How worthy of admiration, how highly exalted above man is this *inner man* of the heart! Faith is his reason and his light; love his heart and his life; the Holy Ghost his soul and strength; Jesus Christ his ego and his nature; God his Father and at the same time his heritage, his glory, his riches, his eternal dwelling-place; God makes him, His work in His own good time, and this through a power whose working corresponds with the riches and the glory of His grace.—Did Christ dwell in us, what would we become to our friends, to our enemies, to the world, to the heavens!—Only the Spirit of God in us can disclose to us what God is; only faith, through the Holy Ghost, can apprehend Christ and His life in us; only pure, holy love in us can comprehend what is transcendent and blissful, the wonders of the love of God in Jesus Christ.—There is a breadth and length and depth and height; for this no worlds are too broad, no paths too long, no space too wide, no abyss, no hell too deep, no heaven too high, that it may not reach thither, and penetrate there with might and almightiness, with light and life, with comfort and salvation and peace from eternal compassion—"fulness of God" the destination and end of man, the aim and end of all the decrees of God, of all the mysteries of Christ. Canst thou not satisfy man? Must he still fill himself with a thousand trifles besides, that his happiness may be complete?

STIER:—The *higher* his petition seeks to ascend above all understanding to Him, who is able to do above all, the *deeper* he bows himself.—The indwelling of Christ: Its *beginning*—through faith; *means*—Christ's love, which becomes ours; *aim*—according to the widest extension of the plan (knowledge) and inmost depths of the foundation (Christ's love).

GERLACH:—The love of Christ to us precedes all our love and knowledge.

NITZSCH:—*The essential petition,* which we, each for all and all for each, should bear in our hearts, during the varieties and vicissitudes of our life-path. 1. *Its purport: a*) To become strong in the inner man; *b*) To have vital fellowship with the Redeemer; *c*) To know His love. 2. *The effect.*

WOLTERS (*Dedication sermon at Godesberg*): The proper prayer for a young congregation: 1) that its members become strong in the inner man: 2) that Christ lives in their hearts; 3) that they understand His love in its greatness and blessedness.

GENZKEN (*Preparatory Lecture** on Eph. iii. 13–21): St. Paul our example in prayer. 1) He bows his knees, so we under the burden of our guilt; 2) He addresses himself to the Father of our Lord Jesus Christ; so there is no other name for us; 3) He asks power for the inner man to strengthen in faith, in love, and for every good work; so we.

LÖHE:—St. Paul's request to the Ephesians, his prayer to God, his song of praise to Him, all in relation to the great mystery of building the church on earth.

WESTERMEIER:—*The best prayer:* 1) to whom it is addressed; 2) the gifts it desires; 3) the basis on which it rests.

KLUGE:—Seek the kingdom of God, not in external things, but in the inner man—1) in judging of the contest of the gospel against the world; 2) of the blessing of the gospel in yourselves.

RABUS:—A glance into the closet of the Apostle: 1) How we should *approach* God in prayer; 2) how *supplicate* Him; 3) how *praise* Him.

RAUTENBERG:—What Paul does in his tribulations, that his disciples may not become weary in the walk of faith: 1) He is far from them—yet sends them his mighty word; 2) He suffers the contempt of the world—but endures it for their glory; 3) He cannot give them his hand, but he bows his knee for them.

DR. MEIER (*Baptismal discourse* on ver. 18): On the breadth, length, depth, height of the love of God.

PRÖHLE:—Paul's pious wish for the Church at Ephesus: 1. That they might not become weary in their Christian course (ver. 13). 2.

* [The German has a similar paranomasia: *Man soll das Christenthum nicht auswendig, sondern inwendig lernen.*—R.]

* [*Beichtrede* is literally a discourse at *confession,* but among Protestants means the service preparatory to the communion, during the previous week. The etymology confirms the view, that our preparatory lecture is borrowed from the Romanist usage of confessing before the communion, though in reality a proper mode of obeying the injunction: Let a man examine himself.—R.]

That God would give them power to become strong in the inner man (vers. 14-16). 3. That Christ may dwell in their hearts (ver. 17). 4. That they may be able to comprehend with all saints the breadth=the universality, embracing all, the length=the endlessness from eternity to eternity, the depth and height=the immeasurable and incomprehensible greatness of the love of Christ.

[HODGE:—The most beautiful object might be in the apartment of a blind man, and he not be sensible of its presence; or if by any means made aware of its nearness, he could have no delight in its beauty. Christ dwells in us by faith, because it is by faith we perceive His presence, His excellence and His glory, and because it is by faith we appropriate and reciprocate the manifestations of His love. Faith is to this spiritual communion what esteem and affection are to the fellowship of domestic life.—The love of Christ is infinite; not only because it inheres in an infinite subject, but because the condescension and sufferings to which it led, and the blessings which it secures for its objects, are beyond our comprehension.—R.]

[EADIE:—Ver. 15. They lose the cold and official name of subjects in the familiar and endearing appellation of sons, and they are united to one another not dimly and unconsciously, as different products of the same Divine workmanship, but they merge into one family—"all they are brethren."—Ver. 17. When Ignatius was asked, on his trial, by the Emperor, what was the meaning of his name—Theophorus—he promptly replied, "He who has Christ in his breast."—Love is the fundamental grace.—Ver. 19. As the attachment of a man, it may be gauged; but as the love of a God, who can by searching find it out? Uncaused itself, it originated salvation; unresponded to amidst the "contradiction of sinners," it neither pined nor collapsed. It led from Divine immortality to human agonies and dissolution, for the victim was bound to the cross, not by the nails of the military executioner, but by the "cords of love." It loved repulsive unloveliness, and, unnourished by reciprocated attachment, its ardor was unquenched, nay, is unquenchable, for it is changeless as the bosom in which it dwells. Thus it may be known, while yet it "passeth knowledge;" thus it may be experimentally known, while still in its origin and glory it surpasses comprehension, and presents new and newer phases to the loving and inquiring spirit. For one may drink of the spring and be refreshed, and his eye may take in at one view its extent and circuit, while he may be able neither to fathom the depth nor mete out the volume of the ocean whence it has its origin.—R.]

---

3. *Conclusion in the form of a Doxology.*

(CHAP. III. 20, 21).

20 Now unto [to] him that [who] is able to do [above all things], exceeding abun-
dantly above all that [above what] we ask or think, according to the power that
21 worketh in us, Unto [to] him *be* [the] glory in the church by [in][1] Christ Jesus
throughout all ages, world without end [*lit.*, unto all the generations of the age of
the ages]. Amen.

### TEXTUAL AND GRAMMATICAL.

1 Ver. 21.—After ἐν τῇ ἐκκλησίᾳ א. A. B. C. insert καὶ before ἐν Χριστῷ Ἰησοῦ. A few authorities [D.[1] F.] read: ἐν Χριστῷ Ἰησοῦ καὶ (ἐν) τῇ ἐκκλησίᾳ, evidently from doctrinal hesitation about placing the church before Christ; in single minor authorities ἐν τῇ ἐκκλησίᾳ is wanting. This arises from the inappropriate καί, which only disturbs, and although well supported externally, is inadmissible on internal grounds. It may be rejected, and is rejected by Tischendorf, on the authority of a number of important MSS. [These are D.[2] K. L., besides the great majority of cursives, oldest versions, and many fathers. Rejected by Tischendorf, Meyer, and most, bracketted by Alford, accepted by Lachmann, Ellicott (ed. 3. 4 only). Before the discovery of א. the internal grounds were sufficiently strong to outweigh the preponderant uncial testimony in its favor, but now the question is more doubtful. The sense is not affected materially by the variation, though the insertion precludes one interpretation. The word may have been inserted to indicate the other meaning, hence its omission presents a *lectio difficilior*.—R.]

### EXEGETICAL AND CRITICAL.

In general the *doxology* is frequent, either at the *beginning* (i. 3-14; 1 Pet. i. 3-5), or at the *close* of an Epistle (Rom. xvi. 25-27; Phil. iv. 20; 2 Tim. iv. 18; 1 Pet. v. 11; Jude 25; Heb. xiii. 21), or at the close of a section, as here, Rom. xi. 33-36; Gal. i. 5; 1 Tim. i. 17.

Ver. 20. **Now to him who is able to do above all things**—Τῷ δὲ* δυναμένῳ stands emphatically first, because the matter in hand is the manifestation of God's power and almightiness (ver. 16: δυνάμει, ver. 18: ἐξισχύσητε). With the infinitive ποιῆσαι ["to do," to effect], we must closely connect ὑπὲρ πάντα, "above all," under which we should understand

* [ALFORD: "δέ brings out a slight contrast to what has just preceded—viz., *ourselves*, and our need of strength and our growth in knowledge and fulness," but the contrast is not strong enough to justify our rendering the particle: "but."—R.]

creatures, powers and events, which may act in a hindering, disturbing or destructive way.

**Exceeding abundantly above what we ask or think** [*ὑπερεκπερισσοῦ ὧν αἰτούμεθα ἢ νοοῦμεν*].—In this added qualification the Apostle places God's almightiness in comparison with his prayer, and that in a most striking manner. Hence *ὑπερεκπερισσοῦ*, found also in 1 Thes. iii. 10, v. 13 [?]. Similar expressions, strengthening the sense, occur in Eph. i. 21; iv. 10; Rom. v. 20; 2 Cor. vii. 4, 13; xi. 5; xii. 11; 1 Tim. i. 14; Mark vii. 37; xiv. 31; vi. 51. In its comparative signification it governs, as in ver. 19: *ὑπερβάλλουσαν τῆς γνώσεως*, the genitive *ὧν*, which is = *τῶν ἃ αἰτούμεθα ἢ νοοῦμεν*. BENGEL: *Cogitatio latius patet quam preces; gradatio.* God is greater than our heart (1 John iii. 20). CHRYSOSTOM: *ἐγὼ μὲν γὰρ εὔχομαι, αὐτὸς δὲ καὶ χωρὶς τῆς ἐμῆς εὐχῆς μείζονα ἐργάσεται τῶν ἡμετέρων αἰτήσεων οὐχ ἁπλῶς μείζονα ἢ ἐκ περισσοῦ ἀλλ' ὑπερεκπερισσοῦ, τὸ μέγεθος ἐμφαίνων τῆς δωρεᾶς.*

[The relative does not refer to *πάντα;* it introduces a new but related subject. The two phrases are not in apposition, but the second member explains the first. There is no tautology therefore, since subjoined to the expression of God's super-abundant power, we have a definition of the mode in which it displays itself, *viz.*, by conferring spiritual gifts in super-abundance (EADIE). There is no hyperbole as HARLESS thinks, though Paul has such a marked predilection for *ὑπέρ* and its compounds; it "occurs nearly thrice as many times in Paul's Epistles and that to the Hebrews as in the rest of the New Testament; and of the 28 words compounded with *ὑπέρ*, 22 are found in these Epistles, and 20 of them there alone."—R.]

**According to the power that worketh [or is working] in us**, *κατὰ τὴν δύναμιν τὴν ἐνεργουμένην ἐν ἡμῖν*.—This belongs to the phrase: "able to do." The *present* middle participle marks the continued efficiency of His power, while "in us" indicates both the object and the sphere of activity. *Paulus allegat experientiam* (BENGEL) and full of confidence turns from the beginning to the future. Comp. Col. i. 29. Miraculous gifts (MICHAEL) are not referred to, nor should *ὑπὲρ πάντα*, "above all," be limited to *quæ hactenus visa sunt* (GROTIUS), or the preposition *ὑπέρ* be taken adverbially (BENGEL), as in 2 Cor. xi. 23 alone. [The power, so frequently referred to in this Epistle, is the might of the indwelling Spirit. The *middle* (comp. Gal. v. 6) is used mainly in non-personal references; see WINER, p. 242.—R.]

Ver. 21. **To him be the glory**, *αὐτῷ ἡ δόξα*.—The pronoun sums up vigorously and emphatically what is predicated in ver. 20. The dative denotes that the glory is due, will be given to Him (Luke xvii. 18; John ix. 24; Acts xii. 23; Rom. iv. 20; 1 Pet. i. 21; Acts iv. 9, xi. 13; xiv. 7; xvi. 9; xix. 7). [So most commentators]. Accordingly the article, *ἡ δόξα*, does not indicate the "glory," which He has (HARLESS); in that case the pronoun *αὐτοῦ* would occur, as in the interpolated doxology at the close of the Lord's prayer: *ὅτι σοῦ ἐστὶν ἡ βασιλεία, κ. τ. λ.* But it is the glory of the church, which indeed she has first from God, but which as received from Him, properly His and yet appropriated by her, she returns to Him with gratitude and praise. It is not = *ἔπαινος, praise*, which consists in words, nor = *τιμή, honor*, which consists in the judgment of those who praise, but refers to the life, worship, and character of the church. Comp. i. 12, 14: *εἰς ἔπαινον τῆς δόξης αὐτοῦ*, "unto the praise of his glory." It is most natural to supply *ἔστω*.

**In the church in Christ Jesus**, [*ἐν τῇ ἐκκλησίᾳ ἐν Χριστῷ Ἰησοῦ*].—The preposition *ἐν* before *τῇ ἐκκλησίᾳ* points to the sphere in which the glory of God is given back, defining more closely either the omitted *ἔστω* or *ἡ δόξα*. By *ἡ ἐκκλησία*, "the church," we should understand the assembly of those in whom God's power has become efficient and works (ver. 20: "in us"); it is accordingly no external region (MEYER), which is indifferent internally, and beside which an inner spiritual sphere is to be indicated (*ἐν Χριστῷ*); the church is indeed herself such a sphere. Hence the phrase "in Christ Jesus," defines more closely the church, its character and status, in order to explain, in what church the glory can and shall be given to God. Luther has rendered it properly as one notion: *die in Christo Jesu lebendige Gemeinde* (the church alive in Christ Jesus).

[To this interpretation, which is that of OLSHAUSEN, STIER and others, it is properly objected that such a definition of the church is altogether unnecessary. If *καί* be accepted (see *Textual Note*) this exegesis is inadmissible. Nor is the view of MEYER (with HARLESS, DE WETTE, EADIE, HODGE, ALFORD and ELLICOTT) open to the objection urged by Braune that it presents an external region internally indifferent. The sphere of the giving of glory is defined in a twofold manner: "It is offered in the church, but it is, at the same time offered 'in Christ Jesus,' or presented by the members of the sacred community in the consciousness of union with Him" (EADIE); "if any glory comes from us to God it is in Christ." The repetition of *ἐν* seems to point to such a meaning, even if *καί* be omitted. —R.] Hence it is not = to *διὰ Χριστοῦ* (GROTIUS); comp. Col. iii. 17; Rom. i. 18; vii. 25. [CALVIN, BEZA and RUECKERT: *per Christum;* E. V.: "by Christ Jesus;" *σὺν Χριστῷ* (ŒCUMENIUS), all alike objectionable, for even the instrumental sense of *ἐν* is not exactly = *διά*, and the proper sense of the preposition is the more necessary because it occurs for the second time. —R.]

**Unto all the generations of the age of the ages**, [*εἰς πάσας τὰς γενεὰς τοῦ αἰῶνος τῶν αἰώνων, ἀμήν*].—The phrase *εἰς πάσας τὰς γενεάς* designates the successive groups which are added to this church; *γενεαί* designates the groups of living persons. Now, at the time when Paul writes, the beginning has been made, the first *γενεά*, "generation," which reflects Godward the glory, the light in and from His light, is present; and thus it should and will continue, hence *εἰς*, "unto." It is = *εἰς γενεὰν καὶ γενεάν*, or *εἰς γενεὰς γενεῶν* (Luke i. 50, various reading); this repetition expressing the same idea as *πᾶσαι*; "the iterative form of the expression indicated the extension" (HARLESS).

The phrase *τοῦ αἰῶνος τῶν αἰώνων* defines to what these *γενεαί* belong and extend, *in omnes generationes, quæ complectitur ὁ αἰών, qui terminatur in τοὺς αἰῶνας perpetuos* (BENGEL). Ὁ αἰών marks the unity or totality of passing time, which at the same time includes eternity. We have no word which indicates both, as the Greeks had. [True in both English and German]. BENGEL: *αἰῶνες periodi œconomiæ divinæ ab una quasi scena ad aliam decurrentes; hic amplificantur causa utrumque vocabulum, cum metaphora in γενεά, generatio, conjungitur, ut significetur tempus bene longum; nam in αἰῶσι non jam sunt* GENERATIONES. Paul says therefore, that the church now begun shall continue through a long series of generations; begun on earth it will be developed throughout these generations, and even when generations shall cease, shall continue in *æons*, without succession of generations, and these generations and those *æons* (in which new generations are not added, but the constituent ones continue permanently) form a whole, one *αἰών*, the *αἰὼν μέλλων*. Instead of this full formula we find only *εἰς τοὺς αἰῶνας*, Rom. i. 25; ix. 5; xi. 36; xvi. 27; Luke i. 33; 2 Cor. xi. 31; or *αἰῶνας τῶν αἰώνων*, 1 Tim. i. 17; 1 Pet. v. 11. Rev. i. 6, 18; iv. 9, 10, *etc.; εἰς πάντας τοὺς αἰῶνας*, Jude 25; *εἰς τὸν αἰῶνα*, Matth. xxi. 19; Mark xi. 14, *etc.; εἰς τὸν αἰῶνα τοῦ αἰῶνος*, Heb. i. 8. Comp. *Doctr. Notes*, 5, 6.

[Only the most extravagant literalism can exclude the idea of eternity from this cumulative expression, and only the most forced exegesis can include "distinct traces of gnosticism." HARLESS makes a subtle distinction between *αἰῶνες τῶν αἰώνων* and *αἰὼν τῶν αἰώνων*, taking the former as more extensive, the latter intensive, for which there is little room here. MEYER is perhaps too literal in his view of *γενεαί*, which Braune apparently adopts. ALFORD is satisfactory: "Probably the account of the meaning is, that the *age* of ages (eternity) is conceived as containing ages, just as our 'age' contains years; and then those ages are thought of as made up, like ours, of generations. It is used, by a transfer of what we know in time, to express, imperfectly and indeed improperly, the idea of Eternity."—R.]

## DOCTRINAL AND ETHICAL.

1. *God's Omnipotence* is unlimited, if we leave out of view His own *will:* He can do what He will (Ps. cxv. 3).

2. God's power works *in* His people (*ἐν ὑμῖν*, ver. 20), not merely *over* them, and *about* them; for they do not resist Him with that will which He has given from His own will to those created in His image. He will not, with His omnipotence, force any into the Church in Christ Jesus, into salvation. Man has might to resist God's Almightiness within himself. [The limitation or extension of meaning which theologians of different schools may put upon this last sentence, need not be discussed here. Given free-will, the sacred right of personality, and it is true in some sense—awfully true, since this is the fearful price of our privilege as free men. *How* God's Almightiness, notwithstanding, never fails of its purpose, we do not know; *that* it never does, lies at the foundation of all proper theology.—R.]

3. The *Essence of worship* is the thankful return of what God has bestowed and the recipient has accepted and appropriated; hence the approach of the recipient to the Bestower, in gratitude for the gift, praise for the Giver; the deepest ground of adoration is, however, the condescending grace and imparting love of the Almighty God. He who is blessed begins to bless the Blesser (i. 3) and ends in praise of the God of glory (iii. 20, 21).

4. *The true Church, a creation of God* (ver. 20), a living congregation, an assembly of sanctified persons, is *Christian*, having and needing no other Mediator than Christ Jesus, proving and defining the relation to the church according to the relation to Him.

5. *The Christian Church has a history*, a development through a long series of generations even into eternity. HOFMANN (*Schriftbeweis*, II. 2, p. 127) retains the *καί* before *ἐν Χριστῷ Ἰησοῦ* and thinks the glorifying of God "in the church" takes place only in time and on earth, but "in Christ" eternally, as though the church were a temporal thing and nothing more. [EADIE: "The obligation to glorify God lasts through eternity, and the glorified church will ever delight in rendering praise, 'as is most due.' Eternal perfection will sustain an eternal anthem."—R.]

6. The Church of Jesus Christ does not find her final issue in the State (ROTHE), or in a higher grade of culture;* she has a rising without a setting. Rescued through all the changes of national life, she is herself the rescuer of individuals, and of larger groups as well, unto the future of eternity.

## HOMILETICAL AND PRACTICAL.

Prayer is no limit to God's working in thee, but a condition, which He Himself has appointed, without which thou canst not experience His almighty grace.—Thou art a creature of God, and shouldst become a work of His, praising the Master hand in word and deed, and above all in private character and conduct.—"Exceeding abundantly!" Hagar asked a drop and found a well (Gen. xxi. 19); Saul sought his father's asses and found a crown (1 Sam. ix. 3; x. 1); David asked bread and received a kingdom (1 Sam. xxi. 3).

STARKE: God does more than we desire. Joseph wishes only to be free from the iron chains: behold, God not only does what he desires, but gives him golden chains besides.

HEUBNER:—In the synagogues, mosques, and pagodas there is no true praise of God, nor yet in our churches, if Christ be not known.—*The prayer of Paul for the church* (vers. 13–21). 1. It was prompted by the impulse of love (ver. 13). 2. Full of confidence toward God, the Father of all churches (vers. 14, 15). 3. It was holy in its purport (vers. 16-19). 4. Hopeful,

* [When De Wette asks: "Was the Apostle warranted in expecting such a long duration for the Church?" he proves his utter want of sympathy with this Epistle, and abundantly justifies the criticism made on his commentary by ALFORD (see *Introd.* § 3, 5).—R.]

certain of hearing (vers. 20, 21).—*God the true Father.* 1. Exposition: *a*) He is not only the physical Creator and Upholder, but *b*) spiritual Father (vers. 14-16). 2. Ground of our belief in this: *a*) not mere reason and experience, but *b*) the gospel of Christ (vers. 17, 18). 3. Power of this belief: *a*) it attracts our heart to God (ver. 18), so that we understand God's heart, *b*) it strengthens unto obedience, *c*) it gives comfort and hope (vers. 19-21).—The intimate fellowship of the Apostles and their churches as an example for us.—The inner growth of a Christian church.

RIEGER: What occurs to each one at his conversion and during his daily renewal, is as good an evidence of the "exceeding abundant" power of God, as what occurs in the creation, preservation and government of all things.

[EADIE:—The Trinity is here again brought out to view. The power within us is that of the Spirit, and glory in Christ is presented to the Father who answers prayer through the Son, and by the Spirit; and, therefore, to the Father, in the Son, and by the Spirit, is offered this glorious minstrelsy: "As it was in the beginning, is now, and ever shall be, world without end. Amen."—R.]

# III. PART SECOND.

## THE SPIRIT RULING IN THE CHURCH OF CHRIST.

CHAPTERS IV.–VI. 20.

### 1. The Theme of the Whole Part:

*Walk worthy of the calling love and unity.*

CHAP. IV. 1–3.

1 I therefore, the prisoner of the Lord, beseech you [I exhort you therefore, I the prisoner in the Lord,][1] that ye walk worthy of the vocation [calling] wherewith ye
2 are [were] called, With all lowliness and meekness,[2] with long-suffering, forbearing
3 one another in love; Endeavoring [Earnestly striving] to keep the unity of the Spirit in the bond of peace.

#### TEXTUAL AND GRAMMATICAL.

[1] Ver. 1.—Nearly all MSS. have: ἐν κυρίῳ; ℵ.: ἐν Χριστῷ. [The change of order is for the purpose of bringing out the emphatic force of παρακαλῶ (*exhort* rather than *beseech*); the second *I* being required in English. *In* is substituted for *of* as more correct, while *calling* is in itself a better word than *vocation*, serving here to preserve the correspondence between the substantive and verb (aorist: *were* called).—R.]

[2] Ver. 2.—[The spelling πραΰτητος (ℵ. B. C. 17) is considered by Tischendorf, Alford, Ellicott, as the best attested form in the dialect of the New Testament. Comp. Gal. v. 23. Braune apparently prefers πραότητος (*Rec.*, A. D. F. L., most cursives). His rendering of the three terms is very neat: *mit aller Demuth und Sanftmuth, mit Langmuth.*—R.]

#### EXEGETICAL AND CRITICAL.

Ver. 1 *a. The connection.* **I exhort you therefore, I the prisoner in the Lord** [Παρακαλῶ οὖν ὑμᾶς ἐγὼ ὁ δέσμιος ἐν κυρίῳ].—The verb παρακαλῶ, placed first for emphasis, marks what follows as the ethical part. Οὖν, "therefore," joins this practical, hortatory portion of the letter with the previous theoretical part, and that too as a consequence, so that the one forms a foundation for the other; the context indicating the reference more closely.—Ὁ δέσμιος, "the prisoner," resumes what was expressed in iii. 1 and continued further in vers. 13, 14. As Paul in his bonds prays for the Church, so he exhorts it also. Although the paronomasia (παρακαλῶ—κλήσεως) recalls ἐκκλησία, yet the reference is not to ἐν τῇ ἐκκλησίᾳ, ver. 21, but to the whole of what precedes (τῇ ἐκκλησίᾳ has occurred already in i. 22), which is, however, summed up in the concluding doxology. Hence MEYER is incorrect in taking οὖν as an inference from iii. 21 merely.* The exhortation of the Apostle gives special emphasis to ἐγώ, "I," even though it stands after ὑμᾶς, "you," in the Greek. The phrase, ὁ δέσμιος

* [EADIE accepts a reference to the preceding paragraph; ALFORD to all that precedes so (HODGE), but adds: "here perhaps also a resumption of τούτου χάριν of chap. iii. 1, 14, and thus carried back to the contents of chaps. i. ii." ELLICOTT: "To those passages in the preceding chapter which relate to the spiritual privileges and calling of the Ephesians, *e. g.*, vers. 6, 12, but especially to ver. 14 ff., in which the tenor of the prayer incidentally discloses how high and how great that calling really was." The objection to the more general reference in my mind is, that it assumes the Epistle to have been by the Apostle himself purposely divided into two parts, *doctrinal* and *practical*, like the divisions of a sermon. Paul's method is rather that of *concatenation.*—R.]

ἐν κυρίῳ,* "the prisoner in the Lord" (which can be taken together grammatically, and must be taken together in view of the reference to iii. 1), marks the importance of the exhortation of Paul, who as a "faithful member of Christ" bears chains in and for the cause of Christ. CALVIN: *Erant (vincula) enim veluti sigillum honorificæ illius legationis, quam obtinuerat.* THEODORET: Τοῖς διὰ τὸν Χριστὸν δεσμοῖς ἐναβρύνεται μᾶλλον ἢ βασιλεὺς διαδήματι. He is a shining example, and elsewhere he refers to his own walk in agreement with his preaching (1 Cor. iv. 16; xi. 1; Phil. iii. 17); he speaks accordingly *ad excitandum effectum, quo sit efficacior exhortatio* (ESTIUS), but not *ut Paulum obsequio exhilararent* (BENGEL). He wishes to gain attention and efficacy for his παρακαλεῖν, by appealing, not to his imprisonment, which in itself was incapable of strengthening his exhortation, but to his willing, joyful, worthy wearing of the bonds; thus at the same time also strongly urging self-denial. The verb itself means originally *to call hither*, to invite (Acts xviii. 20); then *to address* either hortatively (Rom. xii. 1; 2 Cor. ii. 8) or *consolingly* (2 Cor. ii. 7; i. 6; vii. 6, 7). Ὑμᾶς, "you," designates the Church in its individual members; he always conceives of the Church as a fellowship of particular persons.

*The fundamental exhortation.* Ver. 1 *b*.

**That ye walk worthy of the calling** [ἀξίως περιπατῆσαι τῆς κλήσεως.—The infinitive περιπατῆσαι (see ii. 2), as in Acts xxvii. 33, 34, sets forth the purport of the exhortation. The emphasis, of course, rests upon the closer qualification ἀξίως ("worthy"), which stands first; for the kind of walk is the important matter. The genitive (as in Phil. i. 27; Col. i. 10; Rom. xvi. 2; 1 Thess. ii. 12) τῆς κλήσεως denotes that call of God, to which the walk must correspond, in order to be worthy.

**Wherewith ye were called,** ἧς (instead of ᾗ, 1 Cor. vii. 20) ἐκλήθητε.†—This relative clause joined *per attractionem* (see on i. 8) indicates that the call has already taken place and been accepted. He speaks of a walk corresponding to the call already received, not as though we should walk worthy, in order to be called, but, since we are called through the grace of God without our merit or worthiness, we should not be unworthy of such grace (CALVIN). Comp. vers. 17–30; ii. 10; Tit. ii. 11 ff.; Rom. viii. 4 ff.; Gal. v. 19 ff.

*Closer definition of the Christian walk*; vers. 2, 3.

Ver. 2. **With all lowliness and meekness** [μετὰ πάσης ταπεινοφροσύνης καὶ πραΰτητος. See *Textual Note* [2]].—This clause defines more closely "walk worthy of the calling," joining with it two attendants which belong to the Christian walk (WINER, p. 353).* First stands "lowliness," which has for its opposite "minding high things" (Rom. xii. 16), "thinking one's self to be something" (Gal. vi. 3); it is πάσης ἀρετῆς ὑπόθεσις (CHRYSOSTOM). Comp. Phil. ii. 3; Col. ii. 18, 23; iii. 12, 13. It is belief in our poverty over against faith in Christ, so that we know we have nothing, know nothing, can do nothing, having only an empty hand, yet an open one, to receive what the Lord will give. Accordingly, as in Matt. v. 3, 4, 5, to "the poor in spirit" and "they that mourn" (=οἱ ταπεινοφρονοῦντες) are joined "the meek," so here "meekness," πραΰτης, is added, that mildness which is gentle toward others, because it thinks: Have I been helped, then I do not know, who should not be helped! Comp. Gal. vi. 1; 2 Cor. x. 1; 1 Cor. iv. 21; 2 Tim. ii. 25. [See TRENCH, *Syn. N. T.* § xlii., perhaps the most discriminating essay on these words which can be found.†—R.] The adjective πάσης, "all," denotes all the various relations and situations of lowliness and meekness; the former must manifest itself in both intellectual and ethical spheres, before God and men, the latter toward friend and foe, under violations of our own rights and property as well as those of our neighbor.

**With long-suffering,** μετὰ μακροθυμίας, is co-ordinate in form with the other two, standing closely connected, yet taken up by itself. Long-suffering (Matt. xviii. 26, 29; 1 Cor. xiii. 4; 2 Cor. vi. 6; Gal. v. 22) is a manifestation of meekness; much depends upon it frequently in the life of a church. Hence it accords with the context to distinguish this by a second μετά and to conjoin it to the other terms. [The word means, not taking swift vengeance or inflicting speedy punishment, though it becomes more general in its sense=forbearance of every kind. The pointing of the E. V. is correct, making the phrase a separate clause. Besides the objection which Braune urges below against connecting it with what follows we may add, that thus the phrase would receive undue emphasis and the parallelism of the participial clauses be disturbed.—R.]

**Forbearing one another in love** [ἀνεχόμενοι ἀλλήλων ἐν ἀγάπῃ].—We would expect the accusative here instead of the nominative: παρακαλῶ ὑμᾶς—περιπατῆσαι—ἀνεχομένους. It is not however the ὑμᾶς, "you," which

---

* [The choice of this phrase here, following iii. 1, where the genitive occurs, is overlooked in the E. V. Ἐν is not here =διά or σύν (it is doubtful if it ever is), but denotes the sphere or element of the captivity. As distinguished from iii. 1, this passage gives prominence to the fellowship with Christ and devotion to His cause, while the genitive marks Christ more definitely as the author or originator of the captivity. "In the Lord" seems to be at times, ELLICOTT remarks, little more than a qualitative definition, yet there is far more danger of abridging than extending its profound spiritual significance.—The phrase cannot be joined with the verb, as is done by SEMLER and KOPPE.—R.]

† [MEYER thinks the attraction is from the accusative ἣν, though admitting that a dative might be proper here. DE WETTE denies the propriety of the expression κλῆσιν καλεῖν (*cognate accusative*), though it is defended by WINER, p. 154, and occurs in Arrian, *Epict.*: καταισχύνειν τὴν κλῆσιν ἣν κέκληκεν. The dative gives the simpler grammatical form and through a slight violation of the law of attraction, is sustained by the analogy of 2 Tim. i. 9; 1 Cor. v. 20 is not decisive since ἐν with the dative precedes and the relative *might be* attracted into that case, though it probably *is* not.—R.]

* [Σύν denotes coherence, often with the same idea of assistance; μετά refers to an accompaniment or attendant.—R.]

† [TRENCH properly objects to CHRYSOSTOM's proud humility, which shows itself in his definition of the first term: "making ourselves small when we are great," defining it rather: "the esteeming ourselves small, inasmuch as we are so: the thinking truly, lowlily of ourselves."—The second term is more than *gentleness*, to which Braune and HODGE seem to limit it; it rests on the former as its foundation, accepting God's dealings in humility, and manifesting itself toward men, because they are His instruments.—R.]

is to be more closely defined, but the "walking," not the subject, who should walk, but the predicate, how the walk is to be conducted; the two participles (here and ver. 3) do not then present secondary and additional thoughts. The passage is continued as though, in accordance with the sense, περιπατήσατε were to be read. So i. 18; Col. iii. 16; ii. 2, 10. WINER, p. 532. Ἀνεχόμενοι are those who endure the injuries and sins of others; ἀνοχή is the action of μακροθυμία, "long-suffering," which as the disposition, virtue, is to be perceived in the former. Comp. Rom. ii. 4; 2 Cor. xi. 1; 2 Thess. i. 4. Ἀνέχεσθαι is the active forbearance, ὑπομένειν the quiet endurance. TITTMANN, *Syn.* I. p. 194. The genitive ἀλλήλων, "one another," refers to the fact, that each one, who has to endure from another, gives occasion also for endurance; "long-suffering" is well aware of this.

**In love,** ἐν ἀγάπῃ.—This shows at once that the forbearance should not be mere coldness, indifference, obtuseness. Love should be the element of the endurance (iii. 18). *Aliorum infirmitates æquo animo ferimus, nec ob ea, quæ nobis in proximo displicent, ab ejus amicitia recedimus, sed* PERSONAM *constanter amamus, etsi vitia in odio habeamus* (CALOVIUS). Hence "in love" is not to be joined with what follows (OLSHAUSEN); nor are we besides this qualification of "forbearing," to take "with long-suffering," as still another such (CALVIN, RUECKERT, HARLESS, STIER and others); for the "forbearing" is the act of the "long-suffering," and the latter is not therefore the attendant (μετά) of the former, but its ground, its cause; a forbearing without love is conceivable and actually occurs, but never without long-suffering and yet in love, since love, according to its very nature, "suffereth long" (μακροθυμεῖ, 1 Cor. xiii. 4). Still less allowable is it to join the first μετά with ἀνεχόμενοι (BENGEL). [MEYER properly urges against this view that it makes an abrupt, instead of an easy, transition from the general: "walk worthy," to the special: "forbearing one another."—R.]

Ver. 3. **Earnestly striving to keep** [σπουδάζοντες τηρεῖν].—The participle is to be regarded grammatically like the preceding one. ["This clause is parallel to the preceding, and indicates not so much, as Meyer says, the inward feelings by which the ἀνέχεσθαι is to be characterized, as rather the motive to it, and the accompanying or simultaneous effort" (EADIE).—R.] It describes the zealous striving (LUTHER: be diligent), as Gal. ii. 10; 1 Thess. ii. 19. The present infinitive τηρεῖν denotes the continued maintenance which is necessary every day, since dangers constantly approach. The idea of the verb refers to retaining possession of property, which has not first to be gained. *Etiam ubi nulla fissura est, monitis opus est* (BENGEL).

**The unity of the Spirit,** τὴν ἑνότητα τοῦ πνεύματος, not τοῦ νοός, is the unity which the Holy Spirit effects. So CHRYSOSTOM: τὸ πνεῦμα τοὺς γένει καὶ τρόποις διαφόροις διεστηκότας ἑνοῖ, and most. It is not the unity peculiar to the Spirit, which needs not to be preserved by us (SCHENKEL), but the unity and concord of the Church and its members, and indeed only that which the Holy Ghost works; that accomplished by the spirit of the age is not the object of zealous preservation (τηρεῖν), but only of purification. [The genitive is that of the originating cause (EADIE, ELLICOTT) rather than a *possessive.*—The reference to the human spirit is altogether inadmissible, yet is advocated by ANSELM, ERASMUS, CALVIN, ESTIUS, RUECKERT, and others.—R.]

**In the bond of peace,** ἐν τῷ συνδέσμῳ τῆς εἰρήνης.—This defines more closely the "keeping" which is the object of the "earnestly striving," and in the same way (ἐν) as in ver. 2 ("forbearing"—"in love"), since something depends upon the motive and mode of preserving unity. The very "unity," which is "of the Spirit," required and wrought by the Spirit, can be fostered, furthered and preserved in a carnal manner, from political and egotistical grounds. Against this our phrase is directed. Ὁσύνδεσμος, with the exception of Acts viii. 23, occurs only here and in the Epistle to the Colossians (ii. 19; iii. 14); to vers. 2, 3, Col. iii. 13, 14 are evident parallels. There "love" is "the bond of perfectness," hence a bond well adapted to preserve the unity of the Spirit. "Peace" is indeed itself a condition corresponding alike with "unity" and "love;" it is in spiritual life, and for the Church, first peace with God, and then that peace of heart which is undisturbed by the assaults, temptations and ills of the world and the flesh, not even by the disquiet of the conscience; and further with respect to our neighbor, it is peace with him in love to him, out of love to the Lord of the Church, the Saviour, to the Father of our Lord Jesus Christ and our Father, and to His children through Him. Hence love is the bond which cherishes peace in the Church, and in such love should that unity be preserved, which God's Spirit will work in the Church of Christ; "love edifieth" (1 Cor. viii. 1). Accordingly "the bond of peace" is love itself (so BENGEL). The genitive is, therefore, not epexegetical (BLEEK), nor the genitive of apposition (MEYER, SCHENKEL); else, as RUECKERT aptly remarks, the foundation of the building would be sustained by a perishable roof, the unity of the Spirit be preserved in or through peace with our neighbor, while the Apostle says, that the unity of the Spirit should be preserved in the efficient strength of the power, which fosters this very peace; that is love, which has peace through faith in love, and brings, establishes and retains peace. Where it is wanting, there is carnal nature and discord (1 Cor. iii. 3). Accordingly the preposition "in" designates love as the element in which the unity of the Spirit is to be maintained; hence ἐν is not=διά (BLEEK).

[Braune's view takes the genitive as *gen. objecti.* It is adopted by BENGEL, RUECKERT, HARLESS, STIER, following THEOPHYLACT. But it is open to serious objection. It is far from probable that the Apostle would express the notion "in love" by such a periphrasis, especially as the parallel clauses are not parallel in the *meaning* of their several parts. Certainly the Ephesians would not have the Colossian Epistle at hand to suggest to them this sense, and it is not at all obvious without that suggestion. The assumption that ἐν was instrumental may have led to this view of the phrase (MEYER). On the other hand if the genitive be taken as one of apposition, defining the "bond" as "peace" (so FLATT, OLSHAUSEN, MEYER, EADIE, HODGE, ALFORD, ELLICOTT), we have an obvious and simple interpretation, suiting the sense of ἐν. RUECKERT's objection really applies only to the instrumental sense of the proposition. ALFORD: Peace binds together the Church as a condition and symbol of that inner unity which is only wrought by the indwelling Spirit of God.—Far more than the union of Jew and Gentile is meant. —R.]

## DOCTRINAL AND ETHICAL.

1. *Doctrine and Exhortation.* "The distinction of doctrinal and hortatory parts must not assume the unapostolical character of that modern fiction, according to which exhortation is so severed from doctrinal discussion, as to contain no doctrine at all. As little as an apostolic Epistle is a mere doctrinal discussion, so little is an apostolic, or even a Christian, exhortation without doctrine. What the Apostle requires, are not requirements *in addition to* and *outside of* doctrine, but *requirements of* doctrine, if by doctrine we mean the knowledge of Christian saying truth. This is the very order, which distinguishes Christian ethics from all other." The Apostle now shows his readers, "what the gospel *requires*, after he has called to their memories what it has given them. It requires manifestations of life from those who had been quickened, not from the dead. It expects works of love and righteousness from those who believe and are justified, from him who has been new-created unto good works (comp. on ii. 10). It expects good fruit from a good tree. The opinion that men can gather grapes of thorns, see works of holiness without faith, and make man just before God without the Redeemer; the preaching of morality and the theory of good works without faith, all constitute a perversion of Christian intelligence and of the apostolic order into the futility and confusion of pseudo-Christianity," (HARLESS). [The Apostle's "therefore" rebukes both the dogmatism of dead orthodoxy, and the cry: give us something practical, none of your dry doctrine. At one time the application to the former was more necessary, but the tendency of the present day calls for special attention to the other phase of the matter. When professing Christians or churches tire of the facts respecting God's love in Christ (the real Christian doctrine on which the Apostle's "therefore" rests), they have already ceased to be in earnest about the worthy walk.—R.]

2. *Paul's right to exhort.* The exhortation of the Apostle proceeds rather from the *Christian worthiness* of "the prisoner of the Lord," than from the *apostolic dignity* of the ambassador of the Lord; the latter is more the merely *outward*, the former more the inward authority, both belonging together; the latter could not exist without the former and *vice versa.* The former would have neither courage nor right without the latter, but the latter would lack fervency, sincerity and emphasis without the former. The most winning exordium as well as the most powerful Amen, is still the Christianity of the servant of Christ. *Vita clerici evangelium est populi. Non bene auditur, qui non bene diligitur* (GREGORY the Great). There should be no complaint, because at the present time so much is made to depend on the person, to this first of all men will look.

3. *The calling.* With the calling which God proffers to us, which we have experienced, the Christian life begins. At first we have only to hear (*hören*), then it comes about that we *hearken* (*zuhören*), and finally we *adhere* (*zugehören*). Many are the methods of the call: through God's word sung or spoken in the sanctuary, in the pictures of sacred art, in holy action, in the statements of pious Christians, or in the Scriptures as we read in the closet, from the mouth of a mother or a child, from events in the life of others or ourselves, in the voice of conscience and the immediate suggestion of the Spirit, suddenly, or in the way of gradual consideration, of recollection of what was previously learned and perhaps long-forgotten—thus often is the call addressed to each: every one is more than once, yes many times called by God to Himself. To this the walk should correspond, to this it should give testimony.

4. *The worthiness of the walk* is determined first and chiefly by the relation of him who is called to the revelation of grace which introduces and regulates the spiritually received, personal fellowship of grace with God. Thus the foundation of the Christian life is laid. In the received benefits and possession lies the germ of all the blessings of eternity. The great matter is constancy, fidelity, personal fidelity to the inwardly efficient word of God, to the personal fellowship with God wrought by the Holy Ghost who calls us, not to a precept, a law, rule, maxim, not even to one's own nature and soul; this comes in as a result of the first, which is the cause, the basis, the foundation work, followed by a superstructure of fidelity to the renewed soul.

5. *Lowliness* is the first attendant (μετά) of the Christian walk, beginning after the call of God: He who hears the call, recognizes Jesus as the Christ, feeling, He has more and is more, His heavenly and Divine fellowship is beyond all our experience, He knows and explains and presents the Father's will in overpowering clearness, strength and beauty, and thus he who is called ever feels himself to be more insignificant, sinful and needy. In listening to and looking unto Jesus, lowliness springs up within him; he became a Christian not having this, he did not need to bring it to Christianity or as a price for it, but by becoming a Christian he becomes humble, and that too in the most profound earnestness and lively sorrow over his own sin and poverty and weakness. The more the Christian knows and feels himself to be exalted as a child of God, as a member of the body whose Head is Christ, so much the more does he feel himself to be exalted without any desert or worthiness, only through the fellowship of grace with his Creator, Redeemer and Comforter. He rejoices in his peculiar gifts, but only as given, not as profitable or abused. He well knows, that he is of worth before God, but also that what he is and has is little in comparison with what he should and might be and have, that he is an unprofitable ser-

vant and yet is a child of God, a joint heir with Christ.

6. *Meekness* is joined with lowliness. This is not a soft, yielding natural disposition, nor a prudent bridling of a passionate nature, but it is humility applied to the world, not taking offence at the offences of the world, even though misunderstood, mercilessly treated, oppressed and persecuted. This does not estrange her, for she knows herself. The knowledge and experience of corruption and of salvation through Christ in our own heart, produces either no permanent feeling, or else a common feeling, a fellow-feeling, which looks upon him who gives or prepares offence, as one who is suffering under sin, as unfortunate, rather than as evil-minded and rejoicing in sin; accordingly she remains without bitterness, because she has herself experienced the rich grace of God, and perseveres in patience, because she knows God's patience. [It is also exercised toward God, in submission, which is the foundation of its manifestations toward men. —R.]

7. *Long-suffering* is added as an especial attendant of the Christian walk in social life. It is meekness towards the sins of others, whom we can punish, meekness, keeping its ground against a long series of these. She knows out of her own experience of the long-suffering of God, that sin is misery, out of which condemning and judging never helps us, but rather grace and mercy, if one will let himself be helped. Long-suffering refrains from punishment, that rejects, cuts off, expels from fellowship and friendship, having instead entreaty, exhortation, instruction, discipline in word and deed. She can lovingly hope, is lovingly spirited and brave. She bears with her neighbor, does not weakly yield, does not stand by coldly and stolidly, nor yet embittered and in carnal anger; she is not whimpering and feeble, but strong and heroic in her love, like a mother or a friend.

8. *Unity* should be the object of zealous striving, but only that unity which the Holy Ghost works. It is not first to be made, is not factitious, but unity, wrought from above, which we have only to preserve. Over against this, the Christian must keep at a distance from all party combinations, which in effect introduce discord and schism into church-life. But he must also avoid jumbling together the great variety and wealth of gifts and powers, and seeking to unite all under external form and letter. No carnal strife, but also no slothful peace, no patched-up, hypocritical or dead unity.

9. *The impulse* under which we must endeavor to keep this peace, is *peaceable love*, which can have foes, but is a foe to none, rejoicing in every gift and creature of God, embracing such and leading them into the life of the church, employing and enjoying them, as a nation in time of peace with its various classes, labors and powers, strives in every direction to perform its task, not from the motions of the flesh, but from the basis which God has given, out towards the appointed goal.

10. Paul conceives of the Church of Christ above all as a living company of Christian persons, not as an institution with all its regulations. But the sacredness does not rest upon the individuals, but inheres in the whole organism, which the Holy Ghost animates.

### HOMILETICAL AND PRACTICAL.

Suffer as a Christian, in order to be able to work in the service of the Master.—Show thyself in deed a servant of Christ, in order in such service to be able to direct aright in word, those who are directed to thee.—Loosen doctrine from the precept which it contains, but do not sever them from one another; distinguish, but do not divide them. There is no Christianity without Christ, and no religion without morality, but at the same time those ethics are of no value which have no doctrine behind them. True the conscience is the *voice* of God, but what were that, if it were without the Word of God?—He who walks unworthy of his vocation is doubly culpable, more than a heathen; do not despise the calling.—As a child of man, a son of earth, no one stands alone and solitary, but with others, as child of God also dost thou belong to a family; take heed thereto! Thou belongest not merely to the visible, but also to the invisible church.—The three chief virtues of a Christian: Lowliness, meekness, and long-suffering [*Demuth, Sanftmuth, Langmuth*].—Humility is the basis of all Christian virtue; without it all is wicked, however praiseworthy it may otherwise appear. It is nothing more than evangelical truth applied to all cases; a doctrine which does not make us humble is of no account.—Christian practice in walk and conversation is indispensable; it is more important to be skilful in this, than to have special insight respecting the theory.

STARKE:—Christians have a great and important calling, to walk worthily according to the commands of their Saviour. O that we ever had this calling before our eyes in all our doings!—Where there is much cross, there much light is. Tribulation brings experience; he preaches best who preaches out of his experience.—What God gives and how He gives should satisfy us. Bread and honor are the twin-portions of our calling.—He lives in no shame, who has an unpleasant calling, for God has set him in it. Has God ordained, our pleasure's gained!—Without lowliness, gentleness and patience the unity of the Spirit cannot be maintained. All discord, heresy and schism come from the vices which are opposed to these virtues.—A gentle spirit is the garden in which patience grows.—Unity of the Spirit, the highest ornament of Christians. How? should those live in discord, who are members of one body, of one Head, Jesus Christ? But that is the very sign of a corrupted Christianity, that there are so many sects, so much discord and strife among Christians.

RIEGER:—Paul has just prayed so heartily, now he can exhort so profitably. Have you never found that after secret intercourse with God in prayer, your neighbor's heart also inclines more to you, and is more willing to receive a word which is redolent of prayer?—The call entitles us indeed to the kingdom and glory of God, but it obligates us also to sanctification, and to adorn the doctrine of God and our Saviour.—*Humility* stands in the feeling of her own defects, and knows how slowly the growth of the inner man proceeds; hence in *meekness* she does not exact too much of others, and in *long-suffering* does not lose patience, when an enduring love is necessary in meeting others. *Endurance* is keenly felt, but love sweetens it, as we see in the case of our children, what we can endure in them, in order in love to help them out of their infirmities. *Endeavor* overcomes all difficulties: only ever revert to confidence in God.—Unity in the Spirit we dare not make, but only keep it.—To maintain peace is better than to maintain right.

HEUBNER:—The Christian should be and remain conscious of the fellowship to which he belongs: it is a calamity in the Christian church, that this consciousness has been so greatly extinguished. This consciousness should not be maintained proudly but humbly, because the higher the aim, the greater the required perfection, so much the more should each one be conscious of his distance from it and his weakness. The principle of the Christian communion is: to humble ourselves, to become the least, to serve; out of this grows meekness, which shows itself towards those who make the fulfilment of the duty difficult for us.—*Endurance* presupposes, that every one has something that is obnoxious to others. It is necessary, because we ourselves are troublesome to others, and because we are all members of one body, and because it is God who places others by our side.—The unity in the Spirit is something very different from corporate, external, conventional, superficial unity; it dwells deep within, in the entire will and disposition, it is holy, proceeding from the Spirit, not from mere prudence, concerning itself about essentials, not about non-essentials. From this we infer what real union is; the Spirit alone can create it, that made by man is as a rule of no value.—SPANGENBERG says: "I hold that no one is a child of God merely because he belongs to this or that religion [*i. e.*, Christian confession]; to him who receives Jesus Christ, power will be given to become a son of God. In Christ Jesus nothing avails save faith, which works by love. He in whom I find this faith is my brother. Is he of another religion, that makes no difference, he is still my brother and nearer to me than my fellow-professors who have no faith. Indeed, because he is of another religion, in which the gospel does not shine so brightly, he is to me a miracle of grace."—The Moravians have been very unjustly accused of narrow-heartedness.

PASSAVANT:—*The calling of men* was from the beginning, to live innocently and holily, thankfully and obediently toward their God. *The calling of the sinner* is: to repent, to forsake the ways of sin, to seek pardon, grace and peace; to turn to the holy and living God, whom he has long forsaken. *The calling of the Christian* is this: internally and externally, with word and work, with his whole life, in all things, at all times in the church, before believers and unbelievers, to give glory to God the Father in Jesus Christ.—One may endure the faults of his neighbor from want of feeling, from mildness of temperament, from human good-nature, from earthly politeness, from temporal policy, from pharisaical hypocrisy; nothing is so common; but it is rarely done out of real Christian love.

STIER:—What is not rooted in humility does not deserve the name of a virtue.—Always and everywhere this alone is of avail, to cherish the unity of *the Spirit;* thus out of every desolation a new edifice is formed, without this the most beautiful structure becomes rotten and finally breaks.

GERLACH:—Patience manifests itself in the quiet endurance of injuries, long-suffering, more in the active maintenance of others in necessities, even when criminal.

SERMONS *on the Epistle for the 17th Sunday after Trinity* (iv. 1-6). WESTERMEIER: *Unity in the Spirit:* 1. What is it? 2. By what means is it preserved? *a*) in general (ver. 1); *b*) in particular (vers. 2, 3); 3. On what grounds should it be maintained (vers. 4-6).

ZIEL:—Endeavor to keep the unity of the Spirit! 1. On what this admonition is based (vers. 4-6). 2. How we obey it (vers. 1-3).

AHLFELD:—*Walk worthy of your Christian calling!* 1) Your calling as children of God; 2) your calling as brethren to each other; 3) your calling, to derive the power for such a walk from the right sources.—*Our joy in the congregation of the saints.* 1) Who are these saints and how far does this fellowship extend? 2) What is the bond which encircles them? 3) What blessing and what joy do we derive from this fellowship of the saints?

RAUTENBERG:—*The unity of the children of God.* 1) How the Divine call requires it; 2) in what it consists; 3) from what it proceeds; 4) to what it obliges every one.

KAPFF:—Endeavor to keep the unity in the Spirit! 1. Let go what disturbs unity. 2. Hold fast what confirms it.

HEUBNER:—*The unity of the Christian Church.* 1. Oneness of life: *a*) Worthy walk, *b*) brotherly love, *c*) peaceableness. 2. Oneness of faith: *a*) in *one* Holy Ghost, *b*) in *one* Saviour, *c*) in *one* God and Father.—*The duties of Christian church-membership.* 1. A walk which is worthy of the call into the church (ver. 1). 2. Specially fraternal walk in humility and love (ver. 2). 3. A concordant, harmonious walk, not mere external but internal unity (ver. 3), for the fellowship of the Church is not merely a body, but a Spirit (ver. 4); it is founded upon one faith in Christ and *one* confession (ver. 3) and is perfected in God the Father.—*The communion of the saints.* 1. A description: not of a place, nor of a form, but of love and of faith. 2. How is it established: not by force, by human power or act, but by the Spirit of God. 3. Its importance. *The equality of our fellowship in Christianity.* 1. Proof: we have *one* calling, one Saviour, one Father. 2. Application: Thanksgiving to God, caution against pride, consolation for the lowly and poor, awakening endeavors after this fellowship.

PRÖHLE:—Endeavor to keep the unity in the Spirit! 1. Only in sorrow can we receive this exhortation now-a-days. 2. May it knock loudly upon the conscience of every one. 3. And may it bind anew in firm union our hearts and hands.—Forbearing one another in love. 1. *Meaning:* *a*) We should follow after peace, as husbands, wives, kinsmen, masters, servants. *b*) This is possible through lowliness, meekness, long-suffering. 2. *Motive:* *a*) The duty of brotherly love, *b*) our own defects; to-day I must bear with you, to-morrow you must bear with me.

### 2. Three motives to the preservation of the unity in the Spirit.

CHAP. IV. 4–16.

*a. The working of the Triune God in the Church.*

(CHAP. IV. 4–6.)

4 *There is* one body, and one Spirit, even as ye are called [as ye were also called]
5, 6 in one hope of your calling; One Lord, one faith, one baptism, One God and
Father of all, who *is* above [over] all, and through all, and in you all [in all].

TEXTUAL AND GRAMMATICAL.

[1] Ver. 6.—[The *Rec.* inserts ὑμῖν (with very slight authority), while D. F. K. L., good versions and a few fathers, 40 cursives, read ἡμῖν; no pronoun occurs in ℵ. A. B. C., 10 cursives. Most fathers also sustain the omission, which is accepted by nearly all editors and commentators since Lachmann, the pronouns being regarded as exegetical glosses to confine the assertion to Christians.—R.]

EXEGETICAL AND CRITICAL.

*Connection.*—These three verses are joined to what precedes without any connecting particle, and, as parallel clauses, follow each other without any such particle, since the context, being quite clear, requires none. THEODORET: πανταχοῦ τὸ ἓν καὶ εἰς τέθκεικεν εἰς συμφωνίαν συνάπτων τὴν ἐκκλησίαν. BUGENHAGEN: *omnia, unde Christiani sumus, unitate nobis commendantur.* The exhortation to maintain the unity of the Spirit has mainly occasioned these verses; they give a reason for it; γάρ is wanting however, on account of the liveliness of the discourse, and for emphasis.* The *objective bases* for unity in the Spirit, to which they have been exhorted, the motives for such exhortation are stated.† Hence we should supply ἐστίν, and not ἐστέ, as though it were continued exhortation (*Syriac*, CALVIN, HOFMANN, *Schriftbeweis*, II. 2, p. 127, and others). [Braune's view is that generally received, and by far the most tenable.—R.]

Ver. 4. *The nature of the fellowship.*—**There is one body and one Spirit** [ἓν σῶμα καὶ ἓν πνεῦμα].—Ἓν σῶμα (i. 23; ii. 16; Rom. xii. 5; 1 Cor. xii. 13, 20) designates the totality of Christians as a *corpus mysticum;* it is not=ἐκκλησιά, *church*, which is to be viewed as the external *phenomenon*, the *body* of Christ is hidden, but a reality, like the body of nerves, a hidden reality, which can be traced, making itself perceptible, the invisible church, the unity of which is emphasized by the Apostle and to be held fast.—Καὶ ἓν πνεῦμα is added to designate the soul of this body, the Holy Ghost, which forms and moulds the body, and to show that this σῶμα of Christ is no πτῶμα. He is not speaking therefore of an ideal invisible church, which does not actually exist, but of the actual, real essence of the church, which is internal, but comes into being continuously. It is foolish to explain here, we should be united *penitus, corpore et anima, non ex parte duntaxat* (CALVIN and others).

Since Christ's body and the Holy Ghost are perceptible, not in their essence, but only inwardly and in their effects and consequences, Paul refers next to their own experience:

**As ye were also called in one hope of your calling** [καθὼς καὶ ἐκλήθητε ἐν μιᾷ ἐλπίδι τῆς κλήσεως ὑμῶν].—According to the calling (καθὼς καὶ ἐκλήθητε), by means of which he who is called has obtained or can obtain knowledge and perception of the "body" and "Spirit" just mentioned! This calling points likewise (καί) to the unity, because it is consummated "in one hope;" as soon as a man is called of God, he is in the hope of salvation (σωτηρία, κληρονομία) and this hope is one and the same for each and all who are called, by right, in tendency and effect. This "hope" belongs so especially to the being called (ἐκλήθητε) that it can be termed all along "of your calling;" hope and calling are not to be separated from each other. BENGEL is excellent: *Spiritus est* ARRHABO, *atque ideo cum ejus mentione conjungitur* SPES HEREDITATIS. They belong together from the beginning; Paul here however refers to the history of the origin of church-fellowship which is to be maintained, whether one looks at the unity of the church, or of principle, or of aim. It cannot be said that the calling consists *in hope* (BENGEL: ἐν *exprimit indolem rei*, HARLESS and others), still less that it takes place *by means* of hope (MEYER), or that ἐν is=εἰς. WINER, p. 385.

[See EADIE for a list of prepositions used with καλέω in the New Testament. He, with ALFORD

* [So EADIE with more correctness than ALFORD and ELLICOTT, for though γάρ is not to be supplied, yet the logical connection of the assertion is argumentative. It is one of the rare cases where the grammatical nicety of the commentator last named has led him somewhat astray.—R.]

† [So MEYER: "Objective relations of unity, to which the non-observance of the precept in ver. 3 would be opposed. These are: 1. *The Church itself constituted as a unity*—one body, one Spirit, one blessed consummation, ver. 4; 2. *That by which this constitution of the same as a unity has and does come to pass*—one Lord, one faith, one baptism, ver. 5; 3. *The supreme Ruler, Administrator and Preserver of this entire unity*—one God and Father, etc., ver. 6. Notice the triple tri-partite division."—R.]

and ELLICOTT, rightly supports the usual meaning of ἐν here: the element in which the calling took place. ELLICOTT speaks of this sense of the preposition as being, "so to say, its theological meaning." He takes the genitive as one of originating cause, but it is rather that of possession, "the genitive of the correlative noun, suggesting what belongs to the call and characterized it, when they received it. The 'hope' is 'one,' for it has one object, and that is glory; one fountain, and that is Christ" (EADIE). Ἐλπίς is of course subjective.—R.]

Ver. 5. *Christ and the union with Him.*—**One Lord, one faith, one baptism.**—This refers to the way and the means of salvation. Εἷς κύριος, "one Lord," is Christ, the Lord *par excellence*. See ver. 1; i. 21. The word found in Deut. vi. 4 is now applied in the New Testament to Christ (1 Cor. viii. 4-6). His will has authority over all. Each one stands equally near to Him; for there is "one faith," which unites with Him; faith (i. 1, 15; ii. 8; iii. 12, 17) unites inwardly to the one Lord, trusts Him as Lord. Hence there is but **one faith**, and not several kinds: *fides, qua creditur;* it is not then a faith *in abstracto* (HARLESS), nor the doctrine of faith (GROTIUS and others); for this faith is actually and efficiently present and a living power, a believing. [A vast deal of difficulty as well as of error is avoided by bearing in mind that πίστις, "faith," in the New Testament, almost invariably means *subjective* faith (Gal. i. 23 is the only exception, and this perhaps an apparent one). The conception of "faith" as a universal dogma belongs to a later age, and while it has preserved Roman Catholic uniformity, has not "kept the unity of the Spirit." So the Apostle implies: Because there is one faith, keep unity, not because we need unity, lay down one objective Catholic undoubted Christian faith. Dr. HODGE defends the objective sense here, but must make limitations which are of necessity indefinite enough to cast doubt on his own view. Still the context plainly points to the "one Lord" as the object of the "one faith;" and in the nature of things one subjective recognition of this eternal truth respecting Christ, this apprehension of Him in His Person and work, necessarily involves a common objective profession of it, and thus we pass to the third term of the verse, which is to be regarded as the external sign of faith, and in one aspect as a profession objectively made. —R.]

Faith, which is one, begins with baptism, which is also only one; the former is an internal subjective medium, the latter an objective one, from without and above; these two factors make the Lord our own, and us the Lord's own. *Modo baptismus modo fides præponitur*, Mark xvi. 16; Col. ii. 12 (BENGEL). [The order of the words does not justify this view of Dr. Braune's. ALFORD takes the verse as presenting three great facts on which unity rests, the first objective, the second subjective, the third compounded of the two: "the objective seal of the subjective faith, by which, as a badge, the members of Christ are outwardly and visibly stamped with His name." To find a reference to one *mode* of baptism is unwarranted by text or context.—R.]

Why the Lord's Supper is not mentioned, is evident from the context, which contains the motives for the exhortation, to *desire* to preserve the unity of the Spirit. The Lord's Supper is rather an act of the preserved unity, than a motive for its preservation. It is celebrated by those who have been reconciled with God and hold each other to be brethren; it does not so much give an impulse to peaceableness, as it is a result of the same, as a common celebration of those who have become united together, as an attestation of the church which has become one in the Lord. DE WETTE refers to this by intimating that the Lord's Supper is not mentioned, because it is a *representation of unity*.* The reference to the fundamental conditions of the Christian communion at its beginning is an insufficient ground for the omission of this sacrament (HARLESS and others). Still less admissible is it to suppose that it is included in the one sacrament of baptism (CALOVIUS), or in the "one Lord, one faith" (OLSHAUSEN), or to explain historically, that there has been as yet no separate celebration (MEYER), or that this is prophetic foresight, since the unity of the sacred feast would be broken nevertheless (STIER), or because he did not wish to hinder the manifold form of the rite (SCHENKEL), or because a definite expression for it was wanting (BLEEK).

Ver. 6. *The deepest basis of true unity.* **One God and Father of all.**—Here God the Father is referred to, after the Spirit (ver. 4) and the Son (ver. 5) have been made prominent. As little as God can be disunited with Himself, so little should you who are His children be among yourselves. Hence to the phrase "one God," there is added epexegetically: "and Father," the genitive "of all," under which Christ cannot be included, leading us to understand it as the Father of believers, of those who have become God's children in Christ. "Father" cannot then mean merely "creator," according to the heathen conception, nor can "of all" be neuter in this context. *Nam omnes ad unitatem rediguntur* (BENGEL), and the following "all" (πάντων πᾶσι) takes up the first one again, referring to persons, to the members of the Church, who should preserve the unity in the Spirit; on which account ver. 7 continues: "to every one of you." It is accordingly neither neuter (IRENÆUS and others), nor to be extended to men in general (HOLZHAUSEN).

**Who is over all**, ὁ ἐπὶ πάντων, marks the Ruler, Guardian, Guide (WINER, p. 351), governing over all (WINER, p. 390). CHRYSOSTOM: ἐπάνω πάντων, τὴν δεσποτείαν σημαίνει.

**And through all**, καὶ διὰ πάντων, *per omnes operans* (BENGEL); the individuals are instruments, means, as Rom. xv. 18; 1 Cor. iii. 9; Gal. i. 1: δι' ἀνθρώπου—διά Ἰησοῦ. See WINER, p. 390.

**And in all**, καὶ ἐν πᾶσιν, dwelling in all

* [On this question, which seems to have occupied undue prominence from the sacramental tendencies of many commentators, ELLICOTT remarks that if a reason must be assigned, "it must be referred to the fundamental difference between the sacraments. The one is rather the symbol of *union*, the other, from its single celebration and marked individual reference, presents more clearly the idea of *unity*,—the idea most in harmony with the context."—R.]

(Bengel, Winer), filling them, perfecting them (John xiv. 23). All three qualifications refer to "God and Father," hence are not to be interpreted in a trinitarian sense, of the Father, Son and Holy Ghost, so that He who is "through all" is the Head working through all, and He who is "in all" is the indwelling Spirit, yet such a reference lies unmistakably in the background (Rom. xi. 36; 1 Cor. xii. 4-6; 2 Cor. xiii. 13), at all events was not far off, so that Harless can discover here a recapitulation of "one God," "one Lord," "one Spirit," which Stier and others think was intentional. Comp. Hofmann, *Schriftbeweis*, I. p. 201 f.; who doubts any reference to the Trinity, but applying it to the Father not without the Son and the Spirit, excludes no one Person. The reference to Redemption alone is clearer, hence "through all" is not to be understood of the all-pervading creative power, nor of Providence in general.

[While the mention of "one baptism," with its Trinitarian formula, suggests the great probability of a reference to the Trinity in the several expressions of this verse, which is further favored by the first and third prepositions, it is far safer not to press it. The express mention of the "Father" is against it; διά can be referred to the work or office of the Son only by departing from its proper sense or inverting its relation to the rest of the verse ("*per quem omnia facta sunt*," Aquinas, so Olshausen), and as Eadie remarks: "In previous portions of the Epistle triune relation has been distinctly brought out; here the representation is different, for unity is the idea dwelt on, and it is the One God and Father Himself who works through all and dwells in all." Ellicott here confessedly allows doctrinal considerations to outweigh his exegetical convictions, and it is precisely thus, that those who defend the well-grounded doctrine of the church lose in their contests with those who impugn it. They attack our exegesis of a passage like this, and we must defend the doubtful, unimportant outpost at a disadvantage.—One thing is certain that this passage refers to believers alone, neither teaching God's Fathership of all men (though Alford thinks it is referred to as a lost possession), nor pantheism of any kind.—R.]

## DOCTRINAL AND ETHICAL.

1. *The unity of the Church.* Although ἐκκλησία and σῶμα (Χριστοῦ) describe so nearly the same, that of the former it is said (i. 23): "which is his body," while in Col. i. 24 we read of "his body, which is the church," yet the two may be thus distinguished: the former designates the church as an assembly of believers, of saints; the latter as a living organism, the organ of Him who is the Head, thus with the *corpus Christi mysticum*, giving more prominence to the inner concealed side, the unity of the same. Hence there are indeed "churches," but no "*bodies* of Christ." The Nicene creed was right in adding: UNAM *to sanctam catholicam et apostolicam ecclesiam* (the Apostles' has only: *sanctam ecclesiam catholicam*); so the Augsburg Confession, Art. 7: *quod* UNA *sancta ecclesia perpetuo mansura sit.* Strictly there is but *one* Church of Christ, though in groups of congregations with different confessions. No confessional church (though, strictly speaking, the term is a misnomer) is *the* Church of Christ, it is only *a* church by the side of others, through which the body of Christ extends itself.

2. *The distinction of the body of Christ from the Spirit* is indicated definitely enough by their being placed side by side, yet the latter at the same time gives prominence to the church as the working-place of the Spirit.*

3. *The call*, when accepted and effectual, begins within the called, not with a mere promise which he receives, but with a *hope* corresponding thereto, so that the objective call of God and the subjective acceptance of the man come together, and he from the very beginning knows and feels himself to be shown out of the lower sphere of life into the higher one.

4. *Christ is the One Lord*, and no faith in Him is genuine, except it be in Him as Lord. It is not sufficient to believe the Master or Teacher; it is not enough to feel and deem ourselves scholars, hearers, disciples. The Christian must be servant, subject of Christ, not merely to hear or listen to Him, but to belong to Him, to hearken to Him, to obey, to follow Him as His vassal, attendant, servant. No human dignity, in the history of our lives or of the world exceeds the dignity of Christ: He is the one only Lord; who gives Him up, must give up faith and the fellowship of the church.

5. *Baptism*, with which faith begins (*regeneratio præcedit fidem*) imparts the germ of the new life, the beginning of the gift of the Holy Ghost, the principle of faith in the subject, as at birth, upon coming to the light of the world, man is endowed with reason. It is not merely a symbolical act, nor a mere prophecy of the cleansing which begins later, but it is the incorporation into the body of Christ, animated by the Spirit, implantation into the soil of divine life. [This is the Lutheran view, approaching, in its estimate of the objective grace of this Sacrament, the position of Romanism and Anglicanism. Certainly the fact that baptism is mentioned at all, puts it into an exalted position, from which unchurchly Zwinglianism would degrade it. But it is not placed before faith, nor is there here any warrant for the assertion that faith begins with baptism. The Reformed or Calvinistic view is most in accordance with our passage. See *Heidelberg Catechism*, Questions 69-74; *Belgic Confession*, xxxiv.; *Westminster Confession*, xxviii.; comp. especially *Romans*, p. 206, *Doct. Note* 3.—While there is no reference to the one mode of baptism, there is probably an allusion to the fact that baptism is not or should not be repeated. —R.]

* [Hodge: "There are many passages to which the doctrine of the Trinity gives a sacred rhythm, though the doctrine itself is not directly asserted. It is so here. There is one Spirit, one Lord, one God and Father. The unity of the Church is founded on this doctrine. It is one, because there is to us one God the Father, one Lord, one Spirit. It is a truly mystical union; not a mere union of opinion, of interest, or of feeling; but something supernatural arising from a common principle of life. This life is not the natural life which belongs to us as creatures; nor intellectual, which belongs to us as rational beings; but it is spiritual life, called elsewhere the life of God in the soul. And as this life is common on the one hand to Christ and all His members, and on the other to Christ and God, this union of the Church is not only with Christ, but with the Triune God."—R.]

6. *God, the Father of believers*, is not far from them, over them, but near to them, disposing concerning them, working through them, yes, dwelling in them, as in a temple, furnishing His work as in a work-shop. God is a *Person*, who not only rules throughout the universe, but gives to His own a special personality.

7. The *Atheist* denies the Father, the *Deist* the Son, the Pantheist the Holy Ghost, because he substitutes for it the unholy "spirit of the world" (BAADER).

### HOMILETICAL AND PRACTICAL.

Ever return from multiplicity to unity, and in freedom to obligation; but never let your view of the *unities* be disturbed. Do not hold faith higher than baptism, penetrate into the communion of the Church until you reach the Spirit which is its soul, and do not sunder the Lord Jesus and God the Father!

STARKE:—There is but one Church, which receives life and movement from the Holy Ghost, and hence but one ship, with which we can sail into the haven of bliss; all other vessels destroy and drown.—Christians are all equal in the fellowship of heavenly possessions, and no one has a better God, Christ, Spirit, Faith, *etc.*, but what one has, the others have also, although one may have a greater enjoyment of such possessions than another.

RIEGER:—The body of Christ is ruled by one Spirit; one Lord gave Himself for the Redemption of all; out of one Word of truth and of faith are we convinced; one baptism is the door of entrance for us into the kingdom of God. Therefore God administers such a government of love over all, that as much as possible equality is established; out of his property every one can contribute something to the common benefit: as God on the other hand so gives Himself to be enjoyed by each, that he dare not look too anxiously upon others, still less through secret envy render difficult his keeping peace with all.—HEUBNER, see *Homil. Notes* on the preceding section.

PASSAVANT:—There is one path, one goal, one house, one family, one home to which you have been called; you all hope for one heaven, and in the same heaven to obtain a common inheritance, an identical blessedness and glory in the heavenly life.—"I do not know, how it happens, that we glory in being the children of God so confidently and yet at the same time forget brotherly love."

STIER:—Where there is still body, there is also Spirit—that is the Apostle's great thought.—Baptism and Faith belong together: 1. As faith is the subjective appropriation, so baptism is the objective representation of the same; 2. Faith takes out of the Lord's hand, in baptism we have the firm foundation and beginning from the Lord.—I confess that I find the one faith on the Lord in many a [Roman] Catholic with the hearty joy of fraternal agreement, and in many a zealot for the pure Word and Sacrament I might look for it with pain and in vain.

[EADIE:—"One baptism" is the result and expression of the "one faith" in the "one Lord," and, at the same time, the one mode of initiation by the "one Spirit" into the "one body."—All this unity is but the impress of the great primal unity—one God.—Christ's claim for the preservation of unity is upon all the churches—a unity of present connection and actual enjoyment—not a truce, but an alliance, with one living and cognizance—not a compromise, but a veritable incorporation.—HODGE:—All sins against unity are sins against the Holy Ghost.—R.]

[Seven times does the word "one" occur in these verses, but the middle term is "one Lord," next on either side "one hope"—"one faith."—How great a unity results from "one faith," the same trust of the heart on the "one Lord;" one creed often leads and always permits us to chop logic and split hairs, but where the "faith" is "one," hearts are one, and no earnest Christian has failed to notice how quickly this manifests itself.—It is a comfort to come back from the jars of the church of to-day and the wars of the church of the past, to the simple truth: There is one body: but here too faith is required.—R.]

---

*b. The gift of Christ to individuals.*

(CHAP. IV. 7–10).

7 But unto every [to each] one of us is given grace [was the[1] grace given] accord-
8 ing to the measure of the gift of Christ. Wherefore he saith, When he ascended
9 up on high, he led [a] captivity captive, and[2] gave gifts unto [to] men. ([*omit*
parenthesis] Now that he ascended, what is it but that he also descended first [*omit*
10 first][3] into the lower parts[4] of the earth? He that [who] descended is the same
also that [he it is also who] ascended up far [*omit* far] above all [the] heavens,
that he might fill all things.) [*omit* )].

### TEXTUAL AND GRAMMATICAL.

[1] Ver. 7.—[The article is omitted in B. D.[1] F. G. L., a few cursives, by Lachmann; bracketted by Alford; inserted in א. A. C. D.[3] K., accepted by Tischendorf and most recent editors. The omission was probably due to the η which precedes, and some glosses still further sustain its genuineness.—The order of the E. V. is altered for the sake of retaining the article, and *was* substituted for *is*, to bring out the force of the aorist.—R.]

[2] Ver. 8.—[Καί is omitted in א. A. C.[2] D.[1] F., versions and fathers; rejected by Lachmann, Tischendorf (ed. 2), Ellicott. It is found in (*Rec.*) א.[3] B. C.[1 3] D.[3] K. L., nearly all cursives, versions (*Syriac*, etc.), fathers; accepted by Tischendorf (ed. 7), Meyer, Alford, Braune. As it is wanting in the LXX., the internal evidence seems to decide in its favor; an insertion for the sake of connection is not probable.—See *Exeg. Notes* for the text of the original Hebrew and the LXX.—R.]

[3] Ver. 9.—[The *Rec.* inserts πρῶτον, on the authority of א.[3] B. C.[3] K. L., cursives, versions and fathers; it is not found in א. A. C. D.[1] F., and is rejected by modern editors as an explanatory gloss.—R.]

[4] Ver. 9.—[The authority for μέρη is much stronger than for πρῶτον (א. A. B. C. D.[3] K. L., nearly all cursives, a few versions and fathers), though it is open to suspicion as an explanatory gloss, and is rejected by Tischendorf, Meyer and Ellicott (omitted in D.[1] F., most fathers). It is however retained, on account of the strong uncial support, by Lachmann, Scholz, Rückert, Alford and Braune.—R.]

### EXEGETICAL AND CRITICAL.

Ver. 7. *Every one is cared for by Christ.*—**But to each one of us,** ἑνὶ δὲ ἑκάστῳ ἡμῶν.—Antithetical to "through all and in all," in order to explain it and to give prominence to the subjective condition, which is a motive for the preservation of unity; "of us" holds fast to the circle of Christians, of believers; it recalls iii. 20: "in us." After the seventh "one" and the fourth "all," prominence is given to the specializing of what is common to all, to what is peculiar to the individuals. [Hence ἑνὶ in addition to ἑκάστῳ.—R.] It cannot be referred to teachers (PASSAVANT), or to extraordinary Christians (BAUMGARTEN-CRUSIUS), or to the relation of Jewish and Gentile Christians (OLSHAUSEN). Each has a part in salvation, and should prove it in concord; each has a part in salvation, and hence should be treated in a fraternal manner.

**Was the grace given** [ἐδόθη ἡ χάρις].—The verb stands first for emphasis: Every one has *received*, no one has it of himself; each has to recognize that, for himself, in order not to be proud, for another, in order not to despise or avoid him. That which was given by Christ is "the grace," God's grace, which is active and noticeable in Christianity,* and of which he has already spoken in ver. 6 (HARLESS); or the grace imparted

**According to the measure of the gift of Christ** [κατὰ τὸ μέτρον τῆς δωρεᾶς τοῦ Χριστοῦ].—One kind of grace is given, and yet very differently. It is given by Christ; hence the genitive Χριστοῦ is the genitive *subjecti*, on which account we find in ver. 8: "and gave gifts," ver. 11: "and He gave," accordingly that gift which He has given, not received (OEDER in Wolf). He gives to each individual, to one more, to another less, to each the entire grace, but in peculiar form, with differently manifested strength, efficacy and tendency; hence "according to the measure of the gift of Christ." ["In proportion to the amount of the gift which Christ gives" (ELLICOTT), the first genitive being a simple possessive genitive, and the second that of the agent, or both being subjective. STIER tries to combine the ideas of giving and receiving in the phrase: "of Christ." "The rule is not our merit, or our previous capacity, nor our asking, but His own good pleasure" (HODGE).—R.]

* [The aorist points to a definite act: "by Christ, at the time of His exaltation—when He bestowed gifts on men" (Alford).—"The grace," as the article is to be retained, has some shade of a transitive force, denoting the energizing grace which manifests itself in the peculiar gift (ELLICOTT) rather than the spiritual gift itself and the influence, function, or office flowing from it (HODGE).—R.]

*Christ has power thereto*; Vers. 8–10. *a*) The *quotation* (ver. 8). *b*) *The further exposition and application* (vers. 9, 10).

Ver. 8. **Wherefore he saith.**—Διό denotes that in the quotation there is a reference and proof, *i. e.*, for "the gift of Christ;" as will appear. We most naturally supply ἡ γραφή, the Scripture, with λέγει, "saith" (Jas. iv. 6; Rom. xv. 10; Gal. iii. 16; 1 Cor. vi. 16: φησίν), and not ὁ θεός (MEYER, SCHENKEL), or ὁ λέγων (BLEEK: the writer). [The fact that Paul frequently supplies ἡ γραφή (Rom. iv. 3; ix. 17; x. 11; Gal. iv. 30; 1 Tim. v. 18) is against Braune's view; for in some of these passages there is a reason for its insertion (see *Romans*, p. 314), and as the Scriptures are God's Word (MEYER), the natural aim and obvious subject is ὁ θεός. So ALFORD, ELLICOTT and most.—R.] The quotation is from Psalm lxviii. 19: עָלִיתָ לַמָּרוֹם שָׁבִיתָ שֶּׁבִי לָקַחְתָּ מַתָּנוֹת בָּאָדָם: LXX.: ἀναβὰς εἰς ὕψος ᾐχμαλώτευσας αἰχμαλωσίαν ἔλαβες δόματα ἐν ἀνθρώπῳ. In Paul it reads:

**When he ascended upon high he led a captivity captive, and gave gifts to men,** ἀναβὰς εἰς ὕψος ᾐχμαλώτευσεν αἰχμαλωσίαν καὶ ἔδωκε δόματα τοῖς ἀνθρώποις.—The citation is unmistakable up to the last clause: Paul has used the third person instead of the second, because he would mark the application and not merely quote; but in the last clause he substitutes "give" for "receive," and the dative τοῖς ἀνθρώποις for ἐν ἀνθρώπῳ. The article is found in the Hebrew, in the Kamets, and in the singular, the general idea, which Paul expresses by the plural, inheres. Accordingly there remains but three variations of any consequence: לקח, λαμβάνειν, *to receive*, what is in itself inadmissible, διδόναι, *to give;* instead of באדם, the dative, which is not represented by בְּ, but by לְ, and the added καί. What in the glorious Psalm is said of God, whose triumphant doings on the earth are praised, and who takes up His abode on Mount Zion, in His sanctuary, to which the people festively draw near, and whither the Gentiles also will come, this the Apostle here applies to Christ. David sang of the ark of the covenant, which, after a great victory, was transferred (STIER) or brought back (HENGSTEN-

BERG) to Zion. In this fact he sees the principle of the history of the Kingdom of God, appearing in ever widening circles and nobler manner; the fact is to him a type of the method and course of the Messianic kingdom. Hence the general view (vers. 2-7 and 29-36) and the reminiscence of the journey through the wilderness from Sinai to Zion (vers. 8-19). So that the Apostle is perfectly justified in finding the singer's eye directed towards Christ and thus interpreting it. The *height* ("on high") in the Psalm is first of all *Zion* (ver. 16, 17; comp. Jer. xvii. 12, 23; xxxi. 12; xxxiv. 14, where מָרוֹם is spoken of Zion); but this is a type of heaven; of the most holy height, on which account the Apostle has heaven in his mind (ver. 10).* By "captivity," *αἰχμαλωσία*, according to Judith ii. 9; Ezra vi. 5; Rev. xiii. 10, we must understand captives, a troop or group of them, and not prison, captivity (LUTHER). This the parallelism which follows in the Psalm (LXX.: ἀπειθοῦντες, Vulgate: *non credentes*) teaches us; indeed the next clause (ἔλαβες δόματα ἐν ἀνθρώπῳ) indicates plainly enough that the notion of *αἰχμαλωσία* is that of a *turba captivorum*, a crowd of captives, since the passage speaks of gifts in the man (in the human race), in men, presents consisting in men, whom He received and bore with Him into the same sanctuary.† This however the Apostle does not simply take up in his quotation, does not place it after the first clause without any connecting particle, but with *καί*, which denotes advance, something further, passes from the quotation over into the meaning: *and He gave.* For what God conquers, overcomes, leads with Himself, takes to Himself, makes His own, He does not wish to retain for Himself, but He transforms it, endows it, and makes it a gift: His captives become His servants, Israel's servants. He makes the enemies and antagonists of His theocracy its servants. So in a higher sense Christ; He made Saul Paul, the enemy and destroyer of His church an Apostle. God's taking, receiving, points to a subsequent giving, Christ's giving to a previous receiving. Thus the taking of gifts in men passes over into a giving for men, and the citation from David's Psalm the Apostle interprets as referring to Christ. By "men," *τοῖς ἀνθρώποις*, we must understand chiefly men conquered by Him, His men, to whom He has given gifts of grace, that they themselves may and can become gifts for men in wider circles (see ver. 11; Acts ii. 33).

After all this, it cannot be said that the citation is not from Ps. lxviii. 19, but *ex carmine, quod ab Ephesiis cantitari sciret* (STORR, FLATT), or that Paul did not know the exact words (RUECKERT), nor *nonnihil a genuino sensu detorsit, de suo adjecit* (CALVIN), or to invent an exegetical tradition from the Targums (which were made not earlier than the third century, and the Syriac and Arabic versions, altered to accord with the Apostle, and to suppose the Apostle had followed this (HOLZHAUSEN, MEYER and others). Nor should we go beyond the context, and find a reference, as in Col. ii. 15, to Satanic powers, which He has led captive (CHRYSOSTOM, BEZA, CALOV., BENGEL, STIER and others), since this does not comport with the Apostle's interpretation, or to the souls released from Hades (ESTIUS, DELITZSCH, *Psychology*, p. 358, and others), since enemies are spoken of. Finally we cannot infer from this passage in the Psalms and the use Paul makes of it this difference between the Old and New Testaments, that in the former God receives gifts from or among men, but in the latter gives to men (SCHENKEL).

[The real difficulty of this verse lies in the form of the last clause. That Paul quotes from the Psalm which has a Messianic reference, that Christ is represented as returning victoriously to heaven with a crowd of captives, is evident, and occasions no difficulty. But as the point of the section is Christ's *giving to men*, it is singular that the words: "gave gifts to men" are not found in the Psalm, which says: "received gifts among men" (בָּאָדָם, lit., in the man), or as Braune takes it, "consisting in men," *i. e.*, the captives. Dr. J. A. ALEXANDER (*Psalms, in loco*): "To *receive gifts* on the one hand and bestow gifts on the other are correlative ideas and expressions, so that Paul, in applying this description of a theocratic triumph to the conquests of our Saviour, substitutes one of these expressions for the other." If this be deemed satisfactory, and Braune's view, which obviates the difficulty in בָּאָדָם, be accepted, the solution is complete. But if the latter be rejected (see footnote on *αἰχμαλωσίαν*), then we can render the original passage: "has taken gifts among men" (the collective sense is clearly correct) and consider the whole phrase recast by the Apostle to express the correlative idea which is at hand, and which is contained in the further, fuller, and deeper meaning of the Psalm, here succinctly, suggestively and *authoritatively* unfolded (ELLICOTT). This seems to be more satisfactory than to attempt to prove that the Hebrew expresses this meaning. It may be admitted that it is often=*danda sumpsit* (as EADIE clearly proves) but that it means this in the Psalm in question is

* [The inspired and prophetic character of the Psalm, and its antiquity are undoubted (see HITZIG, HENGSTENBERG, DELITZSCH, against DE WETTE and EWALD). It was probably composed after a battle, and quite as probably (against EADIE) "at some bringing up of the ark to the hill of Zion," which took place after a victory (HENGSTENBERG: taking of Rabbah, 2 Sam. xii. 26). ALFORD, with reference to the return of the ark, says: "It is *therefore* a Messianic Psalm. Every part of that ark, every stone of that hill, was full of spiritual meaning. Every note struck on the lyres of the sweet singers of Israel, is but part of a chord, deep and world-wide, sounding from the golden harps of Redemption. The partial triumphs of David and Solomon only prefigured as in a prophetic mirror the universal and eternal triumph of the Incarnate Son of God. Those who do not know this, have yet their first lesson in the Old Testament to learn." Comp. *Doctr. Note* 3.—R.]

† [In the revision by Four Anglican Clergymen, *captives* is substituted for *captivity*. "A captivity" is a literal rendering which points to the concrete sense.—As regards this concrete sense, there is little difference of opinion, the only question being: Who are the captives? Obviously enemies who have been overcome, either (*a*) men who become His servants, those referred to in τοῖς ἀνθρώποις (Braune, following some fathers, HARLESS, OLSHAUSEN and others), who were previously prisoners of Satan (though Braune does not bring this out, or (*b*) Satan, sin, death (CHRYSOSTOM, BENGEL, MEYER, STIER, EADIE, ALFORD, HODGE, ELLICOTT.; CALVIN seeks to combine the two. The former view greatly lessens the difficulty in the last clause of the quotation, helping to justify the substitution of the notion of *giving* for that of *receiving* in the original passage. But this very fact lays it open to suspicion as an exegesis for an emergency. The other view is favored by Col. ii. 15 (though not to be limited by the reference there), it preserves the analogy of the comparison, and gives a forcible meaning. Other views have been suggested, but not very probable ones.—R.]

very doubtful. The same view would render בָּאָדָם, *for men*, which becomes *to men*, after the bestowal of the gift. See EADIE *in loco*.—R.]

Ver. 9. **Now that he ascended,** *τὸ δὲ ἀνέβη*, taken from the *ἀναβάς*.—[Not the *word*, which does not occur in the passage quoted, but the *predicate*, which is contained in *ἀναβάς* (MEYER). The *δέ* introduces a slight explanatory *transition;* not strictly a *proof* (HODGE, ELLICOTT, following HOFMANN and MEYER) of the correctness of the Messianic application of the passage cited, but a further explanation of what it means as thus applied. MEYER now (4th ed.) gives up his former view, remarking that such a proof was unnecessary and illogical, since the subject of the Psalm in its Messianic fulfilment was self-evident, and God Himself is conceived of in the Old Testament as *ὁ καταβάς*.—R.]

**What is it** [What does it imply] **but that he also descended** [*τί ἐστιν εἰ μὴ ὅτι καὶ κατέβη*].—*Τί ἐστιν*=what is thereby expressed (Matth. ix. 13; John xvi. 17 ff.; x. 6)? *Ὅτι καὶ κατέβη*, He has not merely ascended, but has also previously descended; the former presupposes the latter. Thus heaven is indicated as His original dwelling-place (John iii. 13) and His Person as that glorious, helping One, who can and will give gifts. [So MEYER. It is impossible to understand the verse otherwise than as indicating heaven to be the point of departure and the place of return for Him who descends and ascends. The doubt respects only the place whither He descended and whence He ascended. —R.]

**Into the lower parts of the earth,** *εἰς τὰ κατώτερα μέρη τῆς γῆς*.—This closer definition of the descending evidently indicates the depths of the lower world, the subterranean world, which is below the surface of the earth; the genitive is partitive, governed by *μέρη*. The thought occurs in a variety of forms (Phil. ii. 10: *καταχθονίων;* Acts ii. 27, 31: *εἰς ᾅδην;* 1 Pet. iii. 19: *ἐν φυλακῇ*). The expression here corresponds to *κατώτατα τῆς γῆς* (Ps. lxiii. 10), grammatically *τῆς γῆς* might be the genitive of apposition (WINER, p. 494), like *εἰς τὸ ὕψος τοῦ οὐρανοῦ* (Isa. xxxviii. 14). It is also true that the context up to this point would permit us to refer the phrase to the earth alone. But the following *τὰ πάντα* (ver. 10) and the design of the Apostle to show the power of Christ, require the fullest justifiable meaning of the expression, and hence the application to Hades. There is no reference to burial (CHRYSOSTOM and others), nor in accordance with Ps. cxxxix. 15 to the mother's womb (CALIXTUS and others).

[This interpretation of the phrase: "the lower parts of the earth" is the one anciently received, current among Romanist expositors, and adopted more recently by BENGEL, RUECKERT, OLSHAUSEN, STIER, TURNER, WORDSWORTH, ALFORD and ELLICOTT. The other view: the lower parts, *viz.*, the earth, is accepted by the majority of modern commentators, such as CALVIN, GROTIUS, HARLESS, DE WETTE, HOFMANN, HODGE and EADIE (who gives a full statement of views and a good defence of this interpretation). It may be remarked that while one class of expositors may have been led to the one conclusion by a desire to sustain the article of the Apostles' Creed: "He descended into hell," the other may have been quite as much influenced by a fear of favoring the Romanist appendages to that article. Both views are alike grammatical, for while the positive would more naturally express the latter sense and the superlative the former, we have here the indefinite comparative, which may mean either. Doctrinally either view is admissible, while the considerations mentioned by Braune perhaps make the ancient view the preferable one. On Christ's descent into Hades, see Dr. SCHAFF'S note, *Matthew*, pp. 228-229, and LANGE and MOMBERT, *First Peter*, pp. 63 f., 67-72. ZANCHIUS, BARNES and others favor the notion that the phrase signifies, in general, lowliness or humiliation, a view altogether untenable, because opposed to the context, and an unnecessary departure from the literal meaning.—R.]

Ver. 10. **He who descended, he it is also who ascended** [*ὁ καταβὰς αὐτός ἐστιν καὶ ὁ ἀναβάς*].—Both thoughts are here brought together, without *οὖν*, in a lively, joyous manner, marking the identity of the Person. *Καταβάς* stands first, having the emphasis, and *αὐτός* [*He*, emphatic], not *ὁ αὐτός* [*the same*, as in E. V.], gives prominence to the Person, who ascended out of the deepest depths, **above all the heavens,** *ὑπεράνω πάντων τῶν οὐρανῶν;* the strongest antithesis to ver. 9. Under the term "heavens" there is no necessity for reckoning either three (HARLESS and others) according to 2 Cor. xii. 2, or seven (MEYER and others), according to the prevalent Jewish opinion.* Similar expressions: Heb. iv. 14; vii. 26.

**That he might fill all things,** *ἵνα πληρώσῃ τὰ πάντα*.—The Apostle thus gives the motive for what he has presented [in ver. 7]. There is nothing into which He cannot penetrate. Comp. i. 23. *Τὰ πάντα* designates all regions into which He can carry His gifts, can penetrate with His grace and glory, all regions and all persons within them.† There is no reference to a fulfilment of Old Testament prophecy (ANSELM, KOPPE and others), or to the completion of the work of Redemption (RUECKERT and others); nor is it to be limited to Christians (BEZA, GROTIUS, SCHENKEL and others), for He rules also among and in His enemies (Ps. cx. 2). CHRYSOSTOM is excellent: *τοῦτό ἐστι τῆς ἐνεργείας αὐτοῦ καὶ τῆς δεσποτείας*, that He lets none slip, gives to every one, who has permitted himself to be conquered; the gracious and efficient presence of Him, the God-man, is thus established, and ver. 7 explained.

---

* [ALFORD: "It is natural that one who, like St. Paul, had been brought up in the Jewish habit of thought, should still use their method of speaking." But this does not imply an acceptation of such a division of the heavens; rather this: "Whatsoever heaven is higher than all the rest which are called heavens, into that place did He ascend" (BISH. PEARSON in ELLICOTT).—R.]

† [So HODGE, EADIE, ALFORD and ELLICOTT. Even Dr. Braune does not attempt to justify the use made of this passage to defend the doctrine of the ubiquity of Christ's body (*Form. Concord.*). On which ELLICOTT aptly says: "Christ is perfect God, and perfect and glorified man; as the former He is present *everywhere*, as the latter He can be present *anywhere*."—R.]

## DOCTRINAL AND ETHICAL.

1. The *idiosyncracy and freedom of the individual* is as little altered by the gift of Christ's grace as the former is of itself able to replace the latter by its own self-originated development. There must be *giving*, and indeed in this there is necessary a repeated proffering, making receptive or preparing, appropriating and preserving; the Lord offers ten times before we once receive, accept, take; so little does the Lord limit the freedom of the recipient. With the *gift* (*Gabe*), however, a *task* (*Aufgabe*) is at the same time appointed to the recipient: he must use it, gain with it. The gift does not obliterate national, corporate, local, temporal, individual differences, but purifies and ennobles them. Temperament and natural mental powers, talents and inclinations are only refined, directed, moved and used for the Lord's kingdom and our own salvation. "It is self-evident that the gifts of grace are not mere developments of the natural talents of the man,—but this does not deny that they are planted in a natural talent" (KAHNIS, *Lehre vom heil. Geist* I. p. 72).

2. *Christ is the Lord, who gives.* He has fought the fight of Redemption, and stands as a conqueror there; has overcome as the Lion of the tribe of Judah, and as the Lamb of God, who bears the sins of the world. He can give to every one and He is willing to do so. His χρίσμα, by means of which He makes men Christians, is a χάρισμα, grace in a special manner adapted to the individual. Comp. 1 Cor. xii. 8 ff.

3. *Respecting the internal connection of the Old and New Testament*, as well as for *Hermeneutics* and *Homiletics*, much can be deduced from the application of this citation from the Psalms in our passage.

*a.* "The Apostle knows that what the Old Testament contains, the New Testament must also contain, only in a more glorious manner. Comp. 2 Cor. iii. 7-11. He knows that however different according to the different relations, which are indicated in the very character of the Old Testament revelation, it still inheres in the nature of this unity of the two revelations, to bear witness of this unity to those who can and will seek it. All that was written aforetime was written εἰς ἡμετέραν διδασκαλίαν (Rom. xv. 4)." HARLESS. Besides the definite prophecies, there are in the Old Testament enough types and things typical of Christ and what has taken place in and through Him. What occurred in the people of Israel and is narrated as history or sung by holy men of old, is something pointing to the future; while at the time indeed it is accomplished fact or acute sketching of a living person, yet beyond this it has a validity for the Messianic period, so that when this comes in it is related to it as σκιά to σῶμα, shadow to body. In the Old Testament the Logos is concerned, but concealed, in all; in the New Testament manifested openly in all glory, full of grace and truth. The Jehovah of the Old Testament is the Redeemer in the New. Comp. RIEHM, *Lehrbegriff des Hebräerbriefs*, I. p. 131 ff.

*b. Hermeneutics* should perceive and show forth, in the acts of God narrated or sung in the Holy Scriptures, His administration, both going back to seek the preparatory and prophetic types, and forwards to point out the advancing accomplishment. But there must be a distinction made between what the passage to be expounded expresses as the sense and meaning of the writer, and what the deed or person, so simply and transparently described, signifies in the kingdom of God, in His people, of which signification the writer may be entirely unconscious. "The knowledge which looks back to the guidance of youth is the knowledge belonging to Christianity; the guidance of youth is the history of the Old Testament theocracy; the veil which rests on the guidance of youth disappears with the knowledge of manhood in Christ (2 Cor. iii. 4-16)." HARLESS. Every important poet, every skilful artist, may first perceive in the later inspection of his work thoughts therein, of which he neither was nor became conscious in making it. So in the Scripture often enough is there more than the writer had in his consciousness. [Comp. *Exeg. and Doctr. Notes*, *Galatians*, iv. 19-30. Even EADIE, who is most earnest in the effort to prove that the Apostle cites from the Psalm in accordance with its original and exact sense, says: "Our position is, that the same God is revealed as Redeemer both under the Old and New Testament, that the Jehovah of the one is the Jesus of the other, that Psalm lxviii. is filled with imagery which was naturally based on incidents in Jewish history, and that the inspired poet, while describing the interposition of Jehovah, has used language which was fully realized only in the victory and exaltation of Christ."—R.]

*c. Homiletics* may and should place the biblical history of the Old and New Testament, as a concrete manifestation of a Divine thought or of Divine guidance and ways, which enclose love and wisdom for men, besides others in the present life of the world or of individuals, in order to place these latter in that true light, which the former gives. For God and the Saviour Jesus Christ is the same in the Old and the New Testament, and at all times, ours as well, in His Church. GAUPP (*Homiletik* I. p. 174) calls this the *tropological* view. [Admitting both the usefulness of teachings drawn from analogy, since analogy, figure, type, *etc.*, all indicate the harmony of the Divine will in Creation, Providence and Redemption, and the propriety of such extensions and applications of the Old Testament on the part of an inspired Apostle, we must remember that our *tropological* exposition is not authoritative, and that we can base no doctrine or precept upon it, but only use it to elucidate established doctrine or enforce plain precept.—R.]

4. *The Christology of this passage.* It says that Christ is originally in heaven; there is His eternal dwelling-place. But He betook Himself into lowliness and penetrated the universe even to the lower regions, in order to fill all with His glory. He works as King, dispensing victoriously, where He has wrought as champion. His pre-existence is taken for granted, while we are especially taught His eternal activity of grace in all directions and for all times and for every man.

## HOMILETICAL AND PRACTICAL.

Only take what Christ gives thee; thou needst

envy no one.—Thankfully recognize what He has given to another; it benefits thee also.—Do not be satisfied with the natural endowments of your nation, your class, your family, or your intellect; let them be sanctified, purified, penetrated by grace in Christ. The most highly gifted natural man is always smaller and poorer than a living Christian (GOETHE, TERSTEEGEN).—Christ is King, Lord; His sword is His word, but this is a sword.—He has descended into the deep as a Redeemer: thy sin is not too deep and thy heart is not too bad: He can fill it.

STARKE:—Each member must be contented with his measure of gifts, received without pride, shared without envy.—Dear Christian, wilt thou ascend with Christ and reach His glory, then must thou first descend and suffer.

RIEGER:—No one has all, and no one need be concerned lest he come away entirely empty.—The origin of all gifts is to be found especially in the exaltation of Christ, which began with the victory over the rulers of darkness, over the principalities and powers who held us captive, who were themselves taken captive in the deep path of Christ's humiliation, and in the moment of Christ's death, when they believed they had gained the mastery over Him, must find and feel Him to be their Conqueror and Destroyer.

HEUBNER:—The diversity of gifts as respects degree and subject, should not occasion boasting or envy. In working together for the Kingdom of God there can be no envy; where there is envy, there the labor is for personal advantage.—Christ's Kingdom embraces also the invisible Kingdom of God. Would this be conceivable, were He a mere man?

PASSAVANT:—It has ever been the indiscretion and folly of men in the world, that they have forgotten the One Great Giver in the *gifts* and *gifted*, looking with especial astonishment to this teacher, with especial love to this benefactor, with especial admiration to this hero;—a virtual idolatry.—The main blow and the victory for all time and for eternity took place in and with the death of Christ—in and with His Resurrection.

STIER:—Each for himself and all together have to walk the same way in Christ.—The gifts of Christ are themselves at the same time men; all gifts of grace are pre-eminently official gifts.

[EADIE:—Ver. 7. The law of the Church is essential unity in the midst of circumstantial variety. Each gift in its own place completes the unity.—Ver. 9. Reproach and scorn and contumely followed Him as a dark shadow. Persecution at length apprehended Him, accused Him, calumniated Him, scourged Him, mocked Him, and doomed "the man of sorrows" to an ignominious torture and a felon's death. His funeral was extemporized and hasty; nay, the grave He lay in was a borrowed one. He came truly "to the lower parts of the earth."—Ver. 10. But as His descent was to a point so deep, His ascent is to a point as high. His position is the highest in the universe.—R.]

[HODGE:—Ver. 7. To refuse to occupy the place assigned to us in the Church, is to refuse to belong to it at all.—Vers. 9, 10. All other comings were typical of His coming in the flesh, and all ascensions were typical of His ascension from the grave.—It is God clothed in our nature who now exercises this universal dominion; and therefore the Apostle may well say of Christ, as the incarnate God, that He gives gifts unto men.—R.]

---

### *c. The organization and organism of the Church.*

(CHAP. IV. 11–16.)

11 And he gave some, apostles [some to be apostles]; and some, prophets; and
12 some, evangelists; and some, pastors and teachers; For [Unto][1] the perfecting of
the saints, for the work of the ministry [or of ministration], for the edifying [build-
13 ing up] of the body of Christ: Till we all come in [unto] the unity of the faith,
and of the knowledge of the Son of God, unto a perfect [full-grown] man, unto the
14 measure of the stature of the fulness of Christ: That we *henceforth* be no more [To
the end that we be no longer] children, tossed to and fro [tossed as waves], and
carried about with every wind of doctrine [teaching], by [in] the sleight of men,
*and* cunning craftiness, whereby they lie in wait to deceive [in craftiness *tending* to
15 the system[2] of error]; But speaking [holding][3] the truth in love, may grow up into
16 him in all things, which [who] is the head, *even* Christ:[4] From whom the whole
[all the] body fitly joined [framed] together and compacted [,][5] by that which
every joint supplieth [by means of every joint of the supply], according to the effectual [*omit* effectual] working in the measure of every [each several] part,[6]
maketh increase [the growth] of the body unto the edifying [building up] of itself
in love.

## TEXTUAL AND GRAMMATICAL.

1 Ver. 12.—[*Unto* is substituted for the preposition *for*, to indicate the difference in the Greek prepositions. *In order to, with a view to*, would express one view of the meaning of the verse, but *unto* suits the view of Dr. Braune better. *Ministration* is preferable to *ministry*, since the latter is now confined by usage to the office of the preacher and pastor. *Building up* is Saxon, *edifying* Latin.—R.]

2 Ver. 14.—[א. B.[1] D.[1] F. K. L. support the form μεθοδίαν, adopted by Tischendorf (ed. 7); but μεθοδείαν (*Rec.*) is preferable, "as changes in orthography which may be accounted for by itacism or some mode of erroneous transcription must always be received with caution" (Ellicott).—The periphrasis is necessary to express the force of πρός.—R.]

3 Ver. 15.—[See *Exeg. Notes*, especially the additional footnote.—R.]

4 Ver. 15.—[The article is found in the *Rec.*, א.[3] D. F. K. L., most cursives, and is accepted by De Wette; but it is omitted in א.[1] A. B. C., and rejected by Lachmann, Tischendorf, Alford, Ellicott (now by Meyer). It occurs with Χριστός 31 times, and is omitted in 53 instances (Ellicott).—R.]

5 Ver. 16.—[The view of the connection taken in the *Exeg. Notes* requires the insertion of a comma here, to indicate that the subsequent phrases qualify the main verb.—The less usual form: συνβιβασόμενον is sustained by א. A. B. (?) C. D.[1] F. G., adopted by Tischendorf, Ellicott and others. Comp. iii. 6, where the usual euphonic changes in the prefixed preposition are ignored in the best MSS.—*Effectual* is omitted to avoid conveying the impression that the working is God's ἐνέργεια.—R.]

6 Ver. 16.—[A. C., some versions and fathers sustain the reading μέλους, but it is probably a gloss occasioned by σῶμα; μέρους is found in א. B. D. F. K. L., and accepted by all recent editors.—R.]

7 Ver. 16.—[א. D.[1] F. read αὐτοῦ, but ἑαυτοῦ is sustained by most authorities.—R.]

## EXEGETICAL AND CRITICAL.

Ver. 11. *Christ's gift for the Church.*—**And he gave** [καὶ αὐτὸς ἔδωκεν].—"And" joins with what precedes ("that he might fill all things"), what follows, which has the former as its aim. As the clause of design (ver. 10) refers to the beginning (ver. 7: "according to the measure of the gift of Christ"), so the clause "he gave," αὐτὸς ἔδωκεν, refers back also (ver. 10: αὐτός, ver. 8: ἔδωκε, ver. 6: ἐδόθη).* Αὐτός gives emphatic prominence to the Person of the Giver, the Exalted One: He and none other. *Ipse, summa potestate;* and *repetitur ex v.* 10. *Ministri non dedere se ipsos* (BENGEL). It is not=ὁ αὐτός (SCHENKEL), nor is ἔδωκε=ἔθετο (THEOPHYLACT, HARLESS) in accordance with 1 Cor. xii. 28. [EADIE remarks (and ALFORD approves): "The idea is, that the men who filled the office, no less than the office itself, were a Divine gift." —R.] Nor should the aorist be pressed, so as to express only something momentary, passing; Paul is himself included, as one whom the Exalted One gave to be an Apostle; the historical fact is indicated. CALVIN has justly said: *et suscitat interdum prout temporum necessitas postulat*, although he accepts the first three classes of officers as belonging only to the beginning of the Church (*Institutes*, IV. 3, 4).

**Some to be Apostles** [τοὺς μὲν ἀποστόλους].—Τοὺς μέν, τοὺς δέ is not=ἐνίους, some [*i. e.*, some Apostles], since this is only a numeral, while the former expression points as a demonstrative to definite persons, whom He has prepared to be the gift, and given as ἀποστόλους. "Apostles" are those immediately called and equipped by the Lord to extend His work; they were especially endowed by Him, and had personally great advantages and prerogatives. First of all there were twelve; after the apostasy of Judas, Matthias was chosen by the disciples somewhat precipitately, before the day of Pentecost, while Paul was called by the Lord Himself as the twelfth.* Still Barnabas was called an apostle in connection with Paul (Acts xiv. 4, 14) and others also (Rom. xvi. 7; 2 Cor. viii. 23; Phil. ii. 25), hence this is not an abuse of the term (BLEEK), so that one might thus name those men, chosen and specially endowed by the Lord, appointed to found churches, as Boniface the Apostle of the Germans, Egede the Apostle of Greenland, Ziegenbalg and Schwartz the Apostles of India.

**Some prophets.**—"Prophets" are (ii. 20; iii. 5) men, who receive revelation (ἀποκάλυψις) from God, and, perceiving God's will and thought with clearness, announce the same with discretion and power; the prophet is μάντις, as far as he has revelation (1 Cor. xiv. 26); the latter becomes a prophet through interpretation; "glossarily" (to be distinguished from the Pentecostal miracle) is a morbid species of prophecy (1 Cor. xiv. 27 ff.). They appear in Acts xi. 27; xiii. 1; xv. 32; xxi. 10. They are concerned, not so much with the future (BENGEL) as with the eternal. To them correspond in the progress of ages those theologians with more profound insight into God's truth and will, as well as into the character and course of His Kingdom, such as Luther. [Comp. the excellent note of EADIE *in loco*. HODGE: "As the gift of infallibility was essential to the Apostolic office, so the gift of occasional inspiration was essential to the prophetic office."—R.]

**And some evangelists.**—"Evangelists," such as the deacon Philip (Acts xxi. 8; viii. 4-12), περιϊόντες ἐκήρυττον (THEODORET), as travelling missionaries† (NEANDER), but also in per-

* [ELLICOTT: "There is here no direct resumption of the subject of ver. 7, as if vers. 8-10 were merely parenthetical, but a regression to it; while at the same time the αὐτός is naturally and emphatically linked on to the αὐτός of the preceding verse. This return to a subject, without disturbing the harmony of the immediate connection or the natural sequence of thought, constitutes one of the high excellences, but at the same time one of the chief difficulties in the style of the great Apostle."—R.]

* [On the position of Matthias, comp. i. 1 and *Acts* (*in loco*). EADIE thus enumerates the essential elements of the apostolate: 1. That the Apostles should receive their commission immediately from the living lips of Christ. 2. That having seen the Saviour after He rose again, they should be qualified to attest to the truth of His resurrection. 3. They enjoyed a special inspiration. 4. Their authority was therefore supreme. 5. In proof of their commission and inspiration, they were furnished with ample credentials. 6. Their commission to preach and found churches was universal and in no sense limited. This statement, approved by ALFORD and ELLICOTT, involves further: That they have no personal successors, can have none; that no supreme authority exists in any ecclesiastical office, unless that office be the Apostolate. See further, *Galatians*, i. 1-5, *Doctr. Notes; Romans*, p. 59. —R.]

† [Dr. HODGE, in an excellent note here, remarks that the prevalent view at the time of the Reformation (see CALVIN *in*

manent positions (2 Tim. iv. 5; comp. 2 Cor. viii. 18), in consequence of their own view of the facts of the Gospel (John xvi. 26 ff.), or mediate tradition (Luke i. 1-4). It must not be referred to "those writing the Gospel" (CHRYSOSTOM); BENGEL also goes too far in ascribing to them *præterita;* they have to do with the life of the Lord in prophecy and fulfilment.

**And some pastors and teachers,** τοὺς δὲ ποιμένας καὶ διδασκάλους.—JEROME: *Non ait, alios autem pastores et alios magistros, sed alios pastores et magistros, ut qui pastor sit, esse debeat et magister et nemo pastoris sibi nomen assumere debet, nisi possit docere quos pascit.* BENGEL: *Pastores et doctores hic pinguntur, nam pascunt* (and *regunt*) *docendo maxime, tum admonendo, corripiendo, etc.* The pastors are=προϊστάμενοι (Rom. xii. 8), who have the office of κυβέρνησις (1 Cor. xii. 28) and must be "apt to teach," διδακτικοί (1 Tim. iii. 2; 2 Tim. ii. 24; Tit. i. 9), they are "bishops," ἐπίσκοποι (Acts xx. 28). Οἱ κατὰ πόλιν καὶ κώμην ἀφωρισμένοι in distinction from εὐαγγελισταί (THEODORET). BLEEK takes them as distinct; and he is right to this extent only, that the "teachers" are not always "pastors;" it is as "apostles and prophets" (ii. 20; iii. 5); hence despite this distinction, they form one category beside the previous ones.

[There has been much dispute whether these terms refer to two classes of stationary church officers, or to one whose twofold duty is indicated by two titles. The latter view is favored by the absence of the distinctive τοὺς δέ, and is accepted by AUGUSTINE, JEROME, BENGEL, HARLESS, OLSHAUSEN, MEYER, HODGE, EADIE and ALFORD.* The former is accepted by THEOPHYLACT, CALVIN, GROTIUS, NEANDER, DE WETTE, STIER, though the definitions of the distinction vary greatly. ELLICOTT says: "The ποιμένες (a term probably including ἐπίσκοποι and πρεσβύτεροι) might be and perhaps always were διδάσκαλοι, but it does not follow that the converse was true. The χάρισμα of κυβέρνησις is so distinct from that of διδασκαλία, that it seems necessary to recognize in the διδάσκαλοι a body of men (scarcely a distinct class) who had the gift of διδαχή, but who were not invested with any administrative powers and authority." Is the teacher then the parish schoolmaster or the professor of theology? or a preacher who does no pastoral duty? The Reformed Church polity has usually recognized the distinction (*Westminster Directory, Constitution* of Reformed [Dutch] Church in America, *etc.*), but practically it has amounted to nothing, as indeed little good has ever resulted from the attempt to reproduce accurately as *jure divino* those distinctions which expositors discover in the offices of the primitive Church. It may be remarked that while this phrase shows that every pastor ought to be a teacher, putting the former phase of duty first, it will ever be the case that through native endowment some ministers are better adapted for one part of the duty than for the other, though there is no warrant for total neglect of either, or for appointing in one congregation one minister to be pastor and another to be teacher; for the latter would nowadays take undue precedence of the former. Those who are "teachers," in our sense of the word, are also in the most important sense "pastors."—R.]

It is unmistakable that these four categories above named, so divide themselves, that the first three do not belong to a single congregation, but to the whole Church or a number of congregations, the last however is definitely appointed to one congregation. A gradation from higher to lower is noticeable also, in this manner, that the higher includes the lower grade or grades. Thus Jesus is called and calls Himself "Apostle" (Heb. iii. 1, after Jno. xx. 21); "Prophet" (Matt. xiii. 57; Luke xiii. 33; Acts iii. 22 ff., vii. 37); εὐαγγελιζόμενος (Luke iv. 18, 43; xx. 1); "Shepherd," ποιμήν (Jno. x. 11; 1 Pet. ii. 25); "Teacher" (Matt. xxiii. 8; Jno. xiii. 14). Accordingly BENGEL says: *Cum summis gradibus conjuncti poterant esse inferiores; omnes Apostoli simul etiam vim propheticam habuerunt. Sed prophetæ et evangelistæ non simul etiam Apostoli fuerunt.* Finally it must be noticed, that the offices themselves are not named here, and that in distinction from 1 Cor. xii. 28, the official *persons* stand in the foreground as gifts, in Corinthians the *gifts* of office, the offices themselves falling into the back-ground in both cases. See further, *Doctr. Notes* 1, 2.

Ver. 12. *The immediate aim of the activity of the persons in office.* [Note on the *relation and dependence* of the clauses of this verse. There is great difference of opinion, but of the various views those numbered (4) and (5) are most worthy of consideration. Braune adopts (4); but (5) seems to be preferable.

1. The clauses are taken as *co-ordinate* (CHRYSOSTOM, ZANCHIUS, BENGEL, E. V.), but this is opposed by the change of preposition, and in that case we would have a different order, the second clause would come first.

2. The trajection (GROTIUS, KOPPE and others), which actually put that clause first, is altogether unwarranted.

3. The second and third clauses are taken as parallel (by HARLESS and OLSHAUSEN), but as dependent on the first, in a partitive sense: some to teach, others to be edified. But there is nothing to indicate such a sense, and it is logically inadmissible, since the "saints" of one clause and "the body of Christ" of the other are identical.

4. Braune follows ERASMUS, DE WETTE, MEIER, FLATT, RUECKERT, SCHENKEL and many others, in taking the second and third as dependent on

*loco*) regarded this term as applied to "vicars of the Apostles," such as Luke, Timothy, Titus. This is altogether untenable, and no doubt arose from the effort, made by CALVIN and others, to prove that all the offices referred to except that of "pastors and teachers," were of a temporary nature, and thus to establish the principle of "parity of the clergy."—R.]

* [ALFORD remarks that the figure in ποιμένες, if pressed, would imply that they were entrusted with some special flock, which they tended; and then the "teaching" would necessarily form a chief part of their work. EADIE says the former term implies careful, tender, vigilant superintendence and government, being the function of an overseer and elder. The official name ἐπίσκοπος ("bishop"), he adds, is used by the Apostle in addressing churches formed principally out of the heathen world (Ephesus, Philippi, Crete), while πρεσβύτερος ("elder"), the term of honor, is more Jewish in its tinge (Acts, Epistles of James, Peter and John). "Speaking to Timothy and Titus, the Apostle styles them elders (and so does the compiler of the Acts, in referring to spiritual rulers); but describing the duties of the office itself, he calls the holder of it ἐπίσκοπος."—R.]

the first, or rather the second dependent on the first and the third on the second. The meaning then is: "For the perfecting of the saints unto all that variety of service which is essential unto the edification of the body of Christ." As this view is fully presented below, the objections to it alone require mention at this point. These as urged by MEYER are: *a*. That as the context treats of offices in the Church, it is improper to enlarge the meaning of διακονία beyond that of official service (Rom. xi. 13; 2 Cor. iv. 1; vi. 3; comp. Acts vi. 4; 2 Cor. iii. 7 ff.; ix. 12, *etc.*). *b*. That with such a meaning πάντων would have been so essentially necessary with ἁγίων, that it could not have been omitted. These objections are sufficiently strong to lead him to adopt the next view.

5. The second and third clauses are taken as co-ordinate, and dependent on ἔδωκε, "he gave;" the first expressing the more *ultimate* and final purpose (πρός) of the action, the other two the more immediate end (εἰς). This view is adopted by ALFORD, ELLICOTT, HODGE, EADIE (2d ed.), and gives this sense: "He gave Apostles, *etc.*, —to fulfil the works of the ministry, and to build up the body of Christ, His object being to perfect His saints." So HOFMANN substantially. The great objection is the strange order which place the more ultimate end first, but as the difficulty seems to inhere in the Apostle's own choice of prepositions, it is not decisive against this view. While preferring it, I would not insist on its correctness, but, leaving Dr. Braune's notes as they stand, add in footnotes the requirements of this interpretation.—R.]

**Unto the perfecting of the saints** [πρὸς τὸν καταρτισμὸν τῶν ἁγίων].—Πρός marks the end aimed at, *viz.*: "the perfecting of the saints." Καταρτισμός, occurring only here, like κατάρτισις in 2 Cor. xiii. 9 designates the re-establishment of an affair, so that it is ἄρτιος (only 2 Tim. iii. 17, τέλειος, various reading), *integer*, as it should be (1 Cor. i. 10; 2 Cor. xiii. 11; Gal. vi. 1; 1 Thess. iii. 10; Heb. x. 5; xi. 3; xiii. 21; 1 Pet. v. 10). *Non potuit honorificentius verbi ministerium commendare, quam dum hunc illi effectum tribuit* (CALVIN). Through the ministers of Christ the Christians should become complete. perfect.* For what purpose?

**For the work of the ministry** [**or of ministration**, εἰς ἔργον διακονίας].—Hence there is no thought of merely external increase (PELAGIUS, BEZA). Εἰς marks that for which the saints should become expert, complete. The nouns, without the article, have here a more general meaning: ἔργον indicates the efficiency of the διακονίας, and the latter denotes that every work which it does, is a service to our neighbor and then to the whole. Διακονία is a general service (2 Tim. iv. 11; 2 Cor. xi. 8). This meaning is demanded here by the context, the connection with the saints, the members, each one of which has his office (Rom. xii. 4) and needs the other (1 Cor. xii. 21). Comp. 2 Tim. iii. 17: πρὸς πᾶν ἔργον ἀγαθὸν ἐξηρτισμένος. It must not be referred to church service, ecclesiastical office, the diaconate in a technical sense (MEYER).* Comp. on ver. 16.

**For the building up of the body of Christ**, εἰς οἰκοδομὴν τοῦ σώματος τοῦ Χριστοῦ.†—The aim of the "ministry" is again subjoined with the preposition εἰς. So great is the significance of the preparing of Christians through the ministers of the Church to ministering activity in the congregation! The body of Christ is there, it exists, but new members are continually incorporated in it, it extends and increases; hence both of the figures derived from the body (i. 23; ii. 20–22) are included. LUTHER is very good: "that the saints may be fitted to the work of the ministry, that thus the body of Christ may be edified." Accordingly the three clauses are not co-ordinate (CHRYSOSTOM, BENGEL and others); nor are the two subjoined with εἰς co-ordinate (RUECKERT, MEYER, HARLESS and others), nor yet dependent on ἔδωκε, as some think, while others make them dependent on καταρτισμόν. Quite as little can we accept a trajection of the second number before the first (GROTIUS, KOPPE and others). [See above for a classification of opinions.—R.] Comp. *Doctr. Note* 3.

Ver. 13. *The end of the perfecting.* **Till we all come** [μέχρι καταντήσωμεν οἱ πάντες].—Μέχρι denotes the final, highest aim, not the beginning and entrance of the same, ἄχρι, but the presence and enjoyment of it (TITTMANN, *Syn.* I. p. 33 ff.). [Comp. Dr. SCHAFF's note, *Romans*, p. 181.] Καταντήσωμεν, the conjunctive without ἄν denotes simply the future; the verb itself however is= φθάνειν (ŒCUMENIUS), the arriving at the destination, as frequently in the Acts (xvi. 1; xviii. 19, 24, *etc.*), in a local sense; here and Phil. iii. 11 however in the spiritual sense, prominence being given to the free movement, which is occasioned, strengthened and animated by the educating καταρτισμός.‡

Under the term οἱ πάντες, "all,"=οἱ ἅγιοι, as a complete whole, the Apostle includes him-

* [HODGE gives the following meanings which have been suggested here: 1. The completion of the saints ("the number of the elect"). 2. Their renewing or restoration. 3. Their reduction to order and union as one body. 4. Their preparation for service (so Braune). 5. To their perfecting. The last he prefers, as is required by the view taken of the relation of the clauses.—R.]

* [The term is not to be restricted to the *diaconate*, nor to the *ministry*, *i. e.*, the office of pastor and teacher (HODGE), but seems to refer to "spiritual service of an *official* nature" (so MEYER). Hence *ministration* is preferable to the more technical word *ministry*, though Braune extends the signification in accordance with his view. On the absence of the article ELLICOTT remarks: "Διακονία may possibly have been left studiously anarthrous in reference to the different modes of exercising it alluded to in ver. 11, and the various spiritual wants of the Church; ἔργον however seems clearly definite in meaning, though by the principle of *correlation* (Middleton, *Art.* iii. 3, 6) it is necessarily anarthrous in form."—R.]

† [ELLICOTT remarks that this clause is parallel to, but at the same time more nearly defining the nature of the ἔργον. The article is not required, as edifying generally is the object. There is no confusion of metaphors, since both words have a distinct metaphorical meaning, where the original allusion is in a measure lost.—R.]

‡ [All reference to coming together from different starting-points, or coming out of previous wanderings is imaginary (MEYER). ELLICOTT remarks that too much weight must not be laid on the omission of ἄν as giving an air of less uncertainty to the subjunctive, since there was an evident tendency in later Greek to omit it in such cases, adding: "the use of the subjunctive (the mood of conditioned but objective possibility), not future (as Chrysostom) shows that the καταντᾶν is represented not only as the eventual but as the *expected* and *contemplated* result of the ἔδωκεν."—R.]

self; it is therefore implied that those in whom there has been a beginning of πίστις (HARLESS), even the greatest, the Apostles, are in need of progress towards the goal, are not yet there, even although in advance of others, but further their own progress when they labor for others (Phil. iii. 13, 14; Rom. i. 11, 12). Accordingly "all" is not to be extended to all men (JEROME). BENGEL is excellent: *Ne apostoli quidem se putarunt metam assecutos, nedum ecclesia. Semper proficiendum fuerat, non standum, nedum deficiendum. Et nunc ecclesia ideam sui optimæ non a tergo respiciat oportet, sed ante oculos habeat, ut futuram, etiam num assequendum. Notate hoc, qui antiquitatem non tam sequimini, quam obtenditis.*

**Unto the unity of the faith, and of the knowledge of the Son of God,** εἰς τὴν ἑνότητα τῆς πίστεως καὶ τῆς ἐπιγνώσεως τοῦ υἱοῦ τοῦ θεοῦ.—The preposition marks the goal. The repeated article demands absolutely, that "faith" and "knowledge" be kept apart as distinct, independent ideas, although the genitive which they have in common ("of the Son of God") occasions a connection by means of the copulative conjunction. "Faith" designates the immediate possession, "knowledge" the assurance obtained by means of knowing (MATTHIES); the former is applicable to an ethical, the latter to an intellectual sphere; the latter proceeds constantly anew from the former, the former is itself the permanent beginning, the constant principle, not merely an initiatory stage to be surpassed; both belong together accordingly. The unity of both, since "one faith" is presupposed (ver. 5), refers to the various degrees of clearness and power in the individual members (οἱ πάντες), to littleness of faith, weakness of faith, want of maturity, *etc.* Accordingly the genitive, "of the Son of God," defines both more closely, indicating that they are as strong, as He possessed them, and that thus we, being God's children who will grow up and become educated, should possess them; He is the Author and Finisher of our faith (Heb. xii. 2) and knowledge, thus Example and Standard. If He is not the object, there is neither faith nor knowledge at all. Hence it is the genitive *subjecti* (STIER), not *objecti*, as most consider it. But unity of faith and knowledge is not meant, either alone (OLSHAUSEN), or in connection with the other meaning (STIER); we should rather refer it to the unity of the individuals, of the church-members, which is effected by the faith and knowledge of Christ.

[The view of OLSHAUSEN is, that the unity is the state in which faith and knowledge are identified; *fides implicita* developing into *fides explicita* (BISPING). EADIE and ALFORD virtually accept this as included here, the latter citing DE WETTE: "True and full unity of faith is then found, when all thoroughly know Christ, the object of faith, alike, and that in His highest dignity as the Son of God." But the second term is not epexegetical of the first, and faith is not to be lost in knowledge, but abides (1 Cor. xiii. 13).—The strong word ἐπίγνωσις must be noticed. If any prefer the more common view of the genitive as that of the object, the following statement (HODGE) will be satisfactory: "Faith and knowledge express or comprehend all the elements of that state of mind of which the Son of God is the object—a state of mind which includes the apprehension of His glory, the appropriation of His love, as well as confidence and devotion. This state of mind is in itself eternal life." "The unity of faith is now confined to the first principles; the unity of faith contemplated in this place is that perfect unity which implies perfect knowledge and perfect holiness."—R.]

**Unto a full-grown man,** εἰς ἄνδρα τέλειον.—The singular marks the unity of the Church, which grows up into a perfect man.* Here a "development" (*werden*) is spoken of, which is involved in the καταντᾷν; the Church, the body of Christ, becomes a personality educated and completed to the perfect life-degree of Christ. For τέλειος is the opposite of νήπιος (ver. 14); like 1 Cor. iii. 1; ii. 6 and Heb. v. 13, 14, it means one in ripe, full manhood.

**Unto the measure of the stature of the fulness of Christ** [εἰς μέτρον ἡλικίας τοῦ πληρώματος τοῦ Χριστοῦ].—"Unto the measure of the stature" points to a definite measure; it does not therefore extend *in infinitum.* Ἡλικία from ἧλιξ, *qui adultæ et maturæ ætatis est*, certainly designates, as in Luke xix. 2, the stature, the bodily size, elsewhere (Matt. vi. 27; Luke xii. 25; ii. 52; Heb. xi. 11; Jno. ix. 21, 23) however, the age, generally the age of manhood; it is, more fully expressed, the maturity, the full growth, and in accordance with the context the spiritual maturity (STIER).† The genitive: τοῦ πληρώματος τοῦ Χριστοῦ, "of the fulness of Christ," defines more precisely the measure of the maturity: it is conditioned by the fulness, the state of being filled, which comes from Christ, accordingly by Himself, who lives in it and by His gifts and powers. We should become perfect, as He, the Head was, 1 Cor. xii. 12. Hence LUTHER is incorrect: in the measure of perfect age; for πληρώματος is not to be made an adjective quali-

* ["Metaphorical apposition to the foregoing member, the concrete term being probably selected rather than any abstract term, as forming a good contrast to the following νήπιοι (ver. 14), and as suggesting by its 'singular' the idea of the complete unity of the holy personality, further explained in the next clause into which they were united and consummated" (ELLICOTT). As a curiosity ALFORD cites from AUGUSTINE (*Civ. Dei*, xxii. 17): "*Nonnulli. propter hoc quod dictum est, Eph. iv. 13, nec in sexu fœmineo resurrecturas fœminas credunt, sed in virili omnes aiunt.*"—R.]

† [As the word undoubtedly means either *stature* or *age*, the latter being more common, or perhaps includes both, like the German *Erwachsenheit*, the sense here must be determined by considerations drawn from the passage itself. KOPPE, HOLZHAUSEN, HARLESS, MEYER, HODGE prefer the sense: *age*, because "full-grown men," "children" (ver. 14), point to this; the phrase which follows is then a characterizing genitive. But "measure" seems more appropriately used in reference to "stature," and the idea of magnitude is indicated by the words "fulness," "grow up" (ver. 15) and by the figure of ver. 16. This sense is adopted by ERASMUS, GROTIUS, BENGEL, RUECKERT, STIER, EADIE, ELLICOTT, ALFORD. It may be added that πλήρωμα does not refer to the Church (STORR and others), nor to the knowledge of Christ (GROTIUS). The genitive τοῦ Χριστοῦ is a genitive subjective: *Christ's fulness:* "This stature grows just as it receives of Christ's fulness; and when that fulness is wholly enjoyed, it will be that of a 'perfect man'" (EADIE). Some of the Fathers referred this passage to the resurrection, teaching that man shall rise from the grave in the perfect age of Christ, having the form and aspect of thirty-three years of age, the age of Christ at His death. See MEYER, who has a note on the time of fulfilment in which he brings out his favorite views about the Second Advent and Paul's expectation of its speedy coming.—R.]

fying ἡλικία. The explanation: full gracious presence of Christ (HARLESS) is insufficient; still more so the meaning given by RUECKERT: Christ stands *before* us as the *ideal* of manly size and beauty.—Whether this goal will be reached in this life or only in the next, is decided by πίστις in the context, to this extent, that we must refer it to this life also, although indeed many a one first attains unto it in the future life, since this coming to the appointed goal extends through centuries. Comp. *Doctr. Notes* 4, 5.

*The purpose*, vers. 14, 15. *a*) *negatively*, ver. 14; *b*) *positively*, ver. 15.

Ver. 14. **To the end that we be no longer children** [ἵνα μηκέτι ὦμεν νήπιοι].—Ἵνα sets forth the purpose, which aims at the fulfilment of μηκέτι ὦμεν νήπιοι, and this must accordingly take place before the goal is reached, "unto a perfect man." It is not to be joined to ver. 13 (SCHENKEL),* but to vers. 11, 12, more particularly to ἔδωκε, and unfolds wherein the "perfecting of the saints" consists. As the Apostle, who, although the most advanced, still in humble sense of fellowship, bears and suffers in the imperfection of the Church, includes himself (ὦμεν), we must not find here a reproach, but a point or state of transition, which does not continue, hence μηκέτι, which does not recall false teachers in Christendom generally (MEYER). The Gentiles are not yet νήπιοι; Christians in their incipiency are such (Matt. xi. 25; Luke x. 21; 1 Cor. iii. 1; viii. 11; Gal. iv. 13; Heb. v. 13); they should not however remain so, but advance to ripe manhood.

**Tossed to and fro [as waves] and carried about** [κλυδωνιζόμενοι καὶ περιφερόμενοι].—This describes more closely the νηπιότης, with reference to appearances and experiences observed and felt in the churches, inclusive of the false teachers who had appeared and would appear. "Tossed as waves"† (*fluctuantes*, Vulgate), moved as waves, *intrinsecus, sursum deorsum, etiam citra ventum* (BENGEL), "and carried about," *extrinsecus, huc illuc, aliis nos adorientibus* (BENGEL), describes the ready excitability of the unsubstantial, the immature (Jas. i. 6; Heb. xiii. 9; Jude 12); they are dependent on their surroundings, on influences and insinuations, are moved:

**By every wind of teaching**, παντὶ ἀνέμῳ τῆς διδασκαλίας.—The wind has a great variety (παντί), from the *aura seculi, levis aura popelli* to the strong continuing trade-wind, and as to its origin from coarse to refined carnal interests, as well as in its tendency toward aims against the Church or in favor of a false church. [The dative is the dynamic dative, KRUEGER.—R.] "Teaching" is introduced under the figure of the wind, because it is something pneumatic and because, as the wind in proportion to its strength or the free situation of the water, stirs this from ripples to foam, so the teaching sets in motion the spirit of the νήπιος, which is so easily tossed to and fro. The νήπιος will learn, know; that is the proper way to perfection. But beside the one wholesome teaching of truth there appears the multifarious teaching of error as a great danger,* and the greater because it works, moves, attracts and hurries along:

**In the sleight of men**.—Ἐν τῇ κυβείᾳ, belonging to the participles, refers with the article to "teaching;" through the sleight befitting the doctrine, and with the substantive (from κύβος, die), to dice-playing, in order to denote, that the teachers deal with the Scriptures and the truth and men, as players with dice (LUTHER). [Braune agrees with DE WETTE, MEYER, HODGE, and the E. V., in regarding ἐν as instrumental, but as this seems pleonastic after the dative, "and would mar the parallelism with ἐν ἀγάπῃ (ver. 15), the preposition appears rather to denote the element, the evil atmosphere as it were in which the varying currents of doctrine exist and exert their force" (ELLICOTT). So HARLESS, OLSHAUSEN, EADIE and ALFORD.—R.] The genitive ("of men") indicates that the νήπιοι stand under the influence of *men*, instead of their placing themselves under the guidance of *Christ* (MEYER), and also under that of many instead of one. But this is not all; the added parallel clause carries the matter further; there is not only human sleight, *temeritas*, but a plan also:

**In craftiness tending to the system of error** [ἐν πανουργίᾳ πρὸς τὴν μεθοδείαν τῆς πλάνης].—Ἐν connects with the previous phrase. Πανουργίᾳ corresponds with κυβείᾳ, and gives prominence to what the latter does not indicate, the *nequitia*, the conscious malice; hence it is incorrect to find this in the previous phrase (HARLESS, STIER). The article can be dispensed with, since the closer qualification is added. The preposition, as in ver. 12 (πρὸς τὸν καταρτισμόν), denotes toward what the craftiness proceeds (WINER, p. 378). This is τὴν μεθοδείαν (only here and vi. 11, where the plural is used), which is derived from μεθοδεύειν, to follow in order to track up something, then *machinare*, meaning therefore *machinatio*, crafty pursuing (LUTHER: *erschleichen*, to sneak upon), to follow and come upon in a sneaking manner; in this there is found pre-arrangement, system. The principle which μεθοδεύει is indicated by the genitive τῆς πλάνης.

* [SCHENKEL'S view is somewhat novel. He takes our verse as giving the purpose of ver. 13, and to the objection that this places perfection before the state of childhood answers, that the last verse refers to the whole Church, this to individuals. Because the whole Church is perfect, the members should be no longer children. But this is very unsatisfactory. The two leading views are those of HARLESS and MEYER. The former takes our verse as *co-ordinate* with ver. 13, and immediately dependent on vers. 11, 12, giving the purpose of the ministry (so FLATT, BLEEK, HODGE). MEYER, who has a clear statement of the case *in loco*, takes this verse as *subordinate* to ver. 13, and remotely dependent on vers. 11, 12. He holds that ver. 13 defines the "*terminus ad quem*," which characterizes the functions of the Christian ministry, while ver. 14 thus explains the object, our ceasing to be children, contemplated in the appointment of such a "*terminus*," and thence more remotely in the bestowal of a ministry so characterized. To the former view there is the decided grammatical objection that a clause introduced by ἵνα is made co-ordinate with those introduced by εἰς, in that case too ver. 13 would follow vers. 14, 15. The latter view avoids these difficulties without being open to the logical objection which probably led to the adoption of the former.—R.]

† [Not by the waves, like a deserted ship, as MEYER and others hold, but like the billow itself.—R.]

* [EADIE: "The article τῆς before διδασκαλίας gives definitive prominence to 'the teaching,' which, as a high function respected and implicitly obeyed, was very capable of seducing, since whatever false phases it assumed, it might find and secure followers." The substantive is abstract and general; *teaching* is preferable to *doctrine*, because it brings out the active agency employed with more distinctness.—R.]

This is not *error mentis*, but lying, the opposite of ἀλήθεια (1 John iv. 6); hence, especially as τοῦ διαβόλου is added in vi. 11, BENGEL is on the right track when he says: *i. e., Satanæ*.* It is true the πλάνη is in the main only personified (MEYER); but it has a kingdom and a πνεῦμα, that operates through men, the false teachers (τῇ κυβείᾳ τῶν ἀνθρώπων), as through serviceable tools, proper instruments.

Ver. 15. **But holding the truth in love, may grow up into him,** ἀληθεύοντες δὲ ἐν ἀγαπῃ αὐξήσωμεν εἰς αὐτόν, is to be joined with ἵνα (ver. 14) as the antithesis (δέ) to "no longer children." Hence LUTHER is incorrect: "but let us be honest in love and grow." Christians (οἱ πάντες, ver. 13), not merely teachers, are the subject. Αὐξάνειν is simply to grow, not to remain νήπιος, to come out of the νηπιότης. *Hæc αὔξησις, augmentatio* (ver. 16), *media est inter infantes et virum* (BENGEL). Accordingly εἰς points to the goal; hence "into Him" (MATTHIES, STIER); it corresponds to the εἰς ἄνδρα τέλειον, we should become a perfect man, as He is. The phrase "Head" from the following relative clause should not be pressed (HOFMANN, MEYER), in order to make the meaning still more difficult; τὰ πάντα stands between, and this accusative of reference will not allow εἰς αὐτόν to be=grow in respect to Him (MEYER), whatever that may mean. ["Unto and into Him," as the goal and standard of our growth, with a secondary thought apparently of the incorporation of all the Church in Christ, which is developed in the subsequent context. The phrase is not to be joined with "in love" (HARLESS).—R.] Still less can it mean: *ipsius cognitione* (GROTIUS), *virtute et influxu* (A-LAPIDE).

While εἰς αὐτόν denotes the goal of the growth, ἀληθεύοντες ἐν ἀγάπῃ designates the condition under which, the state in which it takes place. Hence the two are to be joined: true in love. Ἀληθεύειν is=ἀληθὴς εἶναι (PASSOW, *sub voce*); the context explains it further. In the New Testament only here and Gal. iv. 16. There ὑμῖν indicates that it means speaking the truth, here the context is a different one. While αὐξήσωμεν forms an antithesis to νήπιοι ὦμεν, ἀληθεύοντες stands in contrast to the manner of such ("tossed as waves and carried about") and to "teaching" in general, as well as that of the deceitful false teachers in particular. BENGEL is excellent: VERANTES, LUTHER (Gen. xlii. 16): if you design truth. The whole personality is spoken of, in walk and nature, and the meaning is more than merely: to be true in speech, *verum dicere* (HOFMANN, *Schriftbeweis*, II. 2, p. 130, MEYER).*

Ἐν ἀγάπῃ sets forth the sphere or element in which the ἀληθεύειν moves; ἀγάπη and ἀλήθεια are correlative ideas.† Comp. 1 Cor. xiii. 6. Love is here entirely undefined, hence general: love for the truth, for the brethren, who come into danger through false teachers, or themselves become false teachers, to the Church as a whole, to God. There is accordingly no reference to forbearance toward error (HARLESS), or love towards those of different profession (MEYER), or something of the same; nor is ἐν=διά (SCHENKEL), or σύν, or merely upright in love (LUTHER and others).

**In all things who is the head, even Christ** [τὰ πάντα, ὅς ἐστιν ἡ κεφαλή, Χριστός].—Τὰ πάντα,‡ without a preposition, as 1 Cor. ix. 25; x. 33; xi. 2, or with κατά (Col. iii. 20) denotes, on account of the article, all, to which reference has been made, into which we must grow: faith, knowledge, truth, love, *etc.* "Who is the Head, even Christ," with great emphasis, in order to furnish a motive for growing up into Him. We might have found τὸν Χριστόν, in apposition to εἰς αὐτόν, but it can either be in apposition to ἡ κεφαλή, or in the first instance still be in the nominative (WINER, p. 495).

Ver. 16. *Comprehensive conclusion.*—**From whom,** ἐξ οὗ, marks the cause, the source, and as the context demands, a continuing one. Christ is the goal (εἰς αὐτόν) and the source of the life-development of the Church (MEYER). If then CHRYSOSTOM says: σφόδρα ἀσαφῶς ἡρμήνευσε τῷ πάντα ὁμοῦ θελῆσαι εἰπεῖν, an exact analysis of the sentence will show what is incorrect (ἀσαφῶς). Col. ii. 19 is parallel.

*a. The subject.*—**All the body fitly framed together and compacted** [πᾶν τὸ σῶμα συναρμολογούμενον καὶ συνβιβαζόμε-

* [On the reading μεθοδείαν see *Textual Note* [2]. As to its meaning, we may remark that the bad sense is not necessarily inherent in the term, which signifies: "a deliberate planning or system." Still here the bad sense is fixed on it by the genitive which follows, and we might render it: *stratagem*, though in the full phrase, "system of error," the meaning is sufficiently evident. EADIE renders "a system," but "the system of error" is one. The force of the preposition can be brought out in English only by a periphrasis: *tending to, leading to*, not *according to*. The word πλανῆς here includes the idea of deceit no doubt, but is perhaps better expressed by *error*, "error in its most abstract nature." The genitive is subjective, the error plans and machinates. That the Apostle meant to characterize "error" as evil, morally as well as intellectually wrong, is evident enough from the context. When RUECKERT says that this was Paul's weak side, to stigmatize those in error, in a spirit of dogmatical defiance, he betrays his usual incapacity for comprehending the Apostle. If truth be not sanctifying, and error demoralizing, then the Scriptures and human experience are alike at fault.—R.]

* [Though the more extended meaning is stoutly denied by MEYER, it is accepted by CALVIN, DE WETTE, RUECKERT, ALFORD, HODGE, EADIE and ELLICOTT. The difficulty is to express the sense in English: *being true* is literal, but not satisfactory; *walking truthfully, walking in truth*, though giving the correct sense, would be inapt here; *holding the truth* is the best rendering, if the care is taken not to give an objective sense to truth."—Comp. the remarks of ALFORD (who renders: *being followers of truth*) and ELLICOTT.—R.]

† [The question of connection is much disputed. Many, perhaps most, join "in love" with the participle (CALVIN, GROTIUS, ALFORD, RUECKERT, HODGE, STIER, BLEEK among others), while HARLESS, MEYER, OLSHAUSEN, EADIE and ELLICOTT connect it with the verb "grow." In favor of the former, the order, the parallelism of structure with ver. 14, the otherwise feeble and awkward position of the participle at the beginning of the sentence, Paul's habit of subjoining his qualifying phrases, and the vital association between love and truth, may be urged. The latter view is supported by MEYER as better agreeing with his rendering of the participle: speaking the truth; he urges also that "in love" ought to be joined with the same verb as in ver. 16, and that thus "in love," at the beginning here and at the close there, receives its due emphasis. Still the other seems preferable, for the connection in verse 16 is equally open to discussion. It is not "a '*fiat justitia, ruat cœlum*' truthfulness: but must be conditioned by love; a true-seeking and true-being with loving caution and kind allowance" (ALFORD).—R.]

‡ [This is the accusative of the *quantitative* object (ELLICOTT); "we are to grow in all those things in which the Christian must advance" (OLSHAUSEN).—R.]

ν ο ν].—"All the body" takes the term "all" (ver. 13) as a unity; the main idea is that of totality. ["All the body," which the E. V. gives in Col. ii. 19, is perhaps preferable to "the whole body," the idea being of the entire body as including every member, rather than of the body as a whole (τὸ πᾶν σῶμα more accurately expresses this). The latter notion becomes the stronger one in the close of the verse.—R.] The double definition, "fitly framed together and compacted," describes the Church in its present development (present participle). The first adjective (see ii. 21; of a building) indicates the individual parts and members (ἁρμός, groove, joint, member), which are printed together (σύν), the other, used more precisely of men who enter into a society, marks these members as individuals, as persons. In this the difference and the reason of the double expression is found. In such a union the Church is conceived of, because it is a building; besides a society is spoken of, a society of persons, a congregation. Accordingly such a two-fold designation sets forth, either the figure and fact (MEYER) or harmony and solidity (BENGEL). ELLICOTT suggests, in accordance with the simple meaning of the words, that the latter term refers to the *aggregatim*, the former to the *inter-adaptation* of the component parts.—R.]

[**By means of every joint of the supply.**—This phrase, which presents more difficulties than any other in our verse, is discussed below by Dr. Braune, who joins it with the *predicate*, not with the *subject* (*i. e.*, as a qualification of the participle) as is done in the E. V. The latter view of the connection is adopted by the majority of commentators (so HODGE, EADIE, ELLICOTT), and is favored by the position of the phrase and the parallel, Col. ii. 19. The former is defended by MEYER, STIER, ALFORD, CHRYSOSTOM, THEODORET, BENGEL). It may be remarked in favor of this, that it gives more perspicuity to the passage, "the whole instrumentality and modality here described belonging to the growth" (ALFORD), the repetition of σῶμα is more natural in an involved predicate, while the complicated subject is much more awkward. As regards the parallel, the position there is totally different. It ought to be added that the earlier defenders of this view advocated a sense of the word ἁφή (=αἴσθησις, the perception of the vital energy imparted from the head), which did not admit so readily of the connection with the participles. Still Braune's view is preferable.—R.]

*b. The predicate.*—**Maketh the growth of the body,** τὴν αὔξησιν τοῦ σώματος ποιεῖται.—Col. ii. 19: αὔξει τὴν αὔξησιν. The repetition of τοῦ σώματος ("of the body") instead of ἑαυτοῦ ("itself") marks the permanent effect proceeding from the cause, and as compared with Christ's continued influence, puts into the background the self-development as an entirely independent one. Only when the principle of life in the Church has grown and been strengthened through Christ, does it become perceptible (εἰς οἰκοδομὴν ἑαυτοῦ); yet it is already indicated by the middle (ποιεῖται). This repetition is therefore not to be explained by the distance of the predicate from the subject (σῶμα) as an effort at distinctness (MEYER), or as negligence (RUECKERT), or as a Hebraism (GROTIUS), or because the interest of individuals is not under discussion (HARLESS, STIER).*

The predicate is then enlarged by a designation of the means: **by means of every joint of the supply** [διὰ πάσης ἁφῆς τῆς ἐπιχορηγίας].—Ἁφή (from ἅπτεσθαι) cannot according to Col. ii. 19, where it is put in one category with συνδέσμων and connected with ἐπιχορηγούμενον καὶ συνβιβαζόμενον, mean the same band, yet must be something similar.† It cannot be=αἴσθησις (CHRYSOSTOM), sensation (MEYER), contact (HOFMANN). Since ἁφὴν ἔχειν means to have something enchaining, enticing (PASSOW, *sub voce*), and the singular is found here, the most natural and correct meaning will be: connection or grasp. Ἐπιχορηγία (from χορηγία) means to lead a choir, to defray the expenses of a choir, to render a public service, the contribution to expenditures, public, common rendering of service; accordingly the growth of the Church is by means of every grasp of contribution or service rendered (genitive *objecti*, and not of apposition, SCHENKEL, nor=πρός, GROTIUS, HOFMANN and others).

[To this view of Dr. Braune it may be objected that it loses sight of the strict anatomical figure without substituting for it the subtler interpretation of Chrysostom and others. It seems better to take ἁφή in the sense indicated by Col. ii. 19, and render it "joints." The qualifying genitive is as ELLICOTT remarks: "a kind of genitive *definitions*, by which the predominant use, purpose, or destination of the ἁφή is specified and characterized." "The joints are the points of union where the supply passes to the different members, and by means of which the body derives the supply by which it grows" (ALFORD). HODGE is undoubtedly correct in interpreting this supply as "the Divine life or Holy Spirit communicated to all parts of the Church" (against Braune, who seems to refer it to the service rendered by the individual members), but it is very doubtful whether he is right in saying that the ἁφαί "are the various spiritual gifts and offices which are made the channels or means of this Divine communication." Most recent commentators have wisely refrained from thus particularizing. Certainly when these ἁφαί are taken as meaning the officers mentioned in ver. 11, despite all saving clauses, a step is taken toward the Romanist and High Anglican view of the clergy. The figures of Scripture, through wrested and strained interpretation, have been made subservient to great error.—R.]

**According to the working in the measure of each several part** [κατ' ἐνέργειαν

* [The repetition is generally regarded as made for the sake of perspicuity, especially as ἑαυτοῦ is found in the next clause. Perhaps however the body as a whole comes more into view now.—The middle is apparently not so much reflexive as *intensive* and indicative of the energy with which the spiritual process is carried on (EADIE, WORDSWORTH, ELLICOTT).—R.]

† [In *Colossians* (p. 55) Braune seems to limit the word to "nerves," in accordance with the view which joins each of the substantives there used with one of the participles. As this is scarcely tenable (see *in loco*), and as the article is not repeated with the second substantive in that passage, the category "joints and bands" decides yet more definitely against any interpretation of this word which removes it out of the general class of the anatomical arrangements.—R.]

ἐν μέτρῳ ἑνὸς ἑκάστου μέρους].—This qualifies the phrase which precedes. Κατ' ἐνέργειαν, without the article on account of the following qualification (i. 19; iii. 7), defines the ἐπιχορηγία as an efficient one, while the proportion of this efficiency rests "in the measure of each several part," in the measure, which every part, the individual member of the Church in himself has from Christ. The service rendered proceeds therefore from the individual parts, from each one, so that it is not to be referred merely to the ministry, the officers of the church (HARLESS). This efficient service of the individuals is to the advantage of the whole and conditions the growth of the whole. Comp. vers. 7, 12. This part of the sentence is therefore to be closely connected with ἐπιχορηγίας, and not joined immediately with αὔξησιν ποιεῖται (MEYER), with which it is connected only through the former.*

**Unto the building up of itself in love,** εἰς οἰκοδομὴν ἑαυτοῦ ἐν ἀγάπῃ.—The aim is thus set forth, and as in ver. 12 it is οἰκοδομή; the self-development is here marked, since the powers of growth thereto are given from Christ. This self-edification is consummated only in love, as the life-sphere rendering it possible. "In love" therefore depends grammatically on "edifying" (BLEEK), not on "maketh increase" (MEYER).† With this so emphatic conclusion ("unto the building up of itself in love") the Apostle is brought back to his starting-point (ver. 1-3), to the bond of peace.

### DOCTRINAL AND ETHICAL.

1. *Christ gives official persons* (ver. 11). It is not so much that Christ established certain regulations binding on the Church, as that He has bestowed on it *persons*, charisms for the endowment of an office, a ministry. He is the Author and Possessor of the office, not only the first, but the only one, who has never relinquished it and never will to the very end. "Christ *gives* the Church's ministers, the Church *takes* those given and sets them in the service of the Church. Accordingly the Church, or he who represents the rights and duties of the Church, never has to choose the subjects arbitrarily, but to know and recognize those endowed by Christ as those given by Him, and to place them in the ministry; hence the highest idea of the ecclesiastical directory is to examine whether those concerned are *given by Christ*, without prejudice however to other requisites which are matters of ecclesiastical polity." MEYER. Concerning the double aspect of the office, which is both *divini* and *humani juris*, a divine institution as well as a human, ecclesiastical arrangement, the passage does not speak more definitely. But three things are plain: 1) It is incorrect to affirm that Christ now raises up no apostolic men, no prophets nor evangelists, but only pastors and teachers. See the *Exeg. Notes*. He does this according to the necessity of the times. 2) It is also erroneous to find no offices at all appointed, and to be unwilling to institute any, as if it were only a human notion to establish a teaching ministry. So the *Quakers* (according to Barclay in GUERICKE, *Christl. Symbol.* p. 626) and SCHENKEL, *Ephesians*, p. 66, 5; the former accept only the authority of the Divine endowment of persons, the latter regards the service alone as from the Lord, but the office as a human regulation. 3) Just as little however should these official persons whom the Lord gave at the beginning and still gives to the Church, be fixed in number, as the Irvingites would do, or be stiffened into a hierarchy as among the Roman Catholics.*

2. The *distinction* between the *official persons*, involving as it does no subordination of one class to the other, since indeed the Apostle Matthew is specially designated as Evangelist, John as prophet and Evangelist, while Peter calls himself "presbyter" (1 Pet. v. 1), is altogether irrelevant as respects the teaching office: this individualizes itself in the other offices. Subordination exists only as respects Christ who gives them. They have no reason for self-exaltation on account of their gifts or special calling, nor has the congregation any for aversion to recognize and respect them and their calling: the Lord works with His word and Spirit in them and

* [It is difficult to decide the question of connection. In favor of the view taken by Braune "is the position of the words, and also the congruity of the figure. It is more natural to say that the Divine influence is according to the working of every part—*i. e.*, according to its capacity and function—than to say, 'the growth is according to the working,' *etc.*" (HODGE). ELLICOTT and ALFORD connect it with the verb however. The "working" is the functional energy of the body, not Divine inworking, as seems to be indicated by the E. V.: "effectual working."—R.]

† [MEYER'S view overloads the verb with qualifications. "Love is just as much the element in which the edification, as that in which the growth takes place" (ALFORD).—In the hope of giving clearness to the exegesis of this verse, a summary is added: *From whom* (Christ) *all the body* (each and every member) *fitly framed together* (jointed together) *and compacted* (forming one whole) *grows* (as if possessed of life in itself) *by means of every joint* (every special adaptation in gift and office) *of supply* (which Christ grants to these joints as means and instruments, the supply being) *according to the working in the measure of each several part* (Christ's vital energy is serviceable only as supplied by the means He has chosen, and He chooses to supply it as the several parts of the body exercise their functions, so that the growth is not only from Him, but symmetrical and organic also) *unto* (the end being) *the building up of the body itself in love* (as the element of edification).—R.]

* [EADIE: "We are ignorant to a very great extent of the government of the primitive Church, and much that has been written upon it is but surmise and conjecture. The Church represented in the Acts was only in process of development, and there seem to have been differences of organization in various Christian communities, as may be seen by comparing the portion of the Epistle before us with allusions in the three letters to Rome, Corinth and Philippi. Offices seem to be mentioned in one which are not referred to in others. It would appear, in fine, that this last office of government and instruction was distinct in two elements from those previously enumerated; inasmuch as it was the special privilege of each Christian community—not a *ministerium vagum*, and was designed also to be a perpetual institute in the Church of Christ. The Apostle says nothing of the modes of human appointment or ordination to these various offices. He descends not to law, order or form, but his great thought is, that though the ascended Lord gave such gifts to men, yet their variety and number interfere not with the unity of the Church." As this Epistle has for its fundamental thought, "*the Church which is in Christ Jesus*," it is remarkable how the Apostle in it scarcely touches upon those points, which seem to fill the minds of many who profess to hold an exalted estimate of the Church: Nothing about the ministry constituting the Church, though enough to show the necessity for the ministry; nothing about the Church maintaining the succession through fixed forms, but a good deal about Christ's giving real pastors and teachers (the Church sometimes fails to receive such through the most ancient order of succession); nothing about Church polity, but much about the means of her advancement toward unity of faith and knowledge, toward perfection, toward the measure of the stature of the fulness of Christ.—R.]

through them (Acts xiii. 21; xv. 28), and this arrangement belongs to the living and animating organism of the Church, in which the life of Christ develops itself. The officers should be called neither *clerics* nor *Geistliche*, nor should the Church be divided into *ecclesia repræsentans* and *repræsentata*. For every Christian belongs to the κλῆρος θεοῦ, has a part in the κληρονομία (i. 11, 15), should be "*geistlich*," and have τὸ πνεῦμα, and the ministers as the Lord's servants must labor in and for the Church, to serve her, not to represent *her*, but the Lord.

3. *The task* of the official persons with their gifts for their special calling, over against the other members of the body of Christ with the general call, is "the perfecting of the saints," and this reaches also to "the work of the ministry," to "the edifying of the body of Christ." As certainly then as the servants of the Lord have to serve the Church and its individual members, hence not in the commission of the Church, as though this were always and everywhere the only efficient impulse, nor yet out of their own authority, so certainly should these ministers be prepared for their special service by their labors in the Church, as they have been called and installed by her. As the Lord works upon the Church, and this should permit itself to be acted upon, so she has the duty of working again according to His purpose, of leading back to Him under His guidance and the help of God, which He will grant and furnish for her welfare. The first link in the chain of congregational activity is the officers, the second is every Christian in healthy activity at his post, and thus the joyous upbuilding of the whole is advanced, which reacts on the ministers and individual members of the Church. Thus it goes from above to below, from the ministers in immediate *rapport* with the Lord to the individuals, the Church, the whole, and from individual to individual, and through them to the whole, and from this back again to the individuals. The lay element must be cultivated, set in motion, sustained, animated and guided. The design is to bless men, to serve the people, the people, the people, as LUTHER (1 *Adv. Kirchenpostille*, ed. Franke I. p. 42) preaches. In avoiding the Scylla of priestly rule, many fall into the Charybdis of congregational or lay rule.* This is of importance for all Church polity.

4. Like all *pedagogy*, the pedagogy of the church also should make itself superfluous and unnecessary. The utility of the ecclesiastical office is appointed to this end, and should be managed accordingly.† But this gives neither right nor occasion to undervalue at the time what will and should cease *after* its time. Fidelity to the Master demands that it should be left to Him, when and how He will break up the form, lest we in doing so should spill and lose its contents and substance.

5. In connection with the prospect that we all (ver. 13) shall attain unto the unity of faith and the knowledge of the Son of God, it must be remarked:

(1.) That this is not spoken of in any way (see *Exeg. Notes*) of the *apocatastasis*: "A communion of the enjoyment of salvation" (SCHNECKENBURGER) is not indicated, but the progress from the militant to the triumphant church, the development, not from unbelief to blessedness, not from eternity to God, to heirship with Him, but from faith to sight, from service according to God's will to participation in the glory of His Nature.

(2.) A *uniformity* of expression, of forms and formulas, is not meant, but that condition is meant which the Lord Himself foretells (John x. 16), when there shall be "one fold" and "one Shepherd," when the church of Christ is developed out of and beyond all "fermentation," is ripened, ministers and members furthering each other's advance, the individual parts and the whole in accord, and on the basis of a deeper unity the proper variety existing in glorious harmony.

It cannot be overlooked, that, although the differences, which divide, will *disappear*, because error attaches to them, or at least immaturity, the *removal* of differences cannot be anticipated, unless the church, instead of growing up unto a perfect man, should become an assembly of offensively over-prudent children. Even the distinction of sex shall be removed (Matt. xxii. 30);

* [All questions of Church polity assume an entirely different aspect, when viewed in the light of the voluntary principle, which totally deprives the State of any control in the internal affairs of the Church. There can be no question that the Erastianism prevalent in Germany has done as much to hinder the development of the lay element in Church work in that country, as the opposite principle has to further that development in America. But the latter state of things has its dangers, *e.g.*, incapable Sunday School superintendents and teachers, elders or deacons or church wardens or whatever they may be called, who, while contributing little to the spiritual advancement of the Church, take advantage of their office, or of the influence of their purse in the annual estimates, to control and annoy him whom God gave to be "pastor and teacher."—R.]

† [EADIE: "The meaning (ver. 13) is, that not only is there a blessed point in spiritual advancement set before the church, and that till such a point be gained the Christian ministry will be continued, but also and primarily, that the grand purpose of a continued pastorate in the church is to enable the church to gain a climax which it will certainly reach; for that climax is neither indefinite in its nature nor contingent in its futurity." On the question whether the goal plainly set before the church in ver. 13, is attainable here in this world there is great difference of opinion. That it will first be reached hereafter is held by THEODORET, CALVIN, HODGE and others, and that it is attainable here is affirmed by CHRYSOSTOM, THEOPHYLACT, JEROME, LUTHER, DE WETTE, MEYER, STIER, SCHENKEL. That πίστις is mentioned does little to decide the matter, nor is there anything to indicate, that the distinction of here and hereafter, entered into the Apostle's mind. He regards the church as one, speaks of the goal set before her on the earth, not stating whether it is to be attained on earth (So HARLESS, OLSHAUSEN, EADIE, ELLICOTT). Besides eschatological views do much to give indefiniteness to the terms "here and hereafter" in our use of them. "In such sketches the Apostle holds up an ideal which, by the aim and labor of the Christian pastorate, is partially realized on earth, and ought to be more vividly manifested; but which will be fully developed in heaven, when, the effect being secured, the instrumentality may be dispensed with" (EADIE). That effect has not yet been secured, that instrumentality may not yet be dispensed with: yet those who are tossed as waves, who are carried about by every wind of doctrine, who according to the Apostle show most clearly the present necessity for the ministerial office, are readiest to cry out that it is useless. Would that the *church* needed ministers less! Then they might go out into the world more frequently to win souls for Christ! Paul here certainly does not prophesy of that "church of the future," in which there shall be neither pastor nor teacher, because each member is able to take care of himself, and there is nothing to be held up to "faith." That "Church" in the view of those who proclaim its coming, will be based on "knowledge;" but it will be γνῶσις not ἐπίγνωσις, perception of some fragments of truth, not the grasping and knowing with "faith and knowledge" all Truth, in the Person "of the Son of God."—R.]

as that of corporealness in general; but that is no reason why we should treat the body as a prison of the soul, and desire to be without sex, before we enter the company of the angels. Let each one be faithful to his own church and to his Lord! Beyond Christ we cannot go, without Him or against Him there is no progress.

6. He who allows himself to be determined by external influences, is still immature, is as yet no man, independent, firm and clear, unless these influences come from the source of truth and life, from Christ: from Him and to Him our life comes and goes. Influences of an unchristian character are brought by the spirit of this world into every age, and many a one may unconsciously serve this spirit against the truth; as in the history of the world there is presented a plan of God, so in these there is a method which points beyond them into the kingdom of darkness and lies.

7. Truth and Love, which belong together, since the former has an ethical character, and the latter is not blind, are the fundamental elements of growth, requiring Christ as the aim and spring of our life, the gifts of Christ and the acceptance on the part of the church, her receptivity and self-activity, the reciprocity of the whole and each individual member. By this we may judge the wrong and error of the separate divisions and generations of the church. The Catholics do not let Christ work as a fresh streaming fountain, nor rightly value the life of the members of the church, but put the apostolic power of the Pope with his hierarchy in the front and centre; they undervalue the Head and members and overvalue the ministers of the church, who become masters. The Lutherans have hampered the lay element, and suffer the consequences of the abridgement: the fellowship of the church is too little developed. The Reformed are wanting in the sacramental element; they foster what is individual and social, rather than that which is formative and established, as the sects proceeding from them plainly show.—By this passage every position and every age regulate itself.

### HOMILETICAL AND PRACTICAL.

Take heed, pastor, that thou not only hast an office and ministry shown to thee, which thou administerest, but that thou art and becomest more and more thyself a gift of Christ to His church.—Rejoice, O church, that the servants of Christ are Christ's gifts for thee and use them according to His will against thy lust and errors.—Thou shouldst not say, that Christ raised up Apostles, prophets, evangelists, only in the first century and never since; nor deny that He raises up the pastors and teachers of His church.—All ministry, even the most important minister is in vain, if he does not labor further into the house and the bye-ways, so that each in his place may do his duty as a Christian; but if the spiritual teachers do their duty, the church will not remain unspiritual.—Do not reckon according to visible results; concealed and gradual is the progress of the work, reaching its mark at last and in glory. But do not think hastily and proudly, now is the time of maturity! You may in the end mistake the impulse of the spirit of the age for the showers of Christ's Spirit and the Shibboleth of party-spirit for the word of life, and this deception would be fearful.—No one is so much a minor as to be without responsibility and strength to resist; have regard to this, proving all things by the truthfulness in love, by Christ, the End and Source of all growth! Preach the word simply and purely! Certainly, but not less: love it in the same way. Love does not, indeed, work by means of injustice, untruth, deception, counterfeiting, intrigue, misrepresentation and pretence. But she creates fellowship, and truth is the cause, not of the isolated individual, but of the fellowship of heaven and earth, of the nations, of the earth, and of centuries, aye of thousands of years.

STARKE: For as rogues so manage dice that they must fall according to their wish, so do schismatics and fanatics act with the sacred Scriptures.—Truth and love must be side by side. True teaching and lovely living. That is the sum of all Christianity. Love and unity edify.

RIEGER: The goal of our growth is a long distance before us, the hindrances are many; but growth is the most certain way thither. For as little as in physical growth is advance made all at once with immoderate rapidity, but as in the use of the ordained means, with proper labor and exercise, in confidence on God and His bestowed blessing, in love and peace with one another, the body grows, not one member only, but one just as another, so we, through God's word, prayer, embracing all the means afforded us in the church, the school and the home, reach the position of men of God furnished for every good work.

HEUBNER: Christ's kingdom embraces even the invisible kingdom of God. Would this be conceivable, if He were a mere man?—The variety of offices should not lead to ambition and place-hunting, but to the service of the church.—The stature of manhood in a Christian consists in this, that he, irrespective of men has spiritual majority and independence. Teachers should not wish to keep the congregation in a state of immaturity, but their task is to render themselves unnecessary.—It is the duty of the Christian to strive after this maturity.—Humanity is capable of an ever-increasing perfection by means of Christianity. Progress in Christianity is, however, no advance beyond Christianity.—The Christian is firm in his faith and free from the miserable dependence on foreign and worldly opinion.—How much is still wanting in the mutual support of all in the Christian church. All should be for the furtherance of the Christian life: for example, the household life should be a school of Christianity, the State should further the church, and the schools of learning educate for Christianity, all arts and sciences should subserve religion.—It is child's play, even when not detrimental, to speculate how far this figure of the body can be carried out into detail, who, for example, is eye, ear, breast, back, *etc.* This can lead to results of as revolting a character, as the Hindoo system of caste.

PASSAVANT: One class, as well as another, is chosen to their particular service by the Master of the church; and He who on earth was in the form of a servant, will regard the more lowly of His servants with special looks of love. He sees the heart, and fidelity in what is little is precious in His sight.—To seek truth always and everywhere, in all things and among all persons; to act in truth with all, towards all, with one's self and before God; to base one's inmost thoughts and impulses always in and on the truth—this keeps the heart, amid all the lies, lusts and illusions of this false world, firm and quiet, as the ship that has escaped the waves and cast anchor in the harbor.—All genuine truth and love come alone from Christ upon us and into us, leading us back again to Christ.

GERLACH: In every false teaching which separates men from Christ and His word, the Apostle shows us also a work of wickedness. Human nature was not created by God so perverse as to choose without the fault of man, a lie instead of the truth.

ZELLER: These are the instruments by which the Lord has chosen to build His Church, not Popes, not Emperors and kings, not princes and great ones, the mighty monarchs of this world, but Apostles, Evangelists, pastors and teachers, men illuminated by His spirit, endued with power from on high, not merely by men, but given and appointed by Himself. It is to take place through the peaceful means of preaching, pastoral care, instruction.

[EADIE: Ver. 12. The spiritual advancement of the Church, is the ultimate design of the Christian pastorate. The ministry preaches and rules to secure this, which is at the same time the purpose of Him who appointed and who blesses it.—Ver. 13. Christians are all to attain to oneness of faith, that is, all of them shall be filled with the same ennobling and vivifying confidence in this Divine Redeemer—not some leaning more to His humanity, and others showing an equally partial and defective preference for His Divinity—not some regarding Him rather as an instructor and example, and others drawn to Him more as an atonement—not some fixing an exclusive gaze on Christ without them, and others cherishing an intense and one-sided aspiration for Christ within them—but all reposing a united confidence in Him—"the Son of God."—The Christian church is not full grown, but it is advancing to perfect age.—Ver. 14. How many go the rounds of all sects, parties, and creeds, and never receive satisfaction. If in the pride of reason they fall into rationalism, then if they recover, they rebound into mysticism. From the one extreme of legalism they recoil to the farthest verge of antinomianism, having travelled at easy stages all the intermediate distance.—Ver. 15. That character is nearest perfection in which the excessive prominence of no grace throws such a withering shadow upon the rest, as to signalize or perpetuate their defect, but in which all is healthfully balanced in just and delicate adaptation.—Ver. 16. The church is built up, for love is the element of spiritual progress. That love fills the renewed nature, and possesses peculiar facilities of action in edifying the mystical body of Christ. Whatever parts it may have, whatever their forms, uses, and position, whatever the amount of energy resident in them, still, from their connection with the one living Head, and from their own compacted union and mutual adjustment, they compose but one growing structure "in love."—R.]

[HODGE: Ver. 12. If Christ has appointed the ministry for the edification of His body, it is in vain to expect that end to be accomplished in any other way.—Ver. 14. Error can never be harmless, nor false teachers innocent. Two considerations, however, should secure moderation and meekness in applying these principles. The one is, that though error implies sin, orthodoxy does not always imply holiness. The character most offensive to God is that of a malignant zealot for the truth. The other consideration is, that men are often much better than their creed: that is, the doctrines on which they live are much nearer the truth than those which they profess. They deceive themselves by attaching wrong meaning to words, and seem to reject truth, when in fact they only reject their own misconceptions.—Ver. 16. The church is Christ's body. The body grows. Concerning this growth, the Apostle says: 1. It is from Him. He is the causal source from whom all life and power are derived. 2. It depends on the intimate union of all the parts of the body with the Head, by means of appropriate bands. 3. It is symmetrical. 4. It is a growth in love.—R.]

---

### 3. General Christian Duties.

CHAP. IV. 17—V. 21.

*a. The principle of the new walk, with reference to the contrast of the old and the new man.*

CHAP. IV. 17–24.

17 This I say therefore [therefore I say], and testify in the Lord, that ye henceforth
walk not [no longer walk] as other Gentiles [the rest of the Gentiles][1] walk, in the
18 vanity of their mind. Having the understanding darkened [Being darkened[2] in
their understanding], being alienated from the life of God [,] through [because of]
the ignorance that is in them, because of the blindness [hardness] of the heart:
19 Who being past feeling have given themselves over unto lasciviousness [to wanton-

20 ness], to work all uncleanness with [in] greediness. But ye have not so learned
21 [did not so learn] Christ; If so be that ye have heard [If indeed ye heard] him,
and have been [were] taught by [in] him, as the truth is [as is truth][3] in Jesus:
22 That ye put off concerning the former conversation [as regards your former way of
life] the old man, which is [waxeth] corrupt according to the deceitful lusts [lusts
23 of deceit]; And be [become] renewed in the spirit [or by the Spirit][4] of your mind;
24 And that ye put on the new man, which after God is [hath been] created in right-
eousness and true holiness [holiness[5] of the truth].

## TEXTUAL AND GRAMMATICAL.

[1] Ver. 17.—[The reading is doubtful: ℵ.[3] D.[2 3] E. K. L., most cursives, Syriac, Chrysostom (*Rec.*, Tischendorf, Meyer, Eadie, Braune), sustain λοιπά; it is wanting in ℵ.[1] B. D.[1] F. G., 5 cursives, Vulgate and other versions, and rejected by Lachmann, Alford, Ellicott. The external evidence against it is slightly preponderating, but internal grounds are in its favor. It was probably misunderstood, and the omission further confirmed by 1 Thess. iv. 5.—R.]

[2] Ver. 18.—[ℵ. A. B.: ἐσκοτωμένοι, which, as more rare, is preferred by most recent editors to ἐσκοτισμένοι (*Rec.*, D. F. K. L.). The comma after "God," is required by the view taken of the construction as a parallelism:

a Being darkened in their understanding,
b Being alienated from the life of God,
*a* Because of the ignorance that is in them,
*b* Because of the hardness of their heart.

The first and third, second and fourth members correspond, the alternation being probably due to the reciprocal interaction which is also implied.—R.]

[3] Ver. 21.—[This rendering is literal, see *Exeg. Notes*.—The aorists in vers. 20, 21 are best rendered by the English past tense.—*In* is substituted for *by*, as is so often necessary.—R.]

[4] Ver. 23.—[The two leading interpretations are suggested by the two readings given above. See *Exeg. Notes*.—*Become renewed* is adopted (from Ellicott) to indicate the force of the present, which here marks a continuing process.—R.]

[5] Ver. 24.—[ℵ.[1] gives: ὁσιότητι καὶ δικαιοσύνῃ.—The hendiadys of the E. V. here (and at the close of ver. 22: "deceitful lusts") must be guarded against.—*Hath been created* is preferable here to *was created*, for though the Greek aorist is historical, the latter rendering "tends to throw the κτίσις further back than is actually intended; the reference being to the new κτίσις in Christ" (Ellicott).—R.]

## EXEGETICAL AND CRITICAL.

Ver. 17 *a*. *The connection.* **This therefore I say** [τοῦτο οὖν λέγω].—Τοῦτο refers to what follows, and with emphasis (WINER, p. 152); οὖν, however, as the subsequent context shows, going back of the digression (iv. 4-16), which contains the motives of the exhortation (iv. 1-3), refers to "walk worthy." THEODORET: πάλιν ἀνέλαβε τῆς παρανέσεως τὸ προοίμιον.* But the simple "I say" is not enough for the Apostle; he adds: **And testify in the Lord**, καὶ μαρτύρομαι ἐν κυρίῳ.—He presents himself in his apostolic authority as a witness, not in his own, but in the Lord's cause. ["By thus sinking his own personality, the Apostle greatly enhances the solemnity of his declaration" (ELLICOTT).—R.] It is similar to Rom. ix. 1; 1 Thess. iv. 1. The Lord is the element in which he lives and in this case bears witness, and at the same time the ground on which he stands in common with the Ephesians; on this account he reckons on their acceptance of his urgent appeal. It is not=πρὸς κυρίου, *per Dominum* (even the *Greek Fathers*, and many others).

*The heathen walk as a type of the natural walk in general;* Vers. 17 *b*-19.

Ver. 17 *b*. **That ye no longer walk** [μηκέτι ὑμᾶς περιπατεῖν.—This infinitive is the object of λέγω (it being unnecessary to understand δεῖν) expressing, however, what ought to be (EADIE) more than what is; ELLICOTT thinks an imperative sense involved ("that ye no longer *must* walk"), as indeed the context indicates (ALFORD).—R.] This says negatively what is expressed positively in ver. 1: "walk worthy." "No longer" denotes their once walking, as they should not and dare not now, being Christians.—**As the rest of the Gentiles walk**.—[See *Textual Note*[1]] Καθώς introduces the kind of walk which they should avoid. Καί is joined with emphasis and admonitory force to τὰ λοιπὰ ἔθνη to which class they belong.* The heathen are those who remained behind, they no longer belong to the heathen who now "walk," and how?

**In the vanity of their mind**, ἐν ματαιότητι τοῦ νοὸς αὐτῶν.—This is the briefest characterization of the natural heathen walk, presenting both its religious and moral side. It is the explanation of THEODORET (τὰ μὴ ὄντα θεοποιεῖν) in accordance with Rom. i. 21; viii. 20; 1 Pet. i. 18. This "vanity" [betokening a *waste* of the whole rational powers on worthless objects (ALFORD).—R.] is, of course, one brought about through sin, another nature as it were. It has penetrated even the will of the human spirit, corrupting this high faculty, the ἡγεμονικόν in the nature of man.† Hence there is no special reference to philosophy (GROTIUS). To this general sketch are added *special* traits in vers. 18, 19.

Ver. 18. **Being darkened in their understanding**, ἐσκοτωμένοι τῇ διανοίᾳ ὄντες.—The masculine form indicates the reference to persons, to particular individuals, and not to the whole, τὰ ἔθνη, as such. The verb (σκοτόω), only here and Rev. xvi. 10, instead of the more usual σκοτίζω, is in the perfect, to denote a state not

* [The οὖν is resumptive rather than illative, but as ALFORD says: "The digression is all in the course of the argument. The fervid style of St. Paul will never divide sharply into separate logical portions—each runs into and overlaps the other." EADIE defends the connection with what immediately precedes.—R.]

* [If λοιπά be rejected, there is still an allusion in καί to the fact that they were once thus walking, *i. e.*, were once Gentiles. The only point of difference is, that the fuller reading implies they are so still. "Though the Ephesians did not walk so now, their returning to such a course is made the logical hypothesis" (ALFORD).—R.]

† [So EADIE and most; HODGE however takes νοῦς as the whole soul, just as on the other hand in Rom. vii. 23-25, he refers it to the renewed nature, in both cases sacrificing exactness to doctrinal considerations.—R.]

previously existing, but having come into being, which the present participle, (ὄντες) designates as present. That to which the darkness clings is set forth by τῇ διανοίᾳ,* which means the intellectual power of the mind, the mode of thought, the character, since the reference is not to the formal faculty, but to its condition. Comp. Rom. i. 21 f.; xi. 10. It is incorrect to join ὄντες with what follows (RUECKERT) [EADIE]; it follows thus in Tit. i. 16 also, and τῇ διανοίᾳ forms one conception, together with the participle in its emphatic position.

**Being alienated from the life of God,** ἀπηλλοτριωμένοι τῆς ζωῆς τοῦ θεοῦ.—See on ii. 12: "alienated from the commonwealth of Israel." The perfect participle must be noted here also; BENGEL correctly remarking: *participia præsupponunt, gentes ante defectionem suam a fide patrum—fuisse participes lucis et vitæ. Conf. renovari ver.* 23.—Ζωή, the opposite of θάνατος (ii. 1), is the intensive spiritual, eternal life, belonging to God (τοῦ θεοῦ), *vita, quæ accenditur ex ipsa Dei vita* (BENGEL), *qua Deus vivit in suis* (BEZA), *vera vita, qui est Deus* (ERASMUS); LUTHER: the life, that is out of God. [Comp. TRENCH, *Syn.* § xxviii.; OLSHAUSEN, STIER *in loco*.—R.] See WINER, p. 175. Thus "the vanity of their mind" is designated as to its two sides, the ethically intelligent, and the ethically practical. [This clause sets forth an "objective result of the subjective 'being darkened'" (ALFORD).—R.] To this corresponds what is immediately added.

**Because of the ignorance that is in them, because of the hardness of their heart,** διὰ τὴν ἄγνοιαν τὴν οὖσαν ἐν αὐτοῖς, διὰ τὴν πώρωσιν† τῆς καρδίας αὐτῶν.—These two clauses are added without a connecting particle, because they refer to the two preceding ones, as their purport requires, and because the one requires and furthers the other. "Because of the ignorance that is in them," points to an ignorance which has become immanent, is now natural and peculiar (Acts iii. 17; xvii. 30; 1 Pet. i. 14), as the ground (διά with the accus., see WINER, p. 372) of the darkening, and which is ever increasing, going from ignorance to ignorance. "Because of the hardness of their heart," renders prominent in the same way the hardness, unsusceptibility of the heart as the ground of the estrangement from the life of God. The two are ever conjoined in the natural man: There is not intellectual obscuration *beside* practical estrangement from God, nor ignorance *beside* hardness of heart; the one conditions the other, working destructively as they reciprocally affect each other. Hence it cannot be affirmed, that the former applies more to the Gentiles, the latter to the Jews (STIER and others); the Gentiles alone are spoken of, as a type of the natural character. But at the same time the "ignorance" is not to be regarded as merely a *consequence*, and these two clauses (with διά) referred to the last participial clause alone (MEYER).

[This parallelism of construction in which the first and third, second and fourth clauses are connected together is accepted, by BENGEL, DE WETTE, OLSHAUSEN, FORBES (*Symmetrical structure of Scripture*, p. 21), SCHENKEL and others. It is opposed by MEYER, HODGE, EADIE and ELLICOTT; but the objection they urge, that "ignorance" is not the cause of "darkness," loses its force when it is remembered that the Apostle is speaking of a *process* rather than a *condition*. Nor is it contrary to the Apostle's style, in which parallelisms abound, far less so than to explain: "Darkness of mind is the cause of ignorance, ignorance and consequent obduracy of heart are the cause of alienation from God" (HODGE), thus trajecting the third and fourth clauses between the first and second. This is the view of MEYER, who makes the last clause subordinate to the third (though both are introduced by διά): a needless complication, which leads to the removal of the comma, while the view of Braune requires the insertion of one after θεοῦ. See *Textual Note* [2].—R.]

Ver. 19. **Who,** οἵτινες [*men who, such as*], introduces the explanation, the proof of this condition.—**Being past feeling have given themselves over** [ἀπηλγηκότες ἑαυτοὺς παρέδωκαν]. — Ἀπηλγηκότες (from ἀπό and ἄλγος, ἀλγέω), unsusceptible of pain, and according to the context, in the heart, the moral consciousness, hence not feeling the unrest and punishment of conscience, the correction of God (Jer. v. 3), they have given themselves over, *ultro* (BENGEL); that is the ἀγαισθησία, *sponte sese in gurgitem omnium vitiorum præcipitans*. CALVIN: *Homines a Deo relicti, sopita conscientia, exstincto divini judicii timore, amisso denique sensu tanquam attoniti, belluino impetu se ad omnem turpitudinem projiciunt.* [The pronoun ἑαυτούς is used "with terrible emphasis" (MEYER).—R.] Self-reprobation is consummated in becoming apathetic, just as Rom. i. 24: "God delivered them over, in the lusts of their hearts." Our passage marks the freedom and guilt of men, the passage in Romans the rule, will and power of God, but both of them indicate the means: the lust corrupting even unto want of feeling; here prominence is given to the consequence, the condition which has arisen and becomes aggravated (ἀπηλγηκότες),* there to the ground, the active power ("lusts").

**To wantonness,** τῇ ἀσελγείᾳ.—The term, apparently from θέλγω, *schwelgen* [allied to the English *swell*, and meaning to over-eat, carouse, debauch], occurs quite frequently (Mark vii. 22; Rom. xiii. 13; 2 Cor. xii. 21; Gal. v. 19; 1 Pet. iv. 3; 2 Pet. ii. 2, 7, 18; Jude 4), almost always in connection with sensual sins, denoting, however, not special sin, but reckless, unbridled, extravagant and excessive character in general.

* [This is a dative of reference, giving the sphere or element in which. On the difference between it and the accusative it may be said that the latter is more objective, denoting that the darkness extended over the mind, the former more subjective, denoting that it has its seat in the mind. The word itself is here=the understanding (*Verstand*).—R.]

† [On the etymology and meaning of πώρωσις. See FRITZCHE, *Rom.* xi. 7. It undoubtedly means *hardness*, *obduracy* (not blindness), used by medical writers of the "*callus*" at the extremity of fractured bones.—R.]

* [Some textual variations occur, but not sufficiently supported to raise any question. From ἀπηλπικότες (D. and others) the sense *desperantes* seems to have come. But it is incorrect; the semi-technical term πώρωσις suggests a continuation of the figure.—R.]

Comp. TITTMANN, I., p. 150 ff., on ἀσέλγεια and ἀκαθαρσία, [TRENCH, § xvi., and *Exeg. Notes* on Gal. v. 19, in this volume.—R.] It is not to be limited to sensual lasciviousness (MEYER).

**To work all uncleanness,** *εἰς ἐργασίαν ἀκαθαρσίας πάσης*.—[The preposition introduces the conscious aim of this self-abandonment.—R.] Ἐργασία marks the managing, the assiduous, connected labor [the working at it as though it were a trade], and ἀκαθαρσία, extended by πάσης,* sets forth what has come to pass in the service of ἀσέλγεια. We should apply it to all kinds of uncleanness, especially libidinous, but also to the lust of the eye and pride, natural and unnatural, refined and coarse, solitary and social, in thought, word and deed (Rom. i. 24–32). Still less is this to be limited to libidinous filthiness (MEYER), or to trade in harlotry, *quæstus ex impudicitia* (GROTIUS, BENGEL and others). The next phrase will not justify this.

**In greediness,** *ἐν πλεονεξίᾳ*.—This word means to want to have more, greediness, avarice, graspingness, limited usually to earthly possession, to money (v. 3; Col. iii. 5; Mark vii. 22; Luke xii. 15); but the limitation arises from the context, not from the word itself. The context here does not admit of any such limitation: ἐν, in, marks the ground on which the "uncleanness" moves, and this is not avarice, but greed in general unto insatiableness. Hence the GREEK FATHERS thus explain it (CHRYSOSTOM: ἀμέτρως, THEODORET: ἀμετρία, ŒCUMENIUS: κωθ' ὑπερβολὴν καὶ ἀνενδότως). Ἐν is not=σύν (LUTHER: together with avarice); there is not a new special vice, avarice, added to another special one, unchastity (MEYER, SCHENKEL); neither the context nor the word itself favors the explanation: gluttony (HARLESS).†

*Reminder respecting Christ and Christian instruction;* vers. 20, 21.

Ver. 20. **But ye,** *ὑμεῖς δέ*, in opposition to "the rest of the Gentiles" [just described].—**Did not so learn Christ.**—*Οὐχ οὕτως* is a very emphatic litotes=entirely otherwise, not at all in such a way that you can live afterwards as you did before. Ἐμάθετε [the historical aorist] τὸν Χριστόν marks Christ as the object, the substance of the preaching of the Apostles and of Christ Himself; His person we must attain to; He Himself must be accepted and appropriated in us (vers. 13, 15; Col. ii. 6; 1 Cor. i. 23; 2 Cor. i. 19). Hence it is not=the doctrine of Christ, as was once almost generally thought. [This use of the verb with an accusative of the person is probably unique (ELLICOTT), and properly so, for in no other learning is a Person so directly and fully the object. Hence the explanation: learnt to know, is inadmissible as without lexical authority and insufficient. BEZA's exegesis is totally unwarranted: "Ye are not so—ye have learned Christ."—R.]

Ver. 21. **If indeed ye heard him** [*εἴγε αὐτὸν ἠκούσατε*]—Εἴγε, as in iii. 2, marks in a fine turn of expression a definite, undoubted fact ("that he heard him"), *particula non minuit, sed auget vim admonitionis* (BENGEL). It is not however="so as" (STIER). Αὐτόν is in emphatic position; "heard" denotes the beginning of the discipleship; hence it is not merely, heard *of* Him (LUTHER), but heard Him Himself in spirit, even though through the instrumentality of others. He is the subject of the very first instruction. Hence Paul adds:

**And were taught in him,** *καὶ ἐν αὐτῷ ἐδιδάχθητε*.—The two designations* correspond to those in Matt. xxviii. 19, 20: "disciple all nations"—"teaching them to observe all things whatsoever I have commanded you." "In," ἐν, is neither=περί, *concerning* (PISCATOR), nor ὑπό (FLATT), nor διά, *by* (BEZA) [E. V.], nor *illius nomine, quod ad illum attinet* (BENGEL), but an instruction not merely having its result, a being or living in Him, but in accordance with the fellowship with Him (WINER, p. 366); *in ipso=ipsi insiti* and *docti* are equivalent (BUCER); *doceri* is *inseri*.

**As is the truth in Jesus** [*καθώς ἐστιν ἀλήθεια ἐν τῷ Ἰησοῦ*].—"As" refers only to the instruction, to its quality; it corresponds to "not so" (ver. 20); what was there negatively and briefly indicated, is here positively expressed, and then given in detail.† "Is truth" gives prominence to the agreement of the teaching with the reality: in the instruction they hear Him really, possess Him as He is. Ἐστιν, coming first, denotes the existence, the reality, and that, too, as a present, now valid and continuing reality.

*Consequens τοῦ audire et τοῦ doceri est τὸ discere* (BENGEL): they have therefore learned, as truth is in Him. "Truth" is here opposed to the heathen "vanity;" as the latter was a self-made foundling, the former is something bestowed, real, excluding the subtleties of human origin or change of any kind. [The notion of the Greek adjective ἀληθινός is thus included by Dr. Braune. The clause setting forth the *manner* of the instruction (the substance follows in vers. 22–24), may be thus explained: If ye were taught so that what you received was according to what is true (true and real) as embodied in a personal Saviour. The literal rendering: "as is truth in Jesus" gives most nearly the exact force.—R.] In the expression ἐν τῷ Ἰησοῦ, the article is significant, pointing to the known Person, the personal name being chosen instead of the official title, Christ. BENGEL: *Expressius ponit nomen Ἰησοῦ. CHRISTI, ideam perfectissime et fulgidissime explevit* JESUS; this preserves the received instruction from obliteration. — The clause is, therefore, not parenthetical (BEZA, RUECKERT and others), "truth" is neither

* [The unusual position of πάσης leads ELLICOTT to render: "uncleanness of every kind."—R.]

† [HODGE renders: "together with covetousness," which is doubly objectionable. The wider sense of πλεονεξία is accepted by EADIE, ALFORD and ELLICOTT. The last named, however, properly objects to obliterating the underlying notion of *covetousness* and *self-seeking* which seems bound up in the word. Comp. Col. iii. 5, p. 64; and TRENCH, *Syn.* § xxiv., who links it most closely with sins of lust.—R.]

* [ALFORD renders: "If, that is, it was Him that ye heard and in Him that ye were taught," following MEYER in regarding both as included in "ye learned Christ," the first clause referring to the first reception, the second to further instruction. So ELLICOTT. Perhaps ALFORD restricts the meaning too much when he explains "heard Him," "if ye really heard at your conversion the voice of the Shepherd Himself calling you as His sheep."—R.]

† [This view properly excludes the interpretation "inasmuch," which Dr. HODGE here, as elsewhere, attaches to καθώς.—R.]

*agnitio Dei* (BENGEL), nor *true doctrine* of Christ (PISCATOR and others), nor true holiness, goodness (ERASMUS, HARLESS [HODGE] and others). We should not connect "in Jesus" with what follows (HOFMANN, *Schriftbeweis*, II., 2, p. 291).

*The Christian walk;* vers. 22–24, *a.* Negative side; ver. 22, *b.* Positive side; vers. 23, 24.

Ver. 22. **That ye put off,** ἀποθέσθαι ὑμᾶς.—This infinitive depends grammatically on the entire thought, that they heard Him and were taught in Him, as the truth in Jesus is (BLEEK), although STIER and BENGEL are not incorrect in connecting it in sense with "I say and testify" (ver. 17); they recognise, however, "a certain reference to the nearest words" (ver. 21). The emphasis rests on the verb, coming first, which has its antithesis in "put on" (ver. 24). It is incorrect to accept a dependence on the last clause alone (MEYER) and a contrast between "Jesus" and "ye" (JEROME, HARLESS, and others), which would be indicated by an emphatic position for ὑμᾶς and the insertion of οὕτως.* In the frequently occurring figures of putting on and off the clothes to represent the external appearance from which the internal state may be inferred, it is not necessary to find an allusion to a race before which, or a baptism (of a proselyte) at which the clothes should be taken off; the context gives no warrant for either. The Lord Himself (Luke xxiv. 49) transferred into the New Testament the usage of the Old Testament in describing an instantaneous, sudden inspiration. Comp. STIER, *Words of Jesus*, vii. p. 323 f. Paul extended the figure (ver. 25; vi. 11, 14; Rom. xiii. 12, 13; Col. iii. 8, 9, 10; 1 Cor. xv. 53, 54; Gal. iii. 27; 1 Thess. v. 8). The verb includes the sense of a decided casting away, not merely a gentle putting off, since this is required of the followers of Jesus, among whom a preserving of the old man and the heathen walk is intolerable.

**As regards your former way of life** [κατὰ τὴν προτέραν ἀναστροφήν].—Κατά introduces that with respect to which the putting off takes place. The substantive (ἀναστροφή), like the verb, includes a course of conduct arising from a corresponding disposition, the manifestation of what is within, as Gal. i. 13; 1 Pet. ii. 11, 12; i. 17, 18 (STIER), and is more than περιπατεῖν, preparing the way for the mention of the internal disposition which should be put off. It is not enough to put off merely the former heathen (προτέραν) walk.† *Antitheton versus 23 totus* (BENGEL).

**The old man** [τὸν παλαιὸν ἄνθρωπον].—"Man" denotes here the Ego (ἐγώ, Rom. vii. 9, 10; 17-21). "Old" designates that it is condemned to be put away, old over against Jesus the second Adam; hence "the old man" (Col. iii. 9; Rom. vi. 6) means the sinful Ego deranged by sin, the natural man in the corruption of his sin.* This condition is then described:

**Which waxeth corrupt according to the lusts of deceit** [τὸν φθειρόμενον κατὰ τὰς ἐπιθυμίας τῆς ἀπάτης].—The present participle denotes the present condition, which is not however a purely passive one: "which is corrupted," but in accordance with ver. 19: "which corrupts himself." It is then neither imperfect: which corrupted himself (BENGEL), nor to be taken as referring to the future judgment (RUECKERT and others); yet it is not merely=morally destroying himself (HARLESS). The antithesis is *creatum* (BENGEL) and the use of φθορά and φθείρεσθαι (Gal. vi. 8; Rom. viii. 20, 21) points to the whole man, body and soul. [MEYER and HODGE refer it to eternal destruction: "which tends to destruction," but this does not do justice to the present participle, the peculiar force of which, as indicating a process not entirely passive, is brought out by "waxeth corrupt" (ELLICOTT). HODGE's objection, that "old" already expresses the idea of corruption, has no force against this description of the *progressive* character, while his own view introduces an objective element into a delineation which is strictly subjective.—R.]

The accomplishment of the corruption is more closely defined by the phrase: "according to the lusts of deceit," The corruption is accomplished in accordance with the lusts, the factors of the corruption; and these are affairs of sin, which are here personified in accordance with the power of deceiving and betraying inherent in it (Rom. vii. 11; 1 Cor. xi. 3; 2 Thess. ii. 9). The genitive, which is that of the *subject*, is not to be resolved into an adjective (GROTIUS [E. V.]) and thus weakened, nor applied merely to *error technicus* (BENGEL). The antithesis is *secundum Deum—in justitia et sanctitate veritatis* (BENGEL).

Ver. 23. **And become renewed** [ἀνανεοῦσθαι δέ].—The contrast is marked by δέ, which introduces the *positive* side (vers. 23, 24), The verb in the passive† points to the fact that a work and operation of God is spoken of (ii. 10; iv. 24; κτισθέντα; see Tit. iii. 5, 2 Tim. i. 9). The present refers to an operation which is not concluded in a moment, but continues. The roots of the word (νέος [*recent*], *new*) points to a becoming rejuvenated, to the beginning, the coming into being, of what was not, or not yet, or no longer; καινός [*novus*] refers to the character of that which exists, as compared with its

*[MEYER insists that ὑμᾶς forbids the dependence on ἐδιδάχθητε, but ELLICOTT suggests that it marks a contrast, not with "Jesus," but with the "Gentiles" and their own previous condition as implied in the next phrase. The infinitive has, not in itself, but from its independence, an imperative force, as in "walk" (ver. 1): "that ye must put off." As an aorist it probably refers to the speedy and single nature of the act. The dependence on the entire preceding thought is a satisfactory solution: The substance of what you heard, were taught, when you heard Him and were taught in Him in the correct way "as is truth in Jesus," was "to put off," "that you must put off," etc.—R.]

†[ALFORD thus indicates the train of thought: "for you were clothed with it (the old man) in your former conversation." The phrase qualified the verb, not the substantive: "That as regards your former way of life you put off."—R.]

*[The reader is referred to *Romans*, p. 203; comp. pp. 235–244. The opinions there advocated are expressed in ELLICOTT'S notes on "the old man:" "personification of our whole sinful condition before regeneration, opposed to the καινος or νέος ἄνθρωπος (ver. 24; Col. iii. 10) and the καινὴ κτίσις (Gal. vi. 15), or, if regarded in another point of view to the ἔσω ἄνθρωπος (iii. 16; Rom. vii. 22)."—R.]

†[The middle form of the verb is active in meaning (HARLESS), so that we must insist on the *passive* here. STIER objects that "to be renewed" is not a proper subject of exhortation. But the Apostle is giving the substance of the teaching (ver. 21), and as ALFORD well remarks: "we have perpetually this seeming paradox of *God's work* encouraged or checked by man's co-operation or counter-action." He renders: "undergo renewal."—R.]

former *condition;* ἀνακαινοῦν is to put away the ruins of the present condition and to supply new powers, to transfer into a condition of newness, as distinguished from the previous one. Hence we never find νέα κτίσις, but καινή, since νεότης is already implied in κτίσις. See TITTMANN, *Syn.* I. p. 60 f. [TRENCH, *Syn.* (§ xviii.; *Colossians*, p. 65,) ALFORD and HODGE *in loco.*—R.] Ἀνά indicates not merely a setting up, but according to the participles in vers. 18, 19, a restitution of the original creation. The infinitive is in the same dependence as ἀποθέσθαι, although in these infinitives there is latent, a hortatory imperative, which comes out in ver. 25. Still this inheres in the thought, not in the form.

**In the Spirit** [or **by the Spirit**] **of your mind** [τῷ πνεύματι τοῦ νοὸς ὑμῶν].—The renewal, the letting themselves be renewed, is accomplished in this. The dative is one of reference, the genitive that of the subject. HARLESS says: ψυχή designates the immediateness of the personal life, καρδία the same as the internal life of a human person, νοῦς is the *habitus* corresponding to this existence and life, πνεῦμα the motive power which calls forth and conditions this *habitus.* To this the organism of the human spirit corresponds. BENGEL: *spiritu mentis*, 1 Cor. xiv. 14. *Spiritus est intimum mentis.* That *inexplicabile* coming from God (OETINGER) must be renewed, is seized by the corruption of sin, needs redemption from "the vanity of the mind." We may not take πνεύματι as instrumental on account of the genitive and understand it of the Holy Spirit (OEKUMEN, and others), nor can both explanations be combined (STIER: through the Spirit yet living in you); in that case the middle, contrary to the usage which gives it an active sense, and contrary to the Biblical view, which never speaks of men renewing themselves, is taken as reflexive. Nor is the "spirit" of man to be regarded as opposed absolutely to the "flesh," as if it could never be subject to the latter (SCHENKEL).

[The view of Braune, which takes τῷ πνεύματι as a dative of reference referring exclusively to the human spirit, is accepted by most commentators. HODGE takes πνεῦμα here as the "interior life—that of which the νοῦς, καρδία, ψυχή are the modes of manifestation,"—a psychological statement inferior to that of HARLESS, and probably resulting from the desire to avoid any *trichotomic* opinion.—MEYER has wavered in his views: adopting in the 1st, 3d and 4th eds. the usual opinion, and in the second that of FRITZSCHE, ALFORD, ELLICOTT and others. This takes the dative as *instrumental*, and as referring to the human spirit acted upon by the Holy Spirit (see *Romans*, p. 235), or to the Holy Spirit in a gracious union with the human spirit (ELLICOTT, 3d ed.). To this view I incline, but not decidedly. The other interpretation is open to objections both of an exegetical and psychological nature. This sense of πνεῦμα is now clearly established, and indispensable in exegesis. In fact as ALFORD says: "the πνεῦμα of man is only then used '*sensu proprio*' as worthy of its place and governing functions, when it is one Spirit with the Lord." The trouble is, that this πνεῦμα would hardly be spoken of as the instrument; the answer being that a *process* is described as going on, the agent being "the restored and Divinely informed leading principle of their νοῦς."—The genitive is then *possessive.* —R.]

Ver. 24. **And that ye put on**, καὶ ἐνδύσασθαι, is an internal act done by us, having an effect upon the walk and thus manifesting itself. —**The new man**, τὸν καινὸν ἄνθρωπον, we have as present, given, outside of ourselves, in Christ; hence Rom. xiii. 14: "Put ye on the Lord Jesus Christ."

**Who after God hath been* created** [τὸν κατὰ θεὸν κτισθέντα].—This marks both the reality and the character of the new man. The designation evidently points to Gen. i. 26, 27; which is even more prominent in the parallel passage, Col. iii. 10 ("after the image of Him that created"). Comp. 1 Pet. i. 15. It should be noticed that this qualification compels us not to take "new man" as exactly= Christ; for He is not "created," but rather "God, the image of Him who creates," after whom (κατά) the new man is created. Hence we should refer it to the new human personality as respects Christ, which the Christian should become. Thus in the Epistle to the Colossians we find: τὸν νέον τὸν ἀνακαινόμενον, the young, tender, newly born, which is renewed, developed in contrast with the previous one. The creation of the protoplast is however merely recalled; the expressions are borrowed from it, to designate the new creation taking place in Christ and to put it in relation to the first.†

**In righteousness and holiness of the truth** [ἐν δικαιοσύνῃ καὶ ὁσιότητι τῆς ἀληθείας].—This characterizes the new man and sets forth the distinguishing marks of its character; the preposition adjoining to "created" that *in* which the created man appears, with which he is endowed, equipped. The Apostle proceeds from without to within. The two notions are united together and applied to God (Rev. xvi. 5), to men (1 Thess. ii. 10; Tit. i. 1; Luke i. 75), ὅσιος is predicated of God (Rev. xv. 4), of Christ (Heb. vii. 26; Acts ii. 27; xiii. 35), of men (1 Tim. ii. 8). Ὁσιότης refers to the inmost nature, the disposition, the immaculate purity of love (i. 4; v. 27; Heb. vii. 26), δικαιοσύνη to the action and mode of dealing, which keeps all relations within the bounds of truth and right (STIER). TITTMANN, *Syn.* I. 25 ff. Here we may not apply the frequent usage of Plato, who joins both notions, of which Philo says: ὁσιότης μὲν πρὸς θεόν, δικαιοσύνη δὲ πρὸς ἀνθρώπους θεωρεῖται. MEYER regards δικαιοσύνη as moral rectitude in itself, ὁσιότης specially in reference to God. SCHENKEL takes the former as respecting the *world*, the latter *God;* the latter is evidently op-

*["Not created in the case of each individual believer, but created once for all (*initio rei Christianæ*, Bengel) and then individually assumed" (ELLICOTT). Comp. *Textual Note* [5]. —R.]

†["The doctrine of the restoration to us of the Divine image in Christ, as here implied, is not to be overlooked. MUELLER, *Lehre von der Sünde*, ii. p. 485 ff., denies any allusion to it here, but on insufficient grounds, as indeed he himself virtually allows. Not the bare fact of Gen. i. 27, but the great truth which that fact represents is alluded to. The image of God in Christ is a far more glorious thing than Adam ever had, or could have had: but still the κατ' εἰκόνα θεοῦ=κατὰ θεόν, is true of both" (ALFORD). Comp. *Colossians*, p. 68.—R.]

posed to "uncleanness" (ver. 19) and the former to "wantonness" and "greediness." [So STIER and ELLICOTT.] The genitive sets forth the ground of both; "the truth" is personified, like "love" (ver. 22), the cause of the righteousness and holiness: out of the eternal Divine basis of truth springs the ethical personal life, which is conditioned by this as true: without this man would lapse into "vanity" (ver. 17). LUTHER incorrectly renders the genitive by an adjective: in real righteousness and holiness. [So CALVIN, BEZA, HOLZHAUSEN and the E. V., while PELAGIUS explains: "in the truth," *καὶ ἐν ἀληθείᾳ* (the reading of D. F. and some fathers). There seems to be an antithesis between "truth" here and "deceit" in ver. 22 (HODGE, EADIE and others), which suggests that the notion "real" is prominent here.—R.] It is incorrect to take the preposition as instrumental (MORUS), or as = *εἰς*. The new man is not created by this ethical quality but by God, nor is this the end, but the accompanying gift of this creation, as is manifest in Christ, to whom this belonged from the beginning, not becoming His in the course of His life.

[OLSHAUSEN's remarks are generally accepted: "*Δικαιοσύνη* betokens a just relation among the powers of the soul within, and towards men and duties without. But *ὁσιότης*, like the Hebrew תָּמִים, betokens the integrity of the spiritual life, and the piety towards God of which that is the condition. Hence both expressions together complete the moral idea of perfection. As here the *ethical side* of the Divine image is brought out, Col. iii. 10 brings out the *intellectual*. The new birth alone leads to *ἐπίγνωσις*: all knowledge which proceeds not from renewal of heart, is but outward appearance; and of this kind was that among the false Colossian teachers. On the other hand, in Wisdom ii. 23 the *physical* side of the Divine image is brought out." ELLICOTT deems the last reference somewhat doubtful.—R.]

## DOCTRINAL AND ETHICAL.

1. *The nature of the heathen life* is "vanity of the mind." This designates the *type* of the natural character among Jews and Christians ["The ethical and religious element of their life was unsatisfactory and cheerless, alike in worship and in practice, the same as to present happiness as to future prospect, for they knew not man's chief end" (EADIE).—R.].

2. The "vanity of the mind" is the result of a fall from a previous possession and enjoyment of original gifts, which is accomplished in a twofold series of acts reciprocally requiring and furthering each other; the intellectual and moral side of man's nature being in turn solicited, and thus roused in selfishness, it is ever further removed from the truth in God and from the God of truth. Indeed, the result, the vanity of the mind, is itself capable of increase and must develop into extreme corruption, if aid does not come and a retrograde movement begin.

3. *The intellectual and moral side* of man require and promote each other. The Reason cannot remain healthy and clear, or susceptible, as from the beginning, if the will is or becomes warped or weakened. The obscuration, weakening of the Reason necessarily enters with the enfeebling and confusion of the will. The Apostle comprises both under the term *πνεῦμα** (ver. 23); the former he designates *νοῦς* (vers. 17, 23), *διάνοια* (ver. 18); the latter *καρδία* (ver. 18). The Apostle Paul places the initiative in the lusts (ver. 22: "corrupted according to the lusts of deceit"), as Luther sharply indicates in his incorrect translation (which corrupts itself through lusts in error). The perverted will, executing what is wrong, makes the understanding a sophistical attorney, a crafty counsellor for its unrighteousness.

4. *The factors of corruption* are three: *God*, who hardens (Exod. iv. 21; vii. 3; xiv. 4, 8; Jno. xii. 40; Rom. ix. 18; i. 24), *man* himself (1 Sam. vi. 6; Ps. xcv. 8; Heb. iii. 8), the *surrounding circumstances*, through which and under which it takes place (Gen. vii. 13; viii. 15; Heb. iii. 13). According to the context man is here described as the cause of the corruption (ver. 19), because personal guilt and the evoking of self-activity is treated of, while in Rom. i. 24 God is termed the Author in the same matter, since there the final and deepest ground is touched upon. Usually its consummation appears as a history, which is pragmatically sketched by the external circumstances, the Power above the man and the concealed doings within him not being brought into prominence. What comes to pass is never loosed from the dealings of God and His holy rule, nor from the consent and opposition of man or without the influences of historical circumstances and persons. Consider, however, that thy guilt is at once God's punishment and thine own guilt, and forget not that the two appear together as a developing history.

5. *The dangerous element* of sin is the deceit of lust, which plays the role of pleasure, and is not really *ἡδονή*, but *φθορά* and *φθείρει*. This is God's appointment, that what is unholy should be unwholesome, as wrong is ill; the lustful one, turning away from God, naturally ruins himself, which is possible only in self-deception.

6. *Renewal* is not accomplished by man in his own strength, but only in the acceptance and use of the vital strength promised and imparted to him with justification, hence in the appropriated power of God, in the strength of Divine life. Comp. *notes* 8, 10.

7. *Renewal* too, like corruption, has its history. As the latter proceeds from *ἀνομία* to *ἀνομία*, even to the end, *θάνατος* (Rom. vi. 19, 21), so in the former advance is made from hearing Christ to being taught in Him, from the scholar to the friend, the intimate of Christ, and from the servant of God, who permits himself to be thus termed, to heirship and participation in His kingdom. [Comp. *Exegetical Notes* on ver. 23.—R.]

8. *The beginning of the Christian walk* is the putting off the previous vices (ver. 28-32), and

*[Whatever view may be taken of ver. 23, or whatever psychological distinctions may be allowable in the exegesis of the New Testament, there is nothing here or elsewhere to indicate that man has a "spirit" unsubdued by the "flesh," unaffected by the fall. The natural state is the more awful, because the "spirit," the higher part, the point of connection with Divine influences, is under the dominion of sin.—R.]

from resistance, even if with feeble result, advance is made to victorious crucifixion of the flesh and its lusts (Gal. v. 16, 17, 24).

9. In this too *knowing* and *willing* stand in reciprocal action conditioning each other: learning Christ and putting on Christ, Christian science and Christian life. Theological faculties and the Church of Christ belong together. No knowledge should sunder itself from life, nor the science of Theology from the Christian Church. Where faith in Christ is not active, the scientific culture of individuals and churches will fare badly enough.

10. *The vital power of faith* must in the moral life-process prove itself real (τῆς ἀληθείας) and permeate the whole mode of life (ἐν δικαιοσύνῃ) from within to without (ἐν ὁσιότητι) and thus manifest itself in the walk. Faith, in itself a moral act, must prove itself in an ethical life-process.

[11. "This passage is of special doctrinal importance, as teaching us the true nature of the image of God in which man was originally created. That image did not consist merely in man's rational nature, nor in his immortality, nor in his dominion, but specially in that righteousness and holiness, that rectitude in all his principles, and that susceptibility of devout affections, which are inseparable from the possession of the truth, or true knowledge of God. This is the Scriptural view of the original state of man, or of original righteousness, as opposed, on the one hand, to the Pelagian theory, that man was created without moral character; and, on the other, to the Romish doctrine, that original righteousness was a supernatural endowment not belonging to man's nature. Knowledge, and consequently righteousness and holiness, were immanent or con-created in the first man, in the same sense as were his sense of beauty and susceptibility of impression from the external world." HODGE.—R.]

### HOMILETICAL AND PRACTICAL.

Deal earnestly with the conduct of those committed to you, as did the Apostle, and take care that none of your children can say: Father and mother have not told me of it.—Much depends upon this, that every one in his circle and place bears witness against the walk of the natural character and in favor of Christian conduct.—Consider, no one is lost except through his own fault; but perhaps through yours too!—Sin binds the will, so that it is not free, and blinds or darkens the Reason, so that it is not healthy. The two faculties act and react upon each other; it is madness for a sinner to boast of a sound reason. It is a fearful truth however, thou wilt have life, enjoy the world and yet thou destroyest thyself, most certainly thy soul at least. Where God's life and gift, peace and pure pleasure of the heart is wanting, there man wastes himself away, grasping in darkness for light, in emptiness for fulness, in apathy for life, aiming at these, and yet, at last, comfortless and unsatisfied.—Hold to Christian instruction and constantly try, whether thou art learning Christ: He is the measure of all truth.—Never forget: He is the Light; whoso is athirst, let him come to Him—and drink! You may know everything in the world, but not knowing Him, thy knowledge is nothing; you may know nothing of the world, knowing Him, trusting in Him, thy knowledge is rich.—The toil of self-denial and denial of the world cannot be spared you; but begin in the centre, in thyself, thy will and heart. What avails external alteration: that is by no means growing better. One must not be ever setting the tools and the plough in order; draw furrows through the field of thy heart and sow good seed therein, thus wilt thou reach the harvest and the harvest home. The sun makes the Spring and rejuvenates the earth, not single sunbeams, however, but the sun itself ever mounting higher, ever working longer. So Christ, who renews thee. Look how Peter with his sanguine temper became the rock-man, became constant, and John with his choleric disposition (Mark iii. 17; Luke ix. 54) was renewed into the Apostle of energetic love.

STARKE:—The natural knowledge of God is not the right one, and is far from sufficing for salvation, 1 Cor. i. 21.—The origin of all our sins is the "vanity of the mind" and the darkened understanding. We do not understand what the true good is, nor how we can attain to it. If we are to be helped, we must be helped in these respects, else a hardening results, and we become at last "without feeling."—All, even the best, in man is corrupted by nature, accordingly nothing is to be expected from his own strength.—Mark, man, the stripes of thy conscience, they are a favor from God; despise them not, lest thy heart be gradually led by the deceit of sin into obduracy.—He who does not live devoutly has not rightly learned or heard Christ.—In Christ Jesus is the truth, not a doctrine merely, but a righteous life, and this truth consists in a putting off of the old man and a putting on of the new.—He who rightly knows Christ, must, to honor Him, live holily.—It is a sheer impossibility to be a Christian and to be willing to continue walking in heathenish lusts.—Through a long habit of sinning, the understanding at length becomes so darkened, the conscience so insensible, the will so stubborn, that the man no longer perceives the danger of his sinful condition, has no more conscience about sin, and no desire to desist from sin.—Where sin began, there repentance must begin.

RIEGER:—The understanding would otherwise be a pre-eminent ornament of man, but it too has suffered much from the inroads of sin.—A proper character begins in us with the knowledge and confession of the might of sin, how it has clung to us from the time of our birth and extended itself as an old man over all our powers and members.

HEUBNER:—Where the will is corrupt, the understanding is darkened; blindness is the result of hardening.—Heathenism is life without God, Christianity life from God.—The Christian must ever begin anew and at the same time afresh. Daily repentance is needed, if we know the weakness, impurity, inconstancy of our hearts.—We will be ever seeing remnants of the old man appearing and returning here and there, and then a putting off of the old and putting on the new man is at once necessary again, and a purging process must be begun as in the case of sick people.—There is no more certain sign of an unspiritual mind, than the question: What then is so bad in me? Am I then so entirely unlike the image of God?

PASSAVANT:—The history of the heathen of all ages and countries is a history of such vanity of mind, and of vanities; and all this vain character and action is renewed, re-decked and increased in the history of the character and doings of the heathen now-a-day, of the unbelieving and God-forsaken in Christendom. In the latter case the guilt is indeed greater, the injury deeper and the vanity worse.—This story of the origin of all heathen character and action, and of all idolatry in the world, repeats itself in every heart, which permits itself to be led through lustfulness and vanity of the mind away from the only true God into unbelief, disobedience and ingratitude. The will becomes perverted and evil, seducing in its turn the understanding and all the senses of man; and the mind, when it has once become false and vain, seduces in turn the impure heart, which has forsaken truth and faith; and here, in this impurity is the damnable ground and beginning of all ignorance and obduracy. That which is most exalted in us, which shall inherit immortality, our most beautiful, thinking, poetizing, loving, that which moves our whole heart and soul, what is inmost and most intellectual, our most profound life, our "spirit" itself must be renewed within us.

STIER:—The natural man in the vanity of his mind chooses what is void, empty and perishing, instead of what is Divinely real. Lust and deceit are akin.—Hearing, learning, becoming learned, are the three orderly degrees.—Man, corrupt by nature, destroys that which was created, God's Spirit in our spirit breaks anew the first creation. Once for all in the *Person of Christ* is that created and prepared for us, which we are to put on.

GERLACH:—The lusts paint joy for us and then bring misery, place man in opposition to his Creator, his eternal destiny, himself, making out of the whole character a lie.

ZIEL: *The heathenish nature in our Christian congregations of to-day.* From the text (vers. 17-32) we may perceive as in a mirror: 1) In what *inward* character of the *heart* (vers. 17-19), 2) in what *outward form* of the *conduct* it still manifests itself among us (vers. 25-32). *Conclusion:* To extirpate it by the roots, each one for himself, puts and must put it away from him.

*On the Epistle for the* 19*th Sunday after Trinity*, iv. 22-28.—LANGBEIN: How it is chiefly shown in social life, that something really new is born within us? When there is found, 1) in our mouth, instead of a lie, the truth, 2) in our heart, instead of wrath, placability, 3) in our hands, instead of unjust property, the gift of mercy.

THOLUCK: The virtue of Christian love of truth. 1. How does it manifest itself *a*) toward God, *b*) toward our neighbor, *c*) towards ourselves? 2. How do we attain to it? *a*) Through the consciousness of the continued presence of that eye, which sees in secret and to which a lie is an abomination, *b*) by taking the right standard, the Word of God.

F. A. WOLF: On the proper conduct of all in authority for the promotion of fidelity and probity in their subordinates. 1. Strict love of truth. 2. Forbearing earnestness in discipline and admonition. 3. Zeal for the public good in our own place and calling.

FLOREY:—A new man, a new life! 1) In words of truth, 2) mastery over the passions, 3) blamelessness in walk, 4) turning away from what is unjust, 5) activity in one's calling, 6) brotherly love in the heart.—Some principles for Christian parents in the education of their children. 1. To convince them of the evil nature of their hearts. 2. To be helpful to the renewal of their mind in the Holy Ghost (Baptism, Home, School, Church). 3. To contend against their darling sins (lying, quick temper, slandering, purloining, tattling) and to help to the opposite virtues.

BRANDT: The new man in Christ. 1. Truthfulness his ornament. 2. His heart breathes love. 3. He allows himself to be guided by benevolence and trustfulness. 4. Faithful and honorable, is his watchword.—A rich harvest blessing is an urgent demand to put off the old man and to put on the new. Without this 1) we do not fulfil the design of God in bestowing this blessing, 2) with all our thanksgiving we cannot please God; 3) we are in danger of turning the blessing into a curse.

SPITTA: Believing and pious Christians should not walk as the heathen. 1. How the heathen walk. 2. Why Christians should not walk thus? 3. How they show proper earnestness in this.

GENZKEN (*Preparatory discourse*): The blessed barter (after Matt. ix. 16 f.). The old ragged mantle of the old man is cast away (the web of lust and error); 2. The Lord Jesus is put on (the garment of righteousness and honor).

[EADIE: Ver. 17. In the case of the heathen, all the efforts and operations of their spiritual nature ended in dreams and disappointment.—Ver. 18. Deep shadow lay upon the Gentile mind, unrelieved save by some fitful gleams which genius occasionally threw across it, and which were succeeded only by profounder darkness. A child in the lowest form of a Sunday School, will answer questions with which the greatest minds of the old heathen world grappled in vain.—There could be no light in their mind, because there was no life in their hearts, for the life in the Logos is the light of men.—Ver. 19. Self-abandonment to deeper sin is the Divine judicial penalty of sin.—Self was the prevailing power—the gathering in of all possible objects and enjoyments on one's self was the absorbing occupation. This accompaniment of sensualism sprang from the same root with itself, and was but another form of its development.—Ver. 20. Once dark, dead, dissolute and apathetic, they had learned Christ as the light and the life—as the purifier and perfecter of His pupils.—Ver. 22. This deceit is not simply error. It has assumed many guises. It gives a refined name to grossness, calls sensualism gallantry, and it hails drunkenness as good cheer. It promises fame and renown to one class, wealth and power to another, and tempts a third onward by the prospect of brilliant discovery. But genuine satisfaction is never gained, for God is forgotten.—Ver. 24. While this spiritual creation is God's peculiar work—for He who creates can alone re-create—this truth in Jesus has a living influence upon the heart, producing, fostering, and sustaining such rectitude and piety.—R.]

[SCHENKEL:—The characteristic marks of heathenish disposition: 1. Darkening of the mind, where the knowledge of what is Divine is concerned; 2. Hardening of the heart, where the repression of their own evil lusts is concerned.—Lust and greed the two fundamental sins of the natural man: 1. Their internal connection; 2. Their external difference.—To learn Christ 1) the Christian's first duty, 2) his highest wisdom.—The seal of true Christianity is the *new birth;* for 1) where this is wanting, all good works are but *seeming*, and 2) where it is present the life with good works must really be *teeming*.—The deceit of sin and the truth of redemption: 1. Sin corrupts man under the deceitful representations of evil lust; 2. Redemption heals man by restoring his original truth in righteousness and holiness.—R.]

---

### *b. Special traits of the new walk.*

CHAP. IV. 25-32.

25 Wherefore putting [having put] away lying [falsehood], speak every man truth
[speak ye truth each one] with his neighbor: for we are members one of another.
26 Be ye angry [Be angry],[1] and sin not: let not the sun go down upon your wrath
27, 28 [irritation]:[2] Neither [Nor yet][3] give place to the devil. Let him that stole
[who stealeth] steal no more [longer]: but rather let him labor, working with *his*
hands[4] the thing [that] which is good, that he may have to give [impart] to him
29 that needeth [who hath need]. Let no corrupt communication proceed out of your
mouth, but that which [whatever] is good to the use of edifying [for the building
up of the need],[5] that it may minister [give] grace unto the hearers [to those who
30 hear]. And grieve not the Holy Spirit of God, whereby [in whom] ye are [were]
31 sealed unto the day of redemption. Let all bitterness, and wrath, and anger, and
32 clamor, and evil speaking, be put away from you, with all malice: And be [become][6] ye kind one to another, tender-hearted, forgiving one another [each other],
even as God for Christ's sake hath forgiven [in Christ forgave][7] you.[8]

#### TEXTUAL AND GRAMMATICAL.

[1] Ver. 26.—[*Ye* is omitted for the sake of euphony, and is inserted in ver. 25 for the same reason.—On the other changes see *Exeg. Notes*.—R.]

[2] Ver. 26.—[The article τῷ is omitted in א.[1] A. B.; rejected by Lachmann, Meyer, bracketed by Alford, but on the authority of א.[3] D. F. K. L., fathers, retained (as in *Rec.*) by most editors. The probability of its being omitted because the substantive was defined by ὑμῶν is very great.—R.]

[3] Ver. 27.—[Instead of μήτε (*Rec.*, a few cursives, Chrysostom) most modern editors accept μηδέ on the authority of all our MSS. (א. A. B., *etc*).—On the grammatical objection to the former reading, see *Exeg. Notes*.—*Nor yet*, see Ellicott's note on the translation of 1 Thess. ii. 3.—R.]

[4] Ver. 22.—[The variations are great: 1. We have the long reading ταῖς ἰδίαις χερσὶν τὸ ἀγαθόν (א.[1] A. D. E. F. G., many versions), accepted by Lachmann, Tischendorf (ed. 1), Wordsworth, Eadie, Ellicott and others; the same words appearing with τὸ ἀγαθόν coming first in K. and some cursives. 2. In many authorities ἰδίαις is omitted, and there is a strong suspicion of its interpolation from 1 Cor. iv. 12. Here too there is variety in the order; א.[3] B. some fathers read: ταῖς χερσὶν τὸ ἀγαθόν (Meyer, Alford, 4th ed.), while the order is reversed in the *Rec.*, L., majority of cursives, many fathers (Griesbach, Scholz, Tischendorf, eds. 2, 7). 3. We have besides two briefer readings, almost wholly conjectural, though each claims a Father in support; the one ταῖς χερσίν alone (regarding τὸ ἀγαθόν as interpolated from Gal. vi. 10), the other τὸ ἀγαθόν alone.—It will be seen then that the evidence strongly sustains the position of τὸ ἀγαθόν at the *end* of the clause; accepting this, the only other question deserving attention is the genuineness of ἰδίαις. The *mass* of authority is in its favor, but very good authorities omit it. The internal evidence seems to be against it, for it may have been inserted from 1 Cor. iv. 12, and the special force attached to it by Ellicott (see *Exeg. Notes*) scarcely amounts to an argument for retaining it.—Braune's preference is rendered uncertain by an evident typographical error, but he rejects ἰδίαις.—R.]

[5] Ver. 29.—[D.[1] F., some fathers read πίστεως instead of χρείας; an evident correction.—*Give* is more literal than *minister*, which at the same time puts upon *grace* the sense of "Divine grace," *hearers* too is somewhat too technical in its present use.—R.]

[6] Ver. 32.—[B. and some minor authorities omit δέ (Lachmann), while οὖν is found in D.[1] F. G., both readings probably due to a misapprehension of the relation between vers. 31, 32.—*Become* is more exact than *be; each other* (ἑαυτοῖς) than *one another*.—R.]

[7] Ver. 32.—[Never was the E. V. more unfortunate in its rendering of the phrase ἐν Χριστῷ.—The aorist requires here: *forgave*.—R.]

[8] Ver. 32.—[B. (according to Alford's personal inspection, not B.[2]) D. E. K. L. and a number of minor authorities read ἡμῖν; accepted by Lachmann. But א. A. F. and other authorities support ὑμῖν. The probability of an alteration from v. 2 has decided most recent editors of the correctness of the *second person*.—R.]

### EXEGETICAL AND CRITICAL.

*The general basis: no lie but the truth* (ver. 25); the special points as respects *disposition* (vers. 26, 27), as respects *work* (ver. 28), word (vers. 29, 30); comprehensive conclusion (vers. 31, 32).

Ver. 25. *The general basis.* **Wherefore,** διό, gives the connection with what precedes ("no longer walk as the rest of the Gentiles walk"), and, as the exhortations with their positive and negative sides show, with special reference to vers. 22-24. Hence immediately: **having put away falsehood,** ἀποθέμενοι τὸ ψεῦδος.—According to Ps. cxvi. 11 ("all men are liars"); lxii. 10; Rom. iii. 4, the first duty of every natural man is to put away the lie, especially as the connection with the kingdom of darkness is thereby indicated. For the devil is the liar from the beginning, who slew man, leading him away out of the truth of life in God (Jno. viii. 44). Hence [the abstract]* τὸ ψεῦδος, which is not τὸ ψεύδεσθαι, nor=lies (LUTHER); it is the opposite of the "truth as it is in Jesus." Comp. 1 Jno. ii. 4; iv. 20; v. 10. It does not occur then, because it is the principal spiritual sin of heathenism and has as its result a darkening of the spirit (SCHENKEL). This requirement is of deeper scope than to allow it to be said that even heathen ethics could designate and forbid this as sin.

**Speak ye truth each one with his neighbor** [λαλεῖτε ἀλήθειαν ἕκαστος μετὰ τοῦ πλησίον αὐτοῦ].—This exhortation is [a reminiscence] from Zech. viii. 16 (LXX.): λαλεῖτε ἀλήθειαν ἕκαστος πρὸς τὸν πλησίον αὐτοῦ. The article is wanting with ἀλήθειαν, in order to mark that not the complete, entire truth is to be spoken; that cannot be done at the beginning; only let what you do say be true. Paul substitutes the preposition μετά for πρός, in order to give special prominence to the intercommunion in the speaking with each other [STIER] and to bring to mind the *Christian* brother, as the context requires. The reference is not to "neighbor" in the wider sense, to all men. The Apostle is treating of the Church of Christ.

**For we are members one of another** [ὅτι ἐσμὲν ἀλλήλων μέλη].—This is the motive: to be members one of another and to belie one another, how contradictory (MEYER)! *Est enim monstrum, si membra inter se non consentiant imo si fraudenter inter se agant* (CALVIN). Christians are "members one of another," not merely members of the body of Christ, but each has to do for the other, to give to him, as well as to receive from him and permit him to do in return. The reciprocal ἐπιχορηγία of speaking the truth (STIER) is marked. It is entirely similar to Rom. xii. 5-8; 1 Cor. xii. 15-27.† The passage is full of significance, not inexact (GROTIUS, RUECKERT and others), and is not to be applied to the Gentiles and the Jews, as is done even by BENGEL.

THE PARTICULAR POINTS: *a.*) *As respects the disposition: anger without sin,* since in the Church so great occasion to anger especially is given to the Christian with his natural man, and the fellowship is so easily disturbed thereby, and the Christian himself corrupted; vers. 26-27.

Ver. 26. **Be angry and sin not** [ὀργίζεσθε καὶ μὴ ἁμαρτάνετε].—The first verb is to be taken as imperative, in this series of imperatives (vers. 25-32). This is further required by the circumstance, that it is a citation (Ps. iv. 5: רִגְזוּ וְאַל־תֶּחֱטָאוּ translated by the LXX. precisely as Paul here writes it): the original and the Greek version are undoubtedly imperative. The passage in the Psalms is rendered by LUTHER: Be angry, so that ye sin not; this passage: Be angry and sin not. The sense is evidently equivalent to ὀργιζόμενοι μὴ ἁμαρτάνετε (WINER, p. 292), which not only states the case in which they would become angry, but also expresses that the anger is allowed, aye commanded and righteous. This is only the more strongly marked by the two imperatives joined with καὶ, the second of which only is negatived (μή); accordingly Paul used this form, this citation.* The original text in the Psalm, in which the main matter is the transformation of the angry *quousque tandem* to rest and gentleness, is correctly rendered by the LXX. (HENGSTENBERG, HITZIG, STIER, against EWALD, HARLESS and others). It can only be affirmed that Paul did not wish to prove anything by the citation (HARLESS); he wishes only to use the words of David, but does not use the words of the LXX. to strengthen those which they are acquainted with; it is incorrect to suppose that nothing depends on the sense of the original passage (RUECKERT). The Sacred Scriptures, which speak of the wrath of God, showing us Christ in anger at the cleansing of the temple (John ii. 13-16; Matt. xxi. 12, 13), do not reject anger: Jas. i. 19, 20; Rom. xii. 19; Eccles. vii. 9. So here, for we do not read: Do not be angry and sin, the negative cannot be moved forward so as to qualify the first verb (WINER, p. 460). Hence we need not accept an unwilling permission of anger (DE WETTE, WINER); in that case ἀλλά would be found in place of καί. Nor is "be angry" in accordance with an assumed Hebraism to be taken *conditionaliter* on account of the connection with a following imperative (RUECKERT, ZYRO, *Stud. u. Krit.*, 1841, p. 690), [HODGE apparently]; that would really mean: if ye are

* [Notice the frequent use of abstract nouns, almost personifications, in this chapter. Here "the vice and habit of lying" is meant, which is a chief characteristic of the "old man," a natural and immediate result of the essential selfishness of sin. The aorist participle is preferred here (= having put away), "because the man must have once for all put off falsehood as a characteristic before he enters the habit of speaking truth" (ALFORD).—R.]

† ["The force of the exhortation does not rest on any mere ethical considerations of our obligations to society, or on any analogy that may be derived from the body (Chrysostom), but on the deeper truth that in being members of one another we are members of the body of Christ."—ELLICOTT. The analogy CHRYSOSTOM draws is striking, however, and deserving of notice: "If the eye were to spy a serpent or a wild beast, will it lie to the foot?" *etc.*—R.]

* [This is perhaps the view now generally received. Both imperatives are jussive; anger is not only allowable, but commanded in certain cases, yet the Apostle forbids the joining of sin with it; in so doing the emphasis resting on the second imperative obscures the jussive force of the first one, rendering it rather *assumptive*: Be angry (for this must be so) and do not sin. So EADIE, ALFORD, MEYER, ELLICOTT and others.—R.]

angry, ye will not sin. The limitation of "sin not" to reconciliation (HARLESS), to the exclusion of enmity against others (ZYRO), is incorrect because not in accordance with the context. The acceptance of an interrogation (GROTIUS: are ye angry?) is inadmissible on account of the quotation.

**Let not the sun go down upon your irritation** [ὁ ἥλιος μὴ ἐπιδυέτω ἐπὶ τῷ παροργισμῷ ὑμῶν].—This thought is occasioned by the citation (Ps. iv. 5) and the matter itself. There is also in the expression "let not the sun go down," a reminiscence of Deut. xxv. 13, 15, according to which the poor man should receive his cloak, given in pledge, and wages should be paid before sundown. There is no reference to the Pythagorean precept to be reconciled before sunset; and quite as little to Christ, the Sun of Righteousness (AUGUSTINE), certainly none to the Reason (LOMBARD). The [non-classical and rare] word παροργισμός occurs only here; it is related to παροργίζεσθαι (Eph. vi. 4; Col. iii. 21; Rom. x. 19), meaning the anger aroused in us, the being or becoming angry, which should not continue, nor be carried about and nourished. *Affectus noctu retentus alte insidet* (BENGEL). Anger thus becomes hate, rancor. What is right towards the occurrence, *viz.*, being angry, should not when that is past, be retained against the person, who remains. The preposition παρά does not indicate something wrong (ZANCHIUS), [WORDSWORTH], and the article, marking the momentary being angry, connected with ὀργίζεσθαι, is not incorrect (STIER). [Comp. *Textual Note* [2]. ALFORD brackets the article, suggesting that the omission gives the sense "upon any παροργισμός." The word *irritation* preserves the reference to occasion given indicated by παρά, and at the same time distinguishes (in English) from the "wrath" which is forbidden in ver. 31.—R.]

Ver. 27. **Nor yet give place to the devil** [μηδὲ δίδοτε τόπον τῷ διαβόλῳ.]—Μηδέ is disjunctive and adds something new (Matt. vi. 25); while μήτε is adjunctive, adding something which belongs to the foregoing (Matt. v. 34-36). Comp. WINER, p. 457.* Besides not sinning by prolonging wrath, they should not sin by giving place to the devil. Δίδοτε τόπον designates, as in Rom. xii. 19, affording free play, wide space, of course in the heart. But to whom? to the devil, as in vi. 11; 2 Tim. ii. 26, even though it does not elsewhere occur in this sense in Paul's writings, but more frequently describes slanderers, or a slanderous manner (1 Tim. iii. 6, 7, 11; Tit. ii. 3).† The antithesis is found in ver. 30. Hence it does not mean: the blasphemer (LUTHER and others) or talebearer, as many hold. Nor is the verse to be applied to social life (HARLESS); the context requires a reference to individuals. Sinful anger brings even the Christian's heart into the power of Satan, from whom he was freed, destroying the fellowship with the Redeemer and His grace.

Ver. 28 *b. As respects work: Honesty reaching to benevolence.* **Let him who stealeth steal no longer** [ὁ κλέπτων μηκέτι κλεπτέτω].—Ὁ κλέπτων, which is neither=ὁ κλέψας, nor =ὁ κλέπτης, marks the act or the action, not the character; hence it is stronger than "him who stole," and weaker than "the thief." Comp. WINER, p. 331. LUTHER is therefore incorrect [rendering as in E. V.]; BENGEL also: *qui furabatur*, adding however: *præsenti hic non excluso.** The notion of stealing, however, must not be limited here by the definition of criminal law and police regulation, but be conceived of from the stand-point of Christian ethics, as in the case of the eighth commandment. That deportment of the natural man over against the possessions of his neighbor, which ought to be overcome, is here treated of. It is incorrect to suppose idle habitual thieves are meant (SCHENKEL).—In the Christian ethical sense there is added: μήκετι κλεπτέτω. Hence it is unnecessary to inquire why nothing is said of restitution (MICHAELIS), and the opinion that this exhortation is unsuitable, because it does not correspond with the Apostle's strictness (DE WETTE), is not pertinent. The Apostle's strictness and the Christian view follow immediately:

**But rather let him labor, working with his hands that which is good** [μᾶλλον δὲ κοπιάτω ἐργαζόμενος ταῖς χερσὶν τὸ ἀγαθόν. See *Textual Note* [4].].—Μᾶλλον δέ gives prominence to the antithesis. With the emphatically placed κοπιάτω Paul includes laziness and idleness as the beginning and ground of theft (BENGEL: *sæpe furtum et otium sunt una*); and all the more decidedly by designating as the antithesis: "working with his hands that which is good." The participle denotes the active, assiduous performance, corresponding slightly with ἐργασία, ver. 19 (STIER); it is not earning, gaining, as the object is not external possessions, or handicraft, trade (MEYER, DE WETTE). BENGEL is excellent: *Antitheton ad furtum, prius manu piceata* (*i. e.*, hands to which whatever comes near sticks as to pitch, *pix*) *male commissum;* on "with his hands" (the hands of the thief), he adds: *quibus ad furtum abusus erat.*† Rom. vi. 19.

* [In addition to the critical grounds for rejecting μήτε, the grammatical objection should be noted. Μήτε here would presuppose another μήτε, while μή precedes. The sequence is therefore abnormal. MEYER suggests that it might occur, if the second member were an after-thought, but it never does occur in Paul's writings. This verse is therefore connected with the preceding, but as an affirmative sentence would be through δέ.—R.]

† [In two of these instances the meaning is: the devil, in the other two, without the article, it may mean *slanderous* (as an adjective applied to women in both cases). MEYER is probably right in affirming that the substantive διαβολος in the New Testament *always* means: the devil. So HODGE, ALFORD and ELLICOTT. "A name derived from the fearful nature and, so to say, office of the Evil One."—R.]

* [EADIE: "Some, shocked at the idea that any connected with the Ephesian Church should be committing such a sin, have attempted to attenuate the meaning of the word." So JEROME, CALVIN, and HODGE who accepts the past sense. But such sinners may yet have been in the Church. See 1 Cor. v. 1; 2 Cor. xii. 21. In the service of the Reformed Church for the ordination of Deacons, this gloss occurs: "Let him that stole (or who hath been burthensome to his neighbor)," as an admonition to those who too long depend on the charities of the Church.—R.]

† [ELLICOTT retains ἰδίαις and says: "The thievish man lives by the labors and hands of others: he is now himself to labor, and with his *own hands*, not at τὸ κακόν, but at τὸ ἀγαθόν." But such an antithesis seems doubtful. The verse is better explained thus: He who steals (whether a thief or a so-called "business-man") should stop this, and go to work, to real labor. The participial clause then adds how: let him

The hands should now do the good, that in its proper time and place must be done; then there will not be wanting something to bestow upon the needy.

**That he may have to impart to him who hath need** [ἵνα ἔχῃ μεταδιδόναι τῷ χρείαν ἔχοντι].—"That he may have" sets forth the purpose, not of him who labors, as if the work should be done on this account, but of the enjoining Apostle, the ruling Lord.* He should have something to give (μεταδιδόναι), for "we are members one of another" (ver. 25). This should take the place of stealing. "To him who hath need," to him from whom recompense is not to be expected. Instead of stealing there is required an honesty and activity, which impels to beneficence. Whether the question about restitution is necessary and ethical earnestness and depth are missed here—is evident enough. See *Doctr. Notes*.

*c. As respects speech: no foul word, but gracious discourse tending to edification;* vers. 29, 30.

Ver. 29. **Let no corrupt communication proceed out of your mouth** [πᾶς λόγος σαπρὸς ἐκ τοῦ στόματος ὑμῶν μὴ ἐκπορευέσθω].—The subject: πᾶς λόγος σαπρός is assumed as present in the mouth of the readers while the predicate forbids: let it not proceed out; not *one* such should be expressed, v. 5; John iii. 16; 1 John ii. 21. [Literally: "let every foul saying not come forth."—R.] See WINER, p. 162 f. BENGEL: *si jam in lingua sit, resorbete.* Σαπρός, from σήπω, σαπῆναι, spoiled by putrefaction, corrupt, used of fishes (Matt. xiii. 48), of fruit (Matt. xii. 33; Luke vi. 43), of a tree (Matt. vii. 17, 18; xii. 33; Luke vi. 43), denotes according to the antithesis (ἀγαθὸς πρός) uselessness, but it is certainly chosen to designate both what is decayed, worn-out, ruined, and what is disgusting and stinking; BENGEL: *vetustatem redolens.* Comp. κενὸς λογός, v. 6; ῥῆμα ἀργόν, Matt. xii. 36. In these passages the emptiness and unprofitableness is more prominent, here however the loathsomeness. THEODORET: αἰσχρολογία, λοιδορία, συκοφαντία, βλασφημία, ψευδολογία καὶ τὰ τούτοις παραπλήσια.

**But whatever is good for the building up of the need.**—Ἀλλὰ (sc. ἐκπορευέσθω), εἴ τις ἀγαθὸς (sc. ἐστί) πρὸς οἰκοδομὴν τῆς χρείας. Over against the prohibition the acceptance of wholesome speech takes a very modest attitude; over against πᾶς we have here εἴ τις. BENGEL: *non postulatur ab omnibus par facundia.* Ἀγαθός, however, as in Rom. xv. 2, designates what is internally, morally good, not merely what is fitting (HARLESS), [HODGE, EADIE, ALFORD, ELLICOTT]; that would be too external. The genitive of reference has been aptly rendered by LUTHER: where it is needed. This refers to the time when, to the place where, to the person to whom, to the method how, and to the purport which, we are to speak. "According to Jerome it applies also *juxta opportunitatem loci, temporis et personæ ædificare audientes*" (STIER). Col. iv. 6: "How ye ought to answer every man." [ELLICOTT also takes the genitive as one of reference; "edifying as regards the need, *i. e.*, which satisfies the need." ALFORD follows MEYER in regarding it as the regular objective genitive="the defect to be supplied by edification," so that the sense is "the edification of the present deficiency or need calling for it." The hypallage of the *Syriac*, BEZA, followed in the E. V., is clearly wrong, also *qua sit opus* (ERASMUS and others).—R.]. It is incorrect to take ἡ χρεία=οἱ χρείαν ἔχοντες (RUECKERT, OLSHAUSEN).

**That it may give grace to those who hear** [ἵνα δῷ χάριν τοῖς ἀκούουσι].—"That" refers to the design of the enjoining Apostle, not that of the obeying member of the congregation. The subject of "give grace" is "good word;" we do not then read "that ye may give." LUTHER presents very well the manner, the esthetic side: "that it may be gracious;" for χάρις means also the gracefulness, agreeableness, of the discourse; just as in Col. iv. 6: "in grace," Luke iv. 22. But the inner side, the matter, must not be overlooked, nor put in a secondary place; it must be a kindness. HARLESS includes this alone, but incorrectly; a befriending, agreeable act of kindness is meant, which should make this impression on the hearers: whether it profits them, is their own affair. STIER seems to be not incorrect, in finding here (δῷ) an echo of ver. 28 (μεταδιδόναι), and a spiritual gift in the seasoned but pleasant word spoken with unction. [ALFORD retains the theological meaning of χάρις: "minister spiritual benefit; be a means of conveying through you the grace of God" (so E. V.). HODGE on the other hand follows HARLESS, holding that the phrase always means to confer a favor; "that it may benefit the hearers." ELLICOTT accepts the non-theological sense of χάρις, but adds that owing to its change of meaning in the New Testament, there seems to be even in this phrase a reference to *spiritual* benefit. He renders: "that it may impart a blessing."—R.]

Ver. 30. **And,** καί, connects closely with what precedes; so much depends on proper speech.—**Grieve not the Holy Spirit of God,** μὴ λυπεῖτε πνεῦμα τὸ ἅγιον τοῦ θεοῦ.—The verb forbids injuring, disturbing, rendering sorrowful, pointing thus to an intimate fellowship, in which joyous love toward and among each other should prevail, and to a tender conduct and intercourse; for it happens *per sermones putres* (BENGEL). The object is "the Holy Spirit of God." This full designation shows the importance of the matter and compels us to recognize the objective reality and Personality of the Holy Ghost. *Shepherd of Hermas*, ii. 10: μὴ θλῖβε τὸ πνεῦμα τὸ ἅγιον τὸ ἐν σοὶ κατοικοῦν, μήποτε ἐντεύξηται κατὰ σοῦ καὶ ἀποστῇ

---

accomplish by assiduous effort with his hands something good, instead of this past evil. The purpose of the effort follows in the next clause. The sum of the whole is: *Honest manual labor*. 1. *Labor*, 2. *better with the hands* than with the dishonest wits; 3. above all let it be honest as to means and good as to end.—R.]

* [This is evidently stated by the Apostle as "the true specific object of all Christian labor, and just to the extent that the work is done on this account, will it be itself Christian." The laborer may be unconscious of this end at times, but it is necessarily *his end* in labor as a Christian. The verse is worth a whole library of volumes on social science. Its precepts would make many a so-called merchant or professional man go to manual labor, while on the other hand this last clause would settle the "workman's question" far more effectually than the whole array of socialistic theories, Agrarian appeals, trades unions and "strikes." But Prudhomme is too often preferred to Paul.—R.]

ἀπὸ σοῦ. He who speaks out the foul thing which comes from his mind to his lips, injures thus the Holy Spirit in himself, and in others also. The plural means also: Ye, each one in himself, or in others too. The Holy Ghost like God is not apathetic, but capable of being affected. Rom. viii. 26. He feels what occurs in us, as a loving Friend, who does not Himself change, but will help us and change us, so long as we grant that He be not rejected. This is a possible final result, in spite of the close connection in which He stands to us, and in spite of the help and blessedness, which He produces in us. Both ideas are added in the relative clause which follows:

**In whom ye were sealed unto the day of redemption**, *ἐν ᾧ ἐσφραγίσθητε εἰς ἡμέραν ἀπολυτρώσεως*.—The first thought is contained in the expression: "in whom ye were sealed," in whom*=in fellowship with whom, ye were sealed (i. 13); the other is marked by "unto the day of redemption" (i. 14); *hic dies est novissimus, cujus representatio quædam est in die mortis; præsupponit dies citeriores* (Rom. ii. 16); *in illo maxime die referet, quis inveniatur obsignatus* (BENGEL). Isa. lxiii. 10 (where the LXX. have incorrectly rendered עִצְּבוּ, *παρώξυναν*; the *Vulgate* is better: (*afflixerunt*) should be compared, not as though this were a citation, but on account of the similar thought.

Accordingly *λυπεῖν* is not to be pared down to a mere troubling (BENGEL: *turbare*), nor is the human spirit to be regarded as the object (DE WETTE; Christian feeling), nor is the capability of being affected which belongs to God and the Holy Ghost to be rejected or regarded as a mere anthropomorphism; the reference to the possibility of being forsaken by the Holy Ghost should not be denied (SCHENKEL). There is both great kindness and earnestness in the warning thus formulated and emphasized: "in the case of the unredeemed sin it is a transgression of the law (Rom. iv. 15, *etc.*), in the case of the redeemed it is a wounding of the Holy Ghost" (HARLESS), whose tempter he is (ii. 22). Not by threatenings respecting the punishment of hell, but by holy dread of grieving the Holy Ghost, and wholesome fear of the day of Judgment, which with Him is only the day of Redemption, does the Apostle seek to persuade and strengthen.†

*Comprehensive conclusion*; vers. 31, 32. *a. The negative side*, ver. 31; *b. The positive side*, ver. 32.

Ver. 31. **Let all bitterness**.—*Πικρία* (Heb. xii. 15; Acts viii. 23; Rom. iii. 14) is ill-temper, animosity, unholy indignation, as *πικραίνεσθαι*, Col. iii. 19. Comp. *ζῆλος πικρός*, Jas. iii. 14. It is entirely internal, concealed in the heart ["the prevailing temperament and frame of mind" (ELLICOTT).—R.].—**And wrath**.—*Θυμός* is excitement, passionate movement of the temper, in selfishness, unrestrained and disorderly.—**And anger**.—*Ὀργή* is the passion concentrating itself, directed against a particular person with the purpose of hurting him. *Ὁ θυμὸς γεννητικός ἐστι τῆς ὀργῆς* (ŒCUMENIUS). According to the context carnal anger is spoken of; hence there is nothing to be inferred respecting ver. 26 from this passage. BENGEL is incorrect: *hactenus descendit climax*; but he properly compares the first with *χρηστοί*, the second with *εὔσπλαγχνοι*, the third with *χαριζόμενοι* (ver. 32) as their respective antitheses. Comp. TITTMANN, *Syn.* I., p. 131 ff. [Also TRENCH, *Syn.* § xxxvii.; DONALDSON, *New Cratylus*, §§ 476, 477; Galatians v. 20.]

We now pass to the breaking out of what was within, to its becoming perceptible in look, mien and gesture: **and clamor**.—*Κραυγή* (Acts xxiii. 9) is wild, rough crying, refers to the voice, improperly strained and sharpened, as in scolding, upbraiding, to the casting about of words uninterruptedly. It is the steed of anger (CHRYSOSTOM).*—**And evil speaking**, *βλασφημία*, pointing to the purport of the speaking, is aspersion of one's neighbor, *λοιδορία* (Col. iii. 18; 1 Tim. vi. 4; Matt. xii. 31; xv. 19), yet sharper than this, not merely like "Raca" (Matt. v. 22), abusing the mental or civil capacity of a brother, but like "thou fool," the moral capacity for God's kingdom, and hence not without a reference to God (STIER), blaspheming possibly or probably. "All," which belongs to all the substantives, refers to the various degrees, from the coarsest among common people to the most refined among the educated; so *θυμοί*, 2 Cor. xii. 20.

**Be put away from you**.—*Ἀρθήτω ἀφ' ὑμῶν* is a stronger conclusion of "putting away" (ver. 25); it must take place with power in the mighty help of One stronger than we, to whom all this clings.—**With all malice**.—*Σὺν πάσῃ κακίᾳ*, the *fermentum* of the bitterness (MEYER) and the rest ["the *active principle* to which they are all due"], refers to malice, *malignitas* and *malitia* (Rom. i. 29; Col. iii. 8), both the quality and its manifestation, in order to sum up in conclusion all that cannot be enumerated.

[EADIE: "This verse contains not only a catalogue, but a melancholy genealogy of bad passions; acerbity of temper exciting passion; that passion heated into indignation; that indignation throwing itself off in indecent brawling, and that brawling darkening into libel and abuse; a malicious element lying all the while at the basis of these enormities."—R.]

Ver. 32. *The positive side*. **And become ye**, *γίνεσθε δέ*.—Thus the antithesis is strongly

---

* [Not *by* whom (whereby, E. V.), HODGE, since God is the Sealer, the Spirit the seal; comp. i. 13.—R.]

† [It is precisely this thought of the Apostle, so correctly stated by Braune, which throws doubt upon the reference to the possibility of losing the seal, found here by HARLESS, STIER, ALFORD and Braune (*Doctr. Note* 6). But the mention of a seal is not suggestive of such a possibility, nor is "grieving the Spirit"=resisting the Spirit, the latter being predicated of unbelievers only (Acts v. 51). Besides had Paul wished to convey this idea *παροξύνετε* (from Isa. lxiii. 10, LXX.) was probably in his memory, and this would have expressed such a thought far better. Of course the caution assumes a logical possibility of falling, which is practical enough, but the appeal is to love not to fear. While the Scriptures always thus exhort men, it seems to be a species of anthropomorphism also, for the more theological and soteriological statements preclude such a possibility. Even here where the verse begins with such a caution, there is at once added a mention of the "seal" and of "the day of redemption" as the end, which suggests the doctrine of "final perseverance" rather than the opposite. Comp. EADIE and HODGE *in loco*.—R.]

* [CHRYSOSTOM adds: "Let women especially attend to this, as they on every occasion cry out and brawl. There is but one thing in which it is needful to cry aloud, and that is in teaching and preaching."—R.]

marked at the very start, as not finished at one stroke, but having a development, a history.*—**Kind one to another.**—Εἰς ἀλλήλους is put first, marking chiefly the fellowship. Χρηστοί (Luke v. 39; vi. 35; 1 Pet. ii. 3; Rom. ii. 4) helping the χρεία; *ingeniosius quam verius* is the reference to the name: Christians (OLSHAUSEN). Comp. TITTMANN, *Syn.* I., 140, 195.—**Tender-hearted,** εὔσπλαγχνοι (like 1 Pet. iii. 8) refers to sympathy, fellow-feeling, hearty compassion. [Comp. *Colossians,* p. 69].—**Forgiving each other,** χαριζόμενοι ἑαυτοῖς (2 Cor. ii., 7, 10; xii. 13), marks the tender, considerate, forbearing, forgiving life among themselves; ἑαυτοῖς points more strongly than ἀλλήλοις to the existing unity, where one deals with another as himself (Col. iii. 13). [The former thought is from STIER, the latter from ORIGEN, but they are not to be pressed too far.—R.]

**Even as God in Christ forgave you** [καθὼς καὶ ὁ θεὸς ἐν Χριστῷ ἐχαρίσατο ὑμῖν].—Καθώς† is as in i. 4 (HARLESS). Καί joins the readers to God, to the clause "God in Christ forgave you." The notion is as in Matt. vi. 12, 14. God's mercy and grace is manifest in Christ, proved itself in Christ, in the death (2 Cor. v. 19) of Him who accomplished the reconciliation of the world with God. "In Christ" belongs to the verb, the predicate, not to "God," the subject. [Either connection presents a truth: God in Christ, manifested in Christ, forgave us, but God forgave in Christ, in giving Him to be a propitiation for our sins. The latter thought seems more appropriate with the aorist which refers to a definite past act; it is neither "hath forgiven" (E. V.), nor "will forgive," a gloss our feeble faith puts on it.—R.]

## DOCTRINAL AND ETHICAL.

1. *The lie* is put first by the Apostle as a fundamental vice. It is the *loveless* misuse of language and the means for communicating the thoughts of the heart, with the design of *deceiving* our neighbor. It injures love, therefore one's own heart, and one's neighbor, it injures fellowship and truth, and thus one's own heart again, which needs these, and our neighbor, who needs them no less. The untruth must be *intentional;* otherwise it is merely not true, an error, not amounting to a lie. The *deception* must be *intentional:* Drama, irony, satire, joke, conventionalities are not lies; for in these it is presupposed that our neighbor understands this language and can translate it into his own. What is conventional is the language of humanity, which should come from the heart and become natural, as in Fenelon. A lie is an *act* of lovelessness against our neighbor, even when not intended to injure him, perhaps only to help or assure ourselves or others, to make preposterous stories, something out of nothing, like all frivolous lies, which, however innocent they may appear, are still the school for turning frivolity into mischief. The word itself does not necessarily make the lie; it may be consummated in silence, in countenance, in gesture or act; but at all events it is an abuse of God's gift for the manifestation of our thoughts and perceptions. Its opposite is *truthfulness,* love of truth, which is at the same time love to mankind. It is indeed not possible without some circumspection and restriction, since it does not consist in having the heart on the tongue, but in having the tongue in the heart.

This vice is less strange among men than many others, so that even the better class of people, the pious world also, has an elastic conscience respecting this point. The conventional mode of life with its illusion and deception makes truthfulness utterly impossible, unless Christ becomes a living power in us. In lying as in stealing, a beginning is made in a little thing, and then come bolder advances, until an extreme is reached: one lie is told to conceal another, instead of forgiveness being sought, and then comes shameless, impudent untruth. It comes from the devil and leads to him; it is the devil's own vice (John viii. 44). The Scripture forbids it unconditionally, especially the Lord Himself (Matth. xii. 36, 37); it does not approve of the untruths of the Hebrew midwives, of Michal, Jonathan, *etc.,* only narrating them as facts. Although lying mainly injures fellowship, yet it is not to be so connected therewith, as to be considered allowable where no fellowship exists; nor is it to be so contra-distinguished from love, that a lie is not to be regarded as such, where the latter is active, even though the untruth is spoken with an intention of deceiving. The former principle applies to robbers, murderers and thieves; the latter to children, lunatics, drunkards and passionate people. In the first case it is not allowable like stratagem in war or in peril of life, and in the other truth should not become poison or poniard.* Over against the sophistry: verbal truth should not stand against hearty love, the rigoristic principle, which allows no lie in an emergency, is justified. It is better inconsistently to deny in books and in the pulpit the right of untruth, and in life and in the household to practise it, than at the expense of truth to serve a false one. To speak an untruth on account of a neighbor's necessity out of love for him is still a lie; personal need, personal interest does not first give it this character; the necessity of a neighbor gives no justification to a lie in a case of emergency.

2. *Anger,* which, in God, is the energy of holy love against sin and corruption disturbing and perverting moral order, is justified in the Scriptures. Affirmed of God more than *three hundred times,* it cannot be wrong of itself in man who is created after the image of God; it is rather a

* [ALFORD is scarcely justified in saying that "become" removes the precept too far from the present. ELLICOTT rightly takes the verb as implying evil elements among them, yet to be taken away; hence the appropriateness of δέ. See *Textual Note* 6.—R.]

† [This particle introduces an example, having at the same time an argumentative force; not=*because,* as HODGE renders it here also.—R.]

* [Lies to children are fearfully common. Surely the motive ("for we are members one of another") in this case has unusual force. To say that such lies are necessary, is to say that it is necessary to blacken a child's heart. In the liveliness of childish imagination they are great romancers themselves, but at the same time sensitive to an untruth told them. How can they have faith in God, when those who stand for the time being in the place of God prove unworthy of belief? What they cannot understand should be declared incomprehensible to them, not misstated. What would we think of our Heavenly Father, if He dealt otherwise with us?—R.]

witness and basis of active love in the surroundings of an unholy world. The *right* to be angry is admitted and granted, but to be angry *rightly* however. Loveless anger is as incorrect as angerless love. Without ardent hatred towards *what* is wicked, there can be no lawful anger towards *those* who are wicked. It is difficult to separate the two; comp. Jude 23; Rev. ii. 6, 15; Rom. xii. 9; Ps. xcvii. 10; Amos v. 15. The Apostle here gives prominence to the pernicious element of that anger which becomes a lingering grudge, and to the danger of thus falling a prey to the devil; it corrupts man inwardly and makes him the slave of Satan; the "irreconcilable remains the unreconciled, incurring the wrath and judgment of God." See PALMER, *Moral*, p. 373.

3. *Property* and *Theft* stand in the closest relation. The latter attaches not only to the lack of the former, but rather to its acquisition, preservation and expenditure. A Christian should have more than he requires for himself; there should be a surplus for others, even though he be a day-laborer. The opposite of thievishness is *Industry*, which leads to opulence; with this many continued and varied exercises of Christian virtue stand connected, and *Benevolence*, personal, private benevolence, both secret and open; this is required, not the public, municipal charity. The emphasis rests on *personal* benevolence, which succors and devotes itself to need, not on police alms. Honesty should proceed toward benevolence, and what hampers and weakens the latter, has the blot of dishonesty upon it. Avarice, dissipation, vanity, laziness, negligence, debauchery and idleness are theft. See BRAUNE, *Die heilig.* 10 *Gebote*, pp. 178–189; PALMER, *Moral*, p. 375.

[The scope of the negative precept ("steal no longer") may be inferred from the positive statement which follows: It forbids idleness in general ("labor") and laziness ("working"), implying also that those who are neither idle nor lazy may yet "steal," because their work is neither "with the hands" nor for "that which is good" (speculation, sinecures, sharp business habits, *etc.*). Further all labor, however assiduous, proper and honest, which does not aim at a *surplus to give away* is not *distinctively Christian.* Though no one has a right to *demand* from capital (*i. e.*, the accumulated surplus of labor), yet here is the responsibility of the Christian capitalist. On the other hand, the positive principle of honesty here set forth bids us labor, that we may have a *capital* for benevolence; so that begging, combining to extort, or even legislating in favor of idleness, is not in accordance with the Apostle's view. Paul by his example (Acts xviii. 3; xx. 34; 2 Thess. iii. 8), as well as by the strongest precepts (Acts xx. 35; 2 Thess. iii. 10) exalts the *dignity of manual labor.* To despise labor is a mark of barbarism, involving as a result either the indigence of savage freedom or the injustice of not less savage slavery. Unless the curse pronounced (Gen. iii. 19) upon the man be accepted and transformed by such acceptance into a blessing, it becomes a worse misfortune. As a working man then Paul appears equally removed from the capitalist hoarding only for self and from those champions of labor who talk too much to work and who ask the same wages for the ignorant and lazy as belongs of right to skill and industry. Appealing to his hands hardened by toil, he says: "So laboring ye ought to support the weak, and to remember the words of the Lord Jesus, how He said, It is more blessed to give than to receive."—R.]

4. The entire scope of speech is here in question: The essential characteristic of Christian speech, well pleasing to God, is "good for the edifying of the need," a furthering in accordance with the necessity of the case. This applies to the preacher and pastor, to the social circle, the popular orator, be he democratic or conservative, and to the statesman as well. To have regard to place, time and auditors, and to regulate both matter and manner accordingly: this is the conscientious scrupulousness of the Christian! The minister should spare all pious phraseology which is not to edification, and not be content with showing and proving his Confession of Faith, without any regard to the necessities of the occasion. *Magna vis est in colloquiis piis* (BENGEL). Much therefore depends on the fitting word; comp. BRAUNE, *Die heil. Gebote*, p. 205 ff.

5. *General remarks: a. Sin is universal;* it attaches not to the heathen only, but to the natural, unregenerate man as a ruling power; nor is it to be found especially in one class, race or period.—*b. Sin* as a *whole* is referred to: sin of thought, word and deed; here too the coarser or finer form, the secret or open manner makes no difference.—The Apostle so sketches the *substance* of sin, that at first glance we are shocked, and can imagine, it exists only in numerous circles, strata and periods, in the heathen or the remarkably degraded; but if we look more closely, we find it everywhere and in all ages, often indeed under the gloss of culture and elegant manners. The *appearance* of sin is in the extremities, but its seat is in the very noblest organs, from which it extends through the whole body of our race, without He helps who is the Head of His Church.

6. The *motives* presented are: God's mercy in Christ over us, the precious gift of the Holy Ghost in us, the thought of the day of decision before us. God's own aim is what is morally good; to injure this is to injure Him, to obstruct, disturb and destroy His working for us and in us. God's unchangeableness is not the impossibility of being affected; that would be imperfection, indolence (Jas. v. 16–18). Our new birth may, like the life of one born, be again taken away, the sealing of the Holy Ghost be again taken from us. He who does not look at the goal not yet attained and still held up, does not preserve what he has received in his spirit from the Spirit of God. We can lose the grace of God, can again fall into condemnation without recovery, much as it is denied.* Heb. vi. 4–6.

* [In the original Dr. Braune adds: "by the Methodists and Baptists," an oversight which is singular enough; it may be accounted for by remembering that these two denominations are almost the only ones which operate among German Protestants as missionaries. The representative of the State Church (Dr. Braune is General Superintendent) naturally classes them together. On the question whether the possibility of falling from grace is here taught, see *Exeg. Notes.* The passage in Hebrews teaches either: *no fall is possible*, or: *the first fall is fatal*, an alternative not usually accepted by the advocates of such a possibility.—R.]

## HOMILETICAL AND PRACTICAL.

Comp. *Doctr. Notes.*—On vers. 22-28 (*the Epistle for the 19th Sunday after Trinity*) see the preceding section.—Virtue helps to cast off vice, and the casting off of vice introduces virtue, both thus acting reciprocally.—Two classes of men sin against the Apostle's precept respecting sinless anger: those who rage and those who can never be angry. Sinful anger is a raging storm which lays waste a planting of God's; righteous anger is a priest, who slays the sacrifice of righteousness and casts all care and anxiety from herself upon the Lord with a Hosanna. As in the Psalm (iv. 5) so here the allusion is to night, to intercourse with one's self, to quiescence about and in us; the day of anger should be the day of reconciliation; in prayer before God let all animosity be still; let not radiant love of God set for us, with the sun in the heaven. With anger we give a lodgement to the murderer of souls, the devil; who does not slay anger, him anger slays. Hot temples are the easiest bridges for the devil into our hearts.—As room can be given to the devil, so is there also a withdrawal of the Holy Ghost.—For the commonest virtues we need what is highest of all: the kindness of God in Christ; without this there is a relapse into the heathen vices.

STARKE:—Truth is a lovely virtue, a glorious ornament, and sparkles brighter than the most beautiful diamond. If you have the truth, speak the truth from your heart, and walk in the truth, then are you certainly a beloved child of God.—Anger must not be taken to bed and allowed to go to sleep with us, lest it become hatred. Where anger takes the upper hand, Christ goes down with His gracious light.—The slanderer and blasphemer has the devil on his tongue, and whoever purposely listens to the slander gets him in his ears, and whoever takes delight in it, has him in his heart.—There is no dignity, no office, in which peculations are not practised by many. It is only a pity that they are so bedecked and behung with the fine show and appearance and well-adorned cloak of right. Not only are the rich bound to have compassion on the needy, but those who maintain themselves by labor, should share with those who cannot work.—See how out of the glow of sin one spark after another rises up, each greater than the last, until a great fire is made out of it.

The enigmatical, mysterious, unfathomable, people, who never let their hearts be seen, do not bear this Divine stamp; it is as if they did not wish their evil tricks to be betrayed.—The Christian should never lay his head unreconciled to rest, and he has no rest, if he has injured any one, or knows himself to be at enmity with any one. Gentle rest belongs only to a heart free from passion. Examine thyself, whether any one sighs over thee. The Pythagoreans, if they had fallen out with each other in words, gave each other the hand before sundown, kissed each other, and were reconciled.—The aim of labor, of earning, should be the weal of others. The worth of labor is this, that it furnishes us the means of doing good and tasting the sweetness of doing good.

*The perceptible alterations of life which must occur in the regenerate.* 1. In general, in the prevailing mind, vers. 22-24. *a*) An entire laying off of the old evil mind, a cessation of the old lust. *b*) Putting on of an entirely new holy mind, of God's likeness, like God to think and will, and daily renewed zeal in reaching after the likeness of God. 2. Specially, vers. 25-28. Through the virtues which the renewed man exhibits: *a*) Purity, chastity. *b*) Truthfulness. *c*) Gentleness. *d*) Inoffensiveness. *e*) Honesty and Rectitude.

The great difference between Christian culture and that of the world. 1. In general. *a*) The world's culture leaves the old humanity untouched, unimproved, only whitewashes it. *b*) Christian culture ennobles man from the foundation up, by substituting the Divine mind for selfishness.

2. Specially. *a.* Culture hinders only the great outbreaks of vice, Christianity makes the heart pure. *b.* Culture teaches to shun great lies, Christianity makes inwardly true. *c.* Culture makes outwardly refined, Christianity gives true gentleness. *d.* Culture guards against coarse injustice, but Christianity makes truly honest, even where one is not remarked.—Real improvement must begin at the bottom of the heart.—Would not the world fare better, if all became real Christians?—Christians are new men.—The speech of a Christian should always have a moral purpose. Paul describes Christian eloquence both as to its matter: it speaks what is serviceable for improvement, awakens good impulses, leaves a sting behind it in the hearts of others; and as to its manner, which is to be kind, so that love is thereby expressed and made perceptible. The Christian is no babbler, does not allow himself to become a mountebank or court-fool!—The Holy Ghost can be grieved: 1. In Himself, one frustrates His work partly in his own heart, and partly in others, which especially happens through evil speeches. 2. In others, when one grieves the pious Christians, who are full of this Spirit. Consider, whom you should respect in such persons, the Holy Ghost dwelling in them!—The Christian should not be bitter, without on this account becoming sweet. Wrath is the full outbreak of hate against others. Clamor is a token of a hasty, vehement, uncontrolled, rough spirit.

PASSAVANT:—All—liars, because all, sinners, for in every sin is falsehood, a denial of the truth, a deception upon and against ourselves and before God.—Better die than lie! says an old Church Father.—In the case of the unconverted every sin is a wrong against the holy law; in the case of the converted it is at the same time a wrong against the Holy Ghost.

GERLACH:—The Holy Ghost is estranged by empty, vain babbling, but grieved by foul talk.—STIER:—To drive out every sin dwelling in the old man, the practice of the opposite virtue must be employed.—Either we slay again, or it slays us. If a man goes to bed with poison, it creeps through all his members during sleep. Anger is a murderer. Who would sleep with a murderer? To be angry is human, but to cherish it long is devilish (HEINRICH MUELLER).

[EADIE:—Ver. 26. Anger is not wholly forbidden; it is an instinctive principle—a species of thorny hedge encircling our birthright. But in the indulgence of it, men are very apt to sin. —"When the curfew bell rings, let us then also quench all sparks of anger and heat of passion" (THOS. FULLER).—Ver. 27. Give the devil "place" but in a point, and he may speedily cover the whole platform of the soul.—Ver. 29. Words so spoken may fall like winged seeds upon a neglected soil. Comp. Prov. xxv. 11.—Ver. 30. All this perverse insubordination is in utter antagonism to the essence and operations of Him who is the Spirit of truth, and inspires the love of it; who assumed, as a fitting symbol, the form of a dove, and creates meekness and forbearance: and who, as the Spirit of holiness, leads to the appreciation of all that is just in action, noble in sentiment, and healthful and edifying in speech. —It may be said to a prodigal son—grieve not your father lest he cast you off; or grieve not your mother lest you break her heart. Which of the twain is the stronger appeal?—Ver. 31. "Anger sets the house on fire, and all the spirits are busy upon trouble, and intend propulsion, defence, displeasure or revenge; it is a short madness, and an eternal enemy to discourse, and sober counsels, and fair conversation; it is a fever in the heart, and a calenture in the head, and a fire in the face, and a sword in the hand, and a fury all over; and therefore can never suffer a man to be in a disposition to pray" (JEREMY TAYLOR).—Ver. 32. In the exercise of Christian forgiveness his authority was their rule, and his example their model. They were to obey and also to imitate, nay, their obedience consisted in imitation.—R.]

[Ver. 25. The ground of Christian truthfulness and its negative and positive sides.—Vers. 26, 27. Anger. 1) may be right; 2) is far more likely to be wrong; 3) certainly is, if it lasts long; 4) becomes worse yet by giving entrance to the devil.—Ver. 28. Obedience here would stop many a business, and deplete the ranks of many a profession, by increasing the number of honest laborers; but how much it would do for the weal of mankind!—Legislative charity is not Christian charity, nor the payment of taxes for the support of the poor, an essentially Christian virtue.—Ver. 29. The Apostle implies here: 1. That corrupt things rise very naturally to the lips, but should never be spoken; 2. That useful things are rarer.—Much speaking is likely to be evil-speaking.—Profitable conversation: 1. How rare; 2. Little sought for; 3. Selfishness the cause.—This verse would shut many a mouth in prayer-meeting, often enough in the pulpit too.—Would that it did, for is it not by unedifying words as well as evil ones, that the Spirit is grieved?—Ver. 31. "Evil speaking," *i. e.*, slander, is "blasphemy" in Greek; it stands last in this catalogue. It always breaks the *sixth* and *ninth* commands, usually the *seventh*, and is an offence against the *third* also.—Ver. 32. Kindness is well, compassion is better, but forgiveness is like God in Christ.—Who forgave us? God in Christ; how did He forgive us? in Christ; whom did He forgive? us in Christ. —R.]

---

### *c. Three points of view for the new walk.*

(CHAP. V. 1–14.)

#### 1) Look above thyself to follow God!

(CHAP. V. 1, 2.)

1 Be ye [Become] therefore followers [or imitators] of God, as dear [beloved]
2 children; And walk in love, as Christ also hath loved us [also loved you],[1] and hath
given himself [gave himself up] for us[2] an offering and a sacrifice to God for a sweet-
smelling savour [savour of sweet smell].

## TEXTUAL AND GRAMMATICAL.

[1] Ver. 2.—[The better attested reading is ὑμᾶς (א.[1] A. B., cursives, versions and fathers). The *Rec.* has ἡμᾶς (א.[3] D. E. F. K. L., most cursives and versions); so Lachmann, Ellicott. See next note.—R.]

[2] Ver. 2.—[B., with some minor authorities, reads ὑμῶν instead of ἡμῶν, which is well supported. The connection with the last clause complicates the critical question however. Tischendorf, Alford and others accept: ὑμᾶς—ὑμῶν; Lachmann, Ellicott and most (*Rec.*): ἡμᾶς—ἡμῶν. If a uniformity in the person of the pronoun is indispensable, then the latter is preferable, but Braune, with Meyer and others, still more correctly accepts the variation ("loved *you* and gave himself for *us*), which is *lectio difficilior*, accounts best for the various readings, and in detail is better supported by diplomatic authority.—R.]

## EXEGETICAL AND CRITICAL.

Vers. 1, 2 *a*. *The exhortation.* **Become therefore,** γίνεσθε οὖν.—This connects with what precedes (iv. 34): γίνεσθε δέ, marking an inference, and at the same time an advance and a distinction, so that it is=διό (iv. 25; ii. 11; iii. 3), and like διὰ τοῦτο (i. 15), τούτου χάριν (iii. 1, 14), indicating a new section, as it does in iv. 1, 17; v. 15. Hence these verses are not to be joined to chap. iv. (SCHENKEL [HODGE]* and

* [Both EADIE and ELLICOTT seem disposed to regard the verses in this light, but ALFORD takes them as transitional, accepting the view of οὖν suggested by STIER and here upheld by Braune.—R.]

others).—**Followers** [or **imitators**] **of God**, *μιμηταὶ τοῦ θεοῦ*.—Like 1 Cor. iv. 16; xi. 1; 1 Thess. i. 6; ii. 14; Heb. vi. 12; 1 Pet. iii. 13. An injunction on the part of the Apostle to the churches, believers, to imitate what is good; we always find *γίνεσθαι*, never *εἶναι*, in this connection; thus the becoming so is marked. LUTHER, [E. V.], (be), *Vulgate* (*estote*) render incorrectly. In what sense this enormous requirement is intended is clearly indicated by the context: *condonando et amando; nam sequitur amati* (BENGEL). [Hence the word "imitators," though a literal rendering, suggests too much, and "followers" is sufficiently correct.—R.]

**As beloved children** [*ὡς τέκνα ἀγαπητά*].—Ὡς, "as," denotes the reality, *τέκνα ἀγαπητά*, "beloved children," the relation in which they are the objects of the love of God* and through Christ His children. THEODORET: *υἱοθεσίας ἠξιώθητε, πατέρα τὸν θεὸν ὀνομάζετε, ζηλώσατε τοιγαροῦν τὴν συγγένειαν*. Comp. 1 John iv. 12; iv. 7-11; Matth. v. 48; Luke vi. 36. *Liberorum est, patrem moribus referre* (GROTIUS).

Ver. 2. **And walk in love.**—Καί, "and," is epexegetical, in order to define the point of the imitation: *περιπατεῖτε ἐν ἀγάπῃ*, "walk in love," "even as God forgave you" (iv. 32). Ἐν ἀγάπῃ is God's characteristic (i. 4, 5), our aim (iii. 17-19); the former makes the latter possible. On *περιπατεῖν*, see ii. 2.

Ver. 2 *b*. *Closer designation*. **As Christ also loved you** [*καθὼς καὶ ὁ Χριστὸς ἠγάπησεν ὑμᾶς*. See *Textual Notes*.]—"In Christ" (iv. 32) is now explained. "As Christ also" binds the Christian walk to Christ and His work. Christ has loved you, in that He became man and dwelt among men, served them, being mighty in word and deed. [While "the Apostle makes no distinction between our being the objects of God's love, and our being the objects of the love of Christ" (HODGE), it is quite as true that *καί*, *also*, marks an advance "from the love of the Father who gave His Son, to that of the Son, the Personal manifestation of that love in our humanity" (ALFORD). The force of the aorists should be preserved.—R.] The *ὑμᾶς* marks the exhortation more strongly than if the reading were *ἡμᾶς*, permitting the general predicate (*ἠγάπησεν*) to become prominent in its independent validity, over against what follows:

**And gave himself up for us.**—*Καὶ παρέδωκεν ἑαυτόν*, over against *ἔδωκεν* (John iii. 16) denotes two things: the voluntary giving and the giving Himself up to suffering, that is, to suffering in the general sense, including the special form, death: so has *He* loved. To this *ὑπὲρ ἡμῶν*, "for us," also points. [The phrase in itself may or may not imply substitution; ELLICOTT and most think the context points indisputably in this case to the sense: *in our stead*.—Comp. *Romans* (v. 6), p. 164; also *Galatians* (ii. 20, and *Doctr. Notes* on iii. 6-14).—R.] The figure is taken from a conflict, in which, against the enemies thronging over a fallen one, a hero, full of noble courage and of love, protectingly contends; similar to this is the use of *περί*, which gives prominence to the being encircled by foes. This reference is found also in the closer definition which follows.

**An offering and a sacrifice**, *προσφορὰν καὶ θυσίαν*.—According to KLIEFOTH (*Liturg. Abhandlungen*, IV. p. 27 ff.) קָרְבָּן (*corban*) is the common name for all sacrifices and offerings, bloody and unbloody, while מִנְחָה (*mincha*) is principally used of the unbloody (*προσφορά*), זֶבַח (*zebach*) for the bloody offerings (*θυσία*). Comp. Heb. ix. 9; x. 5, 8, where both words occur, and x. 10, 14, 18 with x. 12, 26, where they are used promiscuously. Still even there *τοῦ σώματος* is added to *προσφορά*, so that in accordance with the context and *usus loquendi* this distinction is to be maintained, and in the given order also, because He gave Himself here as a *προσφορά*, and became in death a *θυσία*, the former being the soul of the *θυσία ζῶσα* (STIER).—[ALFORD, EADIE, ELLICOTT, all find in the former term a more general reference to the vicarious work of Christ, and in the latter a more special reference to His death. "The great prominent idea here is the *one* sacrifice, which the Son of God made of Himself in His Redeeming love, in our nature—bringing it, in Himself, near to God—offering Himself as our representative Head: whether in perfect righteousness of life, or in sacrifice, properly so called, at His death" (ALFORD).—R.] Accordingly it is not necessary to supply *εἰς θάνατον* in thought (HARLESS [HODGE], SCHENKEL and others); the context includes more.

**To God for a savour of sweet smell** [*τῷ θεῷ* εἰς ὀσμὴν εὐωδίας*].—This is= רֵיחַ נִיחֹחַ לַיהוָֹה (Exod. xxix. 18, LXX.: *τῷ κυρίῳ εἰς ὀσμὴν εὐωδίας*; comp. Lev. i. 9; iii. 16), where *κυρίῳ* in correspondence with the original text is placed last. Hence "to God," which is inserted for the sake of clearness, is not to be joined to the verb (MEYER). The two substantives (both derived from *ὄζω*, *ὀσμή* denoting the smell in so far as it is inhaled, and *εὐωδία* its quality, WINER, p. 562, or its effect, pleasure) give prominence to the fact that God the Father is well-pleased in the self-sacrificing love of the Crucified One, in order to strengthen, through the reference to this, the exhortation, that we too can become well-pleasing to the Father only in self-devoting love. Phil. iv. 18; Rom. xii. 1, 2; 2 Cor. ii. 15.

## DOCTRINAL AND ETHICAL.

1. The *principle* and *impulse* of the Christian walk is *love*—love as it actually exists in God, who is Love in His character (1 John iv. 8), and as it has been felt and enjoyed by us who are beloved (*ἀγαπητοί*), so that we can give more and more what we have received and ever receive again. Now in Christ this love has become our portion, hence it is forgiving, reconciling, peace-

* [The point suggested by the adjective is obscured in the E. V.: "dear;" "as children *beloved*," they should imitate God in love, see ver. 2.—R.]

* [ALFORD, ELLICOTT and others prefer to connect *τῷ θεῷ* as *dat. commodi*. This alters the sense very little, and is favored by the position of the words, though the Old Testament allusion strongly sustains the view of Braune, which is accepted by many commentators. The connection with the verb is out of the question.—R.]

making; to show this in their walk is here required of Christians.

2. God is the original, Christ the express image of the Father, and the ensample of His people, the Christian the likeness and copy. As the imitation of God cannot be absolute, but is to be limited to loving, to forgiving love, so the imitation of Christ cannot be directed toward expiatory sufferings, but only to self-sacrificing love for our fellows, well-pleasing to God.

3. As we are able to walk in love only as beloved of God and as vouchsafed sonship with Him, so we can only, when reconciled to God through Christ, follow Him in filial and hence in fraternal devotion; in His grace we first can walk as well-pleasing to Him. The error of the Socinians and the Rationalists who see in Christ and His self-sacrifice a mere example and nothing more, is great and pernicious. See *Exeg.* and *Doctr. Notes* on ii. 16. As the Bible highly estimates the vicarious sufferings of Christ, which are taught, not in the ὑπὲρ ἡμῶν, but in the θυσία* and the whole Scripture (Matth. xx. 28; 1 Tim. ii. 6), so it occurs in the entire life of human society: the child lives by the mother's sacrifice, and he for whom no one suffers is miserable. So we too should live for others and suffer in their stead; though we cannot make atonement, we can still live and love self-sacrificingly in the strength imparted to us.

* [Eadie remarks: "To warrant the application of the term 'sacrifice' to the death of Christ, it must have been something more than the natural, fitting, and graceful conclusion of a self-denied life—it must have been a violent and vicarious decease and a voluntary presentation." See his full doctrinal note *in loco.* At the same time Alford is perhaps justified in terming the question, as usually discussed, an "irrelevant one here." "It is not the death of Christ which is treated of, but the whole process of His redeeming love. His death lies in the background as one, and the chief, of the acknowledged facts of that process: but it does not give the character to what is predicated of Him." This exegetical view does not however favor any theory of the death of Christ which denies its vicarious, propitiatory character as an atoning sacrifice. —R.]

### HOMILETICAL AND PRACTICAL.

Comp. the foregoing *Doctr. Notes* and *Hom. Notes* at the close of v. 6-14.

Starke:—Wilt thou become like God hereafter, and see Him as He is, then must thou in this life be holy, even as He is holy.—No one can rightly boast himself of sonship with God, who does not imitate Him.—Christ's example is the proper mirror in which to see the true and natural form of love.

Rieger:—The moral instruction of the Apostles is everywhere deduced from the marrow of the gospel, nor can it be put in practice by any one who does not stand in this gospel of peace. It is the character of love, to imitate as it may the Beloved.

Heubner:—This is a powerful precept: who can satisfy its demands? We cannot become like Him, but we can strive to follow Him in holiness and love. Imitating Christ and God is the same thing.—Christ is and remains the original, but we should be copies, the more faithful, the better.

Stier:—The Father gives His children but one command: Love!

Gerlach:—The thank-offering Christ brought for us, that we too might now offer ourselves to God; the sin-offering, that we need not suffer the same punishment.

---

**2) Look into thyself and think of purity.**

(Chap. v. 3-5.)

3 But fornication, and all uncleanness, or covetousness, let it not be once [even]
4 named among you, as becometh saints; Neither[1] filthiness, nor foolish talking, nor
5 [or] jesting, [things] which[2] are not convenient: but rather giving of thanks. For
this ye know [of this ye are sure,[3] knowing] that no whoremonger, nor unclean
person, nor covetous man, who[4] is an idolater, hath any inheritance in the kingdom
of Christ and of [*omit* of] God.[5]

### TEXTUAL AND GRAMMATICAL.

[1] Ver. 4.—[The best established reading as respects the particles is (*Rec.*): καί—καί—ἤ (so ℵ[2] B. D.[3] K. L., most cursives and versions). ℵ[1] has ἤ instead of the second καὶ, while ἤ is found three times in A. D.[1] F., fathers (Lachmann, Meyer, Braune), and in others καί throughout.—R.]

[2] Ver. 4.—[ℵ. A. B., 3 cursives have: ἃ οὐκ ἀνῆκεν (accepted by Lachmann, Alford. and others) instead of τά οὐκ ἀνήκοντα (*Rec.*, D. F. K. L., Meyer, Ellicott, Braune and most). The latter is well supported and *lectio difficilior*, but neither external nor internal grounds are altogether decisive.—R.]

[3] Ver. 5.—[The *Rec.* has ἐστε on the authority of D.[3] K. L., but ℵ. A. B. D. F. G., 30 cursives, good versions support ἴστε, which is accepted by nearly all recent editors. The emendation above conforms to the correct reading.—R.]

[4] Ver. 5.—[The reading ὅ is found in ℵ. B., accepted by Lachmann and Alford. The *Rec.* has ὅς, which has more uncial support. In F. G. the neuter occurs with εἰδωλολατρεία, which helps to account for the change to the neuter.—R.]

[5] Ver. 5.—ℵ. B. and most: Χριστοῦ καὶ θεοῦ. We find also θεοῦ καί Χριστοῦ, Χριστοῦ θεοῦ, and simply Χριστοῦ. The first is not only better supported, but *lectio difficilior*. [The second *of* should be omitted to indicate the close connection implied in the omission of the article before θεοῦ.—R.]

## EXEGETICAL AND CRITICAL.

*The exhortation;* vers. 3, 4.

Ver. 3. **But fornication, and all uncleanness, or covetousness** [πορνεία δὲ καὶ πᾶσα ἀκαθαρσία ἢ πλεονεξία].—"But," δέ, indicates the transition to another part of the exhortation (MEYER). Πορνεία cannot here, where Christians are addressed, be taken in the heathen sense; the Scriptural meaning (in both Old and New Testament) is the prominent one: Hence it refers not to the coarsest exhibition, but to what is within, to the heart. It comes first as something general and comprehensive; applying to act, word, disposition, as indeed the context combines temper and walk in one, to men among themselves and in relation to God. "And all uncleanness" gives prominence to one particular side of this, pointing to every form and mode of the same. "Or covetousness" marks the other side, which is to be clearly distinguished, hence the disjunctive ἤ*, "or," which indicates that πᾶσα, "all," belongs here also. The former refers to impure, unchaste, ungodly, dalliance and contact, solitary uncleanness; the latter to greedy lusting, from a distance and ungratified. This accords with iv. 19, where both substantives are found.

**Let it not be even named among you,** μηδὲ ὀνομαζέσθω ἐν ὑμῖν.—Comp. ver. 12; Ps. xvi. 4. Such a thing should not even be taken up in speech, much less be done. Ἐν ὑμῖν=ἐν μέσῳ ὑμῶν. The prohibition is of course to be limited: *sine necessitate* (BENGEL). It is incorrect to explain: Such a thing should not be told of them, as 1 Cor. v. 1 (GROTIUS, BENGEL).

**As becometh saints.**—Καθώς, as in ver. 2; with πρέπει ἁγίοις, we should compare ἀξίως (iv. 17) and ὁσιότης (iv. 24), with which the introduction of such things into the speech is irreconcilable. ["Were the Apostle to say, Let despondency be banished, he might add, as becometh believers, or, Let enmity be suppressed, he might subjoin, as becometh the brethren; but he pointedly says in this place, "as becometh saints" (EADIE).—R.]

Ver. 4. **Neither filthiness,** αἰσχρότης.—This evidently includes more than αἰσχρολογία (Col. iii. 8). Although the antithesis (εὐχαριστία) points to shameful words (LUTHER), neither the context, which places αἰσχρότης beside μωρολογία nor the word itself require an exclusive reference to speech. Still less is it to be limited to *lewd* talk. BENGEL refers it also to *gestus, etc.*

**Nor foolish talking,** καὶ μωρολογία.—[*Textual Note* 1. Should ἤ be accepted here, we should substitute *or* for *nor*, as is done in the case of the next substantive.—R.] According to the New Testament conception of μωρός, "fool" (Matt. v. 22; Ps. xiv. 1; liii. 2), this means godless discourse; it is not merely *stultiloquium*, insipid talk, silly babbling (CALVIN, [HODGE] MEYER, SCHENKEL). LUTHER hits the meaning with: *Narrentheidinge*, buffoonery, which denotes what is high-flown, pompous, in loose discourse. See JUETTING: *Bibl. Wörterbuch*, p. 189. [TRENCH, *Syn.* § xxxiv.: "The talk of fools, which is folly and sin together."—R.]

**Or jesting,** ἢ εὐτραπελία (from εὖ and τρέπω) means strictly *urbanitas*, a habit of cultivated people, not without adroitness and not without frivolity. LUTHER: *jest.* BENGEL aptly says: *subtilior ingenio nititur;* this refers to the form, the previous term to the purport. The *Vulgate* is incorrect: *scurrilitas.* [Comp. TRENCH, § xxxiv. on this word. He refers to "the profligate old man" of the *Miles gloriosus* (PLAUTUS), who is exactly the εὐτράπελος, and remarkably enough an Ephesian, boasting as though such wit were an Ephesian birthright. See also BARROW's famous sermon on wit from this text (Vol. 1, Serm. xiv.), an extract from which is given by EADIE *in loco.*—R.]

**Things which are not convenient,** τὰ οὐκ ἀνήκοντα.—This gives prominence to the wider range, beyond the lewdness and the coarser forms. In spite of μὴ καθήκοντα (Rom. i. 28) we found οὐκ here, because the negation has coalesced with the word in one conception. See WINER, p. 452. As a predicate we must borrow an *absint* (BENGEL) from μὴ ὀνομαζέσθω. [This phrase is not to be limited to the last of the three substantives, but is "in apposition to the last two words, to both of which εὐχαριστία, as denoting oral expression yet implying inward feeling, forms a clear contrast."—R.]

**But rather giving of thanks,** μᾶλλον δὲ εὐχαριστία—ἀνήκει, as BENGEL aptly supplies out of the preceding context, remarking: *linguæ abusus opponitur sanctus et tamen lætus usus, vers.* 18, 19. *Non conveniunt abusus et usus εὐτραπηλία et εὐχαριστία, concinna paronomasia; illa turbat animam* (*et quidem subtilis aliquando jocus et lepus tenerum gratiæ sensum lædit*) *hæc exhilirat.** As "beloved children" they have ever again to thank God. The reference is not to grace of discourse (JEROME, CALVIN, and others, STIER includes this with the other), nor to *pudicitia* (HEINSIUS).

Ver. 5. *Special motive.* **For this ye are sure, knowing** [τοῦτο γὰρ ἴστε γινώσκοντες].—"For" adds a ground, in order to strengthen the exhortation as a consequence therefrom. Accordingly ἔστε [ἴστε] γινώσκοντες is to be taken as an indicative [MEYER, EADIE, ALFORD and others], not as imperative (*Vulgate*, LUTHER, BENGEL and others). The participle indicates the *mode* of knowing as of their own perception (MEYER), insight. Τοῦτο, "this," placed in advance, points to what is stated afterwards,

* ["The ἢ is not explanatory, but has its full *disjunctive* force, serving to distinguish πλεονεξία from more special sins of the flesh" (ELLICOTT). On the last noun see iv. 19. "It is greed, avarice, unconquerable love of appropriation, morbid lust of acquisition, carrying in itself a violation of almost every precept of the Decalogue" (EADIE). This original notion must not be overridden by the connection with sensual sins.—R.]

* [MEYER and ELLICOTT supply γινέσθω ἐν ὑμῖν; EADIE suggests that ὀνομαζέσθω still guides the construction: "Rather let thanksgiving be named—let there be vocal expression to your grateful emotions." STIER and ALFORD follow BENGEL.—"There is a play perhaps on the similar sound of εὐτραπελία and εὐχαριστία, which may account for the latter not finding so complete a justification in the sense as we might expect: the connection being apparently, 'your true cheerfulness and play of fancy will be found, not in buffoonery, but in the joy of a heart overflowing with a sense of God's mercies.'"—ALFORD.—R.]

the import of which cannot be unknown to Christians. WINER (p. 333) is therefore incorrect: What is said in vers. 3, 4, ye know, since ye perceive, that, etc. [This reference of τοῦτο to what follows is doubtful to say the least. It seems quite correct to refer it, as the object of ἴστε, to what precedes, γινώσκοντες being joined with ὅτι. Braune takes no notice of the correct reading, an inadvertence which probably modifies his opinion of the construction. The combination of finite verb and participle is not to be explained as Hebraistic, since the verbs are different.—R.]

**That no whoremonger, nor unclean person, nor covetous man.**—The concrete terms (πόρνος, ἀκάθαρτος, πλεονέκτης), here occurring instead of the abstract ones mentioned in ver. 3, must be taken in the same sense. [The literal sense is: "that every fornicator or (ἤ individualizes here) unclean man, or covetous man, who is an idolater, hath not inheritance." The negation is transferred to the subject according to English usage.—R.]

**Who is an idolater,** ὅς ἐστιν εἰδωλολάτρης.—This relative clause not only characterizes, but also gives a reason for the fact to be stated. On this account and because "who" is limited to the last term altogether without warrant, the clause is to be applied to "every whoremonger, unclean person, covetous man." It is not the covetous man alone who is an idolater, having this world's goods as his god (Matt. vi. 24; 1 Tim. vi. 10); Paul holds "belly" and "glory" also as "god" for the enemies of the cross (Phil. iii. 19). The proof lacks aptness, if that be not attributed to the first two, which is predicated of the third, who is not an idolater more especially than the former. The clause is incorrectly referred to the "covetous man" alone (MEYER, SCHENKEL, BLEEK); Col. iii. 5 does not prove this, still less can it be said that Paul's self-denial, which unselfishly offered up all, led him to affirm this of covetousness alone, since he was just as free from lust and uncleanness. [In this wide reference of the relative clause Braune is sustained by HARLESS, STIER and others, but the more limited view is that of EADIE, HODGE, ALFORD, ELLICOTT and most. It is more natural and obvious, since all that can be urged in favor of the other view but proves that the reference *may be* thus wide, not that it *is*. And covetousness *is* more specially idolatry, the other sins are but more subtle forms of this. If ὅ be accepted as the correct reading, then the reference is necessarily confined to the last *word*. See ALFORD *in loco*.—R.]

**Hath any inheritance,** οὐκ ἔχει κληρονομίαν.—See i. 11. It is not=οὐ κληρονομήσουσιν, "shall not inherit" (Gal. v. 21; 1 Cor. vi. 9, 10), nor κληρονομῆσαι οὐ δύνανται (1 Cor. xv. 50). It is the fact respecting the status; permanent, prevalent sin excludes from the kingdom of God, effects the repelling of the *arrhabo*, the Holy Ghost (i. 13, 14); "hath an inheritance" is not=inherits the kingdom, since the former marks the heirship, the latter the entrance of the heir. To accept a certain future relation viewed as present, will not suffice (BENGEL). [See WINER, p. 249. "Has no inheritance," can have none, this being a law of God's moral government of the world (EADIE, ELLICOTT), an eternal verity of that kingdom (ALFORD).—R.]

**In the kingdom of Christ and God,** ἐν τῇ βασιλείᾳ Χριστοῦ καὶ Θεοῦ.—Βασιλεία means the kingdom, where God in Christ is the Ruler, and His people belong to Him, and hence to be distinguished from ἐκκλησία, to which the fornicator and such characters belong, without having part in the former. (See *Doctr. Note* 5.) BENGEL is excellent: *articulus simplex, summam unitatem indicans.* The expression here depends on the fact that Christ's and God's kingdom is one (ver. 12), that Christ's kingdom is also God's kingdom; though this first appears at the end in glory (Rev. ix. 15), the development advancing through the Church. Accordingly it is incorrect to explain it as meaning the kingdom of Christ, who is also God (HARLESS) [HODGE and many others] though Christ is termed God (Rom. ix. 5), or can be thus termed [against MEYER].

[ALFORD: "No distinction is to be made, Χριστοῦ καὶ θεοῦ being in the closest union. Nor is any specification needed that the kingdom of Christ is also the kingdom of God, as would be made with the second article. This follows as a matter of course: and thus the words bear no legitimate rendering, except on the substratum of our Lord's Divinity. But on the other hand we cannot safely say here that the same Person is intended by Χριστοῦ καὶ θεοῦ, merely on account of the omission of the article. For 1) any introduction of such a predication regarding Christ would here be manifestly out of place, not belonging to the context: 2) θεός is so frequently and unaccountably anarthrous, that it is not safe to ground any such inference from its use here." So EADIE, ELLICOTT and many others. The inferential proof of the Divinity of Christ thus afforded is well-nigh as strong as, certainly more defensible than, that resulting from the other view.—R.]

## DOCTRINAL AND ETHICAL.

1. The life of the Christian, like Christian ethics, must pursue sin in its coarsest forms and manifestations even into its most secret, refined propensities; it depends upon the substance; this is to be rejected in every form. Christian culture has a sharp eye and delicate perception for evil under its elegant appearance, and a powerful will and apt word for the refusal and overcoming of the same: it can have no pleasure in elegant forms under which wickedness conceals itself.

2. What was of validity in the morals of the Persians (HERODOTUS I., 138): ἅσσα δέ σφι ποιέειν οὐκ ἔξεστι ταῦτα οὐδὲ λέγειν ἔξεστι, every Christian must accept as valid to this extent, that he says: What is more becoming to do or say, that thou shouldst not even think. A word often includes more evil in itself than an act, and a thought than a word; even if the evil thought be less mischievous than the act, because it is only a thought not an act. The sinful act of the non-christian is at all events as a rule less wicked than the Christian sinful word or temper; as the same is true of a neglected Christian child, over

against one carefully trained, or of the same man, as different now and formerly, or on festival or fast day with its elevation and in the press of labor and the throng of the world.

3. The Christian's position is dignity, which preserves the worthiness of the person in a pure life no less than in pure doctrine with tender conscientiousness.

4. Every sin stands connected with idolatry: it remains the same, whether thou makest a god of the goods of this world in covetousness, or of the lust of this world in pursuit of pleasure, or of thine own Ego in pride. Paul terms covetousness not *the* (ἡ) but *a* root (ῥίζα) of all evil (1 Tim. iv. 10). The same is true of the lust of the flesh and the pride of life (1 John ii. 16).

[HODGE is however perfectly correct in saying: "The analogy between this supreme love of riches, this service of mammon and idolatry, is more obvious and more distinctly recognized in Scripture than between idolatry and any other of the sins mentioned. It is well that this should be understood, that men should know that the most common of all sins is the most heinous in the sight of God; for idolatry, which consists in putting the creature in the place of God, is everywhere in His word denounced as the greatest of all sins in His sight. The fact that it is compatible with outward decorum, and with the respect of men, does not alter its nature. It is the permanent and controlling principle of an irreligious heart and life, turning the soul away from God. There is no cure for this destructive love of money, but using it for other than selfish purposes. Riches, therefore, must ruin their possessor, unless he employs them for the good of others and for the glory of God."—R.]

5. The *kingdom* of Christ and of God is not precisely the *church*. The former marks the authority, the latter the *people;* that refers to the *power*, which orders, manages, governs, this to the grace which chooses, attracts, trains, guides and endows; the former has to do with *powers*, which are applied and with laws which are established and administered. Both however have *one end:* God's glory and the creature's salvation. The kingdom of God and Christ is *wider* and *narrower* than the church. It stretches itself over the time *antecedent* to the church, which should become the kingdom of God, and embraces all, who obey and permit themselves to be drawn by the will of the Ruler, God in Christ, so far as the same is known, in His laws given to His creatures in nature from the very creation, in their conscience and in the order about and above them. All moral natures of every kind, childlike, truth-seeking souls belonging thereto (Matt. viii. 12; Mark xii. 34; John xviii. 36, 37). To this belong all historical leadings of nations, all guidance to individuals, all the effects of power and wisdom, which prepare the way for the church. The kingdom is God's as well as Christ's (Matt. xiii. 41; John xviii. 36 f.). As before the church and for the church the kingdom is more extended. But at the same time it becomes *less extended within* the church. There it applies to those called as the people of God, to those who obey the call; those who resist, who are indifferent, who hold only externally to the church, even though they hold in high regard a moral life, as is done without the church as well, who undervalue or despise the faith of the Scriptures or the church, or rely on the latter and neglect the former,—all withdraw themselves from the "kingdom" within the church. The word is to be taken in this latter sense here (ver. 5). At the end of the world both come together: since that will be the *fulness* of time, when the Son of man shall appear in glory.

## HOMILETICAL AND PRACTICAL.

Comp. *Doctr. Notes.*

From the wanderings of the flesh in the insubordination of its appetites and of society in loose talk, we should take occasion, not to run away and forsake the world, but to guard ourselves and so to strive in ourselves, that God's pardoning love is not in vain, and sanctification is not disturbed. Neither happiness, nor pleasure, nor property is the aim and task of life, but the formation of the character, of that stamp with His image received in creation and renewed in redemption. To be covetous in what is noblest, to be impure in what is most exalted, to be disorderly in what is spiritual and heavenly is an abomination of abominations. Such a condition excludes from God and God's kingdom, in the Church, its service and government. Take heed to that, teacher and preacher. Be mindful of it always in prayer and public service.

STARKE:—In Christianity exact bounds are placed upon our words, far more so than is done by mere reason; Matt. xii. 36. Hear this, ye buffoons! ye cannot boast yourselves of Christianity.—You betray by this too well the bottom of your yet unsanctified hearts.—Could we find a register of those whom God as a just Judge will exclude from heaven, the first place as a rule would be given to those who break the Seventh Commandment.

RIEGER:—The world often gives its uncleanness the name of love-affairs; but the word love in the Scriptures is far too good to be applied to any such things.

HEUBNER:—No man has such a horror of all sins of the flesh as the Christian; his destiny, his fellowship, his Exemplar, his future inheritance, all require him to be pure.—Paul describes the Christian's propriety in speech, distinguishing three kinds of obnoxious talk: 1. Such as offends and injures the sense of virtue, that is, impure, indecent, shameless talking; 2. Such as opposes the reason and offends the sense of truth, that is, foolish, silly, senseless, insipid talking; 3. Such as hinders religious earnestness, designed only to raise a laugh.—Every prevailing sin removes us from God. The covetous commit idolatry with their money, the lustful with their flesh. If then it be asked which is more compatible with religion, a disposition to lust or avarice, the latter seems less reconcilable. The covetous man imagines, because he perhaps restrains himself from many vices, that he is better, and covetousness as something relative is more difficult to recognize.—The kingdom of Christ is the medium and condition of the kingdom of God; through Christ the kingdom of God becomes predominant. The kingdom of Christ, in so far as it is an external institution, yields to the kingdom of God.

PASSAVANT:—The Greeks loved a fine joke, seasoned and adorned with wit and grace. But under the jest and its elegant dress, an impure and low sense was often concealed.—Look, wit is a dangerous gift, and to give it play brings discomfort and pain.

STIER:—The worst in front, the obscenities, *double entendres;* there are also obscenities of mammon, nastinesses arising from pride and worldliness, for which the Holy Ghost has the same aversion in His saints.

[EADIE:—Into Christ's kingdom the fornicator and sensualist cannot come; for, unsanctified and unprepared, they are not susceptible of its spiritual enjoyments, and are filled with antipathy to its unfleshly occupations; and specially into God's kingdom "the covetous man, who is an idolater," cannot come, for that God is not his God, and disowning the God of the kingdom, he is self-excluded. As his treasure is not there, so neither there could his heart find satisfaction and repose.—R.]

---

3) Look about thyself and be independent and benevolent!

(CHAP. V. 6–14.)

6 Let no man [no one] deceive you with vain [empty] words: for because of these
7 things cometh the wrath of God upon the children [sons] of disobedience. Be
8 not ye [Become not] therefore partakers[1] with them. For ye were sometime [once
ye were] darkness, but now *are ye* light in the Lord: walk as children of light;
9 (For the fruit of the Spirit [light][2] *is* in all goodness and righteousness and
10, 11 truth;) Proving what is acceptable unto [well-pleasing to] the Lord. And
have no fellowship[3] with the unfruitful works of darkness, but rather [even] re-
12 prove *them*. For it is a shame even to speak of those things which are done of
them in secret [For the things done in secret by them it is a shame even to speak
13 of].[4] But all things that are [being] reproved are made manifest by the light: for
whatsoever doth make manifest [everything which is made manifest][5] is light.
14 Wherefore he saith, Awake [or Up!][6] thou that [who] sleepest, and arise from the
dead, and Christ shall give thee light.

TEXTUAL AND GRAMMATICAL.

[1] Ver. 7.—[Here as so frequently in compounds with συν in Paul's Epistles, συνμέτοχοι is better supported than the usual and more euphonic συμμέτοχοι (*Rec.*). The former is found in ℵ. A. B.[1] D.[1] F. G., accepted by Tischendorf, Alford, Ellicott and many recent editors.—R.]

[2] Ver. 9.—[The reading of the *Rec.:* πνεύματος, is supported by D.[3] K. L., most cursives and some fathers, but is now generally rejected as a gloss from Gal. v. 22, φωτός being sustained by ℵ. A. B. D.[1] F., good cursives, Syriac and other versions, Latin fathers.—The parenthesis is to be retained, see *Exeg. Notes*.—R.]

[3] Ver. 11.—[Συνκοινωνεῖτε (ℵ. A. B.[1] D.[1] F. G. L., Tischendorf, Ellicott).—R.]

[4] Ver. 12.—The E. V. has unnecessarily transposed the order in this verse. A literal rendering would be: "For the things which in secret come to pass by them it is shameful to speak of."—R.]

[5] Ver. 13.—[These alterations are required by the views expressed in the *Exeg. Notes*, and may be accepted as indicating in general the opinions of recent commentators.—R.]

[6] Ver. 14.—The *Rec.* reads ἔγειραι (Lachmann], which has no uncial support. Ἔγειρε is accepted by nearly all recent editors and commentators, since it occurs in ℵ. A. B. D. F. K. L., and other authorities.—R.]

EXEGETICAL AND CRITICAL.

Ver. 6. *The transition.* **Let no one deceive you with empty words,** μηδεὶς ὑμᾶς ἀπατάτω κενοῖς λόγοις.—The precept: "let no one deceive you," is entirely general, but limited by the context to social intercourse; there being nothing to indicate a further extension. Hence "no one" is to be applied to members of the Church and the non-christians who are, or come, near them; "deceive" including unintentional as well as intentional leading astray. Accordingly the reference is not, as in Col. ii. 8, to philosophers and Jewish errorists (GROTIUS), nor merely to frivolous Christians (OLSHAUSEN), or to those heathen who had remained unbelieving (MEYER). The loquacious persons spoken of are false teachers with "empty words." This phrase means discourse wanting in truth, life and spirit; *hoc genus est, species tres* ver. 4. (BENGEL). [ALFORD: "Empty—not containing the kernel of truth, of which words are but the shell—words with no underlying facts."—R.] Comp. 1 Cor. xv. 33. BULLINGER: *Erant apud Ephesios homines corrupti, ut hodie apud nos plurimi sunt, qui hæc salutaria Dei præcepta cachinno excipientes obstrepunt: humanum esse, quod faciunt amatores, utile, quod fœneratores, facetum, quod jaculatores, et idcirco Deum non usque adeo graviter animadvertere in istius modi lapsus.** STIER is not altogether incorrect in find-

* ["The Apostle generally condemns all apologists for vice, whoever they might be. They would of course be most commonly found among the heathen, and to them the passage most naturally points. The palliation or tacit toleration of

ing an ironical opposition in: ἀπατᾷν κενοῖς, exhorting thus: let them speak only in vain (1 Cor. xv. 14, 58).

**For because of these things,** διὰ ταῦτα γάρ, introduces a reason; "because of these things" pointing beyond the genus ("empty word") to the species (ver. 4), just as in the parallel passage, Col. iii. 6 (δι' ἅ). [The context is decisive against the reference either to the ἀπάτῃ of the "empty words," or to this and the sins mentioned in ver. 4. See ELLICOTT and ALFORD.—R.]—**Cometh,** ἔρχεται, marks the fact as present, like "hath not" (ver. 5); it is neither=*venire solet* (ERASMUS), nor a general asseveration without any temporal qualification (HARLESS), nor does it point to the future (MEYER, SCHENKEL, BLEEK); the punishment has *already begun*. See Rom. i. 18.

**The wrath of God,** ἡ ὀργὴ τοῦ θεοῦ.—This also is not to be considered as quiescent until the final Judgment. It already comes both externally and internally as correction and punishment, **upon the sons of disobedience,** ἐπὶ τοὺς υἱοὺς τῆς ἀπειθείας (ii. 2).—This designates more strongly than ἀπειθεῖς those who still or again oppose God and His word within the Church. ["The active and practical side of the ἀπειθῶν (John iii. 36) is here brought out. The word is a valuable middle term between unbelief and disobedience, implying their identity in a manner full of the highest instruction" (ALFORD).—R.]

*Warning against association with wicked men;* vers. 7-10.

Ver. 7. **Become not therefore,** μὴ οὖν γίνεσθε.—Οὖν, "therefore," marks the specializing of the warning and that it rests on "the wrath of God upon the children of disobedience" as its basis, while γίνεσθε, "become," indicates that this state of things is not yet present, and at the same time the danger of its entrance and its quiet, unnoticed and unregarded development.* Vulgate: *Nolite effici!* BENGEL: *Ne ira super vos veniat!*

**Partakers with them,** συνμέτοχοι† αὐτῶν, *i. e.* with the sons of disobedience. It is inappropriate to refer αὐτῶν to vices (SCHENKEL), and to understand συνμέτοχοι (iii. 6) of the portion of the wicked (KOPPE, STIER, who includes this also). The reference to the punishment is the foundation of the warning against companionship with them.

Ver. 8 presents *a new reason,* taken from their experience of grace, their grasp on the Lord and their task · **For once ye were,*** ἦτε γάρ ποτε!—That is, thanks to God, it is past! Hence ἦτε stands emphatically first; and LUTHER with his *weiland* [=to the antique "sometime" of the E. V.] aptly recalls a past condition, referring to a new life.—**Darkness,** σκότος, *abstractum pro concreto, emphasi egregia* (BENGEL). [They were not only living or abiding in it, but themselves actual and veritable darkness (ELLICOTT).—R.]

**But now are ye light in the Lord,** νῦν δὲ φῶς ἐν τῷ κυρίῳ.—This, without ἐστι, is quite as emphatic and brief. "Light," as in 1 John i. 5; John viii. 12, is a comprehensive designation of the Divine life and character, both ethical and intellectual in its meaning, in contrast with darkness (iv. 18; Acts xxvi. 18; Col. i. 12, 13; 1 Pet. ii. 9). These nominatives emphasize the being full, permeated by, and are stronger than ἐν σκότει (Rom. ii. 19; 1 Thess. v. 4), ἐν φωτί. [Comp. USTERI, *Lehrbegr.* ii. 1, 3, p. 229, on the terms φῶς and σκότος.—HODGE weakens the sense into "enlightened," but "light" has here an active sense, which prepares the way for the subsequent exhortation, since they were not only to walk worthy of the light but be light to others (ver. 13).—R.] The added phrase, ἐν τῷ κυρίῳ, excludes the notion of having earned the present condition, marking the operation of the Lord, in order to excite thankfulness for constancy, fear of apostacy and backsliding, without the ability of helping one's self.

**Walk as children of light,** ὡς τέκνα φωτὸς† περιπατεῖτε.—The status is marked by ὡς, "as." What ye are ("children of light"), be in deed and truth ("walk")! Energetically added, without any conjunction, as growing out of what precedes, as its result.

Ver. 9. **For the fruit of the light,** ὁ γὰρ καρπὸς τοῦ φωτός.—This is introduced as a ground (γάρ). The children of the light are referred to the fruit of the light, in order to excite them to a corresponding walk. This fruit consists **in all goodness and righteousness and truth** [ἐν πάσῃ, ἀγαθωσύνῃ καὶ δικαιοσύνῃ καὶ ἀληθείᾳ].—"Fruit" is in the singular, and yet three terms follow, as in Gal. v. 22: "the fruit of the Spirit" is followed by nine, in order to render prominent its unity in contrast with "the works of the flesh" (ver. 19 ff.) in their sundered character, their opposition to each other.

**Goodness,** ἀγαθωσύνη, the opposite of which is κακία, is distinguished from χρηστότης, which is mentioned in connection with it (Gal. v. 22), in this, that it refers to the depth of the disposition, χρηστότης more to the character of its manifestation; both denoting goodness however. Here are designated the character and conduct as regards possessions of every kind,

vice, especially sensuality, was one of the most fearful and repulsive features of heathenism; see specifically Tholuck, *Influence of heathenism*, Part iv. 2."—ELLICOTT. Comp. the citation from Whitby and Gauthey in EADIE. The "vain words" were publicly spoken then, now they come in more concealed form, but the same lies are uttered still on the same subject and with like result, immediate and ultimate. —R.]

* [The force of γίνεσθε is not to be explained away. ALFORD indeed strongly objects to it here as unnecessary and unsuitable, but he seems to entertain a prejudice against it. A German from his familiarity with the distinction between *Sein* and *Werden* in his own language is usually delicate in his perception of the same distinction in other languages.—R.]

† [See *Textual Note* [1] for the authority in favor of thus spelling the word.—R.]

* [This order seems to bring out the emphasis best. Comp. HARLESS and ELLICOTT in justification of the omission of μέν here (against RUECKERT).—R.]

† [The absence of the article with φωτός is regarded by ALFORD as significant: "here it is light, *as light*, which is spoken of." ELLICOTT however thinks the omission is due to the principle of correlation: "if the governing noun is without the article, the governed will be equally so."—R.]

which one has and knows another to stand in need of.

**Righteousness**, δικαιοσύνη, the opposite of which is ἀδικία, respects relations and the ordering of the same, claims which can be made, and obligations, which should be fulfilled, and is just in regard to all these, taking pains that nothing, neither the least nor the most difficult, receives detriment.

**Truth**, ἀλήθεια, the opposite of which is ψεῦδος, concerns the agreement of what is internal and external, of thought and word and deed, of goodness and righteousness, so that one is not served at the expense of the other, and harmony exists. The terms are not to be divided according to the three categories: inwardly, toward man, toward God (B-CRUSIUS), or source, outwardly, inwardly (SCHENKEL).* "All," πάσῃ, denotes the extent of the manifold manifestations (Phil. iv. 6: ὅσα), it is not then=all kinds. Others explain differently, but it is generally agreed, that ἐστι or συνέστηκε should be supplied. [Comp. WINER, p. 173, against the acceptance of a Hebraism here (ἐν=*Beth essentiæ*, Gesenius, *Lexicon*, under ב, C).—R.]

Ver. 10. **Proving**, δοκιμάζοντες.—Grammatically this participle may be the mode of the walking, ver. 9 being taken as a parenthesis. So BENGEL, HARLESS, MEYER, SCHENKEL [HODGE, EADIE, ELLICOTT, ALFORD], and others. But the exhortation may also be regarded as concluded in ver. 8; nor does ver. 9 give in the main the impression of being a parenthesis, while the participle can be, according to WINER (p. 545), taken imperatively with ἐστε supplied, as occurs at least ten times in Rom. xii. 9-13. So KOPPE, STIER, BLEEK and others. [Such a construction is certainly allowable, where the context plainly requires it, but is not to be accepted when a simpler view is so obviously suggested as in this case.—R.] The former view is favored by the connection of "proving" and "walk," since through the walk as a child of the light material and power for the proof grows and ripens. [On the word see TRENCH, *Syn.*, II. § xxiv.—R.] Investigation and discrimination are required of the children of light; independently, not "tossed as waves and carried about—in the sleight of men" (iv. 14), they should prove, **what is well-pleasing to the Lord**, τί ἐστιν εὐάρεστον τῷ κυρίῳ.—"What," τί, defines that all things, even the most refined traits and forms, are to be proved. The question is, Is it "well-pleasing to the Lord," *i. e.*, to Christ, who with His Word is the objective measure. ["The Christian's whole course is a continual proving, testing of the will of God in practice: investigating not what pleases himself, but what pleases Him" (ALFORD).—R.] Comp. Rom. xiv. 23; xii. 2; 2 Cor. v. 9; 1 Thess. v. 21.

*Warning against fellowship with evil works;* vers. 11-13.

Ver. 11. **And have no fellowship**, καὶ μὴ συνκοινωνεῖτε.—"And" connects the imperative with the similar admonition, ver. 7, there "with them" is added, here "with the works," the latter referring to fellowship with the works, the former with the persons. The verb is a strengthened form* (Phil iv. 14, Rev. xviii. 4), from συνκοινωνός (Rom. xi. 17; 1 Cor. ix. 23; Phil. i. 7; Rev. i. 9); it is a compound not usual with the Apostle, denoting however the fellowship on one side alone. Hence συν is not to be referred to the disobedient, and κοινωνεῖν to the works (MEYER).

**With the unfruitful works of darkness** [τοῖς ἔργοις τοῖς ἀκάρποις τοῦ σκότους].—The prominent word ἔργοις, "works," is followed by ἀκάρποις, "unfruitful," distinguished by the article, in contrast to: "the fruit of the light" (ver. 9).† The expression is not without a certain mildness, like "empty words" (ver. 6), yet without being weak, simply denying the fruit, without positively referring to the corruption and condemnation (iv. 22; Rom. vi. 21; viii. 13; Gal. vi. 8). The expressions: "dead works" (Heb. vi. 1; ix. 14), "wicked works" (Col. i. 21), are similar. The added genitive: τοῦ σκότους, "of darkness," appends the positive element (Rom. xiii. 12); Gal. v. 19: τῆς σαρκός.

**But rather even reprove them.**—*Non satis abstinere est* (BENGEL); hence μᾶλλον δὲ καί, "but rather even." Lev. xix. 17. Ἐλέγχετε requires rebuke, punishment, conviction, as in John iii. 20; xvi. 8 The object is not expressed; but the context supplies it: αὐτά (them, *i. e.* the works). The mode is determined by the context, since the evil works are to be punished: through proper conduct in word and work, *verbis et factis luce dignis* (BENGEL). MEYER and SCHENKEL incorrectly apply it to oral rebuke alone, against the passages in John, from which an oral conviction and punishment cannot be deduced. Comp. John viii. 9. The result: conversion, improvement, is in no way indicated, hence not to be accepted (OLSHAUSEN).

[ALFORD, EADIE and ELLICOTT favor the reference to oral rebuke; certainly it seems a prominent thought, but see on the next verse. The last named author thus marks the antithesis: "Do not connive at them or pass them over unnoticed, but take aggressive measures against them; try and raise the Gentiles to your own Christian standard." HODGE takes the verb as meaning: to convince by evidence, deducing from this statement: "The ethics as well as the theology of the Bible are founded on the principle that knowledge and holiness, ignorance and sin, are inseparable." Hence that our duty is simply to let "the light of Divine truth shine into the darkened minds of men, and upon their evil deeds."—R.]

Ver. 12. **For the things done in secret by them it is a shame even to speak of.**—

* [MEYER properly observes that these three words present the whole of Christian morality under its three aspects, the good, the right, the true. It may be added that this verbal triad, presenting the one fruit of the light is less sentimental, but more substantial than the hackneyed cluster of words: the true, the beautiful, the good. "The right" too often gives way to "the beautiful," so-called.—R.]

* [De Wette's rendering: "take no part in," would require a genitive after the verb; the other is more literal, and is now accepted by EADIE, who at first followed DE WETTE.—R.]

† [Comp. especially Gal. v. 19, 22, where there is a similar contrast, on which JEROME remarks: *vitia in semetipsa finiuntur et pereunt, virtutes frugibus pullulant et redundant.*—R.]

[See *Textual Note* [4]]. Evidently a reason (γάρ) for what was said in ver. 11 is here introduced. BENGEL correctly indicates one part of it: *cur indefinite loquatur ver.* 11 *de operibus tenebrarum, quum fructum lucis ver.* 9 *definite descripserit*,* the other is at any rate, why he has expressed himself so briefly, generally, without qualification: ἐλέγχετε. It is incorrect to take γάρ=although (KOPPE), or to insert "although" (RUECKERT).—Τὰ γάρ κρυφῇ γινόμενα ὑπ' αὐτῶν, *i. e*, the children of disobedience (ver. 6), or "those doing the works of darkness" (WINER, p 134), can only be the works mentioned before, but more definitely characterized, in order to give a motive for the propriety of the requirement. Two elements now brought forward, constitute the characteristics of these works: κρυφῇ, "in secret," the main point standing first, and γινόμενα the second. The former marks the works as those to which ever clings something unknown, unrecognized, that may not appear, but will remain in concealment, ashamed of itself however bold; the latter, which is not =ποιούμενα, marks their involuntary, habitual character, not isolated but peculiar, while ὑπό expresses the guilt of those who do them. STIER aptly compares with our passage the profound description of the "rebels against the light" (מֹרְדֵי־אוֹר, Job xxiv. 13-16) and "the hidden things of darkness" (1 Cor. iv. 5; John iii. 20, 21); accordingly it is not to be referred exclusively to sins of debauchery, orgies [HOLZHAUSEN] and the like, although these are included; nor are we to understand only heathen sins of the most objectionable character. The works of darkness are stretched in a way that is universally and continuously valid; of such works "it is a shame even to speak" (vers. 3, 4). Evidently λέγειν is not merely narration, indifferent mention, but includes disapproving, rebuking mention as well. Paul requires an ἐλέγχειν without a λέγειν, "without one's taking all their dirt into his mouth" (*Berlb. Bible*), hence through the walk in word and work, so necessary on this account. Matt. v. 16; Phil. ii. 15.

[The main difficulty here is the question of connection. The views of BENGEL and KOPPE have been already suggested, and seem unsatisfactory. That of Braune (so STIER, PEILE, BLOOMFIELD, following THEOPHYLACT and ERASMUS) depends on the meaning of ἐλέγχετε, and since this seems to include verbal reproof, the restriction here is at least improbable. HARLESS and others connect the verse with "have no fellowship," but this identifies "works of darkness" and "things done in secret" almost too strongly, and as ELLICOTT suggests, gives undue prominence to the negative part of the command, while the phrase "but rather even," as well as the subsequent context makes "reprove" the leading thought. Taking ἐλέγχετε in its proper sense, and accepting the connection of this verse with it by γάρ, two views present themselves: that of ALFORD and others: "I mention not and you need not *speak* of these deeds—much less have any fellowship with them—your connection with them must be only that which the act of ἔλεγξις necessitates:" and that of MEYER, ELLICOTT, EADIE and others: "By all means reprove them, and there is the more need of it, for it is a shame even to speak of their secret sins." This is preferable, and the reproof of the works of darkness can take place without speaking of the more disgusting forms.—R.]

* [So ŒCUMENIUS, BAUMGARTEN, MATTHIES, but the Apostle was not apt to pause thus in his rebuke of sin; comp. Rom. i. 24-32; 1 Cor. vi. 9, 20; Gal. v. 19-21; 1 Tim. i. 9, 10.—R.]

Ver. 13. **But all things,** τὰ δὲ πάντα, denotes what is described in ver. 12. [So MEYER, ELLICOTT and others against RUECKERT and ALFORD, who take the phrase as of general application.—R.]—**Being reproved are made manifest by the light,** ἐλεγχόμενα ὑπὸ τοῦ φωτὸς φανεροῦται.—The light is God's, in His Word, in our conscience, character and conduct; the Christian persons falling into the back-ground behind the "light" which works in and out from them: this must work for its own sake, the efficiency does not enter with reference to our persons. Hence ὑπὸ τοῦ φωτός belongs both to ἐλεγχόμενα and φανεροῦται, as the position indicates also, since otherwise it would be repeated. In ἐλεγχόμενα the success of the ἐλέγχετε is set forth: you do not proceed ineffectually against the works of the children of disobedience, they are rebuked, struck, could not avoid it; your light has become a punishment for them. When this takes place, they are made manifest, what is "in secret" in them, becomes plain and its scandalousness is recognized; ἐλεγχόμενα is therefore a presupposition to φανεροῦται, not an extension of the predicate, but a limitation of the subject, τὰ πάντα. The context however suggests: the reproved acts or conditions become so to the possessor: to him they are now manifest as reproved, as reproved with right, and both reproved and manifested through the light of the truth in Jesus Christ and His people.

[It seems to be an unsatisfactory way out of the difficulty respecting the connection of ὑπὸ τοῦ φωτός, to join it to both the participle and the verb, and Braune is probably led to adopt it by his desire to maintain the thought of a tacit reproof. To join it with the participle (DE WETTE and others) is open to objection, for this gives the ἐλέγχειν a specification not in accordance with ver. 12, while, equally with Braune's view, it makes φῶς entirely too ethical, it being properly metaphorical in both clauses. The connection with the verb is more natural, "by the light" receiving emphasis from the order in the Greek. So MEYER, ELLICOTT, EADIE and most recent commentators. The participle is a predication of manner or time ("being reproved," or "when reproved") joined to the subject. See note at the close of the verse.—R.]

**For everything which is made manifest is light.**—Πᾶν τὸ φανερούμενον, following φανεροῦται, is passive (WINER, p. 242); all, that is illuminated, made manifest, φῶς ἐστιν, itself gives light, has the nature and efficiency of light. This very general proposition is limited by the character of the subject (BENGEL: *sermo de homine ipso*, ver. 14), to the persons who permit themselves to be reproved, who must permit themselves to be enlightened, in order to become manifest, shined upon and illuminated, and finally to become themselves light. BENGEL: *Antanaclasis; nam φανεροῦται est passivum; φανερούμενον medium, quod manifestari non refugit.* With STIER we may find here a recalling of: "once ye were darkness, now are ye light" (ver. 8), in order that in thankfulness and mildness towards those in the same condition in which they formerly were, they may apply the reproving and manifesting walk. Because what is shined upon, illuminated, itself shines, walk then so, that ye shame, reprove, convince those who are busy with the works of darkness, bringing them to the light; thus ye will best help them, as ye yourselves have been helped. The first part of this verse indicates the immediate result, the second the end of the ἐλεγχθῆναι or ἐλέγχειν. BENGEL: *Simul hinc patet facilitas* (STIER: because without speaking, hence without special knowledge of him who is to be reproved), *justitia* (STIER: because to the darkness the judging light is of right due), *salubritas* (STIER: because these can thus become light themselves) *elenchi.*—There is here no reference to the Gnostic light-theory of the Valentinians (BAUR), since these on the contrary wrested and distorted this passage after A. D. 150. Quite as untenable and inapt are those explanations which take φανερούμενον as active and πᾶν as the object—accusative (GROTIUS), or apply the ἐλέγχειν only to oral rebuke (MEYER, SCHENKEL and others), or regard the neuter as masculine merely (STORR and others).

[The view of MEYER is on the whole most satisfactory: "*But all things* (all those secret sins). *when they are reproved*, when that ἐλέγχετε has been effected on them, *are made manifest by the light*, by the light of Christian truth, which is efficient in your reproving, are brought to light as to their true moral quality, unveiled and made clear to the moral consciousness; *by the light*, I say, they are made manifest, *for*—in order to prove by a general proposition, that this cannot take place except by the light—*all that which is made manifest*, that is brought out of its concealment and brought to light in its true character, *is light*, has thus ceased to have the nature of darkness and is now of the *character of light*. The basis of this proof is the syllogism: "*Quod est in effectu* (φ ῶ ς ἐ σ τ ι), *id debet in causa* (ὑπὸ τοῦ φωτός)." This is equally simple and grammatical. It avoids the common mistake of referring the words too definitely. Commentators have run into much perplexity by not accepting occasional general propositions; comp. Gal. iii. 20. EADIE, following CALVIN and others, still maintains an active or middle sense, objecting to the passive that light does not always exercise this transforming influence. But this objection holds only against a too strictly ethical sense of φῶς, to which OLSHAUSEN, STIER, HODGE (and Braune) incline. Objectively taken, it is universally true: "*everything shone upon is* LIGHT." "Whether this tends to condemnation or otherwise, depends on the nature of the case, and the inward operation of the outwardly illuminating influence" (ALFORD, ELLICOTT). See the last named for a clear statement, and comp. HARLESS, EADIE, but especially MEYER *in loco*.—R.]

*The conclusion;* ver. 14.

Ver. 14. **Wherefore he saith** [δ ι ὸ λ έ γ ε ι; Braune: *It is said:* comp. iv. 8.—R.]—"Wherefore" refers to what precedes, and in accordance with the purport of the citation, to all that is said of the walk in the light, not merely to ver. 13 (SCHENKEL), but to vers. 8, 11 also, in order to render the exhortation more complete and forcible through a citation.* Hence λ έ γ ε ι is as in iv. 8. This quotation of the Apostle is not to be weakened, because no corresponding passage is found in the Old Testament, neither Isa. lx. 12 (CALVIN and most) nor xxvi. 19 (BEZA and others) nor lii. 1, 2, or ix. 1; it is not supposed that he cited a saying given directly to him (JEROME) or an apocryphal passage (MORUS and others). Certainly we should not accept a *lapsus memoriæ*, as though he wished to quote from canonical Scripture and happened on an apocryphal passage that could not be authenticated (MEYER, who compares 1 Cor. ii. 9), and quite as little a combination of the passages from Isaiah (SCHENKEL, who refers to Rom. ix. 33; xi. 8, 26).† Least of all is λέγει=φησί, they said, it is said (BORNEMANN). The most probable explanation is, that it is a quotation from a Christian hymn that had grown out of Isa. x. 1, 2. This is confirmed by vers. 18, 19, as well as by the significance of church hymns beside the Scripture. So THEODORET with reference to 1 Cor. xiv. 26; SEVERIANUS in Tischendorf (ed. 7, vol. ii. p. 457). BENGEL: *Simul videtur in mente habuisse formulam, quæ in festo buccinarum adhiberi solita fuerat. Et fortasse illo anni tempore scripsit hanc epistolam.* 1 Cor. v. 7. BLEEK *in loco* and *Stud. und Krit.* 1853, p. 331. STIER and others: A word of God is introduced as speaking to the Christian.

[There is one insuperable objection to these views of Braune, STIER, BENGEL, BORNEMANN, as well as to those of RHENFERD (one of our Lord's unrecorded sayings), WESLEY (the general tenor of Scripture), BARNES (who sees no reason for accepting a quotation at all), and that is Paul's use of λέγει, his formula of citation from the *Old Testament;* especially in conjunction with διό. If we accept a Christian hymn based on the passage in Isaiah the difficulty is not removed, but the way opened for the multiplication of difficulties. If God speaks, (as Braune implies) through a paraphrase in the form of a Christian hymn, much more does he speak, when His Apostle interprets or applies His written word. The best solution is that of ALFORD:

* [ALFORD explains: "Seeing that everything that is made manifest becomes light—is shone upon by the detecting light of Christ—objectively—it only remains that the man should be shone upon *inwardly* by the same Christ revealed in his awakened heart. We have then in Scripture an exhortation to that effect."—R.]

† [The German has an obvious typographical error. It reads *Johanneischen Stellen*, passages from John. SCHENKEL really defends the view, "that the Apostle has freely combined several Scriptural passages in accordance with their sense and from memory," suggesting Isa. lii. 1; xxvi. 19; lx. 1. This view is favored though not definitely adopted by HODGE and EADIE. Undoubtedly, the Apostle combines passages (Rom. ix. 33; xi. 8, 26), but not so loosely. We may defend either a quotation according to the sense, or a literal combination, not both, especially in connection with the notion of free quotation from memory. Paul interpreted the Scriptures, whose words he well knew; a *lapsus memoriæ* was scarcely possible in his case as a man, much less as an inspired man.—R.]

"In the first place, by the introduction of ὁ Χριστός, it is manifestly *a paraphrase, not an exact citation.* The Apostle cites, and had a perfect right to cite, the language of prophecy: and that he is here doing so, the bare word '*Christ*' shows us beyond dispute. I insist upon this, that it may be plainly shown to be no shift in a difficulty, no hypothesis among hypotheses—but the *necessary* inference from the form of the citation. This being so—of what passage of the Old Testament is this a paraphrase? I answer of Isa. lx. 1, 2. There, the Church is set forth as being in a state of darkness and of death (comp. lix. 10), and is exhorted to awake, and become light, for that her light is come, and the glory of Jehovah has arisen upon her. Where need we go further for that of which we are in search?" —The view of ELLICOTT is similar: "St. Paul, speaking under the Inspiration of the Holy Spirit, is expressing in a condensed and summary form the spiritual meaning of the passage." He thinks the prophet's immediate words supply in substance the first part of the quotation, while the latter part is the spiritual application of the remainder of the verse, and of the general tenor of the prophecy. ALFORD'S view is safe, and rests on the Lord's own saying: "Search the Scriptures, they are they which testify of me" (John v. 39).—R.]

**Up! thou who sleepest**, ἔγειρε ὁ καθεύδων.—[The word ἔγειρε is not the active for the middle but is the common form of rousing (FRITZSCHE).—R.]—This can be addressed only to the Christian (Rom. xiii. 11, 12), who at God's call opens his eyes; the Lord has come to him, awakened him, so that he, awake and alive, looks about him. [It is more correct to regard this as addressed to those who are not yet Christians, but about to become so through the effectual call of God.—This is perhaps Braune's view, see *Doctr. Note* 3.—R.] The beginning of knowledge is thus denoted. Still there is yet a struggle with sleep; the eyes close again; the light of day dazzles.—**And arise from the dead**, καὶ ἀνάστα ἐκ τῶν νεκρῶν, is the advance to rising from the couch, standing up and preparing for work. Ἀναστῆναι ἐπὶ ἔργον ἐγερθῆναι ἐξ ὕπνου. The sleeper is inactive, as one who is dead.—The promise incites: **and Christ shall shine upon thee**, καὶ ἐπιφαύσει σοι ὁ Χριστός.—The figure is that of the morning, when day breaks and man meets the sun and daylight. Christ is the light, makes the day that shines upon and enlightens us, in order that we may become light for others, as the context requires. On the forms ἀναστα and ἐπιφαύσει see WINER, pp. 76, 85.

[The question of the connection of this verse deserves some further attention. Braune apparently follows STIER, who thinks the quotation is introduced to exhort: "Become light, that ye may be able to convict others," which accords with his view of silent reproof. But this seems to be stepping aside from the more obvious sense. HODGE takes it as a confirmation of the assertion of the preceding verse: everything made manifest is light. This is true, but scarcely a sufficient reason for its introduction. MEYER paraphrases διό thus: Because the reproof is so necessary, as I have indicated in ver. 12, and so wholesome in its effects as shown in ver. 13, *therefore, etc.*, and then says that the call of God confirms the *necessity* of the reproof, and the promise: "Christ shall shine upon thee," supports the *wholesome influence of the light*, under which the reproof places them. This seems preferable. So that the purpose of the Apostle is to show by a paraphrase from the Scriptures that the effect of the light is such, and that therefore Christians should reprove in order that others may become light through the illumination here promised. In general what is made manifest is light (ver. 15), but Christ's shining makes new light in a spiritual sense. Let your light shine, so as to reprove, in the hope that Christ will shine on the convicted heart. This seems to be the view of ALFORD, and is approached by ERASMUS and RUECKERT.—R.]

What JEROME says is interesting: *scio me audisse quendam de hoc loco in ecclesiam disputantem—testimonium hoc, inquit, ad Adam dicitur in loco calvariæ sepultum, ubi crucifixus est dominus,—illo ergo tempore quo crucifixus dominus super ejus pendebat sepulchrum, hæc prophetia completa est:* surge, Adam, qui dormis et exsurge a mortuis et *non ut legimus* ἐπιφαύσει σοι Χριστός, *i. e.*, orietur tibi Christus, *sed* ἐπιφαύσει, *i. e.*, contingent te Christus, *quia videlicet tactu sanguinis ipsius et corporis dependentis vivificetur atque consurgat.*

### DOCTRINAL AND ETHICAL.

1. One of the weightiest points in the formation of the Christian life is the *conversation* and intercourse with others, the *social life.* Here foresight and circumspection are necessary. Sociality is a gift and has a task, and both of these are twofold: Every one has both for himself and others. *For himself*, that he does not suffer detriment through the idle, flat, empty, useless character of the same. There may enter a somnolence of the awakened Christian impulse and life, of moral endeavor, of zeal in sanctification, through dissipation, gossipping, amusement and jesting, or excitement of carnal zeal, dainty, proud and high-flown character, onesidedness and injustice in opinion and conduct. *For others*, that he promotes their advancement, and in the interchange of sentiment and experience elevates, confirms, clarifies, rectifies, and complements them. Do not enter into more intimate intercourse with him, who cannot and will not be to you what you ought to be to him, or guard against his influence over you, taking heed if you cannot alter him, that you do not at all events conform him in his character. You should not withdraw yourself from others, but so act that you are not withdrawn from God, who has drawn you to Himself. What He has given you hold fast, so that no one deprives you of it. Do not let what He has planted in you be rooted up by the words of others. Let the fruit of His light ripen, and do not allow it to be eaten up by the worms of the world's culture.

2. Consider the two in connection: *proving* what is God's will, and *reproving* your neighbor. The former comes first, the latter is second. The former requires care in intercourse with God through His word, personal growth in His grace and knowledge, intimacy with Him, walk-

ing in His light, as His child. The latter, on the other hand, that you become for your neighbor a conscience outside of and beside him, as your own conscience has borne witness to yourself, or that like Sarah you speak silently in your conduct (1 Pet. iii. 1); very little depends on words, at least on many of them, only on apt ones, without scolding; be free and frank, true in love and lovely in truth (iv. 15). He who is not yet your brother, may and ought to become so; but you should no longer be to him what you were before Christ won you: a companion in his evil works and words.

3. In the concluding verse the grace of God is rendered strongly prominent, but in such a way as to indicate that it is in vain, if man's own act is not also present and he does not lift himself up by applying the power brought nigh and proffered him, his own strength increasing with the use of the power from on high which he appropriates. If he when awakened does not open his eyes and wake up, if when called he does not get up from his couch, he does not reach Christ's light or the walk in the day; this however takes place only in consequence of the initiative of Divine and imparted power.*

4. Finally it may be said, that as Paul immediately afterwards speaks of psalms and hymns and spiritual songs (ver. 19), so he here places on an equality with canonical Scripture the Christian hymn which grows out of God's word. Hence the importance of church hymnology. By this too we must test every hymn and hymn-book, that nothing apocryphal or heretical throws what is Scriptural into the back-ground, but that the truly Christian element of the hymn animates, furthers and subserves the Scriptures in the congregation, in the public service and in the household. [While compelled to object to the premise here laid down for the reason stated in the additional *Exeg. Notes* on ver. 14, we may well approve of the influence, which is valid on other grounds than the supposed citation of a Christian hymn. See further *Doctr. Notes* on the next section.—R.]

HOMILETICAL AND PRACTICAL.

Comp. the *Doctr. Notes.*

You should not fly from men, yet you should not become their admiring slave, nor esteem yourself less than God has esteemed you, nor forsake His truth to accept human errors. Society has her assemblies generally in the evening; how much is there spoken in the artificial life of crowded halls resounding with human voices, with spirit and wit (but generally without this), confidently and with the approval of the mass. But as you go home in the quiet night, under the twinkling light of the stars or the shining of the moon, test what you have heard: Can you still highly estimate it? Have you not oftenest felt its emptiness with inward sadness? You have often thought, I would have got more by staying at home and chatting with my wife and children or with some friend! How then if you test it by God's word, by Christ's life? Prove all thereby!—Let no one say to you: You must believe without examining. But do not let any say of you, that you do so.—The world may ask: what is useful? what is admirable? what is lovely? what is customary? do you only ask: what is right and well-pleasing to the Lord?—Harless very properly says: Punishment is light! But STIER is quite as correct in saying; Light is punishment!—It is good to be convinced by *the light,* whether it breaks forth from the walk and word of a friend or a foe. To change one's way on account of the light is well, but when it comes from an opponent, then to do so is deserving of praise. It really amounts to nothing to accept a rebuke out of fear or gratitude, or any spirit of calculation: it is however a special gift of God, when one receives and is affected by the primitive element of the light, altogether irrespective of the man who bears the light, be he dear, influential, powerful or not. For only thus does the recipient become himself light.—Cherish a spirit of independence not merely *against others* for the truth, but also for others against falsehood; it is the latter that especially needs nurture.—Christ will enlighten thee here, but glorify thee hereafter, if indeed you are really an *enlightened Christian* and not merely a man *shone upon!*

STARKE:—It is an old trick of Satan's to patch up the worst vices with the form of virtue and give them a free pass in the world under a false name. Craftiness is termed prudence, extravagance generosity, vindictiveness high-spiritedness, arrogance neatness, lechery politeness, avarice economy, etc.—True Christians are not credulous, silly and unreasonable people, but lights in the Lord, on the contrary the godless are such, 1 Thess. v. 5.—Where goodness, righteousness and truth cannot be met with, the Spirit of God certainly does not dwell.—Love and goodness must not go so far as to make justice and truth suffer: when these virtues, united together, kiss each other, all goes right. Christian reproof is one of the most excellent obligations of love; from its omission the lack of love and fidelity may certainly be perceived.—As much wickedness is done by the godless in secret, never coming to light; so on the other hand much good is done by the pious, that might be mentioned with praise, yet is concealed out of humility. For them it suffices that God and their own hearts know of it.

RIEGER:—One of the greatest vexations, and at the same time a correct judgment, respecting the world is, that she has so many people who talk to please her and adorn her filthiness. But all these vain words will not cover her from the wrath of God. *Goodness* is the imitator of God in His love, by means of which we avoid anger, hatred, tumult, blasphemy, avarice. *Righteousness* prevents stealing, the unmerciful shutting of the hand against the needy, and avarice which like a weight of lead sinks one into darkness. *Truth* shuns lies, shameful words and buffooneries, foul talk, vain and seductive discourse.

* [Eadie compares the command of ver. 14 to "that given by our Lord to the man with the withered hand—'Stretch it forth.' The man might have objected and said, 'Could I obey thee in this, I would not have troubled thee. Why mock me with my infirmity, and bid me do the very thing I cannot?' But the man did not so perplex himself; and Christ, in exciting the desire to obey, imparted the power to obey." If every man would understand the philosophy of waking up before he gets up, what a world of sleepers we would have!—R.]

Thus Christian prudence is attained, which never seeks to go as far as it can without sin, but after the manner of well-behaved children, is ever concerned to meet God's approval.

HEUBNER:—*With vain words, i. e.*, deceiving talk, as though these vices belonged to things indifferent. This evil, perverted moral sense begets unbelief of morally strict Christianity and thus brings down God's wrath.—The Christian is an interested participant and yet separate and peculiar.—*On the Epistle for the third Sunday in Lent;* vers. 1–9. *The Divine walk of the Christian.* 1. Description. *a*) In general: Imitation of God, ver. 1; *b*) in particular: holy love (ver. 2) and pure, spotless life (vers. 3, 4). 2. Its necessity. *a*. For our own salvation; for without such walk we have no part in the kingdom of God and of Christ (ver. 5); *b*) for the salvation of others: for only such a walk can reprove the evil, corrupt principles of the world, and make out of unbelievers, children of wrath, believers, children of grace. What would the world be without Enochs? (ver. 6). 3. Means. *a*) Separate yourself from the company of the ungodly, leave the path of sinners, else you cannot walk godly (ver. 7). *b*) Accept the light of grace, that your darkness may be enlightened (ver. 8). *c*) Use the light however as you receive it, beginning with God's help to exercise your spiritual strength.—*The imitation of God, to which the Christian is obligated.* 1. In what it consists: *a*) In accepting the temper, which makes us like to Him as children to a Father (ver. 1); *b*) especially in love and holiness (vers. 2-4). 2. What makes this our duty: *a*) Our Christian calling, which should distinguish us from idolaters (ver. 5); *b*) our happiness, our freedom from the wrath of God (ver. 6). 3. What strengthens us thereto: *a*) Holding to the Church and accepting the light of the Word (vers. 7, 8); *b*) seeking the Spirit of God.—The spirit of Christian investigation is nothing else than Christian conscientiousness, with this rule: what pleases God? What pleases man is a matter of indifference.—The Christian is in duty bound to speak earnestly and decidedly against evil; he dare not be silent, where he ought to speak, still less approve with the men-pleasing spirit of the worldly wise.—The ground of this earnestness and reproof is the shamefulness of the world's vices.—What is made manifest through rebuke—is generally brought out of the darkness, in which shameless vice conceals itself, and placed in the light, so that it is thus evident to all as wicked. This is indeed the main matter.—All that is made manifest through reproof, so that the man is really made conscious of his sins,—is *thereby* overcome. This is the only path by which the Divine light rises within man in the place of darkness.—One must be roused, shaken, in order to be brought to consciousness. Out of the sleep of sin, in which he is not aware of the evil, he must be awakened, in order then to see what is in him.

PASSAVANT:—It is indeed an unhappy thing to be a companion of sinners, in follies and vices, in which one becomes a means of annoyance, corruption and distress to another, only to be companion in his shame and pain, hereafter in the despair of the Judgment Day.

STIER:—Words awaken lust, lust bears sin, this is the irresistible and dangerous course of *deceit*, against the *first* appearance of which in *words* we cannot too carefully guard ourselves. —Where there is unbelief, there is also the wrath of God!—Have nothing in common with them, for you are unwilling to have this wrath in common with them!—Not reproving is equivalent to having fellowship.—Darkness can become light only by means of a shining light, and the walk in the light is of itself able to judge and transform the darkness.—Let yourself be enlightened, that you may live, and become alive that the light may ever more fully shine on you!

GENZKEN (*Preparatory Discourse*): *Jesus* my *consolation* (ver. 2), my *love* (vers. 1, 2), my *Shield* (vers. 3–7) and great Reward (vers. 8, 9).

*On the Epistle for the third Sunday in Lent* (Eph. v. 1-9):—KAPFF:—What belongs to the walk in the light? 1. Fellowship with God in Christ; 2. Laying off all ungodly doings; 3. Living according to God's good pleasure (justification, repentance, sanctification).—RAUTENBERG: *That is real love, which goes even unto death for the brethren.* 1) It covers a multitude of sins; 2) is the fulfilment of the law; 3) is well-pleasing to God; 4) brings blessedness.—*How important are the sufferings of Christ for our sanctification!* The Holy Ghost works in us through them 1) powerful, sacred shame, 2) pure, self-sacrificing love.—*The sacrifice of Christ a sweet-smelling savor to God* —on account of the love 1) which brought it; 2) which makes room for it; 3) which is awakened by it.—THYM: The eternal love, 1) in its archetype, 2) its express image, 3) its copy.

[HODGE:—Ver. 6. It is not only among the heathen, but among the mass of men in all ages and nations, a common thing to extenuate the particular sins to which the Apostle here refers. It is urged that they have their origin in the very constitution of our nature; that they are not malignant; that they may co-exist with amiable tempers; and that they are not hurtful to others; that no one is the worse for them, if no one knows them, *etc.* Paul cautions his readers in every age of the Church not to be deceived by such vain words.—Ver. 10. Christ is here recognized as the Lord of the conscience, whose will is to us the ultimate standard of right and wrong. It is thus that the sacred writers show that Christ was their God—not merely the God of their theology, but of their religion.—Ver. 13. According to the Apostle, the relation between truth and holiness is analogous to that between light and vision. Light cannot create the eye, or give to a blind eye the power of vision; but it is essential to its exercise. Wherever it penetrates it dissipates darkness, and brings every thing to view, and causes it to produce its appropriate effect. So truth cannot regenerate, or impart the principle of spiritual life; but it is essential to all holy exercises; and wherever the truth penetrates, it dissipates the clouds of error, and brings every thing to view, so that when spiritually discerned it produces its proper effect on the soul.—Ver. 14. The light which Christ sheds around Him has power to awake the sleeping dead.—R.]

*d. Exhortation to a pure walk, with careful consideration of the Christian position.*

(Chap. V. 15–21.)

15 See then that [how] ye walk circumspectly [strictly], not as fools [unwise men],
16 but as wise, Redeeming the time [Buying up the opportunity], because the days
17 are evil. Wherefore be ye not unwise [on this account do not become senseless],
18 but understanding[1] what the will of the Lord *is*. And be not drunk [made drunk]
with wine, wherein is excess [or dissoluteness]; but be filled with [in] the Spirit;
19 Speaking to yourselves [one another] in[2] psalms and hymns and spiritual songs,
20 singing and making melody in your heart to the Lord; Giving thanks always for
all things unto [to] God and the Father in the name of our Lord Jesus Christ;
21 Submitting yourselves one to another in the fear of God [Christ].[3]

## TEXTUAL AND GRAMMATICAL.

[1] Ver. 17.—[The reading of the *Rec.* (σ υ ν ι έ ν τ ε ς) is supported by D.[3] K. L., nearly all cursives, many fathers and good versions (Tischendorf, Ellicott and most); συνίοντες is found in D.[1] F. G., some versions (Harless, Meyer, Alford, earliest editions); the imperative: συνίετε has good support (א. A. B., 6 cursives, Chrysostom, Jerome), accepted by Lachmann and Alford (ed. 4). The last appears to be a correction, the participle being *lectio difficilior*, so that of the two participial readings the first is to be preferred on external grounds.—R.]

[2] Ver. 19.—[Lachmann and Alford insert ἐν in brackets before ψ α λ μ ο ῖ ς, but as it is found only in B., 5 cursives, some versions, and could so readily enter into an explanatory gloss, it is generally rejected.—Both editors bracket π ν ε υ μ α τ ι κ α ῖ ς on much the same authority, doubting it as a probable interpolation from Col. iii. 16; but it might readily be omitted in a few cases from *homœteleuton* (Meyer).—Ταῖς καρδίαις, instead of τ ῇ κ α ρ δ ί ᾳ (*Rec.* א.[1] B. K. L.) is found in א.[3] A. D. F., but is rejected by Tischendorf, Ellicott, Alford and most, as an emendation derived from Col. iii. 16.—R.]

[3] Ver. 21.—[The reading of the *Rec.* (θεοῦ) has no uncial support; while Χ ρ ι σ τ ο ῦ is found in nearly all MSS., and accepted by all recent editors.—R.]

## EXEGETICAL AND CRITICAL.

*The exhortation;* vers. 15, 16. Ver. 15. **See then** [or **take heed**].—Β λ έ π ε τ ε with ἵνα (1 Cor. xvi. 10; 2 John 8), with the accusative (Phil. iii. 2; Col. iv. 17), here as in 1 Cor. iii. 10 with πῶς. *Sollicitudo etiam* MODUM *spectat* (Bengel). They are enjoined to take heed, and because (ο ὖ ν) as the comprehensive quotation (ver. 14) says, they are awake, have arisen, been enlightened by Christ, to a walk such as has been spoken of (ver. 1: "beloved children," ver. 3: "as becometh saints," ver. 8: "as children of the light"). Calvin is therefore too limited: *Si aliorum discutere tenebras fideles debent fulgure suo, quanto minus cæcutire debent in proprio vitæ instituto*; Meyer limits it also to vers. 10, 11.*

**How ye walk strictly** [π ῶ ς ἀ κ ρ ι β ῶ ς π ε ρ ι π α τ ε ῖ τ ε].—According to the context π ῶ ς is to be confined precisely to the ἀ κ ρ ι β ῶ ς *exacte ad voluntatem divinam* (Luther's rendering: *vorsichtlich* [so E. V.: circumspectly] is not sufficient); marking with the indicative that it is not first to be considered how this shall be taken hold of, but that it already exists in its best feature, the walk being an actual fact (Winer, p. 282). [Alford: "Take heed not only that your walk be exact, strict, but also of *what sort* that strictness is—not only that you have a rule and *keep to it*, but that that rule be the best one." The indicative is not used for the subjunctive or the future; comp. Ellicott *in loco* and *Fritzschiorum Opuscula*, pp. 208 f, note.—R.]

* [Eadie follows Calvin, Hodge follows Meyer, as respects ο ὖ ν, while Alford and Ellicott take the particle as resumptive from the περιπατεῖτε in ver. 8, and what followed it there. This is preferable unless the extended view of Braune be accepted.—R.]

**Not as unwise men, but as wise** [μὴ ὡς ἄ σ ο φ ο ι ἀ λ λ' ὡ ς σ ο φ ο ί].—"As," marking as in i. 8 the actual condition, and not comparative (*Vulgate: quasi*, is apt), designates the subject referred to in "take heed," "walk," as "wise." Hence "not as unwise" (Bengel: *qui præter propter viam ambulant*), which is placed first for emphasis, denotes a subjective notion, which is inadmissible and unexpected as regards Christians. Winer, pp. 442, 567. Paul means Christians, in their walk, as indeed σοφός points to practice, walk, in works and evidences corresponding to the aim (i. 8; Jas. iii. 13), and not philosophers (Grotius), whom he ironically terms ἀσόφους.

Ver. 16. **Buying up the opportunity,** ἐ ξ α γ ο ρ α ζ ό μ ε ν ο ι τ ὸ ν κ α ι ρ ό ν.—This describes the "wise" in their walk. The phrase (Col. iv. 5) recalls Dan. ii. 8 (LXX.: οἶδα ἐγὼ ὅτι καιρὸν ὑμεῖς ἐξαγοράζετε). Nebuchadnezzar says to the Chaldeans, his servants, plainly, that they only want to gain time. Here however *sapienta et ἀκρίβεια præcipitur, non ignavia* (Bengel). In distinction from the passage in Daniel, the article and the middle form are to be noticed. The right point of time, the appropriate time is the object of the ἐξαγοράζειν, the middle denotes that it is to be done *for themselves*, while the preposition ἐ ξ designates the complete entire character of the verb. Christians then should not allow τ ὸ ν κ α ι ρ ό ν, to escape them, should seize the opportunity (χαιρός), though it costs them something in self-denial, after they have properly looked at it, like a skilful merchant, and then redeeming it out of the possession of sin, of slothfulness and pleasure, of the flesh and of darkness, should make it their own and use it for Christian walk. The time is then not to be taken as it is, nor is LUTHER correct: "adapt yourselves to the time." Nor is it, to wait prudently and to temporize (BENGEL), or merely, to use for the ἐλέγχειν (FLATT, HARLESS).

[In regard to this phrase, we may accept as established: 1. That καιρόν means opportunity, not time, hence that the E. V. conveys a wrong impression. 2. That all special references to those *from whom* the purchase is made (bad men, BENGEL; the devil, CALVIN), or to the *price* paid (all things, CHRYSOSTOM and others), are irrelevant and unwarranted. The participle is one of manner, the ἐξ is referred by ELLICOTT and ALFORD to the collecting *out of*, the buying up, "calling your times of good out of a land where there are few such flowers." The exact sense then is: improve the opportunities which occur, looking out for them as a merchant, because the days are evil, and opportunities are rare; not as is often supposed: Be diligent in the use of time, because the days are few. The reference to Gen. xlvii. 9 will not justify this twisting of the next clause.—R.]

**Because the days are evil,** ὅτι αἱ ἡμέραι πονηραί εἰσιν.—See Gen. xlvii. 9; 2 Tim. iii. 1. The days, the present period of life, the αἰὼν οὗτος, in which sin has her glory (OLSHAUSEN), are therefore "evil" on account of sin, creating hindrances and temptations, leading even to apostasy; hence not simply full of difficulties, unfavorable circumstances (RUECKERT).

Ver. 17. *The first point of view as respects the wise: the will of God.* **On this account,** διὰ τοῦτο, refers to vers. 15, 16, not merely as [OECUMENIUS, RUECKERT, DE WETTE, OLSHAUSEN] BLEEK and others think, to the reason ("the days are evil") appended to the designation of the "wise."

**Become not senseless but understanding,** μὴ γίνεσθη ἄφρονες, ἀλλὰ συνιέντες.—This can be said to those who are wise. For ἄφρον is *qui mente non recte utitur* (TITTMANN, *Syn.* I. p. 143), and is joined with νήπιος in Rom. ii. 20. They should not *become* this; they *are* not yet so, since they are "wise." [This is to be maintained against ALFORD, who as usual objects to rendering γίνεσθε, *become.*—R.] The antithesis ("but") is συνιέντες, "understanding" they should become discerning, and that is more than γινώσκοντες. A definite object is treated of, which in every case must be clear to the "wise," but which can however easily remain not understood:

**What the will of the Lord is,** τί τὸ θέλημα τοῦ κυρίου, *i. e.*, of Christ.—*Non solum universo, sed certo loco, tempore, etc.* (BENGEL).* This will reaching to what is least and most peculiar, is the object of the insight of the wise; the further he advances, the less is any thing to him *merely permissible;* everything becomes for him a precept and will from above. Acts xxi. 15.

Ver. 18. *The second point of view: Their own person, its inspiration.* **And be not made drunk with wine,** καὶ μὴ μεθύσκεσθε οἴνῳ.—"And" adds a second point to the first; it is not then=in particular (MEYER), as though it introduced a single vice, for which there is no occasion given by the context, since no general pleasure has been spoken of, the species of which could be named.—[The view of MEYER is accepted by most recent English and American commentators. The objection of Braune is not valid, it would seem; for the thought of pleasure does not enter in this clause either. The general notion is "not senseless, but understanding," and the special and emphatic subordinate thought is "not being drunk," a connection which is obvious enough. The state of drunkenness is viewed not as a sensual pleasure, but as a "senseless" condition. Comp. HODGE.—R.] The precept, after the reference to the will of God and from its position in antithesis to what follows, contains in the special a reference to the general as is allowed and required by the Scriptural view. Luke i. 15; xxi. 34; 1 Thess. v. 6-8; 2 Tim. iv. 5; 1 Pet. i. 13; iv. 7; v. 8. So "the wine of the wrath" (Rev. xiv. 8, 10; xviii. 3; xix. 15). The next clause points the same way.*

**Wherein is excess,** ἐν ᾧ ἐστὶν ἀσωτία.—Ἐν ᾧ refers to the μεθύσκεσθε οἴνῳ;† in this there inheres as on a ground the fact (ἐστίν), which at the same time breaks out as a consequence. Ἀσωτία, the character of an ἄσωτος (ἄσωτος from σόω, σώζω), "past redemption" (Tit. i. 6; 1 Pet. iv. 4), in which one's own character is corrupted (φθείρεσθαι, iv. 22). TITTMANN, *Syn.* I. p. 152 f. [Comp. TRENCH, § XVI. The N. T. sense: *dissoluteness, profligacy*, seems to have arisen from the more common meaning of ἄσωτος: one who does not know how to save, *i. e.*, a spendthrift.—R.] Hence Luther is incorrect in rendering it merely: *unordentlich Wesen.* JEROME incorrectly limits it to lascivious excesses; KOPPE, DE WETTE and others to excess at the *Agapæ*, which are not suggested as in 1 Cor. xi. 21; MEYER and [most] others to the vice of drunkenness.

**But be filled in the Spirit** [ἀλλὰ πληροῦσθε ἐν πνεύματι].—The antithesis is strongly marked (ἀλλά) and is to be found in πληροῦσθε, which stands first, as did μεθύσκεσθε, not in οἴνῳ and πνεύματι. [HODGE (with others) overlooks this in remarking: "To the Christian, therefore, the source of strength and joy is not wine, but the blessed Spirit of God."—R.] The imperative: Be filled! is not to be taken merely as καταλλάγητε τῷ θεῷ (2 Cor. v. 20), because it can be refused (Acts vii. 51) as well

* [The E. V. with its order: "what the will of the Lord is," suggests this definite knowledge in special circumstances, hence to alter it, as some propose, to: "what is the will of the Lord," would be not only unnecessary, but unfortunate.—R.]

* [It is to be feared that the rising from the special to the general renders too indefinite the very important precept of the Apostle. We may well hold fast to the plain literal meaning: "do not be made drunk with wine," this is an injunction deserving all the prominence it receives, even if no general sense be appended.—R.]

† [In which vice, in the becoming drunk (MEYER, ALFORD and most), not in the wine, the use of which is not forbidden (comp. 1 Tim. v. 23; Col. ii. 16, 20–23), although our passage proves that it was intoxicating.—R.]

as requested (Luke xi. 13), but because Christians in the strength of God have to be faithful and to show zeal, in order to increase and become complete; much then depends on themselves. This is an entirely different becoming full from being "drunk with wine." The qualification: ἐν πνεύματι, and not πνεύματι, is not an antithesis to οἴνῳ, but designates in and upon what the becoming full takes place, not in flesh and blood, but in the spirit of man, his better part. It is not instrumental, which cannot be established by i. 24; Phil. iv. 19, as MEYER supposes, nor does it refer to the Holy Spirit (most expositors down to BLEEK) or to our spirit and God's Spirit. That we should be filled with the Holy Ghost is indicated by the context, but not by ἐν πνεύματι. [The instrumental sense of ἐν, if accepted, must not exclude the more usual meaning: "with and in the Spirit" (EADIE, ELLICOTT). Here also, as in iv. 23, the exact sense of πνεύματι, in view of the preposition chosen, is neither the human spirit (Braune), nor the Personal Holy Spirit, but the human spirit as acted upon by the Holy Spirit (ALFORD and others). Comp. *Romans*, p. 235.—R.] FLACIUS: *præclara ebrietas, quæ sobrietatem mentis operatur!* Comp. Ps. xxxvi. 8-10; Acts ii. 15-18.

*Closer definition of becoming full in spirit* [or *the Spirit*]; vers. 19-21. *a. Social Song;* ver. 19 *a.* *b. Singing in private;* ver. 19 *b.* *c. Continual thankfulness;* ver. 20. *d. Proper conduct in one's position;* ver. 21.

Ver. 19 *a.* **Speaking to one another,** λαλοῦντες ἑαυτοῖς.—The participle denotes the most immediate expression of this being filled in spirit by the Holy Spirit, and this result as an exercise re-acts as a means for furthering the fulness. *Spiritus facit fideles* DISERTOS (BENGEL). Ἑαυτοῖς, as in iv. 32; Col. iii. 16, is=ἀλλήλοις. In intercourse, in social circles, they return, in every case, to this point of speaking as is here described. [The reference to both social intercourse and public assemblies is now usually accepted. The reciprocal action on their hearts rather than the antiphonal method with their lips, is implied in the reflexive pronoun.—R.] It is not then=*meditantes vobiscum* (MORUS). The double sense: from inward impulse, with one another (STIER), is inadmissible, as well as the limitation to public assemblies for worship (OLSHAUSEN).

**In psalms and hymns and spiritual songs,** ψαλμοῖς καὶ ὕμνοις καὶ ᾠδαῖς πνευματικαῖς.—LUTHER is incorrect: by Psalms. Since ψαλμός is something historical (Luke xx. 42; xxiv. 44; Acts i. 20; xiii. 33), the word should here retain the meaning of Old Testament Psalms, which were well-known and had been accepted in the public service (*Apost. Constitutions,* II. 57, 5: τοὺς τοῦ Δαβὶδ ψαλλέτω ὕμνους); ὕμνος is a song of praise, according to the context (ver. 19: "to the Lord") and to history (PLINY in GIESELER, *Kirchengeschichte*, I. 1, p. 136: *Carmenque Christo quasi Deo dicere secum invicem*), to Christ, hence more strictly *Christian* hymns, songs of Jesus; ᾠδαὶ πνευματικαί are spiritual songs in general, productions of the Holy Ghost in the department of poetry as regards form, out of the Christian life as regards substance, distinguished from hymns as the spiritual song is distinguished from a song for the church and congregation, by being more general as regards matter and intended more for individual needs and private use. STIER hits it very nearly with his threefold distinction: Scriptural, congregational, private. It is improper to take the first as applicable to Jewish Christians, the second to Gentile Christians, and the third as referring to an expression understood by every one alike (HARLESS) or the last as the *genus*, the first as a hymn with musical accompaniment, the other as a song of praise, improvised, when it is true that out of the head as well as out of the heart only that which is known can be used, or that the heaping of terms is due to the lively and urgent discourse (MEYER and others), since he is not speaking of the day of Pentecost or of the gift of tongues (Acts ii. 4; x. 46; xix. 6; 1 Cor. xiv. 15, 26) but of the orderly and regular course of things in the church; nor should all distinctions be rejected (RUECKERT).* "Spiritual" belongs to the undefined "songs," not to "psalms and hymns" (STIER), which are confessedly productions of the Holy Ghost; the word means precisely this however, and not merely that Christian thoughts and feelings find expression therein (BAUMGARTEN-CRUSIUS). Evidently the Apostle marks that Christians should interweave such into their conversation, often passing in joyous mood into united song, not however that such only should be recited, uninterruptedly said or sung.

Ver. 19 *b. Singing in private.* **Singing and making melody in your heart to the Lord.**—Joined as a co-ordinate clause without a connecting particle. The participle ᾄδοντες καὶ ψάλλοντες designate what is related, singing, the former in melody, the latter in recitative; the added phrase (ἐν τῇ καρδίᾳ ὑμῶν) however marks something different, that is done alone and inwardly. [So HARLESS, MEYER, OLSHAUSEN, ALFORD, ELLICOTT and others. HODGE favors what was once the common view: that the clause is subordinate, defining the mode or moral quality of the preceding one. But HARLESS has shown that such a view is incompatible with the presence of ὑμῶν, and few grammatical commentators have since differed from him.—R.] Here the social song re-echoes, here also is its ground and source. This is even stronger: not merely when excited in the company of others, to become joyously full of the Spirit, but to be that when alone also in disposition and desire "to the Lord" (τῷ κυρίῳ). Acts ii. 47; Jas. v. 13.

Ver. 20. *Continual thankfulness.* **Giving thanks always for all things,** εὐχαρισ-

* [While rigorous distinctions are not to be insisted upon, we may accept in the main the view of Braune. ELLICOTT: "Much curious information will be found in the article, '*Hymni a Christianis decantandi,*' in Deyling, *Obs.* No. 44, Vol. III., p. 430 sq.: for authorities, see Fabricius, *Bibliogr. Antiq.* XI. 13, and for specimens of the ancient ὕμνοι, *ibid.*, *Bibl. Græca*, Book V. I. 24." In the fourth volume of TISCHENDORF'S *Monumenta Sac. Ined.*, some hymns are found at the close of the Psalter, but the MSS. is incomplete, leaving us with a hymn incomplete.—In the face of such testimony there can be no question that the early church was not confined to the Old Testament Psalms.—R.]

τοῦντες πάντοτε ὑπὲρ πάντων.—Thus by the side of the joy is described that circumspect sobriety and thoughtfulness, which at all times and in all things sees and feels God's gracious hand, not merely singing, in public and private, in order to ask, but giving thanks uninterruptedly through the whole life. This is no popular, hyperbolical expression (MEYER); it is an established injunction of the Apostle (vi. 18; Col. iii. 17; iv. 2; 1 Thess. v. 19; Rom. xii. 12). Sufferings are included also (CHRYSOSTOM and others). [HODGE follows MEYER, in needlessly limiting πάντα to blessedness.—R.] It is indeed so difficult, that it is possible only for him who has God in Christ. Hence:

**To God and the Father in the name of our Lord Jesus Christ** [ἐν ὀνόματι τοῦ κυρίου ἡμῶν Ἰησοῦ Χριστοῦ τῷ θεῷ καὶ πατρί].—"In the name" designates the manifested, known and acknowledged Person ("of our Lord Jesus Christ"), in whom, that is: in fellowship with whom the situation in question is experienced: giving thanks (Col. iii. 17), asking (John xiv. 13), commanding (2 Thess. iii. 6), being baptized (Acts x. 48), reproached (1 Pet. iv. 14), saved (Acts iv. 12). We either bear or experience what He permits to be laid upon us or occur to us, or we act in His service, in longing after Him, or in the consciousness of His mediation (*per quem omnia nobis contingunt*, BENGEL); it is=ἐν Χριστῷ (iii. 21); similar to διὰ Χριστοῦ (Rom. vii. 25). Without Him we would have no living God, whom we thanked, least of all in Him the Father. The article (τῷ) points to the God known to us, and the phrase "God and the Father" indicates that the same God is a Father for us, our God and Father. It is incorrect to refer πατρί to Christ (HARLESS, MEYER). [On this august title, comp. i. 3; Gal. i. 4; it seems perfectly proper to accept a reference of a general character: *the* Father, our Father and the Father of our Lord, without limiting it to either or here emphasizing either.—R.]

Ver. 21. *Proper conduct in one's position.* **Submitting yourselves one to another.**—Ὑποτασσόμενοι, a co-ordinating participle [not to be taken as an imperative, CALVIN and others.—R.], refers to the position, also a gift and ordinance of God, in which one should be considerate and contented as regards superiors and inferiors (ἀλλήλοις), in piety, as well as in charity, in service in each direction, but: **in the fear of Christ,** ἐν φόβῳ Χριστοῦ.—According to 2 Cor. v. 11 ("the fear [not "terror," E. V.] of the Lord") and 1 Cor. x. 22 ("Do we provoke the Lord to jealousy? are we stronger than He?"), this means fear before Him, as the present Lord, the Head,* marking the tender awe of the conscientious, the humble and zealous imitation, not the fear before the Judge (HARLESS, MEYER and others).

[HODGE connects this verse with what follows, a view which is very convenient, but not grammatically admissible, though vers. 22 ff. do carry out the thought in detail. He says his view is generally accepted, but the view of Braune is held by KNAPP, TISCHENDORF, RUECKERT, HARLESS, MEYER, ALFORD, ELLICOTT, EADIE, in fact by every recent commentator, who gives due place to grammatical considerations, OLSHAUSEN excepted. The connection is difficult however. ELLICOTT finds here named a comprehensive moral duty in regard to *man* (after the three duties in regard to *God*) the exact connecting link being "thanking God for all things (for sorrows as well, submitting yourselves to Him, yea) submitting yourselves one to another." ALFORD thinks the thought is suggested by ver. 18: "that as we are otherwise to be filled, otherwise to sing and rejoice, so also we are otherwise to behave—not blustering nor letting our voices rise in selfish vaunting, as such men do—but subject to one another," *etc.* So EADIE.—R.]

* ["*Rara phrasis*, Bengel; of Him, whose members we all are, so that any displacement in the Body is a forgetfulness of the reverence due to Him" (ALFORD).—R.]



DOCTRINAL AND ETHICAL.

1. The Christian mode of life is precisely *wisdom*, which has first of all as a pre-supposition the *possession of the truth*, and is essentially the *appropriation* and *acquisition* of truth, or the capacity and readiness, clearly perceiving the truth in every case, position and event, to use it in life, by which use it is not squandered, but increased for the possessor. It is truth becoming or already made practical. It is not a knowing much, but a unity of the knowledge of the truth, a unity referred to the kingdom of God, and hence the doing of the truth; Christian morality is true wisdom, it is of a thoroughly ethical nature, although it never renounces its intellectual character. It is the common bond of truth, love, freedom and rectitude. It takes notice of all, world and nature, the heart itself and men about it, sorrow and joy, circumstances and events, rights and duties, the past and future and present, and above all, what concerns the soul, God's word and counsel, and the course of His kingdom. It learns experience in all and gains a certain tact, which grows in clearness and confidence, so that it readily knows, what it ought to do and why, while at the same time it is willing and able to do it. Accordingly correct life and correct doctrine meet together in wisdom. *Prudence* is a natural gift; a child, an unsanctified man, may be prudent. It is only formal, mainly without regard to a definite object; you *may* be prudent in temporal, even in shameful things, as well as in Divine, eternal things; in the latter you *ought* to be or become so. Prudence is circumspection, insight, intelligence, discrimination, appreciation and estimation; wisdom applies it to what concerns God and the soul, to the department of practical ethics.

2. A principal trait of wisdom and Christian morality is the *improvement of the time*, in which it considers and effects what is eternal. Every moment of time is of value to it to be used for the eternal; it perceives the transitoriness of time, but hastens the more to use it as an opportunity, to improve it for eternity. Like a merchant, it makes traffic in time to gain in eternity. Every year, every greater or smaller portion of time, is viewed and treated with reference to the God-appointed duties, so that time appears as measured out eternity. Wisdom fears to destroy

time, avoids mere pastime,* is unwilling merely to enjoy time, regarding it rather as a season, given of God's eternal grace, in which the power of body and soul bestowed by God, operates for the glory of His name and the soul's own salvation, so that from this no complaint or accusation arises.—Precisely the evil days, which continue as long as sin has power, it views as the set time and urgent occasion to wholesome improvement.

3. The two main points of view for wisdom are: *Understanding of the Divine Will* and *active circumspection of spirit.* The first is the everywhere valid and objectively given foundation of the Divine will, with which nothing that will be moral, Christian, wise, dare enter into opposition. All culture which lacks an intimate, lively regard for the will of God, is without wisdom also, hence foolish, despite all knowledge and clever character. The other however is sobriety. STIER:—"Not only every passion, every merely sensuous pleasure, every dissipation leaving the heart unguarded and lost in the creature, every waste of time called pastime, even the most dutiful, sober 'business,' if it entirely absorbs, has in it something intoxicating; before all however is it the fanaticism of opinion, of error, which the devil will present to us in the most various mixtures, often under the most enticing appearance, out of the great intoxicating cup of the spirit of the age, 'of the power of the air' (Rev. xvii.)." Or one might present a gradation from the common intoxication with wine or brandy, to the "most spirited" form of a "lay-breviary."

[The particular precept must not be overlooked in the general application. EADIE well remarks: "There is in the vice of intemperance that kind of dissoluteness which brooks no restraint, which defies all efforts to reform it, and which sinks lower and lower into hopeless and helpless ruin. There are few vices out of which there is less hope of recovery—its haunts are so numerous and its hold is so tremendous." Especially when the craving opens the door to covetousness on the part of the dealer and manufacturer, so that the victim is poisoned as well as besotted. No wonder that such a tremendous evil has driven most philanthropists and Christians to the advocacy of forcible measures for its prevention. Still the remedy is not *law*, but gospel. And "the freedom of the gospel" should never become a yoke of bondage. The two apparently contradictory principles to be reconciled in Christian practice, are (Col. ii. 16): "Let no man judge you in eating or in drinking," and (Rom. xiv. 21): "It is good neither to eat flesh, nor to drink wine," *etc.*—R.]

4. As a *help to sobriety* the Apostle sets forth *first, the use in common of Christian hymns*, which should be used, though not exclusively, in public service. In this the *Psalms*, as Scriptural songs, with their parallelisms, probably gave rise to *antiphonal* singing between minister and congregation, the *songs of praise* ("hymns"), as ecclesiastical songs to *hypophonal* singing, in which the congregation repeated the last line of the stanza sung by the choir, and the *spiritual songs*, as Christians, to *symphonal* singing. The Holy Ghost, who presides in the Church, wrought beyond the word of Scripture, made art in word and tone serviceable to the Church, exercising His power in connection with public service and even in social intercourse. *So then* beside the use in common there must also be a *solitary* digging into such poetical treasures and a private application of them. *Further, every* gift should be *constantly* esteemed, recognized and used accordingly. *Finally* however in humility every *relation of subordination* ordained by God is to be regarded and maintained unimpaired; social institutions are God's institutions.

[In regard to singing in public worship and social intercourse, ver. 19 plainly shows that other than the Old Testament Psalms were and may still be sung. There is no warrant in the word of God for the exclusion of all hymns composed since the canon of Scripture was closed. Such a view owes its origin to causes quite as much political as religious, and perhaps always more national and local than logical or theological. Still it must be said that this extreme is fostered by a proper antagonism to what is now admitted into the public and especially the social services of Christians. It were better to sing nothing else than the Psalms than to encourage the introduction into congregations of hymn-books, born, not of spiritual feeling, but of pecuniary greed. Especially is it unfortunate that the children in our Sunday Schools are taught bad taste in music, bad morals and worse doctrine by what they sing. The full effect of this mistake has not yet appeared. Comp. *Colossians*, p. 72.—"Christ is the centre of sacred art as well as of theology and religion. From Him music has drawn its highest inspiration. 'The hymns of Jesus are the Holy of holies in the temple of sacred poetry. From this sanctuary every doubt is banished; here the passions of sense, pride and unholy ambition give way to the tears of penitence, the joys of faith, the emotions of love, the aspirations of hope, the anticipations of heaven; here the dissensions of rival churches and theological schools are hushed into silence; here the hymnists of ancient, mediæval and modern times, from every section of Christendom, unite with one voice in the common adoration of a common Saviour. He is the theme of all ages, tongues, and creeds, the Divine harmony of all human discords, the solution of all the dark problems of life" (SCHAFF, *Christ in Song*, preface). To banish Christian hymns is to exclude from this Holy of holies, but to substitute for them unworthy, unspiritual, and unchristian rhymes is to *profane* it.—R.]

5. *The principle, impulse* and *norm* of all Christian morality, of the new, Divine life, is *Jesus Christ*, the Fulfiller of the Law and Divine Will; for He is "the *manifestation of the willing Divinity and fulfilling humanity* (HARLESS, *Christliche Ethik*, p. 362). All other motives adulterate or counterfeit the new life.

* [What relaxation the body demands is certainly not forbidden by ver. 16. If any one thinks that he is better redeeming the opportunity by so overtasking his brain or his conscience either, as to die early or be laid upon a bed of sickness, or unfitted for duty by dyspepsia, melancholy or what not, he makes a great mistake. What God says so plainly in our frames is not to be overborne by seemingly pious principles; if it is, God punishes us.—R.]

### HOMILETICAL AND PRACTICAL.

The Christian has not like a philosopher first

to seek the truth; "as wise," he possesses it and must evidence it in his walk. With the philosopher all depends upon exactness and acuteness in the tide of his thoughts, with the Christian, however, upon his care in the course of his conduct; the former works out a system, the latter a fine character; the former will grow, while his forerunner decreases, the latter will decrease, but his forerunner must grow in him.—Christian wisdom as manifested in the acceptance and application of three proverbs: 1. Time is money! 2. Time gained, all gained! 3. Good fishing in troubled waters!—He who does not become wise in hard evil days, certainly remains a fool in good days.—It is just the evil days that you should not let pass by unimproved, for in the evil days of earthly life in this valley of tears we must gain for the good days in eternal life on God's throne.—The evil days are only the so-called bad weather so needed for the growth of the inner man and God's plants.—There are periodicals and books of all kinds, especially novels, which are like cups full of intoxicating wine, and instead of being bread, they should be burned like the books of magic in Ephesus (Acts xix. 19).—The house and household life should not be isolated from the Church and its services, especially its lovely, consolatory, precious hymns.—Thankfulness and humility are two principal emotions of a glad Christian heart: the former sees the *gifts*, which it has received from the Lord, the latter the *duties* He has appointed. Without serving love that Christian exaltation is not true, but a lie. The Christian must not ask; Who should minister to me, but: to whom should I minister?

STARKE: Foresight and wisdom belong to Christianity: not the cunning of this world, but the prudence of the righteous. It is like a bee, drawing honey from good and bad examples alike.—Redeem the time then, and give good heed to the blessed hours, when the Spirit of God knocks at thy heart. Many men are laden down with so much work in their avocation, that they often do not have the proper time for eating, still less for reading God's word, prayer, and other godly practices: it is especially necessary for these persons to forestall and even to steal time, that they may gain an occasional opportunity for spiritual exercises and collecting their heart before God; and besides this to accustom themselves to lift their heart to God in the midst of business, and to carry on the same in the fear of God.—The will of the Lord is our rule, to know and follow it is the greatest wisdom.—Wine is a good gift of God; but alas! all gifts of God are abused, and so is wine.—In one heart there may not dwell at the same time the fulness of the Spirit and the fulness of the world: God does not enter unless the creature retires thence.—Our Church has a rich treasure of spiritual songs ever increasing; it is a shame that they are so often sung without knowledge or thought.—Great benefits demand great thankfulness.—The fear of God is the bond, which should so unite all Christians together, that they submit to and serve one another.

RIEGER. The evil mixture of light and darkness with which so many are pleased, and in which they seek their wisdom, will, as folly, become their shame. In a wise walk every child of the light looks chiefly to himself and the keeping of his own way.—In the adapting one's self to the time, or redeeming the time, one looks to others also, how they are to be approached, or to be served, which is not the same in one case as in another.—Luxury in eating and drinking hinders true wisdom very much.

HEUBNER: One can permit himself to be robbed of much time. *Amici fures temporis.* Redeeming the time is opposite of whiling away the time. It is a frivolous thought, that of regarding time as an evil. There is a great difference between the worldly wise and the Christian mode of making time profitable. The former seeks to gain as great a pecuniary advantage as possible out of circumstances of time; the Christian regards the pressure and the evil of the time as a means to spiritual gain, as an exercise to faith, and hence places himself in a spiritual attitude to the time; he is for example, prepared for great sacrifices, for privations, sorrows and afflictions, which he has to bear, for difficult duties, disturbances and the like. To the worldly man that time is evil, when his pleasure is interrupted or hindered by sickness, scarcity, *etc.* The Christian holds that for the evil time, when virtue decreases and is made more difficult for himself, when the good have much to suffer, and the enticements to faithfulness and apostasy are great.—There is also a great inward song, when at work, on a journey or a walk, *etc.* Such singing imparts a quiet, glad, godly tone to the spirit. Learn good hymns by heart therefore.—*The Epistle for the 20th Sunday after Trinity;* vers. 15–21: *The Christian disposition—the best help in evil days.* 1. It gives wisdom to understand and to use aright the evil days (vers. 15-17). 2. It gives us cheerful courage, aroused not by wild intoxication, but by God's Spirit, fitting us for proper reflection (vers. 18-20). 3. It teaches the willingness to serve one another in the right way (ver. 21).—*The duty of the Christian, to adapt himself to the time.* 1. What it requires? *a*) Wisdom which bears unavoidable evil as of God's sending, not murmuring, nor resisting, nor walking uncircumspectly therein. *b*) Wholesome use of it for the soul's benefit. 2. Means: *a*) Knowledge of the Divine Will, of the purposes of Divine Providence and of our salvation. *b*) Religious inspiration and meditation. 3. The blessing: *a*) For us; all must serve for our profit, that we give God thanks: *b*) For others, that we serve and help them.

PASSAVANT: It is no easy matter to set the right bounds to our joys; one drop follows another, pleasure entices to sensuality, joyousness to wantonness, forgetfulness to intoxication.—We must give thanks for every gratification even the smallest, which we enjoy from our Heavenly Father through Christ; for every spiritual blessing in the heavenly places and possessions. Whoever understands this, knows how to give thanks to the great Giver for every temporal and earthly good also, even the least.

STIER: The walk of a Christian to his goal is a worthy, exact, correct walking; only thus does he find and follow his path. In continuously increasing exactness and strictness as respects our disposition and conduct, we grow out of folly into complete wisdom.—To gain *the* time is something other than to gain *time*.—To seek and to use opportunities, to make a prudent choice of the point of time, to esteem time and be busy accordingly, to use prudently and circumspectly the time with its circumstances, this is the meaning of redeeming the time.—The special public service should not and must not be something altogether sundered from the private life of the Church.—The *ministry* must always reach the spirit, lay the foundation anew; but the congregation comes in with its praying, responding, singing, praising.—The thankful taking and *returning* of God's grace is itself true gracefulness. —The root of all apostasy and disobedience is ingratitude.

*On the Epistle for the 20th Sunday after Trinity* (Eph. v. 15-21): *Gesetz und Zeugniss*, 1862 [a German theological periodical]: *How does the wisdom of the Christian display itself in walk?* 1. In a *circumspect* walk (strait gate, narrow is the way; the days are evil). 2. In an industrious use of the means of grace (the Lutheran Church, the triumphing one, with large capital of the Holy Ghost). 3. *In humble conduct.* (As the most worthy proof of reason is in sobriety, and the greatest blessedness of a correct walk is shown in a life full of thanksgiving, so in various forms of submission the most delicate tact of this life appears. Thus are added the noblest limitations of life and the purest and most considerate forbearance in all relations.—Löhe.)

Brandt: *Earnest demands of the gospel in an evil time.* 1. It is a time of *ignorance* respecting *Divine* things, and it calls out to us in ver. 17. 2. It is a time of the *dominion of disorderly lusts* and propensities, and we are warned as in ver. 18. 3. It is a time of *ecclesiastical lukewarmness*, and enforces the precept of vers. 19, 20. 4. A time of restless excitement, saying to us as in ver. 21.

Rautenberg. *The prudence of the children of God in the evil time.* 1. They secure to themselves a *free hand*, to seek their safety—amid all the *power* of the evil time; 2. An *open ear* for God's will—amid all *self-will* of the evil time; 3. A *well-prepared heart* for the gift of the Holy Ghost—amid all the *carnal mind* of the evil time, a joyful spirit in the Lord—amid all the complaints of the evil time. Staudt: The life of the *new man* 1) *in foresight*, 2) *insight*, 3) *penetration* (*Durchsicht*).

Pröhle: Rules of Christian practical wisdom. 1. Prudent foresight. 2. Earnest retrospect. 3. Pious insight. 4. Moderation in pleasure. 5. Practice in sacred song. 6. Constant thanks to God. 7. Due subordination.—Become full of the Spirit! 1. Full of the Spirit. 2. Full.

[Eadie: Ver. 15. Wisdom and not mere intelligence was to characterize them; that wisdom which preserves in rectitude, guides amidst temptations, and affords a lesson of consistency to surrounding spectators.—It is a strange infatuation to be obliged in pointing others to heaven, to point over one's shoulder.—Ver. 18. Drunkenness was indeed an epidemic in those times and lands. Plato boasts of the immense quantities of liquor which Socrates could swill uninjured; and the philosopher Xenocrates got a golden crown from Dionysius for swallowing a gallon at a draught.—It is a sensation of want—a desire to fly from himself, a craving after something which is felt to be out of reach, eager and restless thirst to enjoy, if at all possible, some happiness and enlargement of heart—that usually leads to intemperance. But the Spirit fills Christians, and gives them all the elements of cheerfulness and peace; genuine, elevation and mental freedom; superiority to all depressing influences; and refined and permanent enjoyment.—Ver. 19. Mere music is but an empty sound; for compass of voice, graceful execution, and thrilling notes are a vain offering in themselves.—Ver. 20. So many and so salutary are the lessons imparted by chastisement—so much mercy is mingled up in all their trials—so many proofs are experienced of God's staying "his rough wind in the day of His east wind," that the saints will not hang their harps on the willows, but engage in earnest and blessed minstrelsy.—Ver. 21. This Christian virtue is not cringing obsequiousness; and while it stands opposed to rude and dictatorial insolence, and to that selfish preference for our opinion and position which amounts to a claim of infallibility, it is not inconsistent with that honest independence of disposition and sentiment which every rational and responsible being must exercise. It lays the foundation also, as is seen in the following context for the discharge of relative duty,—it should be seen to develop itself in all the relations of domestic life.—Schenkel: The duty of subordination in the Christian Church: 1. It rests on the recognition of natural and historical distinctions, ordained by God Himself; 2. It has its pattern in the relation of believers to Christ, which is not one of servile fear, but of moral reverence.—R.]

## 4. Special Christian duties in domestic relations.

CHAP. V. 22—VI. 9.

*Wives and husbands.*

(CHAP. V. 22–33.)

22 Wives, submit yourselves[1] unto [to] your own husbands, as unto [to] the Lord.
23 For the husband is the head of the [Because a[2] husband is head of his] wife, even
as Christ is the head [as Christ also is head] of the church: [,] and he is [himself
24 *omitting* and he is][3] the Saviour of the body. Therefore, [Nevertheless][4] as the
church is subject unto [to] Christ, so *let* the wives [also] *be* to their own [*omit*
25 own][5] husbands in every thing. Husbands, love your[6] wives, even as Christ also
26 loved the church, and gave himself [up] for it: That he might sanctify [it,] and
cleanse [cleansing] it with the washing [laver] of [the] water by [in] the word,
27 That he might present it to himself a glorious church [That he might himself[7] pre-
sent to himself the church glorious], not having spot, or wrinkle, or any such thing;
28 but that it should [might] be holy and without blemish. So [Thus] ought men
[husbands also][8] to love their [own] wives as their own bodies. He that [who]
29 loveth his [own] wife loveth himself. For no man ever yet hated [no one ever
hated] his own flesh; but nourisheth it, even as the Lord [Christ[9] also *doth*] the
30 church: For [Because] we are members of his body, [*being*][10] of his flesh, and of
31 his bones. For this cause shall a man leave his [*omit* his][11] father and mother,
32 and shall be joined unto his wife,[12] and they [the] two shall be one flesh. This is a
great mystery [This mystery is a great one]: but I speak concerning [I say it in
33 regard to][13] Christ and the church. Nevertheless, let every one of you in particu-
lar [Ye also severally, let each one] so love his [own] wife even [*omit* even] as
himself; and [let] the wife *see* that she reverence *her* husband.

### TEXTUAL AND GRAMMATICAL.

1 Ver. 22.—[The *Rec.*, with K. L., many versions (Chrysostom, Scholz) inserts ὑποτάσσεσθε after ἀνδράσιν, while in D. E. F. G., Syriac it is placed after γυναῖκες. Lachmann accepts ὑποτασσέσθωσαν after ἀνδράσιν on the authority of ℵ. A., 10 cursives, Vulgate, other versions, some fathers. B. omits the verb altogether, and this reading is accepted by Tischendorf. Harless, Meyer, De Wette, Alford, Ellicott and recent editors. While one uncial manuscript would not be decisive for the omission, the variations in form and position suggest an interpolation, (comp. Col. iii. 18) and when to this is added the testimony of Jerome, who asserts that there was nothing in the Greek MSS. to correspond with his *subditæ sint* remarking that it was less necessary in Greek than in Latin, the evidence is conclusive. Still we must supply the verb in English.—R.]

2 Ver. 23.—[The article is wanting in all uncial MSS., the *Rec.* inserts it on altogether insufficient authority. The meaning is not altered by the correct reading, yet the literal form adopted in the above emendation is on the whole preferable.—*His wife* is to be insisted upon, since the article is very definite here. We might render *His Church*, were there any other than *the one Church*.—R.]

3 Ver. 23.—[The briefer reading αὐτός is accepted by nearly all recent editors on the authority of ℵ.1 A. B. D.1 F. Καὶ αὐτός ἐστι (*Rec.*) is found in ℵ.3 D. 2 3 K. L., most cursives, good versions and many fathers; but seems to be an explanatory gloss. As regards punctuation the colon of the E. V. might be retained to indicate the independence of the clause. We can render: *He is Saviour of the body*, or *He Himself is the Saviour of the body*, or *Himself the Saviour of the body*, but the latter which is most literal requires a substitution of a comma for the colon of the E. V.—R.]

4 Ver. 24.—['Αλλά must be thus rendered to give clearness to the sense. The *Rec.* reads ὥσπερ, but on insufficient authority; ὡς is well attested (ℵ. A. D.1 F.) and generally received.—R.]

5 Ver. 24.—[The *Rec.* inserts ἰδίοις on the authority of A. D.3 K. L., many cursives, versions and fathers, but it is omitted in ℵ. B. D.1 F., *etc.*, so that the weight of external authority and the suspicion of an interpolation from ver. 22 are decisive against it. Rejected by recent editors.—R.]

6 Ver. 25.—[The *Rec.* inserts ἑαυτῶν, with D. K. L., most cursives; F. G. read ὑμῶν; while ℵ. A. B., cursives and fathers have simply τὰς γυναῖκας. The briefer reading is accepted by Lachmann, Tischendorf, Alford, Ellicott. Braune, however, follows Meyer in defending ἑαυτῶν, on the ground that ἰδίας would have been a more natural interpolation, if an explanatory gloss were added. This is plausible, but scarcely decisive.—R.]

7 Ver. 27.—[Instead of αὐτήν (*Rec.* D.3 K.) recent editors accept the better supported and emphatic αὐτός (ℵ. A. B. D.1 *etc.*).—The emphasis resting on ἔνδοξον is best presented by the order given above, though Ellicott gives: *in glorious beauty.*—R.]

8 Ver. 28.—[There is a doubt as to the correct order as well in regard to the reading. Καί is omitted in the *Rec.*, ℵ. K. L., nearly all cursives, fathers and versions (Ellicott), but found in A. B. D. F., very good versions, and generally accepted since Lachmann.—The verb ὀφείλουσιν comes first in ℵ. B. K. L. and other authorities (Alford, Ellicott), but Lachmann. Meyer, Eadie, Braune and most put it after ἄνδρες, with A. D. F., good versions, fathers. The longer, noninverted reading: καὶ οἱ ἄνδρες ὀφείλουσιν is *perhaps* preferable.—The inversion of the E. V. need not be altered however.

*Husbands* is more correct here, though in the older English *man* meant *husband* also, as in Greek and German, a philological fact not without interest in the exegesis of this paragraph.—ℵ.$^1$ has τέκνα instead of σωματα, but it is correct.—The E. V. omits *own* twice, apparently for the sake of elegance, but improperly since the emphasis is thus lost.—R.]

[9] Ver. 29.—[The *Rec.* (with D.$^3$ K. L., majority of cursives) reads: κύριος, but the authority for Χριστός is so decisive, that it is accepted by nearly all modern editors.—R.]

[10] Ver. 30.—[Lachmann, on the authority of ℵ.$^1$ A. B., good cursives, a few versions and fathers, omit ἐκ τῆς σαρκὸς—ὀστέων αὐτοῦ. Alford brackets them. They are found in ℵ.$^3$ D. E. F. G. K. L., nearly all cursives, versions and fathers; accepted by Tischendorf (ed. 7), Harless, Meyer, Eadie, Ellicott, Wordsworth. The recurrence of αὐτοῦ would readily occasion the omission, while the citation is not exact enough to suggest an interpolation from the LXX.—We must insert *being*, to avoid the connection: members of his flesh, which the E. V. suggests.—R.]

[11] Ver. 32.—[The articles, τόν, τήν (so LXX. Gen. ii. 24), found in the *Rec.* ℵ. A. D.$^3$ K. L., most cursives, good versions, are rejected by Lachmann, Tischendorf, Meyer. Ellicott, Alford and most, on the authority of B. D.$^1$ F., good cursives, and distinct statements of Origen and Jerome.—So αὐτοῦ after πατέρα on the same authority (ℵ$^1$ in addition) and for the same reason.—R.]

[12] Ver. 32.—[Here instead of τῇ γυναικί (LXX., ℵ$^1$ A. D.$^1$ F) the best editors accept πρὸς τὴν γυναῖκα αὐτοῦ on the authority of ℵ.$^3$ B. D.$^3$ K. L., nearly all cursives, Origen, Chrysostom, Theodoret.—R.]

[13] Ver. 33.—[Lachmann and Alford bracket εἰς, but the external authority (B. K., a few cursives) against it is slight, and it might have been omitted because not understood.—R.]

## EXEGETICAL AND CRITICAL.

To Wives; vers. 22-24. *a. The exhortation*, ver. 22; *b. The basis of it*, vers. 23, 24.

Ver. 22. *The exhortation.* **Wives, submit yourselves to your own husbands,** αἱ γυναῖκες, τοῖς ἰδίοις ἀνδράσιν.—This section with its particular duties is so closely connected to the last sentence: "submitting yourselves one to another," with its general duties, that the form is thus abbreviated. Accordingly the verb to be supplied should be imperative, as in some of the various readings, as is required also by the arrangement of the section itself (vers. 25, 28, 33). Bengel. *Inferiores priore loco ponuntur, deinde superiores* 25, vi. 1, 4, 5, 9; 1 Pet. iii. 1, *quia propositio est de subjectione: et inferiores debent officium facere, qualescunque sunt superiores. Multi etiam ex inferioribus fiunt superiores: et qui bene subest, bene præest.* The term ἴδιος is almost invariably joined with "husbands" in the New Testament (Tit. ii. 5, 17; 1 Pet. iii. 1, 5; 1 Cor. vii. 2: τὴν ἑαυτοῦ γυναῖκα—τὸν ἴδιον ἄνδρα: xiv. 35). We even find ἴδιος αὐτῶν προφήτης (Tit. i. 12) marking in addition to the "their," that no strange (antithesis: ἴδιος) one is to be thought of. From this it follows that ὁ ἴδιος ἀνήρ is not simply=husband (Harless), nor ἴδιος=ἑαυτοῦ, αὐτου (Winer, p. 145). It has elsewhere its definite meaning=*proprius*, as Winer admits in regard to many passages, and the Apostle had in this one precept of obedience for the wife a good and sufficient reason for defining the husband with ἴδιος; this justifies the sharpening by which the command appears a natural one.* At the same time it points to the fact, that the wife is found to the husband in another way than he to her. She has here her calling, the avocation of the husband extends further. It is also to be noticed with Bengel: *Mulieres obsequi debent suis maritis, etiamsi alibi meliora viderentur consilia.* See *Doctr. Notes.*

**As to the Lord,** ὡς τῷ κυρίῳ.—The singular requires according to the context a reference to Christ (vi. 1, 5, 6, 7), and "as" marks a reality; behind the husband stands the Lord Himself. Thus the obedience is characterized. The obedience is to be rendered not to the husband as man, but as "own husband" in and by whose person the Lord is honored who has established the relation, whom the husband himself must obey.* Hence it is not the husband as lord (Thom. Aquinas, Semler and others).

*The basis of the exhortation;* vers. 23, 24.

Ver. 23. **Because a husband is head of his wife** [ὅτι ἀνήρ ἐστι κεφαλὴ τῆς γυναικός].—The foundation of the exhortation is introduced by ὅτι, "because." Ἀνήρ, "husband," without the article, designates generally every husband,† who as such is "head" of the definite wife, chosen and won by him (τῆς γυναικός). The position of the husband is thus marked as of an organizing, managing, controlling and deciding character, which is further set forth by the comparison immediately following:

**As Christ also is head of the Church**—Ὡς καὶ ὁ Χριστός places Him as parallel with the husband (ii. 3; iv. 17). On "head of the Church," see i. 22; iv. 15. The wife and the Church are thus placed as parallels.

**Himself the Saviour of the body.**—This distinguishes Christ from the husband. Αὐτος emphasizes Christ: He and none other. Σωτὴρ τοῦ σώματος, Saviour of the body, the Church, is He and He alone. It is thus explanatory of "Christ," marking His peculiar dignity, and not in apposition to "head." This is not applicable to the husband as respects the wife; for him also Christ is the Redeemer. [Alford thus expands the Apostle's thought: "In Christ's case the Headship is united with, nay gained by, His having *saved* the body in the process of Redemption: so that I am not alleging Christ's Headship as one entirely identical with that other, for He has a claim to it and office in it peculiar to Himself." So most.—R.] It is incorrect to take this as referring to the man also, in order thereby to remind husbands that they should make their wives happy (Erasmus, Hofmann, *Schriftbeweis*, II. 2, p. 133, and others); that thought belongs to the other part

* ["The duty of submission is plainly based on that tenderness, specialty, or exclusiveness of relationship which ἰδίοις implies" (Eadie). So Alford, Ellicott, following Bengel and Meyer, against De Wette, Harless, Olshausen.—R.]

* [Ellicott: "Viewed in its simplest grammatical sense as the pronoun of the relative, the meaning would seem to be, 'yield that obedience to your husbands which you yield to Christ.' As, however, the immediate context and still more the general current of the passage (comp. ver. 32) represent marriage in its typical aspect, ὡς will seem far more naturally to refer to the *aspect* under which the obedience is to be regarded ('*quasi Christo ipsimet, cujus locum et personam viri representant*,' Corn. a Lap.), than to describe the nature of it (Eadie), or the manner (De Wette) in which it is to be tendered. Still less probable is a reference merely to the *similarity* between the duties of the wife to the husband and the Church to Christ, as this interpretation would clearly require ὡς ἡ ἐκκλ. τῷ Κυρ.: See Meyer."—R]

† [Or better "a husband," as an example of the class, ὁ ἀνήρ would be "every husband" in each case, every one of the class (see Winer, p. 113): but the article with γυναικός means "his," in this case.—R.]

of the exhortation (ver. 25 ff.) and would weaken the notion of σωτὴρ very much. STIER is over-refined in discovering in σωτήρ—σῶμα an etymological allusion, as Phil. iii. 20, 21.

Ver. 24. **Nevertheless as the Church is subject to Christ,** ἀλλά ὡς ἡ ἐκκλησία ὑποτάσσεται τῷ Χριστῷ—Ἀλλα, "nevertheless," in spite of the difference between Christ and the husband, the resemblance between the Church and the wife remains. Hence the particle is adversative: *habet quidem id peculiare Christus, quod est, est servator ecclesiæ, nihilominus sciant mulieres, sibi maritos præesse, Christi exemplo, utcunque pari gratia non polleant* (CALVIN, BENGEL and others).* It is accordingly neither syllogistic=ὥστε, οὖν (BEZA [E. V.] and others), nor continuative=δέ (WINER, p. 420), nor resumptive=*inquam* (HARLESS).

**So let the wives also be to their husbands** [οὕτως καὶ αἱ γοναῖκες τοῖς ἀνδράσιν].—The οὕτως καὶ strongly marks the analogy. The verb is to be supplied as in ver. 22. The emphasis rests on the final words: **in everything,** ἐν πάντι (1 Cor. i. 5)=κατὰ πάντα (Col. iii. 20, 22). From such a command we are not to infer that the reference is to Christian wedlock (HARLESS); this must indeed also be thoroughly correct. Neither the one (1 Cor. vii. 12-17) nor the other is to be accepted. "In everything" is limited by the context to that which the husband as such commands and which the wife as such has to do, but in neither contrary to the Lord. [HODGE: "It teaches its extent, not its degree. It extends over all departments, but is limited in all,—first, by the nature of the relation; and secondly, by the higher authority of God."—R.]

TO HUSBANDS; vers. 25-31. *a. The exhortation*, vers. 25-28; *b. The basis of it*, vers. 29-31.

Ver. 25. **Husbands, love your wives,** οἱ ἄνδρες, ἀγαπᾶτε τὰς γοναῖκας ἑαυτῶν. [See *Textual Note* [6]].—Thus the husbands are exhorted, but a closer definition follows: **Even as Christ also loved the Church.**—Καθὼς καὶ ὁ Χριστός places the husbands in emphatic parallelism with Him, and the wives with the Church (τὴν ἐκκλησίαν). *Si omnia rhetorum argumenta in unum conjicias, non tam persuaseris conjugibus dilectionem mutuam quam hic Paulus* (BUGENHAGEN). [Comp. the apt quotation from THEOPHYLACT in ELLICOTT, and the beautiful remarks of CHRYSOSTOM, cited at length by ALFORD *in loco*.—R.] Ἠγάπησεν, "loved" (John xiii. 34; xv. 12; 1 John ii. 8; iii. 14) is more closely defined by proof of fact.

**And gave himself up for it,**† καὶ ἑαυτὸν παρέδωκεν ὑπὲρ αὐτῆς (ver. 2).—Here also we should not supply in thought: *unto death* (MEYER), if by that is meant only the death on the cross; the reference is to the entire suffering including the last act as the extreme point. Thus the love required of the husband, a love self-devoting even unto death, gains a significant depth, while there still remains something important which is incomparable: Christ first created the Church through love, as His love made a reconciliation of the world with God, redemption from sin, and death, eternal life and salvation.

Vers. 26, 27. *The end* of the self-sacrificing love of Christ.

Ver. 26. **That he might sanctify it.**—Ἵνα defines the *end:* αὐτὴν ἁγιάσῃ. There is here indicated a continued action and dealing towards and upon the Church, the result of which is expressed in ver. 27 ("that it should be holy and without blemish"); it is the positive activity, effecting the ethical form and demeanor which is well-pleasing to God. It is not merely *segregare et sibi consecrare* (CALVIN [EADIE, but not to the exclusion of the idea of sanctification as a result.—R.] and others). The modality is set forth in the participial clause: **Cleansing it.**—Καθαρίσας, as in i. 9, 13. This indicates the negative activity directed against the evil which is to be removed; both, the positive and the negative, advance together and undivided. Hence it is not: after he cleansed it (OLSHAUSEN, MEYER and others),* nor, as though it were complete in a moment: and has cleansed it (LUTHER). It continues: it is not a single member of the Church that is spoken of, but the totality of Christians. By what means then is the Church cleansed from sin?

**With the laver of the water,** τῷ λοῦτρῷ† τοῦ ὕδατος.—Unquestionably this means baptism; the readers must have thus understood it (HARLESS); *insigne testimonium de baptismo* (BENGEL). The article (τῷ) denotes something well known; besides ὕδατος and the connection with καθαρίσας. Comp. Tit. iii. 5; 1 Cor. vi. 11; Heb. x. 23; Acts x. 47; xxii. 16. But the water does not give the cleansing which is spoken of, nor the bathing or washing. It is the baptism, not the bath in the water. Hence there is further added: **in the word,** ἐν ῥήματι, in order to designate Christian baptism as to its essence. The notion of baptism, as a means of cleansing beside the sanctifying (see *Doctr. Notes* 5, 6), as well as the position of this phrase require us to take both together, and the usage respecting the word ῥῆμα and the connection by means of ἐν (like vi. 2: ἐντολῇ ἐν ἐπαγγελίᾳ) admit of this. Paul uses ῥῆμα (ver. 17; Rom. x. 8, 17; 2 Cor. xii. 4; comp. Heb. i. 3; xi. 3; 1

* [This view is simple, grammatical and introduces neither a truism (EADIE), nor an unnecessary limitation (WINER). It is accepted by ALFORD, ELLICOTT, HODGE and others. EADIE supposes an ellipsis, which is very objectionable. ALFORD: "But what I do say is, that thus far the two Headships are to be regarded as identical, in the subjection of the body to the Head." *Nevertheless* is on the whole the best rendering of ἀλλα.—R.]

† [It would be more literal and perhaps better accordant with the comparison to substitute the feminine pronoun (*her, she*) for "it" in vers. 26, 27, but our language is very stiff in its rules for gender.—R.]

* [Grammatically the participle may indicate either an act antecedent to or synchronous with that of the leading verb, either *having cleansed* or *cleansing*. The former is the view accepted by ELLICOTT, ALFORD, EADIE and HODGE, mainly on doctrinal or logical grounds derived from the reference to baptism which immediately follows.—R.]

† [This word occurs only here and in Tit. iii. 5. It means not "washing," but "laver," (*lavacrum*, Vulgate); comp. ELLICOTT *in loco*. Dr. HODGE is scarcely justified therefore in finding an argument in favor of a particular mode of baptism in our phrase, which does not mean: a *washing with* water, as he implies. The allusion to the bride's bath before marriage is accepted by EADIE, and most.—R.]

Pet. i. 25) in a similar manner. [In all cases it refers directly or indirectly towards proceeding ultimately or immediately *from God* (ELLICOTT).—R.] The conjunction of καθαρός, ὕδωρ, λόγος, John xiii. 10; xv. 3, is well known. "The washing of water" takes place "in word," consists essentially therein, hence the reference to God's Word in general, and in particular to the name of the triune God and His promise. [ALFORD is quite correct in referring it to "the preached *word of faith* (Rom. x. 8), of which confession is made in baptism, and which carries the real cleansing (John xv. 3; xvii. 17) and regenerating power (1 Pet. i. 23; iii. 21)—so Augustine *Tract.* 80 in Joan. 3, vol. iii. p. 1840, Migne; where these memorable words occur, '*Detrahe verbum, et quid est aqua nisi aqua? Accedit verbum ad elementum, et fit sacramentum, etiam ipsum tanquam visibile verbum.*'" So substantially EADIE, ELLICOTT, HODGE and others. Comp. *Doctr. Notes.*—R.]

Hence it is incorrect to take ἐν ῥήματι, ἵνα as a Hebraism=to the end thereby (KOPPE and others), or as *formula baptizandi* (GREEK FATHERS, SCHOLASTICS and others). Nor is it to be joined with καθαρίσας (BENGEL, HARLESS, HOFMANN, *Schriftbeweis*, II. 2, p. 135, who takes it as the word Matt. viii. 3: καθαρίσθητι), which would then have two means by the side of each other, or with ἁγιάσῃ (JEROME, WINER, p. 130, MEYER and others), for in that case it would of necessity have been immediately subjoined. [The connection with the participle is defended by EADIE, ALFORD and ELLICOTT (who more exactly suggests: "rather with the whole expression"). The absence of the article is strongly opposed to Braune's view, while the participle might well have two added qualifications, one an instrumental dative and the other specifying with ἐν "the necessary *accompaniment*" (ELLICOTT). "Thus *the word*, preached and received, is the conditional element of purification,—the real water of spiritual baptism;—that wherein and whereby alone the efficiency of baptism is conveyed" (ALFORD).—R.]

Ver. 27. **That he might himself present to himself the Church glorious,** ἵνα παραστήσῃ αὐτὸς ἑαυτῷ ἔνδοξον τὴν ἐκκλησίαν.—This second ἵνα depends on ἁγιάσῃ, the end and aim of which it introduces: "He might himself present," *etc.* He and none other (αὐτός), without the co-operation of others for Himself (ἑαυτῷ)* and not for others, the world or anything else, to His own good-pleasure presents the Church gloriously. The figure (παραστῆσαι) is taken, as in 2 Cor. xi. 2, from the adorning of a bride; hence the emphatically placed ἔνδοξον, which in 1 Cor. iv. 10 is the antithesis of ἄτιμος, is like Luke vii. 25 (ἐν ἱματισμῷ) to be applied to the glorious appearance, so that the Church thus appears "worthy of the calling" (iv. 1), or "of the Lord" (Col. i. 10), "of God" (1 Thess. ii. 12; 3 John 6), *respondeat ideæ suæ æternæ* (BENGEL). The result of the ἁγιάζειν is the δοξάζειν, both belong together: *sanctitas est gloria interior, gloria est sanctitas emicans* (BENGEL)*.

* [More literally and correctly "to Himself," He alone presents, He receives (ELLICOTT).—R.]

The second clause beginning with ἵνα is not to be placed as parallel to the first, nor is the figure of an offering to be substituted for that of adorning (HARLESS). But it is to be maintained, that this state of things for the Church is not attained in this life (RUDELBACH), while at the same time we may say with BENGEL: (*id valet suo modo jam de hac vita*). The vital process in the individual and in the whole is indeed that of a development from seed to harvest, is not complete at one stroke, has its stadia and phases. The consummation is really only at the conclusion (Second Advent). [So ALFORD, EADIE and most. HODGE has a full note on the question.—R.]

**Not having spot, or wrinkle, or any such thing,** μὴ ἔχουσαν σπίλον ἢ ῥυτίδα ἤ τι τοιούτων.—Thus the Apostle describes more clearly ἔνδοξον.—Σπίλος† (2 Pet. ii. 13; comp. Jude 12), parallel to μῶμος, designates what clings to her from without, spot and stain, what is loathsome, the remains of the previous walk and conversation; ῥυτίς, wrinkle, refers to internal emotions, which fix themselves in the countenance, and disfigure the face as it grows old. Other antitheses, as those of GROTIUS (the former applying to *carere vitiis*, the latter to *vegetos semper esse*, to what is good) are not justified by the language. The final phrase negatives the least spot or wrinkle or even what is similar, hence in general what can disfigure. ["The terms are taken from physical beauty, health, and symmetry, to denote spiritual perfection" (EADIE).—R.]

**But that it might be,** ἀλλ' ἵνα ᾖ instead of ἀλλ' οὖσαν, in accordance with the liveliness of the Greek, who liked the transition from the participle into the finite verb. WINER, p. 537. This ἵνα is parallel to the second one at the beginning of this verse. [Hence "might" must be substituted for "should" (E. V.), to indicate the parallelism.—R.] The final end of the sanctifying is the *being* **holy and without blemish.**‡—To the "wrinkle" proceeding from within the "holy" corresponds, to the external "spot" ἄμωμος, "without blemish" (i. 4).

Ver. 28. **Thus,** οὕτως, points emphatically to what precedes, on which account HARLESS (with ESTIUS: *digressus nonnihil ad mysterium, nunc ad institutum redit*) incorrectly excludes the definite comparison for wedded life, as though it were inappropriate, when only prudence, moderation are commanded. It is not to be referred to the following ὡς (B-CRUSIUS). [So ALFORD. But ELLICOTT, EADIE and HODGE agree with

* [ELLICOTT: "*The Church glorious;* the tertiary predicate ἔνδοξον (Donaldson, *Gr.* § 489) being placed emphatically forward and receiving its further explanation from the participial clause which follows." The reading of the *Rec.*, giving αὐτήν as the direct object of the verb, necessarily led to the obscuration of the force of the word, disturbing the grammatical structure by making τὴν ἐκκλησίαν the tertiary predicate.—R.]

† [The German editors and commentators (TISCHENDORF and MEYER, Braune also) accent this word: σπῖλος, but EADIE, ALFORD and ELLICOTT adopt: σπίλος. The iota is short apparently, hence the latter is correct. The word belongs to later Greek.—R.]

‡ ["Blameless" (ELLICOTT, ALFORD); but "without blemish" retains the etymological reference, thus according better with the figurative current of the verse.—R.]

Braune, in referring οὕτως to what precedes, *i. e.*, "thus, in like manner as Christ," while ὡς indicates not the measure, but a fact, "as they are," *etc.*—R.]

**Ought husbands to love their own wives** [καὶ οἱ ἄνδρες ὀφείλουσιν ἀγαπᾷν τὰς ἑαυτῶν γυναῖκας].—The comparison with Christ is now especially denoted by καί before οἱ ἄνδρες. Ὀφείλουσιν presupposes a command for this, the "new commandment" (see ver. 25), which corresponds with nature, as God has ordained it,* and, applying to fraternal fellowship, is then certainly valid for marital fellowship, as is indicated by the next phrase which introduces a motive: **as their own bodies,** ὡς τὰ ἑαυτῶν σώματα.—Here ὡς is evidently a designation of a reality, corresponding to the figure, that the man is the head of the wife (ver. 23; 1 Cor. xi. 3). [See EADIE for a lucid statement of the correct view respecting this particle.—R.] It is not comparative (GROTIUS), hence not=as themselves.

The result of the view that the husband is the head of the wife, while the wife is the body of the husband, as the Church is Christ's body is this thought: **He who loveth his own wife loveth himself,** ὁ ἀγαπῶν τὴν ἑαυτοῦ γυναῖκα, ἑαυτον ἀγαπᾷ.—Comp. ver. 33. On this general proposition what follows rests.

*The basis of the exhortation;* vers. 29-31.

Ver. 29. **For no one ever hated his own flesh,** οὐδεὶς γάρ ποτε τὴν ἑαυτοῦ σάρκα ἐμίσησεν.—The ground which follows is introduced by γάρ.† In the first place a general fact is negatively expressed. "No man ever" is not limited; not even *nisi scilicet a natura et a se ipso desciscat* (BENGEL). For all "unsparingness of the body" (Col. ii. 22) rests on self-deception. If he actually injures himself, it cannot even then be said that he "hateth his own flesh." Paul did not choose σῶμα here, because he already had in mind the quotation (ver. 31), which refers to the institution of marriage in Paradise before the fall; there as here all that is sinful is excluded from the σάρξ, which is not of itself subject to sin. Μισεῖν is chosen, because the disposition is spoken of; it is to be understood like 1 John iii. 15. GROTIUS aptly recalls Curtius, vii.: *corporibus nostris, quæ utique non odimus;* SENECA, *ep.* 14: *fateor insitam esse corporis nostri caritatem; De Clem.* 1, 5: *Si quod adhuc collegitur, animus reipublicæ tu es, illa corpum tuum, vides, ut puto, quam necessaria clementia sit. Tibi enim parcis, quum videris alteri parcere.* Comp. Prov. xi. 15, 17.

**But nourisheth and cherisheth it** [ἀλλ' ἐκτρέφει καὶ θάλπει αὐτήν.]—Ἀλλά naturally takes out of οὐδείς the subject ἕκαστος, each one. The first verb, the strengthened τρέφειν, refers to the growing development brought about through nourishment (MEYER); it occurs only here and in vi. 4. The second verb (only here and 1 Thess. ii. 7) is stronger than θερμαίνειν (Jas. ii. 16) which is also more general, and denotes the warming upon and with one's self; hence it is used of brooding, Deut. xxii. 6 (LXX.); it is more than *fovet* (*Vulgate*), *pflegt* (LUTHER). The two expressions are distinguished by BENGEL so far correctly that he remarks on the former *intus*, on the latter *ad extra*, but he is faulty in thinking of *victus* in connection with the former, *amictus* with the latter. The one refers to the strengthening food, renewing the life, the other to the protection and preservation of the life. HARLESS incorrectly denies any distinction, taking both as descriptive of maternal love.

**Even as Christ also doth the Church** [καθὼς καὶ ὁ Χριστὸς τὴν ἐκκλησίαν].—What is of universal validity within the sphere of creation, is found also in the Redeemer as respects His Church (He nourishes and cherishes it). STIER applies it to the Lord's Supper, which is indeed not to be excluded, thinking that after the *nasci* in the baptism (ver. 26) the *pasci* is here spoken of. It is more natural to remember how Christ calls Himself the bread of life (John vi. 48, 51), which "nourishes," not in the Lord's Supper alone, even though it takes place there in its most full and intense form, and also that He compares Himself to a hen (Matt. xxiii. 37) that covereth with her wings, thus protecting and cherishing (θάλπει) at the same time. GROTIUS (*nutrit eam verbo et spiritu, vestit virtutibus*) is correct only in the first part of his comment. Evidently the spheres of Creation and Redemption do not fall outside each other; the former finds in the latter its restoration and consummation, the latter in the former its basis and point of connection. What is unnatural is unchristian.

Ver. 30 proves the action of Christ to His Church through her intimate union with Him:

**Because we are members of his body** [ὅτι μέλη ἐσμὲν τοῦ σώματος αὐτοῦ].—"Because" connects with the foregoing thought: He nourisheth and cherisheth the Church. The Church is now the subject, which inheres in ἐσμέν. Every individual is so, as the plural indicates. The Church as a whole as also individually, the members of the Church are then "members of His body." Here τὸ σῶμα αὐτοῦ is evidently=ὁ Χριστός (1 Cor. vi. 15; xii. 27), on which account BENGEL is correct in saying: *corpus hic dicitur non ecclesia, quæ continentur in subjecto "sumus," sed corpus ipsius Christi;* hence this is entirely like 1 Cor. x. 16 (STIER). The membership, which is designated by the emphatically placed μέλη, and which is conceived of as existing in the word ἐσμέν, is designed to mark Christendom and Christians as "integral parts of His body" (MEYER). A closer definition follows.

**Being of his flesh and of his bones,** ἐκ τῆς σαρκὸς αὐτοῦ καὶ ἐκ τῶν ὀστέων αὐτοῦ.—First of all the repeated preposition must be noticed, marking as it does the origin

---

* [From this passage Dr. HODGE correctly infers the falsity of the Hopkinsian view that all love and all holiness is disinterested benevolence, proportioned to the capacity of its object. We do love ourselves, and our bodies, and it is not only natural, but according to Scripture so to do.—R.]

† [The whole tenor of the argument is thus stated by ELLICOTT: "Men ought to love their wives as Christ loves His Church, as being in fact (I might add) their own (ἑαυτῶν) bodies; yes, I say the man who loves his wife loves himself (ἑαυτόν); for if he hated her he would hate (according to the axiom in ver. 28) his own flesh, whereas on the contrary, unless he acts against nature, he nourishes it, even as (to urge the comparison again) Christ nourishes His Church."—R.]

and the appertaining to. The phrase denotes the personality and corporeality of Christ, in which the Church with her members originates. The connection with and origin from Christ, from the historical, incarnate Christ, from His personal body, is designated in such a way, that we as well as the whole Church are to be regarded as His production and possession; and this is expressed with the Scripture passage, or at least with a reminiscence of the passage, which refers to the creation of the woman out of the first Adam in Paradise (Gen. ii. 23: LXX.: *τοῦτο νῦν ὀστοῦν ἐκ τῶν ὀστέων μου, καὶ σὰρξ ἐκ τῆς σαρκός μου*), because Christ is the second Adam (1 Cor. xv. 45, 47; comp. 1 Tim. ii. 13), and the Church, as well as each of its members, is a creation (1 Cor. v. 19). Comp. the parable of the Vine and the branches (John xv. 1 ff). Our life in Christ proceeds in its inmost nature from holiness, is really strengthened from Him, and affects the resurrection body.

Accordingly it is inappropriate to think only of the close union of Christ with us (KOPPE), or the identity of our nature with His (LATIN FATHERS), or only of spiritual origin (GREEK FATHERS, ERASMUS, CALOVIUS, HOFMANN, *Schriftbeweis*, II., 2, p. 137, MEYER and others), or only of the death of the cross (GROTIUS: *ex carne ejus et ossibus cruci adfixis, i. e., ex passione ejus prædicata et credita ortum habuit ecclesia;* SCHENKEL, who refers to ver. 24), or the Lord's Supper (KAHNIS, HARLESS, OLSHAUSEN, STIER and others), or the glorified body (GESS: *Christi Person*, p. 274 ff.). BENGEL, who is followed, up to a certain point, by STIER, since he also finds in the creation of the woman out of Adam a type of the creation of the Church out of Christ, must be regarded as fanciful despite the several apt remarks he makes: *Moses* OSSA *prius, Paulus* CARNEM *prius nominat; naturalem quippe structuram, de qua ille, ossa potissimum sustinent; ut in nova creatione caro Christi magis consideratur. Porro Moses plenius loquitur; Paulus omittit quæ ad propositum non æque pertinent. Non ossa et caro nostra, sed* NOS *spiritualiter* (STIER: *via spiritualiter in corporationem vergente*) *propagamur ex humanitate Christi, carnem et ossa habente.* RUECKERT is altogether perverted in his notion that the Apostle himself had no definite idea in his mind; if he waives an explanation of the passage, so he must waive first of all his own explanation.

[In agreement with the view of Braune, in the main, the following statement is appended. The Apostle here asserts a *state* (*ἐσμεν*) of Christians, originating from Christ (*ἐκ*), analogous to the physical derivation of Eve from Adam and the consequent union subsequently between them. The direct reference to every nuptial union (EADIE) does not accord with the preposition or the immediate allusion. This is the *mystical* relation, implying as Hodge well contends, something more than that we derive our spiritual life from Christ, as Eve her spiritual life from Adam (ELLICOTT, ALFORD, following MEYER), since the peculiar language seems to involve more; and something else than that we are partakers of the substance of Christ's body, as Eve was formed out of the substance of Adam's body (CALVIN, and with various modifications most strong sacramentalists), a view which tends to materialistic conceptions of the union, and, in attempting to explain one acknowledged mystery, creates confusion instead of clearness. This middle position accepts a connection with Him, "not simply and generally by a spiritual union, but in some close and derivative way, which the Apostle calls a mystery" (EADIE), leaving the matter there. As regards the *secondary* application to the Sacraments, which ELLICOTT and WORDSWORTH (with many German commentators) accept, it may be remarked, that these undoubtedly constitute signs and seals, and in a certain sense means of maintaining this union, but this passage, which speaks not of "body and blood," but of "flesh and bones," does not distinctly refer to these, so that nothing can be deduced from it in regard to the communication with Christ's glorified, or transmuted, body in the Lord's Supper. Comp. the full, clear and excellent discussion of HODGE, who opposes CALVIN's views most strenuously. —R.]

Ver. 31. Paul in this verse proceeds with the passage which follows the saying of Adam respecting the woman brought to him (Gen. ii. 24, LXX.: *ἕνεκεν τούτου καταλείψει ἄνθρωπος τὸν πατέρα αὐτοῦ καὶ τὴν μητέρα αὐτοῦ καὶ προσκολληθήσεται πρὸς τὴν γυναῖκα αὐτοῦ καὶ ἔσονται οἱ δύο εἰς σάρκα μίαν*):

**For this cause shall a man leave father and mother, and shall be joined unto his wife, and the two shall be one flesh.**—The changes are inconsiderable: *ἀντί* instead of *ἕνεκεν*, *πατέρα* and *μητέρα*, according to the best authorities, without the articles and pronouns, *τῇ γυναικί* at least a various reading as Matt. xix. 5. Notwithstanding this, it is not a quotation, since there is nothing to indicate this. He merely continues in the words of Moses, which he uses with slight variations, while the Lord introduces them (Matt. xix. 5) with *εἶπεν*, and Paul himself in 1 Cor. vi. 16, the last clause with *φησίν*. Further, this passage is not a part of Adam's speech, since he could say nothing of forsaking father and mother, unless it be taken as a prediction (STIER) [JEROME: *primus vates Adam*]; in which case, however, he would still in the last clause have prophesied respecting himself. [Comp. *Genesis*, p. 209.—R.] Hence it is not strange that the Apostle passes over the intervening clause, in which HARLESS unnecessarily finds a difficulty.

*Ἀντὶ τούτου* is then, if we compare *ἀνθ' ὧν* (2 Thess. ii. 19; Luke i. 2; xii. 3; xix. 44), *for this*, that the woman is taken from the man, he will cling to her; *εἰς ἀμοιβήν* (WINER, p. 342). Paul unmistakably thus returns to the conjugal state, after he has finished the proof (ver. 30) for "as Christ also" (ver. 29). Hence it is not necessary with BLEEK to supply after ver. 30: we are of His flesh and bones, the following middle term: as the woman is not of the flesh and bones of the man, to which ver. 31 refers. *Τούτου* is not to be referred to our origin from Christ, to whom the forsaking of father and mother does not apply, the forsaking of father not in the future at least (*καταλείψει*), and such a reference is foreign to the purpose, the clinging to the wife, the Church, since either this did not at all exist when He was born a man, or He already clung to it in love, without the necessity of first forsaking the Father. Indeed, the future (καταλείψει) may be regarded here in this saying of *Moses*, analogously to the future [the *ethical* future] of the commandments (Rom. xiii. 9: οὐ μοιχεύσεις, κ. τ. λ.), as the precept corresponding to the relations as established in God's word.

Καὶ ἔσονται οἱ δύο εἰς σάρκα μίαν refers to a gradual coming to pass of unity (hence εἰς with the accusative), and that, too, in the case of two different persons (οἱ δύο, ἄρσεν καὶ θῆλυ, Gen. i. 27), who from within becomes one in all external circumstances, *non solum uti antea, respectu ortus, sed respectu novæ conjunctionis* (BENGEL). Hence it is not necessary to find here only a prophecy of the Second Advent of Christ, who now as Betrothed and afterwards as husband, clings to the Church (MEYER), nor in the Mosaic passage a prophetic type of Christ and His Church (STIER), nor to refer the last clause to the Lord's Supper (CALVIN, BEZA, HARLESS, OLSHAUSEN, KAHNIS).

[The main difficulty is in regard to the connection. MEYER (and many others from CHRYSOSTOM to ALFORD) refers "for this cause" to ver. 30, thus applying our verse to the relation of Christ and the Church. But the Apostle is recalling a passage at the basis of which lies the fact of Eve's being taken out of Adam, and the slight alteration he makes does not show an intent to apply it differently here. Besides the whole section treats of the relation of husband and wife, and this is, therefore, to be regarded as the leading reference unless the other is distinctly marked. This principle the Apostle himself assumes in ver. 32: "But *I* speak concerning Christ and the Church." At the same time we must accept a secondary *application* (ELLICOTT) to Christ and the Church, not simply because most commentators have done so, but because the whole tenor of the passage and the interpretation of ver. 32 seem to demand it. The view of HARLESS, OLSHAUSEN and HODGE, that the last clause alone refers to Christ and the Church, the early part being introduced merely for the sake of that clause, seems to be an exegetical make-shift. As the Apostle had left out a part of the original passage in Genesis, he might just as readily have omitted all that was irrelevant. Still less tenable is the special application, which OLSHAUSEN makes, comparing the Lord's Supper and conjugal cohabitation, showing that allegory may serve to foster the coarsest materialistic conceptions. MEYER'S paraphrase is as follows: "*Wherefore,* because we are members of Christ, of his flesh and bones, *shall a man leave* (*i. e.,* Christ at the Second Advent) *his father and his mother* (*i. e.,* according to the mystical sense of Paul: He will leave His seat at the right hand of God) *and shall be joined to his wife* (to the Church), *and* (and then *the two*) (the husband and the wife, *i. e.,* the descended Christ and the Church) *shall be one flesh.*" Such a view is to be expected from this commentator, whose grammatical exactness is exceeded only by his fondness for bringing in a reference to the Second Advent, but it fails to meet with general acceptance. JEREMY TAYLOR: "Christ descended from His Father's bosom and contracted His divinity with flesh and blood, and married our nature, and we became a Church;" but this confuses our nature with the Church, as well as, impliedly, the Bride and the offspring. ALFORD is safer in regarding "the saying as applied to that, past, present, and future, which constitutes Christ's union to His Bride the Church: His leaving the Father's bosom, which is *past*—His gradual preparation of the union, which is *present,* His full consummation of it, which is *future.*" All these views may be held as partial elucidations of the matter in hand on the side of the application to Christ and the Church, which was doubtless in the Apostle's mind, but we still insist that so detailed a passage, has a primary reference to a union, where a mere man leaves his earthly father *and mother,* and is joined to his wife.—With all these allegorical interpretations, one thought, which inheres in the passage, as referring to the human relation, has been too much overlooked, *viz.,* that it is the *man* who forsakes father and mother. It is remarkable how true this is, and how it comes out in works of fiction, in homely sayings like this: "My son is my son till he gets him a wife, but my daughter's my daughter all her life," in the feelings, since mothers and sisters are rarely jealous of the man, but so often of the woman, who marries into the family. Nor does social custom fail to recognize this. The basis of all is the principle set forth in vers. 28, 29.—R.]

*Comprehensive double conclusion;* vers. 32, 33.

Ver. 32. **This mystery is a great one,** τὸ μυστήριον τοῦτο μέγα ἐστίν.—The position of the words must be noticed. WINER (p. 163) remarks that οὗτος usually comes before the noun, and ἐκεῖνος after, and that accords with the nature of the case. Deviations have their ground in the context. Paul lays the stress here on "mystery," the position after the noun weakens the demonstrative; it is not δεικτικῶς, does not refer to the last point alone. There is here a retrospect over the whole paragraph. BENGEL is correct: *mysterium appellatur non matrimonium humanum* (*ver.* 33), *sed ipsa conjunctio Christi et ecclesiæ.* "Mystery" (i. 9; iii. 3, 4, 9; vi. 19) is a fact, which either entirely or partially transcends the understanding, as the Divine will, a decree of God, the truth in its depth, *etc.* Here it is the union of the man and woman in wedlock, and of Christ and His congregation in the church, which the Apostle so presents that the latter is the pattern, and the former the copy. It is irrelevant to suppose a reference to a concealed sense in the words of Moses, so that εἰρημένον, γεγραμμένον, is to be supplied (GROTIUS, STIER, RUECKERT, MEYER and others). It is termed "great," because Paul himself *plus sensit, quam ii, ad quos scribebat, caperent;* comp. Rom. xi. 33.

[HODGE seems inclined to refer "this mystery" to the union of Christ and the Church, in accordance with his view of ver. 31. EADIE agrees exactly with Braune, while ALFORD refers it to "the mystery of the spiritual union of Christ with our humanity, typified by the close conjunction of the marriage state," alluded to in ver. 31. ELLICOTT applies it to the close conjunction of the married state: He adds: "Ver. 29 states the exact similarity of the relationship; ver. 30 the ground of the relation in regard of Christ and the Church; ver. 31 the nature of the conjugal relation with a probable application also to Christ; ver. 32 the mystery of that conjugal relation in itself, and still more so in its typical application to Christ and His Church." EADIE: "Vers. 25-28 introduce the spiritual nuptial relation, ver. 29 affirms its reality, ver. 30 gives the deep spiritual ground or origin of it, while the quotation in ver. 31 shows the authorized source of the image, and ver. 32 its ultimate application guarding against mistake." On "mystery," see chap. iii. 3.—R.]

**But I.**—Ἐγώ is used only with emphasis (WINER, p. 144), and must have an antithesis, which the context gives; here it is (ver. 33); "you." Δέ, *but*, is merely metabatic (MEYER); therefore: I, the Apostle, the unmarried one.*—**Say it in regard to Christ and the Church** [λέγω εἰς Χριστὸν καὶ εἰς τὴν ἐκκλησίαν].—Λέγειν εἰς marks the aim of the discourse, as Acts ii. 25; Heb. vii. 14; John viii. 26 (WINER, p. 370). Here λέγειν is the expression of the opinion and view of Paul, who refers the mystery to "Christ and the Church" as the archetype and prototype for Christians in the marital fellowship. The repetition of the article is emphatic, containing a caution to consider this on account of the consequence for the copy, marriage. It is incorrect to take λέγω=I apply it (STIER), or, I cite it (MEYER; Luther, too, is wrong: of Christ and the Church, and the *Vulgate: in Christo et in ecclesia.* On the Romanist error, which regards marriage as a Sacrament, to which the *Vulgate* gives occasion, see *Doctr. Note* 7.†

Ver. 33. **Nevertheless ye also.**—Πλήν (from πλέον) precisely: further, beyond this, that is beyond the saying on my part, καὶ ὑμεῖς. There is, therefore, no digression to be accepted, from which he now returns to the subject, ver. 28 (BENGEL: *quasi oblitus propositæ rei nunc ad rem revertitur;* HARLESS, BLEEK), nor is it: in order to enter no further upon this mystery (MEYER).‡

**Severally, let each one,** *οἱ καθ' ἕνα ἕκαστος, vos singuli,* each one without exception; the masculine and the context point to husbands.—**So love his own wife as himself,** *τὴν ἑαυτοῦ γυναῖκα οὕτως ἀγαπάτω ὡς ἑαυτόν.*—Loving as one's self is a conception, which is compared (οὕτως) with the love of Christ to the Church. [Not so love his wife as he loves himself, but: in this manner (like Christ) love his own wife as being himself; comp. ver. 28.—R.]

**And let the wife see that she reverence her husband.**—The construction: *ἡ δὲ γυνὴ ἵνα φοβῆται τὸν ἄνδρα,* presupposes something to be supplied: *volo aut simile quid piam* (Gal. ii. 10; v. 13; 1 Cor. iv. 2; vii. 29; 2 Cor. viii. 7). BENGEL, and answers to an imperative, as indeed one precedes (WINER, pp. 295, 537). It is stronger, however, than an imperative; *ἡ δὲ γυνή* stands first emphatically. [See ELLICOTT, who accepts a nominative absolute, reaching the same conclusion as Braune. "Let the wife see," brings out the emphasis quite well.—R.] *Particula vim habet, vim temperat ellipsis morata* (BENGEL). Thus a special weight for house and husband is laid upon this, that she does her duty, which is summed up in *φοβῆται* and traced to its inmost ground in vers. 22-24. ŒCUMENIUS: *ὡς τρέπει γυναῖκα φοβεῖσθαι μὴ. δουλοτρεπῶς.* See *Doctr. Note* 1, 3, 4. *Optime cohærebit concordia, si utrimque constabunt officia* (ERASMUS). [EADIE well remarks: "What is instinctive on either side is not enforced, but what is necessary to direct and hallow such an instinct is inculcated."—R.]

### DOCTRINAL AND ETHICAL.

1. *The fundamental features of the moral conduct of man and wife towards each other* are the principal points in this section. The Apostle refers the subject, with wholesome words and grand freedom from all casuistry, back to the main point, to its briefest expression: *As regards the wife,* to be *subordinate* to the husband (vers. 22, 24), to *reverence* him (ver. 33); as regards the wife, to love the husband (vers. 25, 28, 33). The former is in force since Gen. iii. 15: "Thy desire shall be to thy husband, and he shall rule over thee;" it is not, however, merely a consequence of the fall and a punishment, but inheres in the position of the woman and her corresponding endowment and nature, since she was to be a help-meet for the man, that he should not be alone (Gen. ii. 18). In this is at once implied that there is here meant no servile subjection, no forced, legal obedience, no loveless, joyless fear, by indicating that the man as the head of the wife, in his mind, character and activity is placed as the representative and provider for his own in circles outside that of the house, the context defines the subordination and fear to this extent, that, as soul, heart, disposition and honor of the household, she submits herself to the regulations established by the husband in virtue of his office, and in tender thought avoids disturbing, injuring or destroying his work. Above the house stands the man's avocation, which is from God, for which God has appointed him; hence it stands higher than the house, the character and life of which should subserve his avocation in the house alone. It is therefore in substance commanded that the wife should be subject, and in tender solicitude should fear to oppose the husband, to undervalue his arrangements, to make him discontented or an-

* [The reference is apparently not so much to his celibacy, as to the subjective character of the application and comparison, while the slightly adversative δέ contrasts it with any other interpretation that might have been adduced: "the mystery of this closeness of the conjugal relation is great, *but* I am *myself* speaking of it in its still deeper application, in reference to Christ and the Church" (ELLICOTT).—R.]

† [Our English and American commentators do not fail to notice this blunder of the Council of Trent, but some people who speak English treat the Authorized Version with the same reverence; ministers preach from the *sound* of the E. V., not the *sense* of the Word of God. The Romanist can cover his blunder by the sanction given to the Vulgate by his church, but Protestants have no such excuse.—R.]

‡ [The view of MEYER is accepted by EADIE, HODGE, ELLICOTT, ALFORD, and seems perfectly tenable. Braune's view results from the effort to maintain a decided antithesis to "I" in "ye," when most commentators find the antithesis to "ye also" in "Christ."—R.]

gry while tarrying in the house to strengthen himself for his avocation.*

The wife who refuses this subordination and considerate respect, who does not see and seek her mission in the house, in the service of her husband, becomes an offensive caricature: from discontent there is bad progress to growling, managing, seeking the mastery, scolding, and finally to "emancipation." Thus is stripped off and destroyed, not only what is Christian, but what is germanic, even what is womanly, especially what is peculiar and individual, the special gift of the Creator. JEZEBEL and HERODIAS are examples of this kind. The true character shines in SARAH (1 Pet. iii. 1-6).—To the husband *one* command is given, and in this one three requirements: *Love* even unto *self-sacrifice*, with the consequence and purpose of *sanctification* (vers. 25-27), and this with such energy, purity and constancy, that more is required of the husband than of the wife. The wife should love the husband, as *the Church loves Christ*, in entire, exclusive, indissoluble and *ministering* love, and the *husband* should love the wife, as *Christ the Church*, in entire, exclusive, indissoluble and *protecting* love. It is more difficult to love the wife, without egotism, without tyranny and despotism, without any severity to be the master in the house in true affection, than to be subject to the man in tender respect for his dignity as husband, and his avocation as man.

2. *The combination of marriage and Church* (*Kirche*), which appears as the main thought in this section, has a twofold reference.

*a.* The two are to be compared with each other: As the wife should conduct herself to her husband, so should the Church to Christ; as the husband should conduct himself to the wife, so does Christ to the Church. Marriage, like the Church (*Kirche*), is a life-fellowship between a head and its body; the former Christ is for the Church (*Gemeinde*) and the man for the wife; the latter, the Church, is for Christ, and the wife for the husband. From the relation and the demeanor between Christ and the Church light falls upon the relation and demeanor of married people to each other, just as from the latter upon the former. Thus marriage and Church serve each other for the rendering clear of that which is normal in the two. But we must guard against descending in this parallelism to small and belittling particulars: such as conjoining winning the bride, baptism, and time of betrothal and the temporal period of the Church, leading home the bride and the Second Advent of the Lord as Bridegroom, sexual fellowship and *unio mystica*. But we may with right speak of the religion of marriage and of the marriage of religion; on this is based, too, the position in the canon of the Song of Solomon, which is a hymn of holy love. The Church should not keep at a distance what appertains to the creature, what is natural, or even turn a disapproving countenance upon it; that would be a wrinkle in the face of the Church, thus despising her Lord's work and so growing old on one side, instead of being glorified. From the wife, who in her husband's house is never to be regarded lightly, but must manage and mould, the Church may and ought to learn how to become at once *deiformis* and *mundeformis*.

*b.* The two, however, stand in such close relation to each other, *that from the Church proceeds the power for the proper direction of marriage, the proper conduct of married people.* The wife should belong to the Church in order to receive from Christ His gifts, that thus she may be to her husband what the Church is to Christ, and quite as much must the husband be sanctified in the Church, taken hold of by Christ and permeated by His love, in order to treat his wife, as Christ does His Church. Thus the Christian Church is the foundation for a normal marriage, as the natural life becomes in the life of regeneration that which is according to God's will.

3. *Marriage and Nature.* Our section points into the sphere of creation. The man is from the beginning made for marriage (Gen. i. 26-28: "male and female"), and in Paradise the first human pair was brought together for wedlock, were wedded pair by the grace of God, before father and mother, and children existed. Marriage is the first union in point of time. And in point of dignity as well: from it proceeds the dignity of father and mother, through it alone comes family life, the basis of all blessing in human life. As to its nature it is the fellowship

* [HODGE: "The ground of the obligation as it exists in nature is the eminency of the husband; his superiority in those attributes which enable and entitle him to command. He is larger, stronger, bolder,—has more of those mental and moral qualities which are required in a leader. This is just as plain from his history as that iron is heavier than water. The superiority of man, in the respects mentioned, thus taught in Scripture, bounded in nature, and proved by all experience, cannot be denied or disregarded without destroying society and degrading both men and women. The superiority of the man, however, is not only consistent with the mutual dependence of the sexes, and their essential quality of nature and, in the kingdom of God, but also with the inferiority of men to women in other qualities than those which entitle to authority. The Scriptural doctrine, while it lays the foundation for order in requiring wives to obey their husbands, at the same time exalts the wife to be the companion and ministering angel to the husband." As a proof that this is the position assigned to woman by her own mind and heart, we may cite the works of imagination written by the most brilliant of the sex. Their *ideal of man*, even when they write, personating the other sex, is one who from his nature *demands* their loving obedience. If it be said that many a woman is joined to a man, whose character does not thus demand the obedience of the superior mind, we must consider how often women accept the relation of wife, with a full knowledge of the right position, as taught by God in nature and in His word, and yet conscious that they neither can nor will occupy that position to the man who becomes their legal husband. Such are punished in this life, and the cry about "the subjection of woman" is often the wail of distress resulting from such punishment.—As regards the relation of the sexes in general, though nothing is expressly said in this section, much may be inferred. No doubt great mistakes have been made in drawing such inferences, but it is perfectly obvious that a distinction between the sexes is here assumed, which distinguishes, if it does not sharply divide, the sphere of duty belonging to each respectively. "Woman's work" is different from man's work, though care should be taken neither arbitrarily to exclude her from certain kinds of labor, nor to deprive her of her just recompense for her work. The Church, too, should find work of a certain kind for many who are not "wives," by constituting them "Bible-readers," "deaconesses;" the mere office of Sunday-school teacher will not satisfy many such, since for that many are not adapted. —In regard to the question of "suffrage," it is a fair inference from our passage, that for a wife to vote independently would be a disturbance of the relation as ordained by God; the question assumes a slightly different phase in regard to unmarried women of full age. Still even in the case of such, the passage at least lays the *onus probandi* on those who advocate the right. One popular argument urged in favor of "women suffrage" is that thus drunkenness could be stopped by force of law. But not only is that method of doubtful justice, legality and expediency, but the question fairly arises how many men are driven to drunkenness by the failure of their wives to heed the spirit of the Apostle's words. —R.]

of one man and one woman, in which both more and more live together (εἰς σάρκα μίαν), chiefly moral, then however sensuous vital fellowship even to sexual fellowship; it is the fellowship of the body and of the worship of God, of all worldly goods, of all intellectual gifts, and, as far as it is possible with personal reason and conscience, of spiritual gifts also; the religious side of the fellowship should predominate, the moral side operate, the sensuous side may never override and repel the others, would enter only but not be repressed.*

4. *Marriage and Bible* are joined together also by our section, since it refers back to the oldest Scripture, deriving thence these thoughts: God has created mankind for marriage; the desire, the initiative, is on the side of man, the being desired is the part of the woman; marriage unites only one man and one woman (Monogamy); is first of all and as to its deepest ground directed to moral fellowship of life, includes in itself sexual fellowship, is directed thus towards the establishment of the family and family life, toward the bringing up and education of children; has such an inwardness and fervor, that devoted conjugal surpasses filial love, even father's and mother's love, that the marriage tie is indissoluble, unless sin should rend it asunder.† *Monogamy* is established from the beginning as self-evident. A Cainite, the bold and sensual Lamech, who first took two wives, Ada (=ornament) and Zillah (=shadow of the head of hair), begetting the master of fiddlers and fifers, and the master of workers in brass and iron, made the transition from monogamy to polygamy, and in the progress of civilization forsook the Divine institution (Gen. iv. 19-24). The impatience of Sarah for an heir caused her to forsake her position and conduct so far as to lead Hagar to Abraham, and the selfishness of Laban made use of the love of Jacob for Rachel, so that he took Leah first, but the promised blessing came only on the child of the legitimate wife (Isaac, not Ishmael) or of the first one (Judah, not Joseph). See HARLESS, *Ethik.*, § 52, p. 5, 7 ff. Hence it should not be said, that in the Old Testament marriage only gradually lifted itself to monogamy (SCHENKEL); on the contrary the latter was recognized as the original institution appointed by God, and the defections from it are referred to sinful tendencies, to the dominion of sin, are not approved. Christianity however has glorified marriage, establishing it firmly and securely in its nature, dignity and blessing. Redemption goes back to the natural institutions established in creation, removing the perversions and degradations introduced by sin into the heathen world and the people of Israel; what is new in Christianity is what is primeval restored. This appears especially prominent in the matter of marriage and family life, so strongly that all which is anti-christian and anti-scriptural is at the same time unnatural and inhuman, just as the impulse of anti-christian Atheism, Materialism, Satanism has led thither. Interest attaches to the view of Melancthon, who, much as he has prized his excellent betrothed, was afraid of married life, lest he might thereby be drawn too much away from his studies, and yet afterwards despite a wife suffering from hypochondria and a numerous family called the marriage state "a kind of philosophy, which required duties the most honorable and most worthy of a noble man." [So JEREMY TAYLOR: "Single life makes men in one instance to be like angels, but marriage in very many things makes the chaste pair to be like Christ" (*Sermon on the Marriage Ring*).—R.]

5. Beside the conduct of married people to each other and the relation between Christ and His church and the husband with his wife, there is also marked, through the purpose of Christ or the aims of the church, *the end of marriage*, viz., *the sanctification of the personality* (vers. 26, 27). This is a process of development, ever deepening and extending through the whole life, with two sides: internal, moral perfection, through growth and unfolding of talent and strength granted (ἁγία) and ever wider and clearer emancipation from all evil imposed and entering or clinging from without (ἄμωμος). The former is based upon the internally and correctly established relation of the person to God and His kingdom, the latter upon the conduct of the same, externally corresponding to the given noun, in all the relations of life from work to word and its source in thought and temper. Hence the sanctification of the sexual appetite can be regarded as only a single purpose, for which there is not even a point of resemblance in the parallel with the church and her Head, not as the principal task of Christian family morals (SCHENKEL), as if marriage were ordained as a safeguard against whoremongery or carnal excess, when this is but a single object, or rather a coincident result, even though the main matter in

* [Dr. HODGE remarks on the true expression of the Apostle "as their own bodies," (ver. 28): (1.) It does not refer to any material identification. (2.) It implies nothing inconsistent with the separate subsistence of husband and wife as distinct persons. (3.) The marriage relation is not essential to the completeness or perfection of our nature in all states of its existence. It is to cease at the resurrection. (4.) It is not however merely a union of interests and feelings. In a certain sense husband and wife complement each other. (5.) There is doubtless involved a oneness of life which no one can understand.—R.]

† [Here Dr. HODGE is excellent: (1.) Marriage is a union for life between one man and one woman; consequently bigamy, polygamy, and voluntary divorce are all inconsistent with its nature. (2.) It must be entered into freely and cordially by the parties, i. e., with the conviction that one is suited to the other (and it may be added, to take the positions involved in the natural and scriptural view of the relation). All coercion on the part of parents is contrary to the nature of the relation; and all marriages of mere convenience are opposed to the design of the institution. (3.) The State can neither make nor dissolve the marriage tie. It may enact laws regulating the mode in which it shall be solemnized and authenticated, and determine its civil effects. It may shield a wife from ill-usage from her husband, as it may remove a child from the custody of an incompetent or cruel parent. When the union is, in fact, dissolved by the operation of the Divine law, the State may ascertain and declare the fact, and free the parties from the civil obligations of the contract. It is *impossible* that the State should have authority to dissolve a union constituted by God, the duties and ordinances of which are determined by His law. (4.) According to the Scriptures, as interpreted by Protestant churches, nothing but the death of one of the parties, or adultery, or wilful desertion can dissolve the marriage contract. When either of the last-mentioned causes of dissolution is judicially ascertained. the injured party is free to contract a new marriage. The greatest social crime, next to murder, which any one can commit, is to seduce the affections of a wife from her husband, or of a husband from his wife: and one of the greatest evils which civil authorities can inflict on society is the dissolution of the marriage contract so far as it is a civil contract (for further the civil authority cannot go), on other than Scriptural grounds.—R.]

this work of sanctification. From the very seeking and consummating of the marriage, the morality of the fellowship not its sensuousness, the religiousness of the married pair not the sexual fellowship, should show itself to be the decisive and impelling feature. The proper sexual pleasure to be allowed by man and wife must like every other pleasure within a social relation find its norm in accordance with the moral end of marriage.

6. On the phrase respecting baptism (ver. 26) rests with full right the explanation of Luther in the smaller catechism, 4 main part, 1: Baptism is not mere water, but it is water taken in God's command and united with God's word. For it is a pledge of the power of the atonement efficient through awakening and growing faith, an assurance of the forgiveness of sins, a guarantee of the new relation to God, of sonship with Him (Matt. xxviii. 19: *εἰς τὸ ὄνομα*; Acts ii. 38; xxii. 16; Heb. x. 22) and an assurance of the power, to be received in faith, of the new life in the gift of the Holy Ghost (John iii. 5; Tit. iii. 5); both together, Rom. vi. 3–11; Col. ii. 12. CHEMNITZ: *Pater salvat, filius emundat, spiritus regenerat* (HARLESS). *Mundatio præcedit donationem gloriæ et nuptias* (BENGEL).—Thus both the mechanical view of baptism as a mere initiatory rite among the Rationalists, and the Baptist sundering of sanctification and cleansing, which makes of baptism merely a seal of entire conversion, are here opposed; it stands at the commencement of sanctification, which begins with it. [The reference to baptism is undeniable, and such a reference seems to contradict at once the very low view of the ordinance which is quite prevalent among many Pedo-baptists, just as the obvious reference to the mystical union of Christ, and His Church in this section implies that the Lord's supper is more than a mere memorial service. As a specimen of the Reformed or Calvinistic views on this subject (though Calvin himself was more of a Sacramentalist than those who moulded the Reformed confessions), the remarks of Dr. HODGE are presented: When the Scriptures speak of baptism as washing away sin, they do not teach (1.) That there is any inherent virtue in baptism, or in the administrator, to produce these effects; nor (2.) That these effects always attend its right administration; nor, (3.) That the Spirit is so connected with baptism that it is the only channel through which He communicates the benefits of redemption. Positively he remarks: (1.) Baptism is a Divine institution. (2.) One of the conditions of salvation, not *sine qua non*, but having the necessity of precept. (3.) A means of grace, that is, a channel through which the Spirit confers grace; not always, nor upon all recipients, nor is it the only channel, nor designed as the ordinary means of regeneration. (4.) Infants are baptized on the faith of their parents; and their baptism secures to them all the benefits of the covenant of grace, provided they ratify that covenant by faith.—R.]

7. Here, as also in i. 8; iii. 3, 9; 1 Tim. iii. 16; Rev. i. 20, the *Vulgate* has rendered *μυστήριον*, *sacramentum*. This translation has been used to support the view of the high dignity of marriage recognized in this section, which exaggerates it to such an extent that the Roman Church, in opposition to her own doctrine of the celibacy of the clergy and the virginity of the saints, proclaims it a sacrament. Comp. *Conc. Triden., Less.* 24, *cap.* 1; *Si quis dixerit, matrimonium non esse vere et proprie unum ex septem legis evangelicæ sacramentis a Christo domino institutum, sed ab hominibus in ecclesia inventum, neque gratiam conferre: anathema sit.*

This church (*Catech. Rom.* ii. 8, 23 sqq.) accepts three gracious gifts [in this so-called sacrament]: *proles, fides, fidelitas quædam und vinculum, quod nunquam dissolvi potest.* As respects the matter and form the schoolmen vacillate in consequence of the novelty of the subject. BONAVENTURA finds the material of the sacrament in the sexual acts, others in the partners themselves, others in their *consensus.* To regard and treat matrimony as a Sacrament, but only for the laity, who do attain to the perfection of the saints, while celibacy is demanded of the monk and priest, that they may be able to boast of sanctity, of actual renunciation of sexual desire, was only possible, because the antithesis between heaven and the world, from which Paul proceeds in speaking of celibacy as respects his own office, age, and individuality (1 Cor. vii. 25–40), was changed into an antithesis of spirit and flesh in such a way that a false dualism was established between Divine and human, spiritual and carnal, moral and natural. This dualism the church has overcome. Very apt are the remarks of HARLESS (*Ethik*, p. 512): "Marriage is the divinely appointed ordinance and form, within which the spirit of Divine love can find on earth according to the nature of the case its most unhampered rule, and in such efficiency can best give a measure of the fulness of the Divine love; *but the marriage itself does not bring or become the medium of this Spirit of pure Divine love.* It is only the vessel which is prepared for this Spirit; the spirit and the power do not come from the earthly copy of the Divine fellowship of love. The Christian perceives rather, that the institution in itself does not at all protect against violation and desecration through selfishness of every kind—but that [the Spirit and the power] come from the graces of the New Testament, that these graces do not come to him by means of marriage, but through the word, baptism, the Lord's Supper, repentance and faith, on which account it is impossible for him, under a misunderstanding of Eph. v. 32 to call the Divine institution of matrimony a sacrament in the sense, in which Baptism and the Lord's Supper are thus termed.—Still the evangelical church down to the latest times has not been free from Romish distortions, of a mystical, theosophic tendency; GOTTFRIED ARNOLD held the marriage state to be incompatible with true wisdom, though he himself afterwards married; with him agreed MICHAEL HAHN, who with his followers remained unmarried, and Pastor CULMANN (*Ethik*, i. p. 42). LUTHER himself did not regard the sexual propensity and its gratification as in itself God-willed (KOESTLIN: *Luther's Theologie*, II. p. 483). On the other hand ZINZENDORF attempted to place the marital obligation under ideal points of view.—If from the Roman Catholic side attacks are still made upon the convenience of Luther and Melancthon for their approval of the bigamy of Landgrave Philip after the example of Abraham, who had however to suffer severely on this account, it may be replied that the Catholic Church not only permitted Abbe Sieyes and Bishop Talleyrand to marry, and dissolved Napoleon's first marriage with Josephine, but even helped him to the second marriage with the Austrian Archduchess.

8. In the 13th century the Old Testament age, and the Old Testament Scriptures were often termed the "*die alte Ehe*" (the old marriage). This points to a mystery of marriage, like that of the communion of Christ and His Church. The former is a mystery on its natural side from the very creation; in it creative powers for soul and body are active; a mystery on the side of redemption: in it wonderful confiding love and consecrated fidelity are manifested; on the side of sanctification: in it operate sanctifying powers for eternity.—Comp. PAUL GERHART: *Voller Wunder, voller Kunst, voller Weisheit, voller Kraft, voller Hulde, Gnad' und Gunst, etc.*

### HOMILETICAL AND PRACTICAL.

Comp. the foregoing *Doctr. Notes* and BRAUNE, *Die heiligen* 10 *Gebote*, pp. 147, 177.—The husband has a great advantage over his wife: he is the older, more mature part, has the choice of the wife, possesses greater power and culture for civil life, must represent his wife and household in these matters (1 Cor. xi. 7–9). So at least it should be. But he has no advantage as regards the Divine image and moral worth over her, the fellow-heir (1 Pet. iii. 7). Both must have patience with each other, but no wife should be ever for having the last word without yielding! She who patiently bears puts to shame the despotism of a husband. Nor should they spoil each other by a weak and false silence respecting unpleasantness; they should inure themselves in the draught of truth, should be confiding without inconsiderateness; neither dare cease to be a lover of the other. Even if the husband should be lacking in what is necessary to fill personally his position, the wife should not in boastfulness despise the social dignity of the husband, but above and beyond him see the Lord. Have you given your "yes," then it must be held good to the end; even if it is hard, the difficulty does not dissolve it; life must fulfil it, death alone dissolve it.—You may be *married* and yet not truly *wedded*, may have one household and yet no matrimonial fellowship; may be with him or her *one flesh*, but not *one heart* and *one soul;* you live together under one roof, but may have no common foundation, may walk united on earth, but heaven is wanting to your union.—No one ought to rejoice so much in Christ and His church as the wife: she and her children have gained most by Christianity; this is a reason why women and children have and ought to have so strong an attraction to Him in the church; there is gratitude involved. Submission, ministering subordination is no misfortune, but a joy, exercising a triumphing, pacifying power.—In one sense every man must die for his wife: he must die to himself, to his sinful Ego, mortify his selfishness and egotism, not his peculiarity, which he should still exercise without self-will. The man is most apt to do this as betrothed and in the honeymoon, as if once were enough. But this should occur throughout life: before death no one is entirely done with it.—Wo to him who chooses before he has to choose, when he knows neither why nor wherefore, or before he knows how to choose, when he does not know what it means, or who chooses arbitrarily, before he has bethought himself what his position requires or proved her whom he chooses! Wo to such, especially if they are or become ministers of the church. Sin separates from God, disturbs the union with Him, grieves the Holy Spirit. Sin does this also to the Divine institution of marriage. All separation of dispositions, all disturbances and discord of soul come from sin, and never merely from that of the other, but from your own sin also. The guilt in unhappy marriages, or even in the disturbance of otherwise happy ones, is on both sides, demands at least an examination of one's own sins. When there is discord and even when the other is wrong, do you listen attentively to what is said against you, and then try it as a judge upon yourself.—Never forget this: what is yours does not merely belong to you, you belong to it also.

STARKE:—How then can a godless man with alacrity be the head of his wife and require obedience of her, when he neither clings nor listens to Christ, his head?—Pious widows, you have lost one head, but the other Head (Jesus) death cannot take from you; He watches and cares for you.—Is Christ the Head of the church, then the Pope cannot be it, else the church would have two heads and so be a monstrosity.—In Christ there is at once a Head and a Saviour; the two characters must unite also in a husband who should use his dominion for the blessing, never for the oppression and damage of those whom he rules.—The fellowship of believers with Jesus gives them that great dignity, noble advantage and blessed consolation.—Without love marriage is a bitter state, with love it is sweet.—The love of Christ to His church is both cause and standard of the love of husbands towards their wives.—Love and fear stand beside each other in a well-ordered marriage: the former must sweeten the latter, the latter must ever more incite the former.

RIEGER:—The Apostle begins with married people, because, if things go wrong between them in the household, the trouble soon extends itself from them to the children and dependents. In each relation the Apostle begins with the weaker side.—Proper distrust of one's self and what is doubtful in one's natural gifts, willingness to be told what to do rather than to lead the other into temptation, is the root of this subjection.—The rule of the household is not to be put on a magisterial footing, but to be conducted by a mild and yet efficient influence, like that of the head upon the members.—What is set before the husbands: love your wives, is not easier than the being submissive. Whoever knows human nature, how loveless, changeful, easily wearied by faults, quickly angered it is, will notice how deep the foundation must be laid for a love which is not puffed up, seeketh not her own, etc.

HEUBNER:—Even with love and similarity of

hearts there must be subordination. The household needs guidance and government. The wife should submit. The wife's government reverses the proper order.—Nothing can frighten a Christian heart from divorce more than this thought: It is as if you separated from Jesus. Unbelief, coldness toward Jesus has terribly wasted our married life.

PASSAVANT:—The Greeks acted more humanly, the Romans and Germans more magnanimously; elsewhere we see everywhere in the history of humanity the mothers and daughters of the nations, the weaker part, despised and oppressed by the stronger, often most cruelly degraded; and we should have, in such traits of ancient and modern heathen, and of all infidel nations and races, enough to perceive how deeply the whole human race has fallen from its original nature and destiny and what rudeness and wickedness of sin has permeated all nations and men, seeing they all have sinned.—With the appearance of the Redeemer, however, a new hour of Redemption struck also for this so misunderstood and oppressed half of the human race.—The more true, wise and manly the husband is in his cherishing of his wife, as *his own body*, the sooner, and if the wife is not altogether unholy in heart —the more faithfully, tenderly and sacredly will all be returned to him by the wife's sacredly affectionate care and solicitude, and he be richly recompensed.

STIER:—The church should never demean itself as merely *parallel* to other circles of fellowship, for she is called to become the inmost of all. —From out of the family, the concentrated life of the household, where a filial spirit is born of wedded love and household dependents regulate themselves accordingly, the moral life of a nation also grows.—The emancipation of the strong-minded woman, that most repulsive miscreation of natural corporealness, destroys not only what is Christian but what is germanic.—Love is the only right dominion; there is then in every house a church *in parvo*.—The Word is the proper, continuing baptism.—The mystery of marriage is a portico to the mystery of the sanctuary; from the latter too a light streams into the former.

SCHLEIERMACHER:—On the Christian conduct of marriage: 1. In marriage there is something *earthly* and something *heavenly*, which are one. There is marriage in an *anxious* form, when only one is satisfied, the other constrained; merely a carefully kept contract. There is marriage in a *repulsive* form, when the parties are accustomed to each other making as few claims as possible on each other, seeking their pleasure outside. There is a marriage in a loathsome form, when there is mutual anger and bitterness.—Ever more aroused in spirit, mollifying each other, and that in household, social life with its possessions, joys and sorrows. —2. In it there is an *inequality*, which *loses itself in perfect equality*—in perfect oneness of life.

BECHER:—Look at your households, fathers and mothers, for you are priests; your congregations impose a hundredfold greater responsibility than mine. Your priesthood is from God's own hand.—HOFMANN (ver. 22-24): The marriage state the school of Christian obedience; its ground, character, measure and aim.—(Vers. 25-29): The marriage state the home of love on earth—of born, free, heavenly love.

[HODGE:—Ver. 22. The obedience of the wife terminates on the Lord, and therefore is religious, because determined by religious motives and directed towards the object of religious affections. This makes the burden light and the yoke easy; for every service which the believer renders to Christ is rendered with joy and alacrity.—Vers. 26, 27. The church the bride of Christ. 1. The object of a peculiar and exclusive love. 2. She belongs exclusively to Christ. 3. The relation more intimate than between Him and any other order of creatures. 4. The church the special object of delight to Christ.—Ver. 29. A man may have a body which does not altogether suit him. He may wish it were handsomer, healthier, stronger, or more active. Still it is *his* body, and he treats it as tenderly as though it were the best and loveliest man ever had. So a man may have a wife whom he could wish to be better, or more beautiful, or more agreeable; still she is his wife, and, by the constitution of nature and ordinance of God, a part of himself.—Ver. 33. The sentiments which lie at the foundation of the marriage relation, which arise out of the constitution of nature, which are required by the command of God, and are essential to the happiness and well-being of the parties, are, on the part of the husband, that form of love which leads him to cherish and protect his wife as being himself, and on the part of the woman, that sense of his superiority out of which trust and obedience involuntarily flow.—R.]

[EADIE:—Ver. 22. In those days wives when converted and elevated from comparative servitude, might be tempted, in the novel consciousness of freedom, to encroach a little, as if to put to the test the extent of their recent liberty and enlargement.—The insubordination of wives has always been a fertile source of sorrow; and yet Christian ladies in early times drew forth this compliment from Libanius, the "last glory of expiring paganism": *proh, quales feminas habent Christiani!*—Ver. 23. There is only one head; dualism would be perpetual antagonism. Each sex is indeed imperfect by itself, and the truest unity is conjugal duality.—Ver. 24. In the domestic economy, though government and obedience certainly exist, they are not felt in painful or even formal contrast; and, in fact, they are so blended in affectionate adjustment, that the line which severs them cannot be distinguished. The law of marital government is an "unwritten law."—Ver. 25. Husbands are not to be domestic tyrants; but their dominion is to be a reign of love.—The church did not crave Christ's love: He bestowed it. It was not excited by any loveliness of aspect on the part of the church, for she was guilty and impure, unworthy of His affection. Who can doubt a love which has proved its strength and glory in such suffering and death?—Ver. 27. As He originally loved her in her impurity, how deep and ardent must be His attachment now to her when He sees in her the realization of His own gracious and eternal purpose!—Vers. 31, 32. So close and tender is the union between Christ and His church that the language of Adam concerning Eve may be applied to it. These primitive espousals afforded imagery and language which might aptly and truly be applied to Christ and the church, which is "of His flesh and of His bones;" and the application of such language is indeed a mystery—a truth, the secret glory and facility of which are known but to those who are wedded to the Lord in a "perpetual covenant."—Ver. 33. "He rules her by authority, and she rules him by love: she ought by all means to please him, and he must by no means displease her" (*Jeremy Taylor*). When this balance of power is unsettled, happiness is lost, and mutual recrimination ensues. "A masterly wife," as Gataker says, "is as much despised and derided for taking rule over her husband as he, or yielding to it."—R.]

[In view of the well-known fact that an immense proportion of the conversation of many women is about their husbands, their children and their servants, showing how their lives are bound up in these relations, it would be well for them to study (and for pastors occasionally to teach in a prudent way) what the Apostle says in this part of the Epistle (chap. v. 22—chap. vi. 9) about their duties as wives, mothers and mistresses.—R.]

---

### *b. Children and parents.*

### CHAP. VI. 1–4.

1, 2 Children, obey your parents in the Lord:[1] for this is right. Honor thy father
3 and [thy][2] mother; which is the first commandment with promise; That it may be
4 well with thee, and thou mayest live long on the earth. And, ye fathers, provoke
[or fret] not your children to wrath: but bring them up in the nurture [discipline]
and admonition of the Lord.

#### TEXTUAL AND GRAMMATICAL.

[1] Ver. 1.—[Lachmann, Rueckert, and Mill omit ἐν κυρίῳ on the authority of B. D.[1] F., some fathers. It is bracketted by Alford; but Harless, Meyer, Ellicott accept it on the strong support of ℵ. A. D. [2 3] K. L., nearly all cursives and versions, express statement of Chrysostom; especially since, as Meyer urges, we would have found ὡς τῷ κυρίῳ in case of an insertion from v. 22, and if from Col. iii. 20, it would have been placed after δίκαιον. Braune's note here speaks of the absence of the phrase in Col. iii. 20, a manifest error.—R.]

[2] Ver. 2.—[The E. V. omits "thy," without reason and unfortunately, for the article occurs in the Greek, and the same emphasis rests on *thy mother* as on *thy father*.—R.]

#### EXEGETICAL AND CRITICAL.

*The precept for children;* vers. 1-3. Ver. 1. **Children**, τὰ τέκνα.—The next step from the married state is the family. The wedded pair become parents through God's gift, which may also be denied. The address to children in a letter to the Church presupposes, that the Apostle regards them as belonging to the Church, present at public worship, understanding the word read to and applicable to them; indeed they must be regarded as baptized, since ver. 1: "in the Lord," ver. 4: "in the admonition of the Lord," obliges us to do so (STIER, HOFMANN, *Schriftbeweis*, II. 2, p. 192.)* See *Doctr. Note* 1.

**Obey your parents in the Lord** [ὑπακούετε τοῖς γονεῦσιν ὑμῶν ἐν κυρίῳ].—The verb coming first has the emphasis: this one precept comprises the main part of filial duty in itself. The word is stronger than ὑποτάσσεσθαι (BENGEL: *id plus etiam dicit quam subordinamini; obedire est imperitioris: subordinari cujusvis inferioris*). To the more mature and experienced persons, who are God's representatives and the child's supporters, and guides in fidelity, love and wisdom, obedience is to be rendered, not because they are Christians, or good and rich, or masters over the child, but because they are the parents ("your parents"), with the duty of bringing up (ver. 4) as they have brought forth. As Christians the children, however, must obey "in the Lord," in Christ (vers. 10, 21; ii. 21; iv. 1, 17; v. 8; WINER, p. 364); analogous to "in the fear of Christ" (v. 21), "as to the Lord" (v. 22). Thus the kind of obedience, not immediately and chiefly the kind of parents, is more closely defined, as specifically Christian in ground, measure and limit. It is incorrect to take it as = κατὰ τοῦ θεοῦ λόγον (THEODORET), or to refer it to God (CALVIN), *in Deo*, or to connect it with "parents," or to take it as merely a designation of the mode of obedience (HARLESS).*

**For this is right** [τοῦτο γάρ ἐστι δίκαιον].—Quickly, briefly Paul presses the proof (γάρ) forward. "This" refers to the whole: the obedience of children to their parents in Christ. In τέκνα and γονεῖς there is a reminder of the μυστήριον (ver. 32), which lies in

* [To this MEYER objects, but in its stead lays down a principle which approaches the strict Reformed view: "The children of Christians through their vital fellowship with their Christian parents were even without baptism ἅγιοι (see 1 Cor. vii. 14; Acts xvi. 15) and should render to their parents obedience ἐν κυρίῳ."—R.]

* [HODGE seems to follow HARLESS, but EADIE, ELLICOTT, ALFORD rightly take ἐν κυρίῳ as indicating the sphere or element of the action. ALFORD adds, in reference to the common view that the Apostle gives a hint as to commands not according to the will of God: "I should rather believe, that he regards both parents and children as ἐν κυρίῳ, and the commands, as well as the obedience, as having that sphere and element. How children were to regard commands *not answering to this description*, would be understood from the nature of the case." Certainly, if the reference be, as is thought by most, to baptized children, then this presupposes the parents ruling "in the Lord." On the limits of obedience, ELLICOTT refers to TAYLOR, *Duct. Dub.* III. 5, Rule 1 and 4 ff.—R.]

the τόκος and γονεία (STIER). Hence δίκαιον, "right," refers to the relations both as given in nature and ordained by Divine law. BENGEL: *etiam natura;* MEYER: according to nature and law. This LUTHER wishes to express with his "it is proper." It should not be referred to the Divine law alone (THEODORET, MEYER, SCHENKEL), to which prominence is given in the next verse. [The natural obligation seems to be brought out here, the enforcement through the Divine law is added in the next verse (so EADIE, ALFORD, ELLICOTT, HODGE, following BENGEL, ESTIUS and THEOPHYLACT).—R.]

Ver. 2. **Honour thy father and thy mother.**—This is the commandment, Exod. xx. 12; Deut. v. 16; Matth. xv. 4. In τίμα there is more included than obedience. *Obedientia testimonium est ejus honoris, quem debent parentibus. Sub voce honoris complectitur officia, quibus serio tuam erga parentes observantiam et pietatem sestantur filius* (CALVIN). In Matth. xv. Jesus deduces from the honor the nourishment, and provision and care. Sirach iii. 8. LUTHER: serve, love and esteem. With emphasis the commandment places on an equality over against the children "thy father and thy mother;" in Lev. xix. 3 the latter even comes first.

**Which is,** ἥτις ἐστίν, introduces a reason, as in iii. 13; it is not=ἥ, *quæ*, but *ut pote quæ.** —**The first commandment with promise.** —Ἐντολη evidently refers to the Mosaic law, the Decalogue, of which what has just been said is one commandment, hence without the article; on the thought that it is a command of God an emphasis rests,† which is strengthened by the added phrase: πρώτη ἐν ἐπαγγελίᾳ: at first; it is not *the* first. According to the context it is as respects the time in which it applies to human beings, a first one: children must first *honor God's representatives*, in order to learn how and to be able to keep those which precede and follow (STIER). And it is indeed placed on the promise, conceived in promise, because thus the obedience to parents becomes joyful, and upon this obedience salvation actually rests both internally and externally (1 Tim. iii. 1, 2). BENGEL: *Honor. parentibus per obedientiam præsertim præstitus initio ætatis omnium præceptorum obedientiam continet.* It is not necessary therefore to say that it is in the series of commandments the first with a promise (HARLESS and others) [see below], as if there were not a promise annexed to the first or second [the Catholic and Lutheran first, our second] (Exod. xx. vers. 9, 10), or as though it were the first with a promise in the second table (AMBROSE and others). It belongs to the first table, and such a distinction is not "a comment of modern theologians, a distinction not founded in the sacred Scriptures" (ERASMUS), since it is definitely stated in Deut. v. 22, and the tenor of the commandments are distinguished accordingly. (Matth. xxii. 37–40; Lev. xix. 18, 34; Deut. vi. 5; x. 12.) Least of all does πρώτη mean the most important, a chief commandment (KOPPE [HODGE] and others). But while it is incorrect to take ἐν ἐπαγγελίᾳ=*annexa, addita promissione*, it is quite as much so to understand it as=in point of promise (WINER, p. 366; and others).

[The view of STIER, advocated by Braune, is not altogether satisfactory, that of KOPPE and HODGE is still less so. Nor is any importance to be attached to the absence of the article with πρώτη. The simplest view, one that usually suggests itself to the children, is that of HARLESS and MEYER, accepted by EADIE, ALFORD and ELLICOTT: *first in order;* in point of, involving a promise, the preposition showing that *in* which the priority consists. The second commandment has attached simply "a broad declaration of the great principles of the Divine government," not a specific promise. As regards the difficulty that no commandment follows in the Decalogue with a promise, we may either accept the explanation of HARLESS that "first" refers only to what precedes in this case, or that of MEYER, which finds the rest of the series in other *Mosaic* commands (so ELLICOTT).—R.]

Ver. 3. **That it may be well with thee, and thou mayest live long on the earth.**—This is the purport of the promise. Exod. xx. 12; Deut. v. 16; LXX.: ἵνα εὖ σοι γένηται καὶ ἵνα μακροχρόνιος γένῃ ἐπὶ τῆς γῆς, ἧς ὁ κύριος ὁ θεός σου δίδωσί σοι. The Apostle only alters: καὶ ἔσῃ μακροχρόνιος, omitting the last relative clause, which as a commandment of God designates, not merely Canaan, but every country appointed by Him as a home, Palestine in the case of the Jews. According to the quotation ἵνα must be retained in the second half with the future, although the conjunctive occurs in the first half. WINER (p. 271) explains the construction with the future as a lapse into a direct discourse, despite similar examples. MEYER finds indicated in the conjunctive the mere actualization, in the future the certain entrance and continuance, hence a logical climax.* Undoubtedly ἵνα is to be taken as telic, and on account of the phrase, "thy father and thy mother," to be applied to individuals, not *toti eorum genti* (BENGEL, who prudently says beforehand: *non tantum singulis;* HARLESS and others). The well being is put in the front rank, the long life in the second. Even among the most decayed people it will go well with him who honors his parents in obedience, and his life will be long, at least *quoad sufficientiam* for eternal salvation (STIER). Godliness has indeed a promise for this life also (1 Tim. iv. 8), but certainly for that which is to come. To limit the promise to the

* [This is the view of MEYER and formerly of ELLICOTT, but the latter now accepts the *explanatory* force of the pronoun, since, as ALFORD intimates, the other view throws "the motive to obedience too much on the fact of the promise accompanying it, whereas the obedience rests on the fact implied in ἐντολῇ, and the promise comes in to show its special acceptableness to God."—R.]

† [ALFORD'S remark *in loco* must be taken with caution. He says the reference is to "the Decalogue, which naturally stands at the head of all God's other commandments; and which, though not formally binding on us as Christians, is quoted, in matters of eternal obligation (not of positive enactment), as an eminent example of God's holy will." —R.]

* [On this ELLICOTT remarks: "The future undoubtedly often does express the more *lasting* and *certain* result (comp. Rev. xxii. 14, where the single act is expressed by the aorist subj., the lasting act by the future); still as the present formula occurs in substance in Deut. xxii. 7 (*Alexand.*), and might have thence become a known form of expression, it seems better not to press the future further than as representing the *temporal evolution* of the εὖ γενέσθαι."—R.]

spiritual possessions of the heavenly Canaan (JEROME, OLSHAUSEN) is incorrect. *Tenerior ætas pro captu suo allicitur promissione longæ vitæ* (BENGEL). The attracting promise is chiefly to be taken in the sense and spirit of children, who hope for a long life; the history of nations and families confirm the truth of the promise. *Hodie æque bene vivunt pii in omne terra, atque Israel olim in illa* (BENGEL).

[We must reject both the generalizing and spiritualizing interpretations of the promise, and accept an individual reference of present validity. On this most recent commentators agree. And the promise is fulfilled in the usual course of providence with obedient children. The only question is: Did the Apostle by omitting the latter part of the commandment, which had a special reference to Canaan, himself apply the promise to obedient children in all lands, or did the original commandment imply this (the given land being the home in every case), so that the Apostle omits the last clause as unessential for his present purpose and really implied in τῆς γῆς? The former is the view of EADIE, ALFORD, ELLICOTT, and HODGE, the latter of Braune and others. Either is preferable to MEYER's notion that the Apostle omitted the clause because his readers were familiar with the passage, and understood it in the general sense, though its original reference was only to Palestine.—R.]

*The precept for fathers;* ver. 4. **And ye fathers.**—Quickly and closely he connects this with καί.* He addresses the "fathers," because he regards the mothers as "submitting to their own husbands" (v. 22, 24, 33), who are their responsible representatives. *Facilius parentes et heri abutuntur potestate sua, quam mariti* (BENGEL); that lies in the freer position of the former. We are not to refer this to grown up children (OLSHAUSEN), since "bring them up" follows; nor is there any oriental depreciation of the mother (RUECKERT), since ver. 2 commands: "honor thy mother," and Gen. xxiv. 67; xxxvii. 10; 1 Kings ii. 19; Judges v. 7; 2 Sam. xx. 19 teach us otherwise.†

*The prohibition:* **Provoke [or fret] not your children to wrath,** μὴ παροργίζετε τὰ τέκνα ὑμῶν.—It is parallel to the παραζηλοῦν, Rom. x. 19; it is explained by Col. iii. 21 (א.: παροργίζετε, others: ἐρεθίζετε—ἵνα μὴ ἀθυμῶσιν). It is the hasty, rough, moody treatment of children, so that, without childish confidence, without joyful obedience, they are repelled and enticed to opposition, defiance and bitterness. Righteous, wholesome parental anger is not excluded, but painful, arbitrary, grumbling treatment, as well as rough, unjust treatment, without sparing the childish nature. [ALFORD: "The Apostle seems to allude to provoking by vexatious commands and unreasonable blame, and uncertain temper, in ordinary intercourse."—R.]

*The command:* **But bring them up,** ἀλλὰ ἐκτρέφετε αὐτά (v. 29).—This points to children who still require care. But it should not be the mere growing up of the proletarians, but spiritual also. Hence:

**In the discipline and admonition of the Lord,** ἐν παιδείᾳ καὶ νουθεσίᾳ κυρίου. Thus the element is denoted in which the bringing up should be consummated.* The former consists in *work,* the latter in *word;* the former is discipline (LUTHER), not merely punishment, also strict ordering of the household, accustoming to self-denial, serviceableness, confession of faults without shuffling. Heb. xii. 6, 7. The latter (LUTHER: admonition) comprises earnest warning (1 Cor. x. 11) and kind exhortation (Tit. iii. 10; Rom. xv. 14; Col. iii. 16; i. 28; 1 Cor. iv. 14; 1 Thess. v. 14; 2 Thess. iii. 15), which evidently predominates over serious rebukes. It is important that the former comes first, and this last. *Harum altera occurrit ruditati, altera oblivioni et levitati; utraque et sermonem et reliquiam disciplinam includit* (BENGEL). [Comp. TRENCH, *Syn.* § xxxii., whose views correspond in the main with those suggested here, and are adopted by EADIE, ALFORD and ELLICOTT.—R.] Hence the first is not general, the training of children in general, the latter special, the reproof for the purpose of improvement (HARLESS, MEYER), nor are they indistinguishable synonyms (KOPPE). The genitive belongs to both words: the Lord does it through the father as His representative; it is therefore a genitive *subjecti.* [So HARLESS, DE WETTE, MEYER, EADIE, HODGE, ALFORD, ELLICOTT and others: the discipline and admonition prescribed by the Lord and to be regulated by His Spirit.—R.] It is not then: to the Lord (LUTHER), nor=well-pleasing to the Lord (FLATT), or=*de Christo* (MICHAELIS), nor are we to accept that the Apostle himself scarcely knew how to explain it (RUECKERT).

## DOCTRINAL AND ETHICAL.

1. The presupposition for the *conduct* of children to parents and parents to children is *the relation of both to Christ.* The children should do their duty "in the Lord" (ver. 1), the parents "in the discipline and admonition of the Lord" (ver. 4), and that too from infancy ("bring them up"). Baptism, infant baptism, is thus presupposed as the basis for the children as well as for the treatment of children. And all the more so, that there is expressed for the children no termination or cessation of their conduct toward their parents and for the parents no beginning of the influence on the children, nor is any hint given of the baptismal act to be effected or experienced, which could scarcely be wanted after iv. 5 ("one baptism"), since the fellowship of the Lord is indicated in the case of children as well as parents. HOFMANN (*Schriftbeweis,* II. 2, p. 193) properly recalls Acts xvi. 15. For before mention was made of the household of the jailer, and without any impression of what had occurred having been made upon his household, it was said to him: "Believe in the Lord Jesus Christ

* [ELLICOTT suggests that the particle "marks that obligation was not all on one side, but that the superior also had duties which he owed to the inferior."—R.]

† [EADIE limits this precept to fathers, urging that mothers are apt to spoil the child by indulgence, while fathers are apt to chastise in a passion. But the other view is preferable.—R.]

* [Dr. HODGE, whose comments on this verse are very clear and instructive, falls into his usual error, in taking the preposition ἐν as instrumental: "developing all their powers by the instruction and admonition of the Lord." The thought is rather that the child shall grow up, be *trained in* an element, sphere, atmosphere, *etc.*—R.]

and thou shalt be saved, and *thy house*." We should therefore with AUGUSTINE (*De Gen.* X. 23, *Serm.* X.) and ORIGEN (*ad Rom.* vi.) regard infant baptism as an ordinance instituted by the Apostles. It was practised in the days of TERTULLIAN, but no mention is made of its having been introduced. Accordingly our passage refers the nurture of children to the basis of baptism and the family: family education and baptismal education are enjoined. [The relation to Christ rests not on the baptismal act, but on the relation to the believing parents, hence children are to be baptized "as members of Christ's Church" (Ref. Church, form of baptism), are thus publicly acknowledged and sealed as Christian children, whose personal piety is to be looked for in faith just as it is prayed for in faith. Despite all abuse of this Christian truth, it is the truth, and holding it fast we may hope for a piety which rests on an educational, not a spasmodic, basis.—In regard to the apostolic origin of the ordinance, the negative proof is overwhelming. Besides the allusion here and in Acts xvi., it is inconceivable that the Jews, who attacked Paul on every actual point of difference, could have omitted opposition here, had he failed to perpetuate in some distinct form the Old Testament doctrine of covenant blessings on the household.—But as negative proof it leaves room for honest adherence to that marked individualistic form of Christianity, which is necessary, it would seem, for many minds of that cast.—R.]

2. The Apostle requires *obedience* on the part of the children to their parents as God's representatives. This is a manifestation of that honor which God requires. It is established, regulated and limited through Christ, and is the foundation of earthly happiness. While ὑπακούειν denotes obedience as a reverent hearing, listening to the parents' will, not merely in order to know it, but rather to be directed by it, so the German word: *gehorchen* [derived from *horchen*=our English *hearken*], related to *hörig, gehörig, zugehörig* [all meaning: belonging to, but strengthened in the longer forms], refers to the internal relation of dependence which finds its answering expression in *gehorsam* [obedience]. Both refer to the relation of piety [*i. e.*, filial piety, since piety toward God and parents are recognized as identical in the Latin word *pius*], and include as the innermost motive love, which devotes itself with recognition of the parental dignity, even when parental worthiness is wanting. Over against the will of the parents the will of the child is illegal; but this statement is valid only so far as the parents exercise their will as the representatives of God, and their will is not opposed to God's will. In this there is a hint that the Fifth Commandment belongs to the first table (BRAUNE, *Die heil.* 10 *Geb.* pp. 85–88). This requirement, to agree to the will of parents, does not cease in the course of years, though it receives limitations from the avocation and position of the children, as in the case of our Lord (John ii. 4)

3. *The blessing of the Fifth Commandment* points to this fact, that in God's world and God's government His law, which is in accordance with the whole as well as with each individual part, is and must be of validity, and because it is valid for life, is given in correspondence with the ordinances of His Creation and Providence. The blessing is not an arbitrarily placed reward, but a result of obedience, actual and true obedience. One cannot creep into the blessing through constrained or feigned obedience. Obedience, this deeply rooted act of a will, growing morally, is not an affair of selfish calculation, still less can an immoral or demoralizing observance of a natural law be spoken of. Nor is the blessing promised for the life of the earthly family and people to be so lightly esteemed, that it must be transferred to the inheritance of the heavenly Canaan. Welfare and long life will be constantly regarded and used by the Christian as a gift of the gracious God; if something is lacking, he will never murmur nor doubt, as if God did not keep His promise, since our obedience of His commandment is never so perfect that it can be brought into an account with Him; it is rather the case that He has always vouchsafed and still vouchsafes to us more than we deserve.

4. *Christian education* must be consummated *in the family*, and if the family, in which children are born, is broken up by death, or destroyed by social, individual or sinful relations, and made incapable of fulfilling the task of education, each child should still be transferred to a family, or every institution which undertakes the task must be formed as a family.—Christian nurture must begin with the *earliest childhood*, with the beginning of the child's life (ἐκτρέφετε). On this account ἐν παιδείᾳ comes first, and νουθεσίᾳ follows. Matters pertaining to the ordering of the household, to habitudes, to treatment without speaking, even to punishment, come first. Comp. Heb. xii. 6; Prov. iii. 11, 12; xxii. 15; xxiii. 13.—But it must add to this and pass over into admonition by word, both alike "of Christ," not in self-will, but under the Lord to whom we are responsible. Hence this education must be Christian.*—Further it connects itself with *baptism;* hence it is *Churchly*. Comp. VON ZESCHWITZ, *System der Christlich Kirchlichen Katechetik*, II. 1, § 2. [More Christian than Churchly however. Hence in those lands where the Church as such must needs control education, there is little gain for the Church or for Christ. Were the family instruction what it ought to be, there is no fear of children becoming irreligious from attending common schools (*i. e.*, schools of the State, not of the Church).—The question of Sunday Schools ought

* [HODGE: "As Christianity is the only true religion, and God in Christ the only true God, the only profitable education is the nurture and admonition of the Lord. That is, the whole process of instruction and discipline must be that which He prescribes and which He administers, so that His authority should be brought into constant and immediate contact with the mind, heart and conscience of the child. It will not do for the parent to present himself as the ultimate end, the source of knowledge and possessor of authority to determine truth and duty. This would be to give his child a mere human development. Nor will it do for him to urge and communicate everything on the abstract ground of reason; for that would be to merge his child in nature. It is only by making God, God in Christ, the teacher and ruler, on whose authority everything is to be believed, and in obedience to whose will everything is to be done, that the ends of education can possibly be attained." But it must still be maintained, that the place where this close contact with Christ as Ruler and Teacher and Saviour is to be brought about is not the school, whether parochial school or Sunday School, but as a rule the *household*, since the command is addressed to "fathers," who, standing *in loco Dei* in the family, should not too readily abdicate from their responsible position.—R.]

to be far oftener studied in the light of this section.—R.]—The *mother* is not excluded, but only subordinated to the *father* (vers. 2, 4). The mother's influence on the formation of character is quiet and deep, reaching both to the tenderest germs and the profoundest depths of the heart. 2 Tim. i. 5.—Finally the individuality of the child must be well considered, and one not be treated as another. Such a difficult task can be performed only in the strength of the Lord, by whom we are ourselves educated.

### HOMILETICAL AND PRACTICAL.

Comp. *Doctr. Notes* and BRAUNE, *Die heiligen* 10 *Gebote*, pp. 84–106.—True obedience is so difficult, that it becomes possible only to the Christian child in the strength of the developed baptismal grace; not the natural, only the spiritual man is capable of proper obedience and becomes more and more so. On the other hand Christian training is so difficult, that only Christian parents can grant it, and this too without having learned the art, often without being conscious of it.—By the child's cradle you still humbly look up to God; you cannot boast that you have given the child life; must indeed confess that you have imparted sin to them.—Eve preferred her first-born Cain (=weapon) to Abel (=shadow, nothingness).—Be sparing of words in your discipline; let your children obey without asking why and punish rather before than after five years of age, else they will punish you.

STARKE: God joins certain promises to His commandments, that we may be the more willing to live in accordance with them. If obedient children have a promise, disobedient ones have a threatening.—The training of children is an art not easily learned. Parents, you must study this, that you may learn it, and implore this grace from God; but especially must you be watchful over all your own conduct, that you give no bad example to your children; and above all implant the true fear of God in their hearts.—If parents bring up their children to the glory of God and the advantage of the world, that is more and better than to leave them great earthly treasures.

RIEGER: The phrase: in the Lord, leads us to perceive that they must be chiefly guided and impelled therein by God's commandment, the walk of the Lord Jesus on the earth; the hope of future recompense from the Lord; but also that it sometimes requires courage to be obedient in all things, and for the Lord's sake to rise above even the parents who stand in the way.—It is often asked how shall we encourage and incite children to their duty? and it is generally thought that the love of honor and the excitement of this feeling are the best means. But he who in accordance with God's word meets their sense of truth with this thought: *for this is right*, proceeds far more securely. There is often in children a far purer feeling than we suppose, we frequently corrupt it by presenting so many frivolous motives.—With the power of self-will love would never suffice for constant obedience, did it not derive support from reverence.—All promises of God must however be treated believingly, *i. e.*, humbly, for they allow nothing to be extorted from them. *Provoking to wrath* takes place not only through unmerciful beating, but also through other unskilful treatment, even though it often has the appearance of right.—God has Himself given us the best pattern of "bringing up." At first without the sharp condemnation of sin designed in the law He led men by His eye and kept them walking before Him. After the stricter imputation of sin through the law, He guided them through His grace in Christ.

HEUBNER: The forbearance, the mildness, the fairness towards children, which Paul enjoins, consists in this, that one neither unmercifully punishes them on account of faults and infirmities, nor teases them with their education and conversion, but leads them with love and earnestness, removing hindrances, and for the rest commending them to the care of the Lord, who loves children. The child has not yet a very lively sense of sin, hence you must not overdo this matter of conversion.—Thus much is certain: religious culture should begin early; the child's heart can be early won and be influenced by love to Jesus. This is the spirit of Christian nurture, which proceeds without constraint and cannot play much with dogmatics.

PASSAVANT: How difficult for a child's heart is *child-like obedience!* for all are sinners, and in all sin there is self-desire, self-will, opposition.—Ill-bred children rarely become good subjects to the king, good citizens for the State, good brethren, good friends, or good parents to their children.

STIER: The obedience of children is due according to natural and revealed right.—The first school of obedience for man is his relation as child.—The mother's love must compensate when the father's character inclines to severity; the father's earnestness and strictness must step in where the mother's natural tenderness is insufficient.

SCHLEIERMACHER: The nature of filial obedience: 1. From what it should arise: neither hold out rewards, nor threaten punishments; nor gratify froward asking for reasons; solely out of filial respect. 2. On what grounds it is recommended: citing the old promise.

ANACKER: To what education must be directed, that it may bear fruit for time and eternity. 1. That the youth learn proper obedience; 2. That they are led through love to obedience; 3. That mildness and strictness be rooted in the nurture and admonition of the Lord.

HOFMANN: The personal work of the parents: anger their greatest hindrance; their surest means: nurture your children into the Lord.—The nurture of the Lord: The fundamental traits and principles of Divine training, presented in the history of salvation from the beginning of our race on and in the conversion of individuals through the training of the Holy Ghost; some applications thence to our training: doing acts of love, blessing (Meyer), preserving from ungodly influences, promising, punishing.—Admonition of the Lord: reminder that Christ should be glorified in the children and that they should become happy men, skilful warriors of God.

ZIMMERMANN: From what you seek in your

children, measure what you owe to them! 1. You desire obedience from them, show yourselves full of love to them. 2. You desire that they honor you, apply to them the right nurture. 3. You desire that they protect and adorn your old age, so help them to inherit the promise: that it may be well with thee and that thou mayest live long on the earth.

[HODGE: Children should obey their parents. This obedience should be in the Lord, determined and regulated by a regard to Christ. The ground of the obligation is: 1. It is in itself right; it is enforced by an express command in the Decalogue, to which a special promise is annexed, vers. 1-3.—Ver. 4. A parent had better sow tares in a field from which he expects to derive food for himself and family, than by his own ill-conduct nurture evil in the heart of a child.—R.]

[EADIE: Ver. 1. The love which Jesus showed to children, when He took them in His arms and blessed them, should induce them, in a spirit of filial faith and fondness to obey their parents, and to regard with special sacredness every parental injunction. And that obedience, if prompted, regulated, and bounded by a sense of religious obligation, will be cheerful, and not sullen; prompt, and not dilatory; uniform, and not occasional; universal, and not capricious in its choice of parental precepts.—Filial obedience, under God's blessing, prolongs life, for it implies the possession of principles of restraint, sobriety, and industry, which secure a lengthened existence.—Ver. 4. Such training leads to early piety, and such is ever welcome to Christ and His Church. For the sun shining on a shrub, in its green youth, is a more gladsome spectacle than the evening beam falling dimly on the ivy and ruins of an old and solitary tower. —R.]

[While ver. 4 does not mean (see *Exeg. Notes*) instruction and admonition concerning Christ, it is still true that a father, who, by proper discipline tempered with love, ever keeps the heart of his children in intimate and trustful allegiance, by his very demeanor teaches lessons concerning Christ and God, that are rarely learned so easily in other ways. Many a son is kept from utter ruin by remembering a mother's love and piety, but happy is he who has had such a father as Paul here sketches in bold outline, for amid every doubt that assails head and heart alike, the reality of that father is an evidence, in kind though not in degree, of what God is to us, which no speculations can overbear.—R.]

---

### *c. Servants and Masters.*

(CHAP. VI. 5–9.)

5 Servants,[1] be obedient to them that are *your* masters [to your masters] according
to the flesh,[2] with fear and trembling, in singleness of your heart, as unto [to]
6 Christ; Not with [or in the way of] eye service, as men-pleasers; but as the ser-
7 vants of Christ,[3] doing the will of God from the heart; With good will doing
8 service, as[4] to the Lord, and not to men: Knowing that whatsoever[5] good thing
any man doeth [each one shall have done], the same shall he receive[6] of the Lord,
9 whether *he be* bond [bondsman] or free. And, ye masters, do the same things unto
[towards] them, forbearing threatening: knowing that your Master also [their
Master and yours][7] is in heaven; neither is there respect of persons with him.

#### TEXTUAL AND GRAMMATICAL.

[1] Ver. 5.—[Literally "slaves;" but as Braune accepts a reference to free servants, and since in any case the injunction has a wider application, the E. V. need not be altered (against Alford). See *Exeg. Notes*.—R.]

[2] Ver. 5.—[Lachmann (א. A. B., a few cursives and fathers) places κατὰ σάρκα before κυρίοις, but Tischendorf and recent editors regard this as a conformation to Col. iii. 22.—R.]

[3] Ver. 6.—[The article before Χριστοῦ (*Rec.*, D.[3] K. L) is omitted by recent editors on the authority of א. A. B. D.[1] F., *etc.*—R.]

[4] Ver. 7.—[The *Rec.* (with D.[3] K. L.) omits ὡς, but it is well sustained and generally accepted.—R.]

[5] Ver. 8.—[The reading of the *Rec.*: ὅτι ὁ ἐάν τι ἕκαστος, is accepted by Griesbach, Scholz, De Wette, Meyer, Tischendorf, Ellicott and others, not so much on external authority (K. L., most cursives, Syriac versions, fathers), as because the very great number of various readings can be best accounted for by regarding this as the original reading. See Ellicott and Meyer, on this point. The second reading in point of preference is that accepted by Lachmann, Rückert, Wordsworth: ὅτι ἕκαστος ὁ ἐὰν ποιήσῃ which is found in A. E. (D.[1] F. G., ἄν); many cursives, Vulgate. B. has ὅτι ἕκαστος ἐάν τι, accepted by Alford; א. has the easiest reading: ἐὰν ποιήσῃ ἕκαστος, while we find in cursives and fathers, ὁ ἐάν τις, ἐάν τις, ἐάν τι, ὁ ἐάν, between ὅτι and ἑκαστος, besides ἄνθρωπος instead of the latter word. The theory of Meyer is simple: The received reading was the original one; but the transcriber passed directly from ὅτι to τι, hence the reading: ὅτι ἕκαστος ποιήσῃ; then came the corrections as above, the greater number tending to prove that ἕκαστος should come last, as in the *Rec.*—The acceptance of the inverted reading of Lachmann or Alford would require this rendering: "that each man if he shall have done any good thing."—R.]

[6] Ver. 8.—[The *Rec.* has κομιεῖται, with א.[3] D.[3] K. L., most cursives, fathers, but κομίσεται is now generally preferred on the authority of א.[1] A. B. D.[1] F. The other reading is regarded by many as taken from Col. iii. 25, where however the same variation occurs.—The article before κυρίου (*Rec.*, K. L., cursives) is generally rejected, not occurring in the best uncials.—R.]

[7] Ver. 9.—[The variations are numerous, but καὶ αὐτῶν καὶ ὑμῶν is accepted by Lachmann, Tischendorf, Alford, Ellicott, Meyer, Harless, because it has good support (A. B. D.,[1] versions and fathers) and best accounts for the occurrence

of the other readings. ℵ.[1] has ἑαυτῶν, while six other variations (in position or through omission) occur. The *Rec.* (ὑμῶν αὐτῶν) is poorly supported, but probably arose early, as a correction, the reference to the slaves being misunderstood; partial attempts at restoration led to changes in position (see Meyer).—The idea presented, that of a *common Master*, seems to be better preserved by omitting the word *both*, which a literal translation would insert before *theirs*.—R.]

## EXEGETICAL AND CRITICAL.

*The precept for* SERVANTS; vers. 5-8. *a. The precept,* ver. 5. *b. Closer definition,* vers. 6, 7. *c. Praise and promise,* ver. 8. Comp. Col. iii. 22-25.

Ver. 5. *The precept.* **Servants,** οἱ δοῦλοι.—In this context this means the domestics, the serving members of the household, as ver. 3: "as the servants of Christ," shows, and ver. 8: "whether bond or free," requires; it includes here the free servants also (BENGEL, STIER, BLEEK), does not refer to slaves alone (MEYER, SCHENKEL).* Thus this section gains its continued validity and importance for all relations of subordination, that of subject and citizen also (GROTIUS: *eadem est ratio in republica et in familia*). The passage says nothing for or against slavery. See *Doctr. Notes.*

**Be obedient,** ὑπακούετε.—Thus the Apostle places the servants on an equality with the children, in the same dependence upon the masters, who are the parents to the children.

**To your masters according to the flesh,** τοῖς κυρίοις κατὰ σάρκα.—Thus the masters are designated as bodily (LUTHER) according to Rom. i. 3; ix. 3, 5, where the last phrase denotes external, temporal, earthly relations. There is also thereby involved at the same time the δεσποτεία πρόσκαιρος καὶ βραχεῖα (CHRYSOSTOM) and the limitation of freedom in external relations (CALVIN).†

The obedience is more closely defined: **with fear and trembling,** μετὰ φόβου καὶ τρόμου.—Comp. Phil. ii. 12; 2 Cor. vii. 15; 1 Cor. ii. 3. This is *sollicita reverentia*, which has in mind as regards the masters the copied majesty of God, remembering the judgment and recompense before Him. [So HODGE]. It does not refer then to anger and rebuke and punishment (BENGEL), nor is it to be weakened into tender, anxious conscientiousness (OLSHAUSEN, MEYER, SCHENKEL). [So ALFORD, ELLICOTT. EADIE remarks: "The Apostle in the following clauses hits upon those peculiar vices which slavery induces, and which are almost inseparable from it: indolence and carelessness."—R.].

To guard against every misunderstanding there is added: **in singleness of your heart,** ἐν ἁπλότητι τῆς καρδίας ὑμῶν.—This not only consists in considering the one interest of the master (HARLESS), but like 2 Cor. viii. 2, 3; xi. 3, includes willingness and the opposite of πανουργία, excluding all untruth. [This phrase sets forth the element (ἐν) of the obedience, as the last phrase expressed its accompanying features. "Singleness" is an apt rendering of the word, which marks that *openness* and sincerity of heart which repudiates *duplicity* in thought or action. On the classical use of the word see HARLESS; comp. TRENCH, *Syn.* II. § vi.—R.] *Quoniam pessimos etiam quosque pœnæ timor cogebat, Christianos servos ab impiis discernit affectu* (CALVIN). It is all to be done: **as to Christ,** ὡς τῷ Χριστῷ, *tamquam* (ERASMUS), not *sicut* (*Vulgate*) *Christo*; v. 22. ["He being the source and ground of all Christian motives and duties" (ALFORD). "As common and secular inducements can have but small influence on the mind of a slave, so the Apostle brings a religious motive to bear upon him" (EADIE). It may be added that if this motive could be brought to bear on the class to whom the exhortation of the Apostle most directly applies in these days when "the workingman's question" is so much discussed, the solution of that question would be less difficult.—R.]

Vers. 6, 7. *Closer definition.* **Not with [or in the way of] eye-service as men-pleasers,** μὴ κατ' ὀφθαλμοδουλείαν ὡς ἀνθρωπάρεσκοι.—The first phrase, as the opposite of "in singleness of your hearts," denotes the mode, method, maxim of the service (STIER).* Paul uses the plural in Col. iii. 22: ἐν ὀφθαλμοδουλείαις. THEODORET explains the word as τὴν οὐκ εἰλικρινοῦς καρδίας προσφερομένην θεραπείαν, ἀλλὰ τῷ σχήματι κεχρωσμένην. ŒCUMENIUS also remarks: μὴ ὅταν πάρεισιν οἱ δέσποται καὶ ὁρῶσιν, ἀλλὰ καὶ ἀπόντων αὐτῶν. The reference is not simply to compulsion, but the appearance of faithful service is designated. They are really "*men*-pleasers," they wish to please men alone, who can only see what is before their eyes; thus they use their master's human weakness to their own advantage. The *studium placendi hominibus* is expressly rejected from the Christian point of view.

The antithesis follows: **but as the servants of Christ, doing the will of God from the heart.**—The first phrase is opposed to: "as men-pleasers," the second, which characterizes the servants of Christ,† to: "with eye-service." The servants of Christ naturally do the will of God, which is also the will of Christ (John x. 30; v. 30), and that too "from the heart," without discontent with their service or murmuring in their service; this necessarily distinguishes them from others, even from those who may be doing the will of God.‡

---

* [Nearly all English and American commentators accept the exclusive reference to slaves, bondmen (CONYBEARE); and with good reason, since the word means "slave" over against a hired servant (Luke xv. 17, 19), and since the greater proportion of servants in those days were slaves. Ver. 8 may be quite as readily urged in favor of the exclusive reference. Still the passage has, and was designed to have, a continued validity, which is better indicated by retaining the word "servants."—R.]

† [On the distinction between κύριος and δεσπότης, which Paul uses in 1 Tim. vi. 1; Tit. ii. 21, see TRENCH, *Syn.* xxviii.; it is neglected here probably because the former word was to be used again (ver. 7) in a higher sense, as indeed κατὰ σάρκα implies. The *deduction* from the latter phrase, that spiritual freedom was left intact is generally accepted, though it is doubtful whether the phrase itself implies this.—R.]

* [The preposition marks the *norm* of the action; ELLICOTT: in the way of; ALFORD: in the spirit of. The substantive is one of Paul's coining, occurring only here and in Col. iii. 22. ELLICOTT says: "the more correct form is ὀφθαλμοδουλία (D. E. F. G. L. ℵ.)," but does not put it in his text.—R.]

† [RUECKERT makes the first phrase subordinate to the second, removing the comma after Χριστοῦ (so TISCHENDORF, ed. 7, against recent editors generally); but this destroys the obvious antithesis.—R.]

‡ [EADIE, HODGE and ALFORD render: "the slave of Christ,"

Ver. 7. One thing more is added, which completes the last designation: **with good-will doing service, as to the Lord.**—Μετ' εὐνοίας δουλεύοντες marks the personal dependence on the masters, in which they serve them (LUTHER, [E. V.]: "with good-will"), so that they serve them, "as to the Lord," *tanquam domino, i. e. Christo.* This is rendered emphatically prominent by the antithesis: **and not to men,** καὶ οὐκ ἀνθρώποις.—On this account "from the heart" is not to be separated from "doing" (ver. 6) and joined to "doing service" (CHRYSOSTOM, JEROME, BENGEL, HARLESS, STIER), which in that case would unnecessarily receive two adverbial qualifications. [So LACHMANN, DE WETTE and ALFORD (who makes a good defence), but the other view is maintained by TISCHENDORF, MEYER, ELLICOTT, HODGE and EADIE. ELLICOTT, however, defends the view of HARLESS (against MEYER), that ἐκ ψυχῆς seems to mark the relation of the servant to his *work*, μετ' εὐνοίας pointing to his relation to his *master.*—R.] Still less is "with good-will" to be joined with what precedes and this verse rendered: Let yourselves think that you serve the Lord and not men (LUTHER). Thus the precept of ver. 5 has been more closely described and a return made to it.

Ver. 8. *Basis and promise.* **Knowing,** εἰδότες. [ELLICOTT: "seeing ye know."]—Thus Paul refers the servants to their faith, to the certain confidence: **that whatsoever good thing each one shall have done, the same shall he receive of the Lord.**—Ὅτι ὃ ἐάν τι ἕκαστος is grammatically clear: ἐάν often is =ἄν in relative clauses (WINER, p. 291) and ὅ—τι is *tmesis* (BENGEL); ἕκαστος is not to be extended to both masters and servants; the context ("whether bond or free") limits it to those addressed; each one of you. [This view assumes that "bondman or free," refers to two classes of servants, but the more commonly received opinion includes the masters under the latter term, thus giving the verse the character of a general proposition. This is the more obvious reference, and has the advantage of giving an easy transition from the exhortation to the bondman to that to the free man (masters, ver. 9).—R.] In ποιήσῃ ἀγαθόν the verb stands first with emphasis; something depends on the doing; the will of God must be done by you, as well as on you. [The rendering: "shall have done," brings out best the relation to the time of recompense, *i. e.*, the Second Advent of the Lord.—R.] Ἀγαθόν, "good," is only what takes place for Christ's sake, in love and obedience to Him. Τοῦτο is the "good," which the servant has done, and which παρὰ κυρίου κομίσεται, "he shall receive of the Lord." The verb is joined with μισθός, 2 Pet. ii. 13; with ἐπαγγελίαν, Heb. x. 36; xi. 39; and with similar expressions, 1 Pet. i. 9; v. 4; it means: *sibi auferet, reportabit* (ERASMUS), *recipiet* (*Vulgate*) [E. V.: receive], from the Lord, from Christ in the Judgment. [ALFORD: "'This in full,' 'this exactly,' he shall then receive in its value as then estimated, changed, so to speak, into the currency of that new and final state."—R.] Thus the complete recompense is marked (τὴν ἀνταπόδοσιν τῆς κληρονομίας, Col. iii. 24).—**Whether he be bondman or free,** added quickly without a verb; it is better to supply: *fuerit* (ERASMUS), than *sit* (MEYER and others). [ELLICOTT: "Whatsoever be his *social* condition here, the future will only regard his *moral* state." Comp. the citation from CHRYSOSTOM in ALFORD.—R.] From this it cannot be inferred that Paul had not conceived of the cessation of slavery before the Second Advent.

*The precept for* MASTERS *and its basis,* ver. 9. *a. Positively; b. negatively; c. basis.*

Ver. 9. **And ye masters,** καὶ οἱ κύριοι, who are thus recognized, just as "and ye fathers" (ver. 4).—The *positive* precept: **do the same things towards them.**—Τὰ αὐτὰ ποιεῖτε refers back both to "the will of God from the heart, with good-will" (RUECKERT), and to "submitting yourselves to one another" (v. 21); as the former should serve (δουλεύειν), so the latter should rule (κυριεύειν). He does not require a δουλεύειν from the masters (CHRYSOSTOM). *Amor officia servilia et herilia moderatur* (BENGEL). "Towards them" denotes the equal footing, as was already required in Deut. xv. 12; Levit. xxv. 42, 43; Job xxxi. 13–15, and enlarged in Christ. [EADIE: "The Apostle had stooped to the slave, and he was not afraid to speak with erect attitude to the master. The language is general, and expresses what Calvin well calls *jus analogum.*"—R.]

The *negative* precept: **forbearing threatening.**—Ἀνιέντες, placed emphatically first, is according to Acts xvi. 26; xxvii. 40: to leave off, cease from; τὴν ἀπειλήν (Acts iv. 17, 29; ix. 1) they should not only moderate; for the singular does not mean a single threat, but threatening, *minatio* (*Vulgate*). ["Your usual, too habitual threatening" (MEYER, following ERASMUS; so ALFORD and ELLICOTT). The last named author says: "St. Paul singles out the prevailing vice and most customary exhibition of bad feeling on the part of the master, and in forbidding this naturally includes every similar form of harshness."—R.] *Deposita fere a dominis sævitia erat, suscepta fide; nunc etiam minæ remittendæ, ne ostentent servis potestatem suam ad terrendum* (BENGEL). Thus Paul defines the action of the masters according to their disposition; in different forms of action the same disposition. *Æqualitas naturæ et fidei potior est, quam differentia statuum* (BENGEL).

*Basis:* **Knowing that their Master and yours is in heaven,** εἰδότες ὅτι καὶ αὐτῶν καὶ ὑμῶν κύριός ἐστιν ἐν οὐρανοῖς. [See *Textual Note* 7].—"Knowing" (as in ver. 8) "that their Master and yours" conceives of both masters and servants as standing on an equality before Him, who helps the latter to their rights and will and can give the former their due. He "is in heaven," *omnipotens*, (BENGEL); before Him earthly power does not appear, is of no value; in His time He comes from heaven as Judge (1 Thess. iv. 16; 2 Thess. i. 7). Hence: **neither is there respect of persons with him,** καὶ προσωποληψία οὐκ ἔστιν παρ'

but this is a harsh expression; ELLICOTT: "bond-servants." The idea of purchase and possession is probably implied.—R.]

αὐτῷ.—The substantive (Rom. ii. 11; Col. iii. 25;* Jas. ii. 1) is used by Paul in every case with reference to the Judgment. This is decidedly excluded, and the phrase suggests what one may expect to receive from Him (παρ' αὐτοῦ, ver. 8). Comp. Wisdom vi. 5-9; Gal. ii. 6.

### DOCTRINAL AND ETHICAL.

1. Paul takes occasion elsewhere also to speak of the relations of service and the state of slavery (1 Cor. vii. 21-24; Col. iii. 22-25; 1 Tim. vi. 1, 2; Tit. ii. 9, 10), as does Peter (1 Pet. i. 18-25), without condemning these relations. But sympathizing, in a specially detailed manner, the gospel instructs those who serve, having for them an affectionate heart, an interesting discourse, a consoling word. It does not without further delay declare the slaves free, but it makes them free from within. Paul sent back to Philemon his escaped slave.† In the Church the master remains a master and the slave a slave. The Apostles see in the service of the bondmen, and in the position of servants, though established by wrong and deformed by sin, the fundamental traits of master and servant, as these are established by God. What the ancients already knew, that the slaves participated in the dignity of humanity and had the rights of humanity as well as their masters (SENECA: *servi sunt? imo homines; servi sunt? imo contubernales; servi sunt? imo conservi, si cogitaveris, tantundem in utrosque licere fortunæ*), that was not first taught by Christianity. But it brought to masters and slaves *one* Redeemer, in whom both are brethren (Gal. iii. 28; Philem. 16); it wrought upon the disposition from the inner life of faith, so that at once the burden was lightened in Christian families, and in the course of centuries the relations were altered and the state of slavery was done away. Still "it must not be overlooked that Paul's mode of viewing the *already present* relation of freedom and slavery cannot be used to justify slavery *introduced* by Christians, the enslaving of free men, the slave-trade," *etc.* (MEYER). The most modern form of slavery, the Helotism of industry, cannot be viewed in the same way as something existing and historical; it remains a disgrace on which Christianity must prove, whether it is antiquated or retains its eternal powers.

2. The care of the Apostle in teaching servants is for every preacher as well as for the Church an earnest exhortation to take up the oppressed.

3. Servants, subordinates, subjects must, irrespective of the example and conduct of their masters, demean themselves according to the commandment and direction of God. *Benevolentiam, quæ in servo est, ne asperitas quidem heri exstringuit, ut in catellis* (BENGEL).—[The general principles underlying this section are applicable to all relations of employer and employee. The latter is warned against eye-service, exhorted to faithful labor "as in God's sight," bid look to a higher recompense than the temporal wages, because serving a higher master; the former is reminded of the equality before God, how position does not avail before Him, and of the duty to Him involved in the duties of an employer. How many then may study these words with profit. Comp. *Colossians*, p. 79.—R.]

4. The following applies to the masters: *ut Dominus vos tractavit, ita vos tractate servos; aut ut vos tractatis servos, ita ille vos tractabit* (BENGEL).

5. The Judgment of God finally awards strict recompense. ["The Christian doctrine of reward is too often lost sight of or kept in abeyance, as if it were not perfectly consistent with the freest bestowment of heavenly glory" (EADIE).—R.]

### HOMILETICAL AND PRACTICAL.

God's service and the master's service.—Eye-servants and God's servants.—Those who serve are a necessary evil for the masters, who are unable by themselves alone to take care of their own, rather than the employers for the servants, who often first learn of them something of order, cleanliness and skill.—*Ernest the Pious* once said: Masters and mistresses can never answer to God, if they keep their domestics away from church-service.—STARKE: Those who murmur and growl in the services, as though weary of them, murmur against God Himself.—Servants can lay up for themselves in continued service a blessing or a curse: a blessing if they faithfully serve in the fear of the Lord, a curse, however, if they act falsely and faithlessly.—A pious serving-man, whose fidelity and industry is not perceived by his employers, and whose wages are improperly withheld or cut down, is known by God, who will give him the best reward.

RIEGER: Compulsory measures, severity and cunning are of no avail. They only make the servants more crafty.—A servant has often nothing in the world but his good name; and anxiety about this can easily lead one into eye-service; but with singleness of heart better progress is made in this direction.—Eye-service spoils the heart, wasting those powers, which would remain united in the fear of the Lord and preserve from weariness also.

HEUBNER: The higher Master frees from slavery. The Lord regards all; servants and slaves are as well-known to Him as masters and princes. Before Him the heart alone gives rank, and even the most trifling services, if rendered with an honest heart, receive their reward. What a transformation the Lord's Judgment will bring about! How much the serving class has to thank

* [In Col. iii. 25, the same thought occurs in the former part of the exhortation, with a slightly different reference therefore. See *Colossians*, pp. 78, 79.—MEYER and ALFORD cite Seneca, *Thyest.* 607: "*Vos, quibus rector maris atque terræ jus dedit magnum necis atque vitæ, Ponite inflatos tumidosque vultus. Quicquid a vobis minor extinescit, major hoc vobis dominus minatur; Omne sub regno graviore regnum est.*"—R.]

† [The reader is referred to the remarks of Dr. HACKETT, *Philemon*, pp. 29 ff., and the extracts there given on the subject of Christianity and slavery. On the general principles which this section implies most commentators agree; and these principles did abolish slavery in the early Christian centuries. Unfortunately there are times when and places where these principles, while theoretically accepted, do not operate toward the desired result; then God's Providence does quickly and retributively what men would not let His gospel do. Still emancipation is not necessarily Christian freedom. The gospel method begins within; the other lays upon Christ's Church the responsibility of so teaching the truth that the "truth may make free" those suddenly released from bondage. That is but the beginning of freedom.—R.]

Christianity! It has made a freer feeling in service and better masters, and effected all this without a violent subversion of relations.—The rough and coarse master makes rough and coarse servants, the gentle master makes gentle servants. The master should not have an imperious, despotic feeling, but a ministering one.

PASSAVANT: This is true, and those who stand high and rule in the world, cannot bethink themselves of it too earnestly and humbly: Before God we are all alike, all of one origin, one nature, one sin—and all partakers of one grace, one redemption, one glory.—You look for so many virtues and perfections in your maid or man; with such conditions do you think you would be worthy or capable of being man or maid-servant?

GERLACH: Obedience to the bodily master should constantly be directed toward Christ.

[EADIE: "And with respect to servants of every denomination, *equity* requires that we treat them with humanity and kindness; that we endeavor to make their service easy, and their condition comfortable; that we forbear rash and passionate language; that we overlook accidental errors, and remit trivial faults; that we impose only such labor as is reasonable in itself and suitable to their capacity; that our reproofs be calm and our counsels well timed; that the restraints we lay upon them be prudent and salutary; that we allow them reasonable time for refreshment, for the culture of their minds, and for attendance on the worship of God; that we set before them a virtuous example, instil into them useful principles, warn them against wickedness of every kind, especially against the sin which most easily besets them; that we afford them opportunity for reading and private devotion, and furnish them with the necessary means of learning the way of salvation; that we attend to the preservation of their health, and have compassion on them in sickness; and, in a word, that we contribute all proper assistance to render them useful, virtuous, and happy" (from LATHROP, *Ephesians*).—R.]

## 5. Concluding exhortation.

CHAP. VI. 10–20.

10 Finally, my brethren, be strong [Finally be strengthened][1] in the Lord, and in the
11 power of his might [in the might of his strength]. Put on the whole armour of
12 God, that ye may be able to stand against the wiles of the devil. For we wrestle
[our[2] wrestling is] not against flesh and blood, but against [the] principalities,
against [the] powers, against the rulers of the darkness of this world [the world-
rulers of this darkness],[3] against spiritual wickedness [the spiritual *hosts* of wicked-
13 ness][4] in high [heavenly] *places*. Wherefore take unto you the whole armour of
God, that ye may be able to withstand in the evil day, and having done [accom-
14 plished] all, to stand. Stand therefore, having your loins girt [girt your loins]
15 about with truth, and having [put] on the breastplate of righteousness. And your
feet shod [having shod your feet] with the preparation [preparedness] of the gospel
16 of peace; Above [In addition to][5] all, taking the shield of faith, wherewith ye shall
17 be able to quench all the fiery darts[6] of the wicked [evil one]. And take[7] [or
receive] the helmet of salvation, and the sword of the Spirit, which is the word of
18 God: Praying always with all prayer and supplication [With all prayer and sup-
plication praying at all times] in the Spirit, and watching thereunto[8] with [in] all
19 perseverance and supplication for all [all the] saints; And for me [or on my be-
half], that utterance may be given[9] unto [to] me, that I may open my mouth
boldly, [in the opening of my mouth, in boldness] to make known the mystery of
20 the gospel,[10] For [or In behalf of] which I am an ambassador in bonds [*literally*
in a chain]; that therein I may speak boldly, as I ought to speak.

### TEXTUAL AND GRAMMATICAL.

1 Ver. 10.—[The *Rec.* reads: τὸ λοιπὸν ἀδελφοί μου, but μοῦ λοιποῦ occurs in ℵ.[1] A. B., 3 cursives, and some fathers; it is accepted by Lachmann, Rückert and Alford, but the other form is retained by Tischendorf, Meyer, Ellicott on the authority of ℵ.[3] D. F, K. L., most cursives and fathers. Most editors, however, reject ἀδελφοί μου, which is found only in ℵ.[3] K. L. (though in others with the omission of μου, and in a different position) most cursives and fathers; besides the good external authority for the omission (ℵ.[1] B. D. E., good versions), the phrase is open to double suspicion: first, as usually following τὸ λοιπόν, and hence likely to be inserted second, as not used in direct address in this Epistle (Olshausen). Meyer holds that the reading τοῦ λοιποῦ is a mechanical repetition from Gal. vi. 17, urging the insertion of the added phrase in favor of τὸ λοιπόν, (see his critical note).—R.]

2 Ver. 12.—[Lachmann and Rückert accept ὑμῖν on the authority of B. D.[1] F. G., a few cursives, a number of versions and fathers; but ἡμῖν is very well supported (ℵ. A. D.[3] K. L., most cursives, versions and fathers), while the change to the second person is an apparent correction on account of the individualizing, hortatory character of the passage as a whole.—R.]

[3] Ver. 12.—[The *Rec.* reads: τοῦ σκότους τοῦ αἰῶνος τούτου, but the words τοῦ αἰῶνος are rejected by all recent editors as an explanatory gloss. They are found in ℵ[3] (but rubbed out) D.[3] K. L., most cursives, a number of fathers (with an asterisk in Syriac-Phil.), but omitted in ℵ.[1] A. B. D.[1] F., good versions, most fathers.—R.]

[4] Ver. 12.—[The emendations in the latter part of this verse are required by the exegetical views adopted in the additional notes. The only variation from the rendering required by Dr. Braune's opinions is in the insertion of *hosts*. See *Exeg. Notes*.—R.]

[5] Ver. 16.—[Instead of the well-supported reading of the *Rec.* (ἐπί) ℵ. B., 10 cursives, a few fathers reads, ἐν, which is adopted by Lachmann, but rejected by nearly all more recent editors as a correction for the ambiguous ἐπί. Alford is in doubt.—The force of ἐπί is correctly given in the above emendation; comp. *Exeg. Notes*.—R.]

[6] Ver. 16.—[In B. D.[1] F., τά is omitted, rejected by Lachmann, bracketted by Alford, but "it seems more probable that the article was omitted by an oversight, than that the transcriber felt any grammatical difficulty, and sought to remedy it by insertion" (Ellicott). So Meyer, and most, with the support of ℵ. A. D.[2] K. L., and most minor authorities. On the effect of the omission on the grammatical construction, see *Exeg. Notes*.—R.]

[7] Ver. 17.—[In D.[1] F. G.; some minor authorities the verb is omitted; in A. D.[3] K., a number of cursives, it is changed into δέξασθαι (Matthies), but the reading of the *Rec.* (δέξασθε) is well supported, and generally accepted. The internal grounds are strongly in favor of it; had the verb been originally wanting the corrector would probably have supplied ἀναλάβετε, while the infinitive form may be ascribed either to itacism or to the presence of an infinitive in the clause immediately preceding (so Meyer.)—R.]

[8] Ver. 18.—[The *Rec.* inserts τοῦτο after αὐτό, with D.[3] K. L., some cursives and fathers, but it is rejected as an explanatory addition by recent editors on good uncial authority, confirmed by variations which are best accounted for on the theory of its spuriousness.—*In* is more literal than *with*, indicating also the variation in prepositions.—R.]

[9] Ver. 19.—The *Rec.* reads δοθείη, but it has no uncial support, found only in a few cursives.—The emendations in this verse are necessary, as the E. V. gives a wrong connection and interpretation.—R.]

[10] Ver. 19.—[The words τοῦ εὐαγγελίου are omitted in B. F. G., and bracketted by Lachmann, but accepted by more recent editors (Tischendorf, Alford, Wordsworth, Ellicott) on the evidence of ℵ. A. D. E. K. L., good cursives and versions.—R.]

## EXEGETICAL AND CRITICAL.

*Summary:* 1. Internal *strengthening*, ver. 10; 2. Necessity of *armor* on account of the enemies, vers. 11-13; 3. The *armor* itself, vers. 14-17 (*a.* the preparation, vers. 14, 15; *b.* the defensive armor, vers. 16, 17 *a*; *c.* the one offensive weapon, ver. 17 *b*); 4. The *prayer* and *intercession*, vers. 18-20 (*a.* prayer in general; *b.* intercession in general, ver. 18; *c.* intercession for the Apostle, vers. 19, 20).

Ver. 10. **Finally,** τὸ λοιπόν.—*Particula sive formula concludendi et ut ad rem magnam excitandi*, 2 Cor. xiii. 11, *formula progrediendi* (BENGEL). Phil. iii. 1; iv. 8; 1 Thess. iv. 1; 2 Thess. ii. 1. LUTHER is good: finally. Τοῦ λοιποῦ [see *Textual Note* [1]] would mean: henceforth, in future (Gal. vi. 17); here it would be unintelligible.

**Be strengthened in the Lord,** ἐνδυναμοῦσθε ἐν κυρίῳ.—What in the active form is ascribed to the Lord, who strengthens (Phil. iv. 13; 1 Tim. i. 12; 2 Tim. iv. 17), is expressed by the passive* here, without further qualification, Acts ix. 22; more closely defined in 2 Tim. ii. 1: "in the grace;" Rom. iv. 20: "in faith;" Heb. xi. 34: "out of weakness" (*ex morbo convalescere*). It cannot be middle (PISCATOR), nor can κυρίῳ refer to God (B-CRUSIUS). The general qualification: in the Lord is then more closely defined: **and in the might of his strength,** καὶ ἐν τῷ κράτει τῆς ἰσχύος αὐτοῦ.—Καί is explicative here. ["This appended clause serves to explain and specify the principle in which our strength was to be sought for, and in which it dwelt" (ELLICOTT).—R.] On the whole phrase see *Exeg. Notes*, i. 19. This gives prominence to what comes to us from Christ (1 Cor. xii. 9): Christ's strength becomes our strength; only in Him are we strengthened.

*The necessity of armor (panoply) on account of the enemies;* vers. 11-13.

Ver. 11. **Put on the whole armour of God** [ἐνδύσασθε τὴν πανοπλίαν τοῦ θεοῦ].—To those being strengthened in the Lord it is said: "put on;" ἐνδύσασθε has something of a paronomasia between ἐνδυναμοῦσθε and δύνασθαι. The internal strengthening must appropriate the proffered means of assistance, in order to become powerful in conflict. For this the Christian requires τὴν πανοπλίαν* τοῦ θεοῦ (here, ver. 13; Luke xi. 22). The figure of a conflict is frequently used by the Apostle (2 Cor. x. 4; 1 Tim. vi. 12; 2 Tim. iv. 7; Rom. vi. 13, 23; 1 Thess. v. 8; comp. Isa. lix. 16-19; Wisdom v. 17-24). The word πανοπλία refers to the entire equipment; it will not suffice to choose, or put on one or another piece of this military equipment; AMBROSE: *universitas armorum;* LUTHER incorrectly limits it to: *Harnesch* [old English *harness*, defensive armor], both here and ver. 13. But it must also be "the panoply *of God*," *arma, quæ offeruntur, suppeditantur a Deo* (CALVIN, CALOVIUS), therefore a Divine armament; the arms should be altogether of a Divine kind, in contrast to the arms of the opponent. The emphasis rests on the whole idea: God's equipment, neither on πανοπλία alone (MEYER), nor on θεοῦ alone (HARLESS).† It is not a detailed and playful imitation of 1 Thess. v. 8 (DE WETTE), but rather an independent reference to Isa. lix. 16-19, which is used in a different way for the Judgment in (Wisdom v. 17-24). Whether a Roman or Jewish warrior was in Paul's mind is in itself an unprofitable question; the former met him constantly, the latter not.

**That ye may be able to stand,** πρὸς τὸ δύνασθαι ὑμᾶς στῆναι. The first verb is repeated in ver. 13 (δυνηθῆτε) and ver. 16 (δυνήσεσθε). Στῆναι πρός τινα is a military phrase, the opposite of φεύγειν, and denotes the acceptance of a conflict with him who attacks. ["To stand one's ground;" ELLICOTT remarks on the sense of πρός in this phrase, that it means

* ["Be strong" does not bring out this passive force; hence "be strengthened" is generally substituted by English commentators and revisers.—R.]

* [The E. V.: "whole armour," is the only possible translation of this word; "panoply" is simply the Greek word with an English termination, and is less readily understood by the ordinary reader. That both offensive weapons and defensive armor are included will appear at first glance from ver. 17.—R.]

† [EADIE, ALFORD and ELLICOTT follow MEYER, urging that the emphasis on τοῦ θεοῦ would imply some other spiritual armor, but Braune's view avoids this objection, and is preferable on account of the double antithesis: "the wiles of the devil."—R.]

*adversus*, with the implied notion of *hostility* ('contra'), which is otherwise less usual unless it is involved in the verb. Comp. WINER, p. 378.—R.]

**Against the wiles of the devil**, πρὸς τὰς μεθοδείας τοῦ διαβόλου.—LUTHER very aptly renders it: "against the crafty assaults of the devil." The plural marks both the multiplicity of the concrete cases, and the obstinacy of the repeated attack (STIER).* Craft and strength are both present in the assault, but the latter is concealed under the former, thus becoming dangerous and destructive. "The devil" is mentioned as the precise enemy, even though it be sin that is to be immediately contended against (Heb. xii. 1, 4). "The panoply of God" and "the wiles of the devil," are thus opposed to each other. The power of the latter is by no means inconsiderable and the contest is difficult, hence the next statement.

Ver. 12. **For our wrestling is not against flesh and blood** [ὅτι οὐκ ἔστιν ἡμῖν ἡ πάλη πρὸς αἷμα καὶ σάρκα.]—"For" (ὅτι) introduces a reason for the proposition: "to stand against the wiles of the devil" is in question. The form οὐκ ἔστιν ἡμῖν ἡ πάλη is remarkable; ἡμῖν includes with emphasis the Apostle; a proposition valid for all is treated of; ἔστιν πάλη denotes the present conflict, while πάλη (πάλλειν, to throw, to swing), the wrestling-match, *lucta* (ERASMUS), *colluctatio* (AUGUSTINE, *Vulgate*), is used in order to characterize the close, personal, struggle. Paul had in view the subject-matter and the readers, not mere rhetorical beauty. The article denotes the contest, which exists and which every one already knows. The Apostle denies the contest "against blood and flesh" because *pone homines, qui nos infestant* LATENT *spiritus* (BENGEL). Underneath and behind what is human and sinful, Satan himself is active (STIER). Paul insists on the final ground, the deepest cause of the contest, the guiding principle, the commanding general; flesh and blood is to him only the division of the army which presses forward, occasioning special danger. Comp. WINER, p. 463. AUGUSTINE: *Non est nobis colluctatio adversus carnem et sanguinem, i. e., homines, quos videtis sævire in nos. Vasa sunt, alius utitur; organa sunt, alius jungit.* We have οὐκ—ἀλλά, hence not= *non tam, non tantum—quam* (GROTIUS, STIER and others). [Most commentators now oppose the softening down of the negation (following WINER and MEYER). The word πάλη (only here) has been generally considered a change of metaphor or taken in a general sense. It undoubtedly marks the hand to hand conflict, and should therefore be taken literally. MEYER, who formerly accepted a change of metaphor, now maintains that this figure enters only in the negative clause, and that some general word is to be supplied after ἀλλά. This avoids a mixing of metaphors, but the learned author does not seem to notice that it weakens the sense just where it ought to be strongest, in the positive clause. He also takes the article as *generic*, but ALFORD suggests that ἡ πάλη refers to "the only conflict which can be described by such a word—our life and death struggle, there being but *one* such," which is better.—R.]

The contest with flesh and blood is not, however, on this account excluded. The usual order is σὰρξ καὶ αἷμα (Matt. xvi. 17; 1 Cor. xv. 50; Gal. i. 16), in Heb. ii. 14 we find as a various reading [probably the correct reading, as it is supported by our best uncial authorities.—R.]: αἵματος καὶ σαρκός. Since the formation of the flesh proceeds from the blood (Wisdom vii. 1, 2), reference is made here to the origin of man and his corrupt nature denoted, according to the context. The position of the two words is not accidental (MEYER). Elsewhere the phrase means human nature in itself (1 Cor. xv. 50), including what is sinful, Matt. xvi. 19; Gen. i. 16. One's own flesh and blood is also included here; it is not to be referred only to the human *persons* about one's self (BENGEL, HARLESS, MEYER, and others).

**But**, ἀλλά supply ἔστιν ἡμῖν ἡ πάλη.—**Against the principalities**, πρὸς τὰς ἀρχάς.—The repetition of the preposition with each term gives prominence rhetorically to the several notions. WINER, p. 392. Ἀρχάς indicates the organization of the kingdom of the devil, denoting the chiefs and heads of the separate groups,—**Against the powers**, πρὸς τὰς ἐξουσίας marks the efficient, attacking powers, comp. i. 21; iii. 10.—**Against the world-rulers of this darkness**, πρὸς τοὺς κοσμοκράτορας του σκότους τούτου.—This term (also in the Hebrew [Rabbinical term] קוֹזְמוֹקְרָטוֹר) denotes the world-ruling power: for "the whole world lieth in darkness" (1 John v. 19; ii. 14) and Satan is "the god of this world" (2 Cor. iv. 4), "the prince of this world" (John xvi. 11; xiv. 30); his angels are under him world-rulers, whose sphere is designated by the genitive: "of this darkness." Κόσμος more closely designates the local extension and region of the dominion, τοῦ σκότους its quality as to origin and corruptness, but it is limited by τούτου, which points to something transient and bounded. On this account we should neither weaken the meaning of κοσμοκράτορες into "rulers" (HARLESS), nor is it necessary (with BENGEL, STIER [E. V.] and others) to read τοῦ αἰῶνος after τοῦ σκότους. BENGEL: *Bene quod non sunt omnitenentes: magna tamen non solum ipsius diaboli, sed etiam eorum, quibus præest, potentia est. Videntur alia esse genera malorum spirituum, quæ magis domi in arce regni tenebrarum manent, imperia, potestates, aliud hoc tertium, quod foris mundanas quasi provincias obtinet munditenentes.** The *power* is made prominent in the first two terms, and in the third the sphere; there follows next a designation which gives prominence to the character:

**Against the spiritual hosts of wicked-**

* [The word is generally used in a bad sense, though Diodorus Siculus uses the verb of geometrical investigations (ALFORD). EADIE renders it: "stratagems;" ALFORD: "schemes." The form μεθοδίας is found in ℵ. A. B.[1] D.[1] F. K. L., many cursives, but not generally received, as the variation is supposed to be due to *itacism* (comp. iv. 14).—R.]

* [ELLICOTT: "The dogmatical meaning is correctly explained by the Greek commentators: the evil spirits exercise dominion over the κόσμος, not in its mere material nature, but in its ethical and perhaps intellectual character and relations, the depravation of which is expressed by τοῦ σκότους τούτου." MEYER's note (mainly adopted by ELLICOTT) *in loco* is interesting and valuable.—R.]

**ness.**—Πρὸς τὰ πνευματικὰ (Vulgate: *spiritualia*) is an abstract term, the concluding antithesis of "flesh and blood," comprising all the spiritualities, which, in contrast with the kingdom of the Holy Ghost, deserve the characteristic: τῆς πονηρίας, as the spirit of revolution; to such belong moral wickedness and malice, which is directed to the destruction of others. It is incorrect to take πνευματικώ=πνεύματα (LUTHER: with evil spirits), or collectively as *Geisterschaft* (MEYER), or to translate the phrase *spirituales nequitias* (ERASMUS). [This view, supported by Braune, is that of STIER, but it is by no means so satisfactory as that of MEYER, accepted by HODGE, EADIE, ALFORD, ELLICOTT and others. This takes the term collectively (see WINER, p. 224, and MEYER), as implying something more than "spirits," rather the bands, hosts, armies, confraternities of spirits, best expressed by the German term: *Geisterschaft.* See ELLICOTT against the altogether untenable rendering of the E. V., as well as against the abstract meaning in general.—R.]

**In heavenly places,** ἐν τοῖς ἐπουρανίοις.—This is to be connected grammatically with τὰ πνευματικά (*omnium doctorum opinio*, JEROME), and, as in iii. 10; i. 3, 20; ii. 6; has a local signification, designating a region in antithesis to the earthly, to what is in any manner perceptible to the sense; here, where angels are spoken of, it means the region assigned to these beings who are purely spiritual over against men, and although there are angels who have not remained in their original fellowship with God, yet there still remains to them a region corresponding to their nature, of course not in nearness to God. It does not then mean *in statu cœlesti* as a moral notion, but only as a physical one, so that it may be taken as parallel to ἀήρ, ii. 1, though it is not exactly equivalent; ἀήρ is spoken of from the stand-point of man, τὰ ἐπουράνια from the nature of angels, marking the dangerous element of the contest with these spirits and their spiritualities. Hence before all we are to reject the explanation: "for heavenly possessions" (GREEK FATHERS, CALOVIUS, MORUS and others), since the position of the words will not permit this phrase to be joined with πάλη in the beginning of the sentence, passing over ἀλλά, nor is ἐν =ὑπέρ, διά, while the signification of the phrase is uniformly local. [Comp. i. 3.] It does not designate the place of the conflict, the kingdom of heaven (MATTHIES),* nor the place, but in a symbolical sense, out into the fathomless air, in order to show that the contest is unequal *Marte iniquo* (RUECKERT), or in such a way that region and subject meet, as though a conflict was spoken of in our souls, but respecting calling and sanctification, our praying and preaching of God's grace (STIER); nor yet are we to think of the spiritual world and its affairs (B-CRUSIUS). Finally with the proper view of the connection we should neither interpolate a "formerly" (SEMLER), as though only the previous condition of the angels was denoted, nor does it suffice to accept the limitation to a locality excluded (HOFMANN, *Schriftbeweis*, i. 455), nor is it admissible to treat the notion of heaven as an elastic one, so that these angels are still relatively in a heaven, the atmospheric one (MEYER). Nor does it at all mean a pretended stay, so that the expression is apt irony in view of the arrogation of equal dignity, power and glory with God (SCHENKEL).

[The connection with the phrase immediately preceding is accepted by nearly all recent commentators, but there is necessarily difference of opinion about the exact force of the term. ELLICOTT objects to any precise specification of locality, though referring to HOFMANN, whose view is properly rejected by MEYER. SCHENKEL'S view is a pure invention. Such irony was not befitting the earnestness of Paul's discourse, and was scarcely so "apt" as SCHENKEL thinks, if no one else but himself has hitherto appreciated it. ELLICOTT aptly expresses the sense: "supernal spirits of evil." The E. V. shows the reluctance to apply the word "heavenly" to evil spirits. See MEYER and EADIE for notice of other shifts. —R.]

* [EADIE adopts this view: "The celestial spots occupied by the Church; on them this combat is to be maintained. Those evil spirits have invaded the Church—and therefore believers must encounter and fight them 'in the heavenly places.'" To this view nothing in the context points, while it seems a too remote connection to join this phrase with πάλη.—R.]

Ver. 13. **Wherefore,** διὰ τοῦτο, because we have to contend against such.—**Take up the whole armour of God.**—Comp. ver. 11. Ἀναλάβετε is a technical term for taking up the arms.—**That ye may be able to withstand.**—Instead of πρός (ver. 11) we here have ἵνα; the goal is denoted there, the purpose here; ἀντιστῆναι is somewhat livelier, indicating the attacks of the spirit, whom he in spirit sees making an assault.—**In the evil day,** ἐν τῇ ἡμέρᾳ τῇ πονηρᾷ.—At all events this means a particular day, immediately impending, but quite as certainly is it not the same for every one, since a common contest is not implied, not a battle, but a πάλη, "wrestling," in which the victory is decisive for "the day of redemption." Therefore the decisive, imminent day of conflict for each one is marked. BENGEL: *bellum est perpetuum; pugna alio die minus fervet; dies malus vel ingruente morte, vel in vita; longior, brevior, in se ipso sæpe varius.* [So HODGE, EADIE, ALFORD, ELLICOTT.] See *Doctr. Notes.* It is neither the day of death (SCHMID), still less the day of Judgment (JEROME), nor in general every day of conflict with its calamity (THEODORET, PELAGIUS, HARLESS and others), [nor the *present life* with the accompanying thought of brevity, CHRYSOSTOM, ŒCUMENIUS, THEOPHYLACT,] nor the particular common day [of the last great Satanic outbreak] before the Second Advent (KOPPE, MEYER, STIER and others), nor is it merely the evil hours (LUTHER).

**And having accomplished all, to stand** [καὶ ἅπαντα κατεργασάμενοι στῆναι].—To ἀντιστῆναι, referring to the conflict, the Apostle appends (καί) στῆναι, which designates the victorious keeping the field on the place of contest; it is the opposite of fleeing, yielding, being thrown down. Ἅπαντα κατεργασάμενοι, placed first, denotes a performing, effecting, the object of which is more fully designated with ἅπαντα, more comprehensible than πάντα, *omnia operati* (JEROME), well executing all (LUTHER); comp. Rom. vii. 13; Phil. ii. 12.

The Apostle here treats of the doing of the Divine will in all directions and relations, the ethical activity and efficiency of the Christian, which cuts its way through all assaults and conflicts from the side of the demons, without being led astray or weakened. It is neither=παρασκευασάμενοι, *omnibus rebus probe comparatis ad pugnam* (BENGEL and others), nor=*debellare, phrasis bellica* (GREEK FATHERS, GROTIUS, KOPPE, HARLESS and others), nor does it refer to the conflict itself (MEYER and others), nor yet is it: *in omnibus perfecti* (*Vulgate*).

[The participle is never used by Paul in the sense of "having overcome;" it is therefore best to accept the usual meaning: "having accomplished," especially as we might expect a masculine object instead of the neuter ἅ π α ν τ α, were the former sense intended. At the same time the view of BENGEL is evidently too restricted for the extended meaning of both participle and object. There remains still another question respecting the scope of the clause. Braune follows LUTHER in referring the infinitive to keeping the field; in that case the participle necessarily refers to all the antecedent action. EADIE, ALFORD, and ELLICOTT however apply the term to standing firm until the end of the combat, which seems preferable in view of the continued reference in context to the conflict itself. The participle, with its object, then means: having done all that the exigencies of the conflict require, "being fully equipped and having bravely fought."—R.]

*The* ARMOR *itself;* vers. 14-17. *a. The preparation;* vers. 14, 15. *b. The defensive armor;* vers. 16, 17 a. *c. The one offensive weapon;* ver. 17 b.

Ver. 14. **Stand therefore,** σ τ ῆ τ ε ο ὖ ν, in the conflict, in order after the conflict to stand as victor. [MEYER, ELLICOTT: "stand ready for the fight;" ALFORD: "whether 'ready for the fight' or 'in the fight' matters very little: all the aoristic participles are in time antecedent to the στῆτε—and the fight ever at hand."—R.]—**Having girt your loins about with truth,** π ε ρ ι ζ ω σ ά μ ε ν ο ι τ ὴ ν ὀ σ φ ὺ ν ὑ μ ῶ ν ἐ ν ἀ λ η θ ε ί ᾳ.—Being girded about their loins, they have on the girdle, or waist-belt (ζωστήρ, ζώνη), which covers the groin and the stomach below the breastplate, the most vulnerable part of the body, the region of the hips and loins; this is the first and a very important piece (Isa. v. 27; xi. 5; Luke xii. 35; 1 Pet. i. 13). [Meyer: "An ungirded soldier would be a contradiction in terms." The girdle kept the armor in place, formed in itself a part of the cuirass, and was also used to support the sword. The latter notion ALFORD regards as confusing here, but it hardly seems so, since the sword was *objective* truth.—R.]—Ἐ ν ἀ λ η θ ε ί ᾳ that with which the loins are enveloped, like καίειν ἐν πυρί, καλύπτειν ἐν ἱματίῳ (WINER, p. 363*); here it means the objective truth revealed in the word, which is appropriated. *Veritas adstringit hominem, mendaciorum magna est laxitas* (GROTIUS). On this account we should neither exclude the former (HARLESS, MEYER), nor understand merely the moral truth of willing (HARLESS) or the agreement of knowledge with the objective truth given in the gospel (MEYER), or sincerity (CALVIN and others), or apply this to ornament (HARLESS). ["Truth" here is *subjective* truth, since the article is wanting and the objective truth is mentioned in ver. 17. Still it is based on the faith and standing of a Christian (ALFORD); "the assured conviction that you believe" (EADIE). It should be noticed that faith (by implication) enters here and in the mention of the sword, as well as explicitly in the figure of the shield.—R.]

**And having put on the breastplate of righteousness** [κ α ὶ ἐ ν δ υ σ ά μ ε ν ο ι τ ὸ ν θ ώ ρ α κ α τ ῆ ς δ ι κ α ι ο σ ύ ν η ς].—Here κ α ί adjoins another piece. Ἐ ν δ υ σ ά μ ε ν ο ι* means putting on like a part of the clothes. Τ ὸ ν θ ώ ρ α κ α is added by the Apostle without a designation of the part of the body (στῆθος) which it covers because that is self-evident. The genitive (τ ῆ ς δ ι κ α ι ο σ ύ ν η ς) is appositional; here it means the righteousness of faith and of life, justification and sanctification before God and men (Rom. vi. 4, 13). *In pectore sedes est conscientiæ, quæ munitur justitia. Hostis per omnia ipsi contraria vincitur* (BENGEL). MEYER finds here the *ethical* rectitude, as in the previous clause the *intellectual*, which is only so far correct, that here we should find an ethical reference, there an intellectual one, as in v. 9; Isa. xi. 5. HARLESS: The righteousness of faith, with which alone one does not stand on the place of conflict, which also passes over into the life. [So ALFORD: "The purity and uprightness of Christian character which is the result of the work of the Spirit of Christ; the inwrought righteousness, not merely the imputed righteousness." The latter reference is defended by EADIE and HODGE; the former pressing the article in support of it, the latter urging that no moral virtue forms part of the armor and then saying that the subjective sense of righteousness was included already in the word "truth." The wider reference is preferable, for the more restricted one belongs to a view of the word δικαιοσύνη, which is too forensic, sundering in twain an indivisible truth. For the correct meaning of the word, see *Romans*, pp. 74, 75, 78, etc.—R.]

Ver. 15. **Having shod your feet,** κ α ὶ ὑ π ο δ η σ ά μ ε ν ο ι τ ο ὺ ς π ό δ α ς.—This adds the third piece, and the terms are again significant. Here we must think of the war-sandals, προκνημῖδας, *ocreæ militares*†, which give firm footing and gait.—**With the preparedness of the gospel of peace** [ἐ ν ἑ τ ο ι μ α σ ί ᾳ τ ο ῦ ε ὐ α γ γ ε λ ί ο υ τ ῆ ς ε ἰ ρ ή ν η ς].—That in (ἐν) which the feet stand, is for the warrior of Christ ἑ τ ο ι μ α σ ί ᾳ, readiness, *promptitudo animi*, internal and external, the ready courage and preparedness for conflict, *firmitas et constantia*, which the gospel gives; hence τ ο ῦ ε ὐ α γ γ ε λ ί ο υ is *auctoris*, the contents and pledge of which is set

* [MEYER, ELLICOTT and others take the preposition as instrumental, but ALFORD is more exact: "not instrumental, but *local;* the girt person is within, surrounded by the girdle; but this is necessarily expressed in English by '*with.*' "—R.]

* [The aorist participles are not used for presents (HOLZHAUSEN), but with propriety; "the different acts specified by the participles were all completed before the soldier took up his position" (ELLICOTT).—R.]

† [The Roman *caligæ* were probably in the Apostle's mind; sandals with soles thickly studded with nails.—R.]

forth by τῆς εἰρήνης chiefly with God, (Rom. v. 1; viii. 31, 38 f.), then in one's self and peaceableness toward men as such.* The Christian fights in peace for the sake of peace, *viz.* the eternal one. That is an *oxymoron* (SCHENKEL): the gospel of peace instils readiness for conflict. We should not then, because *pedum sæpe* (Rom. x. 15; iii. 16 *sqq.*; Luke i. 79) *conjuncta mentio cum evangelis et cum pace* (BENGEL), allow ourselves, contrary to the context to think of the proclamation of the gospel (LUTHER: ready to carry on the gospel, HARLESS and others). [So CHRYSOSTOM and now CONYBEARE, but the Apostle was addressing the whole church as engaged in an individual conflict, mainly defensive too.—R.] Notwithstanding the frequent use of ἑτοιμασία to translate the Hebrew מָכוֹן (LXX. Ezra ii. 68; iii. 3; Ps. lxxxix. 15; Dan. xi. 20, 21), it is not to be rendered as=*fundamentum* (BENGEL and BLEEK and others), although what is positive is not to be excluded. Εἰρήνη is neither to be limited to peace with God (HARLESS, MEYER and others), nor referred to peace between Gentile and Gentile (MICHAELIS). ERASMUS is irrelevant: *evangelium—nontumultu, sed tolerantia tranquillitateque defenditur.*

The *defensive* armor; vers. 16, 17a.

Ver. 16. **In addition to all,** ἐπὶ πᾶσιν (WINER, p. 367), as in Luke iii. 20: "Added this above all;" xvi. 26. ERASMUS: *super omnia*, for a protection over all. Incorrect: before all things (LUTHER). [MEYER, HODGE, ALFORD, ELLICOTT agree with Braune (as does EADIE, who formerly defended the local sense) in taking the preposition as=in addition to, rejecting the local (Bengel and others) and ethical references (E. V.). If ἐν be accepted as the correct reading (see *Textual Note* [5]) the meaning would be: in all things, *i. e.*, on all occasions.—**Having taken up,** ἀναλαβόντες, aptly chosen here:† **the shield of faith.**—Τὸν θυρεόν (from θύρα, originally that which closes an entrance) is chosen by the Apostle because he has in mind the *scutum*, which was four feet long and two and a half broad, צִנָּה (Ps. xxxv. 2; Ezek. xxiii. 24, LXX.) and not ἀσπίς, *clypeus*, מָגֵן, the smaller, round shield. The concern is that the whole person be covered, as indeed faith (τῆς πίστεως, genitive of apposition as in vers. 14, 17) entirely covers and defends the Christian: as God's gift effecting salvation (ii. 8) [MEYER: *fides salvifica*], bringing about forgiveness of sins in the past (i. 7), affording for every moment access to God (iii. 12), assuring in advance of eternal life, by securing to us the gift of the Holy Ghost (i. 13, 14), rendering holy and without blame (i. 4). Comp. Rom. viii. 14-16, 31-39. Man's own holiness is not a shield for him, as in Wisdom, v. 20; God's holiness is his shield; God Himself is our shield (Gen. xv. 1; Ps. xviii. 31; Prov. xxx. 5; 1 Pet. v. 9; 1 John v. 4). It is faith, entirely and constantly giving itself up to God in Christ, on the part of a child and heir, hence not the faith of miracles, nor justifying faith alone (SCHENKEL).

**Wherewith ye shall be able to quench all the fiery darts of the evil one.**—Thus the Apostle describes the protection of faith against dangerous attacks. Ἐν ᾧ is *on* which, not with which (LUTHER and others). [It means either, lighting *on* it and being quenched *in* it, or "as protected by and under cover of which" (ELLICOTT). The former is perhaps preferable. —R.] The figure and the reality are here so much complicated in each other, that we should not think of a shield with wet hides (OLSHAUSEN), but of faith on which the destructive fire from Satan is extinguished, without causing damage. The future (δυνήσεσθε) refers to the impending conflict.* In this are thrown τὰ βέλη τοῦ πονηροῦ τὰ πεπυρωμένα; these are *malleoli* (darts), *falaricæ* (javelins), *tela ignita* (made of reeds, with tow and pitch), which are ignited and then hurled (Ps. vii. 14; LIVY, xxi. 8). The evil one, *i. e.*, Satan† (Matt. v. 37; xiii. 19, 38; John xvii. 15; 2 Thess. iii. 3) throws temptations of many kinds; hence πάντα comes first and τὰ πεπυρωμένα is placed last for emphasis (WINER, p. 127)‡. Certainly we are to understand in part dangerous and corrupting words and speeches which come to one's ears, impart thoughts cast into the heart, the fire of passions, etc. In the σβῆσαι the figure is simply exceeded by the reality. Of course we need not think of poisoned darts (RUECKERT and others), which are not burning, but inflict burning wounds. Yet it cannot be said that we should not think of burning desires (CHRYSOSTOM), because these are present *within* man (SCHENKEL); faith is an affair of the heart, and in the heart the conflict of redemption is fought and won; besides fire and iron could scarcely be two deadly elements, which aptly illustrate the attacks of Satan. [SCHENKEL].

Ver. 17. **And take** [or receive] **the helmet of salvation** [καὶ τὴν περικεφαλαίαν τοῦ σωτηρίου δέξασθε.—This advance is natural. In accordance with the genius of the Greek language a translation is made to the finite construction; it is not simply Paul's lively method (MEYER), but that of the language. The genitive, τοῦ σωτηρίου, is one of apposition, as in vers. 14, 16.] The word is entirely general as in Luke ii. 30; iii. 6; Acts xxviii. 28 (from Isa. lix. 17, LXX. with a reference to the name of Jesus, in which the battle is fought and won,

* [This view of the passage is now generally accepted (MEYER, ALFORD and many others). On the word ἑτοιμασία, used principally in the LXX. and ecclesiastical writers (the classical form was ἑτοιμότης), see MEYER and ALFORD *in loco.* —R.]

† [EADIE: "The pieces of armor already mentioned being fitted on to the body and fastened to it, each by appropriate mechanism, have each its characteristic verb—but shield, helmet and sword need no such special fastening, for they are simply taken up or assumed, and therefore they are joined to the one general participle, ἀναλαβόντες, and the verb δέξασθε."—R.]

* [Not, however, as MEYER thinks, to the last great future fight. ALFORD thinks the future implies the certainty that the shield of faith will thus quench. ELLICOTT regards it as only "a conditioned present."—R.]

† [Should the article be omitted (see *Textual Note* [6]) the participle would be a tertiary predicate; "fire-tipt as they are" (ELLICOTT), "when inflamed, even in their utmost malice and fiery power" (ALFORD).—R.]

‡ [ELLICOTT: "Not 'evil,' τὸ πονηρόν, but in accordance with the individualizing and *personal* nature of the conflict which the context so forcibly depicts—the Devil." ALFORD: "The conflict being personal, the adversary must be, not an abstract principle, but a concrete person."—R.]

whom faith appropriates) and is used for σωτηρία. The salvation of the Messianic kingdom is represented as a helmet, covering the head. For the warrior does not hide himself behind his shield, but looks over it into the face of his opponent.—Δέξασθε, *accipite oblatam a domino. Salute erigitur caput et munitur.* 1 Thess. v. 8; Psa. iii. 3, 4 (BENGEL). Salvation is the subject of the faith, in which the salvation is apprehended (HARLESS). [HODGE: "That which adorns and protects the Christian, which enables him to hold up his head with confidence and joy, is the fact that he is saved." The German has an alliteration here: *Den Helm des Heils nehmt*, which Wickliffe gives in the Old English of his version: "the helme of helthe."—R.]

The *one offensive* weapon; ver. 17 b.

**And the sword of the Spirit**, καὶ τὴν μάχαιραν τοῦ πνεύματος.—There is no mention, in addition, as in 1 Sam. xvii. 47; of the "spear," or of the "bow" (Gen. xlviii. 22; Josh. xxiv. 12; Psa. xliv. 7). The Christian has only to contend *cominus*, personally, not *eminus*. The sword is "of the Spirit;" τοῦ πνεύματος is a genitive *auctoris:* He gives it, makes it. It cannot be appositional (HARLESS and others), as before, since the apposition follows in the relative clause.*

**Which is the word of God.**—Ὅ ἐστι which is neuter by attraction of ῥῆμα θεοῦ, relates to μάχαιραν, and is not to be construed with πνεύματος (OLSHAUSEN), for the Holy Ghost is not the Word of God; the latter is the product, the former is the Producer of what is in the word of God. *Concinne subsequitur mentio Spiritus, adeoque coll. ver.* 13 *habetur mentio s. trinitatis* (BENGEL). The Holy Ghost is meant, in antithesis, both to the letter and to the flesh, hence not the human spirit (MORUS), which in itself is also σάρξ. "The Word of God" is not to be limited to commandments (FLATT), or threatening against the enemies of the kingdom (KOPPE).

This completes the equipment. Two things are to be maintained: 1. The difference of the arms and the ethical or supersensuous realities set forth in them should not be arbitrarily weakened. It should not be said: *universa potius armorum notio tenenda est.* Nor can a proof of this be deduced from 1 Thess. v. 8, where we read: "the breastplate of faith and love, and for an helmet the hope of salvation." From a different stand-point there can be afforded a partially different point of view. 2. The figures are not to be pressed beyond measure and the lively objective metaphor of the Apostle to be dissected in arbitrary subjectivity to practical use.†

*The prayer and the intercession;* vers. 18-20. (*a.*) *Prayer in general,* ver. 18 *a.* (*b.*) *Intercession in general,* ver. 18 *b.* (*c.*) *Intercession for the Apostle,* vers. 19, 20.

Ver. 18. **With all prayer and supplication praying.**—[The connection of this verse is with στῆτε (ver. 15), not with δέξασθε, which is a subordinate thought referring to a definite act, hence inconsistent with the "all," "always" of this verse (MEYER). MEYER is scarcely justifiable in disconnecting διὰ πάσης προσευχῆς καὶ δεήσεως from προσευχόμενοι on the ground of tautology and logical difficulty. Each phrase expresses a proper qualification of the participle, and to pray always with every form of prayer involves no contradiction. HODGE seems to have been led into MEYER's view. CONYBEARE improperly takes the participle as an imperative and begins a new paragraph with this verse.—R.]

The participle (προσευχόμενοι) is closely connected with the summons to the conflict and the putting on of the armor. The summons to prayer did not appear independently. Prayer is rather to be regarded as attending the taking up of the weapons and the conflict, as the present strongly indicates. The phrase: διὰ πάσης προσευχῆς καὶ δεήσεως, placed first, only requires, that prayer should not be neglected and that constant prayer of every form be earnestly offered up. The first term means prayer in general, the second the special request. [So HARLESS, MEYER, FRITZSCHE, TRENCH (*Syn.* II., § 1), ELLICOTT, ALFORD and most recent commentators.—R.] The opinion [GROTIUS] is untenable, that the former refers to the bestowment of a blessing, the latter to the averting of an evil (Jas. v. 16, 17).

**At all times in the Spirit.**—Ἐν παντὶ καιρῷ, gives prominence to the prayer as persevering, despite all change of relations and circumstances, at every opportunity, ἐν πνεύματι to prayer, as fervent and Christian occurring in the impulse of the Holy Ghost.* BENGEL: *Quoties cunque oratis, orate in Spiritu, quippe qui nullo tempore excluditur.*

*Intercession in general.* **And watching thereunto in all perseverance and supplication for all the saints.**—With reference to the already described prayer (εἰς αὐτό) there should also enter (καί), "watching" (ἀγρυπνοῦντες, from ἄυπνος, Mark xiii. 33; Luke xxi. 36), which is elsewhere also joined with prayer (Matt. xxvi. 41; Mark xiv. 38; Col. iv. 2). [ALFORD: "continual habits of prayer cannot be kept up without watchfulness to that very end."—R.] This should take place: "in all perseverance and supplication for all the saints." The feeling of fellowship in the conflict finds its immediate expression in the supplication for all the fellow-combatants, whose standing fast is strength and

---

* ["Still less probably is it a genitive of *quality*, ἡ μάχαιρα πνευματικά (CHRYSOSTOM), or a simple genitive of *possession* in reference to the τιμωρητικὴ ἐνέργεια (Lever. ap. Cram. *Cat.*) of the Spirit, both of which seem to be at variance with the general tenor of the passage, which represents the '*armatura*' as furnished to us by God. Thus then it is from the Spirit that we receive the sword, that sword being the Word of God; the Gospel (ver. 15), which is the δύναμις θεοῦ (Rom. i. 16; 1 Cor. i. 18) to every one who believeth; comp. Heb. iv. 12" (ELLICOTT).—R.]

† [EADIE mentions among the works which are open to this objection: GURNALL, *Christian in complete armour*, Glasgow, 1763; AINSWORTH, *Tactica Sacra*, 1657; LYDIUS, *Syntagma de re militari*, ed Van Til, 1698, Dort.—The best practical commentary on this section is undoubtedly to be found in BUNYAN'S *Pilgrim's Progress*, especially the armory in the "Interpreter's house," and the combat with Apollyon in "the valley of humiliation."—On the arms, comp. SMITH'S *Bible Dictionary*, Arms.—R.]

* ["The Holy Spirit *in* whose blessed and indwelling influence, and by whose merciful aid, we are enabled to pray (Rom. viii. 15; Gal. iv. 6), yea, and who Himself intercedes for us (Rom. viii. 26)." So ELLICOTT, who analyzes the clause thus: "With all prayer and supplication" denotes the earnest, because varied character of the prayer; "at all times" the constancy of it, thus showing that there is no tautology as MEYER asserts and HODGE implies.—R.]

assistance to their neighbor. The Christian should have a clear view about him, to the companions in conflict at other positions, in other places, and besides continue constant in such supplication. [" Perseverance and supplication" here amounts to " persevering supplication," though it is not a grammatical Hendiadys, since the order would be inverted in that case. ELLICOTT says it is " a virtual or what might be termed a contextual ἓν διὰ δυοῖν." EADIE : "In praying for themselves they were uniformly to blend petitions for all the saints."—R.] How much depends on this is exemplified in what follows.

*Intercession for the Apostle*, vers. 19, 20. Ver. 19. **And for me [or on my behalf]**, *καὶ ὑπὲρ ἐμοῦ*.—[Καί brings into prominence a particular instance; WINER, p. 407.—R.] On the change of prepositions (see *Exeg. Notes* on chap. v. 2) it may be remarked: As regards the saints the figure of encirclement by attacking foes is the one, hence *περί*, but in the case of the Apostle in prison, that of a fallen combatant, hence ὑπέρ. Or the former is=on account of, *propter*, the latter=for, *pro* (1 Pet. iii. 18), making known a stronger personal interest.*

**That utterance may be given to me.**—Ἵνα μοι δοθῇ, that there may be given me from the Lord as His gift.† *Non nitebatur Paulus habitu suo* (BENGEL). But what? Utterance, **in the opening of my mouth**, *λόγος ἐν ἀνοίξει τοῦ στόματός μου*.—This is one conception: λόγος without the article, indefinite, is more qualified by the prepositional phrase. Ἄνοιξις τοῦ στόματος is a pregnant expression (Matth. v. 2; 2 Cor. vi. 11), signifying joyful courage, streaming fulness, as well as granted freedom and fit opportunity (STIER). It is an emphatic designation of the inworking of God upon him who should speak in His name (HARLESS). Comp. Exod. iv. 12; Psa. li. 17; Isa. li. 66; Ezek. iii. 27; xxix. 31; xxxii. 22; Matth. x. 19; Luke xxi. 15. CHRYSOSTOM: ἡ ἅλυσις ἐπίκειται τὴν παῤῥησίαν ἐπιστομίζουσα, ἀλλ' ἡ εὐχὴ ἡ ὑμετέρα ἀνοίγει μου τὸ στόμα, ἵνα ἐν αὐτῷ παῤῥησιάσωμαι. CALOVIUS: *Petit sibi sermonem dari, non catenas solvi; petit apertionem oris, non vinculorum; petit sermonis* παῤῥησίαν *in ipsis vinculis, non liberationem ab iisdem.* A word thus uttered in the opening of the mouth effected by God is God's word. He therefore wishes a word, not for himself in his heart, but a word in his mouth for others, in furtherance of the conflict which tends to peace. This differs then from Col. iv. 2, where external opportunity is in question, while here the internal life of the Apostle is treated of. Accordingly it is incorrect to render: *ut aperiam os meum* (BEZA [E. V.] and others); in that case εἰς would occur instead of ἐν. So too: when I speak or open my mouth (MEYER and others) [so substantially EADIE, ELLICOTT, ALFORD and HODGE]; it is not merely a graphic and solemn expression, that would be too flat. Nor is an improvisation referred to (ŒCUMENIUS), or an internal moral quality of Paul, the frankness=ἐν παῤῥησίᾳ (CALVIN, KOPPE [BLEEK, SCHENKEL] and others), or *occasione data* (GROTIUS and others), nor is it to be joined with what follows. [The connection with what precedes (not, as in the E. V., with what follows) is now generally accepted. "The opening of the mouth" most naturally refers neither to the quality nor to the source of the discourse, but to the simple act or fact of speaking, so that the view of MEYER is on the whole preferable. As the phrase occurs here in the purport of a prayer, it *may* refer to an act of God in opening the mouth, as Braune claims, but in that case another form would have made the sense much clearer.—R.]

**In boldness to make known the mystery of the gospel** ["So that with boldness I may make known," *etc.*].—This expresses that for which he wishes that to him " utterance may be given," " in the opening of my mouth." He would gladly " make known," and this was permitted to him in Cesarea (Acts xxiv. 23) and in Rome (Acts xxviii. 30, 31; 2 Tim. i. 16) in spite of his bonds. But he wishes to do it ἐν παῤῥησίᾳ (iii. 12), hence the phrase stands emphatically in advance. What he will gladly make known is the "mystery" (i. 9; iii. 9), which is the substance "of the gospel." [ELLICOTT takes it as a genitive *subjecti*, "the mystery which the gospel has, involves."—R.]

Ver. 20. **For which [or in behalf of which** (ELLICOTT: "*in commodum cujus*, to preach which"); see below on the exact reference.—R.]

**I am an ambassador.**—He thus expresses the reason why he would so gladly stand up and labor for the gospel [not merely why he was in bonds.—R.] As Christ's ambassador he holds that office for all nations, and for the gospel; hence ὑπὲρ οὗ, not ὅν. Πρεσβεύω is: I am an ambassador (2 Cor. v. 20) and that too **in bonds**, ἐν ἁλύσει.—What a contrast: to be an ambassador in a chain! BENGEL: *Paradoxon; mundus habet legatos splendidos.* WETSTEIN: *Alias legati jure gentium sancti et inviolabiles, in vinculis haberi non poterant.* The verb does not however indicate that he was accredited to the Roman court (MICHAELIS), nor does the noun in the singular refer to the single chain with which he was bound to a soldier, to the *custodia militaris* (BAUMGARTEN and others).* GROTIUS is incorrect: *nunc quoque non desino legationem*, for we do not read: καὶ ἐν ἁλύσει πρεσβεύω. Nor is it=πρεσβεύων ἐν ἁλύσει εἰμί (RUECKERT). Finally οὗ does not refer to μυστήριον or to τὸ ἐν παῤῥησίᾳ γνωρίσαι. [EADIE refers it to the whole preceding clause, but this is indistinct; MEYER, ELLICOTT and ALFORD (apparently most correctly) refer it to "the mystery of the gospel," since this was the object of γνωρίσαι, and what he should make known would naturally

* [MEYER, ELLICOTT and others attach little or no importance to the change of preposition here, but HARLESS, EADIE, ALFORD and others are not satisfied with the explanation that the change was occasioned by mere desire for variety. That is unlike Paul. To mark the variation in English, ALFORD renders: "*concerning* all the saints and *for* me." The *Revision* by Four Anglican clergymen gives: "for all the saints and on my behalf." ELLICOTT in his translation gives: and *in particular* for me, but this is a paraphrase of the specializing *καί*.—R.]

† [The reading of the *Rec.* (δοθείη), on which see *Textual Note* [9], would give the purpose a more subjective reference, and represent the feeling of a more dependent reality (ELLICOTT).—R.]

* [The allusion is probable, but as the singular is frequently used in a collective sense, and this word is employed by Paul only in the singular, we cannot certainly infer that there is such an allusion here.—R.]

be that for which he was an ambassador in bonds. R—.]

**That therein I may speak boldly**, ἵνα ἐν αὐτῷ παῤῥησιάσωμαι.—Ἵνα introduces an end, and the final one: "that therein I may speak boldly." ["His being thus a captive ambassador, was all the more reason why they should pray earnestly that he might have boldness" (ALFORD). On the grammatical connection see the concluding note.—R.] The gospel is the immediate task of the free discourse. in this, however, there is also a message of Divine power, is the source and ground of the boldness. When there is first vouchsafed to him "an utterance in the opening of his mouth," then also does he obtain "boldness" in the gospel, and that too: **as I ought to speak**, ὡς δεῖ με λαλῆσαι.—The emphasis rests on the ὡς as in Luke xii. 11 (STIER). Much depends on *how* it is done, hence "as I ought to speak." He must indeed testify; that is his "necessity" (1 Cor. ix. 16); but to him belongs also, beyond the εὐαγγελίσασθαι, the manner worthy of the ambassador of Christ. This defines the fulfilling of his task, his duty. Comp. Col. iv. 4; 1 Thess. ii. 2. Accordingly ἵνα in this verse is not co-ordinate with the first ἵνα in ver. 19 (MEYER, BLEEK and others), since this is the final end of the Church's supplication, to be attained through the fulfilment of the first ἵνα; nor is it dependent on πρεσβεύω (BENGEL), which is inconceivable.

[EADIE, ALFORD, HODGE and ELLICOTT, all agree with MEYER, in taking this ἵνα as co-ordinate with that in ver. 19, thus setting forth a second purpose of the watching and the supplication for the Apostle. This involves no tautology, as HARLESS supposes, since the reference here is to a conditioned boldness, and "therein" indicates not the source or ground, but the sphere of the boldness: "in the matter of, in dealing with the mystery of the gospel;" God is the source. Such a co-ordinate ἵνα occurs in Rom. vii. 13; Gal. iii. 14; 2 Cor. ix. 3. It is true as Braune suggests, that this design is accomplished only through the fulfilment of the previous purpose (ver. 19), but grammatically the clause must be either co-ordinate or subordinate (the view of BENGEL being altogether untenable); if the latter, then it would express the purpose, not of the whole previous context, the supplication and consequent utterance, but simply of the gift of utterance, a view which Braune himself does not accept. We prefer therefore the other construction as more grammatical and not militating against the special point our author would bring out. For convenience a paraphrase of vers. 18–20 is appended: In this conflict therefore stand, not only armed thus, but *with all* (every form of) *prayer and supplication, praying at all times* (perseveringly and under all circumstances) *in the* (Holy) *Spirit, and watching thereunto* (in respect to this varied and constant prayer) *in all perseverance and supplication* (abiding even as you pray in persevering supplication) *for all the saints; and* (in particular) *on behalf of me, that to me may be given* (from God) *utterance, in the opening of my mouth* (when I am called upon to speak), *so that with boldness I may make known the mystery of the gospel* (whose contents are the gospel), *in behalf of which* (gospel mystery) *I am an ambassador in bonds* (a chained ambassador); (praying for me too in view of my office and condition) *that therein* (in the matter of the gospel mystery) *I may speak boldly, as I ought* (as becomes my office) *to speak.*—R.]

## DOCTRINAL AND ETHICAL.

1. *The kingdom of Satan.* There is an organized *kingdom of evil* (HAHN, *Theologie des N. T.*, I. p. 347), opposing the kingdom and people of God. In this there is a head, διάβολος (ver. 11; ii. 2; iv. 27); there are different groups, ἀρχαί, ἐξουσίαι (ver. 12; iii. 10; comp. i. 21), superior and inferior, with dominion over the world, κοσμοκράτορες. The *nature* of the prince and his dependents is pneumatic (ver. 12: τὰ πνευματικά) and super-terrestrial, ἐν τοῖς ἐπουρανίοις (ver. 12); thus prominence is given to their might over against men; they are super-terrestrial, with angelic power. Their character, however, is marked by the terms "wickedness" (ver. 12: τῆς πονηρίας), "darkness" (τοῦ σκότους, ver. 12) and "the evil one" (ver. 16); at his service are multifarious wiles (ver. 11: αἱ μεθοδεῖαι), which perceive the necessities and weakness of the object to be assaulted in all relations, preparing the attacks accordingly. [EADIE: "To rouse up the Christian soldiery, the Apostle brings out into bold relief the terrible foes which they are summoned to encounter. As to their position, they are no subalterns, but foes of mighty rank, the nobility and chieftains of the spirit-world; as to their office, their domain is 'this darkness' in which they exercise imperial sway; as to their essence, they are not encumbered with an animal frame, but are 'spirits;' and as to their character, they are 'evil'—their appetite for evil only exceeds their capacity for producing it."—R.]

2. *The contest* in its essence is a single-handed struggle in wrestling (ver. 12: ἀλλά, sc. ἐστιν ἡμῖν ἡ πάλη), in which each for himself is attacked. The danger lies in the power and character of the enemy and of his wiles (see 1), in which he does not himself openly appear; he casts βέλη, many (πάντα) and fiery ones (ver. 16); as also in the end of the vanquished one, who belongs to "darkness" (ver. 12) as a result of the "deceit" (iv. 14). The means for assault and conflict are afforded to the Evil one by the world, which is at his disposal, and by "flesh and blood" (ver. 12), which war against the soul and become allies in the service of Satan, against whom the contest really is waged, standing behind these as he does with his stratagems and artifices. What is natural and created is not the precise antagonist against whom we must contend. The Apostle sketches the conflict as a present one (ἐστιν, ver. 12), concerning every member of the church, the Apostle and every Christian, having however its history, its various stages up to the day of decision ("in the evil day," ver. 13) for which we must be prepared by opposition from the very start, being practiced in the turns and twists of the contest. Hence we are to understand the temptations and antagonisms, which meet every Christian in this world, which are spared to no period of the Church. They *appear* as contests with flesh and blood, with the world and its influence through its posses-

sions, pleasures and honors, but back of this there stands really and in truth the kingdom of darkness.* At certain times and hours they are intensified into specially decisive conflict. The evil day may be either the most fierce persecution and bitter sorrow, or quite as readily prosperity and undisturbed earthly happiness, in which some may fall even deeper and the Church itself be corrupted into unfaithfulness. This is true in particular for every Christian and his Christian life, and also in general for the Christian Church in its groups and its course of development. As the power of the Evil one is a cosmical one, and not merely a human one, humanly individualized, so the conflict itself is a cosmical one also, and not merely an individual one.

3. *The panoply.* In such a conflict the Christian needs an *equipment*, given by God and covering the whole man (*ἡ πανοπλία τοῦ θεοῦ*, vers. 11, 13). Man of himself, in his own power and strength, is unable to withstand the attacks; he has assailable and vulnerable points, which he must protect against the assaults of the Evil One, but which he alone cannot protect; only with the Lord Christ and in His power can he do it, even though he stands isolated; without God in Christ never!—*The separate pieces* of this armor (vers. 14-17) are: truth, righteousness, zealous but not passionate witness, faith, which concerns the whole personality, hope, which exalts, and God's Word. The first three pieces betoken the garments, the next two the defensive armor, the last the one only weapon of offence and attack adapted only for single-handed and close combat, which belongs to the Christian warrior, to the Christian assailed by the Evil One and yet courageous and assured of victory. No one piece can be undervalued or neglected: each one requires the other; they together form one whole.—The putting on of this armor presupposes a being strengthened, points to an internal and vital appropriation, and requires faithful fulfilment of duty (*ἅπαντα κατεργασάμενοι*, ver. 13). Neither a knowledge which is a matter either of the memory merely or of the reflecting understanding, nor an external mechanical skill in the handling of these spiritual pieces of armor, will suffice for the conflict and the victory. Even the standing ready for the combat is not enough; there must be a solicitous regard as to what is to be done, and performance of the immediate task in peaceable walk. But above all must we cling to the Lord, in order to become inwardly strengthened by Him.—Hence Paul adjoins to the lively sketch of the panoply in close connection soberly without a figure.

4. *Praying and watching* (ver. 18), just as the Lord enjoined it and practiced it in the struggle in the garden of Gethsemane (Matth. xxvi. 36-46); God's Word to and for us teaches and leads us to open our hearts before Him in our word to Him. There must be at length intercourse between Him and our souls, in order to strengthen us more and more and enable us to do our duty. In *prayerful* intercourse, that grows ever more fervent, free, joyous and constant, we obtain God's power. But we must with *true* open look see about and within ourselves, so that our weakness, the motions of the flesh, the surrounding agitation, the state of the times, the assaults of the enemy, God's will and word, do not escape us.

5. We must advance to *intercession* for all saints and for the special warriors of the present. The Christian stands in single-handed combat, but is not isolated; the fall of one may involve the fall of another, perhaps of many. The victory of one preserves many from a fall. The conflict of the Christian is a common concern, the cause of the Church. That is an evidence of watching, when in the supplication for all special thought is given to those who are fighting in the van and most of all exposed to assaults. That is watchfulness, when one sees that the matter is not that the external condition of the assailed one is altered and improved, that the prison should be opened for the prisoner, but rather that he continues internally in joy and boldness to be an unhampered witness of the gospel, especially of the marrow of the gospel, full of life, of the profoundest contents of revelation, thus enabled amid all outward disgrace before the world to preserve the inward dignity of a child and servant of God, of His ambassador.

## HOMILETICAL AND PRACTICAL.

About nothing does man have such indistinct views as about his own strength. Every one, be he never so weak, thinks himself strong: this is proved by his resolutions, his plans, which have been mostly frustrated and shattered. It is with strength as with beauty, which no one even the ugliest thinks is far off. Indeed man is often afraid for himself just where there is nothing to fear, as the miser of unnecessary expense, the ambitious man of renouncing something, not knowing their own weakness. That in the Lord alone, the strong and mighty One, strength is to be sought and found, all those do not consider who are unwilling to ground true freedom in the service of God; only the children of God are strong, and he who stands fast on the soil of Divine precepts, eternal principles, has unconquerable might. He who is overcome by God and holds to Him, overcomes himself and the enemies without him.—The conflict is stirred by a powerful enemy without us, who is the more dangerous, the more allies he finds within us in our flesh and blood, in our natural man. Were there no false friends in us, the enemy, Satan, without us would not have so great power.—The Christian alone is assailed; he who is not assailed is no Christian, either no longer, or not yet. Satan does not attack his own, but rather uses them only in assaulting believers.—In the panoply of God all temptations of the devil turn out to be trials

* [HODGE remarks respecting the conflict: "It is one also in which great mistakes are often committed and serious loss incurred from ignorance of its nature, and of the appropriate means for carrying it on. Men are apt to regard it as a mere moral conflict between reason and conscience on the one side, and evil passions on the other. They therefore rely on their own strength and upon the resources of nature for success. Against these mistakes the Apostle warns his readers. He teaches that everything pertaining to it is supernatural. The source of strength is not in nature. The conflict is not between the good and bad principles of our nature. He shows that we belong to a spiritual as well as to a natural world, and are engaged in a combat in which the higher powers of the universe are involved; and that this conflict, on the issue of which our salvation depends, is not to be carried on with straws picked up by the wayside. As we have superhuman enemies to contend with, we need not only superhuman strength, but Divine armor and arms. The weapons of our warfare are not natural, but Divine."—R.]

from God, in which we become stronger and more invincible.—The girdle of the Christian warrior is a chain of eternal truths, his breastplate is righteousness which avails before God, his war-shoes are skill in Gospel testimony in word and deed without precipitancy in peaceableness; his shield is that faith of the heart which hangs on Christ, securing against seven darts, those of sin, virtue, the world, the cross, despair, calumny and death (H. MUELLER); the helmet is the hope of everlasting salvation, and the short sword is the apprehended word from God, which has the edge and point to parry as drawn by the Lord Himself. Only learn how to choose and use such texts as Matt. iv. 4, 7, 10! See thou hast the sword of the Spirit! 1. The sword which is of the Spirit is a word, God's word, but this word is a sword. 2. The Spirit, whose the sword is, is the Holy Spirit, not theology, not polity, nor confession, neither letter nor man's reason.—Without God's word reason and strength were a leaden banner, a lance without a head, a sword without an edge.—To handle the sword of the Spirit thou needest the strength of God. HAMANN says aptly, the breastplate is no bodice but a breast-plate, to which a champion is as much accustomed as patrons to their loose clothes. From supplication we first learn how to pray for ourselves rightly.—More depends on internal than on external freedom. To be free in chains and bonds, to be full of pure joy in tribulation, to be oppressed and yet free-hearted, is the Apostle's wish and precept.

STARKE: Do you suppose that Christianity comes off without a conflict or that you will receive a crown of glory without having contended? You deceive yourself. Daily must you be in the combat and show good knighthood in faith. Do you ask: who then are my enemies? look into your own breast and there you will find sinful lusts, warring against you; sloth and sleepiness, clouding thy spirit, unbelief and doubt, wounds of conscience, disturbing you, *etc.* Without you are Satan and the world, setting their nets. If you are not properly armed in faith against these enemies, you will go to ruin. —Since artifice is so much more dangerous than force, we must specially protect ourselves against this.—He who is well armed can composedly look the devil in the face and stand up to him foot to foot; he will assuredly conquer.—A good conscience is the Christian's breastwork.—The less sin, the less the power of the devil.—Let a believing Christian take especial care that he guards his heart.—When the enemy is there it is too late to begin to arm; prepare yourself beforehand and be always ready.—Where there is no faith, there is no armor that avails against Satan; all is lost.—The word of God is necessary for all men, even for the overcoming of spiritual adversaries. How can the Romish Church answer for this, that they have refused this to their poor people?—Prating is not praying. He who has not the spirit of prayer, cannot pray aright.—Strong, well-fortified and blessed souls need our intercessions also.—Ye hearers, why is it that your teacher is so dull and that he cannot speak with power to your conscience! The answer is: you do not pray for him! Oh, as often as he enters the pulpit, so often should your mind and your whole heart rise to the Lord, praying earnestly that he may with boldness and great impression speak to your souls.—Oh how much useless stuff is often brought out from the pulpit! Let him who appears before the Lord, see to it that he speaks nothing else than God's word.

RIEGER: A good warrior needs *inward courage* and then *outward armor.*—The devil has a great advantage when his power is denied or deemed trifling. For there is then the less arming against him.—The magnificent names which the Apostle applies to these powers arranged in the kingdom of darkness, we must never look at in themselves, for then they might appear to be expressed only to increase the fear of our hearts; but when we consider in addition the destruction of all these works which is announced in the Gospel, they serve rather to exalt the name of Christ.—In the entire period of life, during which we find ourselves placed on the field of conflict, there still occurs some one occasion which constitutes the *evil day,* and upon which it depends whether the purpose of the enemy be repelled, our will for good, taken from God's word and Spirit, become strengthened and thus God's will toward us be accomplished.—It is really a principal part of the honorable condition of the children of God, that they cannot only present their own concerns in prayer to Him, but also assume those of others in supplication.—There is here however no approval of an indolent leaning upon the intercessions of others, such as Simon sought with a heart "not right" (Acts vi. 24), or of a self-interested application of intercession, such as our Saviour rebuked in the Pharisee (Matt. xxiii. 14), but we are to understand a common contest and mutual help in prayer.

HEUBNER: Weapons of human prudence, the *straw-armor* of our reason, as Luther says, are not sufficient against the evil, spiritual powers. If God is not with us, with His counsel and His strength, all is in vain.—The Christian must ever stand, ever be armed, because there is always a conflict. A fool does not know what kind of a contest there is going to be! He calls the evil powers the fancies of benighted ones.—As among the Spartans the saying was: "either with this or on this," so the Christian should either preserve his shield of faith or die on it.—No one is so strong that he can do without the intercession of others. Even a Paul still needed strengthening and stimulus. The word to be preached is given by the Lord; the Lord opens the mouth. From Him must come the impulse to speak; he who preaches according to his own fancies and pleasure accomplishes nothing. The Gospel is to the perverted heart always a mystery.

PASSAVANT: Paul was a man of God and as such of varied and great experience in all these conflicts.—The more earnestly Paul contended, the more earnestly did his love for the Christians, the brethren, the churches of the Lord, fear and tremble.—Paul is the *ambassador* on behalf of the Gospel and on account of the preaching of it *in bonds.*—This office has its sorrows and dangers; it has heights and also abysses, a destruction, a condemnation, a death.

STIER: As certainly as you can count upon God's help, so necessary is *your own activity* in the use of *means*, which God proffers that you may offer resistance.—To withstand the enemy and to stand is already the entire, difficult triumph.—We are not however once for all done with girding, putting on, grasping our arms and armor; in the midst of the conflict we must constantly look after them and keep them in order.—The contest, the enemies, the field of battle, the equipment,—that is all; but the arms, which the Spirit gives, can be managed only with the prayer of our spirit, can be attained, put on and grasped only through prayer.—*An ambassador in bonds!* But although bound, he can still proclaim unhindered and conduct properly his embassy.—GERLACH: Bound with a chain to a soldier, Paul preached the Gospel and dictated this Epistle, from which the Christian Church in all ages has received so much love and pleasure.

*On the Epistle for the 21st Sunday after Trinity* [vers. 10–17].—HERBERGER: The hand-book (*Enchiridion*) of a Christian knight. 1. What kind of heart and courage such an one must have to appear in the place of review. 2. Who is his chief Captain, to whom he must have regard. 3. What kind of equipment he must have, what is the best armory, the best arsenal. 4. Who are his worst enemies. 5. How he ought and must accustom himself to his armor. 6. What a severe regimen he must carry out. 7. Finally what he has to expect, if he conduct himself in a knightly manner.—LISCO: The sacred combat of the Christian: 1. The cause for which he contends (vers. 10, 11); 2. The enemies against which he contends (vers. 12, 13); 3. The weapons with which he contends (vers. 14–17).—RAUTENBERG: Be strong in the Lord and in the power of His might! How the equipment with the whole armor of God is 1) so indispensable, 2) so accessible, 3) so glorious.—HARLESS: The bond of Christian fellowship consists: 1) in the assurance of the same contest for all; 2) in the possession of the same arms; 3) in the command to accordant love.—*Gesetz und Zeugniss* [a German periodical]: The secret conflict of the Christian. 1) The secret of his danger, 2) of his strength, 3) of his victory.—MUENKEL: The Apostle's war-sermon shows 1) the enemy against whom, 2) the armor in which, 3) the kingdom for which we contend.—PRÖHLE: The Christian warrior. 1. The host of foes against him (ver. 12); 2. The heroic spirit in which he goes forth (vers. 10, 11); 3. The armor he bears (vers. 13–17).

[HODGE: Vers. 10–13. As a conflict is inevitable, the believer should: 1. Muster strength for the struggle. 2. He should seek that strength from Christ. 3. Since his enemies are not human, but superhuman, he needs not only more than human strength, but also Divine armor.—Ver. 10. He who rushes into this conflict without Christ has not strength even to reach the field. When most empty of self, we are most full of God.—Ver. 14. With the flowing garments of the East, the first thing to be done in preparing for any active work was to gird the loins. To enter on this spiritual conflict ignorant or doubting, would be to enter battle blind or lame.—A warrior without his breast-plate was naked, exposed to every thrust of his enemy, and even to every casual dart. In such a state flight or death is inevitable.—Ver. 15. In ancient warfare swiftness of foot was one of the most important qualifications for a good soldier. As the Gospel secures our peace with God, and gives assurance of His favor, it produces that joyful alacrity of mind which is essential to success in the spiritual conflict.—Ver. 16. It is a common experience of the people of God, that at times horrible thoughts, unholy, blasphemous, sceptical, malignant crowd upon the mind, which cannot be accounted for on any ordinary law of mental action, and which cannot be dislodged. There are others which enkindle passion, inflame ambition, excite cupidity, pride, discontent, or vanity. Against these most dangerous weapons of the evil one, the only protection is faith.—Ver. 17. This sword puts to fiight all the powers of darkness; it is true in the individual experience of the Christian, and in the experience of the church collective. All her triumphs over sin and error have been effected by the Word of God. When anything else takes its place, the Church, or the Christian, is at the mercy of the adversary.—Ver. 18. To obtain strength to use this armor aright, and to secure victory, we should pray. These prayers should be: 1. Of all kinds; 2. On every occasion; 3. Importunate and persevering; 4. By the aid of the Holy Spirit; 5. For all saints.—R.]

[EADIE:—Ver. 10. The valor is as spiritual as the armor.—Ver. 11. The great enemy of man, a veteran fierce and malignant has a method of warfare peculiar to himself, for it consists of "wiles." His battles are the rush of a sudden ambuscade.—Ver. 12. It is no vulgar herd of fiends we encounter, but such of them as are darkly eminent in place and dignity.—Ver. 16. The biography of Luther and Bunyan affords apposite examples of these fiery darts.—Ver. 17. The Captain of salvation set the example, and once and again, and a third time, did He repel the assault of the prince of darkness by three brief and simple citations from Scripture.—Ver. 18. "'Praying always'—what does it mean? Being always on our knees? always engaged in the act of prayer? This I believe to be one of the grossest glosses that Satan casts on that text. He has often given it that gloss; monkery, nunnery, abstraction from the world in order to give up one's self to prayer, are but the effects of that false gloss" (EVANS).—"All the saints" pray for us, and in a spirit of reciprocity it becomes us to pray for them.—Ver. 19. "The mystery of the Gospel." It is a system which lay hidden till God's time came for revealing it. To know it there must be a Divine initiator, for its truths are beyond the orbit of human anticipations. The God-man, a vicarious death, gratuitous pardon, the influence of the Spirit—are doctrines which man never could have discovered. This Gospel, without mutilation, in its fulness and majesty, and with all its characteristic elements, the Apostle wishes to proclaim with plain and unfaltering freedom.—Ver. 20. The Apostle's earnest wish was, that he might expound his message in a manner that became him and his high commission, that his imprisonment might have no dispiriting effect upon him, and that he might not in his addresses compromise the name and dignity of an ambassador for Christ.—R.]

# IV. CLOSE OF THE EPISTLE.

## CHAPTER VI. 21-24.

### 1. *Personal intelligence is brought by the bearer of the letter.*

### CHAP. VI. 21, 22.

21 But that ye also may know[1] my affairs, *and* how I do [the things concerning me,
how I fare][2], Tychicus, a [the] beloved brother and faithful minister in the Lord,
22 shall make known to you all things [shall make all known[3] to you]: Whom I have
sent unto you for the same [this very] purpose, that ye might [may][4] know our
affairs, and *that* he might [may] comfort your hearts.

#### TEXTUAL AND GRAMMATICAL.

[1] Ver. 21.—[The order in B. K. L., great majority of cursives, fathers, is: εἰδῆτε καὶ ὑμεῖς (so Tischendorf, Meyer, Alford); א. A. D. E. F. G., Latin fathers: καὶ ὑμεῖς εἰδῆτε (so Lachmann, Ellicott). The former admits of the best explanation of the variation (see Meyer).—R.]

[2] Ver. 21.—[*How I fare* is less ambiguous than *How I do*, while *the things concerning me* is literal and avoids the somewhat uneuphonic juxtaposition: *my affairs, how I fare.*—R.]

[3] Ver. 21.—[The order: ὑμῖν γνωρίσει is accepted by Tischendorf, Meyer, Alford, Wordsworth, Ellicott on the authority of A. K. L., nearly all cursives, good versions, fathers, although א. B. D. E. F. (Lachmann) sustain γνωρίσει ὑμῖν. The probability of a conformation to Col. iv. 7 leads to this view.—The E. V. deviates from the order of the Greek, which would be best brought out by a change to the passive form: "all shall be made known to you by Tychicus, the beloved brother and faithful minister in the Lord, whom I have sent," *etc.* Alford: "Tychicus shall make known all to you, the beloved brother and faithful minister in the Lord, whom," *etc.*—R.]

[4] Ver. 22.—[*May* instead of "might," "in accordance with the law of the succession of the tenses" (Ellicott).—R.]

#### EXEGETICAL AND CRITICAL.

Ver. 21. **But that ye also may know**, ἵνα δὲ εἰδῆτε καὶ ὑμεῖς.—Passing over to another subject (δέ) the Apostle hastens from the intercession for himself to a conclusion. He wishes that in order to make proper intercession for him, they might also know his condition more exactly, referring them, however, to oral communications. The καί before ὑμεῖς points to others (BENGEL; *perinde ut alii*). The immediate antithesis is Tychicus and those who are near Paul in his imprisonment. Not merely those about him (ver. 22: τὰ περὶ ἡμῶν), even those more remote should know respecting him. It cannot be in antithesis to the Apostle himself (RUECKERT and others); this gives no meaning. Even STIER's view: You also on your part should know what I on my part experience and suffer, does not correctly explain the καί before ὑμεῖς. To think of the Colossians (HARLESS, MEYER, BLEEK) or of Timothy (comp. 2 Tim. iv. 12) is not warranted by anything in the passage.*

**The things concerning me, how I fare**, set forth a double object of the communication: τὰ κατ' ἐμέ (Phil. i. 12; Col. iv. 7) denotes the external circumstances, τί πράσσω the personal demeanor and state in the same.*—**Tychicus—shall make all known to you**.—Πάντα comprises what has already been referred to, pointing to the full and detailed deportment (γνωρίσει) of Tychicus, who is mentioned in Acts xx. 4; Col. iv. 7, 8; 2 Tim. iv. 12; Tit. iii. 12, without imparting any further information than that he was a native of Asia and a serviceable companion of Paul, who here characterizes him as:

**The beloved brother and faithful minister in the Lord**.—Ὁ ἀγαπητὸς ἀδελφός designates him as a stout-hearted Christian, καὶ πιστὸς διάκονος as a reliable servant, a servant of the gospel, in accordance with the context, which indicates that Tychicus would come not for personal reasons, but in the interest of the Church (παρακαλέσῃ τὰς καρδίας ὑμῶν), and in agreement with Col. iv. 7 (where "minister and fellow-servant in the Lord" marks him as a servant who with Paul is a δοῦλος of Christ). We should not then think (of the ecclesiastical office of the diaconate (ESTIUS), nor yet of a personal servant to Paul himself (MEYER).† The added phrase ἐν κυρίῳ, "in the Lord," is to be joined with both ἀδελφός and διάκονος, since they are connected without the article, thus confirming the reference to the ministry of the gospel,

*[ALFORD: "As *I* have been going at length into the matters concerning *you*, so if *you also* on your part, wish to know," *etc.* But this is scarcely an obvious antithesis. HODGE explains indefinitely: "You as well as other Christian friends who have manifested solicitude about me in my bonds." The presence of καί here has been used as an argument in favor of the priority of the Epistle to the Colossians, who are supposed to be referred to (antithetically) in καί, but though its presence would be naturally explained were the priority of that Epistle fully established, it scarcely amounts to an argument in favor of that hypothesis.—R.]

*[Not "what I do," for Paul always did one thing (MEYER).—R.]

†[ALFORD and ELLICOTT follow MEYER, in taking διάκονος in the sense of "servant," Paul's servant, not the servant of the gospel; they also join ἐν κυρίῳ with this term alone, as indicating that his service for Paul was yet in Christ. But Braune's view is the more natural one.—The adjective πιστός here means "trusty," "trustworthy," but with no reference to the trustworthiness of his message, as CHRYSOSTOM and BENGEL imply, since he was probably known to the Ephesians, though not to the Colossians (MEYER).—R.]

through which he is a brother; his Christian character he manifests in the service of Christianity. Christ is the sphere of life and effort for Tychicus; hence ἐν κυρίῳ, which refers back to ἀδελφός also.

Ver. 22. **Whom I have sent unto you for this very purpose,** ὃν ἔπεμψα πρὸς ὑμᾶς εἰς αὐτὸ τοῦτο, for the very purpose, which has been already mentioned ["I have sent" is on the whole preferable to "I send" (WORDSWORTH) or "I sent" (ALFORD).—R.]—**That ye may know our affairs.***—Ἵνα must be parallel to the first one, as γνῶτε to εἰδῆτε, Τὰ περὶ ἡμῶν merely extends the circle: the situation, not merely of the Apostle, but of his companions also (Col. iv. 10–14; Philemon 10, 23, 24). Paul does not send there merely in his own interest.

**And that he may comfort your hearts,** καὶ παρακαλέσῃ τὰς καρδίας ὑμῶν.—This denotes the consequence of communication, or the impression which accompanies it. Accordingly it is not necessary to give prominence to ministerial address as the signification here (STIER). BENGEL: *Ne offenderetis in vinculis meis.* ["It is better, however, owing to our ignorance of the exact state of the church, to leave the precise reference undefined, and to extend it generally to all particulars in which they needed it" (ELLICOTT).—R.]

### DOCTRINAL AND ETHICAL.

1. *Personal* and *Congregational interests* stand in close connection. Still the latter are the preponderating ones; the former must fall into the back-ground. 2. *Independency.* The proposition of Robinson in the beginning of the 17th century: *cœtum quemlibet particularem esse totam, integram et perfectam ecclesiam ex suis partibus constantem immediate et* INDEPENDENTEM (*quoad alias ecclesias sub ipso Christo*), cannot be justified from the Apostolic age, in which the local churches stood in active intercourse and received suggestions from various quarters. [Every attempt to carry into practice this extreme view of Robinson has resulted either in ecclesiastical anarchy or a quasi-independency, such as exists in Congregational churches.—R.]

3. Our times are successful in spreading intelligence in many ways from one parish to another. This is well both for those who desire such personally imparted communications, and for those who make a sacrifice in this service, in order to receive as well as give refreshing, revival, consolation and strength. It always happens so, where the inner life is in action, even though the organization and polity are still incomplete, as in the early churches. Care however should be taken, that there be not mixed with this a dissipation of the strength required for the immediate task, or the merest of curiosity. It is precisely the fresh, glad taking root in the local churches which bears flower and fruit to be imparted for the edification of other churches. [These remarks, so pertinent to such an event as the sending of Tychicus, have a bearing on the influence of ecclesiastical bodies on the congregations within whose bounds they assemble, but more especially on the labors of those ministers who travel from place to place as "evangelists," "revival preachers." The good and the evil attendant on their labors are clearly indicated above. Such journeyings find their parallel not in the travel of the Apostles, but in those of Tychicus.—R.]

* [ALFORD, referring to the fact that this verse occurs word for word in Col. iv. 8, except that γνῷ τὰ περὶ ὑμῶν is substituted there, asks: "Does not this variation bear the mark of genuineness with it?" Braune (*Colossians*, p. 82) accepts the reading which conforms exactly to this verse, but the other is defended in the additional notes.—R.]

### HOMILETICAL AND PRACTICAL.

Comp. *Doctr. Notes.* — STARKE: — Preachers should behave to each in a friendly, peaceable, affectionate, brotherly manner.—It pleases God very much, when preachers are concerned for their hearers, and hearers for their preachers.—RIEGER:—More particular intelligence respecting each other awakens also the more fitting intercession for each other.—[It ought to be the aim of the "religious newspaper," to do for churches and families what Tychicus was to do for Paul: Communicate such personal intelligence as would comfort the hearts of those who read. Those editors who do this rather than to minister to pride or to provoke angry discussion, well deserve the title "beloved brother and faithful minister in the Lord."—R.]

---

## 2. *Twofold salutation to the Church.*

(CHAP. VI. 23, 24.)

23 Peace *be* to the brethren, and love with faith, from God the Father and the Lord
24 Jesus Christ. Grace *be* with all them that [those who] love our Lord Jesus Christ
in sincerity [incorruption]. Amen. [*omit* Amen.][1]

### TEXTUAL AND GRAMMATICAL.

1 Ver. 24. [The *Rec.* inserts ἀμήν, with א.3 D. K. L., most versions and fathers, but, as it is not found in א.1 A. B. F. G. 2 cursives and good minor authorities, it is rejected by Lachmann, Tischendorf, Meyer, Alford, Ellicott and most recent editors, as a liturgical gloss. In regard to such concluding words, the obvious rule is that *good* authority is sufficient to warrant a rejection, preponderating external evidence being of itself insufficient to establish the genuineness.

The SUBSCRIPTION in the *Rec.*, with K. L., is: πρὸς Ἐφεσίους ἀπὸ Ῥώμης διὰ Τυχικοῦ B[2] has πρὸς Ἐφεσίους ἐγράφη ἀπο Ῥώμης. ℵ. A. B.[1] D.: πρὸς Ἐφεσίους, to which F. adds ἐτελέσθη. Comp. the subscriptions to the Epistle to the Colossians.—R.]

EXEGETICAL AND CRITICAL.

*The form of the greeting* is altogether unusual; the third person, not the second, is used in spite of the direct address (vers. 21, 22); instead of ὑμῖν we find in ver. 23: τοῖς ἀδελφοῖς, in the usual position of ὑμῖν after the first word of the salutation, and in ver. 24 we read: μετὰ πάντων τῶν ἀγαπώντων instead of ὑμῶν. Thus a general application corresponding with the universal Epistle is strongly marked. Further we find here divided into two salutations what is elsewhere comprised in one. This points emphatically from the actual effects of grace within the Christian heart and life to the ultimate real ground of the same. *Finally*, the first salutation begins with "peace," which elsewhere forms the close, and the second with "grace," which is the usual beginning. See on chap. i. 2. The explanation must accept the sense of the words as used elsewhere, unless other reasons compel a departure from it. In addition this original form supports the originality of this Epistle, its Pauline origin, against the acceptance of a pseudepigraphic work.

Ver. 23. *The first salutation.* **Peace be to the brethren and love with faith.**—Εἰρήνη καὶ ἀγάπη μετὰ πίστεως expresses a wish for *two* things.* Grammatically the three substantives stand in different relations to each other: the first two are connected as co-ordinate with καί, the third is joined to them with μετά, which unites more closely than καί and σύν, the latter denoting external connection, while μετά points to an external one, to a belonging together (WINER, p. 353). This has its influence on the explanation of the substantives, which must designate internal, ethical things. The first is "peace," as the fruit of "grace," out of which it springs (see all the Pauline salutations) [comp. *Romans*, p. 57], communicated through "mercy," as the salutations in Epistles to Timothy conjoin; we must therefore refer it to peace of heart, peace with God, rest of soul. The next, "love," is something springing out of the "peace," hence love to the brethren, who with us have become children of Him who is Love; this love too is in the closest union with faith. "Faith is the characteristic of proper love (as Gal. v. 6), love is the characteristic of proper faith" (HARLESS). "There remains, however, a distinction, inasmuch as faith is the ground and beginning, bringing love with it, not the reverse" (STIER). BENGEL: *Fides præsupponitur ut donum Dei.* By "the brethren" we are to understand Christians in general, not those in Asia (GROTIUS), nor Jewish Christians in particular (WIESELER), nor yet the readers merely (MEYER).† It is incorrect to take εἰρήνη=*concordia* (CALVIN), ἀγάπη as God's love (BENGEL), or μετά=according to (MEYER). It is arbitrary to introduce here, in accordance with the salutations in the Epistles to Timothy, ἔλεος instead of ἀγάπη (RUECKERT), nor is it pertinent either, since "mercy" effects "peace," and would not occur after the latter.

**From God the Father and the Lord Jesus Christ.**—Ἀπό denotes the source, as always in the salutations. *Paulus conjungit* (καί) *causam principem* (θεοῦ πατρός) *cum causa secunda* (κυρίου Ἰησοῦ Χριστοῦ). Comp. i. 2, 22; Phil. ii. 9.

Ver. 24. *The second salutation.* **Grace be with all,** ἡ χάρις μετὰ πάντων.—Elsewhere (Rom. xvi. 20, 24; 1 Cor. xvi. 23; 2 Cor. xiii. 13; Gal. vi. 18; Phil. iv. 23; 1 Thess. v. 28; 2 Thess. iii. 18; Philemon 25) we find ἡ χάρις τοῦ κυρίου Ἰησοῦ Χριστοῦ; the simple ἡ χαρις only here, Col. iv. 18; 1 Tim. vi. 22; 2 Tim. iv. 22 (where, however, ὁ κύριος μετὰ τοῦ πνεύματός σου precedes); Tit. iii. 15. Paul, after the wish which is directed to what is subjective and ethical, points to its objective ground. The article (ἡ) marks the grace as that which is well-known to all, of which the Epistle bears testimony. The single limitation to "all" is given by the following characteristic designation:

**Those who love our Lord Jesus Christ,** τῶν ἀγαπώντων τὸν κύριον ἡμῶν Ἰησοῦν Χριστόν.—Thus Paul gives prominence to what should be the *agens* in every called and baptized Christian. The twofold salutation, bordering on a parallelism, is thus to be distinguished; the first part points to the inner life of the Christian, the second to the principle on which this life is based, with its immediate effect, love to Christ. In this we find then both an advance and a justification of the explanation of ἀδελφοί. [MEYER and most find here alone the wider reference to all real Christians, corresponding to the Anathema in 1 Cor.—R.] So 1 Cor. xvi. 22. Comp. John xiv. 21, 23. Hence the first wish is not for all members of the church, and the second for genuine disciples (STIER); as if the effect were to be wished for the former, and the efficient cause only for the latter! WIESELER finds a most remarkable reference, in the first, to the Jewish Christians, as especially "brethren" after the flesh, in the second to the Gentile Christians, as though they were not brethren; no reader would have thought of this.

**In incorruption,** ἐν ἀφθαρσίᾳ (from ἄφθαρτος, *incorruptus, corruptioni et interitui non obnoxius*, 1 Cor. ix. 25; xv. 52; Rom. i. 23; 1 Tim. i. 17; 1 Pet. i. 4, 23; iii. 4), is used here as in 1 Cor. xv. 42, 50, 53, 54; Rom. ii. 7; 2 Tim. i. 10, where the resurrection of the body is spoken of, and is not to be applied differently. BENGEL:

* [*Two*, not *three*, for the term "brethren" presupposes "faith" there already. The form indicates also, that he wishes for them "peace" and "love" in inseparable connection with the already present "faith." Of course the increase of "love" necessarily *implies* the increase of faith, but the wish is strictly a double one.—R.]

† [MEYER, followed by EADIE, ALFORD and ELLICOTT, takes "the brethren" here as="you," finding in the second benediction a wider reference; Braune, on the other hand, seems to refer to the same persons, *viz.*, all Christians. The former view is the more obvious one, but the latter accounts for the peculiar form of the salutation, and accords with the universal character of the Epistle. Still it lays a great stress upon a form that may have no special significance.—R.]

*ἀφθαρσία dicit sanitatem labis expertem et inde fluentem perpetuitatem.* The phrase is an adverbial qualification of ἀγαπώπτων, as Tit. iii. 15: *τοὺς φιλοῦντας ἡμᾶς ἐν πίστει.* [So MEYER, ALFORD, HODGE, and most recent commentators.] Accordingly it is inadmissible to connect it with χάρις (supplying ἔστω) with the explanation that it is=ἐν ἀφθάρτοις, in whom it manifests itself (HARLESS, STIER and others), still more so, to join it with Χριστόν (SEMLER), as though the glorified Saviour, and not rather the One in the form of a servant, were the object of the love. It is not=in eternity (MATTHIES), that would be εἰς αἰῶνα, nor *in sincerity* [E. V.],* either of love (CALVIN, CALOVIUS and others) or of life (GREEK FATHERS, ERASMUS, ESTIUS), that would be ἐν ἀφθορίᾳ (Tit. ii. 7). LUTHER renders it well: *unverrücht* [immovably]; the phrase denoting that the love is one belonging to incorruption, not succumbing to the fluctuations and changes of the world. BENGEL, who joins it with χάρις, remarks aptly, however: *Congruit cum tota summa epistolæ: et inde redundat etiam ἀφθαρσία in amorem fidelium erga Jesum Christum.* [Comp. the terse and lucid note of ELLICOTT *in loco*, who, after defending the view not commonly accepted, on grammatical and lexical grounds, adds: "*in incorruption, i. e.*, in a manner and in an element that knows neither change, diminution nor decay. Thus then this significant clause not only defines what the essence of the ἀγάπη is, but indicates that it ought to be perennial, immutable, incorruptible." "Not a fleeting earthly love, but a spiritual and eternal one" (ALFORD).—R.] There inheres a mighty earnestness in these closing words, which however may not be spared even with a child; the smallest child can love its mother.

Thus the conclusion returns again to the beginning, and this is the more significant, when one remembers, that Paul, who did not himself write his letters, but always dictated them (Rom. xvi. 22), penned the salutation alone with his own hand, as Col. iv. 18; 1 Cor. xvi. 21; 2 Thess. iii. 17, probably also Gal. vi. 11–18.† See LAURENT, *Neutestamentliche Studien*, pp. 4–9.

## DOCTRINAL AND ETHICAL.

1. The Epistle began (i. 2) and now it closes with the greeting: "grace be with you!" This *grace*, God's condescending love in Christ, is the ground and the goal of all human effort directed toward salvation. 2. From grace there is first brought about in the heart of the Christian, *peace* with God through our Lord Jesus Christ, the reconciliation, which drives away the unrest caused by the re-echo in our conscience of the accusing and condemning law, making real rest of soul. Then in and by the side of peace toward God there enters *love* toward our neighbor; both, peace and love, in the convoy of faith which casts itself upon Christ as Lord. The objective grace works subjectively through faith and peace and love, unfolding and moulding the strength and beauty of the human character in every department of life. Christianity animates and exalts in noble activity the Divine in the human, as a whole and in particular, to a blessed and beatifying permanence. 3. We should not be brethren merely through the external church relation, but prove ourselves such in love to the Lord. This will depend on the healthfulness of our *faith*, which in spite of external "progress," hindrances, dangers, influences, proves itself from the beginning to the very close by incorruptible love to the Lord Jesus.

[4. *The closing benediction* (ver. 24). It differs from all other Pauline benedictions; not in what is wished, but in its definition of those for whom it is wished. This definition makes it a fitting close to our Epistle, the leading idea of which is: "the Church in Christ Jesus." For we thus have a final definition of those who constitute this Church: "those who love the Lord Jesus Christ in incorruption." *Extensively*, then, the Church is not bounded by those external limits necessarily established by ecclesiastical organizations, nor by those logical ones as necessarily defined by detailed dogmatic statement, still less by those empirical ones set up by morbid, fanatical or spasmodic religionism. The empire of love is not co-incident with such boundaries. Still this is not the "broad" territory of indifferentism, ignorance, doubt or unbelief, for the definition is *intensive* also. The love has for its object "the Lord Jesus Christ," whom Paul loved. And those who love as Paul loved, must apprehend this Object in good measure as Paul apprehended Him. No one can define how far speculative doubt about the Person of Christ leaves scope for a real love to Him as "the Lord Jesus Christ," but love seeks to *know* the dear object, and those who seek Him will find Him, here or hereafter, "as He is." Love is the best preceptor in Christology. Mere sincerity is not enough; the love must move in a sphere, partake of a character, "perennial, immutable, incorruptible." That Christ's grace alone can beget such a love is evident both from the Apostle's words and human experience. Those who have it are "in Christ," of His Body, which, in a fuller, higher sense, like the Head, shall live and love "in incorruption," through the same "grace."—R.]

## HOMILETICAL AND PRACTICAL.

Comp. *Doctr. Notes.*

RIEGER: The sum of the whole Epistle was: God in Christ, before the world began in purpose, God in Christ in the accomplishment of our destined Redemption, God in Christ in the saints' appropriation of this salvation provided for us, unto its consummation in glory; hence the benediction at the conclusion concentrates itself upon fellowship with God and His peace and His love. The smallest child in Christ, and he who is the strongest through God's Spirit in the inner man, can unite on the precious heart-point of love to

* [ALFORD, with right, urges that this would make the Epistle end with an anticlimax, "by lowering the high standard which it has lifted up throughout to an apparent indifferentism, and admitting to the apostolic blessing all those, however otherwise wrong, who are only not hypocrites in their love of Christ."—R.]

† [Comp. *Galatians, in loco*, where the additional notes defend the view that the whole of that Epistle was penned by Paul himself. This opinion includes the presupposition that he rarely did so, strengthening therefore, not weakening, the point Dr. Braune here introduces.—R.]

Jesus. The grace remains immovable, and out of this the love also reaches to something amaranthine, which in the heat of the contest does not fade away.

HEUBNER: The love to Jesus must abide, must be immovable, whatever fortunes meet us, however the spirit of the age may change; else it is not pure. *Laus in amore mori.*

PASSAVANT: Here we have an apostolic conclusion. It is a reminder, first, of that *peace*, which comes down from God's heaven alone upon our earth, into our hearts; secondly, of that *love*, which is pure, holy, Divine; thirdly, Paul reminds the Christians of that *faith*, which, inseparable from love, living and active through it, *born of God*, alone is *pleasing to God*, alone gives to God His glory, alone exalts the soul to Him. Fourthly, we are reminded of that *grace*, through which first and alone there comes to us all true, eternal, blessed good, continuing ours out of pure mercy and unto eternity.—The whole of vital Christianity is contained in love to Jesus. Those then who love this Jesus with their whole heart, so that in this love they look to Him alone, desire Him alone, follow Him alone, deny themselves for Him, willingly bear His cross and their cross after Him, living to Him and dying to Him—those are Christians, are God's children, His special, His constant and dear objects of regard.

STIER: If any one loves our Lord Jesus Christ, in vain and in wrong would all the churches pronounce the ban against him, nor are formulas of faith valid against him.

GERLACH: The grace which is the cause of our love to Christ, becomes at the same time the reward of our love to Him; all may be hoped from Him, if one loves Him, all feared, if one does not love Him.

THE END OF EPHESIANS.